FOURTH EDITION

Contemporary International Relations

FRAMEWORKS FOR UNDERSTANDING

Daniel S. Papp

Professor of International Affairs
Georgia Institute of Technology

Macmillan College Publishing Company
NEW YORK

Maxwell Macmillan Canada
TORONTO

Editor: Robert Miller
Production Supervisor: Dora Rizzuto
Production Manager: Paul Smolenski
Text Designer: Jill Bonar
Cover Designer: Robert Vega
Cover Illustration: Tom Post
Photo Researcher: Chris Migdol

This book was set in 10/12 Caledonia by Americomp and was printed and bound by Hamilton Printing Company. The cover was printed by Phoenix Color Corp.

Macmillan College Publishing Company
866 Third Avenue, New York, New York, 10022

Macmillan College Publishing Company is part
of the Maxwell Communication Group of Companies.

Maxwell Macmillan Canada, Inc.
1200 Eglinton Avenue East
Suite 200
Don Mills, Ontario M3C 3N1

Library of Congress Cataloging-in-Publication Data
  Papp, Daniel S.
     Contemporary international relations: frameworks for
  understanding / Daniel S. Papp.—4th ed.
        p.   cm.
     Includes index.
     ISBN 0-02-390881-5
     1. International relations. I. Title.
  JX1395.P36 1994   93-19499
  327—dc20   CIP

Printing: 1 2 3 4 5 6 7 8   Year: 4 5 6 7 8 9 0 1

Preface

Much has changed in the international arena since the third edition of *Contemporary International Relations* was published in early 1991. The East–West conflict has ended, and the Soviet Union, one of the primary antagonists in that conflict, has broken up. A coalition of 33 nations led by the United States expelled Iraq from Kuwait. Less than two years later, in a separate action, U.S. troops were also deployed in Somalia, but this time for humanitarian purposes. Civil war broke out in what once was Yugoslavia, with Serbia, one of the former Yugoslavian republics, pursuing a policy of "ethnic cleansing" in a neighboring former republic, Bosnia-Herzogovina, that many observers considered to be simply another name for genocide. Twelve other European countries agreed to move toward political and economic unity, but many of their citizens had serious reservations about the idea. In South Africa, the government moved to dismantle apartheid, but it was not clear whether the transition to a majority-rule government could be accomplished peacefully. In Rio de Janeiro, the countries of the world tried—but failed—to conclude significant agreements on how to protect the earth's damaged environment. And in the United States, Bill Clinton was elected president, promising to implement new policies to meet new challenges in a new international system.

The implications of these events for the future of international relations were and are immense. They have already changed the way the world works. In subsequent years, these and other events will change it even more.

They also give rise to a number of serious questions. Given the number of events that take place on a daily basis, and the rapidity and magnitude of the changes that they bring about, is there any hope of understanding the complexities and cross-currents that shape contemporary international affairs? Even if we can understand them, can policies be formulated and implemented to shape future trends and events as we desire? Even if humankind can manage to shape future trends and events as it desires, will this lead to improved human conditions and a better international system?

Or rather, are we caught up in events and by forces too complicated to understand, and too powerful to influence? Do we have too limited an understanding of international affairs to fashion policies that can lead to improved human conditions and a better international system? And can we ever reach widespread agreement about what "improved human conditions" and "a better international system" actually are?

In the third edition of *Contemporary International Relations*, these and other questions were examined by focusing on a set of key concepts grouped into six analytical frameworks. Since then, as noted above, much has changed. Nevertheless, *CIR's* analytical frameworks remain valid today, and are used once again in this fourth edition of *Contemporary International Relations*. Together, these six frameworks help provide an overarching structure for *CIR* that enables students to understand the complexities and crosscurrents of today's fast-changing world. Indeed, the underlying theme behind *CIR* is that as students and analysts, our responsibility is to understand change in contemporary international affairs, and to prepare ourselves better to meet and to shape change so that we can improve our common lot in the global community.

With this in mind, the order in which these frameworks is presented is straightforward. *CIR* begins with the assumption that before one can understand international affairs, one must first know who and what the major actors in international affairs are, where they came from, and what their objectives and interests are. Consequently, *CIR's* first framework, completely updated, studies the major types of actors in contemporary international affairs.

Together, the interactions of today's international actors, their objectives, and their interests form an international system. The second framework therefore studies how actors make the policies through which they interact, and explores the dimensions of the international systems that actors and their interactions over time have created and are creating. The fourth edition of *CIR* completely updates this framework, and adds a new chapter that explores how different types of international actors formulate and implement the policies that lead to their international interactions.

The third framework examines the perceptions of major international actors. This is necessary because the policies and actions of all actors, regardless of their place in the international system, are based on how they see themselves, their own situations, the positions of others, and the international system as a whole. This framework has also been updated, with the old chapter on the Soviet Union being replaced by a chapter entitled "Russia and the Other Former Soviet Republics."

Framework four studies the different instruments and tools that international actors have at their disposal to implement policies and undertake actions to achieve their objectives. This framework, updated as are all the others, concentrates once again on economic, military, sociopolitical, diplomatic, and legal parameters of power.

In the fifth framework, several of the more important problems and issues that international actors both create and confront in their international interactions are explored. Given the growing importance of international political economy, two chapters are now devoted to topics in this issue-area, one on population, food, resources, and technology; and the other on economic development and the global distribution of wealth. Subsequent chapters explore emerging global problems such as the environment, drugs, and health; war, peace, and violence; and conflicts of values. All chapters in this framework concentrate on current global policy issues.

Finally, in framework six, *Contemporary International Relations* speculates on the future. This is an important framework because in the final analysis, all actors plan for the future, and implement present policies to try to bring about the future conditions that they desire. With this in mind, the final framework in *Contemporary International Relations* speculates about how the world might change by the end of the twentieth century.

As a result of this approach, actors, their interests, their outlooks and capabilities, and their problems are often examined from several perspectives. This leads to discussions of a number of concepts at several different places in the book. For example, national liberation movements are first studied in Chapter 5 as a separate class of international actor. They are examined again in Chapters 11, 12, and 14 from the respective vantage points of the United States, the former Soviet Union, and China. And the military and sociopolitical parameters of power that national liberation movements employ are studied in Chapters 18 and 19. This approach provides students with an understanding of international actors in their own right. It also shows students how different actors view each other, and how actors attempt to achieve their objectives in the international system. This approach provides a depth of understanding of the complexities of contemporary international relations that a single-faceted approach cannot hope to achieve.

The fourth edition has been completely updated, with current issues and events included throughout the text to provide examples of relevance and immediacy for students and professors alike. Once again, this edition is written with introductory students in mind. It assumes only an elementary knowledge of international affairs, and it steers clear of esoteric language and concepts. It provides a rigorous background in international affairs by consciously blending theoretical academic constructs with the realities of everyday international life.

This edition of *Contemporary International Relations* continues to stress that change is inevitable in international affairs. Events of the last few years have made this exceedingly clear. But it is hoped that change and the forces that lead to change can be understood. Optimistically, they can be influenced and shaped in ways that lead to improvements in the human condition.

Every generation laments that it did not create the problems that confront it. But as Billy Joel observed, even though we didn't start the fire, we must try to fight it. How successful past and present generations have been in this struggle remains a matter of debate. Indeed, in almost every respect, this planet remains a land of confusion, and some peoples and nations find themselves caught between a rock and a hard place.

But some progress has been made as well. The Cold War has ended. Despite the dangers of nearly half a century of the nuclear arms race, no nuclear weapon has been used in anger. And increasingly, peoples of the world recognize that their futures and their interest are interrelated. This third stone from the sun, and the life on it, continues to survive.

So there is hope, hope that with understanding, skill, and perhaps a little luck, we may yet fashion a safer, saner, and more humane world for ourselves, our children, and future generations.

Daniel S. Papp

Contents

CHAPTER 1

Contemporary International Relations

- Why is everything changing so rapidly in international affairs?
- How can international change best be understood?
- How can international relations best be studied?

We live in revolutionary times.

The international system that emerged after World War II has crumbled.

The Soviet Union, one of the world's two dominant superpowers from 1945 to 1991, is no more, torn apart by internal political, economic, social, and nationality problems.

The United States, the other superpower, remains unified and militarily strong, but it faces large economic and social difficulties, and searches for its defining identity in the post–Cold War world.

Western Europe inches slowly and uncertainly toward economic and perhaps political unity, Japan has emerged as a powerful international economic force, and China struggles to regain the international respectability it lost in 1989 when its army killed hundreds, perhaps thousands, of students and workers who were demonstrating for democracy.

In the Middle East, peace may be moving nearer. In South Africa, apartheid is slowly being dismantled. In Latin America, recently created democratic governments struggle to solve the challenges that confront them. Meanwhile, much of the rest of the Developing World remains mired in economic stagnation or decline, giving the people there little to look forward to other than continued poverty, hunger, and ill health.

Where is the world going? With the old international system gone, what comes next? Does the end of the East–West conflict mean that military strength is no longer as important in international affairs as it once was? Has economic strength become the leading measure of national power? Will the nation-state continue as the leading international actor? Or will it be eclipsed in importance by other types of actors as problems arise whose solutions go beyond the reach of individual governments? Indeed, is there any way the international community can solve the many problems that it faces?

These are difficult questions to answer. And for the student of international affairs, they lead to an even more immediate concern. Amid so many variables and changes, how can one ever begin to understand what is happening in contemporary international relations?

One way to begin to develop this understanding is to examine some of the more important forces behind change in today's world. Thus, we begin the task of making sense of the world we live in by studying four of the more significant forces behind international changes in the 1990s.

FORCES BEHIND CHANGE

As the 1990s began, several forces converged that together overturned the old international system that had existed since shortly after World War II. Chief among these forces were the **collapse of communism** in the Soviet Union and Eastern Europe; the rediscovery of economics as a critical concern in international affairs; the renewed nationalistic demands by many ethnic groups and nationalities for their own independent states; and the emergence of global problems as key international issues. These four forces were and are by no means the only causes of international change, but together they have revolutionized contemporary international affairs.

The Collapse of Soviet and Eastern European Communism

Throughout the post–World War II era, one of the main features of the international system was the East–West conflict between the Soviet Union and its communist allies on the one hand and the United States and its allies on the other. Even in times of detente between the superpowers, no one really challenged the fundamental assumption that competition and rivalry remained central to the superpower relationship.

But during the late 1980s, this fundamental assumption began to erode. In March 1985, a new Soviet leader, Mikhail Gorbachev, assumed power and began to put into place a series of social, economic, political, and foreign policy reforms unparalleled in Soviet history. Among other things, Gorbachev's reforms reduced censorship in the U.S.S.R., permitted social and political debate, decentralized the Soviet economy, introduced democracy into the Soviet political system, and promoted "new thinking" in Soviet foreign policy.[1]

Gorbachev had several reasons for undertaking these reforms. For years, even in the late 1970s and early 1980s, it was evident that the Soviet economy was deteriorating and that many of the U.S.S.R.'s citizens had become disenchanted with their lot in life.[2] By the time Gorbachev acquired power, this deterioration and disenchantment had become readily apparent. For Gorbachev, the choice was clear: change past policies radically, or accept the political and economic decline of the Soviet Union.

In some areas, Gorbachev's reforms succeeded. But in others, particularly in economics, they failed. In addition, the Soviet leader's attempt to change his country led to immense political struggles within the U.S.S.R. over his reforms, and contributed to heightened ethnic tensions between the Soviet Union's diverse nationalities. By 1989, even though East–West tensions had declined immensely, it was not at all clear if Gorbachev's reforms were helping or hurting the people of the Soviet Union. Nor was it clear whether Gorbachev himself could withstand the pressures from hard-line party and military conservatives who wanted to end his reforms and return to traditional Soviet policies. Gorbachev also faced pressures from radical reformers who wanted him to accelerate change even more.

By 1989, the impacts of Gorbachev's reforms had also spread beyond the Soviet Union. Nowhere outside the U.S.S.R. itself were the impacts greater than in Eastern Europe. The people of Eastern Europe, who had fallen under communist control following World War II and afterward had twice been subjected to Soviet invasions to maintain that control (Hungary in 1956 and Czechoslovakia in 1968), considered Gorbachev's reforms a godsend. Eastern Europeans took special note of Gorbachev's position that the Soviet Union would no longer use military force to keep other countries under communist rule.

With Gorbachev's rejection of the use of force to impose communism, the long-festering resentment of the peoples of Eastern Europe toward their governments poured out. Thus, in 1989, popular resentment, street demonstrations, and elections toppled governments in all six of the Soviet Union's Eastern European allies. In Poland, the noncommunist trade union Solidarity and its supporters swept to power in a free election, and formed the first noncommunist government in the Soviet bloc. In Hungary, the government and party both formally abandoned the term *communist* even as they dismantled border defenses along the Austrian-Hungarian border and prepared for free elections in 1990. In Czechoslovakia, huge rallies forced communist leader Milos Jakes from power, and noncommunists ran the government for the first time. In Bulgaria, party leader Todor Zhivkov was removed as prodemocracy demonstrators cheered in the streets. In East Germany, long-term German leader Erich Honecker and his successor were forced to resign, and the Berlin Wall was torn down. The communist government in Romania, led for 24 years by Nicolae Ceausescu, fell in December 1989.

These were incredible events that eliminated the Cold War certainty that Eastern European states were subservient to the Soviet Union. These events also led to the unification of East and West Germany; raised questions about the provision of Western economic assistance to Eastern Europe; challenged the rationale behind both the North Atlantic Treaty Organization (NATO) and the Warsaw Pact; and forced reassessment of U.S. interests in Europe.

Indeed, these events shook the entire structure of the international system. With the Soviet Union focusing on internal reform and acting cooperatively internationally, was the Cold War over? Or was it just in remission?

These questions became all the more important as change accelerated in the Soviet Union in 1990 and 1991. As the U.S.S.R.'s economy continued to decline and ethnic conflict worsened, the political struggle over Gorbachev's reforms increased. Finally, in August 1991, conservative communist party and military hard-liners staged a coup and removed Gorbachev from power.

But the coup was short-lived. Thousands of Soviet citizens led by Russian President Boris Yeltsin refused to submit to the hard-liners, and significant numbers of the Soviet military sided with Yeltsin and his supporters as well. The coup collapsed, Gorbachev returned to Moscow, the hard-liners were arrested (one committed suicide), and all that they stood for was disgraced.

After the coup failed, events unfolded even more rapidly. Gorbachev, although still Soviet president, lost considerable prestige and influence because of the coup. Conversely, Russian President Yeltsin gained prestige and influence. In December 1991, Yeltsin and the presidents of two of the other most important Soviet republics, Ukraine and Belarussia (now Belarus), declared that the U.S.S.R. would cease to exist on January 1, 1992. Gorbachev protested, but could do nothing. And the Soviet Union passed into history.

These were momentous events for the people who lived in the former U.S.S.R. And they were momentous events for the world as well. For almost half a century, since shortly after World War II, the East–West conflict, with the East centered around the Soviet Union, and the West around the United States, had defined much of international relations. With the dissolution of the Soviet Union, that conflict was over.

The Rediscovery of Economics

But what might replace it? What might become the dominant organizing concept in contemporary international affairs?

One answer to these questions may be economics. For years, the superpowers and their allies concentrated on military parameters of power, while economic considerations played an important but nevertheless secondary role. Occasionally, world leaders such as former U.S. President Dwight D. Eisenhower emphasized

No two people played more important roles in the collapse of the Soviet Union than Mikhail Gorbachev, the last President of the U.S.S.R., and Boris Yeltsin, the first President of independent Russia. Here, Gorbachev and Yeltsin address the Russian parliament on August 23, 1991, shortly after the failed coup. (Sygma.)

the role of economics as an important component of national strength, but these references were infrequent and quickly forgotten. Newly independent Developing World states focused on economics as a critical issue, but rarely succeeded in elevating it to critical importance. For most of the 1950s, 1960s, and 1970s, then, guns, bombs, and missiles were the stuff of high politics and high importance. Trade, foreign aid, economic development, and debt remained secondary priorities.

Slowly, however, international economic issues during the 1970s and 1980s began to acquire greater importance. The **rediscovery of economics** as a major force in international affairs cannot be traced to a single event or a single trend. Rather, it was the culmination of a series of events and trends that when taken together made it impossible to ignore or overlook the importance that international economic issues have. These events and trends included but were not limited to (1) increased U.S., Western European, and Japanese awareness of their dependence on foreign sources of energy and other nonfuel mineral resources; (2) the burgeoning Developing World debt; (3) the emergence of Japan as a major international economic actor; (4) the transformation of the United States from the world's greatest creditor nation to the world's greatest debtor nation; (5) the economic collapse of the Soviet Union, and the beginning of the integration of the postcommunist Eastern European and Soviet successor states into the Western economic system; (6) the movement of the center of international economic growth to the western Pacific; (7) the decision by Western Europe to create a single European market; (8) the continuing inability of large segments of the Developing World to grow economically; and (9) the transformation by electronic banking of much of the world into a single financial market.[3]

By the beginning of the 1990s, economic concerns had become as important as military concerns on the agendas of many international actors. Thus, when Iraq invaded Kuwait in 1990, many countries feared not only that Iraqi expansionism might threaten their geopolitical interests, but also, as a result of Iraq's control of a large percentage of the world's oil reserves, their economies. This linkage between economic concerns and military concerns was not new, but the Iraqi invasion of Kuwait provided the linkage with a poignancy that it had not had for some time. At the same time, much of the world had become economically linked. American-built aircraft flew Japanese businesspeople to Indonesia to secure oil for Japanese industries, and French financiers tracked their investments in stock markets in London, New York, Tokyo, and Hong Kong. American consumers purchased inexpensive East Asian textile products, forcing U.S. textile manufacturers to lay off workers and invest in high-technology German textile machines purchased with money deposited in Italian banks by Saudi princes. Many people debated whether this economic interdependence was a blessing or a curse, but no one debated its reality. One measure of this economic interdependence was the growth of international trade, as shown in Table 1–1.

The potential for even more rapid growth in international trade increased during the 1990s when, in several geographical regions of the world, states banded together and moved toward the creation of free trade areas. In its purest form, a *free trade area* is a group of states between which all economic and noneconomic barriers to trade such as tariffs and quotas have been removed. By 1992, major free trade areas or near-free trade areas had been negotiated in Europe (the European Community, with twelve members); North America (the North

TABLE 1–1   The Growth of International Trade (U.S. $ millions)

Year	Imports	Exports
1960	139,917	129,919
1965	171,693	162,218
1970	297,075	282,638
1975	816,135	791,391
1980	1,946,400	1,895,500
1985	1,890,200	1,811,200
1990	3,450,600	3,339,600

SOURCE: International Monetary Fund, *Direction of Trade Statistics 1991*.

American Free Trade Area, with three states); South America (Mercosur, with four members); and Southeast Asia (the Association of Southeast Asian Nations, with six states).

Within individual states, supporters of free trade areas asserted that economic benefits of increased production, increased employment, and reduced prices would accompany the introduction of free trade areas. Conversely, critics argued that free trade areas would divide the world into competing trade areas, increasing the possibility not only of trade wars, but of real wars as well.

Clearly, the rediscovery of economics as a critical concern in international affairs raised important questions about the future of the international system. Would the trend toward regionally oriented free trade areas lead to a new era of increased trade and prosperity? If it did, would all states benefit, or just a lucky few? Or would the trend toward free trade areas divide the world into competing economic blocs, increasing the possibility of trade wars and even economically based military conflicts?

Other equally important questions flowed out of economic issues as well. How long could any nation, even one as wealthy as the United States, continue to run huge balance-of-trade deficits? Could individual states maintain their sovereignty in an economically interdependent world? What duty do developed states have to aid economic growth in underdeveloped states? Where do domestic economic concerns end and international economic concerns begin? What responsibility does one state have to citizens of another so that its own citizens and corporations do not take economic advantage of them? And if the first state concludes that it has no responsibility to protect the economic interests of citizens of another state, what actions may that other state take to defend its citizens'—and its own—interests?

The Resurgence of Nationalism

Nationalism also re-emerged in the 1980s and 1990s as a potent force for reshaping international affairs.[4] However, unlike economics, which appeared to be a force that tended to link different states together via trade, **the resurgence of nationalism** appeared to be a force that often—but not always—drove states apart. Indeed, in cases such as Czechoslovakia, the Soviet Union, and Yugoslavia, nationalism in the 1990s even broke up established states when ethnic groups that had long been members of a multinational state demanded—and sometimes fought for—their own independent state.

Nationalism comes from the concept of a "nation," which is simply a grouping of people who view themselves as linked to one another. People who consider themselves to be ethnically, culturally, linguistically, religiously, or in some other way linked may thus be considered a nation. Nationalism in turn is the psychological force that binds such people together. Specifically, nationalism is the feelings of attachment to one another that members of a nation have, and the sense of pride that members of a nation have in themselves and their nation.

Nationalism is not a new arrival on the international scene. It has been a potent force for several centuries, and it remained important during the post–World War II era both in contributing to the dissolution of colonial empires and in adding to the rivalry in the East–West conflict.

But paradoxically, both the struggle against colonialism and the existence of the East–West conflict in some ways also dampened the expression of nationalism. With the struggle against colonialism identifying the colonial country as the primary enemy, national groups in colonial areas sometimes temporarily set aside their differences, concentrating instead on the struggle against the colonial power. And for countries centrally involved in the East–West conflict, the dangers of that conflict often influenced national groups to accept their inclusion in the state in which they found themselves.

As traditional colonial empires disappeared in the 1970s and as the East–West conflict dissipated in the late 1980s, this situation began to change. As a result, long-repressed nationalist sentiment began to emerge in states that included several ethnic, cultural, linguistic, or religious groups.

In several cases, this resurgence of nationalism led to the breakup of established states. This occurred in Yugoslavia and Czechoslovakia. The resurgence of nationalism among its diverse peoples was also one of the leading causes of the dissolution of the Soviet Union.

In other states such as India, Spain, Pakistan, and Iraq, separatist ethnic groups fought the established state government in efforts to establish their own independent states. Even in Belgium, Canada, and Great Britain, separatist ethnic groups made known their desire to obtain independence and establish separate ethnically based states, although in these cases the efforts were usually peaceful.

By the mid-1990s, then, it was not a certainty that the world would move toward large regional blocs based on economic interests. In many regions, a resurgence of nationalism indicated that smaller nationally based rather than larger economically based international actors might be the hallmark of the emerging new international system.

The Emergence of Global Problems

The 1990s also opened with widespread awareness in the international community that problems existed whose solutions had to be global in scope. These problems included terrorism, drugs, and environmental deterioration. As was the case with the rediscovery of economics and the resurgence of nationalism, it is not possible to point to a single event or trend as the beginning of the growth of awareness about the **emergence of global problems**. Nevertheless, growth of such an awareness has clearly taken place, and it is pregnant with implications for contemporary international relations.

Terrorism has been a particularly vexing global problem. As Table 1–2 shows, major terrorist actions against U.S. and other Western interests have been extensive. Although no single source of terrorism exists, U.S. and other Western officials have frequently pointed to North Korea, Libya, Iran, pro-Iranian Islamic fundamentalists throughout the Middle East, and a number of South American drug cartels as centers of the problem. At the same time, it should be pointed out that defining terrorism is a difficult task. Indeed, several countries throughout the world consider the United States, several Western European states, and Israel as undertaking terrorist actions. We will return to the question of defining terrorism later in this text.

Here, we will concentrate simply on the issues of identifying and coping with terrorism, which are two completely different things. Given the necessity to acquire and collate large amounts of timely information about terrorist intentions and movements, and to coordinate responses against planned terrorist attacks or terrorists themselves, an international response to the terrorist problem is clearly required. Single states by themselves rarely have the wherewithal to respond effectively to terrorist activity.

Terrorism can be extremely deadly. When a terrorist bomb destroyed the Pan American 747 "Maid of the Seas," 258 people died. Pictured here is the nose section of the destroyed airliner after it came to earth near Lockerbie, Scotland.   (AP/Wide World Photos.)

TABLE 1–2   Major Terrorist Actions Against U.S. and Other Western Interests—1985 to 1993

Date	Event
June 1985	TWA jetliner is hijacked, with one American killed; complicity of several countries suspected, including Libya, Syria, and Iran.
October 1985	Italian cruiseliner *Achille Lauro* is hijacked, with one American killed; Libyan complicity suspected.
November 1985	Egyptian jetliner is hijacked, with one American killed: Libyan complicity suspected.
December 1985	Terrorist attacks on Rome and Vienna airports kill 20, including 5 Americans; Libyan and Iranian complicity suspected; Qadhafi calls attacks "heroic."
February 1986	CIA says Libyan agents are casing 35 U.S. foreign installations as potential terrorist targets.
April 1986	Bomb explodes on TWA flight, killing 4 Americans; Libyan complicity suspected.
April 1986	Bomb explodes in West Berlin disco, killing two people including one American; United States claims that it has "exact, precise, and irrefutable" evidence of Libya's role in the bombing.
May 1986	Direct Action leftist group attacks Interpol headquarters in Paris with guns and explosives.
September 1986	Paris Police Headquarters bombed by suspected Middle East terrorists; 1 person killed, 51 injured.
September 1986	Bomb explodes outside Paris store killing 5 people; Middle East terrorists implicated.
October 1986	West German Foreign Office official Gerold Von Braunmuehl killed in Bonn; Red Army Faction claims responsibility.
November 1987	115 die as KAL Boeing 707 explodes over Burma; North Korea blamed.
June 1988	Greek leftist terrorists kill American military attaché; say attacks will continue until U.S. bases are removed.
July 1988	Nine killed, many hurt in terrorist attack on Greek ferry.
December 1988	Bomb destroys Pan Am Flight 103 over Lockerbie, Scotland. All aboard are lost.
March 1989	Car bomb explodes 50 yards from British Embassy in Beirut, kills 12, wounds 75.
April 1989	Terrorists firebomb Frankfurt Stock Exchange in West Germany; no deaths, several injuries.
August 1989	Colombia government declares war on drug dealers; by year's end, drug dealers set off 265 bombs and kill 187.
September 1989	UTA airliner bombed over Niger; 171 killed; several Middle East terrorist groups claim responsibility.
November 1989	Car bomb planted by Red Army Faction kills West Germany's most prominent banker.
November 1989	Colombian airliner explodes in flight, killing 107; drug dealers implicated.
February 1990	Islamic Jihad bombs Israeli bus, killing 11.
May 1990	In continuation of wave of attacks against U.S. interests, NPA kills 2 U.S. servicemen outside Clark Air Force Base, Philippines.
October 1990	IRA Provisional Wing sets off car bomb in Londonderry, Northern Ireland, killing 6.
February 1991	Series of bomb attacks against Citibank facilities in Greece cause extensive property damage but no casualties; attacks believed retaliations for Desert Storm.
October 1991	Islamic Jihad claims responsibility for bomb explosion killing American serviceman in Turkey; this third U.S. citizen killed by terrorists in Turkey in 1991, first two killed by leftist group Dev-Sol.
January 1992	IRA begins wave of bombings in Great Britain that last throughout 1992 and into 1993; several killed in these bombings, many injured.
February 1992	Shining Path guerrillas in Peru step up attacks against Peruvian government and Western interests in Peru, leading to April 1992 suspension of constitution by President Fujimori.
March 1992	Bomb kills 14 in Israeli embassy in Buenos Aires, Argentina; radical Palestinian group claims responsibility.
May 1992	Italian Mafia sets off bombing wave against Italian government investigators, several killed as bombings last throughout the year.
August 1992	Antiforeign violence and terrorism increases in Germany; several killed.
September 1992	Islamic fundamentalist groups in Egypt accelerate attacks against Western tourists and businesses; attacks kill several, last throughout 1992 and into 1993.
November 1992	Over 50 bombs set off throughout Colombia in wave of attacks by drug cartels against businesses, law enforcement agencies, and government officials.
February 1993	New York World Trade Center bombed, killing 6; Islamic fundamentalist group suspected.

Even this simple observation gives rise to several difficult questions. When is it legitimate for a state to use military power to defend its interests? What is terrorism, and is it only a weapon that the weak use against the strong? Are terrorists sometimes more powerful than states, or does it only seem that way? To what extent should governments act to protect their citizens living or traveling overseas?

The international drug situation presents similarly difficult issues, and it too transcends national boundaries. Although the United States probably has the world's most serious drug problem, the abuse of drugs is widespread in Europe, Russia, China, and many Developing World states as well.

But once again, identifying the problem is not enough. With drugs originating in South America, Southeast Asia, and elsewhere as well; with billions of dollars involved in illegal international drug traffic; with drug traffickers willing to use both directed and indiscriminate violence; and with demand for drugs apparent in most societies, stemming the tide of drugs is a multifaceted problem that requires the cooperation and integration of domestic and international policies from the entire international community. Whether the international community is up to the challenge remains to be seen.

The international community's response to yet another emerging global problem, environmental deterioration, gives cause for both optimism and pessimism. On the optimistic side of the ledger, within two years of the confirmation that the release of manmade chlorofluorocarbons into the atmosphere played a major role in creating a "hole" in the earth's ozone layer over the South Pole, the nations of the world under the terms of the 1987 Montreal Protocol agreed to limit the production and use of chlorofluorocarbons. Since then, the world's nations have agreed to phase them out completely by 2000. Quick and effective international cooperation on global problems is thus demonstrably possible.

However, on a more pessimistic note, the United States, the Soviet Union, and Japan in 1990 objected to international efforts to limit carbon dioxide emissions into the atmosphere to prevent global warming. The three industrial powers argued that more studies had to be undertaken before a link between global warming and carbon dioxide emissions could be definitely established.

Even more recently, the United States in 1992 was the major stumbling bloc that prevented conclusion of more stringent environmental safeguard agreements at the U.N. Earth Summit held in Rio de Janeiro. And even though Japan emerged as one of the "heroes" of the Earth Summit after pledging over seven billion dollars to help other states fight pollution, Japan itself has an appalling environmental record at home.[5]

Despite these difficulties in moving toward a broad international commitment to environmental protection and improvement, there is widespread recognition that the global environment is deteriorating. There is equally widespread recognition that unprecedented international cooperation will be needed to halt and reverse that deterioration. A certain sense of "global consciousness" may thus be developing, not only on environmental issues, but also on terrorism, drugs, and other global problems.

Does this imply that the concept of national sovereignty may be increasingly challenged? May it even portend that states may curtail their own short-term growth or economic well-being in the interests of securing a greater long-term global good? We are a long way from answering these and related questions, but until recently, these questions could not even be seriously asked.

Taken together, then, the collapse of Soviet and Eastern European communism, the rediscovery of economics, the resurgence of nationalism, and the emergence of global problems are revolutionizing contemporary international affairs. What will emerge as the new international system is not yet clear, but it is clear that the old system is no more.

The purposes of this text flow directly from these forces for change, the questions they raise, and the need to move students of international affairs closer to answers to these and other questions. Before we clarify how this text handles those tasks, we will first discuss other attempts that have been made to make the study of international affairs more comprehensible.

ANALYZING CONTEMPORARY INTERNATIONAL RELATIONS

Without doubt, international relations appear at times bewildering. Students may at times feel that their efforts to understand the complexities of international affairs today are futile.

The task is difficult, but not futile. It requires patience and persistence as well as logical inquiry and flexible perspectives. As the examples just given illustrate, contemporary international events are regularly interrelated; our task of achieving understanding is therefore further complicated because seemingly unrelated events in different areas of the world may over time combine to affect other regions of the globe. Events are demonstrably interdependent, and as we improve our ability to understand the causes of and reasons behind this interdependence, we will improve our ability to understand contemporary international relations.

How can our task best be approached? Throughout history, analysts of international relations have differed in their approaches to their field. For example, during the late nineteenth and early twentieth centuries, the study of international relations centered around **diplomatic history**. Who did what to whom at a particular time and place were the main features of diplomatic history. This methodology concentrated on nation-states as the main actors in international relations and included the study of the major diplomats and ministers of the period. Detailed accuracy was required and obtained, but seldom, if ever, were causal connections or comprehensive analyses sought. As a means for understanding a particular series of events, diplomatic history was (and is) excellent; as a means for understanding broader sweeps of international relations or for developing a theoretical basis for the study of international relations, diplomatic history was (and is) of limited utility.

Whereas diplomatic history sought to explain a particular series of events, other methodologies that were developed during the nineteenth and early twentieth centuries viewed international relations on a global scale. **Strategic and geopolitical analyses**, methodologies in wide use even today, trace their roots to concepts developed by U.S. Admiral Alfred Mahan during the late nineteenth century and British geographer Sir Halford Mackinder during the early twentieth century. To Mahan, the world's oceans were its highways, and whoever controlled its highways could control the course of international relations. Mahan was there-

fore a major proponent of sea power and advocated the development of a powerful American navy and the acquisition of overseas bases to support that navy. Not
surprisingly, Mahan based most of his analysis on Great Britain and its Royal
Navy.[6] Partly because of the urgings of Mahan, the United States strengthened its
fleet during the late nineteenth century and actively sought and acquired territorial possessions in the Pacific Ocean, including Hawaii, Samoa, Guam, and the
Philippines.

Sir Halford Mackinder, on the other hand, emphasized the importance of
land power. To Mackinder, whichever country dominated the center of the
Eurasian land mass would inevitably dominate world politics. Mackinder called
this area the "heartland." The heartland was in turn surrounded by coastal areas
that Mackinder termed the "rimland." The state that controlled the heartland,
Mackinder believed, could exert power as it desired against rimland areas and,
because of its central position, could emerge victorious. Mackinder interpreted
European history as being a record of different countries attempting to achieve
control of the heartland and of other countries in turn attempting to prevent that
from occurring.[7]

Other analysts of international relations in the nineteenth and early twentieth
centuries concluded that diplomatic historians and strategic and geopolitical theorists did not understand the root causes of the problems of international relations. To these analysts **socioeconomic theories of international relations**
provided a more accurate picture of how and why the international system func-
tioned as it did. During the nineteenth century, for example, Karl Marx believed
that the United States expanded to the west because of the pressure of excess
population and urban and rural unemployment and underemployment. American
historian Frederick Jackson Turner developed a similar theory, which eventually
was called "Turner's Frontier Thesis." Other theories were also developed.
Without doubt, however, the most influential socioeconomic theory of international relations was Lenin's theory of **imperialism**, which he set forth in 1912 in
his famous work *Imperialism—the Highest Stage of Capitalism.*

To Lenin, the capitalist economic system was the driving force behind both
colonization and war. Capitalist countries, seeking new markets, inexpensive
resources, and cheap labor, divided the world into vast colonial holdings in their
efforts to increase profits. This imperialist practice in turn led to war as the
European powers sought to divide and reapportion their colonial holdings, again
all in an effort to increase profits. Until recently, communists almost universally
accepted Lenin's views as accurate and legitimate.[8]

The catastrophic trauma of World War I brought forth new methods of analyzing international relations. Diplomatic history remained influential and important,
but geopolitical-strategic and socioeconomic analyses became more influential
than they had ever been before, particularly with Lenin's seizure of power in
Russia in 1917. However, two new schools of thought emerged, one centered
around the question of how best to prevent another major international conflict,
the other centered around the question of how best to assert and establish national
power. These two new major schools of thought were generally labeled **political
idealism** and **national socialism** (or fascism), and they dominated Western analysis of international relations between World War I and World War II.

Both schools of thought were heavily policy oriented, but they reached totally different conclusions. To the political idealists (there were many variations of

them), human beings were basically good and generally sought the welfare of others as well as themselves.[9] The idealists for the most part believed that bad structural and institutional arrangements on a worldwide basis created bad human behavior on an individual basis. Therefore, they argued, war was not inevitable, but was caused by bad structural and institutional arrangements.

War could be prevented and political idealism could be taught only if proper structures could be created. Political idealists, as a result, advocated one or more of a number of policy prescriptions, all of which were implemented to one degree or another during the interwar years. To some, international cooperative institutions would help prevent war. The League of Nations in particular would serve as a forum to which nations could bring their disputes, and in extreme cases all of the nations of the League would act against an aggressor nation to ensure peace. This principle of collective security required joint action and a clear ability to define an aggressor. The events that led up to World War II showed the League could not successfully undertake either task.

To other political idealists, the rule of international law would bring peace. The Kellogg-Briand Pact of 1928 was one such attempt. It declared that all signatory nations had renounced war as an instrument of national policy except in cases of self-defense. Here, it is worth noting that before World War I international conventions such as the Hague Conferences of 1899 and 1907 sought to establish laws *of* war, whereas the postwar political idealists sought to create laws *against* war.

Still other political idealists believed that weapons themselves were the cause of war. A number of studies in the interwar era illustrated that the major arms manufacturers such as Krupp had instigated World War I for profit; in the United States, Senator Gerald Nye chaired a Senate investigation that concluded that U.S. arms makers had garnered immense profits during the war. As a result of these studies, some political idealists argued that if the "merchants of death" could be curbed and the number of weapons reduced, then war would not occur. The Washington Naval Treaties of 1921–1922, the most successful of which established a ratio of capital ships that each nation could have in relation to other nations, were the highwater marks for this approach. Under these treaties the United States, Great Britain, Japan, France, and Italy agreed to a 5-5-3-1.75-1.75 ratio, respectively, for capital ships. This meant that for every five large naval vessels the United States and Great Britain had, Japan could have three, and France and Italy 1.75.

Numerous other political idealists advocated reform of internal social systems, redistribution of wealth and ownership, creation of an international system of free trade, or establishment of universally accepted criteria for self-determination.

Again, however, caution must be exercised, for the political idealist school was neither as unified, as organized, nor as simplistic as the preceding discussion might suggest. Sophisticated men and women, appalled by the horror of modern war, sought ways to prevent its recurrence, and if the competing school of national socialism (fascism) had not developed as rapidly as it did, they might have been successful for a longer period of time.

National socialism was also policy oriented, but it advocated the growth and enhancement of national power. Under national socialism, the German variant of which was called Nazism, the entire industrial and productive capacity of the nation-state and all the energies of its population were to be devoted to strengthening the state. The national leader was deified, and the military was glorified. Territorial expansion was considered proof of the superiority of the system. As a school of analysis of international relations, fascism in all of its variants stated simply that "might makes right," and that the most powerful nation-state should rightfully dictate to weaker nation-states. The fascist leaders of Germany and Italy believed war was inevitable, and if it was inevitable, they meant to win it.[10]

With militarism rampant in Germany, Italy, and Japan, the 1930s became a decade of conflict. Japan attacked Manchuria in 1931, Italy invaded Ethiopia in 1935, and Germany repudiated numerous provisions of the Treaty of Versailles, which formally concluded World War I. By 1939, Germany had remilitarized the Rhineland, taken over Austria, and annexed much of Czechoslovakia following the 1938 Munich Agreement. The appeasement at Munich, where Great Britain and France agreed to the German annexation of the Sudetenland portion of Czechoslovakia, convinced Hitler that neither Great Britain nor France would fight. On September 1, 1939, German forces attacked Poland, and World War II began. Political idealism had proven insufficient to the task of preventing war.[11]

To some, political idealism had failed because it had not been universalized, or because it had not been given a long enough time to succeed. However, to others, political idealism's failure to prevent war was the inevitable result of what they believed were political idealism's naive and erroneous assumptions. Human beings were *not* inherently good, argued the post–World War II **political realists**, led in the United States by Hans Morgenthau, Reinhold Niebuhr, George Kennan, and Henry Kissinger.[12] At best, humans had equal capacities for bad and good; at worst, they had an instinctive desire to dominate each other. War, therefore, was always a possibility and in many instances a probability.

The responsibility of each nation-state, according to this outlook of **realpolitik**, was to provide for its own defense and security. Collective security became a theoretical nicety that could be used in alliances and international organizations to enhance a state's security, but collective security could not be relied on to guarantee a state's security. The measure of the wisdom of a proposed national policy or action, to the political realist, was whether that policy or action furthered the national interest, most often defined by proponents of realpolitik as the acquisition of power in any of its various forms, but most particularly as the acquisition of military power. The logic of realpolitik dictated that peace could never be assured, but it could be attained, because in a world where national policies were based on realpolitik's worldview, a balance of power would result as different states sought to assure their own security and self-interest by aligning against any nation-state that appeared too powerful.

Realpolitik urged primacy of foreign policy over domestic policy, maintenance of large and capable military forces, and emphasis on nationalism. It also asserted the primacy of states as international actors, considered states to be unitary actors with a single decision-making process, maintained that states were essentially rational in their actions, and argued that national security was the most important international issue.

The language and policy prescripts of realpolitik have dominated U.S. government policy since World War II. Every American president since that war, with the possible exceptions of Jimmy Carter and Bill Clinton, has based his policies on its conceptual tenets. But questions were raised about realpolitik in academia, the government, and other circles as well. In a nuclear era, did realpolitik's emphasis on the military make national annihilation a likely outcome? How could realpolitik explain the slow but real move in Western Europe toward transnational economic linkages? In a world in which national borders and national interests were becoming increasingly less well defined, who could tell what did and what did not further the national interest? Indeed, as more and more colonial areas sought and received their independence, and as several major states broke up as a result of internal ethnic demands for national self-determination, the question of whether or not an area was a nation-state became increasingly relevant. In all cases, realpolitik failed to determine who within a nation-state should define the national interest. Realpolitik too often relied on simple assertions, and thus, in more skeptical minds, its shortcomings became increasingly clear. Critics of realpolitik argued that more scientific and less assertive methodologies were needed to enhance the study of international relations.

The new emphasis on the scientific study of international relations was described as the "behavioralist revolution" and accelerated steadily during the late 1950s and 1960s.[13] Proponents of the new methodology all agreed on the need for a more rigorous and systematic study of international relations, but few agreed on how scientific methods should be applied to the study of international relations. To the **behavioralist**, the study of international relations had to include a clear statement of a problem, an analysis of the variables in the problem, additional analysis of the relationships between those variables, and a discussion of the conditions under which those relationships would continue to hold. As in any scientific study, the results had to be replicable and free from biases introduced by external factors. The behavioral revolution demanded that theories derived from behavioral analysis be consistent with all available facts and not solely with those that fit the theories. "The exception that proved the rule" was not acceptable to the behavioralist.

Behavioralism itself has been regularly criticized, at least in part because of the inability of its proponents to agree on anything other than the broadest methodologies. Also, behavioralists have tended to study quantifiable events, a fact that has led some to criticize behavioralists as having limited relevance to the "real world" of international relations. Other critics of behavioralism argue that although the objectives of behavioral analysis are laudable, their findings are irrelevant because the rapidity of change in the modern world has altered the conditions of interrelationships between the variables the behavioralists study even before they complete their analysis. Historical accuracy thus yields policy irrelevance, critics of behavioralism often maintain.

More recently, some scholars have argued that regardless of the approach that is used or the area of international affairs that is studied, the study of the international interactions of states and other international actors should be identified simply as **foreign policy analysis**. This is an all-encompassing approach that has as its central thrust the analysis and understanding of "the intentions, statements, and actions of an actor—often but not always a state—directed toward the external world and the response of other actors to those intentions, statements, and actions."[14] Using diverse approaches and methods including comparative foreign policy analysis and events data analysis;[15] social and political psychology, perception, and culture;[16] bureaucratic politics; the analysis of domestic policies as inputs to foreign policy; area studies; decision theory; economic and strategic analysis; and a host of other analytical methods and tools, foreign policy analysis can be descriptive, explanatory, or predictive.

Nevertheless, critics of foreign policy analysis sometimes assert that it is not a "real" school of analysis because of its eclectic and all-encompassing nature. How can something be considered a "school," they ask, when it is willing to accept virtually any method of analysis? Conversely, defenders of foreign policy analysis as a field of analysis argue that by including all issues pertaining to the interactions of states and other international actors within a single field of study, and by applying a variety of different approaches, methods, and tools to that study, foreign policy analysis provides the best opportunity to understand fully the way international affairs and the international system work.[17]

Historically, then, the last century of the study of international relations has provided no definitive answer to the original question. "How can we best improve our ability to understand contemporary international relations?" Today, as since the late 1960s, numerous methodologies claim to be most accurate but, as before, little empirical evidence supports any of their claims. The methodologies discussed here coexist today, and probably will coexist in the short-term and mid-term future as well. Some political idealists and political realists now prefer to be identified as traditionalists, and some behavioralists believe they have moved into a postbehavioral era, but the fundamental fact remains that analysts of international relations themselves do not agree on how best to improve their own understanding. Nevertheless, Table 1–3 provides a useful representation of the differences between some of the more prominent methods of analyzing international affairs.[18]

LEVELS OF ANALYSIS AS AN ANALYTICAL TOOL

One analytical tool that is widely accepted within the field of international affairs is the concept of **levels of analysis**. In its simplest form, the levels-of-analysis concept forces students of international affairs to recognize that international

TABLE 1–3   Differences Between Several Prominent Methods of Analyzing International Affairs

	Diplomatic History	Marxism-Leninism	Realism	Idealism	Behavioral-ism	Foreign Policy Analysis
Primary actors	Nation-states; Diplomats	Economic classes	Nation-states	Many	Many	Many
Primary issues	Personalities; National security	Economics; Others Subsidiary	National security	Morality	Many	Many
Method of analysis	Historical record	Economic class	Capabilities of state	Values	Quantitative	Many
Perspective	Primarily national	National and global	National	National, regional, or global	National, regional, or global	Many

events flow from many different sources, and that there is rarely a single "correct" way to examine an international event.

A few examples may clarify the point. For example, the Libyan government under Muammar Qadhafi has actively aided and abetted anti-American terrorist attacks around the world. (See again Table 1–2.) Many Americans therefore condemn Libya and all Libyans. But is this actually a valid response? Is Libyan state-supported terrorism a result of the Libyan people's animosity toward the United States, the Libyan government's dislike of the United States, or Muammar Qadhafi's own personal predilections?

Another example is also helpful. In May 1987, the U.S. Navy frigate *Stark*, on patrol in the Persian Gulf, was attacked by an Iraqi warplane. Thirty-seven American sailors were killed, and the *Stark* was severely damaged. Was the attack on the *Stark* intentionally planned by the Iraqi government, perhaps to indicate Iraq's displeasure with earlier U.S. arms sales to Iran? Was it the result of a decision by an individual Iraqi pilot to "get even" with the United States for a real or imagined U.S. slight? Or was it as both the United States and Iraqi governments asserted, simply a "ghastly error"?

A final example is equally poignant. In July 1988, the U.S. cruiser *Vincennes*, also on patrol in the Persian Gulf, mistook an Iranian passenger plane for a hostile military aircraft and shot it down, killing 290 people. Was this action a planned and premeditated U.S. attempt to provoke a confrontation with Iran? Or was it too a "ghastly error," the result of one man making a hurried decision on the basis of information that turned out to be wrong?

These uncertainties are sometimes referred to as "the levels-of-analysis problem."[19] The concept is best viewed and used as a tool to help us understand international affairs. Levels of analysis help us comprehend that all individuals, whether they be the ruler of Libya or the president of the United States, may be acting on purely individualistic motives, or they may be acting on a broad-based statewide consensus on national interest. Between the extremes of action for the individual and action for even a global system, numerous levels exist at which foreign policy can be made and studied. Figure 1–1 illustrates several of these other levels.

At what level, then, should a student view the actions of an international actor, say for example, a state? Should a state's actions be viewed merely as reflections of the individual preferences of the state's leaders? Such a view would force us to conclude that the improved U.S.–Soviet relationship of the late 1980s and early 1990s was not really an American–Soviet success, but rather a

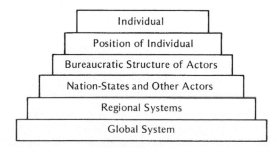

FIGURE 1–1. Different levels of analysis in international relations.

Reagan–Gorbachev and a Bush–Gorbachev success. Or should a state's actions be viewed as the result of domestic bureaucratic, organizational, or political forces? This view would drive us to conclude that Reagan, Bush, and Gorbachev acted neither as individuals nor as representatives of the state, but rather were responding to domestic pressures applied by political parties, business interests, bureaucratic organizations either within or outside of government, ethnic/racial pressures, or other such domestic interests. Or as a third alternative, should the state's actions be viewed simply as the state's actions, that is, as a conscious goal-directed policy that the state undertakes as it seeks to attain its national interests? According to this view, improved U.S.–Soviet relations in the late 1980s and early 1990s served both the U.S. and Soviet national interests, and therefore each government moved in that direction. Or finally, should the actions of a state be viewed as a product of forces operating at the international system level? If so, then the United States and the Soviet Union, as well as every other state and every other national leader, responded to pressures that are the product of the system of states in which they operate. At this level of analysis, states and their leaders may be viewed more as hostages of circumstances beyond their control than as centers of power and calculating decision-makers that determine the fate of the world.

Each level of analysis casts different light on why international actors act as they do. At the individual level of analysis, individual decision-makers are studied. Important factors considered here are the values that a decision-maker holds; the views that a decision-maker has of himself or herself, the actor that he or she acts for, and the world; and how the decision-maker makes decisions. Traditionalists classify these studies as memoirs or biographies, whereas behavioralists class them as studies of "elite ideosyncratic behavior" or "operational codes." At this level of analysis, the unifying factor is that the individual decision-maker is the primary—and sometimes exclusive—unit of analysis. This level of analysis, for example, helps us to understand that Jimmy Carter's strong Christian beliefs and values were important inputs to U.S. human rights policies during the Carter presidency.

A second level of analysis is the position that an individual holds in the decision-making structure. This level of analysis takes into account the fact that positions of responsibility often influence a person's views of life, the world, domestic and international issues, and so on. It recognizes the reality that when it comes to issues, "where you stand depends on where you sit." For example, it is this level of analysis that allows us to understand why Thomas Jefferson opposed an expansion of power by the national government before he became president, but when he became president he sought greater power for the national government so the Louisiana Purchase could take place. Traditionalists and behavioralists both find this level of analysis useful.

A third level of analysis is the bureaucratic structure of actors. This level emphasizes the competition for power and influence between organizations and bureaucracies at the subactor level as a primary variable in understanding the policy of actors. Analyzing policy at the bureaucratic structure level helps the student understand, for example, why the U.S. Army and U.S. Air Force both had long-range missile programs during the 1950s. It also offers one explanation why both Air Force bombers and Navy jets were used in the 1986 U.S. air raid against terrorist training centers in Libya. Traditionalists rarely use this approach, whereas behavioralists use it in a variety of forms, most notably under the terminology of "bureaucratic rivalry" or "linkage politics."

A fourth level of analysis is the international actor itself. In its purest form, this level views each actor as a hard monolithic entity with neither internal divisions nor external attractions. It sees each actor's policy as the result of a rational decision-making process that keeps interests and objectives paramount throughout the decision-making process. Sometimes called the "rational actor" model, this level of analysis is used most often by traditionalists. Behavioralists deride it as the "billiard ball" approach to international affairs.

A fifth level of analysis is that of the regional system. Those who approach issues from a regional system perspective argue that actor level analyses and sub-actor analyses do not allow enough scope to understand the actual dimensions of a given problem. The regional level of analysis, for example, would argue that the Vietnam War could best be understood not as a localized war, but as one that was regional in scope; the El Salvador insurgency of the 1980s and 1990s could also best be understood as part of a regional Central America-wide phenomenon. Regional analysis is not confined to military issues, either. The problem of how to cope with acid rain, for example, may well require regional analyses.

A sixth level of analysis centers around the global system. The global level of analysis asserts that even the regional level is in some instances too confining. For example, a global level of analysis indicates that world hunger is a problem caused not by too little food in the world, but by the uneven distribution of available food. A global level of analysis also would emphasize the global environmental consequences of the "greenhouse effect," or global warming, as well as the global impact of the deterioration of the ozone layer. Traditionalists and behavioralists alike have found this level of analysis useful.

Again, then, each level of analysis casts a different light on why actors act as they do.[20] Thus, for international affairs analysts, an understanding of the levels-of-analysis problem is important because it allows them to improve their understanding of how and why an international actor acts as it does. It allows them to understand, for example, that John Kennedy put a naval quarantine around Cuba during the 1962 Cuban Missile Crisis both because he believed that the United States' national interest demanded that Soviet missiles be withdrawn and because Robert Kennedy, in response to an Air Force plan that the missiles be removed by an air attack, declared that he did not want his brother to go down in history as "another Tojo." (Tojo was the Japanese Minister of War who initiated the attack on Pearl Harbor.)[21] In one sense, then, an understanding of the levels-of-analysis problem is as important for the analyst of international affairs as an understanding of subatomic particles, atoms, compounds, and complex compounds is for the physicist or chemist.

Here, it must be stressed that an understanding of the levels-of-analysis problem is critical if the analyst of international affairs hopes to understand the forces of change that affect contemporary international affairs. The four forces for change with which we began our analysis in this chapter provide excellent examples. Unless an analyst understands that Mikhail Gorbachev had his own perspective on change within the former U.S.S.R. and Eastern Europe (Level 1), that Gorbachev's own perspective was influenced by his position as Soviet leader (Level 2), and that different organizations and bureaucracies within the former U.S.S.R. competed to promote and defend their own positions (Level 3), that analyst cannot hope to understand events in the former U.S.S.R. and Eastern Europe, nor how those events interacted with the international system. Similarly, unless an analyst understands that national economic concerns including employment, debt, and the balance of trade often drive policy at the state level (Level 4), he or she will overlook major forces in international affairs. Finally, unless an analyst understands that acid rain requires at a minimum regional responses (Level 5) and other types of environmental deterioration may require global responses (Level 6), that analyst will not be able to understand emerging regional and global perspectives on contemporary international relations. And importantly, given that all these forces and levels of analysis interact with one another, unless all levels are understood, none can be truly understood.

As important as developing such an understanding is for the analyst, national decision-makers have as pressing a need to understand the levels-of-analysis problem, for they must formulate policy that will allow them to achieve effectively whatever objectives they are pursuing. Unless they have at their disposal overwhelming power and influence, decision-makers must carefully fashion their own policies so that other decision-makers, in responding to that policy, make their attainment of their objectives more probable. Only by being cognizant of the various levels on which his or her opposite numbers may be operating can a decision-maker hope to fashion such a sufficiently subtle policy.

FRAMEWORKS FOR UNDERSTANDING

Students may still feel that their efforts to understand international relations are futile. However, they are not. In reality, students are not much worse off than analysts, and in some ways, they are better off. Students may not yet have a grasp of some of the more esoteric issues and concepts involved in international relations, and in most instances they still may be willing to balance and assess the conflicting types of models, or paradigms, that different schools of analysis use.

For the purpose of improving our ability to understand contemporary international politics, this text borrows heavily from many schools of analysis. It is wedded to none. In avoiding identification with a particular school of thought, this text proceeds from the assumption that many methods of analysis provide useful insights into the state of the world, but none provide perfect insight.

With this assumption in mind, the following 25 chapters are organized into 6 major frameworks based on the questions that were asked following our discussion earlier in this chapter of some of the forces for change in contemporary international relations. Each framework examines a particular set of concepts critical to understanding international relations.

The first framework of chapters identifies and examines the international actors. It discusses who and what they are, how they came to be what they are, and what their objectives are in international affairs. Nation-states, multinational corporations, international government organizations, nongovernmental organizations, and private individuals are all analyzed as actors in the international arena who pursue their diverse interests in various ways. The rationale for this framework is a simple one; one must understand who the participants in international affairs are before international relations in its broader contexts can be understood. Some of the questions that the first framework approaches are:

- Who are the major actors in international affairs?
- What objectives do they seek?
- Who determines those objectives?
- Where did these actors come from?
- How important are they today?
- How are they changing?

Taken together, the actors that we examine in the first framework form an international system that we explore in the second framework. In that second framework, the ways in which major actors interact are first explored in a chapter on how they make their foreign policy. Then, the two major organizing concepts that until recently dominated the international system are examined, the East–West and North–South conflicts. The second framework also explores where the international system may be headed, and studies questions such as these:

- How do states and other international actors formulate and conduct their foreign policies?
- How did the East–West conflict begin and evolve?
- How and why did it end?
- What are the causes of the North–South conflict, and how has it evolved?
- How has the international system evolved?

Unfortunately, understanding who the actors are and how they form and fit into the international system is not enough. Because each of the numerous actors has its own peculiar vantage point, each individual actor views itself—and others—as being somewhat different from other actors. In some instances, perceptions clash to such an extent that it is difficult to realize that the same actor or event is being described. Anyone who seeks to understand world politics must be aware of those differing perceptions and their impacts on the different policies of the various actors. Thus, the third framework stresses the perceptual outlooks of various actors. Although the points of view of all groups of actors are presented, greatest emphasis is placed on the differing outlooks of the larger nation-states. For the most part, they are the major actors in international affairs, and they also have the most significantly differing outlooks. Questions that this framework analyzes are:

- How do actors view each other?
- How do actors view themselves?
- What has influenced the development of these perceptions?
- How do these perceptions affect policy?

The fourth framework analyzes the instruments that the various actors use as they seek to achieve their diverse objectives. It also discusses the utility of different instruments of power in different settings and details what constraints, if any, may operate on the use of a particular instrument. Economic capabilities, military power, and sociopolitical influence, including national will, elite morale, religion, and ideology, are all examined as tools that can be and are employed by various actors as they pursue their objectives. International law and diplomacy are also discussed in a separate chapter as useful elements of power. Among the questions examined in this framework are:

- What are the constituents of power?
- Why is one type of power useful in one instance but not in another?
- What constrains the employment of power?
- What are the differences between military, economic, and sociopolitical parameters of power?
- How do international law and diplomacy affect an actor's power?

The fifth framework presents a series of contemporary global issues both as a statement of concern and as an agenda for discussion. Five of the more widely recognized issue-areas—population, food, resources, and technology; economic development and distribution of wealth; the emerging global issues of the environment, drugs, and health; war, peace, and violence; and global conflicts of values—are all presented and analyzed. Obviously, additional issues could also have been included, but exigencies of space prevent a more comprehensive listing and discussion. This framework discusses questions such as:

- Why are some countries economically underdeveloped, and how can their development be speeded?
- Why do resource shortages exist, and can their impact be lessened?
- How serious are global environmental problems?
- What causes war, and how can war be avoided?
- What types of conflicts of values exist, and why?

The sixth and final framework delves into what is sometimes called "futurology," that is, an effort to delineate the shape of both probable and preferable international futures and how we can move from one to the other. It is the only framework in this text that is speculative. Nonetheless, it is a significant chapter, for without having at least some understanding of the alternative futures we face and can fashion, even a comprehensive and detailed understanding of the present is a sterile and vacuous possession. In some respects, it approaches the most important questions in this or any other book:

- Where is the international community heading?
- Where do we want it to go?
- How can we help it get there?

With study, skill, work, and luck, this and subsequent generations will be able to answer these questions.

KEY TERMS AND CONCEPTS

collapse of communism   **imperialism**
rediscovery of economics   **political idealism**
resurgence of nationalism   **national socialism**
emergence of global problems   **political realism (realpolitik)**
diplomatic history   **behavioralism**

strategic and geopolitical
analyses
socioeconomic theories of
international relations

foreign policy analysis
levels of analysis

NOTES

1. These reforms are discussed in detail in Chapter 12.
2. For example, see Daniel S. Papp, "From the Crest All Directions Are Down: The Soviet Union Views the 1980s," *US Naval War College Review* (July–August 1982), pp. 50–68.
3. These points are discussed in more detail in Chapters 17 and 22.
4. See Chapter 2 for a more detailed discussion of nations and nationalism.
5. See *The International Herald Tribune*, August 1–2, 1992.
6. See Alfred Thayer Mahan, *The Influence of Sea Power upon History 1600–1783* (Boston: Little, Brown, 1890).
7. For Mackinder's own analysis, see Sir Halford Mackinder, *Democratic Ideals and Reality* (New York: Holt, Rinehart and Winston, 1919).
8. V. I. Lenin, *Imperialism–the Highest Stage of Capitalism, Selected Works*, Vol. V (New York: International Publishers, 1943).
9. Most political idealists rejected the outlook that man's selfishness, aggressiveness, or stupidity caused war and international conflict. For a discussion of this outlook, see Kenneth N. Waltz, *Man, the State, and War* (New York: Columbia University Press, 1959). See also Konrad Lorenz, *On Aggression* (New York: Harcourt Brace Jovanovich, 1963).
10. Adolf Hitler detailed his view of the world in *Mein Kampf* (Boston: Houghton Mifflin, 1943).
11. For a superb overview of this entire period of world history, see William R. Keylor, *The Twentieth Century World* (New York: Oxford University Press, 1992).
12. For some of the most prominent works of these political realists, see Hans J. Morgenthau, *Politics Among Nations* (New York: Alfred A. Knopf, 1948); Reinhold Niebuhr, *Moral Man and Immoral Society* (New York: Charles Scribner's Sons, 1947); George Kennan ("X"); "The Sources of Soviet Conduct," *Foreign Affairs*, July 1947, pp. 566–582; and Henry A. Kissinger, *Nuclear Weapons and Foreign Policy* (New York: Harper & Row, 1957).
13. Some of the more prominent analysts of international affairs closely identified with the behavioralist revolution were J. David Singer, James N. Rosenau, and Dina Zinnes. See, for example, J. David Singer (ed.), *Human Behavior and International Politics* (Chicago: Rand McNally, 1965); James N. Rosenau, *The Scientific Study of Foreign Policy* (New York: The Free Press, 1971); and Dina Zinnes, *Contemporary Research in International Relations: A Perspective and a Critical Appraisal* (New York: The Free Press, 1976). See also Karl W. Deutsch and Richard L. Merritt, "Effects of Events on National and International Images," in Herbert C. Kelman (ed.), *International Behavior* (New York: Holt, Rinehart and Winston, 1965), pp. 132–187; Dean G. Pruitt and Richard C. Snyder (eds.), *Theory and Research on the Causes of War* (Englewood Cliffs, NJ: Prentice-Hall, 1969); and Robert C. North, Ole R. Holsti, M. George Zaninovich, and Dina A. Zinnes, *Content Analysis* (Evanston, IL: Northwestern University Press, 1963). This is only a partial listing.
14. Deborah J. Gerner, "Foreign Policy Analysis: Exhilarating Eclecticism, Intriguing Enigmas," *International Studies Notes* (Fall 1991–Winter 1992), p. 4.

15.   For good discussions of the advantages and disadvantages of comparative foreign policy analysis and events data analysis, see for example James N. Rosenau, "Introduction: New Directions and Recurrent Questions in the Comparative Study of Foreign Policy," and Charles F. Hermann and Gregory Peacock, "The Evolution and Future of Theoretical Research in the Comparative Study of Foreign Policy," both in Charles F. Hermann, Charles W. Kegley Jr., and James N. Rosenau, eds., *New Directions in the Study of Foreign Policy* (Boston: Allen and Unwin, 1987). See also Maurice A. East, "The Comparative Study of Foreign Policy: We're Not There Yet But . . ," *International Studies Notes* (Spring 1987), p. 31; and James A. Caporaso et al., "The Comparative Study of Foreign Policy: Perspectives on the Future," *International Studies Notes* (Spring 1987), pp. 32–46.

16.   For an overview of several approaches from the field of political psychology, see for example Eric Singer and Valerie M. Hudson, eds., *Political Psychology and Foreign Policy* (Boulder, CO: Westview Press, 1992).

17.   For a deeper analysis of this debate, see Deborah J. Gerner, "Foreign Policy Analysis: Renaissance, Routine, or Rubbish?" in William Crotty, *Political Science: Looking to the Future* (Evanston: Northwestern University Press, 1991).

18.   For excellent surveys of different theories of international relations, see James E. Dougherty and Robert L. Pfaltzgraff, Jr., *Contending Theories of International Relations: A Comprehensive Survey* (New York: Harper & Row, 1990); and John A. Vasquez (ed.), *Classics of International Relations* (Englewood Cliffs, NJ: Prentice-Hall, 1990).

19.   See, for example, J. David Singer, "The Level-of-Analysis Problem in International Relations," in Klaus Knorr and Sidney Verba (eds.), *The International System: Theoretical Essays* (Princeton, NJ: Princeton University Press, 1961), pp. 77–94.

20.   James N. Rosenau, for example, identifies six levels of decision: (1) individual decision-makers and their personalities; (2) individual decision-makers and their positions; (3) governmental structure; (4) the structure of society; (5) the relations that exist between one nation-state and other international actors; and (6) the international system itself. See James N. Rosenau, *The Scientific Study of Foreign Policy* (New York: The Free Press, 1971), especially Chap. 5.

21.   For a fascinating application of the levels-of-analysis concept to the Cuban Missile Crisis, see Graham Allison, *Essence of Decision: Explaining the Cuban Missile Crisis* (Boston: Little, Brown, 1971).

PART ONE

The Participants' Framework

ACTORS AND INTERESTS IN INTERNATIONAL POLITICS

We are stranded between old conceptions of political conduct and a wholly new conception, between the inadequacy of the nation-state and the emerging imperative of global community.

—*Henry A. Kissinger*

Is it East versus West or man against man?

—*from "Burning Heart," by Survivor*

The international system is in a state of flux.

This is not only because of the end of the East–West conflict, but also because the primacy of the chief actor in international affairs, the state, is increasingly being challenged by a startling variety of relative newcomers to the international arena.

These newcomers include multinational corporations, international governmental organizations, nongovernmental organizations, and even individuals. During the last 30 years, all have steadily increased the roles that they play in the global community. In at least one instance during the early 1970s, the multinational corporation International Telephone and Telegraph (ITT) in Chile played a fundamental role in an internal change in government in a nation-state. As long ago as 1978, General Motors and Exxon individually had more annual income than all but 22 separate nation-states.

International governmental organizations have also challenged the dominance of the state. The European Community (EC), for example, is an international governmental organization consisting of the European Atomic Energy Community (Euratom, created in 1958), the European Coal and Steel Community (ECSC, 1952), and the European Economic Community (EEC, 1958). Since 1967, the EC has been directed by a Council of Ministers, which consists of cabinet ministers of the member states of the EC. The EC Council, by consent of EC members, has the authority to make binding decisions on its members without requiring their approval. Thus, EC member states surrendered some of their national decision-making authority to an international governmental organization. In addition, the EC has sources of revenue that do not depend on member state donations and employs thousands of people who clearly have a stake in the continuing vitality of the EC. In 1979, the EC's European Parliament was chosen by direct elections, and in 1985 the EC adopted a comprehensive program called the Single European Act designed to create a single market throughout Europe at the end of 1992. Even more strikingly, the leaders of the 12 states that made up the EC in December 1991 concluded the Maastricht Treaty, which envisions the EC moving toward political and economic unity by the end of the century. Since then, however, the Maastricht Treaty has run into difficulties as citizens in several EC states made it clear that in their views, rapid movement toward European political and economic unity was premature. Even so, it is clear that the EC challenges the state system in Europe.

Yet another class of actor, the international nongovernmental organization (NGO), also challenges the primacy of the state. NGOs include many types of organizations ranging from national liberation movements, which seek to establish new governments within existing states or to create new states from either the colonial dependencies or internal territory of existing states, to organizations such as Amnesty International or Greenpeace, which seek to mobilize international public opinion to apply pressure to national governments to alter a particular policy or policies.

Even individuals occupy prominent places, as individuals, in contemporary international relations. Until his death in 1989, Soviet physicist Andrei Sakharov's statements and views about the U.S.S.R. had a major impact on Western perceptions of the Soviet Union. Similarly, Mother Theresa's services to the poor in India captured the admiration of the international community throughout the 1980s. Meanwhile, British and American rock stars held concerts for international famine relief, and former U.S. President Jimmy Carter, acting as a private citizen, traveled to Africa and the Middle East to try to end conflict there.

None of this means that the state is dead, in Europe or elsewhere. Indeed, the state as a class of actor still reigns supreme as it has for most of the past three centuries. But new and influential actors have joined it on the international stage, and if an accurate understanding of contemporary international affairs is to be developed, it is also necessary to understand who they are, what their objectives are, and how they seek to achieve them.

The purposes of the next four chapters, then, are to explore the following questions:

- Who are the major actors in international affairs?
- What objectives do they seek?
- Who determines these objectives?
- Where did these actors come from?
- How important are they today?
- How are they changing?

CHAPTER 2

The State, Nationalism, and the National Interest

- What are the differences between a state and a nation?
- How has the international system of states evolved over time?
- What is nationalism?
- What is the national interest?
- How does the balance of power work?
- How secure is the future for the nation–state?

The state has dominated global politics for over 300 years. Arising in Western Europe from the ruins of the feudal system that preceded it, the state's dominance is generally traced back to the **Peace of Westphalia** of 1648. The Westphalian Peace ended the Thirty Years' War in Europe and established a system of sovereign entities that rejected subservience to the political authority of the pope and the Roman Catholic Church. The old system of accepted papal authority over the principalities and fiefdoms of Europe had been overthrown, and a new system of geographically fixed self-ruling political entities that accepted no higher authority than themselves had been born.

The birth of the new state system had been gradual; it evolved over centuries. Whereas previous rulers had accepted their subservience to the papacy in Rome, even in some instances being willing to allow the church to dictate what weapons could and could not be used in combat, the Westphalian system of states placed the newly liberated rulers of states in control of their own destinies. Without a higher authority to dictate their actions or determine their rankings, rulers were free to maximize their power by whatever means they saw fit within the confines of a broadly defined system of international law laid down by the Westphalian treaties.

Central to Westphalian international law were the concepts of legitimacy, sovereignty, and duty. **Legitimacy** meant simply that all states had a right to exist, and that the authority of the king within his country was both supreme and rightfully his. States could fight to rearrange their relative rankings but not to remove an opposing ruler from power.

Sovereignty, by comparison, was the internationally accepted viewpoint that no authority higher than the state existed. States and their kings could pursue the objectives that they thought proper by whatever means they chose and did not have to accept any authority higher than their own. This concept of state sovereignty was a fundamental departure from earlier years when all the rules of the Holy Roman Empire followed the dictate of the pope. Sovereignty, then, asserted the primacy of states and rejected external controls on them.

Nevertheless, certain rules of behavior did exist. Under the developing concept of international law and because of their sovereign status, states had formal **duties** as well—rules were established and followed for declaring and fighting war, for adhering to treaties and alliances, for continuing to recognize the legitimacy of other rulers and the territorial integrity of their states, and for exchanging and treating diplomatic representatives. To a great extent, the Westphalian system's emphasis on legitimacy, sovereignty, and duty formalized international relations. In a certain sense, this emphasis has a tremendous impact even today.

The seventeenth century, however, was a much simpler century than the twentieth. The concepts of legitimacy, sovereignty, and duty on which the Peace of Westphalia was based are no longer universally accepted or meaningfully relevant in the contemporary era. Even the meaning of the concept "state" has been clouded by time and varied usage. Thus, before we continue our examination of the evolution of the Westphalian state system, we must clarify some concepts.

THE MEANING OF STATE, NATION, AND NATION–STATE

The terms *state*, *nation*, and *nation-state* are usually used interchangeably in discussions of international relations. Technically, however, these terms have different meanings. In certain contexts, the differences in meaning may have great significance. Therefore, an understanding of the more precise definitions is important.

A **state** is a geographically bounded entity governed by a central authority that has the ability to make laws, rules, and decisions, and to enforce those laws, rules, and decisions within its boundaries. A state is also a legal entity, recognized under international law as the fundamental decision-making unit of the international legal system. States determine their own policies (at least in theory), and establish their own forms of government, which may differ significantly from state to state. Those people who inhabit the territory of a state may or may not be citizens of that state, depending on the laws passed by the government of that state. Regardless of their citizenship status, inhabitants of the territory of a state are subject to the laws of that state.

A **nation**, by contrast, need not necessarily be either geographically bounded or legally defined. A nation is a grouping of people who view themselves as being linked to one another in some manner. A nation is therefore as much a psychological fixation as anything else. Groupings of people who consider themselves to be ethnically, culturally, or linguistically related may thus be considered a nation. Nations may exist without territorial control, as did the Jewish nation before 1947 (when the *state* of Israel was founded), Ukrainians in the former Soviet Union, and various Indian tribes in the United States. Other groups calling themselves national liberation movements also exist and seek to establish territorial control in a certain area, thereby becoming a state. The Palestine Liberation Organization

(PLO) in the Middle East and the Sendero Luminoso in Peru are examples of self-styled national liberation movements.

The term **nation-state** means a state whose inhabitants consider themselves to be a nation.[1] It is a geographically bounded legal entity under a single government, the population of which psychologically considers itself to be in some way, shape, or form related. The term *nation-state* is historically more recent than either state or nation and reflects the growing convergence in recent years between the two older terms.

However, many countries are commonly called nation-states even though they are not. For example, in Africa, territory included in most states that received independence during the 1950s and 1960s was based on what had been the old colonial boundaries. In some cases, several different ethnic groups were included in one country. Thus, some of these states count many nations as their inhabitants. In other cases, ethnic groups were divided by state boundaries and found themselves inhabiting several different states. The same was true of the former Soviet Union. Technically, such entities that include large percentages of more than one nationality are states, not nation-states.

Despite the extremely important differences between the terms *state*, *nation*, and *nation-state*, these terms are often used interchangeably. This practice is so widespread that in the minds of most casual observers of international affairs, there are no differences among the three terms. However, the significant differences in meaning that are hidden by the modern practice of interchanging terms should be kept in mind.

NATIONALISM

Nationalism is closely related to the concept of a nation. In its most basic form, "nationalism" is a psychological force that binds people together who identify with each other. It refers both to the feelings of attachment to one another that members of a nation have, and to the sense of pride that members of a nation have in themselves and their nation.

Over time, nationalism has in many cases also become closely related to the concept of a state, or more precisely, to a nation-state. But this phenomenon was not always so. When the Westphalian system of states was first emerging in Europe during the mid-seventeenth century, nationalism was only rarely associated with states. Rather, citizens of states pledged allegiance, when they pledged allegiance at all, to the individual who ruled the state. "*L'état, c'est moi,*" ("The state, it is I.") said Louis XIV of France; and he was right, at least in most of Europe until the end of the eighteenth century.

Gradually, however, people who lived in certain states came to believe that the state was theirs as much as the king's. Further, as peoples who lived in a state began to identify more and more with each other as well as—and in some cases, instead of—the king, modern nationalism and the modern nation-state was born.

Nationalism may be expressed in many ways. Efforts to raise standards of living, to win more gold medals than other nations at an Olympics, or to conquer adjoining territories are all different manifestations of nationalism. From these few examples alone, it may be seen that depending on how it is expressed, nationalism may be constructive and helpful, benign and moderate, or destructive and dangerous.

As a psychological force that binds people who identify with one another, nationalism has played and continues to play an immense role in international affairs. Since the eighteenth century, and at an accelerated pace during the nineteenth and twentieth centuries, nationalism has manifested itself most visibly in the desire of the members of a nation to control and govern the territory in which they live. It may thus be argued that in one sense, nationalism is what brought about events and trends as diverse as the American revolution, in which British subjects rejected kingly rule and sought to govern themselves; the collapse of European colonial empires, during which peoples throughout the world struggled against European imperialism and demanded self-government; and the end of the Soviet Union, fomented to a great extent by the demands of different ethnic groups that they, not Moscow, rule themselves.

There is another side to nationalism as well. In its more extreme form, nationalism does more than simply psychologically bind people together who identify with one another, instill them with pride in who and what they are, and lead them to seek self-rule. In its more extreme form, nationalism can also lead a people to ascribe superiority to themselves over others, and create a desire to control and exploit other peoples, their territories, and their wealth. This extreme form of nationalism was one of the main driving forces, along with economics, behind European colonial expansion during the eighteenth, nineteenth, and early twentieth centuries. It also contributed significantly to the national rivalries that led to World War I, and to the German and Japanese territorial expansion that precipitated World War II.

Regardless of how nationalism is expressed, it requires individuals to identify with a larger group. Often, as in Germany, Japan, France, and elsewhere as well, this larger group is based on ethnicity. Sometimes, as in the case of the United States, it is not. In the U.S. case, few would deny that a "U.S. nationalism" exists, but it is a multi-ethnic and theoretically inclusive nationalism, tied to the U.S. government, U.S. citizens, and the ideals that the United States espouses.

Technically, the United States—and other states that have large percentages of more than one nationality living within them—may or may not be nation-states. Nevertheless, citizens of such states may be "nationalists" about the state in which they live. Indeed, in some cases, the United States included, the citizens of multi-ethnic states may exhibit more nationalism toward and about their state than the citizens of "true" nation-states. In these instances, theoretical and definitional differences between "states" and "nation-states" become moot.

Recognizing this, governments of multi-ethnic states often attempt to transfer the loyalty of their citizens from the old group of identification to the new state, thereby creating a sense of state nationalism, and in so doing, the equivalent of a nation-state. Sometimes, it is difficult to tell if this effort has succeeded.

This was the case in the former Soviet Union. For years, the Soviet government and most people around the world believed that the U.S.S.R had successfully created "Soviet nationalism," that is, a sense of Soviet nationhood. But as Soviet citizens became increasingly free to express their real sentiments as a result of Mikhail Gorbachev's reforms, it became clear that most Soviet citizens still identified more with their ethnic nationality than with the U.S.S.R. Hence, "nationalism," in the traditional sense of identification with one's own ethnic group, contributed immensely to the dissolution of the Soviet Union.

Much the same thing happened in Yugoslavia and Czechoslovakia, where ethnic loyalty proved stronger than the loyalty of peoples to either the Yugoslavian or Czechoslovakian states. In the Yugoslav case, ethnic nationalism led to ethnic conflict, civil war, and thousands of deaths. In the Czechoslovakian case, ethnic nationalism led to cordial discussions and the decision by the Czech and Slovak peoples to create peacefully two separate nation-states from what formerly had been one state that included two nations.

Elsewhere around the world, the pull of nationalism remains strong in the 1990s. In many states, some of which have long been considered nation-states, ethnic nationalism has gained new strength, calling into question whether currently established states will survive as presently constituted. In addition to those states already discussed, other states as diverse as Belgium, Canada, India, Iraq, Spain, and Turkey are challenged by internal national groups, some of which call themselves "national liberation movements," that seek to break away to set up their own independent nation-states.

Nationalism, then, has been and remains a powerful force in international affairs. It is a major part of today's international system of states. But it is not a force that necessarily supports the status quo. As the following two sections will show, nationalism has been and remains a powerful force for change in the evolution of the international system of states.

THE EVOLUTION OF THE STATE SYSTEM TO 1870

The Westphalian system of states was a European system that eventually expanded to include all corners of the globe. (See Table 2–1.) However, even before the state system became firmly established in Europe, European powers had begun to expand their empires outside of Europe. By the beginning of the seventeenth century, Dutch, English, French, Portuguese, and Spanish adventurers had explored every inhabited continent. Their parent countries followed their explorations by using military power to create overseas colonial empires.

The First Round of Empire

Almost without exception, European states built their empires during the sixteenth, seventeenth, and eighteenth centuries for the express purpose of increasing their wealth, power, and prestige. Vast colonial empires were created in North and South America, and gold, silver, furs, and other forms of wealth flowed from the New World to the courts of European kings and royalty.

A general pattern of colonization was followed by most European states. After the adventurers proved the feasibility of a journey or the existence of a new (for Europeans) land, European merchants examined the possibility of commercial profit. European governments, aware of the possibility of increasing their own power and wealth and thereby enhancing their position in the competition between states, quickly claimed the new lands as colonies, and chartered and

TABLE 2–1   The Evolution of the Modern State System

1648	Treaty of Wesphalia establishes modern state system.
16th, 17th, 18th cent.	European states establish colonial empires, especially in North and South America; this is the first round of empire.
1775–1780	American and French revolutions challenge the rule of kings; nationalism emerges as a powerful international force.
1804–1815	Napoleon's French empire threatens to overturn European state system.
1815–1870	The Concert of Europe protects the legitimacy of the state and royal rule.
1870–1914	European states divide Africa and much of the Middle East and Asia in the second round of empire; the United States and Japan also acquire overseas colonial holdings.
1914–1918	World War I shakes the world system of states.
1870–1930	The number of states in Europe expands from about 15 to over 35; this is the first proliferation of states.
1918–1939	The coming to power of the Bolsheviks in Russia and the Nazis in Germany challenges the legitimacy of the state system.
1939–1945	World War II.
1945–1990	The second proliferation of states takes place as old colonial empires fall; the number of states increases from about 54 in 1945 to about 170 in 1990; this period also marks the longest uninterrupted time of peace among major powers since the inception of the state system. State formation slows markedly during the last decade of this period as decolonization is achieved on virtually a universal basis.
1991–Today	The third proliferation of states takes place as established states break up. Czechoslovakia, the Soviet Union, and Yugoslavia dissolve and form at least 21 new states, and dissolution threatens other states around the world as well.

funded commercial companies to explore and develop the opportunities for wealth. Inevitably, conflicts between states over colonial holdings broke out, and naval and army forces, financed and manned by the states, became necessary adjuncts of the drive for empire.

The economic philosophy that led to this first round of empire-building was **mercantilism**. First espoused by Jean Baptiste Colbert, Minister of Finance to Louis XIV of France, mercantilism taught that state power was derived from wealth. To maximize power, wealth had to be maximized in any way possible. Gold, silver, and furs were important, but rulers of the day considered it equally necessary to maintain a positive balance of trade, that is to say, to export more than they imported. Colonies became important not only as sources of valuable resources, but also as captive markets.

If mercantilism provided the economic rationale for the first round of empire-building, then scientific-technical innovations in navigation and transportation, as well as in the military, provided the capabilities. In navigation, widespread use of the sextant permitted seafarers to chart their courses accurately, and the European development of the square-rigger allowed ships to point closer into the wind and increased their cargo space. The marriage of gunpower and heavy cannon with the square-rigged sailing vessel permitted European powers, Great Britain in particular, to bring heavy firepower to bear on enemy ships and enemy shores. Although often overlooked, these and other scientific-technical innovations allowed Europeans to travel beyond the confines of their home continent and carry their living requirements and military capabilities with them.

Attacks on Regal Legitimacy

By the end of the eighteenth century, the mercantilist philosophy was decreasing in popularity and persuasiveness and was gradually being replaced by an international trading system that stressed free trade, that is, trade with little or no government intervention. This logic was persuasively argued by Adam Smith in his *Wealth of Nations*. Bullion was not the determinant of national power and prestige, Smith maintained, but capital and goods were. Thus, free trade became a logical adjunct to Smith's laissez-faire economic philosophy.

With the supporting logic of mercantilism removed, colonies became less important. European states continued to maintain their overseas empires, but they became increasingly distracted from non-European affairs by events closer to home. The existence of the European system of states itself was being questioned, first by the French Revolution and then by the revolution's offspring, Napoleon.

During the fifteenth and sixteenth centuries, European explorers ventured to every inhabited continent, and European countries established large overseas empires in their wake. Here, in an 1846 painting by John Vanderlyn currently displayed in the U.S. Capitol, Christopher Columbus lands on the island of Guanahani, West Indies, on October 12, 1492, early in the first round of empire. (© 1977 Instructional Resources Corporation, The American History Slide Collection.)

Following the Peace of Westphalia, the answer to the question of who was to rule the state was considered a given: the king. Within any state, the king's word was law. The regal mantle would be passed from father to son, and the state's fortunes would follow the skills and fortunes of the king. If a king proved unable or unwilling to exercise his authority within his state and was forced to share it, as had occurred in Great Britain, that was acceptable to the royal families of Europe as long as neither the legitimacy of the king nor of his state was challenged, and as long as his realm did not challenge the legitimacy of other kings and their states.

To some extent, the revolt of Great Britain's 13 North American colonies and their Declaration of Independence in 1776 challenged the self-perpetuating continuity of the Westphalian system. By declaring their independence, the North American colonies rejected King George's right to rule them. Some Europeans recognized this challenge. Others did not. In either case, North America was an ocean away, and the actions of the North Americans did not threaten the fundamental stability of the European state system and its rulers. By the early nineteenth century, most Spanish possessions in South America followed the North American lead and declared their independence as well. Regal legitimacy had been rejected in North and South America, but the legitimacy of the state had not been. The European state system was now in the Americas.

The French Revolution was another matter. France was in the heart of Europe, and at the core of the state system. Louis XVI was the legitimate heir to the throne, and he exercised his regal rights as kings had done within their respective states for nearly a century and a half. The French Revolution of 1789 rejected the legitimacy of regal authority, asserted that the people of the state were sovereign, and called on French nationalism to raise France to preeminence in Europe.

France was thus a real and immediate problem for other European states. Louis XVI was beheaded, and a reign of terror swept France. In 1804, after a series of dazzling military victories throughout Europe, Napoleon Bonaparte emerged as Emperor of France.

Napoleon's dream was to create another Roman Empire in Europe. If the French Revolution challenged the legitimacy of kings to govern, Napoleon threatened the very existence of the concept of the state. After establishing his empire throughout most of western Europe, Napoleon overextended his reach and attacked Russia in 1812. Defeated by the Russian winter, Napoleon's empire declined, and within three years a coalition of states destroyed it. Napoleon's last defeat came at Waterloo in 1815.

In Europe, regal legitimacy was again restored, and the state system had been preserved. But in some states, nationalism had been joined to the state, and the era of the modern nation-state was about to begin.

The Second Round of Empire

After the defeat of Napoleon, European states, with the exception of Great Britain, joined together in the so-called Concert of Europe, which consciously sought to preserve and protect the state and regal legitimacy. To a great extent, the concert succeeded for a half century. Great Britain, meanwhile, acted as an independent entity that sought to preserve a balance of power among the states of Europe.[2]

Beginning in about 1870, a second wave of empire-building swept Europe and eventually the United States and Japan. Explanations for the new wave of imperial conquest varied. Diplomatic historians, and later political realists, declared that traditional politics was at work, with states either seeking to improve their status in the international ranking of states or attempting to maintain the European balance of power. Lenin, as we have seen, believed that imperialism was simply the highest stage of capitalism, brought about by capitalism's need for more markets, less expensive resources, and cheaper labor. Whatever the causes, by the early twentieth century, European states again had built colonial empires. The empires were created primarily by superior European military power. By 1900, nearly all of Africa with the exceptions of Liberia and Ethiopia had been divided by seven European states. Asia, including the "Inner Kingdom" of China, had been similarly dismembered. The British Empire was immense. By 1900, Great Britain governed one-fifth of the world's land mass and one-fourth of its population.

Non-European states also joined the rush to empire. The United States annexed Hawaii, leased the Panama Canal Zone "in perpetuity" from the American-created state of Panama, acquired the Philippines from Spain, and granted Cuba its independence only after having an amendment (the Platt Amendment) added to the Cuban constitution that permitted American armed intervention in Cuban affairs when the United States deemed it necessary.[3] Meanwhile, Japan acquired Korea and Taiwan. Imperialism had become the order of the day, and European-style nation-states dominated international affairs.

THE EVOLUTION OF THE STATE SYSTEM: 1870 TO TODAY

At the beginning of the twentieth century, the nation-state's position as supreme arbiter of international affairs seemed secure, and the international state system appeared stable. However, appearances were deceiving. Lurking just below the calm surface of the European state system were forces that soon unleashed the cataclysm of World War I.

The First Proliferation of States

The second wave of imperial expansion inevitably led to economic exploitation of colonial holdings and increased rivalry among the European states themselves. One manifestation of this rivalry was a major arms race among the European powers. For the most part, the struggle for prestige and territory was confined to Asia and Africa. In some instances, however, territorial struggles occurred in Europe as well. Following France's defeat by Prussia in the 1870 Franco-Prussian War, Prussia annexed the French province of Alsace-Lorraine. This annexation, as well as the military defeat itself, was a humiliating blow to French national pride, and revanchist sentiment swelled within the French nation. In addition, particularly in the Austro-Hungarian and Ottoman empires, but to a lesser degree in Czarist Russia as well, national groups accelerated their struggles for national independence from the remaining old and crumbling multinational dynastic empires.

In Europe, a subtle change was taking place in the state system. It was acquiring new members. During the half century before the beginning of World War I, the number of states in Europe grew from about 15 to over 25. This proliferation occurred in two ways. In some cases, as in Albania and Serbia, new states were born as national groupings broke away from traditional empires. In other cases, as in Germany and Italy, smaller territorial units formed modern nation-states. Concurrently with this proliferation of nation-states, the countries of Europe led by the militarily more powerful among them sought to protect themselves and their possessions, and to either maintain the existing distribution of power in Europe or change it by establishing a rather rigid network of alliances that stretched throughout the continent, and as a result of their colonial holdings, beyond.

As we have already seen, alliances had long been a part of the European state system. In the past, however, alliances had been relatively flexible. For example, Great Britain regularly aligned itself with different countries throughout the nineteenth century in an effort to maintain the existing distribution of power in Europe (which, not coincidentally, significantly favored Britain). The two major alliances of the early twentieth century, the Triple Entente including Great Britain, France, and Russia, and the Triple Alliance including Germany, Austria-Hungary, and Italy, were much more rigid in character. In addition, several of the states in the two major alliances were tied by secret treaties to other states not in the Entente or Alliance.

The slide toward World War I would have been comic if its results were not so tragic. Following the assassination of Archduke Ferdinand of Austria-Hungary at Sarajevo, Austria-Hungary demanded that Serbia permit it to enter Serbia to search for the assassins. Serbia refused. Austria-Hungary prepared to march into Serbia anyway, and Russia, committed by secret treaty to Serbia's defense, began to mobilize. Czar Nicholas at first ordered a partial mobilization of Russian forces, intending only to show the Austro-Hungarians that Russia would in fact defend Serbia. However, the Russian military leadership informed him that partial mobilization would hopelessly complicate full mobilization, and urged him to proclaim full mobilization immediately because the Russian mobilization rate was slower than that of any other European power. The Czar complied with his generals' urgings.[4] Germany, viewing the Russian action with alarm, began its mobilization. Meanwhile, Austria-Hungary, fearing that Germany would renege on its "blank check" promise of support for Austria-Hungary in the event of an Austro-Hungarian conflict with Russia, refused to respond to a series of urgent diplomatic communications from Berlin and marched into Serbia. World War I had begun.

The savagery of World War I appalled rational men and women everywhere, but the destruction went on for four bloody years. Blame for the war was variously attributed, depending on which model of international relations was used. Following the war, collective security, international law, and arms control were all proposed as remedies for the scourge of modern war. But by far the most powerful single concept emerging from the war was the principle of national self-determination, espoused most forcefully by the American President Woodrow

Wilson. Henceforth, under this principle, nationalities themselves would determine who would rule them. Theoretically, self-rule would minimize the thrust for territorial expansion and make war less likely. Actually, self-determination further accelerated the growth in numbers of new nation-states.

As a result of the acceptance of self-determination, the number of nation-states in Europe leaped to over 35 by the early 1930s. Six new states—Austria, Czechoslovakia, Hungary, Poland, Romania, and Yugoslavia—were formed from the old Austro-Hungarian Empire alone. Other states were carved from the Russian Empire, which had evolved into the Bolshevik-ruled Soviet Union. Under the League of Nations' mandate system, land in former German-held colonial territories and in the former Ottoman Empire was transferred to other nation-states with the specific intent of eventual self-rule and creation of still additional new states.[5] Thus, in Africa, Great Britain received most of Tanganyika, and shared Cameroons and Togoland with France, whereas the Union of South Africa was mandated Southwest Africa. In the Middle East, France received Syria, whereas Iraq, Transjordan, and Palestine all became subject to the British crown. In the Pacific, Australia, New Zealand, and Japan were all beneficiaries of the league's mandate system. World War I had shaken the state system, but it had also spread the seeds for its further proliferation.

Attacks on Bourgeois Legitimacy

Whereas the collapse of dynastic rule in Austria-Hungary and the Ottoman Empire paved the way for the creation of additional traditional nation-states, the collapse of Czarist Russia led to the formation of a state that proclaimed itself to be of a fundamentally new type. Czar Nicholas II abdicated in February 1917. He was replaced by a provisional government that intended to keep Russia in the war and planned to hold Western-style free elections to form a new government. However, in 1917, the Bolshevik party under V. I. Lenin seized power and proclaimed the creation of a Soviet state under the control of the Russian working class.

Bolshevism was only one variant of Russian Marxism. To Marxists, all history was the record of struggle between classes, and the state was simply the tool that the strongest class used to assure its position and to exploit weaker classes. Under the capitalist economic system of private ownership of the means of production, the strongest class consisted of those who owned the means of production, or the bourgeoisie. The bourgeoisie therefore used the state to maintain its position of power and exploit the working class, or proletariat. Lenin, as we have already seen, further argued that capitalism led directly to imperialism and war. With the overthrow of capitalism, Lenin concluded, exploitation, imperialism, and war would disappear as well.

The Bolshevik party, which eventually became the Communist Party of the Soviet Union, declared itself the spokesperson for the proletariat of Russia. Lenin and his party maintained that their seizure of power marked the first instance that the proletariat class controlled a state. In Russia, Bolsheviks believed, the illegitimate rule of the bourgeois class had been terminated, and the exploitation of man by man would cease.

Some Bolsheviks expected proletariat revolutions to break out across Europe. Indeed, in Germany and Hungary, Marxist governments did seize power briefly, but were soon overthrown. Thus, the Soviet Union remained in the post–World War I world the only socialist state, or as Lenin said, "the only state of a new type." Joseph Stalin, Lenin's successor, reinterpreted this as "capitalist encirclement."

Leaders of other states viewed this "state of a new type" as a new and virulent threat to the international community and acted to suppress it. They extended limited support to Russian groups that opposed the Bolsheviks, and small contingents of Western European, American, and Japanese combat forces landed in the czar's old empire. However, after the four bloody years of World War I, none of the interventionist states were seriously committed to the conflict. All eventually withdrew.

Soviet rhetoric and actions gave other states cause for concern. Asserting clear and active hostility to the "exploitive" governments of other states, Soviet propaganda called for the proletariat of other nations to rise up against their oppressors. In 1920, Bolshevik forces invaded Poland and attempted to establish a "proletariat dictatorship" there but failed. Although Soviet rhetoric and actions became less revolutionary during the 1920s, a fundamental hostility remained between the Soviet Union and most other states throughout the 1920s and 1930s. Bourgeois legitimacy had been challenged, and an allegedly new type of state had come into existence in the Soviet Union. This fact would have tremendous significance for the future of the international system of states.

Similarly, in Germany, another allegedly new type of state came into existence. Based on theories of racial superiority and the subservience of non-Germanic people, national socialism, or Nazism, preached a philosophy of expansion. It was an assault both on all non-Germans and on the system of nation-states, for it sought to reduce Europe and beyond to vassals of Hitler and his minions. From this perspective, World War II in Europe was fought as a result of Nazism's offensive against the state system in Europe.

The Second Proliferation of States

As we have seen, World War I shattered the old European empires of Austria-Hungary, Czarist Russia, and the Ottoman Empire, and led to the creation of a number of new states. Following World War II, a similar phenomenon occurred as the states of Europe gradually granted or were forced to grant independence to their former colonial territories. By 1980, with the exception of some 40 dependencies most of which were inhabited by fewer than 100,000 people, European empires were a thing of the past.

With the end of the Belgian, British, French, Portuguese, and Spanish empires, the European-style state had conquered the world. As Table 2–2 shows, the number of states increased drastically in the post–World War II era. Over 50 states are in Africa alone. Some of the new states remained closely tied to their old colonial masters, sometimes for economic reasons and other times for psychological or cultural reasons. In other cases, the governments of newly independent territories reject any ties with the former colonial ruling power.

Colonialism, then, was the vehicle that led to the second proliferation of states. Colonialism also left its mark in other ways. Almost invariably, former colonial territories, that is, those states that received their independence following

Communism was the brainchild of Karl Marx, pictured here. A Russian variation of communism, Bolshevism, presented an early challenge to bourgeois legitimacy. (Air University Photo Library.)

World War II, are the so-called less-developed countries, the poor nations of the earth. Although perceptions differ as to the causes of that poverty, few analysts anywhere rejected the assertion that the disparity in wealth that exists between the rich "Northern" states (the established industrial states, primarily located in the northern hemisphere) and the poor "Southern" states (the so-called Developing World, primarily located in the southern hemisphere) is a cause both for concern and for potential conflict.[6]

Similarly, in many newly independent states, old colonial boundaries were followed as new states received their independence. In some instances, because of this practice, one nation or tribe sometimes found itself divided among several states, whereas in other instances, one nation or tribe found itself in a multinational state, in the minority, and powerless to influence governmental policy decisions. Thus, colonialism not only led to the second proliferation of nation-states, but also carried with it the seeds of instability and uncertainty that plague so much of the world today.

The Third Proliferation of States

The end of the colonial era led many people to conclude that the number of independent states in the international community by the 1980s had reached a relatively stable maximum of about 170. Indeed, as Table 2–2 shows, during the entire decade of the 1980s, the number of independent states increased only

TABLE 2–2   Independent States, 1945–1993

Year	No. of Independent States
1945	54
1950	75
1955	84
1960	107
1965	125
1970	135
1975	155
1980	165
1985	170
1990	170
1993	190

SOURCE: 1945–1960, from Michael Wallace and J. David Singer, "Intergovernmental Organization in the Global System, 1815–1964: A Quantitative Description," *International Organization*, Vol. 24 (Spring 1970), 272; 1965–1993, United Nations estimates.

Note: These figures are estimates. The international community does not accept a universal definition for "independent state." Therefore, some states are viewed as independent by one government, but not by another.

from 165 in 1980 to 170 by 1990. This was a marked decrease in the rate of growth from the preceding 35 years, when during no decade did the number of independent states grow by fewer than 28 new states.

Many people were wrong. As Chapter 1 has already shown, the struggle against colonialism sometimes influenced national groups to set aside temporarily their differences as they struggled against colonialism, and the dangers of the East-West conflict usually influenced national groups to accept their inclusion in the state in which they found themselves. With traditional colonial empires having disappeared in the 1970s, and with the end of the East-West conflict in the late 1980s and early 1990s, these two factors that held nationalism in check in many areas of the world were removed.

As a result, the early 1990s witnessed yet another significant proliferation of nation-states as the Soviet Union, Yugoslavia, and Czechoslovakia all broke up. The Soviet Union's dissolution led to the creation of 15 nation-states out of the U.S.S.R.'s former 15 republics. The actual breakup of the Soviet Union occurred reasonably peacefully, but violence nevertheless sometimes flared between ethnic groups within individual former Soviet republics as smaller ethnic groups fought for their own independence from several of the newly independent states. Thus, the possibility existed that the collapse of the Soviet Union would lead to the creation of more than 15 new states.

Similarly, in the former Yugoslavia, it was not clear how many new states would finally emerge. Slovenia and Macedonia all seceded relatively peacefully, but when Croatia seceded, civil war broke out, and hundreds of people died in the fighting. It was even worse in Bosnia, where thousands died when warfare erupted following Bosnia-Herzegovina's attempt to withdraw from the remains of the Serbian-dominated former Yugoslavia. Conversely, Czechoslovakia proved able to dissolve itself peacefully into the Czech and Slovak republics.

Thus, by early 1993, at least twenty-one new states had been carved from the territories of what two years earlier had been only three states.

But the struggle by ethnic groups to create their own self-ruled independent states was not confined to the Soviet Union, Yugoslavia, and Czechoslovakia. Many other ethnic groups throughout the world also either launched or accelerated drives for national independence from the states in which they were included. Sometimes these drives were peaceful, as in some Scots' efforts to secede from Great Britain and some Quebecois' efforts to withdraw from Canada. In other cases these drives were violent, as in some Basques' efforts to secede from Spain; the Kurds' efforts to establish their own state out of Iraq, Iran, and Turkey; or the Sikhs' efforts to withdraw from India.

And in still other instances, as in Angola and Afghanistan, it became clear that wars that had once been considered part of the East–West conflict were in fact at least as much—and probably more—civil wars between different ethnic groups or tribes seeking to assert their own national power and identity.

There is reason to believe, then, that the international community has entered an era of a third proliferation of nation-states. This reality has the potential to make the remaining years of the twentieth century a period of considerable change and instability.[7]

The proliferation of states also led to another problem, namely, the multiplication of the number of decision-making units in the world. This often complicated the conduct of foreign policy by states. For example, during the height of European colonial power each European government had to take into account the reaction of only 20 to 30 states to a particular policy. In the 1990s, however, governments need to take into account the reaction of as many as 190 states to a policy.

Obviously, some states are more important than others to a particular government, and many states may even be ignored. Nevertheless, the point to be made is simple: The proliferation of states has tremendously complicated the conduct of foreign policy. In 1918, perhaps 50 states existed throughout the world, and perhaps 1,225 sets of bilateral political relations existed between and among them. If only 150 states existed, then 11,175 sets of bilateral political relations would be possible. With approximately 190 states in existence, the number of possible bilateral political relationship far exceeds even this.[8]

Indeed, then, the world has become far more complex than it has been, if only because so many states now exist.

THE NATIONAL INTEREST

Throughout the history of the evolution of the state, states have recognized no higher authority than themselves. Obviously, then, the state is the entity that defines its own interests and that determines how it will attempt to achieve them. A state's interests are called the national interest, and the methods and actions it employs to attempt to achieve its national interests are called national policy.

Unfortunately, however, the concept of national interest is extremely ambiguous. Who within a state defines the national interest? Do national interests change when governments change either peacefully or by force? Which group or groups within a state define who the friends and enemies of a state are? When serious internal disagreements exist concerning national interests and national policy, which view of interest and policy is truly national? Does a state in fact have long-term interests determined by geography, resource base, population, cultural ties, and other factors that transcend short-term or mid-term definitions of national interest that are influenced by the politics of the day? The ambiguities are many.

These questions are much more than academic inquiries relevant only to the classroom. Throughout history, individuals and groups have appealed to the national interest to justify the policies that they preferred. Hannibal believed that the national interest of Carthage dictated war against Rome; he may have been correct, but because of his failure to defeat Rome in the Punic Wars the Romans eventually sacked and destroyed Carthage. Thomas Jefferson, despite his reputation as pro-French and despite his opposition to a strong central government, upon hearing that Napoleon intended to occupy New Orleans as part of a secret agreement with Spain, informed the French emperor that the United States considered whoever possessed New Orleans to be "our natural and habitual enemy"; Jefferson then promptly expanded the power of the central government by buying not only New Orleans but the entire Louisiana Territory. Nine years later, Napoleon determined that France's national interests dictated he should initiate the disastrous Russian campaign.

National interest is variously defined today as well. Throughout his administration, Ronald Reagan believed that the American national interest was served by a significant U.S. arms buildup. Other Americans disagreed, arguing that Reagan's emphasis on defense actually undermined U.S. economic strength and damaged the U.S. social structure. Meanwhile, Mikhail Gorbachev concluded that the Soviet national interest demanded he implement radical political, economic, social, and foreign policy reforms. Other Soviet officials felt Gorbachev's policies hurt the U.S.S.R., and in 1991 launched an abortive coup to remove the Soviet president. In China in 1989, thousands of students and workers took to the streets to voice their views on where China's national interests lie—in greater political freedom. But the Chinese Communist party's leaders had a different view of what China's national interests were, and with the help of the Chinese army and its tanks, guns, and men, the party's view prevailed.

What, then, is national interest, and who is to define it? What factors should be considered when an attempt is made to define it? With roughly 190 states in the world today, these and other related questions are of great importance. Perhaps the most significant question, however, is what should "count" when national interest is being defined. Inevitably, different individuals give different answers.

To some, *economic criteria* is the answer. Any policy that enhances a state's economic position is seen to be in the national interest. Improving a country's balance of trade, strengthening a country's industrial base, or guaranteeing a country's access to oil, natural gas, or other energy or nonfuel mineral resources may all be considered to be in its national interest. Often, however, economic criteria may conflict with other criteria. For example, should one country continue to trade with another country if the second country uses the materials it buys to subjugate other countries? Such was the dilemma the United States found itself in the years immediately before World War II, both in its relations with Germany and with Japan. Similarly, should one country seek to maintain access to the mineral resources that a second country has if that second country has an internal social system that is repugnant to most of the citizens of the first country? Such was the dilemma in which the United States found itself in its relations with South Africa when apartheid was in place.

Ideological criteria are sometimes used as an important determinant of national interest. Most countries either formally or informally use an ideology (which may be defined as an internally consistent self-justifying belief system that includes both a view of the world and an explanation of that view) to justify both their legitimacy and their policies. For example, until relatively recently, most Marxist-Leninist states generally considered their interests to be quite similar one to another. Likewise, Western liberal-democratic states often saw their interests paralleling one another's, while poverty-stricken Developing World states regularly sided with one another in efforts to restructure the international economic system. But particularly with the collapse of Soviet and Eastern European communism and the rediscovery of economics, ideological criteria have become less influential and less important in the struggle to define national interest in many states. Ideological criteria still influence states to adopt certain ways of looking at the world and of looking at their national interest, and in some states, ideological criteria remain extremely important. But on the whole, the use of ideological criteria to define national interest has declined.

The augmentation of *power* is another method of defining national interest. Power is defined by Hans Morgenthau, perhaps the leading proponent of the realpolitik school of thought, as anything that allows one state to establish and maintain control over another.[9] Any policy that enhances a state's power is therefore in its national interest. Power, of course, may be augmented in a variety of ways, such as by improving economic strength, by using ideological suasion, or by enhancing military capabilities. To Morgenthau, power permits a state to survive, and therefore it is in the interest of all nations to acquire power.

Military security and/or advantage is another prominent criterion for determining national interest. With force playing such a prominent role in international relations, states perhaps only naturally look to military security as a minimum determinant of their national interest. Proponents of military security argue that a chief responsibility of any state is to provide safety for its inhabitants; proponents of military advantage argue that the best way to achieve that safety is through military advantage.

Morality and legality are similarly contentious issues when attempts are made to determine national interest. Although in many instances the "right" or "wrong" of an issue may be at first apparent, closer examination often clouds what at first glance may have been a clear moral or legal conclusion. The December 1989 U.S. invasion of Panama to oust Panamanian leader General Manuel Noriega provides a perfect example of the complexities that spring up when one attempts to define national interest through morality and legality. On the one hand, Noriega was clearly a corrupt dictator deeply involved in drug smuggling. He had stolen the May 1989 Panamanian election, embarked on a campaign to intimidate domestic Panamanian opposition, and had begun to harass and terrorize U.S. citizens living in Panama. Thus, he clearly deserved no sympathy or support. But on the other hand, did his actions, as outrageous as they were, give the United States the right under international law to invade

Panama and remove him from power? Or could it be argued that even in the absence of legal justification for the U.S. invasion, Noriega's behavior had been so repressive, inflammatory, and dangerous that the U.S. invasion to remove him was justified?

Numerous other criteria also exist for determining the national interest. Some people argue that national interest should be determined by *cultural affinity*, that is, by defining a state's interests to coincide with the interests of other states whose language or traditions may be the same as one's own. Others argue that *ethnic* or *race* issues should play a large role in determining national interests. Still other individuals see national interest as any action or set of actions that allow a country to make all its decisions for itself, regardless of what the economic, military, or other implications of that total independence would be.

What, then, "counts" when national interest is being defined? The answer, obviously, depends on who is doing the defining. In the minds of some, so-called objective factors such as economic strength, military capabilities, or the size of the resource base may prove dominant when national interest is being defined. Others may view subjective factors such as morality, legality, or ideology as more important. National interest must therefore be viewed less as a constant set of national objectives than as a changing approximation of what the leaders of a country or other significant individuals or groups within a country view as important. Even this general observation must be qualified, however, for the rate of change of these approximations of national interest may differ considerably from one country to the next.

Even the type of government that a state has may play a major role in determining how a state's national interests are defined. Governments of Western-style democracies, for example, often take into account the wishes and desires of various interest groups that wield domestic political power; more autocratic or dictatorial governments define their national interests with less concern for inputs from domestic interest groups. This does not necessarily mean, however, that the foreign policies of autocratic states have the universal support of those who implement policies; sometimes leaders of autocratic states must accommodate disagreements among themselves to arrive at and implement policy.

National interest, then, is a difficult term with which to come to grips. Within a single state different individuals and different groups define the national interest in different ways, even at the same time. It is a concept that has no universal meaning. Even with those shortcomings, however, national interest is a useful concept, for it provides us with a tool with which we can understand, at least in general terms, the objectives that states seek in international affairs.

THE STATE AND THE "BALANCE OF POWER"

Fashioning an appropriate policy is only part of the problem that national decision-makers face when they undertake international activities. They must also have appropriate means at their disposal to enable them to undertake their policy. Put simply, they must have *power* to implement their policy.

Unfortunately, the exact meaning of power is a matter of considerable debate. It is discussed in detail throughout Framework IV (Chapters 16–20).

Here, however, we must detail the concept of the "balance of power," for it has played and continues to play a major role in the relations between and among states.

"Balance of power" has been used to denote several types of interstate relations. In some cases, it means that two states have approximately equal capabilities. Thus, the statement that "a balance of power existed between the United States and the Soviet Union" meant just that—U.S. and Soviet capabilities were approximately equal. This balance of power relationship is depicted in Figure 2–1(a).

In other cases, "balance of power" means that an imbalance exists! Thus, the statement that "the balance of power is in the U.S. favor over Iraq" implies that U.S. capabilities are greater than Iraqi capabilities, and no "balance" exists. This balance of power relationship is depicted in Figure 2–1(b).

Both these meanings of balance of power envision a relatively static and non-changing relationship. But the concept of balance of power may also be used to envision a dynamic and changing international relationship. Thus, when Israel

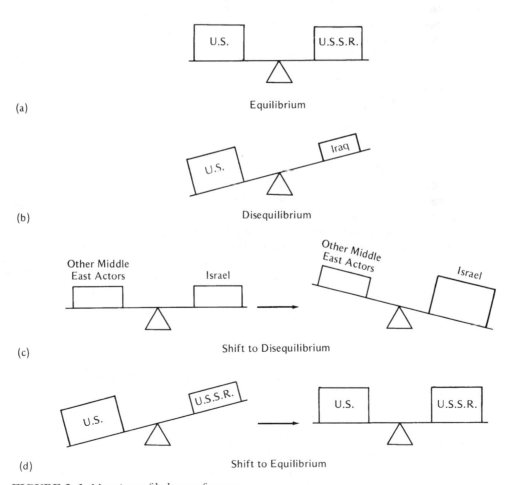

FIGURE 2–1 Meanings of balance of power.

moved into Lebanon during the summer of 1982 and destroyed much of the Syrian military there and forced the Palestine Liberation Organization out of Lebanon, "the balance of power in the Middle East shifted toward Israel." Imbalance replaced relative balance. This meaning of balance of power is illustrated in Figure 2–1(c). Of course, the dynamic nature of this third meaning of balance of power can also be used to describe a movement from imbalance to balance. For example, as the Soviet Union strengthened its military forces during the 1960s and 1970s, "the balance of Soviet-American power moved toward equilibrium." Figure 2–1(d) depicts this transformation.

The concept of *balance of power* need not apply only to the relationship between two individual actors. Several actors or groups of actors may be included. Thus, it is possible to have a balance of power between organizations, as existed between the North Atlantic Treaty Organization (NATO) and the Warsaw Pact through most of the post-World War II era. Similarly, regional and even global balances of power may exist. Thus, in the Middle East, a regional balance of power is sometimes said to exist between Israel and neighboring Arab states.

The nature of the concept of a balance of power system in international affairs warrants closer examination. Following Napoleon's final defeat at Waterloo in 1815, a balance of power system existed in Europe until World War I. Fundamental to this balance of power system was the acceptance by each government of the legitimacy of governments of other countries; a desire on the part of all governments to maintain the equilibrium of the system despite attempts to maximize their own individual power; a willingness by most governments to enter into alliances to create a balance of power; and a flexibility on the part of at least some governments to switch their alliances to the weaker side as the balance of power system began to grow imbalanced. Under this balance of power system, Great Britain in particular acted as the balancing agent in the international system, switching from one group of European states to another group of European states on a case-by-case basis to keep the European state system in equilibrium, that is, in "balance." International relations in Europe were conducted as a "balance of power system" from the nineteenth century until the beginning of World War I.

World War I pointed out a fundamental flaw in the balance of power system: when the system failed, results could be catastrophic. The incredible levels of destruction in the war led most states to reject a balance of power system as the basis for international security in the post–World War I world. Instead, the victorious states sought to institutionalize a system of **collective security** via the League of Nations in which aggression by any one state would bring response from all other states. Collective security would thus be achieved.

Collective security as a replacement for the balance of power system had many flaws. Who would define aggression? What would happen if some states refused to act against aggression? What would happen if some states refused to join the League? What if some states denied the legitimacy of governments ruling other states? All these uncertainties came to pass. In retrospect, it was probably not too surprising that World War II in Europe broke out in 1939, only 21 years after World War I had ended.

Following World War II, a new international system emerged, based primarily on a simple balance of power model. This system, depicted in Figure 2–2, was a **bipolar world** in which two separate blocs, one centered on the United States

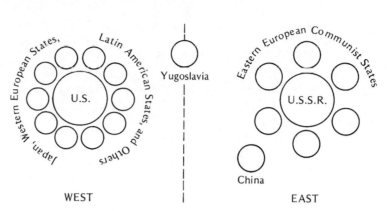

FIGURE 2–2 The bipolar world of the late 1940s and 1950s. (This and subsequent figures depicting the evolution of the post–World War II international system will be presented again in Chapter 7.)

and the other on the Soviet Union, each sought to affect the power and capabilities of the other. This bipolar world existed throughout the 1940s and 1950s, and was dominated by ideological rivalry, nuclear rivalry, and mistrust and hostility. This period is examined in greater detail in Chapter 7.

The bipolar world of the 1940s and 1950s, as dangerous as it seemed at the time, remained relatively stable as it evolved into the **muted bipolar world** of the 1960s. Even the muted bipolar world, however, remained essentially a balance of power system between the Soviet-dominated East and the U.S.-dominated West. The muted bipolar world is depicted in Figure 2–3. It too is discussed in greater depth in Chapter 7.

But the days of the muted bipolar world were numbered, too, as new power centers emerged on the world scene—specifically Japan, Europe, China, and even to a certain extent the disparate states of the Developing World. Significantly, however, none of the new power centers rivaled the United States or the

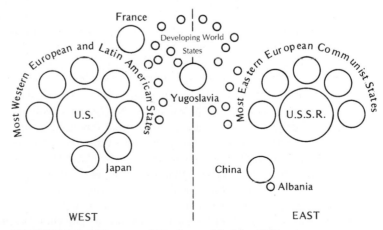

FIGURE 2–3 The muted bipolar world of the 1960s.

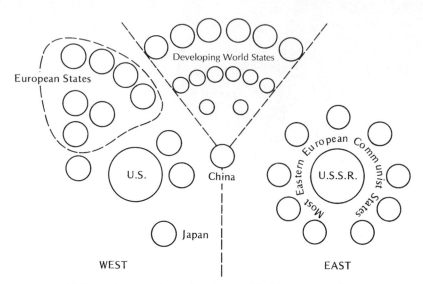

FIGURE 2–4   The multipolar world of the 1970s and 1980s.

Soviet Union in military capabilities; they were rivals in economic, ideological, and numerical senses of power. This fact led some analysts to conclude that the **multipolar world** actually signified an end to the bipolar, post-World War II balance of power system based on military strength and ideological identification; it led others to conclude that the multipolar world was more fiction than fact. One version of the multipolar world of the 1970s and early 1980s is shown in Figure 2–4. It, too, is discussed in Chapter 7.

By the beginning of the 1990s, the reality of a multipolar world had become apparent for all to see. Indeed, the multipolar world of 1989–1991 promised to be more complex than that of the 1970s and 1980s as a result of improved U.S.-Soviet relations, new policy directions of Eastern European states, the economic growth and independent course of China, the emergence of an integrated Europe in 1992 under the Single European Act, the rise of Japan to economic superpower status, and the division of the Developing World into regions some of which were advancing economically and others of which were not. Together, these changes altered the old post-World War II bipolar system almost beyond recognition. The multipolar world of 1989–1991 is depicted in Figure 2–5.

But this version of the multipolar world proved short-lived. There was widespread agreement that the collapse of the Soviet Union in 1991 left Russia and the 14 other post–Soviet successor states that emerged from the wreckage of the U.S.S.R. too weak to play meaningful roles in the new international order that was emerging, but what that order was proved to be a matter of considerable debate.

Some observers believed that the collapse of the Soviet Union led to the emergence of a **unipolar world**, with the one pole being the United States. These observers argued that the United States was now the only country that could project large quantities of military power anywhere in the world, that the United States had far and away the world's single largest national economy, and

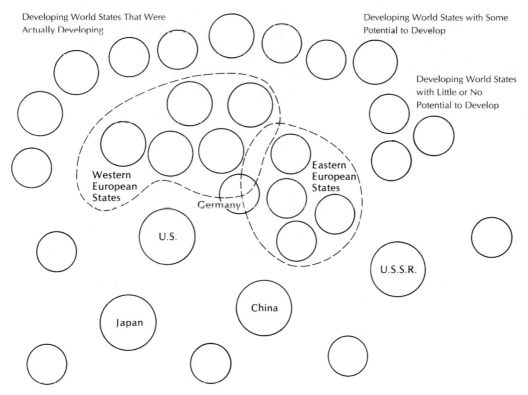

FIGURE 2–5 The multipolar world of 1989–1991.

was now the focus of global affairs. Most observers who took this viewpoint were Americans, and their outlook of American dominance is reflected in Figure 2–6.

Other analysts argued that with the collapse of the Soviet Union and the end of the East–West conflict, military capabilities had become less important and economic strength more important. Many concluded that as a result, the new international order of the middle and late 1990s and beyond would be based on regional economic blocs, in the Americas centered on the United States; in Europe centered on the European Community and its member states; and in East Asia centered on Japan. Their perspective on such a **regionalized world** was bolstered by the emergence of the European Community as an increasingly unified actor; by the movement toward a North American Free Trade Area consisting of Canada, the United States, and Mexico in the Western hemisphere; and by the growth of the economies of Japan and other states in East Asia. This perspective is shown in Figure 2–7.

Still other analysts believed that an extremely diffuse world order existed, with the United States, the European Community, Japan, and China all continuing to play major roles, but with other states and other international actors also on occasion using different types of power to rise to prominence on a case-by-case or issue-by-issue basis. This outlook is depicted in Figure 2–8.

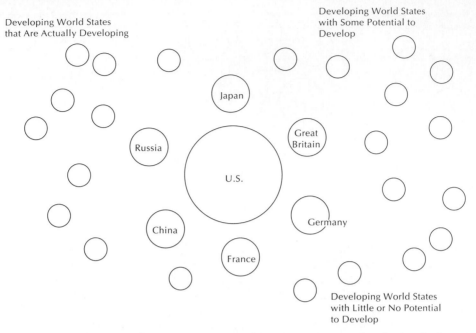

FIGURE 2–6   One version of what may emerge as the "New International Order" in the late 1990s and the twenty–first century: A unipolar world based on military power.

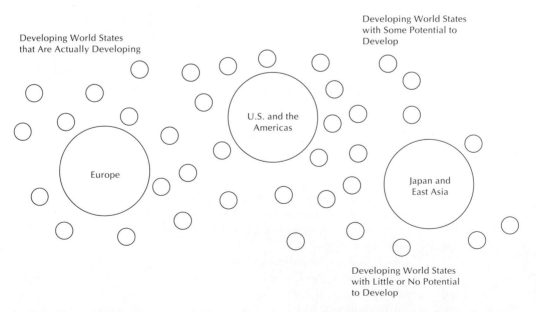

FIGURE 2–7   A second version of what may emerge as the "New International Order" in the late 1990s and the twenty-first century: A regionalized world based on economic trading blocs.

This then leads us directly to the question, "How is power measured?" Chapter 16 studies that question in detail, but we must recognize here in our discussion of the balance of power that no single answer exists to that question. Under the balance of power system that existed in the nineteenth century, the balance of power was almost universally assumed to mean military capabilities; the same assumption prevailed during the post–World War II eras of bipolarity and muted bipolarity. Now, however, economic strength, moral and ideological example, and other factors are often assumed to be important ingredients in determining whether a balance of power exists.

One final point must be made about the concept of *balance of power*. Regardless of which definition of the concept is used, the fulcrum (i.e., the balancing point) is almost always viewed as a single point, as shown in Figure 2–9(a). Envisioned in this manner, the addition of even a small quantity of "power" to one side or the other may change the balance, as illustrated in Figure 2–9(b). However, if the fulcrum is viewed as a widely based central area rather than a single point, as in Figure 2–9(c), even significant additions of "power" to one side or the other may be insufficient to change the balance. Figures 2–9(d) and (e) illustrate this change. The degree of threat that analysts and policy-makers see when one side in a balance of power relationship enhances its power is thus a function not only of power, but also of the width of the fulcrum. A conceptual model, that is, the type of balancing device that we mentally create, may therefore determine

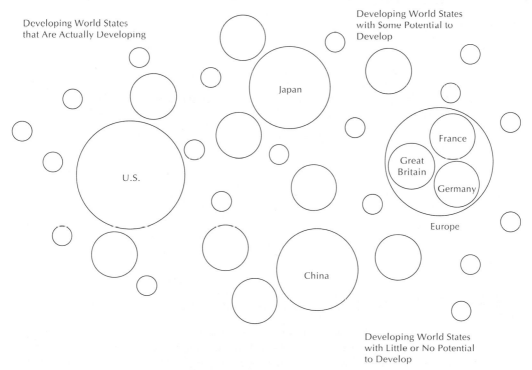

FIGURE 2–8 A third version of what may emerge as the "New International Order" in the late 1990s and the twenty-first century: A multi-polar world based on multiple parameters of power.

(a)   Equilibrium on a Narrow Fulcrum

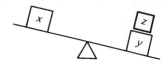

(b)   Disequilibrium on a Narrow Fulcrum

(c)   Equilibrium on a Wide Fulcrum

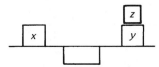

(d)   Equilibrium on a Wide Fulcrum

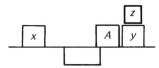

FIGURE 2–9   The balance of power and
the fulcrum.

the degree of balance or imbalance that we see. Unfortunately, however, no
objective method exists to determine how wide the fulcrum should be in a "balance of power" construct. Nevertheless, the "balance of power" has been and
continues to be widely used by analysts and policy-makers as an analytical tool.
Despite its shortcomings, no replacement has found wide acceptance.

CHALLENGES TO THE STATE

The state has dominated international political affairs for over 300 years. In
recent years, however, the utility of the state as we currently know it has been
increasingly questioned. As we have already seen, some groups identify the state
as the cause of war, whereas others maintain that increased global economic
interdependence has rendered the state an obsolescent if not obsolete organizational concept. In other cases, transnational ideological or religious movements
assert that their preachments and outlook supercede the parochial interests of

mere states. Other groups attack the state from within, maintaining that contemporary states are in fact multinational states; these groups argue for further fragmentation of the international system. On many occasions, these organizations, companies, movements, and groups have themselves become significant international actors, and in the following three chapters we will examine them in depth.

However, the point to be made here is that the dominance of the state *is* being challenged. The most significant challenges may be grouped into five broad categories: (1) economic interdependence; (2) military technologies; (3) international governmental organizations; (4) transnational movements and thought systems; and (5) internal fragmentation.

The Challenge of Economic Interdependence

In the not-too-distant past, one of the primary objectives of states was to attain as great a degree of economic self-sufficiency as was feasible. Within the past 30 years, however, fewer and fewer states have pursued economic self-sufficiency as a primary objective of national policy.

This has led to a situation where **economic interdependence** exists between and among most states, that is to say, a situation where states do not produce everything that they need for themselves, but rather, depend on other states to produce some of the goods and services that they need. The reason that this situation has developed is in many instances one of simple economic self-interest. Goods and services may be obtained more cheaply elsewhere than they can be obtained domestically.

As Table 1–1 illustrated, international trade multiplied roughly 25 times between 1960 and 1990 from a total of about $270 billion in 1960 to $6800 billion in 1990. Some countries depend heavily on foreign trade, whereas others do not. For example, Great Britain's trade turnover in 1990 totaled about 48 percent of its gross domestic product (GDP), and Canada's totaled 47 percent. The Netherlands is a particularly startling case, with trade turnover reaching fully 95 percent of its gross domestic product in 1990. By comparison, only 17 percent of the United States' GDP was trade-related in the same year, and 8 percent of the former Soviet Union's GDP was associated with trade.

However, these statistics do not tell the full story. The United States is perhaps the best example to use. Despite the fact that the U.S. economy is only 17 percent trade dependent, the United States imports large shares of vital raw materials and fuels, including about 23 percent of the oil that it uses, over 90 percent of the bauxite and manganese that it consumes, and much of its chromite, cobalt, nickel, platinum, tin, and potassium.[10] Without these imports the American GNP would decline precipitously. On the export side, U.S. agriculture, the aircraft industry, and other manufacturing ventures are heavily export dependent. Japan's economy is even more reliant on external trade relations than is the economy of the United States, both on the import and export sides.

In addition, few finished products in today's world are made entirely in one country. Whether it be automobiles, computers, aircraft, or almost any other manufactured product, raw materials, component parts, and even final assembly often come from and take place in many countries. Economic interdependence has become a present-day reality. Indeed, given the increased volume of world trade, the vital nature of much of that trade, and the international linkages that have developed in manufacturing processes, the challenge of economic interdependence is a serious one for the contemporary state. Why, critics of the state ask, need the state continue to exist if trade is so vital, if economic self-sufficiency is a thing of the past, and if economic and manufacturing efficiency can be improved by an international division of labor?

As already noted, in Western Europe, North America, South America, and Southeast Asia, some trade barriers created by states to assure national economic autonomy have already been removed, and more will follow. Before its collapse, even the Soviet Union was beginning to become integrated into the world marketplace. Its successor states are attempting to accelerate that process. In an economic sense, then, an argument exists that the world may be moving toward a post-state phase.

There is another side to the coin. The leaders and citizens of states are in many instances unwilling to become even more dependent on external sources for critical economic needs. Economic and political considerations both play a role here, as was driven home to much of the industrialized world in 1990 when Iraq conquered Kuwait. The Iraqi action placed that Middle Eastern country in the position where it could direct if not determine oil prices for OPEC states, thereby in effect giving Iraq the ability to play a major role in the economies of industrialized states. Not surprisingly, industrialized states, led by the United States, were not pleased by this situation, and they sent military forces to the Middle East to prevent further Iraqi expansion. (Economics was not the only reason the United States and other countries deployed military forces to the Middle East. Many were also incensed and concerned by Iraq's blatant disregard for Kuwait's sovereignty.)

Equally forebodingly, the periodic recessions of the 1980s and 1990s led many states to favor import restrictions to protect their own economies. Japan never reduced trade barriers as fully as other industrialized nations, and domestic content legislation and other forms of barriers to free trade were introduced to both houses of Congress in the United States in an effort to protect American workers and industry from inexpensive foreign competition.

Nor should it be overlooked that some states are "more interdependent" than others. For example, Japan must import almost all its raw materials, and in turn must export finished products to pay for these imports. In comparison, the Soviet Union was self-sufficient in most resources, and therefore was less reliant on foreign raw materials. Degree of interdependence is thus an important factor in conditioning the international behavior of a state.

Thus, although the world may be moving toward a poststate era in economic relations, the state can marshal persuasive arguments of its own that economic autarchy and independence are still desirable objectives. The challenge of economic interdependence to the state is a real challenge, however, and will not easily be overcome.[11]

The Challenge of Military Technologies

There is no doubt that the state is militarily vulnerable as never before. Barring the perfection of a new "exotic" technology defensive system that would render nuclear weapons and intercontinental ballistic missiles (ICBMs) ineffective, the advent of nuclear weapons and ICBM delivery systems removed forever the state's rationale that it could provide effective security for its citizens.[12] Even at the conventional level, modern weapons are appallingly effective and have a long reach; it is doubtful that even the victorious side in a large-scale war could assure its civilian population's security.

The state's response to the challenge of military technologies has been uncertain. Weapons continue to be procured, and alliances continue to be formed, but the key fact remains that states can no longer guarantee their citizens' security. Indeed, despite the U.S. Strategic Defense Initiative, the central tenet of American defense planning remained mutual assured destruction up until and even after the final collapse of the Soviet Union. Mutual assured destruction, or MAD, was the situation that claimed that if the Soviet Union launched a nuclear attack against the United States, the United States would be unable to defend its own cities and population, but enough U.S. nuclear weapons and strategic missiles would survive the Soviet attack to decimate the U.S.S.R. in retaliation. The Soviet Union would be in a similar position in the event of an American first strike, the logic continued. The conclusion was, therefore, that neither side would attack.

Even with the end of U.S.-Soviet animosity, uncertainty remains about whether states can defend their citizens from external attack. More and more countries are obtaining the capability to build nuclear weapons, even if they have not yet built them. Similarly, many countries already have the ability to make chemical and biological weapons as well.

Just as in the case of nuclear weapons, there is no definite and certain defense against these other weapons of mass destruction. The question thus remains for states, how well can they actually protect their citizens given the challenge of advanced military technologies?

The Challenge of International Governmental Organizations

Although international governmental organizations (IGOs) are not new, the challenge they present to established states is. Many of the political, economic, social, and military problems that confront contemporary states cut across national boundaries, and in response to this reality, governments of states created IGOs to enable them better to meet their problems. In some cases, primarily in Western Europe, states have surrendered effective decision-making and policy-implementing powers to IGOs. Both the European Council and the Nordic Council, for example, can determine export and import prices for selected products. With the European Community's Single European Act, the EC itself will also oversee European technical standards, value added and excise taxes, and other regulations. Even more strikingly, EC leaders in December 1991 concluded the Maastricht Treaty that laid out plans for movement of the EC toward political and economic unity.

Although there was and is extensive concern in Europe about the Maastricht Treaty, the treaty is clearly a massive challenge to the primacy of the state in Europe. As we have already seen, the concepts of the nation-state and national sovereignty were first born in Europe in the seventeenth century. It is ironic that the most serious peaceful challenge to their continuation is also in Europe.

The Challenge of Transnational Movements and Thought Systems

The state system that currently dominates international affairs arose from the ruins of a European-wide religious empire that pledged its allegiance to the pope. It is somewhat ironic, therefore, that one of the most serious challenges confronting the current state system is the existence of a variety of transnational movements and thought systems that claim the allegiance of individuals and groups. Some of these movements are specifically religious, as is fundamentalist Shiite Islam, whereas others are specifically antireligious, as is Marxism.

The resurgence of fundamentalist Islam may be traced to the fall of the shah of Iran and the coming to power of Ayatollah Khomeini in 1979. After a series of fits and starts, Khomeini proclaimed Iran an Islamic republic, and announced that he and his followers would seek to convert other states to Islamic republics. Although territorial designs on neighboring states were officially denied, other Arab states interpreted Khomeini's message as a direct assault on their legitimacy and sovereignty. To them, Khomeini's Iran represented a direct and immediate threat. Khomeini's continuing calls for a return to fundamentalist Islamic teachings only solidified their perception that he sought to establish a transnational political-religious entity following the tenets of his version of the Shiite Islamic faith.

In a theoretical sense, Marxism also rejects the legitimacy of the state. In the *Communist Manifesto* Karl Marx and Friedrich Engels argued that the nation-state and nationalism were simply tools of the ruling bourgeois class to divide and weaken the proletariat. Eventually, Marx believed, the proletariat would develop a sense of international class consciousness and see through the sham of nationalism perpetuated by the bourgeoisie. Following the proletariat revolution, Marx concluded, the state would eventually "wither away."

Even today, Marxists maintain that the state will eventually disappear in communist states. Although communism itself has disappeared in Eastern Europe and the former Soviet Union, and most of these states have themselves instituted capitalist economic reforms, the leaders of China, Cuba, and the Indochinese communist states continue to assert that traditional Marxist outlooks on the eventual withering away of the state are accurate, if not imminent.

In a practical sense, proponents of both fundamentalist Islam and revolutionary Marxism found it necessary to create their own bases of power in states. Both, however, deny that their states are traditional. To Khomeini, Iran was subservient to Allah and the Koran; to the Soviet leadership, the U.S.S.R. was subservient to its working class. Even more strikingly, Soviet ideologues saw fit to declare that communism could develop differently in different countries, taking into account local history, culture, levels of economic development, and other factors.

Indeed, the combination of events in the Soviet Union and Eastern Europe as well as the movement toward moderation in Iran following the 1989 death of Khomeini led some observers to conclude that both Marxism-Leninism and Islamic fundamentalism were ideas whose time had come and gone. But even if that judgment is accurate in regard to these two transnational thought systems, the general point remains valid: religion and ideology continue to have appeal across national boundaries, and their challenge to the state continues.

The Challenge of Internal Fragmentation

As defined earlier in this chapter, a nation-state is a geographically bounded legal entity under a single government, the population of which psychologically considers itself to be in some way, shape, or form related. As shown earlier, there are many indications that nationalism, the very force that led to the existence of nation-states, remains strong and is growing. It is ironic that this very nationalism is leading to further fragmentation of states, and the creation of new "ministates,"

ICBMs threaten the nation-state's ability to guarantee security to its citizens   (United States Air Force.)

which by themselves may not be viable political-economic units. In a certain sense, then, nationalism itself presents a challenge to the state because of its potential to fragment existing states and create nonviable new ministates.

To one extent or another, countries on every continent are beset by separatist pressures. Africa has been particularly affected. In Nigeria during the late 1960s, the Ibo tribe attempted to secede and establish the state of Biafra. A bloody civil war ended the Ibos' effort. The Angolan Civil War was and is as much the product of tribal conflict as ideological antipathy. In Zimbabwe in the 1970s, Robert Mugabe's rule was challenged by Joshua Nkomo; both men based their prestige and influence on their own ethnic groups within Zimbabwe. In Ethiopia, Eritrean secessionist movements fought for over 30 years against two different governments in Addis Ababa. Finally, in 1993, a referendum was held in Eritrea and the Eritreans voted nearly unanimously for independence. In the Western Sahara, the Polisario guerillas began their struggle for independence from Morocco in the 1970s, and fought on into the 1990s until the United Nations arranged a precarious peace.

In recent years, many European countries have also experienced extensive growth of separatist pressures. Since 1991, these pressures have already led to the dissolution of Czechoslovakia, the Soviet Union, and Yugoslavia. But these were not the only countries where the impacts of nationalism within established states have been felt. In Great Britain, Scotland and Wales have local self-government, and Italy established an autonomous provincial government in South Tyrolea. The Basques seek independence from Spain, and some Normans seek independence from France. Belgium has changed its constitution so that the Flemings and the Walloons now enjoy cultural autonomy.

In Asia, Bangladesh received its independence from Pakistan after India defeated Pakistan in full-scale warfare. Meanwhile, in Australia the sporadic Westralia movement again flickered to life during the 1970s and 1980s.

Even North America is not immune to this challenge of fragmentation. Quebec, during the 1970s, 1980s, and 1990s, flirted with secession from Canada, and has consuls in a number of European and American cities. Puerto Rican nationalists periodically demand independence from the United States, and perhaps most interestingly and subtly, by 1993, many American states had established trade offices overseas to seek external foreign investment. Although this last example presents no threat of secession, it does indicate that even within the United States concern for state identity and wealth is influencing changes in policy.

Internal fragmentation, then, is a genuine challenge to many states. In some states, the challenge is a crisis. In others, it is little more than a joke. The point, however, is that the state must face another challenge to its three centuries of international domination.

Despite these challenges to the dominance of the state in the international arena, nothing indicates that the state is in imminent danger of demise. Questions are being raised, however, about the reasons for its existence; if it can no longer offer economic independence, provide military security, or cope with transnational problems, why then does it continue to exist? One answer to that question is that the state may provide a sense of identity to its inhabitants, but even that is not a satisfactory response by itself. Ayatollah Khomeini was not alone in giving his allegiance to a movement, thought system, or organization that transcends the state, and the Ibos, Basques, and Quebecois are not alone in their resentment of and opposition to the governments of the states in which they currently reside.

Perhaps Hans Morgenthau had the best and simplest answer to the question of why the state continues to exist despite its obvious shortcomings—*power*, defined in its broadest terms. Except for those in Antarctica, every person on the earth lives on land that is controlled or claimed by a state, and all the land on the face of the earth, Antarctica again excepted, has been divided by states. International law and common practice recognize the right of states to use force both internationally and domestically, to control their own citizens and citizens of other states living within their territorial confines (except diplomats), and to make laws that determine how and whether other actors will operate on their territory. The sovereignty of states may be less absolute than it once was, but states still dominate the international system.

KEY TERMS AND CONCEPTS

Peace of Westphalia

state

nation

nation-state

legitimacy

sovereignty

duties (of states)

nationalism (also in Chapter 19)

first round of empire

mercantilism

regal legitimacy

second round of empire

first proliferation of states

bourgeois legitimacy

second proliferation of states

colonialism

third proliferation of states

national interest

balance of power

collective security

bipolar world (also in Chapter 9)

muted bipolar world

multipolar world (also in Chapter 9)

unipolar world (also in Chapter 9)

regionalized world (also in Chapter 9)

challenges to the state

economic interdependence

NOTES

1. The United Nations Charter theoretically commits the UN to support the "self-determination of peoples." This would imply that the UN seeks to create a world of nation-states. Political realities intrude into theory, however, and the United Nations has never sought to achieve this theoretical objective.

2. René Albrecht-Carrie's *A Diplomatic History of Europe Since the Congress of Vienna* (New York: Harper & Row, 1958), pp. 3–144, uses the methodology of diplomatic history to detail this period. It also examines the second round of empire, pp. 145–298.

3. American expansionism during this period is chronicled in Foster R. Dulles, *Prelude to World Power: American Diplomatic History, 1860–1900* (New York: Macmillan, 1965); Walter LaFeber, *The New Empire: An Interpretation of American Expansion 1860–1898* (Ithaca: Cornell University Press, 1963); and H. Wayne Morgan, *America's Road to Empire* (New York: John Wiley, 1965).

4. For details of the Russian fiasco, see David MacKenzie and Michael W. Curran, *A History of Russia and the Soviet Union* (Homewood, IL: The Dorsey Press, 1977), pp. 434–436.

5. See "Covenant of the League of Nations," Article 22, in *Essential Facts about the League of Nations* (Geneva: League of Nations, 1935).

6. No less an authority than Henry Kissinger proclaimed in 1975 that "poverty levels may be more of a threat to the security of the world than anything else."

7. For several recent studies on this third proliferation of states, see for example Anthony W. Birch, *Nationalism and National Integration* (New York: Unwin Hyman Academic Press, 1989); Uri Ra'anan et al., eds., *State and Nation in Multi-Ethnic Societies: The Breakup of Multinational States* (Manchester: Manchester University Press, 1992); and R. B. J. Walker and Saul H. Mendlovitz, eds., *Contending Sovereignties: Redefining Political Community* (Boulder, CO: Lynne Rienner Publishers, 1990).

8. The mathematical formula that determines the number of bilateral relations x that may exist between n variables is $x = n!/r(n-4)!$ where r is the number of members in each combination. Thus, for a world in which 50 states exist, $x = 1{,}225$. In a world in which 150 states exist, $x = 11{,}175$.

9. See Hans J. Morgenthau, *Politics Among Nations* (New York: Knopf, 1948), especially Chap. 3.

10. U.S. Department of Defense, *Military Posture FY 1989*, p. 13.

11. For further discussion of interdependence, see Lester Brown, *The Interdependence of Nations* (New York: Foreign Policy Association, 1972); Robert O. Keohane and Joseph S. Nye, *Power and Interdependence* (Boston: Little, Brown, 1989); Robert O. Keohane and Joseph S. Nye, "International Interdependence and Integration," in Fred Greenstein and Nelson Polsby (eds.), *Handbook of Political Science: Vol. VIII, International Relations* (Reading, MA: Addison-Wesley, 1975), pp. 363–414; and Bruce Russett et al., *Choices in World Politics: Sovereignty and Interdependence* (New York: W. H. Freeman, 1989).

12. Most proponents of President Reagan's Strategic Defense Initiative accepted as early as 1985 that they would not be able to perfect an impenetrable "Astrodome" defense shield, as Director of the SDI Office, General James Abrahamson, admitted to a Georgia Tech audience on November 15, 1985. Abrahamson made this comment at a conference on SDI, entitled "SDI: The Pros and Cons of Star Wars."

CHAPTER 3

International Governmental Organizations

THE UNITED NATIONS AND OTHER STATE-CREATED ORGANIZATIONS

- What is an IGO, and what does it do?
- How have IGOs changed over time?
- What does the UN do, and how is it structured?
- How effective has the UN been?
- What do NATO and ASEAN, two other prominent IGOs, actually accomplish?

International governmental organizations (IGOs) are so named for a basic reason: They are organizations that are created by two or more sovereign states. They meet regularly and have full–time staffs. They are organizations in which the interests and policies of the member states are put forward by the representatives of the respective states. Membership in IGOs is voluntary, and therefore in a technical sense, IGOs do not challenge state sovereignty. In an actual sense, however, they may in fact challenge sovereignty.

IGOs may be categorized according to breadth of membership or scope of purpose. Membership may be globally, regionally, or otherwise defined. Thus, for example, both the League of Nations and the United Nations sought to be global organizations with as wide a membership as possible. Regional IGOs are geographically defined, such as the Organization of American States (OAS), the Organization of African Unity (OAU), or the Association of Southeast Asian Nations (ASEAN). Otherwise defined IGOs include the British Commonwealth, which is restricted to former colonies of the British Empire, and the International Wool Study Group, whose membership includes only those states that seek to cooperate in improving their wool production.

IGOs may be described as broad-purpose or limited-purpose. Broad-purpose IGOs operate in a variety of political, economic, military, cultural, social, technical, legal, or developmental milieus; their membership may be globally, regionally, or otherwise defined. The United Nations is an example of a global broad-purpose organization; the North Atlantic Treaty Organization (NATO) is a regional broad-purpose organization, although its primary function is generally viewed as military in nature; and the British Commonwealth is an otherwise-defined broad-purpose IGO. Limited-purpose IGOs, also called functional IGOs, concentrate their activities in a single area; their membership may again be globally, regionally, or otherwise defined. The World Health Organization (WHO), for example, is a global narrow-purpose IGO; the Desert Locust Control Organization of East Africa is a regional narrow-purpose IGO; and the International Wool Study Group is an otherwise-defined narrow-purpose IGO. Table 3–1 schematically groups these IGOs. It must be stressed, however, that this is an extremely simplistic scheme for grouping them.

Why do states find IGOs so useful and continue to create them despite the fact, as we saw at the end of Chapter 2, that some IGOs challenge the dominance of the state? A number of answers exist and are explored in the following section. In addition, the next section examines some institutional structures of modern IGOs.

THE STRUCTURE AND FUNCTION OF MODERN IGOS

As a rule, IGOs are established by treaty or executive agreement between two or more states. States create IGOs to provide a means and a forum for cooperation among states in functional areas where cooperation offers advantages for all or most of the member states. These areas of cooperation may be political, economic, military, cultural, social, technical, legal, or developmental in nature; there is practically no area of human endeavor that could benefit from cooperation from which IGOs have been excluded.

IGOs are therefore sometimes called transnational institutions; that is, they are institutions whose membership transcends traditional state boundaries, but which have no clear authority to enforce their decisions on their members. A very few IGOs have moved from transnational status to supranational status and do have authority over even member states who disagree with the IGOs' decisions. Such supranational IGOs are discussed at the end of this section.

TABLE 3–1   Examples of Types of International Government Organizations

Membership	Broad-purpose	Limited-purpose
Global	UN	WHO
Regional	NATO, ASEAN, OAU	COMECON, Desert Locust Control Organization of East Africa
Other	British Commonwealth	International Wool Study Group

As a rule, IGOs share a number of institutional characteristics regardless of which areas they function in. All have permanent offices, often headquartered in major Western cities such as Brussels, Geneva, London, New York, Paris, Rome, or Zurich. Regional IGOs are headquartered most regularly in a major city within the affected region's domain, such as Bangkok, Buenos Aires, or Moscow. In several regional IGOs such as the Organization for African Unity, IGO headquarters is located in one city, and council meetings are rotated among cities. The leadership of organizations such as the OAU is also rotated among the leaders of member states.

IGOs have professional staffs, generally called secretariats. These staffs are expected to develop loyalty to the IGO rather than maintain loyalty to their original state of origin. The long-term objectives of IGOs are debated and determined by conferences or assemblies, which are scheduled to meet at regular intervals. IGOs also have executive councils whose responsibilities include developing operational plans that reflect the long-term objectives determined by the assembly. In turn, the secretariat is to implement the operational plans developed by the executive council. For the most part, IGOs are relatively small. Their budgets average slightly over $10 million per year, and their staffs average approximately 200 people. The United Nations and its associated organs, with a budget of about $15 billion and a staff of 50,000 people, dwarfs most other IGOs.[1]

IGOs perform several separately identifiable cooperative services for nation-states. This service performance is what accounted for the proliferation of IGOs in recent years. IGOs provide a forum for communications for states; serve regulative functions; distribute scarce goods and services; offer potential for collective defense and peacekeeping; and in a few instances, provide a rudimentary regional or otherwise-defined governmental function. Indeed, in at least some of these areas, states expect IGOs to act for them, and even argue that IGOs are the proper actors to undertake actions that in earlier eras were the domain of the state.[2]

As *forums for communications*, IGOs may serve as convenient locations for representatives of states to meet informally and discuss issues or items that, for one reason or another, they cannot discuss elsewhere. For example, the United States in the late 1970s held a series of discussions at the United Nations with the Palestine Liberation Organization, even though the United States did not recognize the PLO. Although the first series of these meetings led to the eventual resignation of then U.S. Ambassador to the United Nations Andrew Young, the existence of the UN made such meetings both practical and possible. Alternatively, IGOs serve as formal arenas for communication between states, and many even provide mechanisms for mediating disputes. As Winston Churchill once said, "Jaw-jaw is better than war-war," and the case can be made that although IGOs such as the United Nations and the Organization for African Unity have not prevented war, they have multiplied the opportunities for countries to air their grievances and make an effort to achieve peaceful conflict resolution, even if they are not always successful.

As *regulators*, IGOs serve in a number of capacities ranging from health and postal services to meteorology and atomic energy. The World Health Organization, for example, establishes international health regulations to "ensure the maximum security against the international spread of disease with the minimum interference of world traffic." Similarly, the African Postal Union establishes regulations to improve and facilitate the movement of mail in Africa, and the World Meteorological Organization is tasked to "ensure the uniform publication of observations and statistics" on weather. The International Atomic Energy Agency, meanwhile, establishes regulations for the transfer and use of nuclear technologies. Although one may again question the degree of success that these and other regulative IGOs have achieved, it is difficult to deny that what inter-state cooperation does exist has been greatly enhanced by their existence. Indeed, in some cases, such as the WHO's efforts against malaria and smallpox, the efforts of IGOs have been startlingly successful. The incidence of malaria has been sharply reduced, and smallpox has been eradicated.

Much the same may be said for the *distributive functions* that some IGOs serve. For example, the World Bank and the International Monetary Fund distribute scarce financial funds to a number of states that meet differing criteria of need. Similarly, the United Nations Children's Fund (UNICEF) distributes goods and services to some of the world's needy children. As distributive agents, IGOs are praised as being indispensable adjuncts for services rendered too rarely by nation-states and condemned as costly bureaucracies that consume a disproportionate amount of the goods and services they are supposed to be distributing.

IGOs have long been created to enhance the *military capabilities* of states. As long ago as the fifth century B.C., Greek city-states formed the Delian League to fight the Persian invasion, and in Thucydides' *The Peloponnesian War* formal alliance systems play a major role.[3] More recently, the League of Nations and the United Nations both sought to provide collective security for their member states, and certain regional IGOs such as NATO are predominantly military in nature.

IGOs also provide *peacekeeping services* that may not be strictly described as collective security. The United Nations and the Organization of African Unity have on numerous occasions created multinational military forces to enter areas of high tension to separate hostile or potentially hostile forces, or to quiet domestic disturbances when they threaten to disrupt the international community. UN and OAU peacekeeping operations are generally undertaken only when widespread consensus exists on a particular issue within the involved organization.[4]

In rare instances, IGOs perform what may be described as a *supranational political function*. That is, they have acquired power to make decisions that are binding on member states even if unanimous consent has not been achieved. In these cases member states maintain that their sovereignty has not been abridged because the IGO receives its power by consent of the member states. Even so, in a functional sense the IGO determines policy. The European Community's various bodies, such as the Coal and Steel Community and Euratom (the European Community's agency whose purpose is to develop nuclear energy technologies for peaceful purposes) are good examples of supranational IGOs. But the best example may be the European Community itself, which with the Maastricht Treaty of December 1991 pledged to move toward political and economic unity, thereby for all practical purposes supplanting the sovereignty of European states.

However, it must be stressed that there was and is considerable opposition to this, and the Maastricht Treaty itself may be renegotiated. Indeed, the desire of states and their citizens to maintain national sovereignty is undoubtedly the primary reason why there are so few supranational IGOs.

THE EVOLUTION OF IGOS

IGOs, particularly those whose primary function is military-related, are not new. As we have seen, the Greek city-states had formal organizations that linked them for military purposes over 2,500 years ago. However, the modern IGO is of more recent origin and owes its birth to the industrial revolution and the French Revolution.

Before the industrial revolution, trade in Europe was relatively limited, mass production did not exist, communications were poor, and markets were small. The industrial revolution brought about mass production, improved communications, and a drive for expanded markets. It therefore promoted the establishment of transnational links and functional integration for economic purposes.

Such trends did not proceed in a vacuum. Whereas the industrial revolution tended to encourage international linkages, the French Revolution discouraged them. The French Revolution based its appeal on nationalism, and in turn evoked nationalistic responses throughout Europe. The states of Europe demanded both autonomy of action and control over the flow of goods, services, people, and even ideas. How then were the economic pressures for integration to be resolved with the opposing political pressures for autonomy?

One answer was the international governmental organization, which provided both mechanisms for international cooperation and protection for national sovereignty. Indeed, the Congress of Vienna in 1815, called to create a post–Napoleonic order in Europe, also created what some have described as the first modern international governmental organization, the Central Commission for the Navigation of the Rhine. The commission's task was to provide safe and secure transportation on the Rhine; its charter not only outlined its duties, but also promised no infringement on state sovereignty. A compromise had been reached, and the modern IGO was born.

The number of IGOs increased slowly throughout the nineteenth century. Two levels of nineteenth-century organization may be usefully discussed, one described as a "high-politics" system of negotiating institutions and the other described as a "low-politics" system of functioning institutions. The high-politics system was the Congress System, which eventually evolved into the Hague Conferences and, in a certain sense, the League of Nations and the United Nations. The low-politics system consisted of functional organizations such as the Central Commission for the Navigation of the Rhine.

Although the Congress System was not an IGO in the strictest sense of the term, as it had no permanent administrative staff, the great powers of the day clearly viewed it as an institutional mechanism to which they could turn to communicate with other powers, impose their will on smaller states, solve their own minor disputes, and seek approval for whatever new departures in policy they were contemplating. Meetings were not scheduled regularly, but from 1815 to 1900, only 36 years passed without a Congress being held.

Functional IGOs of the nineteenth century have been classified as river commissions, quasi-colonial organizations, and administrative unions; they existed both in Europe and the Americas. River commissions are exemplified by the Rhine Commission. Quasi-colonial organizations were called into being by European states to provide or supervise services in non–European states. Questions of health and finance in China, for example, were decided by

European commissions that may be described as IGOs. Finally, many of the global or regional postal, telegraph, rail, scientific, and economic unions of today trace their lineage to IGOs created during the nineteenth century.

Even so, by the beginning of World War I, fewer than 50 IGOs existed. World War I precipitated a rapid growth in the number of IGOs, even as it did with nation-states. By 1935 nearly 90 IGOs could be identified. Although this number dropped slightly as World War II approached, the conclusion of that war ushered in an even more rapid growth in the number of IGOs than had occurred in the interwar period. Indeed, according to the United Nations, over 400 IGOs existed by 1990, as Table 3–2 shows.

What accounted for the rapid growth in numbers of IGOs after World War I and their even more rapid increase after World War II? The answers are several. First, the devastation of the two wars, and most particularly the destructive power of nuclear weapons, created a subtle psychological shift in the minds of many policy-makers, who slowly realized that international problems had the potential to become so destructive that increased international cooperation was a necessity for survival. Many of the IGOs created in the post–World War II era as a result addressed themselves to issues of war and peace, disease prevention, and economic development.

A second reason that the number of IGOs increased so rapidly is the increased ease of international travel and communication. The mere fact that it is now possible to travel between Europe and North America in five hours instead of five days served as an impetus for governments to cooperate on solutions to issues and problems that were formerly most easily approached on a national level. Nearly instantaneous global communications systems accelerated this trend even more markedly.

Humanitarianism provided a third impetus to IGOs. Poverty, underdevelopment, starvation, and disease have long blighted human societies, but only recently have governments involved themselves in attacking these problems on a cooperative global level. In part, these problems are tackled today because they

TABLE 3–2   The Number of International
Governmental Organizations

Year	No. of IGOs
1956	132
1960	154
1964	179
1968	229
1972	280
1976	252
1980	337
1984	365
1987	381
1990	390+
1993	400+

SOURCE: *Yearbook of International Organizations
1985/86*, p. 1587; *Yearbook of International Organizations
1987/88*, p. 1531; and United Nations estimates.

are threats to world peace, and in part they are approached because requisite capabilities have only recently become available. Nevertheless, humanitarianism provides a definite motivating factor.

A fourth explanation for the growing number of international organizations is the expansion of the international civil service itself. As more individuals are drawn into the bureaucracy of IGOs—and as of 1993, over 150,000 people worked for IGOs on a full-time basis—more issues and problems are identified that can be approached by IGOs. Woodrow Wilson once concluded that "legislation unquestionably generates legislation";[5] it appears that his observation applies equally well to IGOs.

THE UNITED NATIONS AND ITS RELATED ORGANIZATIONS

The United Nations is the most famous and the most important IGO. Even before the United States entered World War II, Winston Churchill and Franklin Roosevelt agreed in the eighth point of the Atlantic Charter that a "permanent system of general security" should be created after the war. The 1943 Moscow Conference of Foreign Ministers affirmed that a new international organization should be created to regulate the postwar world, and after a number of other meetings were held, representatives from 50 countries met in San Francisco during April and May 1945 at the United Nations Conference. The conference drew up both the United Nations Charter and the Statutes of the International Court of Justice.[6]

During the years since then, the UN has undertaken a host of different activities throughout the world. But throughout that time, many UN activities, including its efforts to help create a "permanent system of general security," were complicated by U.S.-Soviet rivalry and the East–West conflict. However, many of those complications disappeared in the late 1980s and early 1990s with the emergence of American-Soviet cooperation, the ensuing collapse of the U.S.S.R., and the end of the East–West conflict. By the early 1990s, then, the United Nations had begun to play a more sizable role in international affairs than it had during its first 45 years of existence.

The UN's Structure

The final organizational structure of the United Nations was basically the creation of the victorious Great Powers of World War II. (See Figure 3–1.) Of the six major segments of the United Nations, the **Security Council** was most reflective of the Great Powers' concerns that their voices be predominant in the new UN. The Security Council consists of five permanent members, not coincidentally the five major victorious powers of World War II—China (before October 1971, the Republic of China on Taiwan, and since then, the People's Republic of China in Beijing), France, Great Britain, Russia (before 1992, the Soviet Union), and the United States—and 10 other nonpermanent representatives elected by the General Assembly to two-year terms. Each of the five permanent members can veto any important action brought before the council; that is, for the council to take any action the five permanent members must be in agreement on that action.

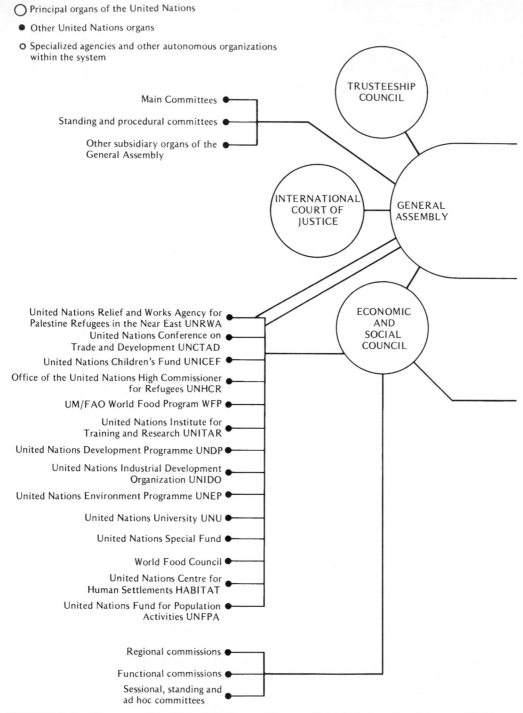

FIGURE 3–1   Structure of the United Nations.   (Source: United Nations, Department of Public Information, *Basic Facts about the United Nations*, 1989.)

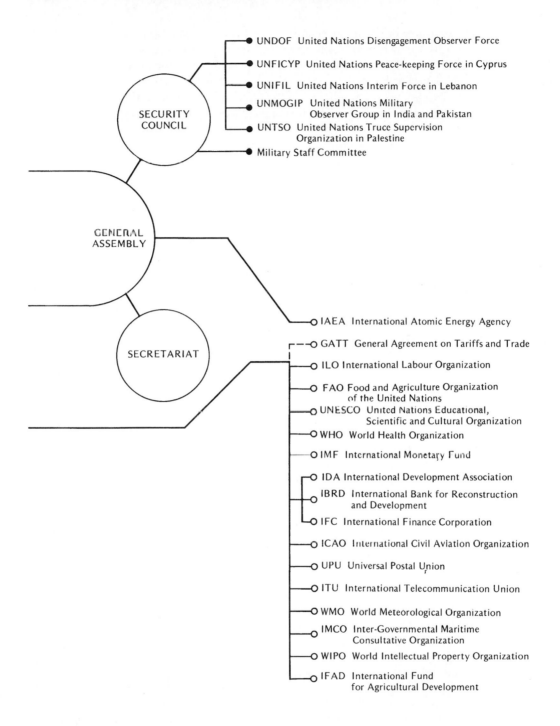

SECURITY
COUNCIL

● UNDOF United Nations Disengagement Observer Force

● UNFICYP United Nations Peace-keeping Force in Cyprus

● UNIFIL United Nations Interim Force in Lebanon

● UNMOGIP United Nations Military
                Observer Group in India and Pakistan

● UNTSO United Nations Truce Supervision
              Organization in Palestine

● Military Staff Committee

GENERAL
ASSEMBLY

SECRETARIAT

○ IAEA International Atomic Energy Agency

○ GATT General Agreement on Tariffs and Trade

○ ILO International Labour Organization

○ FAO Food and Agriculture Organization
        of the United Nations

○ UNESCO United Nations Educational,
                  Scientific and Cultural Organization

○ WHO World Health Organization

○ IMF International Monetary Fund

○ IDA International Development Association

○ IBRD International Bank for Reconstruction
            and Development

○ IFC International Finance Corporation

○ ICAO International Civil Aviation Organization

○ UPU Universal Postal Union

○ ITU International Telecommunication Union

○ WMO World Meteorological Organization

○ IMCO Inter-Governmental Maritime
              Consultative Organization

○ WIPO World Intellectual Property Organization

○ IFAD International Fund
            for Agricultural Development

At least four of the nonpermanent members must also agree to that action. The Security Council begins actions on collective security issues and economic sanctions, and authorizes deployment of UN peacekeeping forces. It also recommends candidates for the secretary-general's position to the General Assembly.

Two interesting sidelights on the Great Powers' role in the Security Council may be instructive here. The first sidelight concerns the introduction of combat troops under the United Nations' flag to the Korean War in 1950. Ordinarily, because UN forces were to be used against communist North Korea, the Soviet Union would have vetoed the Security Council's action. However, the Soviet Union boycotted the sessions of the Security Council when the Korean action was taken, not because of the Korean action itself, but because the United Nations had refused to remove Nationalist China from the Security Council and give its seat to Mao Zedong's People's Republic of China. Since that incident, the five permanent members of the Council have all faithfully attended meetings when major actions were to be taken.

The second sidelight concerns trends in the Great Powers' use of the veto. As Table 3–3 illustrates, the former Soviet Union used its veto power most frequently. However, the U.S.S.R.'s use of its veto declined dramatically, whereas the frequency of American and British vetoes increased dramatically. There are two explanations for these trends.

First, many of the Soviet Union's vetoes between 1945 and 1955 were cast to block admission of new states supported by the United States to the UN. In 1955, the two superpowers agreed to admit members from both alliance blocs. The U.S.S.R.'s use of its veto therefore became less frequent.

Second, as more and more states achieved independence during the 1960s and 1970s, and as these states joined the United Nations and voted in the UN's General Assembly, the United States and the United Kingdom found fewer and fewer of their allies, close friends, or dependents being elected by the General Assembly to the nonpermanent positions on the Security Council. More and more frequently, the United States and the United Kingdom were faced with situations in which at least four and even five or six of the nonpermanent members opposed American or British interests. Thus, to protect their interests, the United States and Great Britain found it increasingly necessary to resort to the veto.

The second major segment of the United Nations is the **General Assembly**, which consists of representatives from all governments that have ratified the UN Charter. As of 1993, 179 states had membership in the General Assembly. Additionally, certain nongovernmental organizations such as the Palestine Liberation Organization have acquired nonvoting observer status in the General Assembly.[7] The General Assembly approves the UN's budget, acts with the Security Council to select the secretary-general and judges of the International Court of Justice, and passes resolutions on myriad issues ranging from self-determination and colonialism to the new international economic order and the global distribution of wealth.

Although the General Assembly itself has no recognized authority to enforce its conclusions on anything other than internal UN matters, it makes its viewpoints on issues that are brought before it known in one of three ways. A General Assembly *declaration* is a broad statement of general principle, such as the Universal Declaration of Human Rights, passed in 1948. Declarations are often put

TABLE 3–3 Vetoes at the United Nations, 1945–1990

State	1945–50	1951–60	1961–70	1971–80	1981–90	Total
China°	0	1	0	2	0	3
France	2	2	0	7	7	18
U.S.S.R.	47	45	13	9	2	116
U.K.	0	2	2	13	15	32
U.S.A.	0	0	1	21	47	69
Total	49	50	16	52	71	238

SOURCE: U.S. Department of State, Bureau of International Organization Affairs, *Use of the Veto in Meetings of the Security Council of the United Nations*, SO/A/C.1/112/REV.21 (May 1980), for statistics to 1980. United Nations for statistics since 1980.

°Until October 25, 1971, the Chinese seat on the Security Council was occupied by the Republic of China (Taiwan). After that date, the Chinese seat was occupied by the People's Republic of China, which cast both Chinese vetoes during the 1970s.

forward as an expression of an ideal; in practice they are regularly ignored. A General Assembly *resolution* is essentially a document that recommends that member states take a particular policy action. States claim sovereignty and make their own decisions as to whether they will follow a General Assembly resolution. In some cases, however, if many states implement a particular resolution, other states that may not wish to act on the resolution may feel themselves pressured to do so anyway. At the very least, a resolution has the effect of legitimizing the policies of those states that wish to comply with the resolution. Finally, a General Assembly *convention*, or treaty, has two meanings. The more comprehensive convention refers to multilateral treaties voted on by the General Assembly that, upon passage by the General Assembly, are carried back to the capitals of member states for ratification by whatever means each state uses domestically. In other cases, a General Assembly convention refers specifically to a treaty signed between the United Nations and the government of a nation–state, as when in 1956 Egypt agreed to allow United Nations peacekeeping forces to enter Egyptian territory.

The third major segment of the UN is the **Secretariat**, which administers the UN under the leadership of the secretary-general, who is appointed by the General Assembly for a five-year term. The secretary-general has always been from a neutral or nonaligned state; his primary responsibility is to attempt to resolve international disputes and serve as mediator. For example, when American hostages were held at the U.S. embassy in Teheran, Kurt Waldheim, who served as secretary-general from 1972 to 1982, flew to Teheran to mediate between the United States and Iran.

The Secretariat also consists of a sizable staff, numbering over 5,000, which organizes conferences, collects and publishes statistics on global societal, economic, and cultural trends, administers UN peacekeeping missions, and provides others with information about the UN and its activities.

The fourth segment of the UN is the **Economic and Social Council** (ECOSOC). It is an umbrella organization that loosely oversees the activities of the UN's specialized agencies, conferences, and funds such as the United Nations Development Program (UNDP), the United Nations International Children's Fund (UNICEF), and the Office of the United Nations High Commissioner for

Refugees (UNHCR). ECOSOC also concerns itself with human rights, world trade and other related issues. ECOSOC has 54 members, each elected for a three-year term by the General Assembly.

The fifth segment of the UN is the **International Court of Justice** (ICJ). Each of the 15 judges is elected by the General Assembly and the Security Council together. No two judges may be from the same country. The court hears cases that are referred to it by members of the General Assembly or Security Council. In actuality the court hears few cases, and given the claims of national sovereignty and the inability of the court or the UN to enforce its rulings, those rulings are sometimes ignored. Thus, even though the ICJ decided in favor of the United States when American hostages were captured at the U.S. embassy in Teheran, Iran rejected the ICJ's ruling.[8] Similarly, when in 1986 the ICJ found merit in Nicaragua's claim that U.S. economic and logistical support for the Contras was a violation of international law, the United States declared the ICJ had no jurisdiction because of the "political nature" of the case. The United States then downgraded its participation in the ICJ.

The sixth and final segment of the UN is the nearly moribund *Trusteeship Council*. Following World War II, territories formerly held by defeated countries were entrusted to the victor states to prepare those territories for eventual independence. Only one of the 11 original trust territories, the Trust Territory of the Pacific administered by the United States, has not yet received independence. It is scheduled to obtain independence in the near future.

THE UN IN ACTION: PEACEKEEPING[9]

Here it may be useful to provide a detailed examination of one specific area of UN effort, peacekeeping. When all is said and done, peacekeeping, after all, was the real reason for which the United Nations was created.

But since the UN has come into existence, there have been at least 150 major conflicts. Some of these conflicts have pitted nation against nation, and others have been civil wars. In some cases, fewer than a thousand people have been killed, but in others the casualty toll has exceeded a million people. Clearly, the United Nations has not prevented conflict and warfare.

But does this mean that the United Nations has been a failure as a peacekeeper? Despite the tensions and dangers of the Cold War, since 1945, half a century has passed without a third world war. No nuclear weapon has been used in warfare. How many more lives would have been lost during the decolonization process of the 1940s, 1950s, and 1960s had there been no United Nations? How many more conflicts would there have been had the United Nations not existed? There is no way to answer these questions. Nevertheless, the United Nations' success or failure as an international peacekeeping agency cannot be judged in black-and-white terms.

Tools of Peacekeeping

The United Nations has several tools at its disposal with which to try to keep the peace. As a first step, once the Security Council determines that a threat to the peace exists or an act of aggression has occurred, it may seek to resolve the situation via discussion in the Security Council. Occasionally, such discussion serves to defuse an impending conflict as one or both sides give vent to their charges before an international audience. On other occasions, the Security Council may pass a resolution or make a recommendation concerning the crisis. Usually, it is then up to the involved parties to adhere to or ignore Security Council recommendations or resolutions.

Closely related to Security Council discussions, resolutions, and recommendations is the imposition of **comprehensive economic sanctions**. When it imposes comprehensive economic sanctions, the Security Council attempts to influence a country's policy actions by applying economic pressure on it. However, because of the difficulty of getting widespread support for such sanctions within the Security Council and especially among its five permanent members, comprehensive economic sanctions are rarely imposed. Indeed, after comprehensive economic sanctions were imposed against the minority white government of Rhodesia (now Zimbabwe) in 1967 in response to its racial policies, the UN has only imposed economic sanctions three times, against South Africa in 1977 because of apartheid, against Iraq in 1990 because of its invasion of Kuwait, and against Serbia/Yugoslavia in 1992 because of its warfare against Bosnia-Herzegovina. Even when comprehensive economic sanctions are put into effect, individual UN member states decide whether or not they should abide by them.

Beyond rhetoric and economic sanctions, the Security Council may also ask UN members to make military forces available to the UN. As is the case with economic sanctions, however, this is rarely done. Only twice in the UN's entire history has there been a **military enforcement action**. The first time was in 1950, when under U.S. leadership the Security Council recommended that UN members "furnish such assistance to the Republic of Korea as may be necessary to repel [North Korea's] attack" against it. A "unified command under the United States" was created, and the UN forces—mostly American, but from 16 other UN member states as well—were deployed to Korea. They remain there today. The second time was in 1990, when under Resolution 678, the UN Security Council approved "all necessary means" including military force to expel Iraq from Kuwait. Within weeks, under American leadership, the 30 countries that had sent military forces to the Middle East to oppose Iraq's takeover of Kuwait launched "Operation Desert Storm."

Usually, however, instead of military enforcement actions, the Security Council opts to place **peacekeeping operations** into areas of conflict. To begin peacekeeping operations, three informal but very real conditions must be met. First, all parties to the conflict must accept the presence of UN operations. Second, broad segments of the UN, and most particularly all five permanent members of the Security Council as well as at least four of the other ten Security Council members, must support the operation. Third, UN members must be willing to provide the forces needed for peacekeeping operations and pay for their deployment.

As a concept, peacekeeping operations does not appear in the UN Charter. Rather, it has evolved over time, flowing from former UN Secretary-General Dag Hammarskjold's idea of "preventive diplomacy." To Hammarskjold, one of the primary purposes of the UN was to prevent wars from occurring, and if they did

During the late 1980s and early 1990s, the UN sent peacekeeping forces to many locations of conflict around the world. Sometimes the peacekeeping missions were successful, and sometimes they were not. UN troops are shown here in Sarajevo, Bosnia, in June 1992. (The United Nations.)

occur, to prevent them from becoming worse. Hence "preventive diplomacy" helped foster the UN's move into peacekeeping operations.

Traditionally, there have been two major types of UN peacekeeping operations. The first, **peacekeeping forces**, consists of lightly armed troops that are authorized to use force only in self-defense. The second type, **military observer missions**, is usually unarmed, and is authorized only to observe events.

Recently, though, two new forms of UN peacekeeping operations have been initiated. The first new form is a **transition assistance group**, which is designed to help bring new governments into power in countries that are receiving their independence or undergoing a major change in governmental structure. As of 1993, the UN had deployed three transition assistance groups in Namibia, Cambodia, and Western Sahara. The second new form of UN peacekeeping operation for want of a better term might be described as **peacekeeping forces for humanitarian purposes**. As of 1993, the U.N. had deployed two such forces, in Bosnia and Somalia.

Usually, UN peacekeeping operations employ at most a few thousand troops. However, on rare occasions, they may become rather sizable. For example, the UN effort in the Congo from 1960 to 1964 at one time deployed over 20,000 troops; the transition assistance effort that began in 1992 in Cambodia was nearly as large when it began; and the UN deployment that began in Somalia in the same year at one time totaled over 40,000 troops, almost all of which were temporarily U.S. Troops. Table 3–4 lists past and present UN peacekeeping operations.

TABLE 3–4 United Nations Peacekeeping Operations

	Peacekeeping Forces
Africa:	
ONUC	French initials for the 1960–1964 effort in the Congo (now called Zaire)
UNSOM	UN Force in Somalia included 4,000 troops to help keep peace in Somali Civil War; force approved in April 1992; augmented by 38,000 U.S. troops under U.S. command in December 1992; objective expanded to include protection of humanitarian assistance deliveries; still in field in 1993
Asia/Pacific:	
UNSF	UN Security Force in Indonesia during 1962–1963 to help transfer West Irian to Indonesia
Europe:	
UNFICYP	UN Forces in Cyprus, placed there in 1974 to maintain peace between Cyprus' Greek and Turkish communities; 2,150 troops from Australia, Austria, Canada, Denmark, Finland, Ireland, Sweden, and Great Britain remain deployed today
UNPROFOR	UN Protection Force deployed in 1992 in Bosnia-Herzegovina and Croatia, two republics of former Yugoslavia; as many as 15,000 Canadian, French, Russian, and other peacekeepers were deployed to try to keep peace between Serbs, Croatians, and Moslems; also had as an objective protection of convoys delivering humanitarian aid; still in field in 1993
Middle East:	
UNEF I	UN Emergency Force served as a buffer between Egyptian and Israeli forces from November 1956 until June 1967
UNEF II	UN Emergency Force served as a buffer between Egyptian and Israeli forces from October 1973 until July 1979
UNDOF	UN Disengagement Observer Force helps maintain Israeli-Syrian ceasefire since 1974; 1,330 UN troops from Austria, Canada, Finland, and Poland remain deployed today
UNIFIL	UN Interim Forces in Lebanon from 1978 until today to police Lebanese Israeli border, 5,800 UN troops from Fiji, Finland, France, Ghana, Ireland, Italy, Nepal, Norway, and Sweden remain deployed today

	Military Observer Missions
Africa:	
UNAVEM	UN Angola Verification Mission monitors Cuban withdrawal from Angola; 90 observers from Algeria, Brazil, Congo, India, Jordan, Norway, Spain, and Yugoslavia arrived in 1989 and stayed until 1991
UNAVEM II	Second UN Angola Verification Mission deployed 440 troops in 1991 to continue to oversee ceasefire, remained deployed in 1993
Asia/Pacific:	
UNMOGIP	UN Military Observer Group in India and Pakistan observes ceasefire in Kashmir; established in 1948, 38 observers from Belgium, Chile, Denmark, Finland, Italy, Norway, Sweden, and Uruguay remain in the field today
UNAMIC	UN Advance Mission in Cambodia; observers of ceasefire between Vietnamese-backed Cambodian government and three different guerrilla groups including Khmer Rouge first deployed 1992
UNIPOM	UN India-Pakistan Observation Mission oversaw ceasefire in Rann of Kutch during 1965
UNIIMOG	UN Iran-Iraq Military Observer Group oversees Iran-Iraq ceasefire; established 1988, 347 observers from 26 different countries remain in the field today
Europe:	
UNMOG	UN Military Observer Mission in Greece from 1952 to 1954 to check on border tensions with Albania, Bulgaria, and Yugoslavia
Latin America:	
DOMREP	Mission of the Representative of the secretary-general accompanies Organization of American States' Peace Force to Dominican Republic in 1965–1966
ONUCA	UN Observer Mission in Central America sent to Nicaragua in 1989 to observe ceasefire and elections between Sandanista government and Contras

TABLE 3–4   United Nations Peacekeeping Operations (*cont*)

ONUSAL	UN Observer Mission in El Salvador; 543 troops from several states deployed in 1991 to observe ceasefire between government and FMLN guerrillas; remained deployed in 1993

Middle East:

UNTSO	UN Truce Supervisors in Palestine established in 1948 remains in place today with 299 observers from 17 countries
UNOGIL	UN Observer Group in Lebanon sent in during 1958 to monitor the Lebanese-Syrian border
UNYOM	UN Yemen Observer Mission operated in 1963–1964 to report on Saudi and Egyptian withdrawal
UNIKOM	UN Iraq-Kuwait Observer Mission, first deployed in July 1991; includes 549 troops from several nations; remained in the field in 1993

Transition Assistance Groups	
UNTAG	UN Transition Assistance Group in Namibia, created in 1978 but not deployed until 1989, oversaw ceasefire, election, and independence process for Namibian freedom from South Africa; several thousand peacekeepers from several countries were in the field
UNTAC	UN Transition Assistance Group for Cambodia oversaw ceasefire, election, and creation of new government in Cambodia to replace Vietnamese-installed government; over 19,000 troops including the first Japanese forces used overseas since World War II were deployed
MINURSO	UN Transition Assistance Group in the Western Sahara created in 1992 to help transition of Western Sahara from Moroccan rule to independence

UN peacekeeping operations try to accomplish several purposes. Whereas unarmed observer missions almost exclusively serve as on-the-scene reporters, the lightly armed peacekeeping forces patrol buffer zones between hostile forces, block resupply efforts from outside the areas of conflict, provide emergency medical service, supervise troop withdrawal, investigate ceasefire violations, help resettle refugees, and serve as a reminder to hostile parties that their conflict is a global concern. The role of a UN peacekeeper is a difficult, frustrating, and dangerous job, but there is little doubt that UN peacekeeping efforts have helped prevent some conflicts from becoming more violent than they might otherwise have become.

Namibia as a Case Study

Sometimes, UN peacekeeping efforts take many years to implement, and occasionally the UN finds it must create new tools to help it maintain or bring about peace and other objectives that it establishes. This proved to be the case in Namibia, a large arid territory in southwest Africa bordered by Angola, Zambia, Botswana, and South Africa.

A former German colony mandated to South Africa by the League of Nations following World War I, Namibia became the object of international controversy in 1966, when the UN formally ended South Africa's mandate. South Africa refused to recognize the end of its mandate, however, and retained administrative control of the territory despite United Nations and international protests. Meanwhile, as happened elsewhere in the colonial world, a national liberation movement formed in Namibia, the leftist Southwest Africa People's Organization (SWAPO), and struggled against South Africa's control over Namibia. By 1976, the United Nations recognized SWAPO as the only legitimate claimant to power in Namibia, which further strengthened South Africa's resolve to ignore the UN. Besides the political support it received from the UN, SWAPO received material aid and assistance from a variety of other sources.

Many of SWAPO's bases and training centers were in Angola, Namibia's neighbor to the north. Consequently, South Africa invaded Angola from Namibia on several occasions in an effort to destroy SWAPO bases and eliminate SWAPO's operations there. As complex as the Namibia–South Africa–Angola situation was, it was further complicated by U.S., Soviet, and Cuban involvement in the on-going Angolan Civil War and by South Africa's internal racist policy of apartheid.

In 1978, 12 years after the UN ended South Africa's mandate over Namibia, the UN Security Council passed Resolution 435 that created the United Nations Transition Assistance Group (UNTAG), a body whose purpose was to assist the secretary-general's special representative in bringing about Namibian independence via a UN-supervised and controlled election. Despite the best efforts of the special representative and UNTAG, for a decade little progress was made on resolving the Namibian conflict and bringing about an election. The combination of South African intransigence over Namibia, civil war in Angola and Namibia, East–West rivalry, and racial politics proved too difficult a knot to untie.

Gradually, however, a variety of forces led all parties concerned with Namibia to seek a resolution to the conflict. With the United States leading the way and the Soviet Union providing significant positive contributions, Angola, Cuba, and South Africa inched toward a solution to the Namibia problem throughout 1988; for the most part, the United Nations played no role in this phase of negotiations, a fact that some African states resented. Finally, on December 22, 1988—22 years after the UN ended South Africa's Namibia mandate and 10 years after UNTAG was created—Angola, Cuba, and South Africa signed a tripartite agreement, and Angola and Cuba signed a bilateral agreement at UN headquarters in New York, designed to bring about Namibian independence. The parties then recommended to the secretary–general that April 1, 1989, be the date on which UN Resolution 435 be implemented. On January 16, 1989, the Security Council adopted Resolution 629, which affirmed April 1, 1989, as the date on which Resolution 435 would be implemented. A month later, the Security Council passed Resolution 632, which stated that Resolution 435 would be implemented in its original form.

Finally, then, 11 years after it was created, UNTAG began to carry out the mission for which it was formed. Directed by the secretary-general's special representative, UNTAG civilians were based at over 50 locations throughout Namibia, while UNTAG military personnel moved around the country monitoring the ceasefire that went into effect on April 1, 1989. They also observed South Africa's military withdrawal. In addition, as many as 500 UNTAG police helped enforce law and order throughout Namibia. All told, UNTAG forces numbered several thousand people.

Additionally, UNTAG personnel set up procedures to hold an election in late 1989 to establish a "constitutional assembly" to govern Namibia upon its formal independence. UNTAG personnel also registered voters, watched polling places, and tabulated and published election results, all in the name of peacekeeping. Eventually, upon successful completion of Namibia's transition to independence and self-rule, UNTAG was withdrawn and disbanded.

The experience of UNTAG shows that peacekeeping can be a time-consuming and uncertain effort. But despite years of frustration, the bottom line is that in Namibia, the UN eventually was in a position to help resolve conflict and help bring about what it called for in 1966, Namibian independence.

Indeed, the UNTAG effort proved so successful that the United Nations in the 1990s moved to create similar transition missions to help resolve conflict and oversee elections in Cambodia (UNTAC) and in Western Sahara (MINURSO). UNTAC was particularly notable since Japanese soldiers were among its 19,000 troops. This was the first overseas use of Japanese armed forces since World War II.

Issues of Peacekeeping

Finally, several issues must be addressed concerning UN efforts to maintain peace and prevent escalation of wars. Many issues could be raised, but three are most important: (1) Why has the United Nations not been more successful in preventing wars and escalation of wars? (2) How can UN peacekeeping operations be improved? (3) Is the UN a success or a failure as a peacekeeping organization?

1. *Why has the United Nations not been more successful in preventing wars and escalation of wars?* There are several answers to this question, but none looms larger than the American-Soviet rivalry and the East–West conflict. From 1945 until the late 1980s, this rivalry and conflict often made it impossible for the United Nations to undertake successful efforts to prevent wars and to slow or prevent their escalation. As has already been noted, the end of this rivalry and conflict has provided the UN with more opportunities to act as a peacekeeping institution. As a result, in the late 1980s and early 1990s, new UN peacekeeping missions were sent to Angola, Cambodia, Namibia, Yugoslavia, and elsewhere as well.

But in reality, the impact that American-Soviet rivalry and the East–West conflict had on UN peacekeeping operations was simply the most glaring example of the primary difficulty that UN peacekeeping efforts face: the continued worldwide primacy of national sovereignty. Despite everything that the United Nations has become, it remains an international governmental organization. The countries of the world, and particularly the five permanent members of the Security Council, have reserved for themselves the right to act whenever they see fit, and to frustrate actions that the United Nations might undertake when those actions might interfere with their own objectives or interests.

"National sovereignty"—the insistence by individual countries that they themselves have the right to determine their own courses of action and defend their own interests—has thus been the major reason that UN peacekeeping operations have not been more successful. "National sovereignty" dictates that the UN can undertake peacekeeping operations almost exclusively when all parties to a conflict as well as most of the rest of the international community support the peacekeeping operation. This occurs infrequently.

There are also other reasons why the UN has not been more successful. Chief among these is the basic reason that for a peacekeeping mission to have a realistic chance of keeping the peace, all sides in a conflict must want peacekeeping forces to succeed. This situation does not always exist, as the UN's experience in Yugoslavia in 1992 and 1993 showed. There, Serbian forces continued to attack Moslems and others living in Bosnia-Herzegovina despite a series of ceasefire agreements and the presence of UN peacekeeping forces.

In other instances, UN members have not wanted to commit their own forces to peacekeeping operations because of fear of adverse domestic reaction, because of concern about potential casualty levels, or because they perceive no advantage to themselves. Obviously, without peacekeeping forces or observers, there can be no peacekeeping operation.

Similarly, arranging financing has complicated UN peacekeeping efforts. In each case where peacekeeping operations are contemplated, financing must be arranged. This has slowed and sometimes prevented the deployment of peace-keeping forces and military observer missions. Even in those cases where difficul-ties in arranging funding only slowed deployment of peacekeeping personnel, situations in the field sometimes deteriorated while financing was being arranged. The UN's peacekeeping operations were thus further complicated.

Another reason that UN peacekeeping efforts have not been more successful is that the art of peacekeeping is new, and new methods and ideas are continually being put into effect. In essence, peacekeeping has been and remains a trial-and-error undertaking. Unfortunately, sometimes mistakes are made. The key, how-ever, is to learn lessons from past mistakes.

2. *How can UN peacekeeping operations be improved?* One obvious answer is to limit national sovereignty, but there is little likelihood of this occurring. Indeed, the entire United Nations Charter was worded to allow states to defend their sovereignty. (Had it not been, there is little likelihood that the United Nations would ever have come into being.) There are few if any indications that countries have become willing to submerge their sovereignty in the United Nations.

At the same time, it must be recognized that in the late 1980s, UN members began to show a greater willingness to cooperate with one another in peacekeep-ing efforts. In 1988 alone, for example, the UN helped arrange the Soviet with-drawal from Afghanistan, a ceasefire between Iran and Iraq, the Angola–South Africa–Cuba accords on Namibia, a peace initiative in the western Sahara, and an agreement between Greece and Turkey to begin talks on unifying Cyprus. None of these initiatives limited national sovereignty, but a new aura of cooperation was apparent.

At the same time, it has been suggested by people as diverse as former UN Undersecretary-General Sir Brian Urquhart and former Soviet leader Mikhail Gorbachev that the UN's Military Staff Committee be revived. Established by the UN Charter, the UN Military Staff Committee theoretically consists of the chiefs of staff of the militaries of the five permanent members of the Security Council. It was originally hoped that the Military Staff Committee could ease international tensions and provide the basis for international military cooperation and under-standing. However, primarily because of the East–West conflict, it has done little since the United Nations was founded. Nevertheless, both Urquhart and Gorbachev believe that it could be used to smooth out certain aspects of UN peacekeeping operations, and feel that the international political climate is now conducive to the Military Staff Committee's effective operation.

Other concrete proposals have also been made to improve UN peacekeeping efforts. One proposal is that UN members designate a certain part of their armed forces to be "on call" to the United Nations. These forces would remain part of each respective country's national military force but be assigned immediately to UN peacekeeping operations when such operations are put in place. Some countries—for example, Norway, Sweden, Denmark, and Finland—already have taken steps in this direction. If more countries would do this, it is argued, the UN would have what amounted to a "standby force" ready for short-notice deployment.

Similarly, it has been proposed that the United Nations develop and maintain a $1 billion "contingency fund" that would enable the UN to organize and deploy peacekeeping forces and military observer missions quickly without waiting to arrange funding. The problem with such a suggestion is that it is first necessary to convince member states to contribute to the fund.

Two controversial proposals to improve UN peacekeeping efforts are to arm UN peacekeeping forces more heavily and to allow UN personnel to use force more readily. Proponents of these positions assert that UN forces would become more influential and more assertive if these concepts were implemented, thereby aiding peace efforts. Opponents maintain that either proposal would make it more difficult to gain approval for peacekeeping missions, fundamentally alter the nature of UN peacekeeping operations, and turn UN personnel into combatants instead of peacekeepers.

Another controversial proposal advocates consciously moving UN activities from "peacekeeping" to "peacemaking." Advocates of this proposal argue that the end of the East–West conflict has opened opportunities for the United Nations to become a forceful and active defender of human rights on a global basis, and to allow it to prevent future cases of "extreme human rights abuse" such as the genocide that occurred in Cambodia under the Pol Pot regime in the 1970s; the "ethnic cleansing" campaign implemented by Serbia in Bosnia-Herzegovina in 1992 and 1993; and the use of food as a political weapon such as occurred in Somalia in 1992 before the deployment of U.S. troops there. Others oppose the idea, arguing that the UN should not become a global police force, that it would be difficult to draw a line between "human rights abuse" and "extreme human rights abuse," that the cost in resources and human lives of using such a force would be high, and that few nation-states would be willing to devote the necessary resources to developing, maintaining, and deploying a UN peacemaking operation.

3. *Is the UN a success or a failure as a peacekeeping organization?* How one answers this question depends on expectations. If someone began with extremely high expectations about the UN's ability to prevent war and to stop wars from escalating, he or she is probably disappointed with the UN's performance, and may consider the UN a failure. If someone began with the expectation that wars could not be prevented and their escalation could not be controlled, then he or she from the outset would have concluded that the UN was doomed to fail.

But if one's expectations were less extreme—that is, somewhere between the position that the UN could prevent all future wars and the position that the UN was preordained to fail—then it is possible to reach a more optimistic conclusion about what the UN has accomplished in peacekeeping. Even if it has not prevented all wars and stopped all escalation, the UN has prevented some wars from occurring, stopped some wars from escalating, and helped others come to an end. And there is no doubt that the end of the East–West conflict has removed one of the most significant barriers to more successful UN efforts in peacekeeping.

But problems still remain. It is therefore still highly probable that future UN peacekeeping efforts will require widespread international approval, and that funding will continue to be difficult to arrange.

For both cynics and idealists, then, the UN's future in peacekeeping, like its past, is likely to be a disappointment. But for those who begin with more modest expectations, the UN has made many useful contributions to world peace, and promises to make even more.[10]

THE UN AND ITS OTHER ACTIVITIES AND PROBLEMS

The saga of the UN's peacekeeping efforts goes a long way to pointing out the strengths and weaknesses of the organization. Via peacekeeping efforts, the UN has on occasion brought together much of the international community on select international issues.

The UN has done this on issues other than peacekeeping as well, as Tables 3–5 and 3–6 show. Both the special sessions of the UN General Assembly and the major world conferences sponsored by the UN are notable UN achievements and services. On some occasions, assembly and conference objectives are even achieved.

But more often than not, concerns of state sovereignty, security, politics, and economic loss or gain frustrate attainment of UN objectives, not only at General Assembly special sessions and world conferences, but in the UN's other objectives as well. Concerns of sovereignty and national interest frequently arise as some nation-states claim that they fear the UN may move toward supranational status, that is, a status in which the majority of UN members grant the UN

TABLE 3–5　Special Sessions of the UN General Assembly

Topic	Year
Palestine	1947
Palestine	1948
Tunisia	1961
Financial and Budgetary Problems	1963
Peacekeeping and Southwest Africa	1967
Raw Materials and Development	1974
Development and International Cooperations	1975
Financing UN Interim Forces in Lebanon	1978
Namibia	1978
Disarmament	1978
International Economic Cooperation	1980
Disarmament	1982
Africa's Economy	1986
Disarmament	1988
Apartheid	1989
Narcotic Drugs	1990
Economic Cooperation	1990

TABLE 3–6   Selected UN-Sponsored World Conferences

Topic	Year	City
Human Environment	1972	Stockholm
Law of the Sea	1973–82	Caracas, Geneva, and New York
Population	1974	Bucharest
Food	1974	Rome
Women and Development	1975	Mexico City
Employment	1976	Geneva
Human Settlements (HABITAT)	1976	Vancouver, British Columbia
Water	1977	Mar del Plata, Argentina
Desertification	1977	Nairobi
Agrarian Reform and Rural Development	1979	Rome
Science and Technology for Development	1979	Vienna
New and Renewable Sources of Energy (UNERG)	1981	Nairobi
Least Developed Countries	1981	Paris
Exploitation and Peaceful Uses of Outer Space (UNISPACE)	1982	Vienna
Aging	1982	Vienna
Population	1984	Mexico City
Women	1985	Nairobi
Drugs	1987	Vienna
Disarmament and Development	1987	New York
Copper	1989	Geneva
World Disarmament	1989	Dagomys, U.S.S.R.
Environment and Development	1992	Rio de Janeiro
Geographical Names Standards	1992	New York

authority over and above nation-states. Realistically, however, there is no likelihood that the UN will attain supranational status in the foreseeable future.

Even so, states sometimes believe that they have legitimate reason to be concerned about the UN's actions, activities, and attitudes. Sometimes, states take action against the UN and its agencies when they believe the UN has taken positions or actions that they believe are aimed against them. For example, in 1985 and 1986, the United States and Great Britain both withdrew from the United Nations Educational, Scientific, and Cultural Organization (UNESCO) because of that organization's perceived anti–Western bias. As far as both the United States and British governments were concerned, UNESCO had become a forum used exclusively for the vilification of Western values, attitudes, and ideas, and neither believed it in their national interest to remain members. As a result, both left, leading to a net loss to UNESCO not only of two prominent members, but also 29.6 percent of its annual budget of $382 million (25 percent provided by the United States, 4.6 percent by Great Britain).

Indeed, even the UN itself has had its funding levels reduced because certain states felt it did not serve their purposes. For years, the Soviet Union was far behind on its payments to the UN. It began to make amends only in the late 1980s under Gorbachev. At the same time, resentment in the U.S. Congress

The United Nations' record as a peacekeeping institution is far from perfect, but it has achieved several notable successes. Here, the United Nations Security Council votes on a measure. (The United Nations.)

about anti-Americanism in the General Assembly and in associated UN agencies and about an oversized UN bureaucracy led Congress in 1985 to pass a law that threatened to reduce U.S. funding of the UN by 5 percent unless the UN changed its rules to permit voting according to level of financial contribution. Thus, in 1987 the United States intentionally fell far behind in its payment to the UN to illustrate its displeasure.

U.S. financial pressures on the UN brought about some changes in procedures at the United Nations. The UN cut staffing levels about 15 percent, and a new budgetary system was adopted in which all major budget decisions had to be made unanimously. Some U.S. government observers also believed the General Assembly became less overtly anti-American. In any event, by September 1988 the Reagan administration declared that the UN had made "striking progress" on budgetary and political reforms, and announced that the U.S. would restore its full level of funding to the UN. Nevertheless, at the beginning of 1993, the United States still owed the United Nations over $500 million in back dues and unpaid contributions to peacekeeping missions.

If the UN's record as a keeper of the peace may be described as mottled, so too may its record as a distributor of goods and services. The UN's problem here is one of resources; put simply, nation-states have been unwilling to support the United Nations at a level that would permit its specialized agencies and other bodies to affect significantly on a global scale those issues that they confront. Again caution must be exercised, for the UN's specialized agencies have undertaken some impressive programs. The United Nations Development Program, for example, has extended over $2 billion in development aid during its existence, and by 1993 the number of UN developmental experts working in the Third World exceeded 12,000. In addition, the World Health Organization reduced the frequency of malaria and eradicated smallpox. More examples on both sides of the argument could be used, but an objective observer is driven to the conclusion that the UN's record as a distributor of goods and services is mottled. If there were no UN or specialized agencies the world's condition would be worse. How much worse is a matter of debate.

The two areas where the United Nations and its related organizations have most clearly succeeded are in the regulation of certain international activities and in the production and dissemination of information. A number of specialized agencies such as the Universal Postal Union, the International Telecommunications Union, and the General Agreement on Tariffs and Trade exist within the United Nations system, and have as their specific purpose the international regulation of various forms of relations between states. Although it would be an overstatement to declare that all the world's states accede to the regulations put forward on, for example, the mail, telecommunications, and tariffs, almost all states recognize the benefits that such regulation brings, and consequently have accepted the specialized agencies' regulations. Similarly, the United Nations system has had great success in compiling and disseminating statistics on the economic and social performances of its member states. Until the late 1980s, and in some cases the early 1990s, the greatest UN shortcoming in this area stemmed from the national policy of Soviet–bloc states that considered such information to be a state secret. Now, however, the Soviet Union's successor states as well as Eastern European states are increasingly a part of the UN's statistical network.[11]

Under the auspices of the United Nations Environment Program (UNEP), the UN has also developed an international network through which it can obtain and disseminate vital environmental information. UNEP's activities include maintaining a Global Environment Monitoring System (GEMS), establishing an International Register of Potentially Toxic Chemicals, and creating Infoterra, a worldwide environmental network. Although considerations of sovereignty and national interest played a major role in limiting the results of the 1992 UN Rio de Janeiro Conference on the Environment and Development, UNEP's operations have been hampered more by limited funding than anything else.

Another area of UN operations that is the subject of much debate and political disagreement is decolonization. Frequently, the United Nations receives credit for the wave of decolonization that swept the world during the 1950s, 1960s, and 1970s. The two United Nations "tools" to which decolonization is attributed are the Declaration Regarding Non-Self-Governing Territories (Chapter 11 of the UN charter) and the International Trusteeship System (Chapter 12).[12] As we saw in our discussion of the Trusteeship Council, 10 states received their independence because of the trusteeship procedures. Little debate is possible about the importance of the trusteeship system; clearly, the involved states received independence as a result of the procedures outlined by the United Nations. Considerable disagreement exists, however, when Chapter 11 is discussed. Proponents of the United Nations argue that Chapter 11 and its requirements, which demand that colonial powers recognize the "sacred trust" to promote "the well-being of the inhabitants of these territories," including eventual self-government, were major factors that led to the massive decolonization phenomenon of the post–World War II era. More cynical observers believe that the costs of colonization began to outweigh its benefits, and therefore old colonies became new sovereign states as the colonial powers no longer saw advantage in having colonies.

Another aspect of colonialism that the United Nations sometimes approaches is "internal colonization." Internal colonization occurs when one state has within it a number of nationalities, at least one of which asserts its desire to establish its own independent nation-state, or when one state has removed a nationality from territories that the nationality alleges are its homeland. The United Nation's record on these issues is erratic. In some cases, as with the PLO, the UN has not formally recognized the claims of the nationality for statehood, but has granted the group representing the nationality observer status at the General Assembly. In other cases, as with Eritrea, the United Nations ignored the claims of nationality groups. The United Nations is clearly in a difficult position on such cases, because to support the claims of all such groups would win for the United Nations the animosity of all states that had internal groups seeking independence. Thus, on any particular case involving potential "internal colonization," the United Nations' position is the product of a variety of political, social, economic, and military factors.

All things considered, the United Nations during its first 45 years of existence did not live up to the hopes of its founders in taking "effective collective measures for the prevention and removal of threats to the peace," in developing "friendly relations among nations," nor in achieving "international cooperation in solving international problems." As we have already seen, much of the UN's frustrations were caused by the East–West conflict.

But even during that conflict, the UN served as an effective forum for debating, discussing, and in some instances acting upon and even solving some of the international community's problems and conflicts. With the East–West conflict over, new possibilities are emerging for the United Nations to become a more effective actor in contemporary international affairs.

OTHER IGOS: AN OVERVIEW

The United Nations is a global broad-purpose IGO. Other IGOs have neither the global membership nor the broad purpose that the United Nations aspires to. As the archetypical IGO, the UN must of course be studied. However, because of the combination of global membership and broad purpose, it is atypical as well. This section therefore briefly examines two IGOs that have more narrowly defined memberships or purposes: the North Atlantic Treaty Organization (NATO), a regional IGO primarily concerned with the security of its member states; and the Association of Southeast Asian Nations (ASEAN), a regional IGO concerned primarily with the economic well-being of its member states, none of which are superpowers or even second-rank powers.

NATO

The North Atlantic Treaty was signed in 1949 by Belgium, Britain, Canada, Denmark, France, Iceland, Italy, Luxembourg, the Netherlands, Norway,

Portugal, and the United States. Greece and Turkey joined in the alliance in 1952, and West Germany in 1955. In 1982, Spain also became a member of NATO.[13] In the treaty, the signatory nations agreed to consult together if the security of any member state was threatened and to regard a military attack against one of the members as an attack against all. Further, the treaty committed the allies to use military force "to restore and maintain the security of the North Atlantic area."

Obviously, the primary purpose of NATO was and is to provide security for its members. Although it was not specifically stated in the North Atlantic Treaty, NATO countries were primarily concerned about the threat of Soviet aggression, and NATO designed its policies to counter the U.S.S.R. But with the demise of the U.S.S.R., many people argue that NATO is an IGO whose time has passed, and that it should be disbanded. Others argue that even though the Soviet threat is over, threats to North Atlantic security remain, and NATO therefore still serves a useful purpose.

Organizationally, the governing body of NATO is the North Atlantic Council, which meets twice a year and consists of ministers from each of the NATO countries and of an ambassador from each country. The ambassadors are in permanent session in NATO's Brussels headquarters.

The council is advised on political-military matters by the secretary-general and his staff, also headquartered in Brussels. The Secretariat also discusses financial, economic, and scientific aspects of defense planning with the council. A separate Military Committee consisting of the chiefs-of-staff of all member countries except France and Iceland, neither of which have military forces incorporated within NATO's military command structure, recommend military policy to the council. NATO also has a separate civilian structure that deals with nonmilitary matters. (See Figure 3–2.)

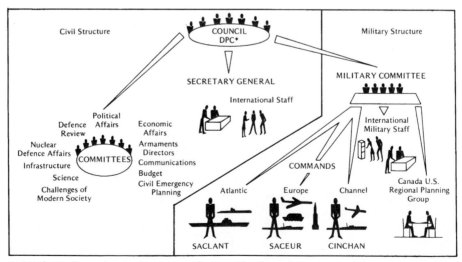

*DPC: the Defense Planning Committee, dealing with military policy, meets at the same levels as the council.

FIGURE 3–2   Civil and military structure of the North Atlantic Treaty Organization. (Source: NATO, *NATO Facts and Figures.* Brussels: NATO Information Service, 1978, p. 204.)

The Defense Planning Committee of NATO meets at the same level as the council and plans the defense of Europe in the event of war. All NATO members except France are members. Indeed, the only reason that the Defense Planning Committee exists is that in 1966 France chose to remove its armed forces from the integrated military organization of NATO, but still desired to sit on the North Atlantic Council. By exercising this right of national sovereignty within an IGO, France forced NATO to create a new committee, the Defense Planning Committee, which would meet at the same level as the council to discuss all matters in which France, by reason of its withdrawal from the integrated military structure, would not participate.

Another separate committee of NATO is the Nuclear Planning Group (NPG), which meets twice a year at ministerial or ambassadorial levels, to prepare NATO's nuclear policy. It has 12 members. (France, Iceland, Spain and Luxembourg are not members because of their own national policies and attitudes regarding nuclear weapons.)

Operationally, NATO has three major military commands. Allied Command Europe (ACE) has its headquarters at Casteau, Belgium. It is responsible for the defense of all NATO territory on the European continent except France and Portugal. The commander of ACE, who has always been an American, is responsible to the Military Committee, although he also has direct access to the council, the Defense Planning Committee, and individual heads of government. NATO's two other major military commands are Allied Command Atlantic (ACLANT), which is responsible for the security of the North Atlantic Ocean from the Tropic of Cancer to the North Pole, and Allied Command Channel (ACCHAN), whose duties include controlling the English Channel and the southern North Sea. ACCHAN is scheduled to be phased out in the mid-1990s.

NATO's history as an IGO points out both the strengths and weaknesses of IGOs as a class of international actors. On the one hand, NATO's military structure provides a degree of security for its member states that they, acting as individual sovereign entities, could not attain for themselves. On the other hand, because of the continuing demand on the part of individual states for their rights of sovereignty, policies undertaken by NATO are often hesitant and uncertain. Thus, when France decided to withdraw its military forces from NATO commands, the alliance was temporarily thrown into disarray. More recently, the December 1979 Soviet invasion of Afghanistan led NATO member states to adopt widely diverging viewpoints and policies in response to the Soviet action. No unified NATO policy was forthcoming. NATO states also disagreed on the types of restrictions that should exist on technology transfer to the Soviet Union and over how best to respond to terrorism.

On the whole, though, NATO states have disagreed more over how best to achieve their objective—collective security—than over what that objective should be. But as noted earlier, the demise of the Soviet Union raised for NATO and its member states a new and fundamental question concerning NATO—namely, with the Soviet threat gone, did NATO still serve a purpose?

NATO's defenders argued that it did, and pointed to NATO's rapid creation of the North Atlantic Coordination Council (NACC) as proof that NATO still could play a vital role in helping provide for European and North Atlantic security. NACC was created in response to many former communist states' desires to join NATO once they overthrew their communist governments.

NATO states were not willing to let the newly noncommunist states into NATO as full members, but they did establish NACC as a forum at which NATO states and former communist European states could discuss mutual security concerns. Thus, NATO proponents argued, NATO still served an extremely useful security function.

"Not so," NATO's critics replied. NACC was nothing more than a transparent attempt to maintain a reason for existing when no security threat remained. They argued that NATO itself should be disbanded. So the battle over NATO's continued existence was joined, with no clear outcome in sight.

ASEAN

The Association of Southeast Asian Nations was founded in 1967 to "accelerate the economic growth, social progress and cultural development in the region" and to "promote regional peace and security."[14] Indonesia, Malaysia, the Philippines, Singapore, Thailand, and Brunei are the six members. ASEAN holds Ministerial Conferences of Foreign Ministers at least once a year, and appoints a standing committee that meets more often. The Secretariat of ASEAN is in Kuala Lumpur, Malaysia.

ASEAN has successfully lowered some of the tariff and trade barriers that existed between its member states, but as is the case with all IGOs, demands for national sovereignty have lessened the effectiveness of ASEAN. This was well-demonstrated in January 1992 when the leaders of ASEAN agreed to form a free trade area known as AFTA, the "ASEAN Free Trade Area," but because of concerns over national sovereignty and domestic politics, decided not to implement it for 15 years. Thus, even in the absence of great power rivalry, the functioning of an IGO has been impaired by states' claims for sovereignty. On the other hand, unlike NATO, ASEAN has only rarely been accused of being a tool used by one or more of its members to achieve a national objective.

Disagreement exists about the degree to which ASEAN policies served as the catalyst that fueled the region's impressive economic growth during the 1970s and 1980s. ASEAN detractors assert that the organization played little or no role, whereas ASEAN supporters claim that it played a major role. Nevertheless, at a minimum, it appears that ASEAN did help establish a climate of confidence about the region that helped attract external investment to Southeast Asia. This was an impressive achievement, especially because it came on the heels of the American defeat in Vietnam when confidence in the stability of the region was at a low ebb.

ASEAN states also played a significant role in bringing about Vietnam's 1989 withdrawal from Cambodia. The six ASEAN countries presented the Vietnamese with a relatively unified noncommunist Southeast Asian perspective on the conflict, and they worked behind the scenes to set up conditions and contests to aid the Vietnamese withdrawal.

Nevertheless, despite its successes, all is not perfect within ASEAN. Some ASEAN states have occasionally expressed concern about the intentions of their fellow members within ASEAN. For example, Indonesia has implied concern that Thailand wants to use ASEAN as a tool to provide it security from Vietnam, and most other ASEAN states are concerned that Indonesia's sheer size will allow it to dominate ASEAN. Even so, despite these concerns, ASEAN must be regarded as a reasonably successful IGO.

THE FUTURE OF IGOS

The numbers, roles, and importance of international governmental organizations in contemporary international relations have expanded tremendously, and all indications are that their numbers, roles, and importance will continue to expand in the future. The ability of IGOs to approach, analyze, and propose solutions to problems and issues that transcend national boundaries is in most cases unequaled by any other international actor. Indeed, in the eyes of many, it is unfortunate that IGOs do not have more resources at their disposal so that they may better cope with the problems and issues that they face.

With this being said, the importance of IGOs as actors in the international arena should not be exaggerated. All IGOs, even those few such as the European Community that have moved from transnational to supranational status, are careful to guarantee the powers of sovereignty to their member states. (Here it should be remembered that the EC receives its supranatural authority from its member states and therefore, at least in theory, can have that authority revoked by them.) IGOs therefore remain creations of states, and as a consequence are less influential than their creators.

In addition, different states have different views of IGOs, and consequently pursue different policies toward them. The general American attitude toward the United Nations, for example, was supportive during the early years of the UN's existence. However, as more and more Developing World nations entered the United Nations and as more and more UN votes opposed preferred American outcomes, American support for the UN cooled. Then in the early 1990s, U.S. attitudes toward the UN reversed again as U.S. and UN positions on many issues again coincided.

Conversely, the Soviet Union's perception of the United Nations was that the UN reflected the dominance of the United States in international affairs and therefore on most issues was a tool of American policy that should not receive significant support from the U.S.S.R. That Soviet viewpoint changed, however, as the Kremlin adopted a more cooperative international posture in the late 1980s.

The desire of states to maintain national sovereignty remains the most significant threat to the future of IGOs and to the continued growth of their global influence. As discussed earlier in this chapter, IGOs do provide services for states, and it is because of these services that states have seen fit to bring them into existence and to grant them whatever powers they do have.

A last point should be made concerning the role of IGOs in the 1990s and beyond. Although a clear relationship exists between major wars and the growth in number of IGOs, analysts have been unable to agree whether the amount of violence in the international arena has been reduced by the increased number of IGOs and the increased international interaction that they bring about. Similarly, analysts have not agreed whether IGOs perform other tasks that may lead to a more stable and just international environment. As in so many other aspects of international affairs, then, the answer to the question of whether IGOs are a force for improvement in the global community is open to debate. What is not open to debate is that international governmental organizations, although more powerful, influential, and numerous today than they have ever been in the past, are still subordinate to states as actors in the international arena.

KEY TERMS AND CONCEPTS

structures of IGOs	military enforcement action
functions of IGOs	peacekeeping operations
evolution of IGOs	peacekeeping forces
UN Security Council	military observer missions
UN General Assembly	transition assistance groups
UN Secretariat	peacekeeping forces for
UN Economic and Social	humanitarian purposes
Council	Namibia
International Court of Justice	peacekeeping issues
(ICJ) (also in Chapter 20)	problems the UN faces
comprehensive economic	NATO (also in Chapter 13)
sanctions	ASEAN

NOTES

1. These figures are for 1992, furnished by the United Nations.
2. For more detailed discussion of IGOs, see Harold K. Jacobson, *Networks of Interdependence: International Organizations and the Global Political System* (New York: Knopf, 1979). See also Clive Archer, *International Organizations, 4th Ed.* (New York: Routledge, 1992).
3. Thucydides, *The Peloponnesian War* (Baltimore: Penguin, 1954).
4. For discussions of UN peacekeeping efforts, see *The Blue Helmets: A Review of UN Peacekeeping* (New York: United Nations Publications, 1985); Henry Wiseman (ed.), *Peacekeeping: Appraisals and Proposals* (New York: Pergamon Press, 1983); and F. T. Lin, *United Nations Peacekeeping and the Non-Use of Force* (Boulder, CO: Lynne Rienner Publishers, 1992).
5. Woodrow Wilson, *Congressional Government* (New York: Meridian, 1956, p. 194).
6. For a detailed history of the birth of the United Nations, see Ruth B. Russell, *A History of the United Nations Charter: The Role of the United States 1940–1945* (Washington: Brookings Institution, 1958).
7. As might be expected, granting observer status to nongovernmental organizations implies a certain degree of political recognition. Therefore, observer status is rarely awarded, though often hotly debated.
8. See Dana D. Fischer, "Decisions to Use the International Court of Justice: Four Recent Cases," *International Studies Quarterly*, Vol. 6 (June 1982): 251–277.
9. Much of the following section is taken from Daniel S. Papp and John Diehl, *The United Nations: Issues of Peace and Conflict* (Atlanta: Southern Center for International Studies, 1990).

10. For other views on the future of the UN, see Peter R. Baehr and Leon Gordenker, *The United Nations in the 1990s* (New York: St. Martin's, 1992); and James N. Rosenau, *The United Nations in a Turbulent World* (Boulder, CO: Lynne Rienner Publishers, 1992).

11. For an interesting pre–Gorbachev Soviet view of the UN, see V. Petrovsky, "The UN and World Politics," *International Affairs (Moscow)*, no. 7 (July 1980): 10–20. For Gorbachev's own views on the UN, see *Pravada*, September 17, 1987, and Gorbachev's December 7, 1988, UN speech.

12. The UN charter may be found in A. LeRoy Bennet, *International Organizations: Principles and Issues* (Englewood Cliffs, NJ: Prentice–Hall, 1977), pp. 400–425.

13. For detailed discussions of the organization and roles of NATO, see Kenneth A. Myers (ed.), *NATO: The Next Thirty Years* (Boulder, CO: Westview, 1980); and *NATO: Facts and Figures* (Brussels: NATO Information Service, 1992).

14. For additional views on ASEAN, see Kernial S. Sandhu et al., eds., *The ASEAN Reader* (Singapore: Institute of Southeast Asian Studies, 1992); Hans Christoph Rieger, ed., *ASEAN Economic Cooperation: A Handbook* (Singapore: Institute of Southeast Asian Studies, 1991); and Pearl Imada et al., *A Free Trade Area: Implications for ASEAN* (Singapore: Institute of Southeast Asian Studies, 1991).

CHAPTER 4

Multinational Corporations

- How are MNCs different from other corporations?
- Why are MNCs so widely praised and condemned?
- Do MNCs really challenge state sovereignty, and if so, how?

Few actors in the contemporary international arena evoke stronger praise or condemnation than multinational corporations (MNCs). On the one extreme, the MNCs' most ardent defenders argue that MNCs provide opportunities for global economic advancement and employment, establish a rational and efficient way to maximize the quantity and minimize the cost of international production, and offer a realistic opportunity to move beyond the parochial national allegiances fostered by the state. On the other extreme, the MNCs' most zealous critics maintain that MNCs are agents of economic imperialism and political control, seek to maximize profit without regard to environmental or human consequences, and are under the control of elitist managers and technocrats who seek to expand their own power and influence. Between these two extremes lie other interpretations of the roles, purposes, and objectives of today's MNCs, interpretations that, to one degree or another, see these multinational corporations as mixed blessings that are neither as angelic nor as evil as their defenders or detractors make them out to be.[1]

Regardless of the accuracy of the claims of and charges against the MNCs, the massive impact of the productive capacities of the multinationals on the world's economy guarantees MNCs important roles in international relations. In 1978 alone, $1,886 billion of the world's gross product was produced by the largest 430 multinational corporations. By 1991, the world's 44 largest multinational firms by themselves produced $2,008 billion. This totaled almost 10 percent of the world's entire economic output! And in the same year, those 44 MNCs were among the world's largest 100 economic units, as Table 4–1 shows. Perhaps even more surprisingly, every one of the world's largest Fortune 500 corporations in 1991 produced more than the world's 61 smallest state economies.[2]

TABLE 4–1   The World's 100 Largest Economic Units, 1991 ($U.S. Billions)[a]

1.	U.S.A.	5,465		Thailand	79	69.	New Zealand	40
2.	Soviet Union	2,660	36.	Denmark	78	70.	**E.I. DuPont De**	
3.	Japan	2,115		**Toyota**	78		**Nemours**	38
4.	Germany	1,157	38.	Finland	77		**Texaco**	38
5.	France	873	39.	Greece	76	72.	**Chevron**	37
6.	U.K.	858	40.	Norway	74		Egypt	37
7.	Italy	844	41.	Romania	70	74.	**ELF Aquitaine**	36
8.	Canada	516	42.	**IBM**	65		**Nestlé**	36
9.	Spain	435	43.	**IRI**	64	76.	Iraq	35
10.	China	413		Hong Kong	64		Singapore	35
11.	Brazil	388	45.	Hungary	61	78.	Ireland	34
12.	Australia	254	46.	**General Electric**	60	79.	**Toshiba**	33
	India	254	47.	**British Petroleum**	58	80.	**Honda**	31
14.	South Korea	238		Portugal	58	81.	**Philips Electronic**	30
15.	Mexico	236	49.	**Daimler Benz**	57		North Korea	30
16.	Netherlands	218		**Mobil**	57	83.	**Renault**	29
17.	Turkey	178	51.	**Hitachi**	56		**Chrysler**	29
18.	Poland	158	52.	Algeria	54		**Boeing**	29
19.	Taiwan	150	53.	**Matsushita Electric**			**ABB ASEA Brown**	
20.	Belgium	144		**Industries**	49		**Baveri**	29
21.	Sweden	137	54.	**Philip Morris**	48	87.	**Hoechst**	38
22.	Switzerland	126	55.	**Fiat**	47		**Peugeot**	28
23.	**General Motors**	123		Bulgaria	47		**Alcatel Alstham**	28
24.	Czechoslovakia	120	57.	Israel	46		**BASF**	28
	Yugoslavia	120		Volkswagen	46		Chile	28
26.	Austria	111	59.	Siemens	45	92.	Nigeria	27
27.	**Royal Dutch/Shell**			Philippines	45		**Procter & Gamble**	27
	Group	104	61.	**Samsung Group**	44		**NEC**	27
28.	**Exxon**	103	62.	Pakistan	43		**Sony**	27
29.	South Africa	102		Malaysia	43	96.	**Amoco**	26
30.	Indonesia	94		Colombia	43		**Bayer**	26
31.	**Ford Motor**	89		**Nissan Motor**	43	98.	**Total**	25
32.	Argentina	82	66.	Venezuela	42		**Morocco**	25
33.	Iran	80	67.	Unilever	41		**Daewoo**	25
34.	Saudi Arabia	79		**ENI**	41			

[a] Figures for states are gross domestic or gross national products as provided by the U.S. Central Intelligence Agency, *The World Factbook 1991* (Washington, DC: U.S. Government Printing Office, 1992). Figures for corporations are for total sales as provided by *Fortune*, July 27, 1992.

MNCs are important not only because of their size, but also because of their global presence. Scarcely a country in the world does not serve as a host to a multinational corporation or one of its subsidiaries. In some cases multinational corporations are permitted full control of their subsidiary units in host countries, but in other cases host countries require some degree of control by local economic interests or even by the government itself. Nonetheless, the fact remains that multinational corporations have penetrated most if not all of the countries in the world today.

The control that MNCs have over many advanced technologies and raw materials is also worth noting. IBM, General Electric, ITT, and Daimler-Benz all deal heavily in advanced technical applications, and the so-called Seven Sisters corporations of the oil and petroleum industry dominate that field in the Western industrialized world. MNC dominance of these and other economic sectors so critical to industrialized societies has led some critics of MNCs to charge that the multinationals have obtained a stranglehold over the economic well-being of the industrialized Western world and the Developing World alike. This charge is openly and hotly denied by spokespersons for MNCs.

What, then, is a multinational corporation? How is it structured, how does it operate, and from where does it obtain its influence? What are the origins of MNCs as a class of international actors, and what may the future hold for MNCs? May their influence be expected to rise or wane? Are they in fact so powerful and influential that they have placed state sovereignty at bay? These and other issues concerning multinational corporations will be discussed throughout this chapter.

AN OVERVIEW OF MULTINATIONAL CORPORATIONS

In its simplest form, a multinational corporation is a corporation that has its head-quarters or center of operations in one country and owns and operates other corporations, or subsets of itself, in other countries. These other corporations or subsets are generally called **subsidiaries**. A multinational corporation is there-fore exactly what its name implies: a corporation that operates in more than one country.

Drawing on this basic definition, some observers posit that there are actually three stages in the development of a multinational corporation. In the first stage, an MNC creates a separate business strategy for each country in which it oper-ates. At this stage of development, a multinational corporation may best be described as a "multidomestic" corporation. In the second stage, an MNC strives to dominate a global market, but it nevertheless concentrates much of its efforts in its home country. Such MNCs have been described as "global" corporations. In the third stage of development, an MNC draws on global resources, man-agement, production, and other capabilities to assume the stature of a "transna-tional" corporation. Few MNCs have actually made this transition to transnational status. IBM is one corporation that has. For our purposes in this chapter, we will consider all MNCs together, regardless of the stage of develop-ment they may be in.

MNCs produce a variety of goods and services. Some MNCs such as Nestlé and Fiat produce consumer-oriented products; others such as IBM and ITT deal in high technology and capital goods. Still other MNCs such as Anaconda or Royal Dutch deal in raw materials. Most MNCs are large and most operate in a number of different product areas. At least through the 1980s, the combined effect of large-size, diversified product fields, and global operations permitted most MNCs to weather the economic vicissitudes that beset smaller corporations operating in a single national market. Indeed, during the 1970s and 1980s the growth rate of world sales of most MNCs far exceeded the growth rate of sales of nationally oriented firms as well as the growth rate of gross national product of individual nation-states.

On some occasions, MNCs produce goods from components that are made in several countries, thereby making it difficult to say with certainty whether a given product is "Made in America," "Made in Japan," or made somewhere else. Chrysler Corporation's "Dodge Stealth" is a perfect example. Although the markings on the automobile make one think that it is made in the United States, much of the car is in fact made in Japan under a Chrysler Corporation co-production agreement with Mitsubishi Motors.

Although at first blush it might appear not important where in the world a product is produced, the reality is that production creates jobs for workers, profits for companies, and economic strength for countries. Thus, even though MNCs may argue that they are only economic entities, their decisions have immense national and international political importance, as we will see throughout this chapter.

The **organizational structure of multinational corporations** can and does vary. Before World War II, when national differences in consumer preference were large, differences in industrial standards were numerous, and governmentally created barriers to international trade were high, multinational corporations were obliged to operate on a predominantly national and decentralized basis. In other words, MNCs established their foreign subsidiaries so that each subsidiary operated on its own with little or no guidance from the parent corporation. Such a structural organization, known as a mother-daughter arrangement, was requisite for operating in the international political-economic environment of the era. Most MNCs that were organized as mother-daughter arrangements were European.[3] Figure 4–1(a) illustrates the organizational structure of these types of firms.

Following World War II a new international global economic order was created by the victorious Western powers. Over time, differences in consumer preferences were reduced (but not eliminated), industrial standards slowly became more uniform, and governmentally created barriers to trade lessened. These gradual occurrences had an impact on the organizational structure of MNCs. Larger markets became available because of reduced barriers to trade, increased standardization, and more homogeneous consumer tastes, so economies of scale could be brought to bear. With fewer barriers to trade, the productive benefits of comparative advantage could be made an operational reality. And larger corporations, with their new potential for global reach, could scan the world for the least expensive raw material and labor inputs for their products. The era of the modern multinational corporation had come.

All this took a number of years. Nevertheless, MNCs adapted their organizational structures to take advantage of the opportunities afforded them by the new postwar international economic order. The old mother-daughter arrangements, created to allow decisions to be made individually in each unit and to allow differentiated products to be made by each unit, could not take fullest advantage of the new international economic environment. Gradually, new organizational structures for MNCs were created.

American firms were among the first and the most aggressive corporations to seek and find alternative structures. Many U.S. MNCs developed organizational structures based on product divisions with one division designated an international division. Thus, a single firm making products A, B, and C within the United

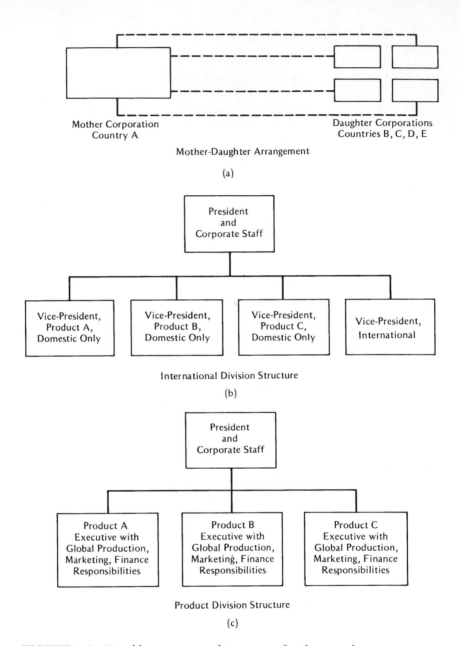

FIGURE 4-1   Possible organizational structures of multinational corporations.

States would have a separate domestic division for each of its three products, and a fourth division for its international operations. Figure 4–1(b) illustrates this type of arrangement.

However, as international operations of MNCs accelerated during the 1950s and 1960s, more and more corporations both inside and outside the United States changed their structures to ones of product divisions that operated on a global scale. This change was necessitated in many cases by the astronomical growth of the international movement of goods and materials that took place during this period; put simply, the international divisions of many MNCs became more important than all other divisions of operations combined. Globally oriented products divisions thus became the most logical and efficient managerial structure. This organizational trend, begun during the 1950s, has continued into the 1990s.[4] Figure 4–1(c) diagrams this organizational structure.

An extremely subtle shift in **perspectives of MNC management** accompanied this structural shift. In many cases, the perspective of the top management of MNCs changed from an outlook that viewed MNCs as national companies with international operations to an outlook that considered MNCs to be truly international corporations. In essence, then, at least in the minds of many corporate managers, many MNCs are now international rather than national firms. The implications of this subtle change of emphasis are potentially massive.

Before we examine these implications, we must first further examine MNCs themselves. As a general rule, MNCs prefer to have full ownership of their foreign subsidiaries because full ownership allows maximum control. To achieve full ownership, MNCs must often invest large sums of money directly in countries outside their home country. Money that MNCs—or other companies and individuals as well—invest directly outside their home country is called, aptly enough, **foreign direct investment**.

Sometimes parent MNCs share ownership of a foreign subsidiary through either public or private groups in the host country. This is called a **joint venture**. In some cases, the public group that the parent corporation shares ownership with is the government of the host country itself. Indeed, one of the major changes instituted in the Soviet economy before the U.S.S.R. collapsed was the legalization of joint ventures between Western businesses and Soviet government-owned firms.[5] In communist China, such joint ventures were also legalized during the 1980s and remain legal today.

There are a variety of reasons why MNCs may participate in a joint venture even though they lose some control of their subsidiaries. First, a multinational may find that public or private groups in the host country have capital or expertise without which the subsidiary would fail. Second, an MNC may view a particular market as requiring host-nation participation to reduce the political risk of having a foreign corporation operating within that market. Finally, in some states, laws require host-nation participation.

This is not to say that MNCs are willing in all cases to allow other groups or individuals to have partial control of their subsidiaries. On occasion, MNCs view joint ventures as unacceptable or consider other strictures on their operations in a particular country too serious to permit continued operation. One of the most celebrated examples of the latter situation involved the Indian government and the Coca-Cola Corporation. The Indian government demanded that if Coca-Cola wished to continue operating its subsidiary in India, it had to provide India with the composition of the closely guarded secret formula for the cola syrup that the American corporation used in its most famous product. Coca-Cola refused and ended its Indian operations.

Sometimes MNCs choose not to invest directly in foreign countries, but opt instead to conclude **licensing agreements** with foreign companies or governments. Under a licensing agreement, an MNC—or other company as well—agrees to allow a foreign company to produce one or more of its products, with the MNC receiving payment from the foreign company for allowing it to produce its wares. Licensing agreements reduce the amount of risk that a company takes because it has little or no foreign direct investment in the country of the corporation with which it has a licensing agreement. MNCs and their licensing partners may also choose this form of relationship over a joint venture because of company policy preferences, tax laws, political or cultural considerations, or insufficient funds to acquire a wholly-owned or partly-owned subsidiary through foreign direct investment. The disadvantage of licensing from an MNC's perspective is that licensing greatly restricts the flexibility of decision-making and the central control that MNCs so often prefer.

Since multinational corporations are in business to make money, their leading objective is the maximization of profit. MNCs have a number of strategies available to them to achieve this objective. Because of their size and their global access to resources, material, and information, MNCs can maximize profits by minimizing the cost of their inputs, by dominating the market for a specific product in a particular country or a particular region, or by moving their operations to a country where the economic or political environment is more favorable to their operations.[6]

On occasion, MNCs have actively intervened to alter what they perceive as unfavorable economic or political environments. The leading example of the **political influence of MNCs** took place between 1970 and 1973 in Chile when ITT in conjunction with the U.S. Central Intelligence Agency helped overthrow the government of Salvador Allende, all in the pursuit, from ITT's perspective, of establishing a more favorable environment in which it could do business.

ITT's major investment in Chile during the early 1970s was Chiltelco, a telephone subsidiary valued at $153 million. ITT had maintained good relations with a series of Chilean governments, made respectable profits, and expected that the future would remain favorable. Although some Chileans discussed eventual nationalization of Chiltelco, ITT believed that in such a situation it would be reimbursed for the full value of Chiltelco.

The only blot on ITT's Chilean horizon was Salvador Allende. Allende, a Marxist candidate for the presidency in the 1970 Chilean election, had campaigned on a platform of nationalization. Allende appeared to be the leading contender for the position, and he did not support compensation for nationalization. ITT feared its $153 million was at risk and intervened in the Chilean political process to prevent Allende's election.

At first, ITT sought to funnel campaign money to the conservative Jorge Alessandri. A former director of the CIA, John McCone, was at the time a member of the Board of Directors of ITT. McCone arranged a meeting between the president of ITT, Harold Geneen, and the CIA's Western Hemisphere head of clandestine operations, William Broe. Geneen offered to arrange funding for Alessandri's campaign and allow that money to be controlled by the CIA. The CIA rejected ITT's offer.

Despite this, ITT funded conservative newspapers that opposed Allende. Even with this opposition, Allende emerged victorious with 36.3 percent of the vote compared with Alessandri's 34.9 percent. The Christian Democratic candidate Radomiro Tomic received 27.8 percent of the vote.

According to the Chilean constitution, in elections where no candidate received over half of the votes, the Chilean congress determined the next president. Having been frustrated in its effort to elect Alessandri at the popular level,

ITT now turned to Congress. Geneen and other ITT directors planned to spend $1 million to influence congressional voting. ITT again approached the CIA, and again was rejected.

The CIA, meanwhile, was attempting to implement its own plan to keep Allende out of office by undermining the Chilean economy through a combined program of credit and loan terminations, shipment delays, and informal product boycotts. The CIA requested ITT support for its programs. ITT rejected the CIA proposals, but offered to present them to other corporations to get their opinions.

Meanwhile, the Chilean congress elected Allende president. This action did not end the anti-Allende activity of either ITT or the CIA. Rather, ITT continued to seek to undermine and overthrow Allende. Perhaps the most outstanding indication of ITT's continuing effort was an October 1971 ITT memorandum in which ITT advocated economic warfare against Chile involving credit restrictions, copper boycotts, delays of fuel and weapons shipments, and a global anti-Allende propaganda effort. These and other ITT and CIA activities against Allende were publicized in 1972, and eventually a U.S. Senate inquiry examined ITT's role in Chile. Although debate over the role of ITT and the CIA in the collapse of the Chilean economy between 1970 and 1973 continues even today, it was and is evident that ITT consciously and actively intervened in the political process of a sovereign state. Although the ITT-Chile case is an extreme one, it illustrates the role that multinationals can play in host state politics. On October 11, 1973, Allende was overthrown in a military coup.[7]

The moral questions raised by MNC intervention in political affairs of host states are significant questions, but other moral questions about the operation of MNCs exist that are not at the level of the "rightness" or "wrongness" of overthrowing governments. If, for example, common business practice in one country dictates large up-front cash payments to guarantee the conclusion of a contract, but in the home country of the involved MNC such payment is considered a bribe, are MNC executives acting morally or immorally if such payments are made?[8] Similarly, if the leadership of an MNC decides that operations in one country must be curtailed or eliminated to take advantage of less expensive material or labor costs elsewhere, what responsibility does the MNC have to its former employees?[9]

These and similar questions are part of the decision-making dilemma of the multinational corporation. Other parts of the dilemma include whether an MNC should remain in a given market if it is operating at a loss there. Although a short-term assessment of the economic return may imply that an operation should be closed, the hope that future profit may be forthcoming in that market may dictate continued operation. Coca-Cola serves as a useful example. For years, Coca-Cola's operations in Japan cost the company money, but the decision was made to continue operations there. During the 1970s, that decision was justified as Coke's Japanese subsidiary steadily increased its profitability. Small financial losses over an extended period eventually led to a major profit. Currently, in China, Coca-Cola is pursuing the same strategy of accepting losses in hopes of developing a long-term profitable market.

Again, however, it was the global size and overall profitability of Coca-Cola that allowed it to absorb losses for an extended period of time. Similarly, it was the centralized control of overall operations that allowed that decision to be made. Indeed, when the contemporary multinational corporation is examined in detail, these two ingredients—size and centralization of operations—are what make the MNC a significant force in international relations today.

SIZE, CENTRALIZATION, AND MNCS

Globally, there are at least 10,000 privately owned corporations operating at least 90,000 subsidiaries in other countries. (These figures exclude state-owned corporations such as Italy's ENI.) Many of these corporations are huge. Table 4–1 has already illustrated this. Even more impressive is the fact that their economic growth rates regularly exceed national growth rates; indeed, by the year 2000, some estimates conclude that the MNCs will produce over two-thirds of the *world's* gross economic product.[10]

Because of their size, MNCs wield impressive economic, political, and social power. It does not matter whether that power is sought or unsought . . . it exists. And the fact of that existence of power and concern over how it is used has made the contemporary MNC the subject of heated debate.

In an economic sense, multinational corporations can make or break a local economy and in the cases of smaller states, even a national economy. MNCs provide investment funds, jobs, advanced technologies, and educational services. They can also remove that which they bring on the basis of decisions taken in corporate headquarters. With their ability to move production facilities from high labor-cost areas to low labor-cost areas, MNCs have proven to be the groundworks on which several national economic "miracles" such as Singapore, Hong Kong, and Taiwan have based their prosperity. Indeed, the economic power of MNCs is such that when visiting foreign states, corporate heads often receive treatment generally reserved for visiting governmental dignitaries and heads of state.[11] For example, when Nissan and Toyota let word out in the 1980s that they intended to build plants in the United States, governors from at least eight U.S. states contacted corporate headquarters to try to attract the Japanese firms to their states. And when the Japanese site-visit teams arrived in the United States, they were treated like royalty. Regardless of whether this practice is desirable, it is understandable because MNC investment means jobs.

Because of the size of their aggregate holdings of currency, MNCs collectively even have the ability to influence exchange rates. As long ago as 1973, a U.S. Senate Finance Committee report concluded that it was "beyond dispute" that the $268 billion held by the MNCs, a figure "more than twice the total of all international reserves held by all central banks and international monetary institutions in the world," could generate "international monetary crises of the sort that have plagued the major central banks in recent years."[12] And as we have already seen, MNCs are much larger today—and hold much more currency— than they did in 1973. Thus, by delaying payments in some countries and accelerating payments in others, MNCs may profit by influencing exchange rate variations.

Equally vexing is the problem that MNCs cause for state security. There are several different aspects to the problem. First, home-based MNCs may develop products useful for defense, and then sell those products to potential enemies. For example, many U.S., British, French, Japanese, and German firms sold materials to Iraq that allowed Saddam Hussein to develop the large and well-equipped military force that he used to invade Kuwait in 1990. Similarly, the United States government remains concerned about the sale by MNCs—and other firms as well— of advanced nuclear, chemical, and missile technologies to other unfriendly states.

Second, with the globalization of the world economy brought about by MNCs and the accompanying free flow of investment capital, critical components of military equipment must frequently be imported. Thus, by the early 1990s, the United States could not build a single first-line fighter aircraft without Japanese technology. And third, even under the best of conditions, few countries want domestic firms vital to defense production to be owned by foreign business interests. Thus, in 1987, the United States refused to allow Japan's Fujitsu electronics corporation to buy Fairchild Semiconductor, which made computer microchips.

Similarly, because some MNCs deal in materials requisite for modern society or have cornered a product market, they are often accused of monopolistic or oligopolistic behavior. For example, during the gasoline shortages that accompanied the Iraqi occupation of Kuwait during 1990 and 1991, many Americans believed that international oil companies were withholding gasoline so that prices for the consumers and profits for the companies would be driven up. Although such allegations were never proved, it was true that the oil corporations were collectively large enough to undertake such action if they desired.

How better to illustrate the global reach of the modern multinational corporation than with the McDonald's in Moscow? When McDonald's opened its first restaurant in Moscow in 1990, it was hailed as a major breakthrough. Now, there are three McDonald's in Moscow, with more on the way!   (AP/Wide World Photos.)

Closely allied with the economic power of "bigness" is the political power of "bigness." We have already examined the moral question of the intervention of MNCs in the internal political affairs of host states, specifically of ITT in Chile. The fact is inescapable, however, that the size of many MNCs means that they will have a political impact on a host country even if they do not seek such an impact. If the economic operation of an MNC is critical to the political survival of the host government, that government is inevitably pressured—unless it can provide its own expertise through alternative sources—to grant favorable concessions to guest MNCs. In Zaire, extremely favorable mining concessions were granted to a number of MNCs for exactly this reason. Zaire is not unique.

Even in the United States, MNCs sometimes are seen as exerting extensive political influence. Thus, when the United States clamped an economic boycott on Libya in early 1986 in response to Libya's support of anti-Western terrorism, U.S. oil companies operating in Libya were exempted. This caused many Americans to accuse the oil companies and even the U.S. government of allowing economic profit to dominate national interest. Oil company executives and government officials asserted that oil company operations in Libya were not ended for different reasons: to prevent Libya from getting all the profits of oil extraction in Libya, which would have given Libya even more money to fund terrorism, and to protect the oil companies' long-term large-scale capital investment in Libya. The public outcry over this issue was nevertheless sufficient that operations were cut back and negotiations begun in several cases to sell U.S. oil holdings in Libya. Despite this, the key point is that in many people's eyes, MNCs had been allowed to continue to seek economic profit, thereby endangering national interest.

In a social sense, the global marketing capabilities of MNCs have influenced and homogenized consumer tastes. Regardless of whether this is viewed as an advantage or disadvantage—an issue that will be discussed in the concluding section of this chapter—multinationals benefit from the reduction in national distinctions because they are able to sell to a more extensive market with uniform tastes. MNCs are both a beneficiary and a cause of this phenomenon, but the fact remains that MNCs, because of their size, influence international social behavior.

To take fullest advantage of the opportunities that their size and their worldwide operations afford them, MNCs in most instances have evolved a highly centralized decision-making structure. Foreign subsidiaries are closely integrated in that structure and rarely have the latitude of action that the old mother-daughter arrangements had. The purposes of close oversight of operations and centrality of decision-making by the headquarters office are to allow the MNC to respond quickly to changing international political and economic situations and to prevent the firm from competing with itself. To the MNC manager, then, oversight and centralization improve the opportunity for profit.

To host nations, however, oversight and centralization imply a loss of control over their own political, economic, and social destinies. With operations overseen and decisions made for a subsidiary in a corporate headquarters that may be half a world away, the governments and peoples of a host state may legitimately question whether the decisions made by the MNCs' management have the interests of the host state and its inhabitants at heart. For example, during the 1970s and 1980s, Ford, Chrysler, and General Motors moved more and more of their automotive production overseas as the "Big Three" sought less expensive labor and cheaper raw materials. The U.S. Congress, American labor unions, and many other Americans condemned the companies' managements for actions "not in the American interest." From the companies' perspective, however, good decisions had been made. None of the "Big Three" were—or are—in business to further "the American interest."

During the 1980s, the American textile industry and computer industry fell victim to this same phenomenon—or phrased somewhat differently, took advantage of lower production costs elsewhere. By the late 1980s, the flight of jobs formerly done in the United States to other countries was so extensive that a variety of protectionist legislative measures were introduced in the U.S. Congress to deny MNCs the ability to produce goods outside the United States and then ship them back into the United States. Congress maintained that it was acting in the American national interest, and domestic American producers applauded Congress' efforts. Meanwhile, MNCs argued that protectionism could lead to international trade wars and would inevitably raise the price of goods to consumers. The Reagan administration, with its advocacy of free trade, sided with the MNCs.

This series of events only strengthened the arguments of those who posit that in today's world, the interests of governments (or at least the executive branch of governments) and interests of corporations are similar if not identical. Thus, the interests of an MNC with headquarters in the United States are often equated with the interests of the United States itself, and the interests of a French-headquartered MNC are equated with the interests of France. Indeed, in some cases this perception has been strengthened both because of a government's effort to use the subsidiary of an MNC headquartered on its territory to achieve policy objectives and because of a sometimes existing willingness of governments to protect the foreign investments of its citizens. The CIA's willingness to cooperate with and use ITT in Chile has already been discussed, and there are numerous other examples of governments using MNCs to achieve their objectives. Similarly, again using a U.S. governmental action as only one of numerous possible examples, the Hickenlooper Amendment, passed by the U.S. Congress, in the 1960s, directed the U.S. government to terminate aid programs to any country that nationalized American-owned property without fair compensation.[13]

Nonetheless, numerous examples also exist to illustrate that national interest and corporate interests often do clash. American-headquartered firms continued to operate in Germany during World War II even after the United States and Germany were fighting. More recently, several U.S. firms opposed the embargo of high technology trade with the U.S.S.R. that President Carter imposed in retaliation for the Soviet invasion of Afghanistan. In Europe, the European Community ended all trade with Argentina in April 1982 in response to Argentina's capture of the Falkland Islands. European MNCs operating in Argentina objected bitterly. Again, in 1982, when Ronald Reagan demanded that all U.S. firms and their foreign subsidiaries terminate their cooperation with the U.S.S.R. on the gas pipeline to Western Europe, U.S. firms, not to mention Europeans, were outraged. And throughout the 1980s, even with the improvement in East–West relations that marked the end of the decade, the U.S. government sought to maintain tight controls on high-technology trade with the Soviet Union and Eastern Europe. Obviously, companies that dealt in high-technology products condemned this U.S. government effort as an unwarranted constraint on trade.

Another aspect of multinational corporations related to their size and centralization that sometimes creates problems between MNCs and host governments in the Developing World is the simple fact that most large MNCs are based in the developed industrialized world. For example, of the world's 44 largest MNCs (see Table 4–1), only one, Samsung, a South Korean electrical corporation, has corporate headquarters outside the United States, Western Europe, or Japan. Some Developing World states thus see MNCs as instruments of economic imperialism, also known as neocolonialism.

Size and centralization, then, have their downside as well as their upside for MNCs. Whereas MNC managers look on size and capitalization as tools to use to expand corporate size and wealth, host countries sometimes view size and centralization as proof of colonialism and challenges to their authority. It is to this latter point—MNCs as challenges to the authority of the state—that we now turn.

MNCS AND STATES: SOVEREIGNTY AT BAY?[14]

The global operations of multinational corporations present a real challenge to governments of states. Corporate decisions taken in MNC headquarters can raise or lower unemployment levels within a country, compromise or enhance the security of a country, and lead to greater or lesser dependence of one country on another. A state's economic growth rate can be accelerated or retarded by corporate decisions, and it need not matter whether a country is the seat of headquarters for an MNC or host country for a subsidiary of an MNC. When General Motors or Ford decides to close a plant or reduce the operations of a plant in Detroit because of high labor costs and open a plant in Mexico City, the Michigan economy and American automotive workers suffer even though General Motors or Ford is an American-based company. Conversely, when the copper content of ore mined in Peru declines below that available in, say, Australia, Kennicott may close that Peruvian mine. The Peruvian economy and workers suffer, whereas the Australian economy and workers benefit. Again, a firm headquartered in the United States will have made decisions affecting the economy and social structure in two countries in which it has subsidiaries without the governments of those host countries playing a decision-making role in those decisions.

Because of the MNC, then, governments of states have lost some of their ability to influence and control decisions within their own states. Naturally they resent this loss of ability to control events within their borders, and in some instances have moved to reassert their control over their domains. The methods that states have chosen to harness MNCs have varied.

In some cases, governments have passed laws that require that over half of a subsidiary be owned by nationals of the host country or perhaps by the host country's government itself. From the perspective of a host country, such laws are desirable because they return control of operations to the host country. Conversely, MNCs oppose such laws because their power of decision over joint venture subsidiaries is reduced or removed.

Another method through which states attempt to exert control over multinational corporations is by limiting or forbidding the repatriation of profits. For example, during much of the 1970s and 1980s, Argentina and Columbia limited how much profit could be removed, and in Brazil, all profit had to remain there for two years, after which only 5 percent could be repatriated. These and other governments hoped to keep MNC profits in the country, but frequently the result was to drive MNC investment elsewhere. As a result, this practice declined in the late 1980s and early 1990s.

Another method that some governments use to try to control MNCs, also closely related to controls on profit repatriation, is governmental refusal to allow currency to be exported. Because of this type of restriction, MNCs in many cases attempt to export their profits from host nations by buying a product produced domestically within a host nation, exporting it, and selling that product overseas. In a certain sense, then, MNCs may serve as marketing agents for host countries. Thus, because the former U.S.S.R. did not permit rubles to be exported, Pepsi Cola used the rubles that it made within the U.S.S.R. by selling Pepsi to buy Stolichnaya vodka, made in the U.S.S.R. Pepsi then sold Stolichnaya in the West. The bottom line was that Pepsi could repatriate only the dollar value of Pepsi Cola that it sold in the U.S.S.R. equal to the dollar value of Stolichnaya it could sell in the West.

Other states have taken other measures to assert their control over MNCs. In the United States, the president and Congress have legal authority to control export of certain types of capital and products, such as state-of-the-art computers and oil extraction technologies. On several occasions during the 1960s, the U.S. government attempted to block the sales of transportation equipment to China from foreign subsidiaries of U.S.-headquartered MNCs. In one case, the U.S. government intended to bring the French subsidiary of the Fruehauf Corporation to court in France to block the sale of trucks to China. Faster legal action by French citizens who opposed the sale made the U.S. action unnecessary. In another case, the U.S. government applied political pressures to Ford Motor Company to force it to prevent its Canadian subsidiary from selling trucks to China. Neither the Canadian government nor Canadian labor unions were pleased by the U.S. government's action because it cost Canadians jobs.

Some governments have opted for blacklists or embargoes in an effort to influence the sales practices of MNCs. Until recently, Arab states blacklisted any corporation that trades with Israel, although considerable evidence exists that the blacklist is less than totally effective. Similarly, just after the Arab-Israeli War, Arab members of the Organization of Petroleum Exporting Countries (OPEC) announced that they would not sell oil to corporations that in turn sold that oil to countries that supported Israel. In some cases, the threatened oil embargo influenced the MNCs to change policies. Although OPEC's objectives were clearly to alter the policies of states, it was nevertheless evident that OPEC sought to exert its influence over the multinationals.

Impressive as these successes may appear, governments often believe that the MNCs still act as they choose. In 1972, Robert Bork, then Solicitor-General of the United States, observed that ITT was so powerful that it could ignore American laws, sometimes with impunity. A group of developing states reached the same conclusion about MNCs during the mid-1970s and approached the United Nations, requesting that the UN set up an international commission to develop regulations and a code of conduct for multinational operation.[15]

Although states for their part decry MNCs as being in many cases beyond the control of governments, MNCs regularly view states as regulative interlopers that complicate the operation of legitimate business and raise prices (and reduce profit) by those very regulations. Carl A. Gerstacker, former Chairman of Dow Chemical Company, dreamed of "buying an island owned by no nation and establishing the World Headquarters of the Dow Company on the truly neutral ground of such an island, beholden to no nation or society." George Ball, former U.S. undersecretary of state and chairman of Lehman Brothers International, considered the state to be "a very old-fashioned idea and badly adapted to our present complex world." The MNC, by comparison, was a "modern concept, designed to meet modern requirements."[16]

Who, then, is correct, MNC managers who chastise government intervention and control and who view their corporations as being targets of senseless and costly state regulation, or the states' governmental authorities, who believe that MNCs can and do have the size, flexibility, and centralization to successfully sidestep governmental regulations? Not surprisingly, depending on the case chosen, both sides can prove their points.

Coca-Cola's international operations again provide an excellent example.[17] Throughout the 1970s, Coca-Cola sold its products in Bulgaria, exporting whatever profits it made in Bulgarian peaches, wines, and jams. In 1977, however, the Bulgarian government approached Coca-Cola with what amounted to an ultimatum: Provide Bulgaria with additional expertise and Western technologies or Coke sales in Bulgaria would be terminated.

Although Coca-Cola was not making a significant profit in Bulgaria, Coke management deemed Bulgaria enough of a lucrative future market that it decided to meet the Bulgarian demands. For three years, the U.S.-based company attempted to develop and market a dairy product based on local Bulgarian yogurt cultures, finally determining in 1980 that the experiment was a failure. Nevertheless, the Bulgarian government continued to demand that a Coca-Cola–Bulgarian government joint venture be initiated if Coke were to remain in the Bulgarian market.

Coca-Cola's next effort was to develop a dairy-based fruit drink to be produced with primarily Bulgarian products. Coca-Cola was to provide a few key elements such as product stabilizer and, of course, technology. Had the Bulgarian–Coca-Cola dealings been restricted to only Bulgaria and Coca-Cola, little more need be said about the situation. In short order, however, Israel, Arab states, and the U.S. government became involved.

Bulgaria, it turned out, intended to market its coproduced fruit drink in several Arab states, including Kuwait and Saudi Arabia. Coca-Cola, however, sold its products to Israel, which meant that Coke was on the Arab blacklist. Both the Kuwaiti and Saudi governments required that distributors of new products fill out questionnaires concerning the newly imported product. If the new product was in any way connected with a blacklisted company, it could not be imported.

Complicating matters further were U.S. antiboycott laws that, among other things, forbade U.S. corporations to participate in any exchange that included filling out blacklist questionnaires. Coca-Cola was therefore in a position to break an American law if it participated in a joint venture with Bulgaria, inasmuch as the Bulgarian government intended to fill out a blacklist questionnaire. Bulgaria, meanwhile, could not sell its fruit drink to Arab states if Coca-Cola participated.

What had been a relatively simple business proposition had become a complex international issue.

The solution to the business partners' problems was relatively simple: Coca-Cola would sell its technology, packaging equipment, and expertise to a newly created, wholly owned Bulgarian company. Bulgaria could therefore answer the questionnaire by denying that a blacklisted company was engaged in producing the fruit drink. Coca-Cola, meanwhile, was forced by U.S. antiboycott laws to purchase everything that it sold to Bulgaria from non-U.S. sources. Only after this series of events could Bulgaria then sell its fruit drink to the Arabs; a Coca-Cola product, in the final analysis, was to be sold in Arab states.

This example well illustrates the conflicting objectives and perceptions of states and MNCs. From the states' perspective, an MNC had successfully circumvented both blacklist and antiboycott laws and sold its product in Arab states. From Coca-Cola's perspective, the states' meddling had complicated a simple business proposition. Both sides, surprisingly, were correct.

MNCs, then, can and do present challenges to the state. In a certain sense, though, they also present challenges to any group or individual viewing the world in less than global terms, for the MNCs' perspective is, in fact, global. It is this advocacy of globalism as much as anything else that arouses much of the furor over multinational corporations.

MNCS AS WORLD CITIZENS: CLAIMS AND COUNTERCLAIMS

Multinational managers, as we have seen, claim to have the expertise and resources to structure a more efficiently productive world, and therefore improve

The Coca-Cola Corporation is one of the world's most successful multinational corporations, and even though its world headquarters is in Atlanta, Georgia, it has vending machines in downtown Tokyo, Japan.   (The Coca-Cola Corporation.)

global living standards. Only the unique blend of size, centralization, and internationalism peculiar to MNCs, they argue, can bring about the global reality of comparative advantage. As espoused by British economists David Ricardo and John Stuart Mill during the nineteenth century, the concept of **comparative advantage** posits simply that products should be produced wherever they can be produced least expensively, and that products produced elsewhere should be imported and paid for with excess internal products.[18] As an economic theory, comparative advantage has been operationalized by MNCs.

Multinational managers do not end their advocacy of their corporations with their assertions that MNCs will raise living standards. They also argue that MNCs help less developed countries modernize and industrialize by introducing technology, job opportunities, and expertise to struggling underdeveloped economies. The benefits of economic plenty would therefore not be restricted to the industrialized countries, but would be extended throughout all human societies.

Finally, according to those who believe in the vision of a brighter future through multinational corporations, MNCs by their very nature make war obsolete. In a future world with all states and regions dependent on other states and regions for economic well-being, no sane person or government would initiate a war. MNCs bring about an interdependent world, the argument goes, and in so doing make war unthinkable. Using Western Europe, Japan, and the North American states as examples, advocates of MNCs point out that so many overseas investments exist between and among those states and their economies are so intertwined through the operations of MNCs that war among them would be virtually economic suicide.[19]

Critics of MNCs have a different outlook. In addition to governments of both industrialized and developing states that lament that they cannot control the actions of MNCs, labor unions criticize the multinationals for their tendency to relocate in regions where labor is unorganized and inexpensive. By building plants with excess capacity MNCs can even insulate themselves from labor's most useful weapon, the strike. When unions in one state strike against an MNC, that MNC can simply expand its production in one of its nonstrikebound plants.

Nationalists also frequently criticize MNCs, often in concert with their governments. As we have already seen, most MNCs are based in the United States, Western Europe, and Japan, and this has led many Developing World states to condemn MNCs as tools of imperialism and neocolonialism. But nationalist resentment of MNCs goes far beyond Developing World hostility. For example, in the United States, the late 1980s and early 1990s witnessed a significant growth in anti-Japanese sentiment as more and more Japanese MNCs set up operations in the United States. At the same time, this sentiment has not lessened the desire of American cities and states to attract Japanese investment.

Other critics of MNCs argue that MNCs use managerial expertise and technical know-how available only in the industrialized West and cheap labor and inexpensive resources available primarily in the nonindustrialized Developing World to increase their profits without making significant contributions to the economies in which they operate. Indeed, Barnet and Muller continue, multinational corporations do not bring in large quantities of external capital but rather use existing capital that could best be devoted to other purposes within developing countries. With their superior capital-intensive productive capabilities, MNCs drive other labor-intensive local market competitors out of business, thereby actually increasing unemployment in a host country. In addition, MNCs are accused of destroying traditional cultures by use of sophisticated advertising techniques, and replacing them with local versions of American and Western European consumer societies. As profit on the global levels is the MNCs' primary objective, the multinationals are often accused of ignoring local questions such as environmental quality, resource conservation, and health and nutrition.

The early 1980s' efforts of the Nestlé Corporation and other international distributers of powdered dry baby formula to market their product to developing countries provide a good case in point. The MNCs argued that dry baby formula was as good or better than mothers' milk in providing the nutritional needs of infants and marketed the formula as the "modern" way to care for an infant. Unfortunately, none considered the quality of Developing World water supplies, which are often undrinkable. By mixing formula with water (as is required), mothers in those area would in fact be exposing their infants to numerous diseases that they otherwise would have avoided by remaining on mothers' milk. Another and perhaps graver danger to infants occurred when, in efforts to economize, mothers put too little formula into each measure of water. Widespread malnutrition among infants resulted. Only after an extensive worldwide publicity campaign including efforts at the United Nations did the MNCs reduce their baby formula marketing efforts in the Developing World.

According to critics of MNCs, continued unbridled operation of MNCs in developing countries will inevitably lead to more unemployment, more environmental degradation, poorer nutrition and health standards, and more inequitable distribution of wealth in those countries. As more and more MNCs invest outside North America and Europe, they maintain, unemployment rates will go up there as well. At the same time, as more developing countries form producer cartels to protect their resource interests against the MNCs, the multinationals will charge higher prices for their products in the developed world. Thus, in the developed world as well, critics assert that MNCs cause unemployment, inflation, and economic stagnation, at least according to critics of the multinational corporation.

Obviously, the most ardent advocates and the most vocal critics of the multinational corporation are separated by a wide chasm. They agree that the size, centralization of decision-making, and global flexibility of multinational corporations give those corporations an almost unprecedented opportunity to act in the international arena, but they disagree as to the results of those actions. MNC advocates see improved living standards, more employment, and a less violent world, if only MNCs could operate in a world with less governmental intervention and a more widely accepted set of international standards. Thus, when MNC advocates favorably discuss regulation of MNCs, they mean global regulation that would enhance the operating environment for the multinationals.

Conversely, MNC critics see higher unemployment, worse living conditions, and a more elitist world with increasingly inequitable distribution of wealth if MNCs continue to operate without increased subnational, national, and supranational control. Thus, when MNC critics favorably discuss regulation of MNCs, they mean regulation that would curtail the ability of multinationals to make decisions on their own without government control at some level.

As the debate between advocates and critics of multinational corporations should make clear, the role of multinational corporations in contemporary international relations is significant. Although the more extreme claims of both advocates and critics of MNCs can probably be safely ignored, it is nonetheless true that a conflicting body of evidence exists concerning the role of MNCs in today's world. For students and scholars of international affairs, MNCs must remain a centerpiece of inquiry for years to come.

KEY TERMS AND CONCEPTS

subsidiaries

organizational structures of MNCs

perspectives of MNC managers

foreign direct investment

joint ventures

licensing agreements

political influence of MNCs

ITT in Chile

impact of MNCs on state sovereignty

impact of states on MNC operations

reasons for criticism of MNCs

reasons for praise of MNCs

comparative advantage

NOTES

1. For a critical approach to MNCs, see Richard J. Barnet and Ronald E. Muller, *Global Reach: The Power of the Multinational Corporations* (New York: Simon & Schuster, 1974). For more favorable approaches, see Raymond Vernon, *Sovereignty at Bay: The Multinational Spread of U.S. Enterprises* (New York: Basic Books, 1971), and Raymond Vernon, *Storm Over the Multinationals: The Real Issues* (Cambridge: Harvard University Press, 1977). See also Abdul A. Said and Luiz R. Simmons (eds.), *The New Sovereigns: Multinational Corporations as World Powers* (Englewood Cliffs, NJ: Prentice-Hall, 1975).

2. These figures are taken from or derived from John M. Stopford, John H. Dunning, and Klaus O. Haberich, *The World Directory of Multinational Enterprises* (New York: Facts on File, 1980), p. xxv; U.S. Central Intelligence Agency, *The World Factbook 1991* (Washington: U.S. Government Printing Office, 1992); and *Fortune*, July 27, 1992.

3. Vernon (1977), pp. 31, 34.

4. For discussions of various organizational approaches to MNC operation, see Stefan H. Robock et al., *International Business and Multinational Enterprises* (Homewood, IL: Richard D. Irwin, 1977), especially chap. 19.

5. The Soviets hoped Western MNCs would invest in the U.S.S.R. and aid the Soviet economy.

6. As satellite communications and computer technology continue to improve, opportunities for instantaneous global communication of critical business information will multiply. Large MNCs are ideally situated to take fullest advantage of the price and cost information that such instantaneous communication can provide on a global scale.

7. For a more detailed account of the Allende-ITT-CIA affair, see Joan Edelman Spero, *The Politics of International Economic Relations*, 4th Ed. (New York: St. Martin's Press, 1990).

8. This situation was faced by executives of Lockheed as they attempted to sell their aircraft to Japan.

9. U.S. automakers faced this dilemma as they moved production to Canada, Mexico, and elsewhere.

10. This estimate is taken from United Nations sources, 1992.

11. See Christopher Tugendhat, "Transnational Enterprise: Tying Down Gulliver," *Atlantic Community Quarterly*, Vol. 9 (1971/72): 499–508.

12. As quoted in Barnet, p. 29.

13. Some observers argue that such identity of interest proves that the state is a tool of business interests, and quote expressions like "What's good for General Motors is good for America" as proof.

14. This phrase is taken from Ray Vernon's 1971 book, as are many of the thoughts in this section. See also Robert L. Heilbroner, "The Multinational Corporation and the Nation-State," in Steven L. Spiegel (ed.), *At Issue: Politics in the World Arena* (New York: St. Martin's Press, 1977), and Patrick M. Boarman and Hans Schollhammer (eds.), *Multinational Corporations and Governments: Business–Government Relations in an International Context* (New York: Praeger, 1975).

15. See Werner J. Feld, *Multinational Corporations and U.N. Politics: The Quest for Codes of Conduct* (New York: Pergamon, 1980).

16. As quoted in Barnet, pp. 16, 19.

17. This account has been pieced together from a series of conversations with several Coca-Cola executives.

18. See David Ricardo, excerpts from "The Principles of Political Economy and Taxation," and John Stuart Mill, excerpts from "Principles of Political Economy with Some of Their Applications to Social Philosophy," in William R. Allen (ed.), *International Trade Theory: Hume to Ohlin* (New York: Random House, 1965) pp. 62–67, 68–69.

19. For a relatively sympathetic treatment of the role of MNCs in contemporary international affairs, see C. K. Prahalad and Yves L. Doz, *The Multinational Mission: Balancing Local Demands and Global Vision* (New York: The Free Press, 1987).

CHAPTER 5

Nongovernmental Organizations, Individuals, and Other International Actors

- What is an NGO, and what does it hope to accomplish?
- What role do individuals play in international affairs?
- What is a national liberation movement, and what does it seek?
- What does a terrorist hope to achieve, and why?
- How does religion influence international affairs today?
- Do political parties make contacts across international boundaries, and what effect does this have on international affairs?

To this point, our examination of the actors in the contemporary international arena has centered on states, those international organizations that states create, and multinational corporations. The roles that these actors play in contemporary international affairs are dominant. Numerous other actors, however, also play roles in today's world that cannot be overlooked. In many instances, these other actors are not officially recognized by states, IGOs, or MNCs. Nevertheless, they often influence and sometimes determine the course of international relations.

Nongovernmental organizations (NGOs) are among the most organized of these other actors in international affairs. NGOs are extremely diverse in size, composition, objectives, and influence, and include bodies such as the International Olympic Commission, Amnesty International, the Committee for Nuclear Disarmament, the International Federation of Airline Pilots' Associations, the International Red Cross, the International Chamber of Commerce, and the World

Federation of Trade Unions. The *Yearbook of International Organizations 1987–88* lists over 5,000 such NGOs. To the *Yearbook*, NGOs are all structured organizations operating internationally without formal ties to government.[1]

But there are many unstructured or minimally structured organizations that operate internationally without formal ties to governments that also play major roles in contemporary international relations. Ethnic and national liberation organizations such as the African National Council and the Palestine Liberation Organization have had and continue to have a major impact on international affairs. So too have terrorist organizations such as Italy's Red Brigade and West Germany's Red Army Faction. Therefore, they must be included in our discussion as well.

Certain transnational religious movements and groups are also significant international actors. In the Christian world, the transnational impact of Catholicism, the Catholic Church, and the pope is immense. The pope is ruler of the Vatican State in Rome, but his domain extends far beyond the Eternal City. Similarly, in the Islamic world, the resurgence of Islamic fundamentalism has altered the course of world affairs. Colonel Muammar Qadhafi of Libya and Ayatollah Ruhollah Khomeini of Iran were two of the most prominent figures leading the resurgence of Islam.

Transnational political parties and movements must not be overlooked as international actors, either. Western European Social Democrats have forged links that transcend national boundaries, and although communism as a global ideology has been discredited, until relatively recently communist parties appealed to their international solidarity and unity.

Finally, the role of the individual in international affairs remains significant. Prominent individuals such as Richard Nixon after his resignation from the American presidency, Jean Monnet following his tenure as head of the European Coal and Steel Community High Authority, and even Muhammad Ali and U-2 have had some influence on policies and perceptions in the international arena; less individually notable personages such as tourists, businesspeople, refugees, and soldiers stationed overseas may well have had a cumulative impact on international affairs more significant than their more famous counterparts.

Again, it must be stressed that these diverse actors grouped in this chapter as nongovernmental organizations, individuals, and other international actors can be and often are significantly different in size, composition, influence, and objectives. However, unless they are considered in some detail, we cannot obtain an accurate picture of contemporary international relations.

This chapter, then, examines six diverse groupings of international actors. The individual's role in international affairs is examined first, followed by ethnic/national liberation organizations. Terrorist organizations and movements are discussed separately, as are religious movements and political parties. Finally, several types of traditional NGOs are examined.[2]

INDIVIDUALS IN INTERNATIONAL AFFAIRS

The **role that a private individual may play in international affairs** is often difficult to determine because of the role that that same individual may have had in an organization, agency, or government participating in international affairs. Thus, when Richard Nixon traveled to China during the Carter administration, he traveled as a private citizen but very clearly was viewed by the Chinese as much more than a private citizen. Similarly, when at the behest of Ronald Reagan three private American citizens attended the funeral of slain Egyptian President Anwar Sadat, they were accorded high honors of protocol by the Egyptians. It was also helpful that the three private citizens were Richard Nixon, Gerald Ford, and Jimmy Carter. And when in 1989 Jimmy Carter as a private citizen tried to bring peace through mediation to the Ethiopian civil war, it helped that he was a former U.S. president.

At the other extreme from prominent individuals are the large numbers of more obscure people who move from country to country for a host of different reasons, but who nevertheless may have a significant impact on international affairs. For example, there are millions of refugees throughout the world who for one reason or another—war, famine, drought, and so on—have chosen to or have been forced to leave their homes.

The role of refugees is an often overlooked human aspect of international affairs, but as Table 5–1 makes clear, the world refugee problem is immense, and growing. For example, in the 18 months between the time when Tables 5–1 and 5–2 were compiled in January 1991 and mid-1992, the world's refugee population grew by at least another 3 million people as a result of civil wars in Yugoslavia (2.5 million refugees) and Somalia (another half million people beyond those shown in the tables). The toll in human suffering exacted by the tribulations of the world's refugee population is immeasurable but immense, and the cost to the countries that harbor and provide aid for refugees is also sizable.[3]

Nor can the role of something as elementary as **tourism** be overlooked. Every year, millions of people cross the Atlantic and Pacific Oceans as tourists, as Figure 5–1 shows. On an individual basis, these people play almost no role in international affairs. But on a cumulative basis, their impact is considerable not only because of the effect they may have on the perceptions of those whose coun-

TABLE 5–1   Refugees Displaced Outside Their Own Countries

Afghanistan	6,027,100[a]	Burundi	186,200
Palestinians	2,428,100	W. Sahara	165,000[a]
Mozambique	1,427,500	Vietnam	122,200
Ethiopia	1,066,300[a]	China (Tibet)	114,000
Liberia	729,800	Bangladesh	75,000[a]
Iraq	529,700	Laos	67,400
Sudan	499,100	Mauritania	60,100
Somalia	454,600[a]	Guatemala	57,400
Angola	435,700[a]	Burma	50,800
Kuwait	385,500	Zaire	50,700
Cambodia	344,500	Nicaragua	41,900
Sri Lanka	228,000	S. Africa	40,000[a]
Iran	211,100[a]	El Salvador	37,200
Rwanda	203,900[a]	Chad	34,400

SOURCE: *World Refugee Survey 1991* (Washington, DC: U.S. Committee for Refugees, 1991)

[a]Indicates that sources vary significantly in number reported.

TABLE 5–2   Refugees Displaced Within Their Own Countries

Sudan	4,500,000	El Salvador	400,000
South Africa	4,100,000	Nicaragua	354,000
Mozambique	2,000,000	Uganda	300,000
Afghanistan	2,000,000	Cyprus	268,000
Sri Lanka	1,000,000	Burma	200,000
Ethiopia	1,000,000	Peru	200,000
Lebanon	800,000	Cambodia	140,000
USSR	750,000	Guatemala	100,000
Angola	704,000	India	85,000
Liberia	500,000	Colombia	50,000
Iraq	500,000[a]	Turkey	30,000
Philippines	900,000	Honduras	22,000
Somalia	400,000		

Source: *World Refugee Survey 1991* (Washington, DC: U.S. Committee for Refugees, 1991)

[a]The number of displaced Iraqis increased considerably in 1991, to as many as two million people.

try they visit, but also because of the perceptions that they develop about the countries they visit. The "ugly American" syndrome of the 1950s and 1960s was as much the product of American tourist behavior as anything else, and the "ungrateful European" viewpoint of the same era was the product of perceptions the "ugly Americans" acquired during their European visits. In the 1980s and 1990s, the "ugly American" syndrome has been increasingly replaced by an "ugly Japanese" syndrome, but the overall point is the same. in their various travels, tourists pick up impressions of the countries they visit, and in turn leave impressions of their country behind in the minds of those whom they encounter.

Between the extremes of a few past presidents and millions of refugees and tourists, private citizens engage in a variety of other significant activities in international affairs. Muhammad Ali, for example, proclaimed himself America's unofficial ambassador to Africa during the Carter administration and on another occasion was even asked by the Carter government to engage in formal diplomatic activity. During the hostage crisis in Iran, the Carter administration turned to private French and Colombian citizens who had contacts in the Iranian

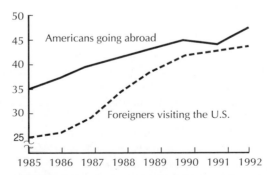

FIGURE 5–1   Comparison of outgoing and incoming travel in millions. (Source: U.S. Department of Commerce.)

government to attempt to attain the hostages' release. During the Johnson presidency, private individuals were used on a number of occasions to attempt to open separate channels of communications between Washington and Hanoi.[4] More recently, when the U.S. Congress banned official U.S. arms sales to the Contras in Nicaragua, the Reagan government turned to private U.S. citizens (as well as certain U.S. government employees and non-Americans) in an effort to develop private support for the Contras.

Other types of private individual contacts also play definite but undocumentable roles in international affairs. Student exchanges, foreign teaching and research, long-term job-related migration or permanent settlement, and similar activities all yield personal-level interactions between citizens of different countries. Nor can the role of businesspeople be overlooked. Indeed, as the Soviet Union and Eastern Europe changed their economic organization in the late 1980s and early 1990s, the flow of businesspeople to these countries increased dramatically. They carried with them different business practices and attitudes than those that up until that time prevailed in the U.S.S.R. and Eastern Europe.

Generally speaking, private individual activities in an international context are supportive of or neutral toward the government of one's country of citizenship. However, this is not always the case. Although cases of spying or outright treason are the extremes, there are other actions that private individuals take in international affairs that can conflict with the policies of their state. Jane Fonda's trip to Hanoi during the Vietnam War was undertaken as a private American citizen, and she was heavily criticized by the Nixon administration for both her trip and her statements on the war. A few years later Nixon himself was criticized within the Carter White House for his trip to China. To the Carter White House, Nixon's trip complicated conduct of American policy toward China. More recently, throughout the Reagan administration, private American citizens traveled to Nicaragua to provide assistance to the Sandinista government, and other Americans provided the Sandinistas with medical aid, food, and clothing. These Americans obviously disagreed with their government's policy of trying to overthrow the Sandinistas.

Nor should the economic impact of large numbers of individual travelers be overlooked. During the 1970s, following the murder of several terrorists in the U.S. Virgin Islands and political unrest in Jamaica, tourists by the thousands changed their travel plans, avoiding not only the U.S. Virgin Islands and Jamaica but the rest of the Caribbean as well. The economies of every Caribbean island were seriously hurt by these decisions of individual travelers. Similarly, in 1989, many tourists once again changed their vacation plans in the wake of Hurricane Hugo's devastation of the Caribbean, thereby unintentionally hurting the economies of the Caribbean islands even more. And in 1991, fearing Iraqi-sponsored terrorist attacks against Americans in Europe, many U.S. citizens once again refused to travel overseas, as shown in Figure 5–1.

A single individual can also have an immense impact on the human side of the international community, regardless of whether that person is someone like Mother Teresa, a Catholic nun, with her compassion for the poor and homeless in India; Bob Geldof, lead singer for the Boomtown Rats, with his concern for the starving people of Africa; or Ted Turner, owner of Cable News Network and other communications and sports enterprises, with his stated concern for world peace. Mother Teresa's compassion won the world's admiration. Geldof's concern galvanized British rock stars into forming Band Aid, American rock stars into forming USA for Africa, and as many as 20 million runners around the world via Sport Aid in May 1986 to express their concern and raise money to combat African starvation. Although some dismissed Geldof's efforts as "showbiz glitz," Band Aid, USA for Africa, and Sport Aid raised as much as $250 million for food aid to Africa. And Ted Turner's desire to improve U.S.–Soviet relations led him to organize and broadcast the 1986 and 1990 Goodwill Games, a sort of "between-the-Olympics Olympics." Without Mother Teresa, the poor and homeless of India would be worse off; without Bob Geldof, none of the "Aid" programs would have taken place; and without Ted Turner, the Goodwill Games would not have occurred. The point is clear: individuals can matter.

On another level, it is also instructive to speculate on the impact that different individuals with different values may have had if they had been in critical locations at crucial times in the course of international events. How would international affairs have been changed if George Washington had less of a sense of country and more of a sense of self, and decided not to step down after two terms in office? What would have happened in the U.S.S.R. if instead of Joseph Stalin, Lenin's successor had been a humane individual with a sense of human values? More recently, what would have happened in Eastern Europe if Mikhail Gorbachev had concluded like his predecessors that the U.S.S.R. must dominate those countries? Would there have been a Soviet invasion and a military bloodbath? Obviously, we will never know. Washington had a sense of country, Stalin had few human values, and Gorbachev adopted a policy of nonintervention. The point is obvious: individuals can matter.

Individuals, then, do play diverse roles in contemporary international affairs. For better or worse, we form our opinions about other nationalities, about businesspeople, about military officers, and others, on the basis of our experiences with them; also for better or worse, they form their opinions about us. Individuals also play major roles in transmission of cultures and values, in policy formulation and implementation, and even in economic affairs. And it is perhaps at the human level where individuals are most important.

Unfortunately, however, it is difficult to assess the level of importance that should be attached to their actions. No accurate picture of the conduct of contemporary international relations can be obtained without their inclusion. Perhaps all that can be safely said is that such actions form an integral part of the fabric of contemporary international relations.[5]

ETHNIC/NATIONAL LIBERATION ORGANIZATIONS

Ethnic/national liberation movements may be divided into three types. The first we encountered in our discussion of nation-states, when we discussed certain ethnic or national groups that sought to break away from the countries of which they were a part to establish their own nation-state. The Basques of Spain, the Biafrans of Nigeria, the Eritreans of Ethiopia, and the Québecois of Canada are just a few of the many ethnic/national groups that have sought or are seeking independent statehood. Indeed, in the final analysis, the breakup of the Soviet

Union was a result of the demands of ethnic and national groups for national independence.

Ethnic and national groups have different levels of power and influence, and different organizational structures. They may use nonviolent means to achieve their objectives of national independence, as has the *Parti Québecois* in Canada, or they may choose violence that results in civil war or terrorist attacks, as have the Eritreans and Basques. Although all national liberation movements have as their objective the establishment of a nation-state under their own rule, they seldom have anything else in common.

The second type of ethnic/national liberation movement seeks to overthrow a government that it views as dictatorial, exploitive, or under the control of an external influence. In this type of liberation, the objective of the liberation movement is not the creation of a new state, but rather the creation of a new government for an old state. Political change rather than political fragmentation is sought. The Sandinistas in Nicaragua, the Contras in Nicaragua after the Sandinista takeover, the Vietcong in South Vietnam, the Mujahadeen in Afghanistan, the ANC in South Africa, and UNITA in Angola since Angolan independence are examples of this second type of ethnic/national liberation movement. The organizational structures and capabilities of these movements are as diverse as those of the first type of movement, but because of the type of political change they are attempting to initiate, violence is their most frequently used tool.

The third type of ethnic/national liberation movement pits colonial peoples against colonial powers. Colonial peoples struggle for attainment of independence whereas colonial powers struggle for maintenance of empire. The struggle of the Mau Maus against the British in Kenya, of Frelimo against the Portuguese in Mozambique, and of the MPLA, FNLA, and UNITA against the Portuguese in Angola are typical examples of this third type of ethnic/national liberation movement. As in the preceding typology, structures and strengths of movement differ, and the objective sought necessitates violence in most cases. Perhaps the leading example of a nonviolent national liberation movement was Mahatma Gandhi's program of civil disobedience that he unleashed against Great Britain during India's struggle for independence.

Ethnic/national liberation movements are not new arrivals on the international scene. Biblical history is replete with stories of the Jewish people's efforts to establish and maintain an independent state under their own control, and the eventual collapse and fall of the Ottoman Empire in the early twentieth century was but the final chapter of a centuries-long drama that saw Bulgars, Greeks, Romanians, Serbs, and Turks achieve their own political states. The American and French revolutions were two different types of ethnic/national liberation conflicts of the eighteenth century, in the American case against a colonial power, and in the French case against an oppressive internal government. The revolts of the South American states against their Spanish and Portuguese masters are yet other instances of pre–twentieth-century national liberation activities.

In the post–World War II twentieth century, ethnic/national liberation movements play important roles in international affairs not only because of their obvious impact on nation-states, but also because of the relationships they develop with particular states. Inevitably, an ethnic/national liberation movement that concludes that it must resort to violence must have weapons and must find a source for those weapons. Private weapons merchants are one source of weaponry, but so are countries that either wish to see colonial empires dismantled, political power thrown into disequilibrium, or a particular government overthrown. Ethnic/national liberation movements may therefore turn to states for weapons and for political or economic support.[6] Given the sentiments that nationalism, imperialism, and claims of exploitation evoke, it is little wonder that ethnic/national liberation movements are as controversial as multinational corporations.

TERRORIST GROUPS AND MOVEMENTS

Depending on one's perspective, a fine line may or may not exist between terrorist groups and movements and other actors such as ethnic/national liberation groups, religious extremists, and other movements that resort to violence.

To a great extent, whether an organization is defined as a terrorist group depends on one's perspective. When seen from an American perspective, the "Indians" of the Boston Tea Party were American nationalists making a political point; when seen from a British perspective, they were terrorists destroying property and endangering life. As a general rule, if an observer agrees with the objectives of someone who employs violence, the observer considers the person a "freedom fighter"; if the observer disagrees with the objectives, that same individual is a terrorist.

Some analysts have attempted to move beyond this extremely subjective method of defining terrorism by arguing that violence perpetrated against state institutions and other organs the state uses for control should not be considered terrorism, whereas all other forms of violence are terrorism. Under this type of definition, placing a bomb in a police station or a court building would not be terrorism. Placing a bomb in a school or a passenger plane would be.

Although such efforts to define terrorism are laudable, they are nevertheless fraught with problems. For example, if a bomb is set off at a police station but happens to kill innocent passersby as well, was the bombing a terrorist attack or not? Such an event happened in South Africa in 1985, with the perpetrators of the bombing arguing that the deaths outside the police station were unintended and that they were therefore not terrorists but freedom fighters seeking to overthrow apartheid. Similarly, when a U.S. Navy diver was executed by airline hijackers who claimed to be members of the PLO during a 1985 incident, their response was that the diver, even though on leave, was a part of the U.S. military establishment that helped Israel subjugate territory that was, they claimed, rightfully Palestinian. Thus, they argued, they were not terrorists.

Obviously, defining terrorism presents problems. Some cases are relatively straightforward and can clearly and easily be categorized as terrorism. For example, the murder of an elderly American man confined to a wheelchair during the 1985 hijacking of the Italian cruise liner *Achille Lauro* and the bomb blast that destroyed Pan American Flight 103 over Lockerbie, Scotland, in December 1988 fall into this category. But there are many shades of gray, and no universally accepted definition has yet been fashioned.

In its simplest form, terrorism denotes the use of violence to achieve a political objective. Ordinarily, the death and destruction caused by terrorism are limited, at least in comparison with the death and destruction caused by war. However, the specter lurks that terrorists will escalate their level of violence. The most feared scenario is that a terrorist group will obtain a nuclear weapon and threaten to destroy a city unless its demands are met.

Terrorism has been and is used by groups of all ideological persuasions. In El Salvador, the political right wing employed "Death Squads" to silence proponents of change, and the political left used similar tactics to foment revolution and undermine the existing social structure. Similarly, left-wing and right-wing terrorists both assaulted the social structure of Lebanon throughout the 1970s and 1980s.

Objectives of terrorists vary and may include eventual political independence for a state, a changed social or economic structure within a state or region, maintenance of an existing socioeconomic structure, or simple publicity for a cause. Targets of terrorist groups are often highly visible individuals, prominent corporations, government buildings, or military bases that newspapers and the media deem newsworthy. Bombing, abductions, murders, hostage taking, and hijacking are all methods that terrorists employ. The Islamic Jihad Organization's destruction of the American Embassy in Beirut in 1983, the truck bombing of the U.S. Marine barracks in Beirut the same year, the 1985 Abul Abbas-inspired hijacking of the *Achille Lauro*, the 1986 bombing of a West Berlin disco by Libyan-supported terrorists, the bombing of Pan American Flight 103 over Lockerbie, Scotland, in December 1988, and the numerous aerial hijackings of the past 20 years are all manifestations of terrorist groups seeking to target newsworthy items that guarantee great publicity. So too was the 1993 bombing of the World Trade Center in New York. Such attacks, if carried out successfully, also have a disproportionate psychological impact on the opponents of terrorist groups, because potential victims never know where or when the next attack will occur.

During the 1980s, a new phenomenon gained increased notoriety—state-supported terrorism. In simplest form, state-supported terrorism occurs when certain states for reasons of their own provide funding, training, and support for terrorist groups and movements. Libya, Syria, and Iran all have been indicted by the U.S. and other Western states as prominent supporters of terrorist activity.[7] Notably, however, a campaign of international sanctions against Syria influenced Syria to change its attitude toward supporting terrorism. Implicated in 34 terrorist attacks in 1985, Syria was involved in only 6 in 1986, one in 1987, and none since then.

State-supported terrorism presents a quandary to those who seek to combat terrorism; namely, if it is well documented that a particular state supported a specific terrorist action, how should other states respond? Should war be declared? Should a retaliatory raid be launched? Should a retaliatory raid be launched even if innocent bystanders may be killed? Should diplomatic channels, economic boycotts, or other paths be followed? Should international law be ignored if terrorists can be apprehended? What sorts of risks are acceptable to forces that are retaliating against state-supported terrorism? And if the evidence linking a particular state to a specific terrorist action is not completely reliable but only 90 percent reliable, what then?

Terrorist organizations exist around the world. In Europe, Turkey's Gray Wolves, Ireland's Provisional Wing of the Irish Republican Army, Italy's Red Guard, and Germany's Baader-Meinhof Gang all have been or are among the leading terrorist organizations. In the Americas, Peru's Shining Path, Uruguay's

Tupamoros, the United States' Aryan Nation, and a variety of left- and right-wing terrorists in El Salvador have been or are prominent. In Asia, certain of India's Sikhs, Japan's Red Army Faction, and Sri Lanka's Tamil separatists have all pursued terrorism. And in the Middle East, various factions of the PLO, led by Abu Nidal and Abul Abbas, are among the foremost terrorists.

Because of the threat presented by terrorist groups, states in particular have undertaken a number of steps to attempt to combat terrorism. Several Western governments have developed specially trained military forces to combat terrorist groups. West Germany's Group Nine, Great Britain's Special Air Services, and Israel's 269 Headquarters Reconnaissance Regiment all have counterterrorist responsibilities. The United States' elite Delta Team was designated to handle antiterrorist planning for the 1984 Los Angeles Olympics, and elite South Korean and Spanish military units had the same task respectively for the 1988 Seoul Olympics and the 1992 Barcelona Olympics. The Delta Team will be responsible for the 1996 Atlanta Olympics once again as well. Similarly, in general, security has been strengthened at most airports, and international cooperation between national counterterrorist intelligence units has been improved. Even with these steps, however, terrorism remains a major international problem, as Figure 5–2 indicates. Given the nature of the problem and the draconian methods that would probably be required to eliminate it, it is likely that terrorism will be with the international community for the foreseeable future.[8]

TRANSNATIONAL RELIGIOUS MOVEMENTS AND GROUPS

Religious movements have played major roles in international affairs for centuries. The Christian Crusades to the Holy Land and the Muslim jihad through northern Africa are but two of many examples of religious wars against "infidels," and the inter-European wars of the sixteenth and seventeenth centuries are examples of conflicts brought about by differing interpretations of the same religion.

The impact of religious groups or movements on international affairs is not, however, limited to violence and conflicts. During the late nineteenth and early twentieth centuries, at least part of the U.S. affinity for China was the product of the efforts of U.S. missionaries to spread Christianity in that country. Centuries earlier, Buddhist monks traveled about China and Southeast Asia spreading their own version of peace and godliness. More recently, South Korean religious figure Sun Myung Moon and his Unification Church have had a significant religious impact within the United States.

Major religious movements by and large have either made their peace with the governments of those states in which they operate or have combined their religious authority with the secular political authority of the state to create a government headed by a combined religious–political symbol of authority. In much of the industrialized world, church and state made their peace through separatism; the U.S. doctrine of the separation of church and state is a prominent example. In other cases, however, as in Western Europe during the preindustrial era and particularly before the Treaty of Westphalia, and in revolutionary Iran today, the unity of church and state was and is the rule.

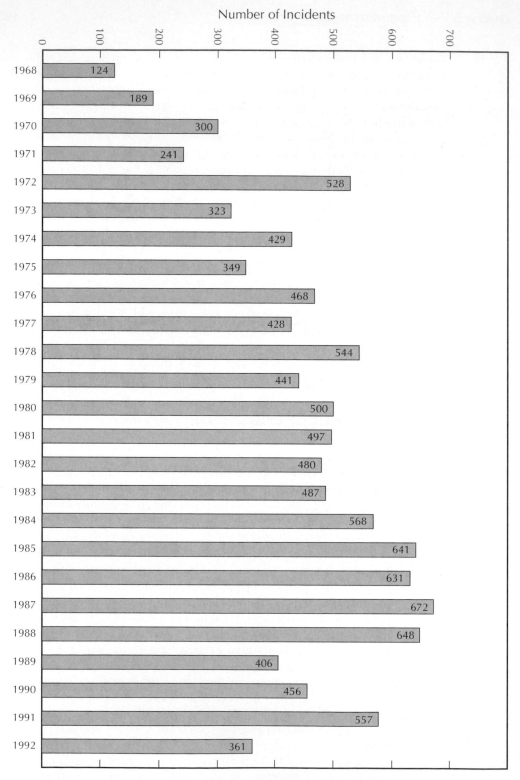

FIGURE 5–2 International terrorist incidents, 1968–92. (SOURCE: U.S. Department of State Dispatch, May 18, 1992, p. 392. The 1992 statistic was also provided by the U.S. Department of State.)

Even in those states where church and state are separated, religion may play a role in international affairs. Formally organized religious groups such as the World Council of Churches may take a conscious stand on an international issue, as the council did on black majority rule in Namibia and apartheid in South Africa. Conversely, less organized groups or movements such as the "moral majority" in the United States may seek to influence governmental policies across a wide range of international issues.

Perhaps the most prominent religious actor in the Western world in international affairs is the Catholic Church. Seated in Vatican City and headed by the pope, the Catholic Church plays a unique role in the contemporary international arena. It is both a territorial state and a religious movement, and its influence reaches into every continent on earth. Although the actual territory that it rules is limited today, only a few centuries ago it held political control throughout and beyond Europe. Kings, princes, and lords did not act until they had cleared their actions with the pope. As the secular state moved to the forefront in Western Europe following the Treaty of Westphalia in 1648, the papacy's territorial control receded.

Even so, the Catholic Church's religious influence remained immense. In many cases, bishops and priests accommodated themselves to whatever government was in power. The Catholic Church has survived and prospered in Western industrial democracies such as the United States, in communist states such as Poland between 1945 and 1989, and in military states such as Argentina during the 1970s and early 1980s. In some cases, bishops and priests have seen fit to criticize governments of states in which they reside.

In the Catholic Church in Latin America during the 1980s, the "theology of liberation" was widely influential. This version of Catholicism taught peasants that they had a right and even a duty to better their lives. Not surprisingly, the entrenched upper classes saw this "liberation theology" as a threat emanating from the Catholic Church, which for centuries had supported the status quo in Latin America. Although not all priests subscribed to this new and revolutionary approach to Catholicism, enough did to make the role of the Catholic Church a political issue. The governments in Latin America—as well as the pope in Vatican City—had to decide whether and how to respond to the challenges that the theology of liberation presents to their authority. Perhaps surprisingly, the pope and the Vatican took a stand, in the April 1986 "Instruction on Christian Freedom and Liberation." According to the instruction, it was "perfectly legitimate that those who suffer oppression on the part of the wealthy or the politically powerful should take action." Even armed struggle was ruled appropriate as a last resort against entrenched tyranny. Additionally, private property rights were deemed subordinate to "the higher principle that states that goods are meant for all."[9] The Catholic Church, it seemed, had opted for change.

In the United States, religion increased its public policy role in the 1980s and 1990s as well. The fundamentalist "Moral Majority" played a major role in the 1980 presidential campaign, and in 1982 Catholic bishops in the United States moved to the forefront of the antinuclear movement with their criticism of U.S. nuclear policy.[10] The Reverend Jesse Jackson played a major role in the 1984 and 1988 Democratic presidential race with his Rainbow Coalition. On the Republican side, evangelist Pat Robertson ran in the 1988 presidential primaries, and in 1992, the "religious right" figured prominently in President George Bush's reelection efforts.

Religion's role in other societies has also expanded, evidenced most clearly in Iran. There, Ayatollah Ruhollah Khomeini concluded during the 1960s that the shah of Iran was secularizing the Iranian state and destroying fundamental Islamic lifestyles in Iran. From his headquarters in exile in Paris, Khomeini preached the overthrow of the shah and the creation of an Islamic state that would be guided in its policies by the Koran. To Khomeini, his version of Islam, Shiite fundamentalism, provided the guidelines on which policy could be formulated. After the shah's overthrow, Khomeini sought to bring his own beliefs into practice. Most of the secularized Western practices that the shah sought to introduce to Iran during his rule were outlawed, and the tenets of fundamental Shiite Islam again ran private and public life in Iran. After Khomeini's death in 1989, a degree of religious moderation surfaced in Iran, but the country remained an Islamic republic.

Other instances of the political activity of religious groups, movements, or individuals abound. Self-immolation by Buddhist monks during the Vietnam War carried a political as well as individual message, and Billy Graham's 1982 trip to the U.S.S.R. was widely viewed as a propaganda coup for the U.S.S.R. Even Pope John Paul II cannot avoid undertaking actions pregnant with political implications. His clear support for the trade union Solidarity in his native Poland and his meeting with Soviet leader Mikhail Gorbachev in late 1989 are two cases in point.

In any event, it is evident that religious groups and movements from the Catholic Church to Shiite fundamentalists to moral majority members influence and in some cases determine the conduct of international affairs. Although simplistic generalizations about the roles that such groups and movements play are impossible to make if an accurate understanding of international affairs is to be developed, the fact remains that they have been neglected for too long as major actors in the international scene.

TRANSNATIONAL POLITICAL PARTIES AND MOVEMENTS

As with many other international actors, transnational political parties and movements are difficult to specifically define. To some, certain ethnic/national liberation movements may be described as political movements, whereas others may consider them terrorist groups. Thus, depending on one's point of departure, the Palestine Liberation Organization could be described as a political movement, a national liberation movement, or a terrorist group. Similarly, supporters of the Polish trade union Solidarity were described as belonging to a political movement, a nationalist organization, and a revolutionary group. Indeed, the chameleonlike qualities of the labels we are trying to attach to different organizations, groups, and movements so that we may better conceptualize how the world works are well illustrated by Solidarity: after its stunning 1989 election victory, Solidarity became the Polish government!

For our purposes, however, we will define a political party as any group that seeks to obtain political power and public office by supplying its candidates for office with labels—party "identifications"—by which they are known to the electorate. They must also have a formal structure and a policy "platform." Obviously, this is a broad definition, and it implies that political parties are willing to participate in elections. It does not necessarily mean that those elections are impartial by Western democratic standards or that parties will not resort to means of obtaining political power other than the ballot box.[11]

Some political parties and movements transcend national boundaries and appeal to an international clientele. Western European Social Democrats regularly coordinate and discuss their national party platforms with each other and share a political philosophy that includes equitable distribution of jobs, income, and property. Although national identities of the European Social Democratic parties remain clearly discernible, the international connections of these parties in European politics are a force to be reckoned with.

Similarly, in an earlier era, the international communist movement could have been described as a major global transnational political movement and/or party. Three separate Communist Internationals (Cominterns) were formed during the

Throughout Eastern Europe in 1989, individuals and groups went to the streets to bring down communist governments. But were they acting as individuals, nationalist organizations, political parties, or revolutionary movements? Here, Lech Walesa and other strikers protest in Gdansk, Poland.   (AP/Wide World Photos.)

late nineteenth and early twentieth centuries to aid communists in their avowed goal of uniting the workers of the world and wresting political power from the hands of the workers' "class enemies." However, following the collapse of communism in Eastern Europe and the Soviet Union and despite the continuation of communist governments in China and a few other isolated locations, communism can no longer be said to be a global political party or movement.

While communism has disintegrated as an international political movement, major American political movements and parties of the twentieth century have never become really internationalized. To be sure, both the Democratic and Republican parties have a major impact on international affairs, particularly when a member of their party is in the White House, but neither party has sought to build systematic links with ideologically kindred parties in other countries. The Democratic and Republican parties are not international parties.

NONGOVERNMENTAL ORGANIZATIONS (NGOS)

Although NGOs are not historically new actors in international affairs, they have received only a semblance of legal and formal recognition as actors since World War II. In contrast to the League of Nations, where representatives of NGOs competed daily with tourists for seats, the United Nations has recognized the roles that NGOs play in international affairs. This recognition is in part the result of the precedent established in 1945 by the U.S. government when it designated representatives of various national groups "special consultants" to the U.S. delegation to the UN's Conference on International Organizations.[12]

Although the precise definition of NGOs is open to debate, general agreement exists that they have proliferated numerically since World War II. Their newly acquired international status, the increased volume of international interactions, and the increased ease of international travel and communications are all causes of this proliferation, even as they are for the increased numbers of IGOs, which we discussed in Chapter 3.

NGOs operate in a variety of areas of human activity. Some, such as the Committee for Nuclear Disarmament (CND) or Greenpeace, seek to change policies of national governments. Both CND and Greenpeace have had a degree of success in obtaining their objectives. The willingness of the Reagan administration to begin nuclear weapons talks with the U.S.S.R. first evidenced itself only after CND and other antinuclear activist groups (some of which could be described as NGOs) organized massive antinuclear protests in North America and Europe. Similarly, in 1982, the states of the world agreed to permit the "harvesting" of only 12,000 whales per year, owing in no small part to the "Save the Whales" campaigns initiated by Greenpeace.

On occasion, actions taken by an NGO may even complicate policies that a state would like to pursue to the extent that the state feels it must respond against the NGO. Perhaps the classic example occurred in 1985 when the French Secret Service decided that it must act against Greenpeace's efforts to disrupt French nuclear testing in the South Pacific. French agents placed a bomb on the *Rainbow Warrior*, a Greenpeace vessel that was to lead a flotilla of antinuclear ships into the French testing area, when it was anchored in Auckland Harbor in New

Zealand. The *Rainbow Warrior* was sunk, one person was killed, and French–New Zealand relations deteriorated dramatically. Although French nuclear testing went on, it was clear that the actions of an NGO—Greenpeace—had influenced a state—France—to undertake a rash and precipitous action.

NGO activities may also coincide with attitudes and even policies of nation-states. Thus, within weeks of the changes in governments in Eastern Europe in 1989, the American Federation of Teachers, several U.S. and Western European labor unions, and the International Bar Association had dispatched members to Eastern Europe to help teach people there how democratic institutions operated.

Some NGOs such as the International Red Cross undertake humanitarian efforts. Amnesty International's programs of investigating, pointing out, and publicizing human rights abuses around the world are particularly noteworthy in this regard. So too are the programs of Americas Watch, which undertakes similar activities pointing out human rights abuses in the Western hemisphere. Still other humanitarian efforts are undertaken by organizations that evolved from NGOs into IGOs as governments recognized the importance of the work they were doing. Included in this category are the International Relief Union and the International Refugee Organization of the United Nations.

Still other NGOs may best be described as professional organizations that seek to further the interests of their members. The International Sugar Office, the International Chamber of Commerce, the World Veterans Association, and the International Federation of Airline Pilots' Association (IFALPA) are all examples of NGOs. Not surprisingly, there is no uniform record of success or failure for these NGOs in their efforts to further their members' interests. A former Secretary of the International Chamber of Commerce lamented the dearth of publicity that NGOs receive and noted that their efforts in international affairs are generally ignored.[13] By contrast, IFALPA had a major impact on how states handle skyjacking. IFALPA members agreed to boycott all states that took ineffective antiskyjacking measures or that clearly supported skyjackers. When IFALPA called for a boycott of all flights to Algeria in August 1968 because of the Algerian government's detention of a hijacked El Al aircraft, crew, and passengers, the Algerian government quickly ended the detention.[14] More recently, in 1986, IFALPA again threatened to boycott all states that supported terrorism aimed at commercial airline flights or facilities. The 1986 declaration was aimed at Libya.

Scientific organizations are themselves often NGOs, although they regularly find themselves in a complex web of governmental, IGO, NGO, and MNC relations. The International Council of Scientific Unions (ICSU) is perhaps the leading scientific NGO. ICSU members include the major scientific academies of the world, national research councils, and associations of scientific institutions from many countries. Its activities have included organization of the International Geophysical Year and the International Year of the Quiet Sun, and it has specialized international committees on ocean research, space research, and science and technology in developing countries, to name only a few. One of its other committees is the Scientific Committee on Problems of the Environment, which in 1985 issued a major report on the environmental consequences of nuclear war, specifically on the concept of nuclear winter.[15] Given the scope of its activities, ICSU often cooperates with governmental agencies, proposes programs to IGOs and other NGOs, and seeks funding support from private corporations and MNCs. It is not the only NGO that finds itself in such a complex web of interactions; it is simply an excellent example.

A variety of international sports federations also qualify as NGOs. The International Olympic Committee (IOC) and the International Rugby Union (IRU) are of particular note because of their extreme involvement in politics between states. Although both groups (as well as other athletically oriented NGOs) maintain that politics should have no role in international sports, both have become inextricably entwined in political issues that they would prefer to avoid. The IOC has been forced to decide whether the Republic of China (Taiwan) or the People's Republic of China (mainland China) should participate in the Olympic games, whether New Zealand should be excluded from participation in the Olympics because a non-Olympic New Zealand sports team competed against a South African team, whether an Olympic site should be changed because a host country (the Soviet Union) had militarily occupied a neighbor (Afghanistan), and how many if any Olympic events should be held in North Korea when the host country was South Korea. And the IRU has been forced to decide whether it would permit member teams to play against the South African national team, one of the best in the world, or refuse matches because of South Africa's apartheid policy. These issues were clearly political and had little to do with sports as such, but nevertheless, because of the issues at stake, athletically oriented NGOs intruded into the political domain of states.

A final type of NGO is the private foundation. Some authorities, it should be cautioned, do not consider foundations legitimate NGOs because they are generally chartered under the laws of one state, have a board of directors consisting of

The nongovernmental organization Greenpeace has protested against nuclear weapons and disrupted whaling activity throughout the world. Here a Greenpeace motorized dinghy carries a banner protesting nuclear weapons as it sails past the U.S. carrier *Forrestal* in New York harbor.   (AP/Wide World Photos.)

a single or very few nationalities, and operate primarily in the domestic sphere. Here only those foundations that devote significant shares of their resources to international programs will be considered.

Two foundations in particular have had major impacts on international relations in recent years. The Ford Foundation, the world's largest, centers its international projects on developmental assistance, population studies, and European and international studies. The Rockefeller Foundation, the world's third largest foundation, has concentrated on health, population, biomedical, and nutritional projects. Together, the Rockefeller and Ford Foundations have contributed extensively to the so-called "green revolution" through their funding of the International Rice Research Institute in the Philippines, the International Center of Tropical Agriculture in Colombia, the International Wheat and Maize Improvement Center in Mexico, and the International Institute of Tropical Agriculture in Nigeria. Like the scientific NGOs, foundations have interacted regularly and closely with a variety of states. Ford and Rockefeller programs are often closely coordinated with programs run by the U.S. government's Agency for International Development and the Canadian government's Canadian Development Agency. Cooperation has also been effected between the foundations and IGOs such as the Organization of American States, the United Nations Development Program, and the International Bank for Reconstruction and Development.

So far the impression may have been created that NGOs regularly cooperate effectively with nation-states, IGOs, and MNCs. This is only part of the picture. Although the lament of a former secretary of the International Chamber of Commerce that other international actors regularly ignore NGOs has been noted, relations between NGOs and other actors do on occasion deteriorate even more. The International Olympic Committee's experience with the 1980 Moscow Olympic Games is a good case in point.

The IOC, like many NGOs, has a central committee that acts as an administrative and policy-making body to which national sports federations can apply for membership. The IOC decides upon sites for Olympic games several years in advance; the various national sports federations then send their representatives to participate in the games. Other than providing some funding in some states, national governments theoretically are in no way connected with either the IOC or the national sports federations.

However, because of the immensity of the spectacle of the international competition and cooperation of the Olympics, the games also evoke tremendous displays of national pride. Like it or not, political nationalism runs rampant at the Olympic games, not only in the competition itself, but also in the international media. Host countries now use the Olympics to showcase not only their athletes but also their social system.

Thus, when the Soviet Union invaded Afghanistan only seven months before the 1980 Moscow Olympics were scheduled to begin and Jimmy Carter responded by declaring the United States would boycott the games, the stage was set for a clash of wills between states as well as between international nongovernmental organizations and states. Carter could not order a boycott. Only the U.S. Olympic Committee with the acquiescence of its member federations could take such an action, which it eventually did. Carter also requested that other Western states and the Developing World boycott the games. In some cases comparable to that of the United States, governmental desires to boycott were acceded to by national Olympic committees. West Germany and Australia followed this model. In other cases, particularly in the Developing World, national Olympic committees had little choice but to boycott when governmental funding was revoked. In still other cases, national Olympic committees decided to participate in the Olympics despite the desire of the national government to boycott the Olympics. Thus, even though Margaret Thatcher's British government sided with the boycott, the British Olympic team went to the Moscow Olympics and won four gold medals.

The IOC, meanwhile, condemned the American–led boycott as an unwarranted intrusion of politics into the Olympics. The U.S. government, for its part, requested that the IOC change the site of the 1980 games because, to the United States, the Soviet invasion of Afghanistan was proof that the U.S.S.R. did not adhere to Olympic ideals. The IOC responded by threatening to change the site of the 1984 Olympics, scheduled for Los Angeles, because of the U.S. boycott of the Moscow games. Despite this threat, the 1984 Los Angeles games went on as scheduled, this time boycotted by the Soviet Union and most of its allies. And in 1988, the IOC received immense pressure to allow some competitions to be held in North Korea as well as South Korea. NGOs, it seems, cannot avoid state-to-state politics even when they prefer to.

Nongovernmental organizations, individuals, and the varied array of other international actors that have been examined in this chapter have only one common denominator: they are regularly overlooked and ignored in the study of international relations. Although it is true that their impact on international affairs in most cases is not so great as the impact of states, IGOs, or MNCs, there are numerous cases to prove that if these "less significant" actors are ignored, contemporary international politics cannot be understood. Pope John Paul II captured the imagination of the world not only because of his position, but also because of his humanity, his individuality; the international power and prestige of the Catholic Church has been enhanced because of a single man. On another level, Ayatollah Khomeini's Islamic fundamentalism was a force that led not only to the collapse of the shah's government, but also to a restructuring of the entire international balance of power in South Asia. And the whaling profession throughout the world is on the brink of extinction because of a crusade launched by some relatively isolated and nondescript nongovernmental organizations. The individual, the religious movement, the ethnic/national liberation movement, the political movement or party, the terrorist group, and the NGO can and do play major roles in today's world. Their contributions as actors to contemporary international relations must be increasingly studied and understood.

KEY TERMS AND CONCEPTS

role of private individuals in
   international affairs
impact of refugees
impact of tourism
ethnic/national liberation
   organizations
terrorist groups and movements

state-supported terrorism
transnational religious movements
   and groups
transnational political parties and
   movements
NGOs

NOTES

1. See *The Yearbook of International Organizations, 1987–88*.
2. Few analysts agree on how these "other actors" should be typed. For different typologies of these "other actors" in introductory international relations texts, see Theodore A. Couloumbis and James H. Wolfe, *Introduction to International Relations: Power and Justice* (Englewood Cliffs, NJ: Prentice-Hall, 1990); Walter S. Jones, *The Logic of International Relations* (Boston: Little, Brown, 1988); Charles W. Kegley, Jr., and Eugene R. Wittkopf, *World Politics: Trend and Transformation* (New York: St. Martin's Press, 1992); and Bruce Russett and Harvey Starr, *World Politics: The Menu for Choice* (San Francisco: W.H. Freeman, 1992).
3. For an important study of the role of refugees in world affairs in the 1990s, see Gil Loescher, *Refugee Movements and International Security: Adelphi Paper 268* (London: International Institute for Strategic Studies, 1992). See also the journal of the UN High Commissioner for Refugees, *Refugees*.
4. See David Kraslow and Stuart H. Loory, *The Secret Search for Peace in Vietnam* (New York: Random House, 1968).
5. For several different approaches to the role of individuals and individual behavior in international affairs, see Joseph H. De Rivera, *The Psychological Dimension of Foreign Policy* (Columbus, OH: Charles E. Merrill, 1968); Robert A. Isaak, *Individuals and World Politics* (North Scituate, MA: Duxbury, 1975); Otto Klineberg, *The Human Dimension in International Relations* (New York: Holt, Rinehart and Winston, 1966); Ralph Pettman, *Human Behavior and World Politics* (New York: St. Martin's Press, 1975); and Kenneth N. Waltz, *Man, the State, and War* (New York: Columbia University Press, 1965).
6. Many ethnic/national liberation movements turned to the Soviet Union for arms during the 1960s and 1970s. Soviet objectives—the reduction of Western influence and the expansion of Soviet influence—coincided with national liberation movement objectives—the elimination of Western colonialism. Hence the U.S.S.R. provided weapons.
7. There is an opposed school of thought that argues that the United States itself engages in state-supported terrorism. See Alexander George (ed.), *Western State Terrorism* (New York: Routledge, 1991).
8. For further discussions of terrorism and terrorists, see Peter C. Sederberg, *Terrorist Myths: Illusion, Rhetoric, and Reality* (Englewood Cliffs, NJ: Prentice-Hall, 1989); Edward F. Mickolus et al., *International Terrorism in the 1980's* (Ames, IA: Iowa State University Press, 1989); and Charles W. Kegley (ed.), *International Terrorism: Characteristics, Causes, Controls* (New York: St. Martin's Press, 1990). For an excellent study of a single terrorist movement, see David Scott Palmer (ed), *The Shining Path of Peru* (New York: St. Martin's Press, 1992).
9. See "Instruction on Christian Freedom and Liberation," released by the Vatican, April 1986. For other discussions of the theology of liberation from earlier years, see R. J. Sider, "Evangelical Theology of Liberation," *Christian Century*, Vol. 97 (March 1980): 314–318; J. H. Cone, "Gospel and the Liberation of the Poor," *Christian Century*, Vol. 98 (February 1981): 162–166; C. Krauthammer, "Holy Fools," *New Republic*, Vol. 185 (September 1981): 10+; C. P. Conn, "Where the World Council of Churches Went Wrong," *Saturday Evening Post*, Vol. 254 (May–June 1982): 12+; and J. M. Wall, "Liberation Ethics: Insisting on Equality," *Christian Century*, Vol. 99 (November 1982): 1123.
10. See "Bishops and the Bomb," *Time*, November 29, 1982, pp. 68–77.
11. This definition is taken from James Q. Wilson, *American Government: Institutions and Policies* (Lexington, MA: D.C. Heath, 1980), pp. 132–134.
12. Donald C. Blaisdell, *International Organization* (New York: Ronald Press, 1966), p. 374.

13. Pierre Vasseur, "The Difficulties of International Non-Governmental Organizations,"
     International Associations, No. 9 (1968): 620–624.

14. A. LeRoy Bennett, *International Organizations: Principles and Issues* (Englewood
     Cliffs, NJ: Prentice-Hall, 1977), p. 356.

15. A. B. Pittock et al. for the Scientific Committee on Problems of the Environment of
     the International Council of Scientific Unions, *Environmental Consequences of
     Nuclear War* (New York: John Wiley, 1985).

PART TWO

The Systemic Framework

THE ACTORS IN THE INTERNATIONAL SYSTEM

All events, wherever they occur, react upon each other.

—*Raymond Aron*

We're in the same boat
On the same sea
And we're sailing south
On the same breeze

—*from "Rock and a Hard Place,"*
by the Rolling Stones

International affairs would be a simple subject if each actor interacted only with identical actors, and if all shared similar objectives, outlooks, and capabilities. Unfortunately, however, this is not the case. States interact not only with other states, but also with intergovernmental organizations, multinational corporations, nongovernmental organizations, and a multitude of other actors. The objectives, outlooks, and capabilities of these various actors and classes of actors are seldom closely matched. In some contexts, the military power of a state may provide a more effective means of influencing a situation than the economic might of a multinational corporation, but in other contexts the relationship may be reversed. Similarly, the efforts of the United Nations to quiet a potentially dangerous source of international conflict may be utterly futile in one context, but a resounding success in another.

Together, all international actors plus their interactions with one another form an international system. Over time, as these actors and their capabilities and interests change, the international system changes. Simultaneously, the system influences the way actors act and the way they view themselves and others.

Raymond Aron likened the international system that these various actors create to a vast echo chamber. According to Aron, "the noises of men and events are amplified and reverberated to infinity. The disturbance occurring at one point of the planet communicates itself, step by step, to the opposite side of the globe. . . . All events, wherever they occur, react upon each other."[1] And Aron is correct; the interrelationship of actors and their interests creates an ever-changing international system that defies simplistic explanations.

To understand these complex interrelationships, it is sometimes helpful to formulate a mental picture of these trends and relationships that dominate the international system during a particular era. The late eighteenth century is often regarded as an era of revolutionary nationalism, whereas the late nineteenth and early twentieth centuries are described as years of colonial and imperial rivalry. All these descriptions are gross oversimplifications; other trends and relationships were continuing at the same time as the development of nationalism and imperialism. Nevertheless, as analytical concepts, nationalism and imperialism are useful descriptors of the dominant features of the international system of earlier eras.

For the first step in our analysis of the international system, it will be useful to develop an understanding of how states and other international actors formulate their interactions. In the case of states, the process that leads to most international interactions is called the *foreign policy process*, and the output from this process is *foreign policy*. In the case of other international actors, this process may be called *international decision-making* or a similar term, with the output identified as *international operations, international business policy*, or something similar. However, regardless of what the terminology used is, international actors must decide what they want to do in their interactions with each other, and how they want to try to do it. Thus, the first chapter in this framework studies the foreign policy process, foreign policy, and other forms of formulating and implementing international interactions.

Together, the actors and their interactions create an international system. Until recently, two major conflicts dominated the international system. The first was the East–West conflict, which pitted the United States and its friends and allies against the Soviet Union and its friends and allies. Although the East–West conflict centered on states, IGOs, MNCs, NGOs, and other actors all influenced, and in turn were influenced by, the conflict. In many ways, the East–West conflict was the central feature of the international system from shortly after World War II until the early 1990s.

Even though it is now over, the conflict's impact on our world today remains immense. Thus, it remains important to understand the origins and evolution of that conflict. The second chapter in this framework undertakes this task.

The second major conflict is the North–South conflict between the wealthy industrialized countries, most of which are in the northern hemisphere, and the poor nonindustrialized developing countries in the southern hemisphere. While the East–West conflict was, among other things, a debate over the preferred way to organize society, the root of the North–South conflict is the global inequity in the distribution of wealth. The third chapter in this framework examines the North–South conflict.

The East–West and North–South conflicts played major roles in shaping today's world. But at most, they were and are convenient concepts that help us order our thinking about how the international system works. They were not and are not perfect descriptions of the system. Since we live in an era in which the international system is undergoing revolutionary change, it is therefore appropriate that the final chapter in this framework explores the directions in which the international system may be headed.

The purposes of the following four chapters, then, are to examine the following questions:

- How do states and other international actors formulate and implement their interactions with one another?
- How did the East–West and North–South conflicts begin, and how did they evolve over time?
- How has the international system changed during the twentieth century?
- What are the dominant features of today's international system?
- Where is today's international system headed?

NOTE

1. Raymond Aron, *Peace and War* (Garden City, NY: Doubleday, 1966), p. 373.

CHAPTER 6

Foreign Policy and Other International Interactions

- How do states make foreign policy?
- What are the stages in a state's foreign policy process?
- How do other international actors make foreign policy?

To this point, our study of contemporary international relations has concentrated on different types of international actors and their objectives. In this chapter, we turn our attention to how the actors formulate their interactions with each other.

In the case of states, the process of formulating external actions is called the **foreign policy process**. The output from this process is called **foreign policy**. In the cases of other types of international actors, other terms are used. For example, international governmental organizations have a decision-making process that leads to their international operations. Multinational corporations engage in international strategic planning, international business, or international operations. NGOs, individuals, and other international actors also must decide what activities to pursue in their interactions with other actors, but there is little uniformity in the terms that are used to describe their decision-making processes.

In this chapter, we will first concentrate on the ways that states formulate and implement their interactions with each other. In other words, we will study the foreign policy process and foreign policy formulation. We will then discuss similar activities of IGOs, MNCs, NGOs, and other types of international actors. Our primary purpose is to develop a better understanding of how international actors formulate their international interactions.

THE FOREIGN POLICY PROCESS AND FOREIGN POLICY: AN OVERVIEW

The foreign policy process and foreign policy are both complex concepts. As a result, people rarely agree completely on what the terms mean or what the terms include. For our purposes here, we will consider very basic definitions. The foreign policy process will be defined as the entire set of actions that a state goes through as it formulates and implements its foreign policy. Foreign policy will be defined as the goal-directed set of actions that a state takes in its efforts to achieve its foreign policy objectives. Defined in these ways, foreign policy may be considered the output of a state's foreign policy process.

Different states have different foreign policy processes. Some countries may allow only their institutional version of the U.S. Department of State, often called the Ministry of Foreign Affairs, to participate in the foreign policy process. Other countries may allow their institutional versions of the U.S. Departments of Defense or Commerce to have a role in the process. Some countries may have their equivalent of the U.S. Secretary of State, usually the Minister of Foreign Affairs, make foreign policy decisions, while others may restrict final decision-making authority to their equivalent of the U.S. president. And some countries may spend billions of dollars on intelligence collection so they can have the best and most current information available upon which to base their decisions, whereas other states may have neither the money, the skill, nor the inclination to gather extensive up-to-date intelligence.

Obviously, potential exists for significant differences in the foreign policy processes of different states. Not surprisingly, then, different analysts and scholars have also developed different ways to study and understand these processes. For example, some analysts and scholars believe that the best way to study and understand the foreign policy process is to use the concept of levels of analysis that we studied in Chapter 1.[1] Other analysts and scholars prefer to concentrate their study on *rings of power*, a term used to describe the degree of influence that different individuals and groups may have on the foreign policy process.[2] Still other analysts and scholars emphasize the different steps that lead to the final formulation and implementation of foreign policy.[3]

All of these approaches—and others as well—are useful. Each provides a different type of insight into the foreign policy process. Nevertheless, in this chapter, we will examine only the third method that we have noted—that is, the different steps that virtually every country has in its foreign policy process. However, before we begin this study, four cautions must be added.

First, even though the foreign policy process is the primary means by which states formulate and implement the policies through which they interact, not all of the interactions that a state or its agents have with other international actors are necessarily outputs of a state's foreign policy process. Sometimes interactions are the result of spontaneous actions or chance encounters that were not expected. On other occasions, global trends in technology, economics, or culture develop that are the result of forces beyond the control of states, but that nevertheless affect states and their interactions. And in still other cases, policies are not implemented as planned, or they unfold in ways that are unanticipated, unexpected, or unwanted.

The tragedies of the *U.S.S. Stark* and the *U.S.S. Vincennes*, already detailed in our discussion of levels of analysis, provide perfect examples. The 1986 Iraqi attack on the *Stark* was not an output of Iraq's foreign policy process. At the time when the unfortunate event occurred, it was Iraqi policy in the Persian Gulf to attack merchant vessels, especially tankers, that were going to or from Iranian ports. It was not Iraqi policy to attack U.S. warships. The entire unfortunate episode was the result of a pilot's error. Nevertheless, the attack happened, and it had a major impact on U.S.-Iraqi relations.

Similarly, the *Vincennes'* destruction of an Iranian airliner was not an output of the American foreign policy process. Rather, it was the result of an incorrect interpretation of too limited an amount of data by the captain of the *Vincennes*. Nevertheless, the Iranian airliner was destroyed, and its destruction had a significant impact on U.S.-Iranian relations.

The key point here is that although the foreign policy of a state is the most important portion of a state's international interactions, not all the international interactions of a state or its agents are necessarily foreign policy. Put differently, not all international actions by states or their agents are outputs of the foreign policy process. Students and analysts of international affairs alike must be careful to differentiate between the foreign policy of states, and actions that may appear to be foreign policy but that in reality are not. Differentiation is often a challenging and difficult task.

A second caution is that students and analysts of the foreign policy process must not ascribe too much rationality to the foreign policy process. Although the concept of "process" brings to mind the image of a well-reasoned and logical approach to an issue, factors often intervene that make the foreign policy process less than completely rational, at least if rationality is measured in terms of planned and reasoned efforts to move toward a defined foreign policy objective.

Third, students and analysts of the foreign policy process should not ascribe too great a degree of order to the foreign policy process. Although the process described here is sequential, real-world pressures of time, politics, and money often dictate that the steps in the foreign policy process be undertaken simultaneously, with less than sufficient information or analysis, or in a different order than presented here. In certain cases, some steps may even be bypassed completely.

Finally, in every case, different people, different situations, different capabilities, and different perceptions combine in different ways to make the foreign policy process dynamic and ever-changing. This reality of constant change is one of the things that makes the study of the foreign policy process so fascinating—and so difficult.

THE FOREIGN POLICY PROCESS

As countries develop and implement their foreign policy, they regularly go through certain procedures. These procedures are called the *foreign policy process*. Not all countries follow identical steps. Even so, most countries include goal setting; intelligence gathering, reporting, and interpreting; option formulation; planning and programming; decision-making; policy articulation; policy implementation; policy monitoring; policy appraisal; policy modification; and memory storage and recall as steps in their foreign policy processes.[4] Table 6–1 lists these steps and identifies the purposes of and difficulties inherent to each step.

Goal Setting

Goal setting refers to the task of identifying national interests and foreign policy objectives, and arranging them by order of priority. More often than not, goal set-

TABLE 6–1   Major Steps in the Foreign Policy Process

Tasks	Purposes of the Task	Difficulties of the Task
1. Goal Setting	Identifying national interests and foreign policy objectives; Assigning priorities to interests and objectives	Agreeing on identity of national interests, objectives, and priorities
2. Intelligence Gathering, Reporting, and Interpreting	Gaining the most accurate information available upon which to base decisions, understanding what it means, and getting it to the people who need it	Incomplete information; Distortion of information; Delay in information; Interpreting information incorrectly; Information overload
3. Option Formulation	Developing choices about what to do	Limiting options too much; Developing options on the basis of predispositions, groupthink, or politics
4. Planning and Programming	Identifying and weighing costs and benefits of each option	Predisposition, groupthink, or politics will influence cost-benefit identification and weighting
5. Decision-Making	Deciding upon the proper policy option	Predisposition, groupthink, or politics will influence cost-benefit identification and weighting; Deciding upon proper time frame
6. Policy Articulation	Effectively stating policy and its rationale to gain domestic and foreign support	Too many spokespersons; Contradictions, confusion, and concern for personal image; Media distortion
7. Policy Implementation	Allocating resources to ensure effectiveness of policy elements; Clear command and control of policy elements; Decisive action	Communication problems; Unclear lines of authority; Organizational interests; Bureaucratic politics; Changing situations; and Counter-actions by others
8. Policy Monitoring	Staying abreast of the policy and its effects as it is implemented	Gaps in monitoring; Feedback failures; Unclear linkages between cause and effect
9. Policy Appraisal	Assessing whether the policy is having its intended effects; Assessing unintended effects	Predisposition, groupthink, or politics will influence policy appraisal
10. Policy Modification	Changing policy to better achieve goal	Policy inertia; Insufficient resources; Organizational interests; Bureaucratic politics; Image damage
11. Memory Storage and Recall	Learning from experience; Improve future policy	Partial and unreliable storage and recall; "Lessons" applied poorly or remembered selectively

SOURCE: Adopted, with significant alterations made by the present author, from John P. Lovell, *The Challenge of American Foreign Policy: Purpose and Adaptation* (New York: Macmillan, 1985), pp. 27, 32.

ting in the foreign policy process is the task of a few senior people in the executive branch of a state's national government. The president and the secretary of state or their equivalents usually figure prominently in this process.

The degree of difficulty inherent in goal setting depends to a great extent on a state's type of government and the structure of its society. For example, authoritarian governments rarely must take public opinion into account to the same extent that democratic governments do. For authoritarian regimes, aside from taking into account the ruling elite's own outlooks and priorities and settling disagreements that may exist within the ruling elite, goal setting in foreign policy is relatively uncomplicated.

By contrast, democratic societies often find it difficult to reach agreement on what national interests actually are and what foreign policy goals should be. Democratic countries also often find it difficult to assign priorities with national interests. This is because in democratic societies, many different parochial interest groups have opportunities to make known their own views on the national interest, foreign policy goals, and national priorities. They also often have an ability to influence the decision-making process. As a result, goal setting is often a more complex task in democratic societies than in authoritarian societies.

Nevertheless, decision-makers in democratic states and authoritarian states alike must set goals and assign priorities to them if their states are to have successful foreign policies.

Intelligence Gathering, Interpreting, and Reporting

Intelligence gathering, interpreting, and reporting are all important parts of the second step of the foreign policy process. After goals have been set, it becomes important to find out as much as possible about the issues at hand, the factors that affect the issues, and what others think about and plan to do about them. Governments typically seek information about what others can do, what others plan to do, and what impact the policies that they themselves are implementing might have or are having. These three aspects of intelligence are sometimes called intelligence about *capabilities*, *intentions*, and *feedback*.

As important as acquiring information is, by itself it is not enough. Information must be interpreted accurately, and it must also be provided in a timely manner to those who need it to make decisions and implement policy. A country may have the best intelligence gathering capabilities in the world, but unless the intelligence it gathers is interpreted correctly and reaches those who need it in a timely manner, intelligence is absolutely useless.

Intelligence analysis and interpretation is a difficult task, requiring among other things familiarity with the issues and events under consideration, an open mind and a good memory, an ability to identify causal relationships, and an ability to anticipate future events. Another skill needed to analyze and interpret intelligence is the ability to sift through the immense quantity of information that is frequently available to find truly meaningful data.

Indeed, one way that states and other international actors sometimes try to confuse foreign intelligence analysts about their real capabilities and intentions is to provide them with too much information, much of it incorrect. The rationale behind this approach, relying on "information overload" to frustrate intelligence efforts, is to hide the "real" and "important" information behind a blizzard of "noise," or misleading information. This is exactly the technique that the Allies used during World War II to confuse Germany about where the D-Day landings would occur.

States gather intelligence in a variety of ways. Most is acquired from readily available open sources. A surprising amount of information is acquired from newspapers, magazines, and other open sources. Diplomats and other government employees also acquire extensive amounts of information for their country from the people they talk to and the contacts that they have. Sometimes governments also "debrief" citizens who travel abroad or who have foreign contacts. They may include businesspeople, journalists, scientists, professors, and occasionally even tourists who may have ventured into sensitive areas. In addition, technologically advanced countries often employ "national technical means" of intelligence gathering such as monitoring radio and telephone conversations or using satellites to gather information.

A surprisingly small percentage of intelligence is actually gathered by traditional cloak-and-dagger undercover work, or "spying." Nevertheless, covert methods, as spying is also called, sometimes uncover extremely useful and important information.

Different states devote different amounts of resources to intelligence gathering, interpreting, and reporting. Some states with limited resources have virtually no intelligence capability. Others spend immense amounts of money on intelligence. For example, the budget for the U.S. intelligence community in 1992 was estimated as over $29 billion dollars.

Option Formulation

Option formulation is usually the third step in the foreign policy process. Although decision-makers in some states sometimes simply make decisions about what they intend to do without formulating options, in most states, different policy choices are developed for decision-makers about what can be done about a given issue.

The purpose of this step is straightforward: to provide decision-makers with choices about how to achieve the goals that they have established in light of the information available on the issue at hand. At first blush, this seems like an easy task, but in fact it is not. Those who formulate options must be careful not to limit the range of choices that they develop in light of their own predispositions. They must also avoid *groupthink*, that is, the human tendency to go along with what someone else thinks. At the same time, they must try not to take political considerations into account as they formulate options; taking political considerations into account is more the task of planners, programmers, and decision-makers. The task of those who formulate options is to provide planners, programmers, and decision-makers with choices on policy that have a realistic chance of succeeding, and they must not present those choices in ways that predispose planners, programmers, and decision-makers to certain conclusions.

Different states pursue the formulation of options in different ways, with different parts of the government bureaucracy becoming involved in the process. Many states use variations of what the United States government calls *inter-*

agency working groups. Inter-agency working groups bring together people from various governmental departments and agencies that might be affected by a particular issue. These groups then formulate policy options, and present them to their superiors, sometimes accompanied by assessments about the costs and benefits of each option, thus overlapping responsibilities with the next step in the foreign policy process—planning and programming.

Planning and Programming

Planning and programming comprise the fourth major step in the foreign policy process. In this step, first policy analysts and then more senior governmental officials identify and weigh the costs and benefits of the options that have been developed. Factors that are considered in this step include how many resources each option will require, the length of time that an option may require to succeed, the amount of time that is available before a particular problem must be resolved or ameliorated, the political impacts that an option may have, other secondary and tertiary effects that an option might have, and the likelihood of success for an option.

Planning and programming efforts are usually undertaken by inter-agency working groups or their equivalents. The major pitfalls that planners and programmers face are the same as found in their primary task—to properly identify and weigh the costs and benefits of each policy option proposed. In many respects, this is more art than science.

Like those who formulate options, planners and programmers must strive to minimize the influence of their own predispositions and of groupthink. Unlike option formulators, they must also assess the political fallout that given options might have. And perhaps most difficult of all, planners and programmers must then communicate their analyses to decision-makers in clear, concrete, concise, and nonconfusing language.

Decision-Making

Decision-making is the fifth step in the foreign policy process. Who makes the final decision on which policy option will become national policy more often than not depends on the degree of importance of the issue at hand. Extremely critical decisions that involve options such as the use of military force are usually made by the national leader. Less critical decisions like the naming of ambassadors are often made by the secretary of state or the equivalent, although the national leader may sometimes also become involved. Relatively minor decisions such as deciding whether or not a visa should be issued are more often than not left to government bureaucrats such as consular officials. As a practical matter, such decisions rarely enter the policy process, but they are foreign policy decisions nevertheless.

Decision-makers face the same problems that were identified in the preceding steps, but these people also have the ability to recognize when they are receiving skewed information and analysis. Put differently, skilled decision-makers must have the ability to "ask the right questions" to uncover errors or omissions in the policy process.

National decision-making is often a complicated and difficult task that requires input from many people. Here, President Bill Clinton meets with his National Security Council in May 1993 to discuss U.S. policy on the Bosnia crisis.   (Sygma.)

It is at this point in the foreign policy process that we must return to the levels-of-analysis problem that we examined earlier. Will the decision-maker ask the right questions, thereby uncovering any bureaucratic biases or personal predispositions that may have altered the information and analyses that he or she received? Even if the decision-maker asks the right questions, will he or she make a decision on the basis of the national interest and national objectives? Or will she or he make a decision based on personal values, her or his own political future, or his or her perceived place in history? The answer to these questions depends on the individual leader, not the policy process.

Indeed, some prominent analysts argue that foreign policy decisions in the final analysis are rarely made on the basis of how a problem may best be solved. For example, Charles Lindblom argues that decision-makers more often than not have as their primary objective not the national interest or some higher concern, but rather the minimization of uncertainty and risk, the reduction of the number of unknowns, and the maintenance of the familiar.[5] This theory, called **incrementalism**, argues that even if earlier steps in the foreign policy process indicate that major changes in policy are warranted, decision-makers prefer to make small changes that do not significantly alter policy directions. Lindblom asserts that the incrementalist approach to decision-making reduces risk and danger for the decision-maker, and allows him or her to change course quickly if newly implemented policies appear to be bringing about undesirable change.

Lindblom's analysis fits closely with Herbert Simon's observation that decision-makers do not seek the "best" solution to a problem, but rather one that "satisfies," that is, meets a minimum level of acceptability.[6] Simon accepts the argument that most people try to act rationally, but he also maintains that everyone's rationality is unavoidably "bounded" or "limited" by the simplified mental images that they hold of how the world is structured and how the world works. Thus, Simon asserts, despite even the best efforts to make rational decisions, decisions that in retrospect may appear irrational are sometimes made.

The debate over how and why people in positions of authority make the decisions that they do is of course not limited to the foreign policy process. But in foreign policy, with war and peace sometimes being the issue at hand, the stakes of decision-making are sometimes immense.

Policy Articulation

The sixth step in the foreign policy process—policy articulation—refers to the need to state effectively what a country's policy is once it has been decided upon. The need to explain the rationale behind the policy is also a critical goal of policy articulation.

Policy articulation is an extremely important part of the foreign policy process in a democratic state because of the need for domestic public support for foreign policy implementation. But even in an authoritarian or totalitarian state, policy articulation is important. Every country, regardless of governmental type, finds the implementation of foreign policy easier if its domestic population supports its policies.

At the same time, governments of all types also find foreign policy implementation easier if foreign publics support—or at a minimum do not oppose—their policies. Governments consequently also see foreign publics as important targets for their policy articulation efforts.

Like the preceding steps in the foreign policy process, policy articulation is a difficult task. Among the pitfalls that confront it are the dangers of multiple spokespersons who may inadvertently offer contradictory rationales for a policy, or who may present confusing information about their government's policies or intentions. Indeed, contradictions and confusion frequently crop up in this phase of the foreign policy process even when there are only a few government spokespersons. Concern for personal image on the part of government officials sometimes also complicates policy articulation. So too does unintended—and sometimes intended—media distortion.

Despite its difficulties and regardless of the nature of a state's regime, policy articulation is an extremely important part of the foreign policy process. The reason for this is straightforward. It is simply easier for a government to undertake foreign policy initiatives if domestic and foreign publics understand what they are and why they are being undertaken, and support their objectives and implementation.

Policy Implementation

Policy implementation is the seventh step in the foreign policy process, and it is the first step in which a state actually attempts to move toward the goals that it identified earlier. It is here that traditional foreign policy begins.

As a concept, policy implementation refers to the actions that a state undertakes to put into practice the policy decisions that it has made (or more accurately, that its decision-makers have made for it). In many cases, these actions will be designed to move a country toward the goals that it set for itself (or once again more accurately, that its decision-makers set for it). However, in other cases, factors such as personal ambition and concern, bureaucratic politics, misinformation, and faulty analysis will have intervened. In these cases, policy goals and policy actions will be less directly related.

States have at their disposal a variety of economic, military, sociopolitical, diplomatic, legal, and other instruments to pursue their goals and to implement their policies. These instruments will be examined in detail in Framework Four, and will not be examined here.

Policy Monitoring

The foreign policy process does not end with policy implementation. Since states must stay abreast of the progress of their policy and must determine what effects their policies once implemented are having, states must also engage in policy monitoring.

Sometimes it is quite easy to monitor the progress and observe the effect that a policy is having. But on other occasions, gaps in monitoring capabilities may exist. In some cases, especially where policies are implemented with the goal of changing another international actor's intentions, it might not even be possible to observe the impact of a given policy. Similarly, unclear linkages between cause and effect may exist, complicating the monitoring effort still further.

Nevertheless, unless a country is willing to implement a policy without caring about whether it succeeds or fails, policy monitoring is a requisite step in the foreign policy process. With policy monitoring, one may fail to alter or to fine tune a policy to achieve a desired goal. In the absence of policy monitoring, it is a virtual certainty that alterations or fine tuning will not be undertaken.

Policy Appraisal

Policy appraisal is the process of assessing whether a policy is having its intended effect and determining what unintended side effects, if any, may be occurring. More often than not, policy appraisal is undertaken at the inter-agency working group level or at senior levels of government.

As with option formulation and planning and programming, policy appraisal may fall victim to the predisposition of analysts and decision-makers, to group-think, and to considerations of politics. If this happens, then policy appraisal will not be effective. Without effective policy appraisal, it is difficult to modify or change policies that are in place in ways that increase the likelihood of achieving the goals set in step one of the foreign policy process.

Policy Modification

Once policy appraisal has been completed, national decision-makers may choose to modify policies that are in place so that policy objectives can be better met. This is a straightforward and logical step. Nevertheless, efforts to modify policy frequently run into significant difficulties in the "real" world.

The most significant difficulty is often policy inertia; unless a particular policy is glaringly wrong or is rapidly worsening a country's situation, it is often easier just to let policies that are underway run their courses. Also, additional resources are frequently needed to initiate significant changes in policy. This sometimes leaves decision-makers open to the charge of "throwing good money after bad," a charge that is warranted less often than it is made.

Frequently, the biggest obstacles to policy modification are organizational interests, bureaucratic politics, and harm to the images of the decision-makers who decided upon the policy that is being modified. Domestic and even foreign opponents of those who decided upon the policy that is being modified sometimes are able to argue that a policy modification indicates that a policy in place has failed, when in fact the policy is only being modified. From the perspective of a decision-maker, policy modification therefore carries with it the risk of charges of failed policy. The larger the contemplated modification in policy, the greater the possibility that such charges may be credible and accurate.

Despite the work and effort that goes into the foreign policy process, perfect policy is rarely implemented. Consequently, policy modification is an extremely important step. States that are willing and able to undertake this step successfully can significantly increase the chances of achieving the foreign policy goals that they set out to achieve in the first place. Nevertheless, it is an often overlooked and sometimes ignored step.

Memory Storage and Recall

The final step in the foreign policy process is memory storage and recall. Its purpose is to help states learn from experience so that future policies can be improved.

Different states store and recall information and data in different ways. Some rely on the memories of people involved in the foreign policy process. Others use archival materials. Still others employ sophisticated information storage and recall technologies. And still others use a combination of some or all of these methods. But in all cases, the purpose of storage and recall is to improve future policy.

No single level of government has exclusive responsibility for memory storage and recall. Archivists at the Department of State and its equivalents elsewhere may have responsibility for maintaining paper and electronic data on foreign policy and foreign policy issues, but secretaries of state, presidents, and their equivalents all find it useful to store mentally and recall as needed information about foreign leaders, economics, security concerns and threats, and other issues.

There are several potential flaws in any memory storage and recall system. Information may be stored incorrectly or incompletely. Lessons that are learned may be applied poorly or remembered selectively. But even if the memory storage and recall system is less than perfect, it is an extremely useful step for all countries that intend to continue to have interactions with other states and with other types of international actors. At a minimum, with successful storage and recall, states do not have to begin anew when old issues reappear or when new items move up the priority list to become part of the current foreign policy agenda.

FORMULATING THE POLICIES OF OTHER INTERNATIONAL ACTORS

In the international arena, states are not the only international actors that interact with others and that must formulate policy. IGOs, MNCs, NGOs, and all the other actors we examined in the first framework must also decide what to do and how to do it.

Given the diversity of actors involved in the international system, it should not be surprising that other decision-making methods exist in addition to the foreign policy process of states. We turn our attention to those other methods in this section. However, to begin with, it is useful to repeat the four cautions that began our discussion of foreign policy and the foreign policy process, modified as appropriate for the "foreign policies" and "foreign policy processes" of IGOs, MNCs, NGOs, and other international actors.

First, as with states, not all of the international interactions that IGOS, MNCs, NGOs, and other international actors have with others are necessarily outputs of a policy process. Sometimes interactions are the result of spontaneous actions or chance encounters that no one expected. On other occasions, global trends in technology, economics, or culture develop that are the results of forces beyond the control of any international actor, but that nevertheless affect actors and their interactions. And in still other cases, policies are not implemented as planned, or they unfold in ways that are unanticipated, unexpected, and sometimes unwanted.

Second, again as with states, too much rationality should not be ascribed to the decision-making process of non-state actors. Although the concept of process often conjures up images of a well-reasoned and logical approach to an issue, factors often intervene in the decision-making processes of IGOs, MNCs, NGOs, and other international actors that make them less than completely rational, at least if rationality is measured in terms of planned and reasoned efforts to move toward a defined objective.

Third, students and analysts of policy formulation in non-state actors should not assume that there is a great degree of order in the various policy processes. Although such processes may be sequential, real-world pressures of time, politics, and money sometimes dictate that the steps in the policy process of non-state actors, like states, be undertaken simultaneously, with less than sufficient information or analysis, or in a different order than presented here. In some cases, some steps may be bypassed completely.

Finally, in every sense, the policy process of non-state actors is dynamic and ever-changing. In non-state actors (as with state actors), different people, different situations, different capabilities, and different perceptions combine in different ways to make the decision-making process dynamic and ever-changing.

Formulating Policy in IGOs

Because of their structures and functions, IGOs are continually and unavoidably involved in one form or another of international interaction. More often than not, states are the primary type of actor with which IGOs interact.

Because of their structures and functions, except in rare cases where all of an IGO's members agree on a policy and provide resources sufficient to pursue it, IGOs often have an extremely complicated and difficult task in formulating effective policies. A primary reason for this is that even though the member states of an IGO may agree on an IGO's objectives, they often disagree on which policies to implement to achieve the objectives. IGO policies are thus often the result of compromises.

In a few cases, IGOs may temporarily espouse positions or undertake actions that run counter to the goals of member states. On rare occasions, a persuasive IGO secretariat may even convince member states to alter their agendas to be more in accord with those that the secretariat of the IGO prefers.

But if the IGO secretariat fails to do this, IGOs then run the risk of having their member states resign. In more extreme cases, IGOs may even be disbanded. Thus, because states create them and are their chief members, most IGOs have a more limited ability than states have to set and give priority to goals.

As for intelligence, IGOs again often find themselves in difficult positions. All IGOs—and indeed, all international actors—require good data to formulate and implement effective policy. Many IGOs have the collection of data as one of their primary responsibilities. But this does not necessarily mean that IGOs can obtain the information they seek to acquire. In those instances where states fully agree with the activities of IGOs of which they are members, or do not see a potential threat to their own interests as the result of sharing information with the IGO and its other member states, IGOs may gather information to the fullest of their ability. But in cases where an IGO member state does not fully agree with the IGO's activities or sees a threat to its own interests as the result of sharing information, states may actively oppose IGO information-gathering activities.

Once IGOs acquire whatever information they can, they, like states, must also interpret and report it. Here, IGOs face many of the same problems that states face. Too much information may be available, thereby creating noise. Information may be distorted, delayed, or misinterpreted. And in addition to distortions, delays, or misinterpretations brought about by accident, bureaucratic politics, or personal agendas, IGOs may find that national predispositions or biases slant the interpretation and reporting of information.

Option formulation, planning and programming, and decision-making in IGOs are often complicated political processes for which each IGO member state seeks to identify, defend, and promote its own interests. Whereas in state actors it is often possible to differentiate between these steps, in IGOs, these steps often merge, sometimes becoming indistinguishable.

Coalition building is often an important part of the decision-making process in IGOs. This in itself can be a time-consuming and difficult task, in part because of the differing perspectives different states may hold on an issue. As noted earlier, states may agree on an IGO's objectives, but hold widely varying views on how best to achieve that objective. As a result, option formulation, planning and programming, and decision-making are all often affected, especially since these tasks are usually undertaken by teams of people from two or more of the IGO member states.

The decision-making process in many IGOs is also complicated by the need for national representatives to interact with their home governments. Depending on each country's own foreign policy process and the given issue at hand, state representatives at IGOs may be required to check with their home government for guidance on almost a daily basis. For example, the United States generally grants its representatives to IGOs very little discretion, and requires them to check back with Washington frequently. In comparison, smaller countries often grant their representatives to IGOs much greater leeway in stating their country's positions. As a result, home governments can sometimes actually be surprised by the positions that they have adopted on a given issue in an IGO.[7]

As with states, IGOs must also articulate their policies effectively once a decision has been reached. IGOs by definition have an international audience, with their immediate and most important target audiences being the governments and populations of their member states. This is because if the IGO is to undertake any action based on its policy, it needs its members' support and resources.

Here, IGOs face a complicated task. It may seem like a foregone conclusion that when an IGO such as the UN gains the support of a country for the UN's preferred actions and positions, resources will be forthcoming. However, this is not always the case. Even though a country may support a given IGO policy, that country has additional uses for its resources aside from the needs of the IGO. Therefore, a country might not provide anything beyond declaratory support for an IGO's actions and positions even though it agrees with them. In addition, a country's representatives to an IGO may disagree with their own government about the IGO and its policy preferences. Even if this is not the case, a country's government may be unable to develop support for an IGO action or position among its own population. In either event, the IGO will receive little or nothing from the state in question.

Thus, for IGOs, policy articulation is extremely important. Consequently, many large IGOs have their own press and media relations offices, often staffed by skilled professionals. Frequently, however, these professionals face the daunting task of convincing governments to provide resources for IGO activities that governments place low on their priority list. Not surprisingly, they frequently fail.

Throughout the rest of the policy process, from policy implementation to memory storage and recall, IGOs remain hostage to the need for states to provide resources. Neither policy implementation, nor policy monitoring, nor any of the following steps in the policy process can proceed in the absence of state-supplied resources. Obviously, this limits the ability of IGOs to interact with other actors in ways that run counter to the desires of the more influential member states of IGOs.

In addition, the problems that confronted states in these steps also confront IGOs. In the case of IGOs, these problems are complicated by the need of IGO member states to protect their own national interests and objectives within the context of IGO policy.

In sum, then, IGOs are more constrained than other types of actors are in their interactions with others in the international system. Although they perform services for states that states either cannot perform for themselves, or that they can perform better than states, IGOs are an extremely dependent type of actor in the international system. This dependence is often reflected in their decision-making processes.

Formulating Policy in Multinational Corporations

Unlike states and IGOs, MNCs have a single very distinct and well-defined objective. They are in business to make money. Thus, the first stage in the foreign policy process of multinational corporations—goal setting—must be considered a given. But from this point on, the decision-making process of MNC executives is in every respect as complicated as, and in some ways even more complicated than, the comparable processes in states and IGOs.

To make money, MNC executives must make the right decisions about what business practices and strategies to pursue, and about which countries to do business in.[8] This requires accurate and timely information. Not surprisingly, then, MNCs devote considerable quantities of time, talent, and resources to gathering, reporting, and interpreting intelligence about factors as diverse as market size, market preference, the capabilities and strategies of real and potential competitors, host government attitudes and policies toward foreign firms, present and

Like leaders of states, executives of multinational corporations must make complex decisions about the international activities of their companies. Here, Lee Iacocca, Chairman of the Board of Chrysler Corporation, ponders a decision about how Chrysler should respond to foreign competition.   (Bettman Archive.)

future political risk, labor cost, capital cost, level of capitalization, quality and reliability of infrastructure in a host or potential host country, technological inputs, one's own corporate culture, and the timeframe of analysis. Only when such information has been gathered, reported, and interpreted can the leadership of a corporation begin to develop options about how and where business should be pursued.

MNCs sometimes find that gathering pertinent information is a challenge. There are several reasons for this. Competitors and governments might conceal needed information. Helpful data may simply never have been compiled. Public attitudes, political situations, and markets might be subject to wildly unpredictable fluctuations. The reliability of information may be questionable. Or sometimes, MNCs may simply not understand the cultures in which they are operating or contemplating operating, and as a result may ask the wrong questions or interpret data incorrectly.

Once they have sufficient information, MNC executives must try to use that information to answer questions about international business as it relates to their firm. Consequently, MNC managers may formulate several sets of options concerning their future business activities. Ideally, MNC leaders might lay out several different business strategies within each country or region in which they are doing business or planning to do business. In each strategy in each country, they may alter one or more of the factors that they control that might affect their company's profitability. If done comprehensively, this can be a complex, time-consuming, and costly process.

After laying out options in each of the countries or regions in which they are doing or contemplating doing business, MNC decision-makers might then determine how to weigh factors beyond their control that are nevertheless important to them. These might, for example, include host government policies, social cost, projected market growth, and so on. This too can be a complex, costly, and time-consuming effort. For example, in the single area of MNC relations with host governments, some of the more important variables that MNCs must consider are permissible ownership levels of domestic corporations by foreign interests, tax schedules, depreciation schedules, infrastructure support, repatriation levels, duties and quotas on imports, export levels, employment levels, capital structure, debt sources, import protection, and labor laws.

At this point, MNC executives might then assess the impact of these on the projected profitability of each strategy. After completing this, MNC managers might then compare the most profitable option in country X with the most profitable option in country Y or region Z, and on the basis of these steps (i.e., option formulation, and planning and programming), find themselves better equipped to make decisions than they were at the beginning of the process.

Firms that are just entering the international marketplace at this point might find themselves facing a difficult decision. On the basis of the just-completed steps of option formulation and planning and programming, should they in fact pursue a global business strategy? Would a regional strategy be best, and if so, which one and in which regions? Would it be better to concentrate on two or three countries or pursue a broader and more comprehensive strategy? Might it even be better to forego international activity and concentrate instead on one's own home country?

Even firms already involved in international business face difficult decisions about whether to expand or contract their activities, about whether they should alter the locations of their production or sales activities, and about the repercussions that such expansion, contraction, or alteration might visit upon them. As one pair of observers noted, the multinational corporation is continually facing the tension between its global vision and local demands.[9]

Once MNC decision-makers have decided upon a business strategy and all of its various elements, they must then begin to implement it. An MNC's leadership must articulate its conclusions to the MNC stockholders, and to other important publics as well. Chief among these other important publics are its work force, but other publics such as the host government, consumers, and potential consumers may be important depending on the strategy and location of MNC operations.

Despite these complexities, MNCs enjoy an advantage over most states and IGOs at the implementation stage of their international interactions. Because of the ability of senior MNC officers to set policy directions, and because of the primacy of a single objective, MNCs often have a greater ability than states and IGOs to implement their policies with a singleminded focus.

This is not always the case. Sometimes, as during war, states demonstrate a great ability to focus their efforts in a single direction on a single objective. Similarly, when IGOs are fortunate enough to have all of their members agree on a single policy to achieve a single objective, IGOs also are able to focus their efforts. Nevertheless, as a general rule, MNCs enjoy an advantage in this regard in comparison to other types of actors.

MNCs as a class of international actors also suffer from several disadvantages when they attempt to implement policies. More often than not, they must seek and obtain approval from a state to operate within the state's territories. Depending on the prevailing practices and philosophy of the government that rules a state, this may create problems for MNC operations within a state. For example, a state may demand access to a proprietary technology or process to allow an MNC to operate within the country. Conversely, as we saw in Chapter 4, MNCs with economic clout sometimes find themselves in positions to influence the policies of states.

Like states and IGOs, MNCs also monitor, appraise, and modify their policies. In the cases of all three types of actors, the purpose of these steps is to determine whether or not the policy being implemented is achieving the desired results. If possible, the policy might have to be improved. Because MNCs have a single dominant objective and more often than not can be directed by senior management more easily than states or IGOs, these steps can usually be accomplished more easily in MNCs than in states and IGOs.

Information storage and recall is vitally important for MNCs as they attempt to change present policies and plan future ones. Poor information storage and recall can affect profitability, and in extreme cases, even determine whether or not a corporation will survive. In addition to industry and corporate data banks that most major MNCs maintain, the "institutional memory" of executives is frequently an important source of data storage and recall.

All told, then, even though MNCs have the single primary objective of making money, their interactions with the rest of the international community must take many factors beyond making money into account. As the preceding discussion shows, MNC decision-makers must take this into account throughout their company's decision-making process if their company is to be successful.

Formulating Policy in NGOs and Other Types of International Actors

NGOs and the other international actors that we have not yet examined in this chapter often do not have a well-defined structure in their policy formulation and decision-making processes. All, to one extent or another, set goals and establish priorities. But once one moves beyond goal setting, other steps in the policy formulation and decision-making process of NGOs and related international actors are usually peculiar to the individual actor—not the type of actor—under consideration.

For example, some NGOs have a well-defined decision-making process, while others proceed on a completely ad hoc basis. Similarly, some NGOs place high priority on intelligence, but others either find intelligence virtually useless or have little or no ability to collect it. These actors must ignore intelligence out of necessity.

These observations lead to the unsatisfying but accurate statement that there is no truly useful way to describe or analyze the decision-making process for NGOs and the other international actors we have not yet examined. This does not mean that their decision-making processes are unimportant. It means simply that they are idiosyncratic, that is, peculiar to the individual NGO or individual other actor, not to the type of actor.

Nor does this mean that the international interactions that result from these idiosyncratic processes are unimportant. Indeed, as we have already seen, NGOs and other actors that were examined together with them sometimes play extremely important roles in the international system.

Perhaps in the future, a general pattern may become evident concerning the decision-making processes in NGOs and related international actors. But for the present, their decision-making processes can best be understood on a case-by-case basis.

THE ACTORS AND THEIR INTERACTIONS

In the first framework of this book, we studied the major types of international actors in today's world. In this chapter, we examined the ways in which these actors decide how they will interact. Together, the actors and their interactions form the international system. This system is not only formed by the actors and their interactions, but also in turn influences the way the actors act and interact. This feedback is based primarily on the way that the actors see the international system, their own role and position in the system, and the role and position of others in the system.

This international system changes over time. Already this century, there have been three different international systems, and the international community is now on the verge of the emergence of a fourth. In the next two chapters, we will examine the two most dominant aspects of the international system that collapsed in the late 1980s and early 1990s, and assess whether any dimensions of the dominant aspects of the recently ended system will carry over into the next international system. The final chapter of this framework will speculate on the likely shape of the international system that is now emerging.

KEY TERMS AND CONCEPTS

foreign policy
foreign policy process
goal setting
intelligence
option formulation
planning and programming
decision-making
incrementalism

policy articulation
policy implementation
policy monitoring
policy appraisal
policy modification
memory storage and recall
coalition building

NOTES

1. As discussed in Chapter 1, see Graham Allison, *Essence of Decision: Explaining the Cuban Missile Crisis* (Boston: Little, Brown, 1971).
2. For example, see Roger Hilsman, *The Politics of Policy Making in Defense and Foreign Affairs* (Englewood Cliffs, NJ: Prentice Hall, 1993).
3. See John P. Lovell, *The Challenge of American Foreign Policy: Purpose and Adaptation* (New York: Macmillan, 1985).
4. The steps discussed in this section are taken from Lovell, pp. 27, 32, with some adaptation by the present author. The explanation and discussion of each step is the present author's own, except as noted.
5. Charles Lindblom, "The Science of 'Muddling Through,'" *Public Administration Review*, Volume 19 (1959), pp. 79–88.
6. Herbert Simon *Models of Man* (New York: Wiley, 1957). See also Herbert Simon, "Human Nature in Politics," *American Political Science Review*, Volume 79 (June 1985), pp. 293–304.
7. This information was developed from discussions the author had in 1992 with several representatives from different delegations to the United Nations.
8. For discussions of MNC business strategy, see Kenichi Ohmae, *The Mind of the Strategist: Business Planning for Competitive Advantage* (New York: McGraw Hill, 1982); Peter Schwartz, *The Art of the Long View; Planning for the Future in an Uncertain World* (New York: Doubleday, 1991); and William H. Davidson, *Global Strategic Management* (New York: John Wiley, 1982).
9. C. K. Prahalad and Yves L. Doz, *The Multinational Mission: Balancing Local Demands and Global Vision* (New York: The Free Press, 1987).

CHAPTER 7

The Rise and Fall of the East–West Conflict

- What was the East–West conflict?
- How did the East–West conflict start?
- How did the East–West conflict evolve?
- How and why did the East–West conflict end?

Even before the end of World War II, it was clear that the old international order had ended, and a new one was about to begin. Europe lay in ruins for the second time in a generation, and the old European powers were either weakened or destroyed. The Soviet Union's armies had swept halfway across Europe from the east, while American and British armies had marched across Europe from the west. Fittingly enough, the most colossal war in recorded history was ended by the most colossal military weapon ever used in warfare, the atomic bomb. Politically and technologically, a new age had dawned, but its outlines were still vague.

Expectations for the new era ran the gamut from hope for a new cooperative international order made manifest in the United Nations to fear of an inevitable conflict between the United States and the U.S.S.R. Nuclear weapons made the possibility of such a conflict all the more terrifying. To optimists, the United Nations presented a hope for peace if only the great powers were willing to seek accommodation instead of confrontation. Optimists hoped that the allies of World War II could build on the platform of cooperation established during the war to devise a safer world. Pragmatists, including Winston Churchill and Franklin Roosevelt, hoped that the United States and the U.S.S.R., and to a lesser extent Great Britain, would exercise their powers within their own respective spheres of influence, thereby avoiding confrontation. Churchill was even so bold as to travel to Moscow during the fall of 1944 to propose to Stalin a formal division of Europe into spheres of influence. Only pessimists predicted confrontation, and they were correct.

The almost half-century long confrontation that emerged after World War II pitted the Soviet Union and its allies, known collectively as **the East**, against the

United States and its allies, known together as **the West**. This **East–West conflict** was also called the **Cold War** for the very basic reason that although everyone agreed that the two sides were locked in conflict, few shots were ever fired. It was, indeed, a cold war.

ORIGINS OF THE COLD WAR

At least five explanations have been advanced for the gradual slide into hostility that marked post–World War II relations between the United States and the Soviet Union. The explanations are not mutually exclusive. Indeed, according to many analysts, they complement one another. The historical record, national objectives, opposed ideologies, the personalities of the decision-makers of the postwar world, and differing perceptions of the international environment have all been used to explain the growth of U.S.-Soviet hostility.

Historically, relations between Washington and Moscow before World War II were coolly formal at best, and openly hostile at worst. In the Kremlin, memories of the U.S. intervention in Russia in 1918 bore out the Marxist-Leninist prediction that capitalist states would seek to destroy Bolshevism. Indeed, the United States did not even recognize the Bolshevik regime until 1933. In Washington, the Red Scare of the early 1920s and the fears of international communism dur-

Churchill, Roosevelt, and Stalin, the leaders of the "Big Three," met at Yalta in 1945 in an effort to shape the post–World War II world.   (The National Archives.)

ing the 1930s created an equally pallid climate for good relations. Soviet unwillingness to repay czarist debts to external creditors added an extra dimension to U.S.-Soviet animosity. This record of mistrust continued until World War II drove the two countries into an alliance of convenience.

Even the record of U.S.-Soviet cooperation during World War II was scarred by mistrust. U.S. and British delays in invading Hitler's "Fortress Europa" were interpreted by Stalin as proof that the Western allies desired Germany and the Soviet Union to bleed each other to death while the United States and Great Britain stood on the sidelines. Stalin also resented Truman's unannounced termination of military aid to the Soviet Union. For its part, the United States believed that the U.S.S.R. circumvented promises for free elections in Eastern Europe and pushed its political control into Eastern Europe. Consequently, at war's end, an underlying current of mutual mistrust and suspicion remained.

Postwar objectives of both countries may also be viewed as a cause of U.S.-Soviet animosity. Regardless of whether the U.S.S.R. established governments in its own image in Eastern Europe for expansionistic reasons or out of a desire to obtain defensible Western boundaries, American policy-makers interpreted Soviet actions as a conscious thrust into the European heartland. Conversely, as the United States argued for free trade and free elections, Soviet policy-makers believed that the United States was acting as Marxism-Leninism decreed it must, as an expansionistic political-economic system. National objectives, then, or rather opposed perceptions of national objectives, played an integral role in undermining U.S.-Soviet relations.

The opposed ideologies of Soviet-style Marxism-Leninism and American-style democracy were also causes of postwar U.S.-Soviet animosity. To many Americans, communist ideology was an expansionist, atheistic, militaristic form of social organization that presented a threat of immense proportion to the West. Any cooperation with such an ideology was dangerous and abhorrent. Conversely, to the dedicated Soviet communist, Western democracy, particularly as evidenced in the United States, was a threat to the survival of the Soviet state and Marxism-Leninism. Advocates of the view that different ideological outlooks caused the Cold War therefore maintained that Soviet communism defined the United States as the enemy, and the United States had no choice but to respond. U.S. foreign policy thus became an anticommunist crusade, thereby proving to the Soviet leadership the accuracy of Marxist-Leninist ideological preconceptions.

In addition, according to some, the personalities of the leaders of the era contributed to the slide into Cold War hostility. Winston Churchill, the British prime minister, was the ultimate advocate of realpolitik and spheres of influence. He did not trust Joseph Stalin or the wisdom of the U.S. leadership. Stalin, meanwhile, feared that his own domestic base of power was eroding. He also bordered on the paranoid concerning U.S. and British intentions. Although Stalin and Franklin Roosevelt had apparently arrived at some degree of grudging but cautious mutual respect, Roosevelt was no longer alive to help fashion the postwar world. The new U.S. president, Harry Truman, had no use for Stalin, and trusted him even less than did Churchill.

Perceptually, then, Soviet and U.S. leaders found it possible to choose selectively from among the historical record, real and imagined objectives, ideological preconceptions, and their own personal biases to arrive at an image of the other that was malevolent and evil. Events were interpreted in light of expectations, and both sides had ample evidence to "prove" the worst intentions of the other. Given these different perspectives from which Soviet and U.S. leaders viewed the world, the Cold War may not have been inevitable, but only an inordinate combination of fortuitous circumstances could have prevented it.[1]

THE EVOLUTION OF THE U.S.-SOVIET RELATIONSHIP

Nevertheless, the U.S.-Soviet relationship changed over time. Six distinct periods may be identified, although no clear boundaries exist between them. Indeed, foreign policy analysts themselves often differ when they seek to define periods in the evolving U.S.-Soviet relationship.

Skeptical Cooperation

The first period, an era of skeptical cooperation, extended through early 1947. Throughout this period, the twin thrusts of conflict and cooperation that would become hallmarks of U.S.-Soviet relations were concurrently followed. The United Nations became a functioning reality during this period. In addition, although the U.S.S.R. and the United States disagreed about more issues than they agreed on concerning the future of Europe, a postwar equilibrium was established in Europe that was not ideal from any perspective but was acceptable to almost everyone. Two of the essential features of this postwar European equilibrium were a divided Germany and the maintenance of spheres of influence by the superpowers—the Soviet Union's in Eastern Europe and the United States' in the West.

Even so, during this first postwar period, the seeds for future hostility continued to be planted. Communist-led insurrections developed in Greece, China, and Southeast Asia, and from the perspective of Western policy-makers who viewed communism as a monolithic transnational political movement directed from Moscow, the Kremlin's hand was apparent. This view was further strengthened by overt Soviet pressures on Turkey and Iran and by the creation of communist governments in Eastern Europe. Stalin himself reasserted the accuracy of the Marxist-Leninist tenet of inevitable communist-capitalist conflict in his February 9, 1946, preelection speech. Truman, meanwhile, told the Russians that they could "go to hell" if they chose not to cooperate with the United States. From the viewpoint of two Russian historians, the United States during 1945 and 1946 sought to create a world "in which the U.S.S.R. would be weakened and isolated. . . . , in which the liberated peoples of Europe and Asia would pursue . . . an antisocialist route."[2] Despite these sentiments, both sides maintained negotiating contacts. By 1947, even that pretense ceased.

Outright Hostility

The second period, one of outright hostility between the United States and the Soviet Union, extended from 1947 to 1955. Both sides set about consolidating their respective spheres of influence with military alliances and economic ties. By the end of this period, the world system could accurately be described as bipolar. (See Figure 7–1.) All countries, with only a few exceptions such as Yugoslavia, which had been ousted from the Soviet-created Council for Mutual Economic Assistance, and Finland and Switzerland, which chose to remain nonaligned because of geopolitical or traditional reasons, were closely tied to either the United States or the Soviet Union.

For all practical purposes, two worlds existed, the **First World** of the Western industrial democracies and their colonial holdings, and the **Second World** of the so-called socialist commonwealth of nations. The First World centered on the United States, with its global military might and massive economic strength. The Second World centered on the U.S.S.R., with its powerful army and growing economic base. This led to a classic balance of power in the international system, with the economically powerful United States, armed primarily with its arsenal of nuclear weapons, confronting the economically destroyed Soviet Union, employing the world's largest army. U.S. nuclear weapons held the Soviet Union hostage, whereas the Soviet army held Western Europe hostage. Both sides feared the other, and neither side dared to act.

In the First World, that is, the West, the United States had moved to a position of clear and unchallenged leadership following Great Britain's February 1947 realization that it no longer had the economic might to combat insurrectionist forces in Greece. In rapid succession, the Truman administration formulated the Truman Doctrine, in which the American president stated that America's policy would be one of giving support to "peoples who are resisting attempted subjugation by armed minorities or by outside pressures," and the Marshall Plan, in which the United States sent billions of dollars of economic aid to Western Europe to restore Europe's war-shattered economy and to prevent communist expansion.[3] Within two years, the United States and several other countries had concluded the North Atlantic Treaty Organization. Eventually, 16 nations joined NATO. Over the next six years, the United States expanded its alliance system to include NATO, the Organization of American States Treaty (the Rio Pact), the Southeast Asian Treaty Organization (SEATO), the Central Treaty Organization (CENTO), and the Australia-New Zealand-U.S. pact (ANZUS). Nearly 50 states belonged to these and other U.S.-initiated treaty organizations.

U.S. policy toward the Soviet Union during this period was based on the doctrine of **containment**. The brainchild of George Kennan, one of the leading U.S. State Department experts on the Soviet Union, containment postulated that Soviet leaders were insecure about their hold on domestic political power and hostile to and fearful of foreign nation-states. To Kennan, this meant that Soviet policies would continue to be repressive domestically and hostile internationally. Kennan's conclusion was simple: "In these circumstances, it is clear that the main element of any United States policy toward the Soviet Union must be that of a long-term, patient but firm and vigilant containment of Russian expansive tendencies." To Kennan, such a policy would defend the West and lead over time to a Soviet willingness to accept the international status quo.[4]

In the Second World, that is, those countries in which communist governments held sway, the Soviet Union enjoyed preeminence. Few actions were taken and few speeches were given without prior clearance by the Kremlin. Economically, what remained of the industrial capacity of Eastern Europe was

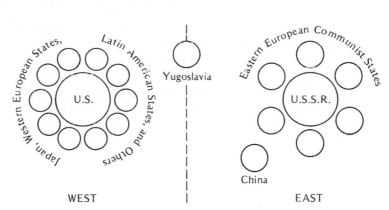

FIGURE 7–1 The bipolar world of the 1940s and 1950s.

dismantled and moved to the U.S.S.R. as the Kremlin sought to repair the ravages it had suffered during World War II. The U.S.S.R. also initiated formation of the Council for Mutual Economic Assistance (CMEA) during this period. Militarily, the U.S.S.R. constructed its own system of bilateral treaties with its Eastern European neighbors, concluded a mutual defense pact with China after Mao Zedong's 1949 victory, and capped its treaty system with the Warsaw Pact in 1955.[5]

By 1955, then, the world was divided into two hostile camps. The communist world viewed Western companies and multinational corporations as agents of Western and particularly American expansion. Both sides in this bipolar system viewed other international actors as being either Soviet or American surrogates.

Rapprochement and Confrontation

Even as the world was frozen into Cold War bipolarity, forces were at work that undermined the seemingly static bipolar system and unleashed global trends that are only beginning to be understood now in the 1990s. The clarion calls of nationalism and independence increasingly were heard in the old colonial empires and the new alliance systems alike, and the growth of international trade brought about by the newly created international economic system of the First World promised both economic plenty and interdependence. Not surprisingly, East–West relations moved into a third phase which lasted for 15 years, until 1969.

This third phase of East-West relations was one of rapprochement and confrontation. Throughout the 1955 to 1969 era, periods of thaw and accommodation followed periods of renewed Cold War tension. The opening event of this period was the first meeting in ten years between an American president and a Soviet premier. Occurring in Geneva in 1955, this first summit between Eisenhower and Khrushchev accomplished little. Nevertheless, the **Spirit of Geneva** indicated a new willingness of both sides to discuss issues, and indicated to many observers of the time that the Cold War was finally thawing.

However, the Geneva thaw lasted only a short time. In 1956, Soviet tanks rolled into Hungary, brutally repressing an anticommunist movement that had developed there, and putting in place a new government under Soviet control. At the same time, in an unrelated action, British, French, and Israeli forces invaded Egypt. The "Spirit of Geneva" had disappeared.

The following year, in 1957, the Soviet Union launched Sputnik I, the world's first satellite. This encouraged Khrushchev to increase the frequency of his missile-rattling threats. The Berlin situation reached crisis proportions in 1958 and early 1959, but by September of that year Khrushchev had visited the United States, and U.S.-Soviet relations were once again cordial.[6] Plans were laid for Eisenhower to visit the Soviet Union.

Eisenhower's trip to the Soviet Union was shot down along with Francis Gary Powers' U-2 over the Soviet Union in May 1960. The Paris summit meeting of that month between Eisenhower and Khrushchev also fell casualty to the downing of the American spy plane. For the next two years, U.S.-Soviet relations remained tense, even though a new American president was elected. In June 1961, Khrushchev met with John Kennedy, the new president, in a summit meeting in Vienna. The net result of that meeting was that both leaders returned to their respective countries and began military buildups. Shortly thereafter, the Soviets and East Germans built the Berlin Wall.

The rollercoaster of U.S.-Soviet relations continued downward in 1962. In October, the Soviet effort to deploy intermediate range ballistic missiles (IRBMs) in Cuba and the American response to that effort brought the world closer to a nuclear exchange than it had ever been before or since. The aftermath of the Cuban missile crisis, however, was another period of rapprochement between the United States and the U.S.S.R. The Partial Test Ban Treaty of 1963 and the "hot line" agreement were the two most significant accomplishments of the new thaw.

President Kennedy, speaking at American University's June 1963 commencement exercises, added his voice to those who sought to improve relations between the world's two foremost nuclear powers:

> We (the United States and the Soviet Union) are both caught up in a vicious and dangerous cycle in which suspicion on one side breeds suspicion on the other and new weapons beget counterweapons.
>
> In short, both the United States and its allies, and the Soviet Union and its allies, have a mutually deep interest in a just and genuine peace and in halting the arms race. . . .
>
> So let us not be blind to our differences, but let us also direct attention to our common interests and to the means by which those differences can be resolved. And if we cannot end now our differences, at least we can make the world safe for diversity.[7]

Kennedy's presidency came to an abrupt end five months later. After Kennedy's assassination, Lyndon Johnson assumed the presidency and vowed to continue Kennedy's policies, including improving relations with the U.S.S.R. U.S.-Soviet relations remained cordial even following Khrushchev's removal from power in 1964 as the new general secretary of the Communist Party of the Soviet Union, Leonid Brezhnev, promised to work for friendly U.S.-Soviet relations. However, only four months after Brezhnev took power, U.S.-Soviet relations began to deteriorate as U.S. involvement in **Vietnam** escalated.

Inevitably, U.S.-Soviet relations soured. Soviet promises to send "necessary assistance" to North Vietnam were followed by Soviet warnings that Soviet "vol-

Cold War summit meetings did not always reduce tensions between the United States and the Soviet Union. After the 1961 Vienna summit between John Kennedy and Nikita Khrushchev, the Cold War heated up considerably.   (John F. Kennedy Library.)

unteers" might travel to Southeast Asia.[8] As American involvement in the war increased throughout 1965, Soviet attitudes toward the United States worsened. On September 29 Brezhnev declared that "normalization of [U.S.-Soviet] relations [was] incompatible with the armed aggression" in Vietnam. U.S.-Soviet relations, he declared, would again "freeze."[9]

For four years, at least on a formal level, relations between the United States and the U.S.S.R. did freeze. But below the formal level, contacts remained and communications continued. Lyndon Johnson met with Soviet Premier Alexei Kosygin at the Glassboro Meeting in 1967, an Outer Space Treaty was concluded in the same year, and the multilateral Nuclear Nonproliferation Treaty was concluded in 1968. Despite the "freeze," cooperation remained evident.

Unfortunately for both the United States and the Soviet Union, both countries found it increasingly difficult to cooperate with certain of their allies throughout the 1955–1969 period. The diversity to which Kennedy had alluded in his 1963 American University address became an increasingly significant force throughout this period as countries on both sides of the bipolar equation more and more regularly questioned the wisdom and policies of the respective bloc leaders and embarked on actions and policies of their own.

In NATO, France questioned and challenged American dominance. Not trusting American guarantees of coming to Europe's assistance in the event of a war in Europe, France developed its own nuclear capabilities, exploding its first nuclear weapon in 1964. In 1966, France withdrew its forces from NATO's military command.

In the socialist world, the U.S.S.R. was having even greater difficulty keeping its allies in line. Anticommunist and anti-Soviet sentiment swelled up in Eastern Germany in 1953, in Poland and Hungary in 1956, and in Czechoslovakia in 1968. In the latter two cases, Soviet and Warsaw Pact forces crushed the rebellions. Albania formally withdrew from the Warsaw Pact in 1968, although it had ceased participating in the pact five years earlier. Meanwhile, Romania refused to allow the Warsaw Pact to conduct maneuvers on Romanian soil.[10] Soviet-Chinese relations began to deteriorate in 1960, and by the end of the decade, Soviet and Chinese forces were engaged in open conflict along the Sino-Soviet border. Clearly, the bipolar system was no longer as tightly structured as it had been.

In addition, as more and more colonies escaped their colonial yokes and joined the ranks of sovereign states, a **Third World** of developing states was created, separate and distinct from the First World of Western industrial democratic states and the Second World of communist central economy states.

The **impact of decolonization on East-West relations** was immense. Many Developing World states were willing to accept economic and military aid and technical assistance from whoever offered it, but chose to remain politically nonaligned. Thus, even outside the military and economic alliances of the First and Second Worlds, the post-World War II bipolar structure of world politics was breaking down.

The **breakdown of bipolarity** that occurred between 1955 and 1969 should not be interpreted as a collapse of the bipolar system. Indeed, during times of heightened international tension such as the Berlin crises, the Cuban missile crisis, and the Czechoslovakian crisis, the fundamental bipolar nature of the international system reasserted itself. During each of these crises (and others as well), most of the established nation-states made clear their allegiance to one or another of the major poles.

The key point, however, is that during the decade and a half of this period, fundamental structural changes were altering the international system. The North-South conflict, the weakening of discipline within the established political-economic-military blocs, and the growing quantity and strength of nonstate international actors all played major roles in complicating international affairs during the 1970s and 1980s. Nevertheless, the East–West conflict predominated throughout the 1960s, even if the bipolarity that that conflict created was no longer as well defined as it had been. Thus, this third phase of East–West relations has been called an era of "muted bipolarity." Figure 7–2 schematically diagrams this period.

Detente

The fourth major phase of East-West relations, the era of detente, extended from 1969 to 1979. The period began when Richard Nixon assumed the American presidency in 1969. In his inaugural address, Nixon declared that the time had come to move from "an era of confrontation" to an "era of negotiation." Gradually, over the next few years, that transformation occurred.

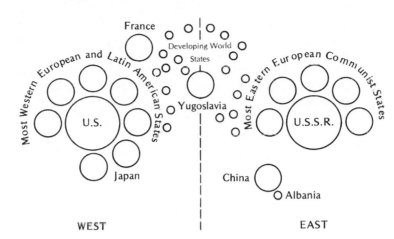

FIGURE 7–2 The muted bipolar world of the 1960s.

The changed atmosphere of U.S.-Soviet relations was best illustrated by Soviet-American **summitry**. Between 1945 and 1971, the men at the pinnacle of power in the United States and the U.S.S.R. met only three times (Geneva in 1955, the United States in 1959, and Vienna in 1961; the 1960 Paris Summit was aborted, and Kosygin, not Brezhnev, attended the 1967 Glassboro Meeting for the U.S.S.R.). Now, in the space of only four years, Brezhnev and Nixon met three times (1972, 1973, and 1974), and Brezhnev and Ford twice (in Vladivostok in 1974 and Helsinki in 1975). In 1979, Brezhnev met yet another American president, Jimmy Carter, in Vienna.

Detente was marked by more than summitry. Cultural exchanges, growth in U.S.-Soviet trade, technical cooperation including a joint space flight, and other manifestations of improved U.S.-Soviet relations abounded. The most significant U.S.-Soviet agreement of the period was the first Strategic Arms Limitation Agreement (SALT I), which constrained certain aspects of the nuclear arms race. Other efforts such as the Mutual Balanced Force Reduction talks and the Indian Ocean negotiations were also undertaken to decrease the possibility of a U.S.-Soviet military confrontation, but met with little success.

Detente witnessed not only improved U.S.-Soviet relations, but also better East–West relations as both sides sought to expand so-called confidence building measures (CBMs) between East and West. West Germany initiated *Ostpolitik*, a policy in which Germany actively sought to improve relations with its eastern neighbors. Other Western European states soon followed, and by the middle 1970s, East–West relations in Europe were better than they had been at any time since World War II. Trade and tourism expanded rapidly, Western European investments in Eastern Europe and the Soviet Union rose sharply, and the Cold War rhetoric of both sides was greatly curtailed. Most impressively, in 1975 a meeting was held in Helsinki, Finland, that the heads of government of almost all of the states of Europe and North America attended. Called the Conference on Security and Cooperation in Europe (CSCE), the meeting heralded a new era in East–West consultation and cooperation. Indeed, to many, it appeared as if a new era had dawned in international affairs.

What caused this change in East–West relations? In part, detente must be attributed to the realization throughout the world, but particularly in the United States and the Soviet Union, that a Soviet-American war would probably destroy the world as it existed. By the late 1960s, the U.S.S.R. had developed a nuclear capability sufficient to devastate the United States and Western Europe; the United States had already had such a capacity to devastate the U.S.S.R. In part, the "balance of terror" led to detente.

Both sides also maintained that mutual advantages could be obtained by collaboration. For example, Western technology and investment could develop Soviet raw materials with both sides benefiting. Less tension also meant that resources formerly devoted to the military could be diverted to social needs and concerns if detente proceeded far enough. Detente was thus also the product of claimed optimism on both sides.

Finally, detente was the product of the continuing collapse of the old bipolar international system. By the beginning of the 1970s, it was clear that the Developing World, although itself internally divided, had become a major actor on the international scene. In addition, the old First and Second Worlds had become internally divided. A variety of economic, geopolitical, and social differences separated Western Europe from the United States, and Japan increasingly followed its own economic and foreign policy directions. In the Second World, China and the Soviet Union denounced each other almost daily, and certain Eastern European communist states increasingly asserted their independence from Soviet policy dictates. Some analysts declared the old bipolar international system dead and proclaimed the birth of a multipolar world system with the United States, the Soviet Union, China, Western Europe, and Japan acting as poles. Other analysts included parts of the Developing World as potential poles.

Summitry was a high point of the Nixon–Brezhnev detente. Here, Nixon and Brezhnev are shown with Soviet President Nikolai Podgorny in Moscow in 1972.   (Nixon Presidential Papers Project.)

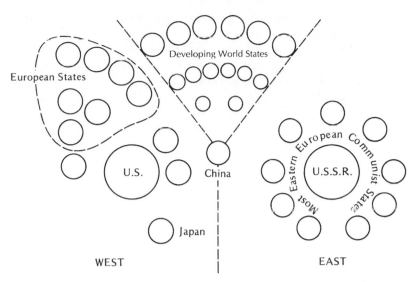

FIGURE 7–3 The multipolar world of the 1970s and 1980s.

In either event, from the viewpoint of Moscow and Washington, the result was the same: The U.S.S.R. and the United States could no longer dominate international affairs as they had in the past. A new international power relationship had arisen, and detente was, at least in part, an indication of the Soviet and American realization of that fact. Figure 7–3 diagrams this new relationship.

However, the euphoria of detente was destined to be short-lived, for many of the fundamental disagreements that caused the Cold War still existed. Historical animosities remained, as did ideological differences and conflicting national objectives. The leaders of both sides had obviously changed since the time of Roosevelt and Stalin, but differences in perceptions continued between the new leaders. Thus, even while European and North American leaders met at Helsinki, other events unfolded outside Europe that brought the fourth period in postwar East–West relations to a close.

Many of these events were in the Developing World, where the United States and the Soviet Union for years had struggled to expand their own influence and limit that of the other. Before the middle 1970s, however, the Soviet Union had rarely sent large numbers of its own or its allies' military forces into Developing World areas.

This began to change when the Kremlin helped Cuba deploy 80,000 troops to Angola, in southern Africa. As Angola moved toward independence in late 1975, three separate national liberation movements, each of which based its political and military strength on a different tribal group, struggled with one another for the right to become the new government of the south African state, and Angola was drawn into the cauldron of East–West competition.[11]

The introduction of Soviet-supplied Cuban combat forces into the Angolan Civil War during early 1976 not only determined the near-term outcome of the war, but also cast a pall across U.S.-Soviet relations. U.S. leaders accused the U.S.S.R. of "breaking the rules" of detente. For their part, Soviet leaders maintained that they would support groups that they defined as national liberation movements in any way they deemed proper. Detente remained, but its luster had been dimmed.

Detente was damaged further by the Soviet-supported introduction of Cuban combat forces into Ethiopia in 1978. As in Angola two years earlier, Cuban troops won the victory for their allies.

Detente had again been traumatized. Jimmy Carter, who had assumed the presidency in January 1977, spoke of the necessity to link Soviet actions throughout the world to continued cordial U.S.-Soviet relations. According to this concept of linkage, if Soviet behavior anywhere in the world challenged American interests, then the Soviet-American bilateral relationship would be correspondingly cooled.

Challenges to detente emanated from the American side as well, at least as seen from the Soviet perspective. Carter's "human rights doctrine" was vigorously condemned by the U.S.S.R. as an unwarranted American intrusion into the internal affairs of other sovereign states. Similarly, the gradual improvement in relations between the United States and China throughout the 1970s caused clear consternation in the U.S.S.R. One analyst reported that the 1971 announcement of Nixon's 1972 trip to China "stunned" Moscow.[12] By the end of the decade, with the 1979 establishment of diplomatic relations between the United States and China, the U.S.S.R. had become convinced that a Sino-American anti-Soviet alliance had been forged.

The decade of detente, then, was a period of cooperation and competition. For most of the decade, cooperation predominated, but tensions remained throughout the period, growing more serious as the 1980s approached.

Measured Confrontation

Finally, on December 27, 1979, an event occurred that was the break point between detente and the subsequent period of measured confrontation. That event was **the Soviet intervention in Afghanistan**.

According to Carter, the Soviet intervention was "the most serious strategic challenge (to the entire world) since the Cold War began." In response to the Soviet action, the U.S. government spearheaded an attempted worldwide boycott of the 1980 Moscow Olympics, terminated American exports of grain and high-technology products to the U.S.S.R., withdrew the SALT II Treaty from the Senate, and reduced the frequency of other U.S.-Soviet contacts. Carter also put forward a new American "doctrine," eventually called the Carter Doctrine, which declared that the United States would regard any effort by any external power to gain control of the Persian Gulf region as "an assault on the vital interests of the United States of America." Carter further declared that "such an assault will be repelled by any means necessary, including military force."[13]

Other Western nations believed that Carter had overreacted and did not support the boycott of the Olympics or the curtailment in East–West trade that the American government espoused. The Soviet Union, meanwhile, claimed it had entered Afghanistan at the request of the Afghan government to help it extinguish a "reactionary counter-insurgency movement" supported by the United States and China. The Soviet claim was less than persuasive because the Afghan

Gorbachev; in New York in December 1988 between Reagan, Gorbachev, and President-elect Bush; and in Malta in December 1989 between Bush and Gorbachev. Two more summits were held in 1990, in Washington and Helsinki. Superpower summitry had become institutionalized. This institutionalization helped improve significantly the political atmosphere of East–West relations.

So too did Mikhail Gorbachev's willingness to redefine Soviet outlooks on how the international system operated. Dissatisfied with old Soviet approaches, the Soviet leader emphasized that "**New Thinking**" was necessary in foreign policy, a "New Thinking" that stressed the importance of interdependence rather than class conflict, global issues rather than ideology, and national self-determination rather than externally imposed social systems. Gorbachev also stressed the need for a new security formula that emphasized political rather than military solutions to problems, recognized the need for mutual security, and constructed military forces on the basis of "reasonable sufficiency" and "defensive defense." These new Soviet perspectives were further underlined by Gorbachev in his December 1988 address to the United Nations, during which he announced that the U.S.S.R. would reduce its armed forces by a half million men, cut back its tank force stationed in Eastern Europe by 50 percent, and decrease significantly its forward-deployed artillery.

Arms control was another area in which East–West relations improved, and again the beginning of the improvement may be traced back to 1985. Although

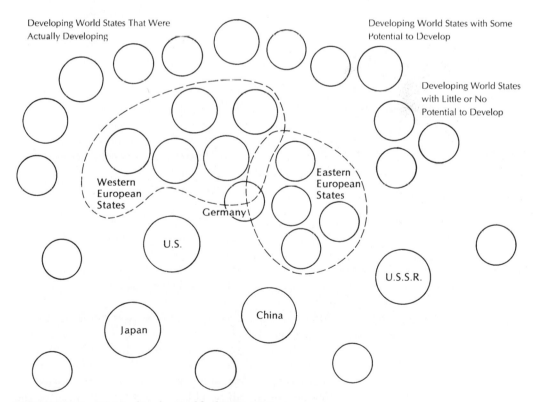

FIGURE 7–4 The multipolar world of 1989–1991.

the only major breakthrough in the 1980s was the December 1987 INF Treaty, the record of accomplishment—and of changed Soviet positions and attitudes— was a long one: an 18-month unilateral Soviet nuclear testing moratorium (1985–1986); disconnecting INF negotiations from "Star Wars" and British and French nuclear forces (1987); the INF Treaty, with Soviet acceptance for the first time of asymmetrical reductions and intrusive on-site inspection (1987); Soviet withdrawal of one division from Mongolia (1988); Soviet withdrawal of all combat troops from Afghanistan (begun in 1988, completed in 1989); Soviet acceptance of the "Atlantic to the Urals" concept for the Negotiations on Conventional Armed Forces in Europe (accepted in 1988, begun in 1989, and continuing into the 1990s); Soviet force drawdowns in Eastern Europe (announced in 1988, begun in 1989, and continuing into the 1990s); and the Soviet termination of chemical weapons and fissionable materials production (1989). In addition, nego- tiations continued at the Nuclear and Space Talks, and the Conference on Disarmament, and bilateral U.S.-Soviet consultations were held on chemical weapons and missile technology proliferation.

The two sides also made considerable progress in their efforts to defuse regional conflicts in the Developing World. The United States and the Soviet Union made major contributions to the December 1988 Angola-Namibia settle- ment that removed South African troops from those two countries; achieved a phased withdrawal of Cuban troops from Angola; and led to Namibian indepen- dence. The United States and the U.S.S.R. also cooperated in arranging condi- tions that led to the Soviet withdrawal from Afghanistan. And behind the scenes, the Kremlin applied pressure on Vietnam that helped end in 1989 Vietnam's military occupation of Cambodia. Admittedly, conflict dragged on in Angola, Afghanistan, and Cambodia, but the superpowers nevertheless collaborated to deescalate these regional conflicts.

As amazing as all these events were, they paled in comparison to the trans- formation that took place in 1989 in the Soviet Union's relations with its commu- nist neighbors. For nearly three decades, the U.S.S.R. and China had reviled each other, and for over four decades, the Soviet Union reserved for itself the right to determine the course of events in Eastern Europe. Suddenly, in the space of fewer than eight months in 1989, all this changed.

The transformation in Sino-Soviet relations was not unexpected. As early as 1982, the U.S.S.R. sought improved relations with China. However, the road to rapprochement was rocky, foundering on the Soviet military buildup on the Sino- Soviet border, the U.S.S.R.'s military occupation of Afghanistan, and Soviet sup- port for Vietnam's occupation of Cambodia. Gradually, however, these three problems were removed or ameliorated, and Sino-Soviet relations improved. Finally, in May 1989, Gorbachev visited China. A new Sino-Soviet relationship— cordial but careful—had been forged.

The transformation in Soviet-East European relations was different; no one expected it. At first tentatively but then more forcefully, the peoples of Eastern Europe voiced opposition to the communist governments that had ruled them since the 1940s. Emboldened by Soviet declarations that the Kremlin would no longer use military force to keep governments in power and encouraged by Gorbachev's assertions that people should be able to choose for themselves the type of society in which they lived, the peoples of Eastern Europe overthrew one communist government after another. In Poland, a free election brought the noncommunist trade union Solidarity to power. In Hungary, the Communist party and government declared itself noncommunist and prepared for free elections. In East Germany, Czechoslovakia, and Bulgaria, massive demonstrations forced communist governments to resign. In Romania, a bloody revolution toppled the communist government, and the long-time communist leader Nicolae Ceausescu was executed.

Thus, when the 1990s opened, new faces were in power in almost every Eastern European capital. Even the political map of Europe changed as East and West Germany unified in 1990. And these new faces and changes in the political map of Europe, in conjunction with all the other changes in 1988 and 1989, had completely transformed U.S.-Soviet and East–West relations. These transformations and the impact that they had on the structure of the international system are depicted in Figure 7–4. But even these transformations paled in comparison to what occurred in 1991 in the U.S.S.R. itself.

By 1991, Gorbachev had been in power for six years. During that time, the domestic reforms that he had instituted had had an immense impact on Soviet society. In some cases the impact was beneficial, and in other cases harmful. *Glasnost*, Gorbachev's policy of opening Soviet society to greater debate and freedom of expression, had worked well and been readily accepted by many Soviet citizens. Gorbachev's political reform effort, democratization, had also been readily accepted by most Soviet citizens. However, *perestroika*, Gorbachev's conception of economic reform that he had put in place to try to revitalize the failing Soviet economy, had failed. According to most analyses, by 1991 the Soviet economy was much worse than it had been when Gorbachev assumed power in 1985.

This mixed record of success and failure caused Gorbachev's reforms to be the subject of considerable debate and disagreement within the U.S.S.R. What is more, some senior Soviet officials, especially conservative party members, government bureaucrats, and military leaders, strongly opposed Gorbachev's policies for ideological reasons. Furthermore, Gorbachev's ideas challenged their own power. Conversely, other prominent Soviet leaders such as Russian President Boris Yeltsin criticized Gorbachev for proceeding too cautiously with his reform programs.

By 1991, then, Soviet society had become substantially polarized over Gorbachev's reforms. But Gorbachev's reforms had unleashed an additional force within the U.S.S.R.: ethnic nationalism. Unfortunately for Gorbachev and the Soviet Union, this newly unleashed ethnic nationalism saw people identifying themselves not with the Soviet Union, but with their own nationality groups. Indeed, by 1991, all 15 of the U.S.S.R.'s nationally based republics declared that their own laws took precedence over those of the Soviet Union.

Recognizing that the U.S.S.R. was in the process of unraveling, Gorbachev negotiated a new treaty of union with the presidents of most of the Soviet Union's republics. This new treaty gave the republics unprecedented power. Had the treaty been implemented, the entire nature of the Soviet Union would have changed. But the new union treaty was too much for conservative party members, government bureaucrats, and military leaders to accept. Already alienated from Gorbachev and his reforms, a small group of Gorbachev's conservative opponents launched a coup in August 1991 and temporarily removed Gorbachev from power.

Yeltsin and other reformers, as well as tens of thousands of Soviet citizens, rallied to Gorbachev's support and the defense of reform. Within days, the coup collapsed and its leaders were arrested.

But the impact of the coup was immense. Gorbachev's already shaky authority was further undermined, the remaining credibility of the Communist party of the Soviet Union was destroyed, and Yeltsin and other radical reformers benefited from an immense surge of popular support for their role in defeating the coup. Emboldened by his new strength and popularity, Yeltsin met in December with the presidents of Ukraine and Belarus, two other Soviet republics, and declared that the Soviet Union would cease to exist on January 1, 1992. Gorbachev protested, but could do nothing to stop the flow of events. And so on January 1, 1992, the Soviet Union disappeared, replaced by 15 newly independent states, 11 of which were loosely linked together in a so-called Commonwealth of Independent States.

The end of the Soviet Union also ended the debate about whether the transformations in Eastern Europe and the improvements in East–West relations that had taken place in the late 1980s and 1990 had ended the Cold War. With no Soviet Union, the Cold War could scarcely continue. And more significant for our purposes here, the end of the Soviet Union also eliminated whatever remaining utility there had been to characterize the East–West conflict as an organizing concept for international affairs.

THE LEGACY OF THE EAST-WEST CONFLICT

Before its demise, the East-West conflict had gone through several phases (see Table 7–1). During the late 1940s and early 1950s, the world had been divided into two hostile camps, one centered around the United States and the other around the Soviet Union. By the 1990s, this bipolarity had disappeared and had been replaced by a multipolarity that saw both superpowers unable to control their former allies. China, Japan, Western Europe, Eastern Europe, and several Developing World states all formulated their own policies and had enough power to influence the policies of the two superpowers. On occasion, they could even chart their own policies with little regard for American and Soviet desires.

In addition, as we have seen in Chapters 3, 4, and 5, other actors had become more important between the late 1940s and the early 1990s. Multinational corporations, viewed by the Soviet Union as tools of capitalist expansion and exploitation during the 1940s and 1950s, had come to be regarded in the Kremlin as potential providers of needed investment capital and technology. First World states, meanwhile, lamented their inability to control the activities of MNCs. International governmental organizations, nongovernmental organizations, and other international actors also operated against the backdrop of international change, no longer sure of what the flow of events might bring.

Today's world is much more complicated and uncertain than the world of earlier decades. The East–West conflict of the 1940s and 1950s, so easily represented conceptually by a bipolar world system that created a balance of power, is over. One of the chief protagonists in that conflict, the Soviet Union, no longer exists. The other, the United States, has military capabilities that remain unrivaled anywhere in the world, but also has the world's largest economic debt, suf-

TABLE 7–1 Some of the Major Events in East–West Relations

Period	Events and Trends
Skeptical cooperation (1945–1947)	UN established Germany divided Eastern Europe communized Communist-led insurrection in Greece, China, and Southeast Asia Western Europe established democratic governments
Outright hostility (1947–1955)	Truman Doctrine Marshall Plan U.S. containment policy Czechoslovakian coup First Berlin crisis and Berlin airlift Mao victorious in China NATO formed Korean War SEATO, CENTO, ANZUS, and other Western treaty systems formed Warsaw Pact formed Franco-Vietminh War in Southeast Asia
Rapprochement and confrontation (1955–1969)	Eisenhower and Khrushchev at Geneva Taiwan Straits crisis Soviet troops invade Hungary Britain, France, and Israel enter Egypt Khrushchev's missile-rattling and Sputnik I U.S. Marines land in Lebanon Second Berlin crisis Khrushchev visits United States U-2 and the failed Paris Summit Kennedy and Khrushchev at Vienna Berlin Wall put up Cuban missile crisis Test ban treaty and hotline agreement Kennedy assassinated, Khrushchev removed United States enters Vietnam War U.S. Marines land in Dominican Republic Glassboro meeting Sino-Soviet rift widens France withdraws from NATO's military structure Nonproliferation Treaty Warsaw Pact invades Czechoslovakia Many former colonies attain statehood throughout the period
Detente (1969–1979)	United States withdraws from Vietnam Six meetings between U.S. presidents and Brezhnev SALT I and SALT II Many other East–West agreements on trade, culture, science, etc. Confidence-building measures and *Ostpolitik* Helsinki Conference (Conference on Security and Cooperation in Europe) U.S.-China ties established Sino–Soviet hostility worsens Soviet military buildup continues Cuban troops deployed to Angola Cuban troops deployed to Ethiopia Americans taken hostage in Iran U.S. "human rights" policy

TABLE 7–1   Some of the Major Events in East–West Relations (*continued*)

Period	Events and Trends
Measured confrontation (1979–1988)	Soviets invade Afghanistan
	United States and U.S.S.R. increase criticism of each other's policies
	United States begins military buildup
	Warfare in El Salvador
	INF and START negotiations begin
	United States accuses U.S.S.R. of using chemical warfare in Afghanistan, Laos, and Cambodia
	Brezhnev dies and triple succession begins: Andropov, Chernenko, Gorbachev in 28 months
	"Star Wars" strategic defense program proposed
	U.S.S.R. shoots down KAL 747
	United States invades Grenada
	U.S. opposition to Nicaragua increases
	INF deployment in Europe begins
	Soviets walk out of Geneva arms talks
	Reagan reelected
	Arms talks resume
	Reagan-Gorbachev summit in Geneva
	Terrorism worsens
	United States attacks Libya
	Chernobyl nuclear disaster in the Soviet Union
	Reagan-Gorbachev summit in Reykjavik
	Reagan-Gorbachev summit in Washington
	INF Agreement
The End of the East–West Conflict (1988–1992)	Soviets withdraw from Afghanistan
	Reagan-Gorbachev summit in Moscow
	UN plays more active peacekeeping role in several conflicts
	U.S.S. *Vincennes* shoots down Iranian airliner
	United States and Soviets help arrange Angola-Namibia accords
	Nationality unrest in the U.S.S.R.
	Iran-Iraq war ends
	Gorbachev's UN speech
	Reagan-Bush-Gorbachev summit in New York
	Gorbachev visits China
	Tianenmen Square massacre
	Free Polish election brings Solidarity to power
	Vietnam withdraws from Cambodia
	Hungary declares itself an ex-communist state
	Communist leaders in Bulgaria, Czechoslovakia, Romania, and East Germany overthrown
	Berlin Wall torn down
	Bush-Gorbachev summit in Malta
	United States invades Panama
	Bush-Gorbachev summit in U.S.
	German unification
	Iraq invades Kuwait
	Multinational forces deployed to Middle East in response to Iraqi invasion
	Bush-Gorbachev summit in Helsinki
	Iraq expelled from Kuwait in Persian Gulf War
	New Soviet Treaty of Union formulated
	Gorbachev attends G-7 meeting of major Western industrial countries in London
	Soviet Coup
	Breakup of the Soviet Union

fers from serious domestic social problems, and is searching for its role in the post-Cold War world.[15] Japan has become a leading global economic power, and Western Europe is forging a single economic market. China sets its own independent political and economic course, and Developing World states struggle to survive. Meanwhile, MNCs invest in the former Soviet Union, Eastern Europe, and China, while civil wars, national liberation conflicts, and ethnic warfare continue in much of the world. Fundamentalist Islam rejects both communism and Western solutions to social problems.

The bipolar world that was based on the East-West conflict has clearly been relegated to the dustbin of history, but what will replace it remains unclear. Several different models have been suggested, and we will explore them in more detail in the last chapter in this framework.

KEY TERMS AND CONCEPTS

the East
the West
East–West conflict
Cold War
reasons the Cold War started
period of skeptical cooperation
period of outright hostility
First World
Second World
containment
period of rapprochement and
  confrontation
Spirit of Geneva, and what
  happened to it
impact of Vietnam on
  East–West relations

impact of decolonization on
  East–West relations
Third World (*also in Chapter* 8)
impact of nuclear weapons on
  East–West relations
breakdown of bipolarity
detente
summitry
measured confrontation
impact of Afghanistan on
  East–West relations
arms control
regional conflicts
Gorbachev's New Thinking
reasons the Cold War ended

NOTES

1. For just a few of the many views and interpretations of who caused the Cold War, and of the events that occurred during it, see Gar Alperovitz, *Atomic Diplomacy* (New York: Simon & Schuster, 1965); Stephen E. Ambrose, *Rise to Globalism: American Foreign Policy 1938–1980* (New York: Penguin Books, 1981); Seyom Brown, *The Faces of Power* (New York: Columbia University Press, 1969); Herbert Feis, *From Trust to Terror: The Onset of the Cold War, 1945–1950* (New York: Norton, 1970); William L. Gaddis, *The United States and the Origins of the Cold War, 1941–47* (New York: Columbia University Press, 1972); Lloyd C. Gardner, *American Foreign Policy: Present to Past* (New York: The Free Press, 1947); Louis J. Halle, *The Cold War as History* (New York: Harper & Row, 1967); John Herz, *Beginnings of the Cold War* (Bloomington: Indiana University Press, 1966); Townsend Hoopes, *The Devil and John Foster Dulles: The Diplomacy of the Eisenhower Era* (Boston: Little, Brown, 1973); David Horowitz, *The Free World*

Colossus (New York: Hill & Wang, 1965); George F. Kennan, *American Diplomacy, 1900–1950* (New York: New American Library, 1951); Gabriel Kolko, *The Roots of American Foreign Policy* (Boston: Beacon Press, 1969); Walter Lippmann, *The Cold War: A Study in U.S. Foreign Policy* (New York: Harper & Row, 1947); Vojtech Mastny, *Russia's Road to the Cold War* (New York: Columbia University Press, 1979); James A. Nathan and James K. Oliver, *United States Foreign Policy and World Order* (Boston: Little, Brown, 1976); Thomas G. Paterson, *On Every Front: The Making of the Cold War* (New York: Norton, 1979); John Spanier, *American Foreign Policy Since World War II* (New York: Congressional Quarterly, 1988); William Appleman Williams, *The Tragedy of American Diplomacy* (New York: Delta Books, 1972); and Daniel Yergin, *Shattered Peace: The Origins of the Cold War and the National Security State* (Boston: Houghton Mifflin, 1978).

2.   N. Sivachyov and E. Yazkov, *History of the USA Since World War I* (Moscow: Progress, 1976) p. 195.

3.   See Joseph Marion Jones, *The Fifteen Weeks* (New York: Harcourt Brace Jovanovich, 1964).

4.   George F. Kennan ("X"), "The Sources of Soviet Conduct," *Foreign Affairs*, Vol. 25 (July 1947): 566–582.

5.   For a detailed and balanced account of Soviet foreign policy behavior during this and other periods, see Adam B. Ulam, *Expansion and Coexistence: Soviet Foreign Policy 1917–1973* (New York: Praeger, 1974). See also Joseph L. Nogee and Robert H. Donaldson, *Soviet Foreign Policy Since World War II* (New York: Pergamon Press, 1988); and Alvin Z. Rubinstein, *Soviet Foreign Policy Since World War II: Imperial and Global* (Cambridge, MA: Winthrop, 1988).

6.   *Khrushchev in America* (New York: Crosscurrents, 1960) contains all of the speeches the Soviet leader gave during his historic American tour.

7.   *The New York Times*, June 11, 1963.

8.   *Pravda*, March 24, 1965, and April 11, 1965.

9.   L. I. Brezhnev, *Leninskim Kursom, Vol. 1* (Moscow: Izdatel'stvo Politicheskoi Literatury, 1970); 228.

10. See Robin Alison Remington, *The Warsaw Pact: Case Studies in Communist Conflict Resolution* (Cambridge: MIT Press, 1971) for a presentation of Soviet difficulties with other Warsaw Pact members.

11. For fascinating accounts of this conflict, see Arthur Jay Klinghoffer, *The Angolan War: A Study in Soviet Policy in the Third World* (Boulder, CO: Westview Press, 1980); John Marcum, *The Angolan Revolution: Exile Politics and Guerrilla Warfare (1962–1967)* (Cambridge: MIT Press, 1978); and Daniel S. Papp, "Angola, National Liberation, and the Soviet Union," *Parameters*, Vol. 8 (June 1978): 57–70.

12. Gene T. Hsiao, *Sino-American Détente and Its Policy Implications* (New York: Praeger, 1974), p. 141.

13. President Jimmy Carter, "President Carter's 1980 State of the Union Address," January 25, 1980.

14. For just a few examples, see *Pravda*, June 25, 1982; September 18, 1982; and September 19, 1982.

15. For an interesting treatment of the implication of the end of the Cold War for the United States, see John Lewis Gaddis, *The United States and the End of the Cold War: Implications, Reconsiderations, Provocations* (New York: Oxford University Press, 1992).

CHAPTER 8

The North–South Conflict

CAN IT BE RESOLVED?

- What is the North–South Conflict?
- How did the North–South Conflict evolve?
- What are the objectives of Developing World states?

The **North–South conflict** derives its name from the simple fact that, almost without exception, the wealthy nations of the world are in the northern hemisphere, and the poorer nations lie to their south. Generally speaking, **the North** consists of the United States, Canada, Europe excluding Albania, Israel, Russia and the other newly independent former Soviet republics (although this is a matter of debate), Japan, South Africa, Australia, and New Zealand. The remaining states of the world, numbering over 110, are the South.

The South has been and is described by many terms—**the Third World**, the **Developing World**, and the **Less Developed Countries** (LDCs), to name just a few. Again speaking in general terms, the countries of the South share two attributes: (1) They have had a colonial past dominated by European powers; and (2) they are poor. Exceptions do exist. Ethiopia and Thailand were never included in European empires, and OPEC countries are usually not impoverished. Nevertheless, they are considered countries of the South.

In many respects, terms such as *South* and *Third World* are misleading, for they conjure up images of a unified group of states. Although many of the objectives that these states seek may be similar or even identical to the objectives of other Developing World states, an incredible diversity exists within the Developing World states of the South. This diversity exists in political form, social structure, and economic organization. Table 8–1 provides one view of the political-economic diversity that exists in the Third World. Some Developing World states purport to be Western-style democracies. India, for example, advertises itself as "the world's largest democracy." Other Developing World states such as Idi Amin's Uganda or Jean Bokassa's Central African Empire were dictatorships of the most repugnant type. Hereditary monarchies exist in several Developing World states. Socially, some states seek to emulate Western values

TABLE 8–1   Examples of the Political–Economic Diversity of the Developing World

Government Type	Level of Economic Development		
	Great Potential to Develop	**Some Potential to Develop**	**Little Potential to Develop**
Constitutional Monarchy		Malaysia, Thailand	
Democratic	Argentina, Brazil, Chile	Barbados, Bolivia, India, Philippines	Bangladesh, Namibia
Hereditary	Bahrain, Brunei, Saudi Arabia	Morocco	Jordan
Military	Indonesia, Iraq, Libya	Congo, Ghana, Nigeria, Myanmar	Burkina, Chad, Haiti, Mauritania
Nonmilitary Autocratic	Iran	Cuba, Egypt, Kenya, Vietnam	Ethiopia, Gambia, Tanzania

and mores, as did Iran under the shah, whereas others such as Tanzania strive to protect traditional local values and customs. Economically, some—Sri Lanka and Kenya, for example—are proponents of capitalist-style private enterprise, whereas others, such as Mozambique and Angola, until recently advocated state ownership of the means of production.

No single level of economic development exists in the South. Indeed, some analysts have argued that the concept of "Third World," when it is used, should be supplemented by a Fourth World and even a Fifth World.[1] According to this typology, the Third World would consist of such states as Argentina, Brazil, Nigeria, and Saudi Arabia, which have sufficiently developed economic infrastructures, resources, and/or skills of the population so that they could become industrialized in the foreseeable future. The **Fourth World**, by comparison, would comprise countries that had the potential for eventual economic development. Bolivia, Zaire, Zambia, and Thailand fall into this category. Finally, the **Fifth World** would consist of countries that have little hope for economic development because of a dearth of infrastructure, resources, and skill. Niger, Chad, Somalia, and Bangladesh represent this poorest of all classes of economic conditions. Table 8–2 lists the average per capita incomes of various developing countries, and contrasts them with the average per capita in-comes of selected First and former Second World countries. A quick perusal of Table 8–2 gives an adequate overview of selected national per capita incomes, but a simple global statement may be more helpful in understanding the extreme maldistribution of global wealth. In simple terms, 75 percent of the world's population receives less than 20 percent of the world's gross national product.

The concept of the Third World is criticized by analysts who believe that the term hides the diversity of the poverty-stricken regions of the world. Many governments of poorer nations also criticize it because it carries with it, from their perspectives, an image of a third-rate country. Despite these criticisms of the concept, the term remains in widespread use today. However, for our purposes, we will use primarily the term *Developing World*.

TABLE 8–2   Average Annual Per Capital
Income of Selected First, Second,
and Developing World States

	Per Capital Income in Dollars, 1990
First World States	
France	19,490
Great Britain	16,100
Japan	25,430
Switzerland	32,680
United States	21,790
West Germany	22,320
Former Second World States	
Bulgaria	2,250
Czechoslovakia	3,140
Hungary	2,780
Poland	1,690
Yugoslavia	3,060
Developing World States	
Algeria (OPEC state)	2,060
Bangladesh	210
Brazil	2,680
Central African Republic	390
Ecuador	980
Ghana	390
India	350
Kenya	370
Madagascar	230
Pakistan	380
Panama	1,830
Somalia	120
Tanzania	110
Thailand	1,420
United Arab Emirates (OPEC state)	19,860
Zaire	220

SOURCE: The World Bank, *World Development Report 1992*, pp. 218–219.

Existent poverty, a shared colonial history, and a fear of continuing political and economic dependency are consequently three of the forces that give the Developing World its very tenuous sense of self-identity. Not surprisingly, the South seeks to rectify the political-economic exploitation of its colonial past and to overturn what it perceives as an international economic system biased against newly independent or poor states. Similarly, during the Cold War, many Developing World states actively pursued a foreign policy of nonalignment, that is, they refused to become closely associated with either the Eastern or Western blocs. However, with the demise of Soviet and Eastern European communism, it is no longer clear exactly what nonalignment means. As a result, a few developing states, most notably Argentina, left the nonaligned movement.

Even so, political-economic independence, political-military nonalignment, and economic-social advancement remain primary objectives of most Developing World states today. Thus, the continued fixation of most Developing World states on these objectives continues to provide a sense of solidarity, of almost a "Developing World nationalism," to many Developing World states.[2] Therefore, it remains important in the post-Cold War world to understand how and why the Developing World evolved as it did.

THE EVOLUTION OF THE DEVELOPING WORLD

As we have already seen, Western European colonial empires began to disintegrate following World War II. This disintegration was an uneven process, proceeding as a general rule most rapidly in those colonial empires that had been the most liberal and most slowly in those that had been the most restrictive. It was no accident that the Portuguese Empire, which had been arguably the most restrictive of all empires, was not liquidated until 1975 when Angola and Mozambique finally received their independence.

The metropolitan European powers also bequeathed different levels of modernization to their colonial empires. In former British colonies, for example, the transition from colony to sovereign state was often eased by the gradual absorption of more and more indigenous people into the colonial administration. In many colonies, rather extensive school systems were also established. India served as a primary example for both policies. The French, meanwhile, maintained a tighter rein on their colonial holdings. By 1930, for example, there were as many French colonial officials in Vietnam as British officials in India, even though Vietnam's population was only one twelfth of India's. By 1940, Vietnam had only 14 secondary schools, whereas India had several hundred.[3] Although French colonial policy in Vietnam and elsewhere changed following the French defeat at the battle of Dienbienphu in 1954, historically induced differences persisted.

The lesser Western colonial powers—Belgium, the Netherlands, Portugal, and Spain—did even less than Great Britain and France to prepare their colonies for independence. Although all colonial regimes were exploitive, the lesser colonial powers were generally the most extreme. The Dutch government ran the East Indies as an enormous sugar plantation, blatantly exploiting land, labor, and what little capital there was for the improvement of the Dutch economy. Belgium exploited the Congo's mineral resources. The Belgians went further than most metropolitan powers in guaranteeing minimum wages, housing, and medical care to their colonial peoples, but they permitted little political development or education. When the Congo received its independence in 1960, there were fewer than a dozen university graduates in the entire country, and the new Congolese leader, Patrice Lumumba, had held no responsibility greater than postmaster. Portugal, meanwhile, fought until 1974 to maintain its grip on its colonial empire. Only then, following a military coup, did Portugal consent to grant independence to Guinea-Bissau (formerly Portuguese Guinea), Angola, and Mozambique.

The European colonial record is not a proud one, at least in light of most late-twentieth-century values and attitudes, and it is understandable why resentment lingers in the minds and hearts of many former colonial peoples against their former masters. Often, because of the United States' close political, economic, and social identity with Western Europe; because of its leadership role in the Western world; and perhaps more important because of the United States' vast wealth and global power, Developing World countries identify the United States as a colonial exploiter as well. Inevitably, then, as the second proliferation of states brought more and more sovereign states into being, Developing World resentment of and hostility toward the West became a major force on the international political scene.

On occasion, less-developed countries met among themselves to discuss their problems. The first major gathering of Developing World states was the **Bandung Conference**, held in Bandung, Indonesia, in April 1955. Twenty-nine Asian and African states met to condemn colonialism and its effect as "an evil which should speedily be brought to an end."[4] Since Bandung, other conferences of Developing World states have taken place, most notably the series of conferences of non-aligned nations. More often than not, however, Developing World states have turned to the United Nations and other regional IGOs that they have created to make their voices heard. Indeed, if one examines both the composition of the United Nations and the quantitative growth in IGOs, one is driven to the conclusion that Developing World states have become, as a group, an increasingly prominent force in international affairs despite their continuing economic poverty.[5]

In the United Nations, the Developing World has been particularly effective in using the General Assembly to attract attention to issues of colonialism and imperialism and in mobilizing the UN's specialized agencies to address its needs. One of the major reasons Developing World states have had these successes is because of their numbers. A formal coalition of Developing World states known as the **Group of 77** wields a sizable influence in UN affairs. Although the Group of 77 by 1993 numbered 123 states, it still retained its original name.

The Group of 77's quantitative growth at the United Nations is important because it can now pass any action that it chooses in the General Assembly if it can maintain its cohesiveness. Not surprisingly, then, the United Nations became as much a forum for North–South conflict as a forum for East–West conflict during the 1970s and 1980s. It will probably remain a center of North–South disagreement during the 1990s.

Because the North, and particularly the United States, pays most of the support costs of the UN, the Group of 77 seeks both to articulate its viewpoint and to refrain from antagonizing the North to such a degree that it terminates its support for the United Nations. It is not always successful, as illustrated by the U.S. withdrawal in 1985 from the United Nations Educational, Scientific, and Cultural Organization (UNESCO). Great Britain withdrew in 1986. In both cases, Developing World criticism of Western attitudes, values, and policies precipitated the withdrawals.

The Developing World had also used the United Nations to push for a series of international conferences to address specific issues of concern such as the environment, population, food, the law of the sea, disarmament, women, industrialization, desertification, technology transfer, rural development, and the role of science and technology in development. These conferences have rarely led to concrete actions. For example, the United Nations Conference on the Law of the Seas (UNCLOS) met sporadically from 1973 until 1982 and finalized a treaty, but the United States refused to sign the treaty. With U.S. preeminence in ocean exploitation technology, any Law of the Sea treaty without U.S. acquiescence verges on being meaningless.[6]

Developing World states have also opted for their own regional IGOs to approach the problems that beset them. The Organization of African Unity, the Association of Southeast Asian Nations, the Arab League, the Caribbean Common Market, the Latin American Integration Association, and the Economic Community of West African States are just a few of the many Developing World IGOs. Their records, by and large, have been mixed.

Nevertheless, a sense of community has developed among many of the states of the South, a community brought about by shared history, objectives, and injustice. For states as disparate as those that make up the Developing World, this is a notable achievement. All seek a future of change.

THE OBJECTIVES OF THE DEVELOPING WORLD

In general, states of the South share three objectives: political-economic independence, political-military nonalignment, and economic-social modernization.[7] There are, of course, exceptions. Some Developing World governments seek political-economic integration with First or former Second World power centers, as Vietnam until recently did with the Soviet Union. Others seek political-military unity with one or another center, as Cuba until recently did with the former U.S.S.R. And still others eschew economic-social modernization, as Iran does. It must also be cautioned that independence, nonalignment, and modernization are in many ways interrelated. Political-economic independence may be unobtainable if modernization is not achieved. Conversely, strict adherence to the principle of nonalignment may mean that modernization cannot be attained. Thus, as in all aspects of international affairs, interrelationships exist that should not be obscured by dichotomies established for analytical purposes. The key point is that as a general rule, political-economic independence, political-military nonalignment, and economic-social modernization are objectives shared by most Developing World states.

Political-Economic Independence

Despite obtaining formal independence, many Developing World states have discovered to their chagrin that they remain economically and even politically dependent on their former colonial masters. Trade ties and investment patterns established during decades of colonial rule were rarely terminated by the simple attainment of political sovereignty. From the viewpoint of Developing World countries, this economic dependence carried with it unavoidable political subservience. Thus, even though a Developing World state may have sought to establish its own political-economic independence, it could not.

Such a relationship between former colonial metropoles and their putatively independent former colonies is termed **neocolonialism**. Although interpretations of neocolonialism differ on a case-by-case and region-by-region basis, a unifying thrust of the South is to escape this neocolonial relationship.

In part, the Developing World's desire to escape the vestiges of colonial dependency explains its animus toward both the West and Western institutions, including multinational corporations. Having had numerous occasions to witness the linkage between economic strength and political power, governments of the less-developed states often were skeptical of the claim promulgated by Western state actors and nonstate actors alike that no political concessions would be sought if investment opportunities were awarded.

The South, then, was on the horns of a dilemma as it sought to achieve political-economic independence. Full political and economic independence could be achieved only if Developing World states could strengthen their economic autonomy. In most cases, however, that required increased reliance on external sources of finance and expertise. To many Developing World countries, such external economic reliance implied continued political dependence. Indeed, on the basis of the historical record, this was a view with at least as much fact as fiction.

Developing World states pointed particularly to their ongoing debt problem as proof of their continuing neocolonial status. Table 8–3 shows both the total international debt of selected Developing World countries and the size of that debt as a percentage of their gross national products. Obviously, when foreign debts make up sizable percentages of gross national products, prospects for repayment are not good. From the perspective of First World lenders, some bad lending decisions had been made. From the perspective of Developing World governments, economic indebtedness and accompanying high interest rates were simply new ways that the First World had found to continue to plunder what little wealth the Developing World had.

Nevertheless, by the 1990s, most Developing World states concluded that they had no choice other than to seek external investment from MNCs and other private and public sources. Political-economic independence remained an objective, but most developing states had not achieved it. And in some Developing World states, as global economic interdependence became more and more a reality, the concept of political-economic independence became little more than an unobtainable ideal.

This did not mean that Developing World states were pleased with the course of events. As India's Prime Minister Rajiv Gandhi said to the Ninth Nonaligned Summit Meeting in Belgrade in September 1989:

> Dominance by military strength has been successfully resisted, but dominance by subversion and proxy continues. It is dominance by economic pressure which is emerging as the single most important threat to the independence and stability of nonaligned countries.[8]

Political-Military Nonalignment

Despite the end of the East–West conflict in the early 1990s, many Developing World states consider it critically important to achieve and maintain political-military nonalignment. This objective flows from one of the same motivations as

TABLE 8–3   International Debt of Selected Developing World States, in Billions of
Dollars and as a Percentage of Gross National Product, 1970 and 1990

Country	Debt in Billions of Dollars		Debt as Percentage of GNP	
	1970	**1990**	**1970**	**1990**
Argentina	1.9	46.1	8.6	61.7
Bolivia	.5	3.7	48.2	100.9
Brazil	3.2	82.1	8.2	25.1
Egypt	1.8	34.2	22.5	126.5
Ethiopia	.2	3.1	9.5	54.2
India	7.9	61.1	14.9	25.0
Madagascar	.1	3.7	10.4	134.1
Mexico	3.2	76.2	8.7	42.1
Nicaragua	.1	8.1	19.5	NA
Nigeria	.5	33.7	3.4	110.9
Philippines	.6	24.1	8.8	69.3
Somalia	.1	1.9	24.4	276.9
Syria	.2	15.0	10.8	118.1
Sudan	.3	9.2	15.2	NA
Tanzania	.3	5.3	19.5	282.0
Thailand	.3	12.6	4.6	32.6
Zaire	.3	8.9	9.1	141.0

SOURCE: The World Bank, *World Development Report 1992*, pp. 258–259, 264–265.

the Developing World's desire to achieve political-economic independence: having achieved political sovereignty, Developing World states do not want to be subjected to another form of external control.

The **nonaligned movement** dates specifically to the 1955 Bandung Conference. Since then, the nonaligned movement has established a widely recognized role for itself in the modern world. Two of the leading early spokesmen for the nonaligned movement, India's Jawaharlal Nehru and Yugoslavia's Josef Broz Tito, sought to guide the nonaligned movement on a path equidistant from East and West. But given the historical legacy of colonialism, that proved difficult.

What, then, is the nonaligned movement? To begin with, it is a grouping of extremely diverse states, just as is the Developing World. Some nonaligned states, such as Venezuela, Peru, and Bolivia, are tied to the United States through the Organization of American States; other nonaligned states, such as the Philippines and Thailand, have had formal defense alliances with the United States. On the other hand, Ethiopia, Angola, Afghanistan, Yemen, and Mozambique were tied to the U.S.S.R. through "Treaties of Friendship and Cooperation." In the case of Cuba, formal agreements in the past were superseded by Cuban willingness to undertake policy actions supported, sponsored, and supplied by the U.S.S.R.

Throughout the early and middle 1980s, the nonaligned movement continued to be pulled and tugged by its internal divisions between pro-Soviet radical states, pro-Western conservative states, and legitimately nonaligned states. The first two groups sided with the blocs with which they were more closely identified, and the third group voted its mind at the UN and in other international forums on issues as diverse as the Soviet invasion of Afghanistan, the American invasion of Grenada, and the international debt crisis.

As East–West tensions eased in the late 1980s and early 1990s, maintaining a nonaligned status became less problematic for most Developing World states. And with the collapse of the Soviet Union in 1991, the traditional concept of non-alignment in many respects became moot. Indeed, Argentina and one or two other states even left the nonaligned movement, observing that with the collapse of the Soviet Union, nonalignment had lost its meaning.

Other Developing World states saw things differently. Despite the growing recognition in many Developing World states that they needed investment and other sources of capital from the West, they still remained concerned that they might become subservient to Western interests and objectives.

Economic-Social Modernization

Above all else, Developing World countries see their plight of poverty and dependence as the result of past colonial exploitation and current economic inequities in international trade, pricing, and exchange mechanisms. As a result, the South seeks both expanded aid from the North and a restructuring of the existing international economic order. In short, the South desires a **New International Economic Order** (NIEO).

The NIEO's origins may be traced to the first United Nations Conference on Trade and Development (UNCTAD) held in Geneva in 1964. At UNCTAD I, Developing World states formed the Group of 77 to unify and articulate their objections to trade, aid, and development practices of the mid-1960s. UNCTAD became a permanent organization of the United Nations in December 1964, with the self-defined responsibility of speaking for the world's poor.

Members of the Group of 77 also used their numerical advantage in the UN General Assembly to struggle for a NIEO. Algeria first convened a special session of the General Assembly specifically for the purpose of developing methods to transfer wealth from rich states to poor ones. Specific proposals that the Group of 77-dominated General Assembly passed included the Charter of Economic Rights and Duties of States, the Declaration of the Establishment of a New International Economic Order, and its associated Action Program. Developing World states have also urged the UN Task Force on Multinational Corporations to finalize a code of acceptable business practices for MNCs.

The basic outline for the Group of 77's concept of a New International Economic Order has at least six components. First, developed states of the North should increase their economic assistance level to Developing World states to at least .7 percent of their GNP. As Table 8–4 shows, only Denmark, France, the Netherlands, Norway, and Sweden reached this level in 1990. If all Western developed states expanded their assistance to at least .7 percent of their GNP, then as much as $55.6 billion of additional economic assistance would flow to the Developing World, most from the United States and Japan.

The second component of the proposed New International Economic Order is tariff reductions and quota increases on all end products produced in the

TABLE 8–4 Official Development Assistance from Northern States (Organization for Economic Cooperation and Development Members), 1990, and the Impact that NIEO Proposals Would Have on Development Assistance

Country	Actual Development Assistance, 1990, in Billions of Dollars	Actual Development Assistance, 1990, as Percentage of GNP	Proposed Billions of Dollars of Development Assistance, 1990, at NIEO .7 Percent GNP Level	Billions of Dollars Increase in 1990 Development Assistance if .7 Percent Adopted
Australia	1.0	.34	2.0	1.0
Austria	.4	.25	1.1	.7
Belgium	.9	.45	1.4	.5
Canada	2.5	.44	4.0	1.5
Denmark	1.2	.93	now above .7	—
Finland	.8	.64	.9	.1
France	9.4	.79	now above .7	—
Germany	6.3	.42	10.5	4.2
Ireland	.2	.16	.4	.3
Italy	3.4	.32	7.4	4.0
Japan	9.1	.31	20.5	11.4
Netherlands	2.6	.94	now above .7	—
New Zealand	.1	.23	.3	.2
Norway	1.2	1.17	now above .7	—
Sweden	2.0	.90	now above .7	—
Switzerland	.8	.31	1.8	1.0
United Kingdom	2.6	.27	6.7	4.1
United States	11.4	.21	38.0	26.6

SOURCE: World Bank data, obtained September 1992.

Developing World. This action would drive up the demand for Developing World products, thereby decreasing unemployment in the Developing World.

The third component of the NIEO is a proposed change in the decision-making process of international economic organizations such as the World Bank, the General Agreement on Tariffs and Trade, and the International Monetary Fund. The proposed change would allow Developing World states to have an increased role in the financial decisions that will influence and perhaps determine their futures.

Fourth, the major international economic organizations should be less intrusive in their demands for financial information on which to base their decisions for loans and grants. This, it is argued by Group of 77 members, will enhance North–South trust.

Fifth, the International Monetary Fund and other international banking institutions should undertake a massive redistribution of the international credit system, making more credit available to less-developed countries. This action would theoretically allow Developing World states to develop their domestic economic base over a longer period of time without having to be concerned with short-term loan repayments, thereby permitting Developing World states to better reach the elusive economic take-off point.[9]

Sixth, and finally, technical and financial assistance from the North to the South should be increasingly redirected toward processing facilities, transportation systems, and distribution systems, not only those internal to Developing World states, but also those external to Developing World states that are under the control, management, and ownership of Developing World governments, corporations, or individuals. This, it is argued, would permit Developing World countries to retain more of the "middleman profits" in their own national treasuries, thereby again strengthening Developing World economic bases.

Not surprisingly, the industrialized North rejects most of the proposed tenets of the NIEO. In the United States, Western Europe, Japan, Australia, Israel, South Africa, and New Zealand, the NIEO is rejected as being economically and politically unrealistic, pragmatically unworkable, and founded on inaccurate economic premises.[10] None of the Developing World states accept the West's rejection of the NIEO, although there is little they can do but argue for additional negotiations.

The North–South conflict, then, is a real conflict. The dangers that it generates are not so readily apparent as those that arose from the East–West conflict. Nevertheless, the dangers are real, even as the conflict itself is real, and they are dangers that present challenges to the entire world.

DANGERS OF THE NORTH–SOUTH CONFLICT

Several dangers may be derived from the continuation of present levels of unequal distribution of wealth between North and South. Before they are discussed, however, it is first necessary to point out the elementary fact that the gap between rich and poor is, in most cases, expanding. Table 8–5 lists those countries that have experienced economic growth rates greater than Western industrialized states between 1965 and 1990; these are the only Developing World states that are closing the gap. Obviously, even for most of them, no opportunity exists to eliminate the gap during the next several generations. Thus, the North–South gap will inevitably continue, and in most cases grow, at least if present policies and current rates of growth hold.

The continued growth of the rich-poor gap may be effectively expressed in another way as well. In 1850, the ratio between industrializing societies' incomes and those of the rest of the world was 2 to 1. By 1950, the ratio was 10 to 1, and by 1960 it was nearly 15 to 1. Projections for the year 2000 reach as high as 30 to 1.[11]

Quality of life, it may be argued, is not necessarily reflective of either per capita income or income ratios between two societies. This is a legitimate observation in societies where the population has had its basic needs for food, water, shelter, clothing, and health care met, and where possibilities exist for effective

TABLE 8–5   Developing World States Whose Economic Growth Rates Exceed That of the Combined Western Industrialized OECD States

Country	Average Annual GNP per Capita 1990 in Dollars	Growth Rate, 1965–1990	Number of Years until Gap Closed if 1965–1990 Growth Rate Continues
OECD Countries	20,170	2.4	—
Burundi	210	3.4	over 100
China	370	5.8	over 100
Pakistan	380	2.5	over 100
Sri Lanka	470	2.9	over 100
Lesotho	530	4.9	over 100
Indonesia	570	4.5	over 100
Egypt	600	4.1	over 100
Cameroon	960	3.0	over 100
Ecuador	980	2.8	over 100
Congo	1,010	3.1	over 100
Paraguay	1,110	4.6	over 100
Colombia	1,240	2.7	over 100
Thailand	1,420	4.4	over 100
Tunisia	1,440	3.2	over 100
Turkey	1,630	2.6	over 100
Botswana	2,040	8.4	48
Mauritius	2,250	3.2	over 100
Malaysia	2,320	4.0	over 100
Mexico	2,490	2.8	over 100
Syria	2,640	3.3	over 100
Brazil	2,680	3.3	over 100
South Korea	5,400	7.1	30
Oman	6,800	6.4	23
Saudi Arabia	7,050	2.6	over 100
Singapore	11,160	6.5	15

SOURCE: Derived from the World Bank, *World Development Report 1992*, pp. 218–219.

Note: These statistics do not take into account internal distribution of income. See Table 8–6 for wealth distribution.

Hunger and starvation are immense problems throughout much of the world. Somalia has been particularly hard hit during the 1990s, and even the intervention of the United Nations has not solved the problem.   (AP/Wide World Photos.)

education and gainful employment. In most Developing World societies, however, those basic needs are not met for the population as a whole. Indeed, in many Developing World societies, per capita income and comparative income ratios present an overly optimistic picture of actual conditions. Just as wealth is distributed unequally in international affairs, so too is wealth distributed unequally within countries. This is particularly true in many Developing World countries. Table 8–6 illustrates this point by listing the percentage of national income received by the wealthiest 10 percent of society and the percentage of national income received by the poorest 20 percent of society. Although it must be cautioned that this is neither a listing of all countries nor are data compared from the same year, it is worth noting that in no developed industrialized state does the wealthiest 10 percent of the population have more than 30 percent of the wealth. By comparison, in the 31 developing states listed, only in Bangladesh, El Salvador, India, Indonesia, and South Korea do the wealthiest 10 percent of the population have less than 30 percent of the wealth. Equally startlingly, the poorest 20 percent of the population have less than 5 percent of the wealth in only two developed industrialized states, Australia and the United States, whereas in 18 of the 31 developing nations listed, the poorest 20 percent of the population receives less than 20 percent of the national income. Interestingly, Latin American states seem to offer their poorest people the least income. Of the nine states in which the poorest 20 percent of the population receive less than 4 percent of the national income, five are in Latin America (Brazil, Chile, Costa Rica, El Salvador, and Panama.)

TABLE 8–6   Wealth Distribution Within States

Country	Years Data Compiled	% National Income to Richest 10%	% National Income to Poorest 20%
Mauritius	1980–81	46.7	4.0
Nepal	1976–77	46.5	4.6
Zambia	1976	46.3	3.4
Brazil	1983	46.2	2.4
Kenya	1976	45.8	2.6
Panama	1973	44.2	2.0
Ivory Coast	1985–86	43.7	2.4
Sri Lanka	1985–86	43.0	4.8
Turkey	1973	40.7	3.5
Mexico	1977	40.6	2.9
Malawi	1967–68	40.1	10.4
Costa Rica	1986	38.8	3.3
Sierra Leone	1967–69	37.8	5.6
Peru	1985–86	35.8	4.4
Tanzania	1969	35.6	5.8
Argentina	1970	35.2	4.4
Malaysia	1987	34.8	4.6
Chile	1973	34.8	3.5
Sudan	1967–68	34.6	4.0
Venezuela	1987	34.2	4.7
Thailand	1975–76	34.1	5.6
Portugal	1973–74	33.4	5.2
Egypt	1974	33.2	5.8
Philippines	1985	32.1	5.5
Trinidad	1975–76	31.8	4.2
Hong Kong	1980	31.3	5.5
Switzerland	1982	29.8	5.2
El Salvador	1976–77	29.5	5.5
New Zealand	1981–82	28.7	5.1
Sweden	1981	28.1	7.4
South Korea	1976	27.5	5.7
India	1983	26.7	8.1
Yugoslavia	1987	26.6	6.1
Indonesia	1987	26.5	8.8
Australia	1985	25.8	4.4
France	1979	25.5	6.3
Italy	1986	25.3	6.8
Ireland	1973	25.1	7.2
United States	1985	25.0	4.7
Spain	1980–81	24.5	6.9
Canada	1987	24.1	5.7
West Germany	1984	23.4	6.8
Great Britain	1979	23.4	7.0
Bangladesh	1985–86	23.2	10.0
Netherlands	1983	23.0	6.9
Norway	1982	22.8	6.0
Israel	1969–80	22.6	6.0
Japan	1979	22.4	8.7
Denmark	1981	22.3	5.4
Finland	1981	21.7	6.3
Belgium	1978–79	21.5	7.9
Hungary	1987–88	20.7	10.9

SOURCE: The World Bank, *World Development Report 1992*, pp. 222–223.

What dangers exist because of real and growing differences in the distribution of wealth between North and South? One danger is that North and South may find themselves even more deeply entwined in the rhetoric of confrontation and hostility. Do the economically wealthy countries have a duty and responsibility to help less fortunate states improve themselves economically? Developing World states unequivocally answer yes, whereas the wealthy states respond hesitatingly and uncertainly on both sides of the question. Even in those instances where the North extends aid and assistance, disagreement exists over what development strategy to use. At the same time, the South closely guards its newly won independence, fearing that economic ties to the North through either state agencies or private firms may increase economic dependence and political subservience. The danger of allowing the current North–South dialogue to move toward confrontation and hostility is that constructive action may end, thereby allowing the South to slip even more deeply into the abyss of abject poverty and influencing the South to take action with whatever tools it has at its disposal against the North.

Despite its poverty, the South is not without tools. Many of the resources that the industrial North requires are available primarily in the South. Realizing this, the South could turn to a strategy of resource deprivation and price increases in raw materials. So far only the OPEC states have employed this strategy successfully, but their impact on the industrialized world has been immense. Although other raw material cartels would not have the same advantages that OPEC enjoyed during the 1970s, a policy of cartelization could appear a useful strategy to Developing World governments. Obviously, the virtual collapse of OPEC that occurred in 1986, bringing with it sizable reductions in oil prices, pointed out that cartelization is not a guaranteed answer to the Developing World's problems. Nevertheless, even with the difficulties inherent in cartelization, it could prove attractive.

Developing World governments, however, need not be the only representatives of the Developing World to act because of frustration over the distribution of global wealth. Nonstate actors such as terrorist groups or transnational ideological or religious movements may conclude that resorting to violence or terror is the key to goading the North to action or to overturning an unfair international economic system. Given the weaponry available on the international arms market, and given the integrated nature of modern industrial society, a small group could terrorize a much larger organization or society. With little to lose under current conditions, resort to violence or terror may become a preferred option for some nongovernmental actors, and perhaps even for some governments as well. Indeed, in the mid-1980s reports circulated in New York that terrorists of unknown origin had entered the United States to shoot down domestic aircraft with surface-to-air missiles unless the United States expanded its aid commitment to developing nations. Similarly, in 1990, Iraq's leader, Saddam Hussein, argued that one of the justifications for Iraq's invasion of Kuwait was that it was not proper for Kuwait's people to be rich while many other Arabs were poor.

A more subtle effect of the continued disparity in wealth between North and South is the psychological impact that the effects of that gap may have on the collective psyche of the North, particularly in situations where starvation occurs. Whereas proponents of the "lifeboat" theory of international relations urge that the North jealously provide only for itself,[12] others have concluded that the industrialized societies are gradually eroding their own humanity by neglecting the needs of the developing world.

Perceived potential threats, then, are diverse: resource deprivation and price wars through cartelization, violence and terror against Northern societies and interests, and the gradual erosion of the North's very humanity are but three of the projected scenarios that may eventuate unless the North–South conflict is somehow ameliorated.

The question that must be answered for that amelioration to occur, however, is how does economic development itself occur? Various answers to this question will be presented in Chapter 22. Even at this point, it should be obvious that many answers to the question exist. Despite the disagreement over how best to approach and solve the plight of the South, agreement appears to be growing that unless some steps are taken to change a situation where 75 percent of the world's population have only 20 percent of the world's gross national product, the North–South conflict can only pose heightened dangers for the entire global community.

KEY TERMS AND CONCEPTS

the South	Group of 77
the North	political-economic independence
North–South conflict	neocolonialism
Developing World	political-military nonalignment
Third World (also in Ch.7)	nonaligned movement
Fourth World	economic-social modernization
Fifth World	New International Economic
Less Developed Countries (LDCs)	Order (NIEO)
conditions in developing countries	dangers of the North–South
at independence	conflict
Bandung Conference	

NOTES

1. For example, see Hollis B. Chenery, "Restructuring the World Economy," *Foreign Affairs*, Vol. 53 (January 1975): 258–263.

2. See, for example, Dawa Norbu, *Culture and the Politics of Third World Nationalism* (New York: Routledge, 1992).

3. George McTurnan Kahin and John W. Lewis, *The United States in Vietnam* (New York: Delta Books, 1969), pp. 8–10.

4. Coral Bell, "China: The Communists and the World," in F. S. Northedge, *The Foreign Policies of the Powers* (New York: The Free Press, 1974), p. 128.

5. See, for example, *Third World Cooperation: The Group of 77 in UNCTAD* (New York: St. Martins, 1991).

6. For a discussion of the treaty and the U.S. position on it, see Leigh S. Ratiner, "The Law of the Sea: A Crossroads for American Foreign Policy," *Foreign Affairs*, Vol. 60 (Summer 1982): 1006–1021. See also Marvin Soroos, *Beyond Sovereignty: The*

Challenge of Global Policy (Columbia: University of South Carolina Press, 1986), pp. 261–293.

7. Some analysts add a fourth factor that may be termed psychological independence. See Franz Fanon, *Black Skin, White Masks* (New York: Grove Press, 1967); and Franz Fanon, *The Wretched of the Earth* (New York: Grove Press, 1968).

8. Rajiv Gandhi, "Speech to the Ninth Nonaligned Summit Meeting," September 1989.

9. It should be noted that as of 1992 Developing World debt to Western banking institutions alone exceeded $1 trillion.

10. See Robert H. Donaldson, "The Second World, the Third World, and the New International Economic Order," in Robert H. Donaldson (ed.), *The Soviet Union in the Third World: Successes and Failures* (Boulder, CO: Westview, 1981), pp. 358–383.

11. Lester R. Brown, *World Without Borders* (New York: Vintage Books, 1972), p. 42.

12. For an interesting treatment of "lifeboat ethics," see Richard J. Barnet, "No Room in the Lifeboats," *The New York Times Magazine* (April 16, 1978), pp. 32–38. See also Garrett Hardin, "Lifeboat Ethics: The Case Against Helping the Poor," *Psychology Today*, Vol. 8 (September 1974).

CHAPTER 9

Systemic Change

WHERE IS THE WORLD GOING?

- With the East–West conflict over, are "North" and "South" still useful analytical concepts?
- What international systems have existed in the twentieth century?
- What kind of international system is most likely to emerge next?

Having viewed the contemporary international system in terms of the two conflicts that dominated the evolution of post-World War II international relations, and having seen that one of those two conflicts is over and that the other is not a completely accurate description of the present-day international system, we must now ask the inevitable questions. Are *North* and *South* still valid as analytical concepts, or has too much changed to allow us to use these terms to try to understand the world in which we live? With the Cold War and the East–West conflict over, what kind of international system is most likely to emerge next?

We will take three separate approaches to try to answer these questions. First, we will explore the dimensions of change in the current international system. Second, we will explore previous major changes in the international system that took place during the twentieth century. Finally, we will speculate about what type of international system may be most likely to emerge from the current situation. Taken together, these approaches will provide us with a better understanding of where the world may be going.

SHORTCOMINGS OF CURRENT PERSPECTIVES

As we discussed earlier, the international system is formed by all the international actors plus their interactions with one another. Over time, as actors, their capabilities, and their interests change, and so too does the international system. But simultaneously, the system influences the way the actors act and the way they view themselves and others.

For most of the post–World War II era, analysts, academics, and policy-makers alike used the convenient shorthand concepts of the East–West and North–South conflicts to order their thinking on international affairs. Nevertheless, throughout the post-World War II period, certain international actors and international situations did not fit neatly within either conflict. For example, following Ayatollah Khomeini's 1979 revolution that overthrew the shah in Iran, Iran opposed both the East and the West, and maintained that the emphasis on increased wealth that the shah sought for the country degraded the quality of religious life so dear to Khomeini and his followers. Revolutionary Iran, then, was a state actor that did not fall neatly into either the East–West or the North–South framework. Nevertheless, because of its strategic location and oil wealth, it had a major impact on both conflicts.

Certain national liberation movements, transnational religious and ideological movements, terrorist organizations, and other nongovernmental organizations and individuals also fell outside the purview of the East–West and North–South conflicts, although few were not affected by one or both conflicts. For example, the International Political Science Association (IPSA), a nonideological professional NGO of political science specialists, played no functional role in either conflict under discussion. However, when it decided to hold its 1979 convention in Moscow, some conservative Western circles criticized IPSA for its alleged communist sympathies. During the convention itself, several panels slated to discuss human rights issues were scheduled in extremely small rooms with inoperative translation facilities, quite probably because of the Soviet government's apparent opposition to such discussions. Thus, even though IPSA itself was a party to neither the East–West nor the North–South conflicts, it clearly was affected by the East–West conflict.

Similarly, the International Olympic Committee (IOC) is an NGO that played no role in and of itself in the East–West or North–South conflicts. Nevertheless, the IOC and the Olympics were used by Eastern, Western, Northern, and Southern states for their own political purposes. Again, however, the point is that neither the IOC, nor IPSA, nor Iran, nor any of a number of other international actors may be categorized. Even multinational corporations, long the purported bane of East and South as agents of Western imperial and colonial expansion, are now viewed in a somewhat different light in the Developing World. Some Developing World states such as Singapore, Hong Kong, India, and Nigeria even serve as bases of operations for locally owned MNCs.

In addition, Australia and New Zealand do not fit into the North–South scheme. Both are southern hemisphere states that enjoy standards of living associated with Northern industrialized states. Clearly, the North–South model is not completely accurate.

The People's Republic of China (P.R.C.) presents perhaps the best example of the inadequacy of the East–West and North–South schemes for explaining international relations. As a communist state, the P.R.C. had been viewed as a member of the Eastern bloc since Mao Zedong wrested control of the mainland from Chiang Kai-shek in 1949. By 1960, however, Western analysts of Chinese affairs noted that serious strains had developed in the Sino-Soviet alliance. Less than ten years later, the P.R.C. and the Soviet Union were actively engaged in open warfare along their mutual boundary, and during the 1970s, China and the United States gradually improved relations. By the end of the 1970s, China and the United States were closely aligned on many international issues in opposition to the U.S.S.R. In addition, the P.R.C. undertook "punitive military actions" against a close Soviet ally, the Socialist Republic of Vietnam, and urged the United States and Western Europe to strengthen NATO. According to the East–West model of the international system, China's internal political system mandated that the P.R.C. be an Eastern country, but most of its external actions aligned it with the West. Clearly, the East–West model was inadequate to explain China.

The P.R.C. also does not fit into the North–South model well. Although the P.R.C. is obviously a poor state that played a major role in initiating the non-aligned movement at Bandung and that regularly puts itself forward as spokesperson for Developing World states, other Developing World states some-times view the Chinese claims of Developing World membership with skepti-cism. China simply has too much potential, they believe, to be a legitimate Developing World state, even though, economically speaking, it obviously deserves membership.

If China serves as a good example of a state that did not fit neatly within the confines of the East–West or North–South conflicts, then the **Angolan Civil War** is a good example of a situation that defies categorization. As already noted, three tribally based national liberation movements received support from various external sources in their struggle for independence against the Portuguese. When a new government in Portugal announced that it would grant Angola independence in November 1975, the national liberation move-ments' struggle against the Portuguese increasingly became a struggle against each other, with the Soviet-backed MPLA fighting against the American and Chinese-backed FNLA and UNITA. UNITA also received military backing from white-ruled South Africa. In addition, a fourth movement, the Federation for the Liberation of the Enclave of Cabinda (FLEC) sought to win autonomy and sovereignty for that province of Angola. Whoever won the civil war among the MPLA, UNITA, and the FNLA would become the new government of Angola.

By early 1976, the Soviet Union had helped Cuba introduce approximately 20,000 soldiers to Angola to support the MPLA. South Africa, meanwhile, sent an armored column into southern Angola to support UNITA. China stepped up its aid to both the FNLA and UNITA. The U.S. government also attempted to increase its aid to the FNLA and UNITA, but congressional action (the Clark Amendment) prevented the United States from sending additional aid to any fac-tion in Angola. Meanwhile, the Organization for African Unity, was almost evenly divided over whether the MPLA or UNITA should govern.

The MPLA, with its Cuban and Soviet backing, established a government in Luanda, although it would be too much to say that the MPLA won the civil war. UNITA continued to struggle to gain control militarily of Angola until 1992, when national elections were finally held. UNITA lost the elections, then claimed that they were unfair, and renewed the civil war.

Throughout much of this time, the MPLA sought to attract external technical aid and financial assistance from any willing source. As part of this effort, the American-based Gulf Oil Corporation was granted a concession in Cabinda, where it had been drilling before Angolan independence. The U.S. government, still seeking to weaken the MPLA, forbade Gulf to make payments to the MPLA for its drilling operations. After additional legal maneuvering, however, the MPLA received payment from Gulf. Throughout these proceedings, FLEC sought to disrupt Gulf's drilling by conducting terrorist attacks against its operations. Paradoxically, Cuban troops armed with Soviet weapons were used to protect Gulf's investments.

The Angolan Civil War was in part a product of the North–South struggle and the East–West struggle, but it was also more than that. National liberation movement fought against national liberation movement. Communist sided with anticommunist against communist, and white racist sided with black and yellow against black and white. Western multinational corporations defied Western governments to obtain profits won under the protection of Soviet-supplied guns wielded by troops of an allegedly nonaligned nation against a local liberation movement. An international governmental organization found itself hopelessly deadlocked over which of two national movements should rightfully form a government. Elements of the North–South and East–West conflicts pervaded the entire struggle, but the conflicts by themselves could not explain the struggle. It was too complicated a situation for such helpful but simplistic models.

The Iranian revolution, China, the Angolan conflict, and the other situations discussed above had for some time made it apparent that the East–West and North–South models were insufficient to explain all international interactions. Nevertheless, despite their shortcomings, the East–West and North–South conflicts explained enough about what went on in the world between 1945 and 1989 that they were accepted by most people as accurate descriptions of how the international system operated.

This began to change in 1989 as revolution swept Eastern Europe and as the Soviet Union deepened the alterations in its international outlook and domestic and foreign policy behavior. It eroded even further in 1990 and early 1991 as a result of the international community's response to Iraq's invasion of Kuwait. While Iraq's President Saddam Hussein called for a *jihad*, or holy war, to expel U.S., Western, and other non-Islamic influences from the Arab world, the industrialized West, the Soviet Union, and other states—including several Arab countries—condemned the Iraqi invasion. The U.S.S.R. even verbally supported the deployment of a multinational military force including American units to Saudi Arabia and the Persian Gulf.

Later in 1991, after a coup attempt in the Soviet Union failed and the U.S.S.R. itself dissolved, there was no longer any room for debate. The East–West conflict was over, and the East–West model of the international system that had been so useful a construct for understanding the way the world worked for almost half a century was no longer relevant.

At the same time, the North–South conflict continued, although it too was changing. The Middle Eastern events of 1990 and 1991 well illustrate both points. Saddam Hussein's call for a holy war was directed not only against non-Islamic influences in the Arab world, but also against conservative and wealthy ruling classes in other Arab countries. His call for a holy war fell on receptive ears among the lower classes in several Arab states.

But simultaneously, in the Middle East and throughout the world, more and more Developing World states sought to attract external investment from developed states and MNCs rather than exclude it as they had done during earlier decades. They also increasingly appeared willing to work with international financial institutions to put development plans into place that had a chance to succeed. Thus, even though the North–South conflict remained, it too was in the process of changing.

Clearly, then, with the East–West conflict gone and the North–South conflict remaining but changing, the international system is in the midst of a fundamental transformation. Although the precise nature of this transformation is not yet clear, it will usher in the fourth major systemic era of the twentieth century. We turn now to a discussion of those earlier eras in the hope that through understanding them, we may better grasp the dimensions of what the emerging international system may be like.

The East–West conflict was one of the main features of the international system from 1945 to 1990. The Eastern European revolutions of 1989 provided strong evidence that the conflict was ending and that the international system was changing. Here workers in Prague rip down a hammer and sickle sign, long one of the banners of communism. (AP/Wide World Photos.)

TWENTIETH-CENTURY INTERNATIONAL SYSTEMS

One after another, three international systems have dominated international affairs since 1900. The international community is now on the verge of creating a fourth.

The first international system of the twentieth century carried over from the nineteenth century, and extended until 1914. In general terms, it was a **balance of power system** in which flexible groupings of states altered their relationships with one another to maintain a semblance of international peace and stability. Its hallmarks were the economic dominance of European states, the maintenance of global European empires, and the functioning of a militarily based balance of power in Europe to maintain the peace.

One of the extremely important but often overlooked preconditions for the successful operation of the system was the widespread acceptance by the actors within the system of the system's legitimacy. At the same time, while there was widespread acceptance of the system's legitimacy, the legitimacy of two of the major state actors, the Austrian-Hungarian Empire and the Ottoman Empire, was being challenged by internal ethnic groups that sought to dissolve the empires in which they lived. These groups hoped to establish their own nation-states.

In addition, other pressures had long been building that challenged the balance of power system's stability. As early as 1868, dissatisfied but increasingly powerful nation-states sought to reapportion colonial holdings, upset existing military balances, and otherwise challenge the existing system. Chief among these unsettling influences were Japan following the Meiji Restoration (1868) and Germany following unification (1871). Even the United States, which itself joined the rush to assemble overseas empires in the 1890s, had a role in destabilizing the balance of power system.

However, it was not until World War I (1914–1918) that the balance of power system collapsed. Not surprisingly, the unprecedented death and destruction of World War I caused many people to reject the system that had led to the war. Thus, when World War I ended, the victorious side, urged on by American President Woodrow Wilson, created a new international system based on **national self-determination** and the nation-state in Europe, and on collective security throughout the world.

To obtain self-determination and create nation-states in Europe, the old Austrian-Hungarian and Ottoman Empires were broken up. New nation-states were created out of the remains. This process was aided by the fact that both Austria–Hungary and the Ottoman Empire were on the losing side in World War I, and by the ethnic unrest that had plagued both before World War I. Albania, Austria, Bulgaria, Czechoslovakia, Hungary, Romania, Turkey, and Yugoslavia all owed their existence to this process. In addition, those territories of the Ottoman Empire that were at the Eastern end of the Mediterranean Sea were given to Great Britain as the Palestinian and Iraqi mandates.

The process of creating new states based on national self-determination went even further. Although Russia had been on the winning side in World War I, the strains of the war had been more than the old Czarist empire could endure. It too collapsed, replaced by V. I. Lenin's communist state, the Soviet Union. The combination of Soviet weakness, mutual hostility between Russian communists and Western capitalists, and legitimate aspirations for independence by ethnic minorities that had been included within the old Russian empire made it inevitable that new states would be created out of the remains of the Czar's empire as well. Therefore, with the Soviet Union retaining the core of the old Russian empire, the new nation-states of Estonia, Finland, Latvia, Lithuania, and Poland were all created out of the fallen Russian Empire by the victorious Allied powers following World War I.[1]

Here, it is important to note that the Allies applied the concepts of national self-determination and the nation-state to Europe, not to other continents. European colonial holdings outside Europe remained European colonial holdings. Nevertheless, in the years following World War I, more and more people in European colonies outside Europe asked why they too could not have self-determination and their own nation-states. These questions planted the seeds that developed into many colonial independence movements in subsequent years.

However, those who were attempting to rebuild the international system after World War I had a more pressing problem, namely, what sort of system should replace the failed balance of power system? Their answer was a **collective security system**. Such a system relied on the belief that if one state acted as an aggressor, then other states had a responsibility and duty to act against and if need be punish the aggressor. This system again relied on the major actors within the system accepting its legitimacy and responding together to punish those who did not.

Unfortunately, however, few major states chose to follow the rules needed for the collective security system to prosper and survive. After a decade of relative success in the 1920s, one state after another abandoned the pretense of accepting collective security. First Japan and then Germany, Italy, and the Soviet Union in the 1930s invaded neighboring states. Meanwhile, first the United States, and then Great Britain and France, all decided that the potential costs of collective security were too high to pay, and did little or nothing to counter aggression.

Consequently, by the early 1930s, the collective security system had failed. However, the dimensions of its failure did not become apparent until 1939, when Germany and the Soviet Union invaded Poland. Immediately, Great Britain and France declared war on Germany. After almost six years of fighting, World War II finally ended, and once again international actors were faced with decisions about what kind of international system they intended to create.

Some hoped to fashion an improved collective security system based on the United Nations. But events moved too rapidly for that to occur as the American-Soviet cooperation of World War II broke down and as old colonial empires disintegrated. What emerged from the destruction of World War II was a **bipolar system** based on the East–West conflict, as we saw in Chapter 7, with a second conflict, the North–South conflict, playing a less prominent but nevertheless important role.

Both the East–West and North–South conflicts themselves evolved over time, as we saw in Chapters 7 and 8. However, with the East–West conflict over and the North–South conflict remaining but changing, the international system is today in disarray. Will the North–South conflict surge to a new prominence and shape the international system that ushers in the twenty-first century? Or are other forces at work that will overshadow the North–South conflict, relegate it to history, and bring about a new international order? These are difficult questions to answer.

THREE MODELS OF THE NEXT INTERNATIONAL SYSTEM

At least three different models of the next international system have been put forward by analysts, policy-makers, journalists, politicians, and other observers of contemporary international affairs. These three models—a unipolar world based on American military might, a regionalized world organized around three economic trading blocs, and a multipolar world based on several measures of national and international capabilities—were briefly introduced in Chapter 2. It is now time to analyze each in more detail.[2]

A Unipolar World

Throughout most of the years of the post–World War II bipolar international system, military strength was the primary measure of national power. To be sure, economic strength was almost always a major component of an international actor's ability to develop and maintain military strength, but military capabilities were nevertheless the foremost measure of national strength in most observers' eyes.

Given this emphasis, it therefore was not too surprising that when the Soviet Union collapsed, some people concluded that a unipolar world had emerged, with that one pole being the United States. These observers argued that the United States was now the only country that could project large quantities of military power anywhere in the world, that the United States had far and away the world's single largest national economy, and that the United States was now the focus of global affairs. Most observers who adopted this viewpoint were U.S. citizens, and their outlook of U.S. dominance is reflected in Figure 9–1.

This outlook received additional support as a result of the 1990 U.S. buildup of military forces on and around the Arabian peninsula in response to the Iraqi invasion of Kuwait, and the ensuing 1991 Persian Gulf war in which the United States and an international coalition of countries expelled Iraq from Kuwait. Proponents of this perspective argued that no country except the United States could project so much military power so far and so fast, and win so large a conflict so quickly and easily. They also observed that the United States was the only country diplomatically positioned to bring together and keep together such a large and diverse coalition of countries as that which opposed Iraq's aggression.

These were persuasive arguments. Nevertheless, by concentrating on military might and diplomatic positioning, the arguments tended to overlook several important issues. Could the United States maintain its military might given its own economic problems? In the post-Cold War world, would military might remain the most important dimension of national power, or was economic strength becoming most important? Indeed, were issues emerging on the international scene that could not be readily solved by either military might or eco-

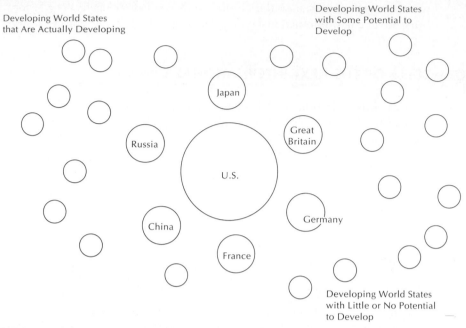

FIGURE 9–1.   One version of what may emerge as the "New International Order" in the late 1990s
and the 21st century: A unipolar world based on military power.

nomic strength? Most people who asked these questions rejected the unipolar
world as the most likely model of the new international order.

A Regionalized World

A second model of the new international order was based on regional economic
blocs, in the Americas centered on the United States; in Europe centered on the
European Community and its member states; and in East Asia centered on
Japan. To proponents of this viewpoint, the collapse of the Soviet Union and the
end of the East–West conflict had relegated military capabilities to a less important place in international affairs, and had elevated economic strength to the
highest importance. Many concluded that as a result, the new international order
of the late 1990s and beyond would be one of competing regional economic
blocs. This perspective is shown in Figure 9–2.

This view of the emerging international system was bolstered by the emergence of the European Community as an increasingly unified economic actor in
Europe; by the movement toward a North American Free Trade Area consisting
of Canada, the United States, and Mexico in the Western hemisphere; and by the
growth and interdependence of the economies of Japan and other states in East
Asia. It is a view that is further supported by the creation of a South American
free trade area called Mercosur that links Argentina, Brazil, Paraguay, and
Uruguay; the revitalization of a Central American common market; similar activities in West Africa; and a move toward a further reduction and eventual elimination of internal trade barriers between member states of the Association of

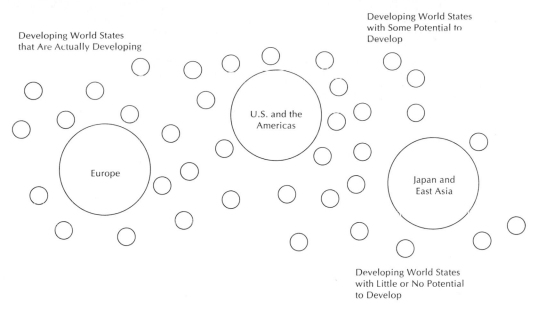

Developing World States
that Are Actually Developing

Developing World States
with Some Potential to
Develop

U.S. and the
Americas

Europe

Japan and
East Asia

Developing World States
with Little or No Potential
to Develop

FIGURE 9–2   A second version of what may emerge as the "New International Order" in the late
1990s and the 21st century: A regionalized world based on economic trading blocs.

Southeast Asian Nations. Proponents of this perspective argue that economics is
becoming the dominant force in international affairs as the twentieth century
ends, and that world will soon be divided into three major trading blocs centered
on Europe, East Asia, and the Americas.

But this outlook also has its detractors. Critics of this perspective maintain
that it overlooks the continuing importance of military capabilities and national
aspirations in contemporary international relations. They argue that military
strength remains an important tool of state power, and point to the difficulties of
the Maastricht Treaty in Europe as proof that moving toward economic cooperation does not mean that economic cooperation will enable people to overcome
national pride and national identity.

In addition, critics of the regionalized world model insist that such a world
is unstable and dangerous since it could lead to economic warfare and trade
restrictions like those that contributed to the onset of World War II. If this
becomes the direction in which the new international order is heading, they
insist, the international community should do everything in its power to change
directions.

A Multipolar World

Still other observers believe that the next international system will be an extremely diffuse world order, with the United States, the European Community,
Japan, and China all continuing to play major roles, but with other states and
other types of international actors also, on occasion, rising to prominence on a
case-by-case or issue-by-issue basis. This outlook is depicted in Figure 9–3.

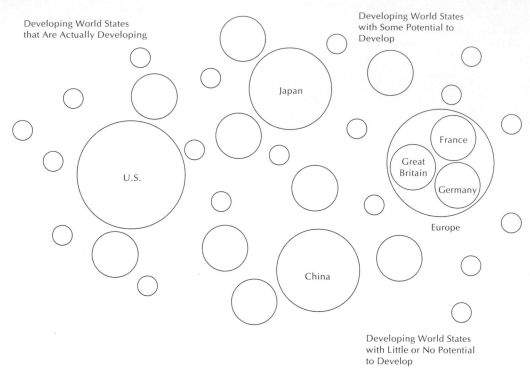

FIGURE 9–3   A third version of what may emerge as the "New International Order" in the late
1990s and the 21st century: A multipolar world based on multiple parameters of
power.

Proponents of this perspective more often than not see economic strength
growing in importance in the next few years. However, they also believe that military strength will continue to play an important role in contemporary international affairs. Often, they point to the collapse of the Soviet Union as proof of the
growing importance of economics, and the 1991 Persian Gulf War as proof of the
continuing importance of military power. But they also stress that measures of
national power in addition to economic capabilities and military strength are
extremely important. Sometimes termed **soft power**, these other measures
include but are not necessarily limited to beliefs, ideas, and culture. (These
measures are discussed in Chapter 19, "Sociopolitical Parameters of Power.")
Proponents of this perspective emphasize that "soft power" dimensions of national strength can not be overlooked.[3]

As already noted, this third perspective of the emerging international order is
extremely diffuse. Some of its critics assert that it underplays the importance of
economic capabilities and military strength, as well as the continued importance
of traditional actors and issues in contemporary international affairs. Other critics
argue that it is so diffuse a model of the emerging international order that it is not
really a model at all, but rather a refusal to create a model of what the new international order will become. Nevertheless, its proponents believe that it provides
the most accurate representation of what the emerging international system will
be like.

CONCLUSIONS

What, then, will the emerging international system be like? Can the international community complete a systemic transformation without resorting to catastrophic conflicts such as those that ended the balance of power and collective security systems? These are vitally important questions, but at this point in our study of contemporary international affairs, we do not yet have enough information or understanding to answer them.

Assessing the shape of the emerging international system is made even more difficult because regardless of what system actually emerges, its creation will in the short run be partially a function of decisions that result from the foreign policy and other decision-making processes of today's and tomorrow's international actors. For example, if the United States decides that it will use military force to achieve its objectives and take what it needs, then at least in the short run, the likelihood of a unipolar world emerging as the next international system increases. Similarly, if states opt to form restrictive regionalized economic trading blocs, then the second model becomes more likely in the short run. And if international actors strive for the third model, then the possibility of that model emerging as the last international system of the twentieth century and the first one of the twenty-first century will increase.

Regardless of which international system international actors attempt to create, and regardless of which system actually emerges, the next international system will be the creation of those that exist and act within it. Thus, especially in this era of international change, it is vitally important that we understand how the actors in the system see themselves and others, for it is on the basis of those perceptions that actors decide which actions to take. With this in mind, we now turn to the perceptual framework for varying views of the global community.

KEY TERMS AND CONCEPTS

shortcomings of current systemic
   perspectives
Angolan Civil War
balance of power system
national self-determination
collective security system
bipolar world (also in Chapter 2)

unipolar world (also in
   Chapter 2)
regionalized world (also in
   Chapter 2)
multipolar world (also in
   Chapter 2)
soft power

NOTES

1. For an excellent treatment of these and other related events, see William R. Keylor, *The Twentieth Century World* (New York: Oxford University Press, 1992).
2. For several different views on the emerging international order, see Jeffrey T. Bergner, *The New Superpowers: Germany, Japan, the United States, and the New World Order* (New York: St. Martins Press, 1991); Michael T. Klare and Daniel C. Thomas, *World Security Trends and Challenges at Century's End* (New York: St. Martins Press, 1991); Wayne Sandholtz et al., *The Highest Stakes: The Economic*

Foundations of the Next Security System (New York: Oxford University Press, 1992); and Donald Snow, *Distant Thunder: Third World Conflict and the New International Order* (New York: St. Martins, 1992).

3. For an in-depth discussion of "soft power," see Joseph S. Nye, Jr., *Bound to Lead: The Changing Nature of American Power* (New York: Basic Books, 1990).

PART THREE

The Perceptual Framework

VARYING VIEWS OF THE GLOBAL COMMUNITY

We see . . . through the eyes of one participant after the other. Each vision is so different, so contradictory, that in the end we can never be certain of what it is that has transpired . . . the images . . . not only vary widely from one power to another but also from one period to another. The same is true of the images which the involved powers have of each other's actions and motivations.

—*Harrison Salisbury*

O wad some poer the giftie gie us
To see oursel's as ithers see us!

—*Robert Burns*

"**J**ust the facts, ma'am." Sergeant Joe Friday repeated that famous phrase innumerable times on the old television program "Dragnet." Invariably Sergeant Friday found that different witnesses had different versions of the same fact, and only after a long and detailed investigation was one version of events finally accepted as true.

The uncertainties of Joe Friday's investigation apply equally well to our study of international affairs. For years, the United States viewed the Soviet Union as bent on international expansion and conquest, and the Soviet Union claimed the United States sought imperial growth and economic domination. Who was right, if anyone? In April 1986, the United States bombed five targets in Libya, arguing that the attack was a legitimate response to Libyan support of terrorist actions against U.S. interests. However, much of the rest of the world community con-

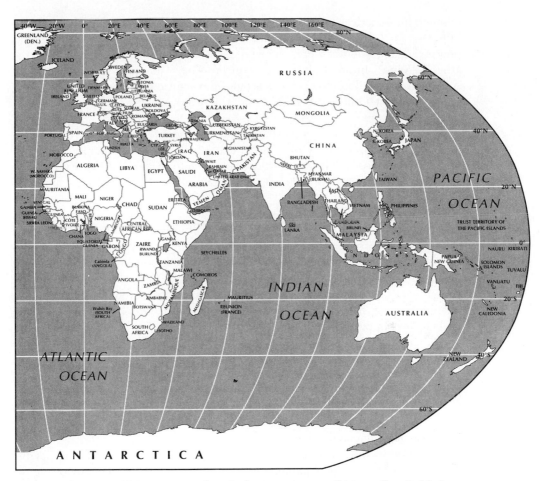

Nations of the world. (Reprinted with the permission of Macmillan Publishing Company from *Geography* by Arthur Getis, Judith Getis, and Jerome Fellman. Copyright © 1981 by Macmillan Publishing Company, updated 1993.)

demned the American action as either an overreaction that would only win more influence for Libya or as proof of U.S. President Reagan's own militaristic tendencies. Again, who was right, and who was wrong? And in December 1989, the United States invaded Panama, overthrowing General Manuel Noriega. Americans applauded the action as a rightful response to Noriega's drug-dealing and harassment. Others, especially Latin Americans, saw the U.S. assault as proof that the "Colossus of the North" still lived.

What, then, are the facts? How should they be interpreted? In the international community, a variety of answers exists to these rather simple questions. The answers differ as one moves from one capital to another capital. Even within a single capital, facts and their interpretations differ depending on whom one talks to or listens to.

Answers vary not only according to location of respondent or source of answer, but also according to time of answer. Between 1941 and 1945 Japan and the United States were avowed enemies, but after World War II, the two countries developed a close alliance. Now, however, trade tensions have introduced strains to the relationship. Similarly, at least on the surface, China and the Soviet Union were on friendly terms between 1949 and 1960. However, by 1969 the relationship had deteriorated into open hostility and border fighting. By 1989, Beijing and Moscow had again established a cordial but careful relationship.

Perceptually, then, enemies can become friends and friends enemies as time passes. Other, more subtle variations of perceptions may also occur over time, as they did in the United States during the Vietnam War. During the early years of American combat involvement (1965–1966), most Americans supported the U.S. involvement. Gradually, however, as losses mounted and success seemed no closer, more and more Americans opposed U.S. efforts in Vietnam. Perceptions had changed, and a policy change soon followed.

Differences in perceptual outlooks are therefore major contributing factors to the complications of contemporary international affairs. The following six chapters offer insight into various perceptual outlooks on international affairs. Chapter 10 discusses the role of perceptions in international affairs and analyzes the types of perceptions that are held by international actors other than nation-states. Chapters 11 through 15 examine differing national perspectives on international affairs. These chapters are based on the observation that states remain the central actors in international affairs, and that it is the perceptions of their government that are most significant. Specific questions that will be examined include:

- How do actors view each other?
- How do actors view themselves?
- What has influenced the development of these perceptions?
- How do perceptions affect policy?

CHAPTER 10

Perceptions and Policy in International Affairs

- Why are perceptions important in international affairs?
- How were U.S. and Soviet perceptions of the Vietnam War different?
- How did Soviet and U.S. perceptions of the Soviet occupation of Afghanistan differ?
- Are the perceptions of international actors additional to states important?

Many volumes have been written about the importance of perceptions in human affairs. Philosophers, psychologists, politicians, and social scientists have all pointed to the role of perceptions as guides to actions and to the different factors that determine how each of us views reality. Their points of departure and methods of analysis may differ, but all have concluded that, inevitably, no universally shared set of experiences exists that would influence diverse observers to view a certain situation in the same way.

Within the realm of international affairs, authors as diverse as Kenneth Boulding, David Easton, Robert Jervis, K. J. Holsti, Anatol Rapaport, Richard Snyder, and John Stoessinger have analyzed various ramifications of perceptions.[1] Their work and the work of other analysts of foreign policy and international affairs has cast new light on, and led to additional understanding of, relations among the various international actors. In this chapter, we first examine theoretical discussions of the role of perceptions in international affairs, and then the perceptions that nonstate actors in the international system hold.

THE ROLE OF PERCEPTIONS IN INTERNATIONAL AFFAIRS

Students of perceptual analysis often identify three separate components of perceptions—values, beliefs, and cognitions. A **value** gives rank and order to conditions, situations, individuals, and objects. Thus, most people rank health as better than sickness, and life as better than death. However, in some people's eyes, sickness may be preferable to health (one's ability to withstand suffering may be proved), and death may be preferable to life (one may escape suffering through death). On a less dramatic level, some people value a good book more than a good television program, or think that beef tastes better than pork. In all of these examples, an individual's values are what leads that individual to prefer one condition, situation, person, or object over another.

A **belief**, by contrast, is the acceptance of a particular description of reality as true or legitimate. An observer may believe that colonialism is repugnant because it usually retards economic, social, and cultural advancement. Or one may believe that dictatorships are more likely to go to war than democracies because in a dictatorship only one person makes decisions, whereas in a democracy many people share in making a decision. A belief is usually an effort to explain in a consistent manner a pattern of activity consisting of several pieces of information. It is, in the simplest terms, an analytical answer to a stated question.

A **cognition** is any piece of information that observers receive about their surroundings that they use to arrive at a value or belief. Cognitions may be either sensory or factual inputs to our value or belief systems and are the basis for our values and beliefs. If we value health more than sickness, it is because we have seen or felt both conditions. Seeing or feeling those conditions were cognitive inputs. If we saw Hitler take over the European continent and Saddam Hussein kill his countrymen, those were our cognitive inputs from which we concluded that dictatorship was a less desirable form of government than democracy.

How do values, beliefs, and cognitions influence international affairs? In the limited space available here, we discuss only two ways. First, given the vast array of cognitive information that everyone receives, it should be evident that the values and beliefs that we form, and that in turn are then used both to receive and interpret new cognitive information, are highly individualized. Inevitably this leads to a wide diversity of perceptions, and these diverse perceptions have impact on international affairs.

Second, since perceptions are guides to actions, values, beliefs, and cognitions influence what actions we take. Thus, regardless of whether perceptions are accurate or inaccurate, the actions we take are grounded in our perceptions. In the international arena, the implications of this reality are many.

The Diversity of Perceptions

As we have already seen, there is no universal point of perceptual departure. Put more simply, different individuals see the same event or situation in different ways. As Bertrand Russell said:

> we cannot escape from perception with all its personal limitations. . . .
> Individual percepts are the basis of all our knowledge, and no method exists by which we can begin with data which are public to many observers.[2]

A perception is thus a relative concept, determined by previous experience, present expectations, current fears or desires, and the influences of others;[3] other factors are also undoubtedly involved. The key point is the realization that another person's interpretation of a situation may be different from one's own. It may be "determined by a different frame of reference, or shaped by other sets of values and presuppositions."[4]

Anatol Rapaport stated this in a different way, declaring:

> Thus, without falsifying a single fact, entirely contradictory descriptions can be and are given of persons, situations, social orders, etc., by selecting (often unconsciously) only the features which support preconceived notions. . . .
>
> Controversial issues tend to be polarized not only because commitments have been made but because certain perceptions are actively excluded from consciousness if they do not fit the chosen world image.[5]

K. J. Holsti agreed with Rapaport and added several additional observations. As not all relevant factors influencing a situation could be known, perceptions differed from reality. Preconceived values, beliefs, or expectations often determined which factors are viewed as relevant to a situation.[6] Dean Pruitt stressed this point in his work on threat perception, noting that the stronger the predisposition to perceive a threat, the more likely it was that a threat will be perceived.[7]

These observations are directly applicable to the study of international relations. In their examinations of foreign policy decision-making, Richard Snyder and Graham Allison regularly pointed to perceptual differences among American decision-makers as a significant variable in U.S. foreign policy determination.[8] Given the preceding discussion concerning the diversity of perceptions, the existence of such perceptual differences within a given nation is not surprising. Even less surprising is the fact that perceptual differences exist between nations. Students of international affairs have increasingly realized this and have examined individual events not only from the perspectives of individual actors within a state, but also from the viewpoint of several of the involved states.[9] The remaining chapters in this framework are based on this, and provide differing views of contemporary international relations as seen from different countries in the international community.

Perceptions as Guides to Action

Differing perceptions by themselves would be of limited interest to us if they did not also serve as a basis for explaining human action and reaction. In his classic work *The Image*, Kenneth Boulding argued that "behavior depends on the image."[10] More recently, K. J. Holsti observed that "man acts and reacts according to his images of the environment."[11] It is because of this linkage between perception and action that perceptual analysis has come to occupy so prominent a place in contemporary international relations.

When international actors formulate an action or a policy, perceptions of situations, events, and other involved actors form the bases of those actions and policies. Thus, an actor's perceptions must be examined and understood if that actor's actions and policies are to be understood. To an extent, understanding the perceptions that actors hold at the time they undertake an action or implement a policy enables observers to comprehend why a particular action is taken or policy implemented. The way in which a state views itself is critical to its national pride, whereas the way in which a state views others is critical to its national policy.

Indeed, when studying actions of actors in the international arena, analysis of events and personalities is seldom sufficient to yield understanding of those policies. Rather, as policies are made on the basis of the "appearance of things" rather than on "subjective reality," those appearances *as seen by the actors* must be studied as well. One question that students must keep constantly in mind as they examine international affairs is, "How did the different actors see a particular situation?"

This is not an easy task. Among the pitfalls confronting any perceptual analysis of any action or policy is the accurate determination of perceptions. At least two levels of problems exist when one is assessing the accuracy of perceptions. The first level concerns obtaining sources that are privy to the actual perceptions held by actors. This problem exists in most societies. In the United States, for example, the analyst is faced with uncertainty as to which of several potential sources he or she should believe. Before glasnost swept the former Soviet Union, the problem in the U.S.S.R. was one of finding a single worthwhile and accurate source. After glasnost, analysts of Soviet affairs were faced by a problem similar to that faced by analysts of American affairs, which of several sources should one believe? This analytical problem was further magnified by the breakup of the U.S.S.R.

The second level of problem concerns reliability of sources. International actors often find it to their advantage to have both other actors and analysts of international affairs believe that their outlooks on a particular situation are something other than what they really are. For example, even if the United States did not intend to use nuclear weapons to defend Western Europe in the event of a Soviet attack there, it was clearly in the U.S. interest to convince the U.S.S.R. that such weapons would be used in the event of a Soviet invasion. Similarly, a multinational corporation that believes it will garner large profits in a particular country would clearly find it advantageous to have that particular country think that the MNC's operations would be barely profitable. In all probability, the MNC could then negotiate a much more favorable contract agreement.

Perceptions, then, are diverse, and they are guides to action. Unfortunately, they are also difficult to determine. However, before we examine the perceptions of some of the nonstate actors in the contemporary world, it may be instructive if we first analyze some of the differing global perceptions of two recent international actions, namely the U.S. involvement in Vietnam and the Soviet intervention in Afghanistan.

CASE STUDIES: VIETNAM AND AFGHANISTAN

Vietnam

From August 1950 when the first 35-member U.S. Military Assistance Advisory Group arrived in Vietnam until April 1975 when the last U.S. Marines were lifted by helicopter from the soon-to-be-captured U.S. embassy in Saigon, the

United States attempted to create a viable noncommunist state in Vietnam.[12] During that same 25-year period, the U.S. military commitment in Vietnam gradually escalated until by 1968, over one-half million U.S. troops were in Vietnam. During that 25-year period, over 50,000 American lives were lost, and over $200 billion was spent on the war effort. Ultimately, these expenditures and sacrifices proved futile as North Vietnamese forces overran South Vietnam during March and April 1975.

Why had the United States become so deeply involved in Vietnam? What convinced the U.S. leadership that Vietnam was worth so great an outlay of human and material resources? The answers to these questions were complex, and they changed over time. Nevertheless, at the very least, a general outline of U.S. perceptions can be presented here.

The early phases of the United States' involvement in Vietnam occurred during the depths of the East–West Cold War of the 1950s. As has already been seen, U.S. policy-makers viewed the world in bipolar terms during this era; they saw states and other international actors as either members of the Eastern bloc or the Western bloc. Thus, as Ho Chi Minh and his Vietminh continued their struggle against France to end colonial rule in Vietnam, and as Ho's linkages to the Soviet Union and China became more widely known, U.S. policy-makers concluded that the struggle in Vietnam was not between a colonial power and freedom fighters, but rather between anticommunists and communists. Given the way in which U.S. policy-makers looked at the world at this time, no other alternative was possible. In the words of Dwight D. Eisenhower, during the early 1950s the war in Vietnam began to

> assume its true complexion of a struggle between Communism and non-Communist forces rather than one between a colonial power and colonists who were intent on attaining independence.[13]

Although the Vietnam conflict was viewed through bipolar binoculars, it was also seen as part of a larger strategic picture that pitted East against West in geopolitical terms. In 1953, Congressman Walter Judd headed a study commission on Vietnam that issued a report that gave birth to what became another driving force behind U.S. involvement in Vietnam, the so-called domino theory. According to the Judd Commission:

> The area of Indochina is immensely wealthy in rice, rubber, cork, and iron ore. Its position makes it a strategic key to the rest of Southeast Asia. If Indochina should fall, Thailand and Burma would be in extreme danger. Malaya, Singapore, and even Indonesia would become more vulnerable to the Communist power drive. . . .[14]

U.S. Secretary of State John Foster Dulles seconded this outlook, stressing the importance of Indochina as a producer of food, and pointed an accusing finger at the Soviet Union:

> If they [the Soviets] could get this peninsula of Indochina, Siam, Burma, Malaya, they would have what is called the rice bowl of Asia. . . . And you can see that if the Soviet Union had control of the rice bowl of Asia that would be another weapon which would tend to expand their control into Japan and into India.[15]

The U.S. involvement in Vietnam, then, was originally undertaken with the specific purpose of preventing the expansion of Soviet-controlled monolithic communism into the vital geopolitical and resource areas of Southeast Asia, at least as portrayed by U.S. leaders of that era.

It is somewhat ironic by way of comparison to note that as seen from Moscow during the early 1950s, continuance of the Vietminh's resistance was probably detrimental to Soviet interests. Although the U.S.S.R. issued its soon-to-be-familiar condemnation of U.S. military adviser presence in Vietnam and U.S. assistance to the French as manifestations of U.S. imperialism, the Soviets probably had at least two good reasons for urging Ho to stop fighting. First, the U.S. government had recently unveiled its massive retaliation doctrine, in which the United States claimed that it would use nuclear weapons against any aggressor. At the time, this policy was credible; the U.S.S.R. doubtless preferred not to be the target of American nuclear wrath, particularly over an issue so far removed from the U.S.S.R.'s primary interests. Second, the French Assembly was debating the European Defense Community proposal; the Kremlin may have reasoned that if the French Assembly perceived a reduced "communist threat" in Vietnam, it may also perceive a reduced "communist threat" in Europe and oppose the European Defense Community.[16]

In either event, the key point is that the United States perceived the Soviet Union as organizing and directing the Vietminh and formulated its policy on that perception. The Soviet Union, meanwhile, saw the conflict as dangerous to its own interests and acted accordingly. Indeed, at the 1954 Geneva Conference, the U.S.S.R. and China both pressured the Vietminh to settle for less than what they could have won on the battlefield.[17] The first four years of American involvement in Vietnam were thus marked by significant differences in perception between the United States and the Soviet Union; 21 more years of differing perceptions followed.

U.S. involvement in Vietnam continued to be predicated on the necessity of preventing communist expansion, but gradually other rationales were also used. By early 1965, an internal U.S. government memorandum pointed not only to containment, but also to American prestige as a significant reason for upgrading the U.S. presence there:

> The stakes in Vietnam are extremely high. The American investment is very large. . . . The international prestige of the United States and a substantial part of our influence are directly at risk in Vietnam.[18]

Not surprisingly, the Soviet Union had a different view of the growing U.S. involvement, which by March 1965 included ground combat forces. According to the Soviets, the United States had now embarked on a policy of active military suppression of national liberation movements undertaken beneath the cover of U.S. strategic nuclear superiority. To the Soviets, U.S. actions in Vietnam were only a segment of a newly conceived global military doctrine. The Soviet media continually lambasted the "aggressive actions of American imperialism" and predicted that the United States could not win the war.

As the Vietnam War became Americanized between 1965 and 1968, the perceptions of U.S. and Soviet policy-makers changed little. Americans by 1968 realized that communism was no longer monolithic, but the belief persisted that

U.S. presence was needed in Vietnam to prevent communism's expansion. Honor, reliability, and commitment were also put forward as prominent reasons for continued U.S. involvement. Meanwhile, the Soviets pointed to Vietnam as a classic case of capitalist imperialism and U.S. expansionistic aggressiveness.

Within the United States, support had eroded for the U.S. war effort. Antiwar demonstrations and sentiment played a major role in driving Lyndon Johnson from the presidency, and his successor, Richard Nixon, promised "peace with honor." However, evidence suggested that all that Nixon changed was the U.S. government's belief that a military victory was possible. As Henry Kissinger, Nixon's newly appointed assistant for national security affairs, declared, the United States had to find a strategy that was "sustainable with substantially reduced casualties" so that "a genuine indigenous political process" could become established in South Vietnam.[19] That strategy was Vietnamization, the equipping and training of South Vietnamese forces so that they could defend their country for themselves. For U.S. policy-makers, the perception persisted that expansionistic communism had to be contained, and that the credibility of U.S. power around the world demanded success in that effort. Policy had changed, but other than with the realization that communism was not monolithic, governmental perceptions had changed little.

Meanwhile, the Soviet leadership viewed Vietnamization and the U.S. withdrawal as preludes to more subtle U.S. efforts to maintain influence in Vietnam. Growing Soviet military might, the strength and resilience of North Vietnam and

When North Vietnam overran South Vietnam in April 1975, many Americans and pro-American South Vietnamese were hurriedly evacuated by helicopter from the top of buildings in Saigon to U.S. Navy ships waiting offshore.   (UPI/Bettmann Newsphotos.)

the Vietcong, and the U.S. antiwar movement had all combined to force the United States to withdraw from Vietnam, the Soviets believed, but their basic perception of U.S. expansionism had not changed.[20]

When North Vietnamese forces overran South Vietnam two years after the final withdrawal of U.S. forces from Vietnam, the U.S. government had not significantly altered its perception of the conflict in Vietnam itself or of the role of the Soviet Union in that conflict. President Ford, for one, argued that the war ended as it did because the Soviet Union and China had "maintained their commitment," whereas the United States "[had] not." At one time, the Ford administration claimed that the Soviet Union and China had poured $1.7 billion of military aid into North Vietnam in 1974 alone.[21] To the U.S. government, then, communist aggression had won out. The enemy was no longer monolithic, but it was still the same enemy as 25 years earlier.

To the Ford administration, the potential damage to the United States' reputation as a reliable ally was as dangerous a result of the collapse of South Vietnam as the expansion of communism. Indeed, events surrounding the *Mayaguez* ship-seizure incident of May 12–15, 1975, suggested that the United States was as much concerned with shoring up its reputation as a reliable ally as it was with rescuing the ship and its crew. A month before the *Mayaguez* incident, Ford had warned other nations that the tragedy of Vietnam was not "an indication that the American people have lost their will or desire to stand up for freedom any place in the world."[22] The U.S. effort to rescue the *Mayaguez* and its crew appeared to be an effort to prove the point.

Meanwhile, some Soviet views of the Vietnam War and the U.S. role in that war had changed, although most had not. In general, Soviet coverage of the Vietnam War became less frequent and less vitriolic following the withdrawal of U.S. combat units from Vietnam in January 1973. In part, Soviet restraint was the product of Soviet desire to "protect" U.S.-Soviet detente, but in part it was reflective of the internal Soviet debate over whether American "imperialism" had changed.

Proponents of the view that U.S. policy had not changed pointed to continuing U.S. support for South Vietnam and to "the guise of rehabilitation" as proof of their position. Other Soviet authorities believed that "U.S. ruling circles [were taking] a fresh look at their foreign policy strategy" and "actively adapting their policy to the changing international situation." Clearly, perceptual disagreement existed within the U.S.S.R. about the impact of Vietnam on U.S. foreign policy.

However, it was still evident that the United States and the Soviet Union viewed their own actions and the actions of the other in considerably different terms. After 25 years of U.S. involvement in Vietnam, the U.S. government still viewed the U.S.S.R. as aiding and abetting aggression, and itself as acting to defeat that aggression. By contrast, Soviet authorities believed that U.S. aggression had finally been overcome when South Vietnam fell, and that the U.S.S.R. had been instrumental in bringing about that defeat. Although disagreement was apparent in the U.S.S.R. about what impact that defeat would have on U.S. foreign policy, no disagreement existed as to who caused the conflict. Clearly, after 25 years, Soviet and U.S. perceptual outlooks remained fundamentally opposed.

Afghanistan

Different perceptual outlooks between the United States and the U.S.S.R. were equally evident over Afghanistan. To a limited extent, the Vietnam and Afghanistan situations were mirror images of each other; it should come as no surprise that U.S. and Soviet perceptions of Afghanistan were similarly mirror images of what they were in Vietnam.[23]

Even under the Czars, the territory of present-day Afghanistan was a center of concern for Russian foreign policy. Throughout much of the nineteenth century, Russia and Great Britain vied for control of the area, Great Britain seeking to create a buffer territory between Russia and the prized British colony of India, and Russia seeking to move one step closer to attaining a warm-water port. Afghanistan itself was formally created as a kingdom in the early twentieth century by an agreement between Russia and Great Britain.

Afghanistan remained a kingdom until 1973, when a new government under Mohammad Daud took power and exiled the king. Daud continued Afghanistan's nonaligned foreign policy but moved politically closer to the U.S.S.R. However, by late 1977, Afghanistan and the U.S.S.R. had become estranged from each other as Daud accused the Soviets of meddling in Afghanistan's internal affairs. In April 1978, Daud was overthrown by Nur M. Taraki.

The new government sought to undertake socialist-oriented reforms throughout Afghanistan, and concluded a "Treaty of Friendship and Cooperation" with the U.S.S.R. as well. Internal opposition to the reforms grew throughout 1978 and 1979. Claiming that the reforms threatened their traditional Islamic culture and values, Afghan tribesmen declared themselves "Mujahadeen"—fighters for Allah—and attacked government officials and military detachments throughout the country. Afghanistan was in a civil war.

Another change in government took place in Afghanistan in September 1979, with Hafizullah Amin replacing Taraki. Amin sought accommodation with the Mujahadeen at first, but still intended to push forward with a socialist program for Afghanistan and follow a pro-Soviet foreign policy. The civil war worsened, and the survival of the central Afghan government became increasingly more doubtful.

To the Soviet Union, the situation had become grave. A pro-Soviet government that followed Soviet policy preferences on many issues was in danger of being overthrown. The Mujahadeen were avowed enemies of Soviet communism, and with their Islamic heritage had religious and cultural affinity with not only the revolutionary Khomeini government in Iran but also potentially with millions of Muslims in Soviet Central Asia. From the Soviet perspective, the situation demanded drastic action.

In late December 1979, Soviet troops invaded Afghanistan; by early 1980 over 100,000 occupied the country. The Soviets claimed that the Amin government had invited them into Afghanistan, but in the midst of the first wave of intervention, Amin was murdered, allegedly by Soviet troops. Babrak Karmal, a member of the Parcham faction of the Marxist-Leninist Khalq party, was flown in by the U.S.S.R. from Czechoslovakia to become the new Afghan head of state.

Why had the Soviet Union intervened in Afghanistan? A number of answers were possible. First, at least some members of the Soviet hierarchy undoubtedly believed that Afghan socialism had to be defended regardless of cost. To a doctrinaire Soviet Marxist-Leninist, this would have been a strong argument. Second, some Soviet decision-makers probably viewed the Mujahadeen's activities in conjunction with the Iranian revolution, and argued that Soviet national security would be jeopardized if the pro-Soviet Afghan government were overthrown and replaced by a government that could ally itself with Iran. To the more paranoid among the Soviet leaders, such an alliance could not only present the U.S.S.R. with a military threat along its southern borders, but also serve as a center of attraction and possibly alternate loyalty for the millions of Soviet Central Asian Muslims. Thus, a third reason for the Soviet invasion of Afghanistan may have been internal Soviet security. Fourth, Soviet military leaders may have believed that a small controlled war in Afghanistan would be the ideal place to test Soviet weapons and tactics, even as the United States had tested its weapons and tactics in Vietnam. Fifth, for any remaining unreconstructed imperialists in the Soviet leadership, sending Soviet troops into Afghanistan offered an opportunity to expand the Soviet empire and take one more step toward obtaining the long-desired warm-water port. Finally, to Soviet leaders concerned with geostrategic implications, a Soviet military presence in Afghanistan put Soviet air power within striking distance of the vital Strait of Hormuz, through which much of the oil imported by Western Europe, Japan, and the United States passed. From this final perspective, the movement of Soviet forces into Afghanistan presented a strategic threat to the Western alliance with little threat to the U.S.S.R.

Although the Soviet invasion of Afghanistan was based on multiple perceptions, the U.S. government's view of the Soviet action emphasized only two: that the Soviet Union sought to add to the territory under its influence, and that the U.S.S.R. sought to place itself in a position where it could cut off the West's oil imports from the Persian Gulf. With the exception of George Kennan and a few other analysts of Soviet policy, the Soviet action was universally decried as a prime example of Soviet expansionism and aggression. The United States condemned Soviet actions in Afghanistan with many of the same terms that the U.S.S.R. had used to describe U.S. actions in Vietnam less than a decade earlier. On a short-term basis, most of the rest of the world criticized the Soviet invasion of Afghanistan as vehemently as they had criticized the U.S. presence in Vietnam.

In the United States, the reaffirmed perception of an aggressive Soviet Union with hostile intent led to several immediate actions. President Carter withdrew the SALT II treaty from the U.S. Senate, where it had been under debate for ratification; ended the shipment of U.S. grains and high technology to the Soviet Union; and began to organize a boycott of the 1980 Moscow Olympics. Additionally, he speeded the formation of a Rapid Deployment Joint Task Force that by the middle 1980s could project U.S. military power into the Persian Gulf area to protect U.S. interests and counter Soviet expansion. Obviously, the U.S. perception of an aggressive U.S.S.R. had had a policy impact. For all practical purposes, detente was dead.

As the 1980s progressed, the Soviet Union continued its occupation of Afghanistan. At first, neither side changed its perceptions of Afghan affairs or the ongoing occupation. Indeed, actions by each side tended to reinforce previously held outlooks. From the U.S. viewpoint, Soviet carpet-bombing of rebel-held territory in Afghanistan, Soviet use of chemical weapons, Soviet border incursions into Pakistan, and Soviet refusal to differentiate between combatant and noncombatant confirmed what many Americans had previously believed: The U.S.S.R. was a brutal, expansionistic, imperialist power. This perception was affirmed again in May 1986 when a new man loyal to and dependent on Moscow, General Muhammad Najibullah, replaced Karmal as general secretary.

From the Soviet perspective, Afghan events looked different. The Mujahadeen proved a much more difficult adversary than first imagined, and the survival of a "progressive" regime had not yet been assured. The United States, China, Egypt, and others supplied the Mujahadeen through Pakistan in a clear effort to overthrow a progressive government and install an anti-Soviet government on the U.S.S.R.'s own borders. The public U.S. aid commitment of at least $100 million was particularly onerous from the Soviet point of view. Thus, Soviet forces had to defend themselves from attacks by Mujahadeen armed with U.S.-provided weapons even as they sought to defend the progression of various pro-Soviet governments. And attacks against Soviet forces could come from any

The Soviet armed forces pulled out of Afghanistan in 1989 after ten years of military conflict there. Thousands of Soviets and hundreds of thousands of Afghans lost their lives during the war, which continued after the Soviets withdrew.   (Reuters/Bettmann Newsphotos.)

quarter. Thus, it was understandable, the Soviets asserted, that on occasion extreme military steps had to be taken. The revolution—and Soviet forces—had to be defended.

Gradually, however, this Soviet outlook changed. In 1986, speaking at the Twenty-seventh Congress of the Communist Party of the Soviet Union, Mikhail Gorbachev labeled Afghanistan a "bleeding wound." Domestic Soviet opposition to the war grew as the number of Soviet combat casualties mounted. On one occasion, a Moscow TV newscaster even departed from his previously prepared pro-involvement remarks to condemn his country's presence in Afghanistan.

Slowly, then, the perception began to develop in Moscow that the U.S.S.R. must leave Afghanistan. A series of U.S. meetings among Soviet, U.S., Pakistani, United Nations, Mujahadeen, and other officials led to the April 1988 Geneva Agreement on Afghanistan, under which the Soviet Union agreed to withdraw its combat forces by February 15, 1989. And on that date, the last Soviet soldier, the commanding general, crossed by foot from Afghanistan into the Soviet Union.

Despite the Soviet withdrawal, the Afghan civil war raged on. The Soviets sent supplies to the government, and the U.S. sent supplies to the Mujahadeen. Clearly, Soviet and U.S. perceptions of Afghanistan still did not coincide. But both Moscow and Washington expressed pleasure that the U.S.S.R. was no longer in Afghanistan.

This state of affairs continued until 1991, when the two sides finally agreed to stop sending military aid into Afghanistan. A year later, the government that the Soviet Union had installed in Kabul finally fell to the Mujahadeen. But by then, the Soviet government had fallen as well. It was rather ironic that after the U.S.S.R. and the United States had spent so much time, wealth, and energy on Afghanistan, by the time the Mujahadeen won in Afghanistan, neither Moscow nor Washington were particularly interested in Afghan affairs. Finally, the two former antagonists in the Cold War—which itself was now over—saw Afghan affairs in the same way.

NONSTATE ACTORS AND PERCEPTIONS

Not only the governments of states base their actions and policies on the perceptions that they hold. All the international actors we examined in earlier chapters also undertake actions and formulate policies on the basis of their views of the international arena. Each has its own unique perspective, even as each state has its perspective. In some instances, perspectives are influenced by the type of entity that an actor is. In other cases, perspectives are influenced more by the endeavors that the individual actor undertakes. Often, the perceptions that non-state actors hold are significantly different from perceptions that states have. Given the significance of nonstate actors in contemporary international affairs, it is important that some of their perceptions be examined. Unfortunately, given the diversity of outlooks within even the broad categories of international governmental organizations, multinational corporations, nongovernmental organizations, and other international actors, only some very general perceptions can be addressed here.

International Governmental Organizations

As creations of states, IGOs may be expected to share many of the perceptions of their state members. Often this is true. For example, throughout most of its existence, the Warsaw Treaty Organization, through its Political Consultative Committee and other associated bodies, viewed the United States and Western Europe as the major threats to peace, even as its member states did. Similarly, NATO through its Secretariat and the North Atlantic Council pointed to the Soviet Union and Eastern Europe as the greatest dangers to peace, even as its member states did.

In other cases, IGOs develop perceptions that may be considerably different from those of member states. Such perceptions are held primarily by members of the permanent Secretariat of IGOs and the IGOs' operational staffs. Often, these perceptions are internationalist and even globalist in nature as an individual's allegiance to his IGO transcends his allegiance to his country of citizenship. Thus, when Arkady N. Shevchenko defected from the U.S.S.R. in 1978, one of the reasons he gave for his defection was that his native country's foreign policy objectives were not in keeping with the ideals put forward in the United Nations Charter.[24] Similarly in the European Community, members of the European Council on occasion support measures that may have an adverse effect on their home countries but may be helpful for the European Community as a whole. In a sense, IGOs foster the development of international citizens.

However, one must be careful not to overstate the case. Although many IGOs and their secretariats and operational staffs decry the dangers of war presented by parochial state interests and the refusal of wealthy states to provide resources sufficient to alleviate Developing World poverty, their viewpoints rarely have much impact beyond the IGOs with which they are associated. One also must not assume that all IGOs, their secretariats, and staffs have acquired an internationalist perspective. Many—possibly most—have not, and remain wedded to the objectives and interests of the states that created them.

Multinational Corporations

Multinational corporations very clearly start with a single, well-defined objective: attaining profit. It is therefore not surprising that MNCs generally consider actions and policies that enhance their profitability as desirable and actions and policies that detract from or complicate their profitability as undesirable. Other factors also determine the shape of the perceptual lenses through which MNCs view the world, but profitability is invariably the dominant determinant.[25]

As we saw in our discussion of the MNCs as international actors, the corporate directorships of MNCs often consider states to be impediments to their operations. With globalist outlooks, MNCs' leaderships maintain that their activities will lead to peace, prosperity, and eventually a more equitable distribution of global wealth. The international mobility of capital and technology controlled by MNCs will benefit all humanity, defenders of MNCs argue, and any actor, whether it be a state or not, that hinders that flow is both shortsighted and wrong.

There are exceptions to this outlook. Smaller MNCs seek government support, defense-related MNCs recognize the necessity for government regulation of exports, and MNCs whose foreign subsidiaries are threatened by expropriation or terrorism desire state protection. Some MNCs emphasize social responsibility; others do not. In general, however, MNCs conclude that the path to world peace is world trade. And that, of course, brings profit.

Nongovernmental Organizations and Other Nonstate Actors

The perceptual outlooks of NGOs and other nonstate actors are as varied as the NGOs and other actors themselves. Given the vastly different objectives, frames of references, values, and other presuppositions and experiences that these actors have, this is to be expected.

For obvious reasons, individuals hold the most diversified perceptions. Little can be or need be said about individual percepts. To paraphrase Bertrand Russell, no method exists by which the many individuals who participate in international affairs can share perceptions. Individual perceptions are widely scattered and often at odds with each other.

In contrast, ethnic/national liberation organizations usually perceive a common category of enemy, either a local government that is believed to be too closely tied to an external interest or an external colonial power that is considered oppressive. In general terms, ethnic/national liberation organizations seek friends and allies where they can find them. The Irish Republican Army, for example, accepts support from U.S. citizens of Irish descent as well as from Libya, even though it is clear that U.S. citizens and Libyans agree on little else. Similarly, UNITA, one of the Angolan national liberation movements, willingly accepted aid from South Africa, a government with which UNITA had nothing in common. For the ethnic/national liberation organization, the drive for national independence renders all other issues of marginal importance. It is therefore not surprising that from the vantage point of an ethnic/national liberation organization, any international actor that will extend military aid and/or diplomatic support is usually a friend.

The perceptions of terrorist organizations and groups may be categorized in two ways. First, terrorists recognize that they are incapable of effecting the changes they desire, given the prevailing social climate at the time they undertake their terrorist activity. Resort to terror is thus a method to maximize what may otherwise be a limited ability to affect events. Terrorists may therefore be said to recognize the limits of their own powers. Second, terrorists more often than not have a well-defined target that they are seeking to destroy. It may be the prevailing social system, as in the case of the Red Brigade or the Bader-Meinhof Gang, which sought to undermine the capitalist system in Europe, or it may be a single individual or institution, as in the case of Mehmet Ali Agca's attempt to assassinate Pope John Paul II.[26] Again, as cautioned in Chapter 5, it should be stressed that because of differing perceptual vantage points, a group or organization that one observer defines as "terrorist" may be termed a "national liberation movement" by another observer. This point does not refer to the perceptions held by terrorists themselves, but rather to the perceptions of those who seek to define terrorism and terrorists.

The perceptions of transnational religious movements or groups and transnational political parties or movements may be discussed together. All, to varying

extents, believe that the religious or ideological outlooks that they hold have widespread applicability transcending established national boundaries. Jesus' disciples were instructed to go forward and teach all nations; Muhammad's followers were told to win converts to the true way. Marx and Engels asked the workers of the world to unite; Mao called for the peasants of the world to rise up and surround the cities. The perceptual outlook of many less-renowned religious movements and political parties are similarly internationalist in content.

Again, however, the degree of internationalist outlook must not be overstated. In many states once ruled by communist governments, local customs and interests colored and transformed what was a universalist political ideology. Similarly, religion has more than once been used by states for their own purposes. The European religious wars of the sixteenth and seventeenth centuries were ample proof that even within a universalist religion, disagreement may exist and flourish, sometimes with tragic consequences.

It should also be stressed that transnational religions and political movements and groups have also found it possible to reach accommodation with national purposes of states. In reaching such an accommodation, an internationalist outlook on some questions may become captive to a more nationally oriented outlook. Communism and Christianity offer poignant examples. In Poland, for instance, the Catholic church and the communist government coexisted for four decades despite the fact that their respective religious teachings and ideological preachments mandated hostility between the two. Tension existed, but both Christians and communists perceived a necessity to coexist on the national level despite their respective teachings about the other on the transnational level. Similarly, in 1989 Pope John Paul II and Soviet leader Mikhail Gorbachev found it possible to meet and work out an accommodation between Vatican City and the Soviet Union.

Nongovernmental organizations are also on occasion caught between national objectives and internationalist outlooks. During the 1982 effort by the International Red Cross to accelerate aid shipments to the victims of tropical storms in Nicaragua, the Soviet Red Cross actively participated despite the fact that the Soviet government and the Nicaraguan governments sought to minimize the role of the Red Cross in disaster relief. (Both preferred government-to-government relief efforts.) Thus, the Soviet Red Cross in fulfilling what it perceived to be its internationalist duty complicated the policy of its own government. Its view of the world was somewhat different from that of the Soviet government. But following the disastrous December 1988 earthquake in Armenia, the Soviet Red Cross and the Soviet government worked together to deliver domestic and international assistance to the unfortunate earthquake victims.

Each nonstate actor, then, views the world somewhat differently. Some of the actors may have similar views or even identical views on a particular situation or issue, or even on a number of situations or issues, but inevitably differences of perception exist. Because states still predominate as international actors despite the challenges to their preeminence put forward by other actors, we will spend the remaining chapters of this framework examining in detail the perceptions of international relations held by several major and a few minor states. As we will see, in some cases perceptions are so different that it is difficult to believe that the same issue, event, or actor is being described.

KEY TERMS AND CONCEPTS

value
belief
cognition
diversity of perceptions

alternate perceptions of Vietnam
alternate perceptions of
   Afghanistan
perceptions of nonstate actors

NOTES

1. Kenneth E. Boulding, "National Images and International Systems," in William D. Coplin and Charles W. Kegley, Jr. (eds.), *Analyzing International Relations* (New York: Praeger, 1975), pp. 347–360; Robert Jervis, *The Logic of Images in International Relations* (Princeton, N.J.: Princeton University Press, 1970); K. J. Holsti, *International Politics: A Framework for Analysis* (Englewood Cliffs, NJ: Prentice-Hall, 1967); Anatol Rapaport, *The Big Two: Soviet-American Perceptions of Foreign Policy* (New York: Pegasus, 1971); Richard C. Snyder et al., *Foreign Policy Decision-Making: An Approach to the Study of International Politics* (New York: The Free Press, 1962); and John Stoessinger, *Nations in Darkness: China, Russia, America* (New York: Random House, 1990).

2. Bertrand Russell, *Human Knowledge: Its Scope and Limits* (New York: Simon & Schuster, 1948), p. 8.

3. Otto Klineberg, *The Human Dimension in International Relations* (New York: Holt, Rinehart and Winston, 1966), pp. 90–92.

4. Ibid., p. 99.

5. Anatol Rapaport, *Fights, Games, and Debates* (Ann Arbor: University of Michigan Press, 1960), p. 258.

6. Holsti, p. 159.

7. Dean G. Pruitt and Richard C. Snyder (eds.), *Theory and Research on the Causes of War* (Englewood Cliffs, NJ: Prentice-Hall, 1969), p. 65.

8. Graham T. Allison, "Conceptual Models and the Cuban Missile Crisis," *American Political Science Review*, Vol. 63 (1969): 689–718; Graham T. Allison, *Essence of Decision: Explaining the Cuban Missile Crisis* (Boston: Little, Brown, 1971); and Richard C. Snyder et al., *Foreign Policy Decision-Making*.

9. See particularly Rapaport, *The Big Two*, and Stoessinger, *Nations in Darkness*.

10. Kenneth Boulding, *The Image* (Ann Arbor: University of Michigan Press, 1956), p. 6.

11. Holsti, p. 158.

12. For a detailed study of Chinese, Soviet, and U.S. perceptions of the American involvement in Vietnam, see Daniel S. Papp, *Vietnam: The View from Moscow, Peking, Washington* (Jefferson, NC: McFarland & Company, 1981).

13. Dwight D. Eisenhower, *Mandate for Change, 1953–56: The White House Years* (Garden City, NY: Doubleday, 1963), p. 167.

14. U.S. Congress, House, Committee on Foreign Affairs, *Report of the Special Study Mission to Pakistan, India, Thailand, Indochina Pursuant to House Resolution 113*, House Report No. 412, 83rd Cong., 1st sess. (Washington: U.S. Government Printing Office, 1953), p. 35.

15. *New York Times*, January 28, 1953.

16. Donald S. Zagoria, *Vietnam Triangle: Moscow, Peking, Hanoi* (New York: Pegasus, 1967), p. 40.

17. U.S. Department of Defense, *United States-Vietnam Relations 1945–1967*, Book 1,

III, D, "The Geneva Accords" (Washington: U.S. Government Printing Office, 1971), p. D9. See also *New York Times*, July 25, 1954.

18. *United States-Vietnam Relations*, Book 4, IV, C, 3, pp. 31–34.

19. Henry A. Kissinger, "The Vietnam Negotiations," *Foreign Affairs*, Vol. 47 (January 1969): 211–234.

20. For the historical evolution of Soviet perceptions of the U.S. involvement in Vietnam, see Papp, pp. 31–48, 59–72, 102–111, 145–158, 188–195, and 207–209.

21. *New York Times*, March 20, 1974; and April 17, 1975.

22. Ibid., April 4, 1975.

23. For just a few of the early articles concerning the Soviet invasion of Afghanistan, see Joseph J. Collins, "The Soviet Invasion of Afghanistan: Methods, Motives, and Ramifications," *Naval War College Review* (November–December 1980), pp. 53–62; Douglas M. Hart, "Low-Intensity Conflict in Afghanistan: The Soviet View," *Survival* (March–April 1982), pp. 61–68; Shirin Tahir-Kheli, "Soviet Fortunes on the Southern Tier: Afghanistan, Iran, and Pakistan," *Naval War College Review* (November–December 1981), pp. 3–13; and J. Valenta, "From Prague to Kabul: The Soviet Style of Invasion," *International Security*, Vol 5 (Fall 1980): 114–141.

24. See *New York Times*, April 11, 1978; April 12, 1978; and April 27, 1978.

25. See Richard J. Barnet and Ronald E. Muller, *Global Reach: The Power of the Multinational Corporations* (New York: Simon & Schuster, 1974).

26. *New York Times*, May 14–25, 1981.

CHAPTER 11

The United States' Outlook

- What are the roots of the U.S. self-image?
- How do U.S. citizens view their country?
- How do U.S. citizens view the rest of the world?
- What factors influence U.S. citizens' views of themselves and the rest of the world?

Throughout their history, U.S. citizens have believed that the United States was different from other states. Immodestly describing their country as the world's "first new nation," U.S. politicians, statesmen, writers, poets—indeed, men and women from every walk of life—have viewed the United States as a country with a special destiny, a sense of mission. Thomas Jefferson called the United States "the last best hope of mankind" and a "barrier against the returns of ignorance and barbarism." Alexander Hamilton, who agreed with Jefferson on little else, predicted that the American Revolution would force Europe to make "inquiries which may shake it to its deepest foundations." As early as 1782, Benjamin Franklin declared that the creation of the United States and the political liberties found within it would not only "make that people happy," but would also "have some effect in diminishing the misery of those, who in other parts of the world groan under despotism, by rendering its more circumspect, and inducing it to govern with a lighter hand." Three years later, John Adams predicted an even more outstanding future, declaring that the United States was "destined beyond a doubt to be the greatest power on earth."

Writers and poets waxed as eloquent as politicians and statesmen in praising the self-proclaimed "first new nation." Ralph Waldo Emerson viewed the formation of the United States as "a last effort of the Divine Providence in behalf of the human race," and Herman Melville considered his countrymen a "peculiar, chosen people, the Israel of our times; we bear the ark of the liberties of the world." The poet Walt Whitman boldly described his assessment of how he believed the rest of the human race viewed the United States:

Thou, too, sail on, O Ship of State!
Sail on, O Union, strong and great!
Humanity with all its fears,
With all the hopes of future years
Is hanging breathless on thy fate!

What was the American mission? Although American interpretations of the specifics of that mission have changed over time, it is instructive to compare Thomas Jefferson's view of the American mission with Harry Truman's view of that mission. To Jefferson, the American mission was "to consecrate a sanctuary for those whom the misrule of Europe may compel to seek happiness in other climes. This refuge once known will produce reaction on the happiness even of those who remain there." A century and a half later, Truman declared in his Truman Doctrine speech that "the free peoples of the world look to us for support in maintaining their freedoms. . . . Great responsibilities have been placed upon us by the swift movement of events."[1] One hundred fifty years had passed, but the sense of mission remained strong.

In a subtle respect, however, the mission had changed. Whereas for the first century and a half of its existence the United States had seen its mission primarily to serve as an example for those who fought for and sought political freedoms, the years following World War II saw the United States adopt a more internationalist role in its efforts to support and aid foreign states and individuals who desired political freedom as defined in the United States.

Despite this altered sense of mission, the American self-image changed little. Most Americans still viewed their country as preferring isolationism rather than internationalism or interventionism, although they recognized that the international situation mandated a more activist foreign policy. Most Americans also believed that their country was on the side of liberty and justice, even as they believed it had always been. Thus, even while America's role in the post–World War II world was expanding and changing, deep-seated perceptions that Americans held about the role and purpose of the United States in international affairs remained relatively constant.

THE ROOTS OF THE U.S. SELF-IMAGE

Any nation's views of its own role and place in the international arena is the product of numerous factors. Even so, it is often possible to isolate the most important factors that influence a nation's image of itself. Through most of U.S. history, at least until World War II, the most important factors influencing the United States' self-image were isolationism, morality, and pragmatism.

Isolationism

Traditionally, the United States has not sought close alignment with other states, nor has it sought to intervene in the political affairs of other states. The causes of this preference for isolation were geographical, emotional, and psychological. Geographically, North America was separated from Europe by a vast ocean that took weeks and even months to cross. Little immediate threat of invasion from Canada or Mexico existed, and the reality of a broad and expanding frontier gave the United States the opportunity to absorb immigrants disaffected with their old lives in Europe and to enhance its own size and strength without challenging the interests of most European states. In short, in a political and diplomatic sense, the United States believed it did not need Europe.

Emotional and psychological isolation went hand in hand with geographic isolation. As "the last best hope of mankind," the United States consciously sought to develop a society devoid of the feudalistic baggage of Europe. With a population of immigrants who had fled the religious, social, and economic big-otry of Europe, the United States developed a new style of government where power was shared among three branches, where church was separated from state, where the worth of individual human beings was equally valued, and where a social contract of justice was declared to exist between governed and government. Even if these ideals were sometimes overlooked and ignored, they were ideals significantly different from those espoused in most of the states of the Old World.

American isolationism, then, was a policy born out of geographic reality and emotional and psychological experience. In his Farewell Address, George Washington set the course that guided most of the United States' pre–World War II foreign policy:

> Europe has a set of primary interests, which to us have none, or a very remote rela-tion. Hence she must be engaged in frequent controversies, the causes of which are essentially foreign to our concerns. . . . Our detached and distant situation invites and enables us to pursue a different course. . . . Why forego the advantages of so peculiar a situation? Why quit our own to stand upon foreign ground? Why, by intertwining our destiny with that of any part of Europe, entangle our peace and prosperity in the toils of European Ambition, Rivalship, Interest, Humour, or Caprice?[2]

U.S. isolationism was also the product of a growing U.S. superiority complex. Although the new Republic was neither a military nor economic match for any of the established European powers, it considered its ideals and its forms of govern-ment far superior to any of its European counterparts. Americans would lead by example and develop their continent to a degree unparalleled elsewhere in the world. A foreign policy of isolationism not only allowed the United States to con-centrate on its own domestic growth, but also permitted Americans to develop their own sense of uniqueness.

Isolationism, became a habit of mind as much as a policy reality. Throughout the nineteenth century, U.S. citizens viewed their country as essentially isolation-ist. Even during the early twentieth century, they advocated isolationism, and generally believed the United States followed such a policy course. Woodrow Wilson was reelected in 1916 under the slogan, "He kept us out of war." Although the argument may be made that the United States, even while at peace, sided more and more with the Allies, the United States succeeded in avoiding active involvement in World War I for two and a half years. World War II was much the same; it broke out in Europe in September 1939, but the United States did not become a combatant until December 1941, fully 27 months after the conflict began. Again, the United States aided particularly Great Britain during that period, but it was clear that the United States pursued a careful path in its foreign policy vis-à-vis the combatants. The tradition of U.S. isolation remained a perceptual reality.

Moralism

Throughout the century and a half of perceived U.S. isolation, the United States in fact actively undertook many international endeavors. U.S. international trade and commercial activity increased throughout the nineteenth and early twentieth centuries, but was rarely regarded as a departure from isolationism. Rather, it was viewed as a logical and natural extension of free enterprise, and therefore beyond the purview of government except for tariff and embargo considerations. The United States' westward expansion was similarly rarely regarded as a departure from isolationism. The doctrine of manifest destiny combined very neatly with the U.S. sense of mission to dictate that the United States should expand across the continent. The expansion was achieved through purchases and military conquests. In all cases, however, U.S. actions were rationalized as being within the U.S. mission. It also helped, of course, that most of the military conquests were in lands inhabited by "uncivilized" Indians.

By the end of the nineteenth century, however, American eyes began to search for trade markets, for foreign sites for naval bases to protect trading lanes, and in the eyes of some, for empire. Manifest destiny could not rationalize the United States' increasingly interventionist actions in Mexico, Central America, and the Caribbean. An answer to the paradox of the reality of increasing U.S. intervention and the self-perception of U.S. support for liberty and justice was that interventions were undertaken in the name of liberty and justice. Instead of spreading its ideals and values by example, the United States would spread them by intervention.

The moral imperative for abandoning isolation was not a new phenomenon in American history. It had been invoked in 1801 to send a U.S. naval squadron to the Mediterranean when the Barbary states persisted in capturing U.S. merchant vessels, in 1812 when British warships impressed American seamen, and in 1846 when the Mexican government refused to acknowledge Texas' desire to break away from Mexico and join the United States. In 1898, however, the moral imperative was used for the first time to rationalize U.S. efforts to expand its influence in territory outside continental North America. The Spanish-American War of 1898 was thus something more than "a splendid little war," as U.S. Secretary of State John Hay called it. It was a significant watershed in U.S. foreign policy. Even so, the entire Spanish-American War and the spoils that the United States acquired from the war, including the Philippines, were explained in moralistic terms. McKinley, speaking in Cedar Rapids, Iowa, posited that "we accepted war for humanity. We can accept no terms of peace which shall not be in the interests of humanity."[3]

Morality had become a watchword for intervention. Throughout the McKinley, Roosevelt, Taft, and Wilson administrations, the morality of U.S. inter-

ventions in the Philippines, China, Central America, Mexico, and the Caribbean
was seldom questioned. Theodore Roosevelt, fearing European intervention in
Latin America and the Caribbean, put forward the so-called Roosevelt Corollary
to the Monroe Doctrine in May 1904, which linked morality, finance, and U.S.
interests:

> If a nation shows that it knows how to act with decency in industrial and political mat-
> ters, if it keeps order and pays its obligations, then it need fear no interference from
> the United States. Brutal wrong-doing, or an impotence which results in a general
> loosening of the ties of civilized society, may finally require intervention by some civi-
> lized nation, and in the Western Hemisphere the United States might act as a police-
> man, at least in the Caribbean region.[4]

Thirteen years later, President Woodrow Wilson couched U.S. entry into
World War I in similarly moralistic terms, declaring that the United States was
fighting to "make the world safe for democracy" in "a war to end all wars." Near
the conclusion of the war, Wilson also unveiled his "Fourteen Points," in which
he appealed for open diplomacy, self-determination, freedom of the seas, arms
reductions, and the League of Nations, a new intergovernmental organization
that would guarantee peace through collective security. Never before had the
U.S. mission so occupied the center stage of international affairs, and seldom
before had U.S. moralism in foreign policy been better represented.

Moralism, then, has been a dominant factor in U.S. foreign policy that both
justified the American sense of mission and legitimized interventionist behavior.
Whereas the British patriot would say, "my country right or wrong," the U.S.
patriot would say, "my country because it is right." From the viewpoint of most
U.S. citizens in the pre–World War II era, U.S. morality in international affairs
was a given, and liberty and justice were part of that morality.

Pragmatism

Although U.S. citizens prefer to couch their foreign policy in moralistic terms,
they also on occasion admit to an underlying pragmatism. A brief survey of the
history of U.S. foreign policy reveals numerous examples of pragmatic national
behavior.

During the last decade of the eighteenth century and first decade of the
nineteenth, U.S. businessmen and traders sought and found profit by selling to
all sides in the Napoleonic wars that raged across Europe. Only when Great
Britain and France interfered with that trade did the United States argue that
moral issues were involved. Jefferson's original solution to British/French interference, the embargo of 1807, proved a disaster for U.S. trading interests.
Jefferson argued for the embargo, which barred U.S. ships from entering any
foreign port, by saying that U.S. commerce was so valuable to Europeans that
"they will be glad to purchase it when the only price we ask is to do us justice."
Especially in the Northeast, Americans ignored the embargo, concluding that the
economic impact of the embargo was worse than either impressment or ship
seizures.

The embargo was removed two years after it was passed and replaced by the marginally effective Nonintercourse Act that banned exports to and imports from Great Britain and France. Impressment and ship seizure remained serious problems and eventually led to public agitation for and Congressional support of war against Great Britain. Westerners, however, seized on the issues for another purpose. Despite their own limited interest in maritime matters, they realized that impressment and seizure could be converted into issues that would legitimize territorial acquisitions from Great Britain in Canada and the West. The War of 1812, then, was not fought over the morality of impressment and seizure alone. It was also a war fought for pragmatic causes of territorial acquisition.

The nineteenth century is replete with other examples of U.S. pragmatism. Americans remember the Barbary War of 1801 as a series of naval encounters that, in a moral sense, were undertaken because "Americans don't pay bribes." They forget that in a pragmatic sense, payments were made to the Barbary states until 1816, although at a much reduced rate. Similarly, they remember that the United States went to war with Mexico in 1846 to defend the U.S. territorial claims in Texas. They forget that acquiring Mexican territory was also part of the war's objectives. Even the Civil War, fought in U.S. folklore for the moral issue of ending slavery, had as its primary objective, as far as Lincoln was concerned, the maintenance of the Union.

The twentieth century also contains numerous instances of pragmatic U.S. foreign policy behavior. The United States may have avoided the first three years of World War I because of its abhorrence of war, but its businesses profited handsomely during those years of American peace and European war. They also found it acceptable and profitable to aid Hitler's industrialization program during the 1930s while the U.S. government looked on quietly. Numerous U.S. interventions in the Caribbean throughout the first three decades of this century were explained in moral terms that smacked of the pragmatic thought that it was better for the United States to intervene than anyone else.

The competing and complementary themes of pragmatism and moralism in U.S. foreign policy gave rise to a major debate in American intellectual circles following World War II concerning the causes of the Cold War. Traditionalists emphasized U.S. morality in their interpretations of the Cold War's origins. As the dominant school of interpretation, they stressed the justness and propriety of U.S. actions, and the obverse of Soviet actions. Conversely, revisionists stressed the pragmatic nature of the United States' postwar actions. Observing that the postwar settlement permitted U.S. economic and military interests to expand throughout the world, revisionists concluded that the Cold War's inception was a product of the United States' pursuit of its own pragmatic interests.

THE UNITED STATES AS A SUPERPOWER: THE U.S. SELF-IMAGE UNTIL VIETNAM, 1945–1969

Obviously, times have changed considerably since before World War II, and they have changed even more in the years since then. In 1939, the United States remained isolated and at peace as Europe exploded in war. In 1945, the U.S. was hailed throughout most of the world as the major contributor to the defeat of the fascist powers in World War II. And fewer than 25 years after that, American youth were marching on Washington condemning their country as an interventionist power that knew no morality save that of military might. What had happened? What had become of the self-perception of isolationism and morality?

The answers to those questions are complex and must be approached from several directions. Again, however, it is possible to isolate three factors that led to a changed self-image of the U.S. role and purpose in the world. The fundamental morality of the U.S. position in the East–West conflict and the necessity for U.S. economic and military strength were both unquestioned during the 1945–1969 era, as was the pragmatic necessity of occasionally supporting governments that were not quite up to U.S. ideals. By the end of the 1960s, however, these three core elements of U.S. foreign policy had been thrown open to question.

The United States in the East–West Conflict

World War II ended with U.S. fighting forces spread across the world. Never before had one state had the ability to project so great a power into nearly every corner of the globe. To Americans, the United States—and the United States alone—had brought victory to the Allies. The U.S. Air Force and Navy were second to none, and only the Soviet Army equaled the U.S. Army. The United States also had a nuclear monopoly. The era of the global superpower had arrived, and the United States, without consciously seeking the position, had become that superpower.

The United States' ability to project global military power may or may not have implied that it had the desire to do so. Deep differences of opinion exist even today among the most informed analysts about the actual intent of U.S. policy at the end of World War II. Some stress continued isolationism and point to the significant reduction of U.S. conventional forces and the rapid withdrawal of U.S. forces from Europe as proof that the United States intended to return to isolationism. Others stress morality and point to U.S. insistence on the establishment of the United Nations as proof that the United States did not seek a wider role in international politics. Still others emphasize U.S. pragmatism, observing that with nuclear weapons the United States did not need a large conventional armed force and that with its highly productive economic base, it could exert its economic presence wherever it desired without regular reliance on military power.

U.S. hopes for peace, prosperity, and security were not easily realized as the cooperative relationship that existed during World War II between the United States and Great Britain on the one hand and the Soviet Union on the other became increasingly strained following the war. The issues were numerous: the Soviet creation of communist governments in Eastern Europe; fear of communist subversion in France and Italy; Soviet pressures on Turkey; communist-led revolution in Greece, Malaya, the Philippines, and Indochina; and resurgence of the communist-Kuomintang struggle in China. Some Americans concluded that

March 12, 1947—President Truman delivers the Truman Doctrine speech, and the United States adopts a new activist foreign policy. (UPI/Bettmann.)

many of these issues were based on local concerns and directed by indigenous peoples. Most concluded that the Soviet Union sought unlimited expansion and global domination.

According to the latter viewpoint, Soviet expansionism and aggression had to be contained and the free countries of the West had to be protected. Once again, U.S. moralism would be called upon. Once again, the United States would fight on the side of liberty and justice against dictatorship and oppression. As Truman said in his March 12, 1947, **Truman Doctrine** address:

> I believe that it must be the policy of the United States to support peoples who are resisting attempted subjugation by armed minorities or by outside pressures.
>
> I believe that we must assist free peoples to work out their own destinies in their own ways.[5]

The policy of **containment** was closely tied to the Truman Doctrine and the dominant American view of an expansionistic Soviet Union. According to the policy of containment, the United States would apply "counterforce" wherever the Soviet Union applied pressure. As postulated by George Kennan in his famous "X" article, "The Sources of Soviet Conduct," U.S. policy could successfully counter Soviet aggressiveness:

> The Soviet pressure against the free institutions of the Western World is something that can be contained by the adroit and vigilant application of counterforce at a series

of constantly shifting geographical and political points, corresponding to the shifts and maneuvers of Soviet policy.[6]

Clearly, such a policy necessitated the abandonment of isolationism and the maintenance of U.S. global presence. It also became the target of criticism from many positions on the U.S. political spectrum. The political left argued that containment worsened the threat of war and that U.S.-Soviet negotiations could bring about amity between the two former allies. Conversely, one segment of the political right argued that by abandoning isolationism and seeking to encircle the Soviet Union, a Soviet-American arms race was inevitable and war probable. Other leading conservative thinkers criticized containment because it "condemned half the world" to live under communist totalitarianism.

Containment was criticized as a policy, but its fundamental philosophical underpinning, that the United States was defending morality, political liberty, and democracy, was rarely questioned by any responsible spokesperson. The U.S. mission in the postwar world became anticommunism, and for 25 years containment was the policy through which that mission was pursued. On occasion, containment dictated that the United States might find it necessary to support dictatorial regimes, but even this could be accepted by the pragmatic side of U.S. policy. The greatest danger was communism.

In the East–West conflict, then, most U.S. citizens pictured the United States as a morally correct defender of liberty and justice, acting pragmatically when necessary but always with restraint to prevent communist expansion. The traditional American view of the United States as an isolationist country had been for the most part abandoned, but few questioned the continuity of U.S. morality or the necessity of occasional pragmatism.

Then came **Vietnam**. Until the middle 1960s, few Americans were either aware of the growing U.S. involvement there or questioned the fundamental morality of that presence. The U.S. presence in Vietnam, as elsewhere, was justified by the necessity to contain communism. But as American deaths in Vietnam mounted, as costs grew greater, and as violence escalated and destruction worsened, increasing numbers of people asked questions that they had rarely asked about their country's foreign policy and its role in the East–West conflict. Was the United States on the side of justice in Vietnam, or had it simply replaced the French there as a colonial power? Was the United States pursuing a respectable and honorable objective with dishonorable and unjustified means? How much killing and how great a cost would the United States bear to prevent the expansion of communism? More fundamentally, was communism still the enemy it had been during the preceding 25 years?

Increasingly, U.S. citizens became less persuaded that their mission in Vietnam was by definition moral or that communism was by definition a dangerous enemy. In addition, the realization that American minorities themselves had been suppressed and exploited within the United States further challenged the legitimacy of the moral crusade against communism. Few Americans altered their view of the Soviet Union to the extent that the U.S.S.R. was viewed as "in the right," but many altered their view of the United States itself. How could a country on the side of liberty and justice allow suppression and exploitation to occur within? The question was difficult to answer. By 1970, Americans were not as sure of their moral superiority as they had once been.[7]

The Growth of Military Might and Economic Strength

U.S. citizens not only viewed their cause as just throughout the Cold War, but also recognized the necessity of maintaining strong military forces throughout the world to implement containment. Whereas before World War II U.S. armed forces had always been small during times of peace, the demands of postwar U.S. commitments led to a rejection of the traditional small peacetime military. One way to compare the prewar U.S. military establishment with its postwar counterpart is through military expenditures. During the middle 1930s, U.S. expenditures on the Department of War averaged about $300 million per year.[8] Only 20 years later, in 1954, defense expenditures had soared to over $34 billion per year. In 1968, defense expenditures totaled $75 billion, and by the late 1980s, they reached $300 billion per year. These expenditures bought a military force unequaled in world history.

U.S. military power was centered on strategic nuclear weapons. Although Americans feared first a bomber gap and then later a missile gap, U.S. strategic nuclear forces were far superior to those of the Soviet Union until the middle 1960s, when the Soviet Union initiated a massive nuclear arms buildup. By the end of the 1960s, the era of U.S. nuclear superiority had ended and the era of parity had begun.

On the conventional level, U.S. military forces saw open conflict in Korea and Vietnam and engaged in smaller-scale "police actions" in Lebanon and the Dominican Republic. Although many Americans expressed regret that military force had to be used in these situations, general agreement existed that such employment was a necessity. Communism had to be contained.

Just as the Vietnam War swept aside the perception of U.S. moral superiority, so too did the war cause new questions to be asked about the U.S. military. Had the military grown too large and become too influential in determining policy? Did the United States try too often to impose a military solution on a political problem? Was a peacetime draft contrary to American principles? If the communist threat was not as great as once believed, why did so much have to be spent on defense? By 1970, the U.S. military as an institution had lost the trust and confidence of wide segments of the American populace, and the United States' pride in its military prowess had been severely shaken.

The United States' international economic role also expanded tremendously during the post–World War II era. The United States played a key role in shaping the new international economic structures that brought prosperity to much of the Western world, and U.S. domestic production far outstripped the nearest challenger. However, Americans often overlooked the fact that their industrial base was the only one in the world that had escaped the destruction of World War II.

As the only state with a fully functioning industrial economy, the United States occupied the preeminent position in the world's economy. Other nation-states needed U.S. industrial production and technical aid, and the United States obliged their needs. In some cases, as with Western Europe and the Marshall Plan, products and aid were provided through the U.S. government for the purposes of containing communism, economic refurbishment, and humanitarian assistance. In other cases, as with the growth of U.S. exports and the movement of U.S. firms from national to multinational status, products and aid were provided by private interests for the purpose of profit. The dominance of the United States economy in the immediate postwar world is easily illustrated; in 1948, American income was 40.7 percent of the world's total income.[9]

Americans were understandably proud of their economic achievements. Particularly during the early 1960s, the combination of U.S. military might and economic strength renewed the belief of more optimistic American nationalists that the world was on the verge of an American century where the United States' armed forces would provide peace and security through a Pax Americana and where the United States' industrial and technical know-how would provide plenty for all.

The United States' economic preeminence declined during the late 1960s. In part, Vietnam may be blamed. Billions of dollars were squandered there, and Lyndon Johnson's decision to fight the war without reducing domestic consumption fueled inflation that had a debilitating effect on the U.S. economy into the late 1970s. But other causes also existed for the reduction of U.S. economic preeminence. First, other states had rebuilt their industrial bases following the war, often with technologies more advanced than those in U.S. plants. Second, U.S. investment lagged as consumerism began to take its toll. Ever higher levels of current consumption reduced the United States' ability to invest for future production. Thus, by the end of the 1960s, U.S. economic optimism was on the wane. The "American century" had become the "American decade."[10] Militarily and economically, the United States had no equals, but the euphoric sense of optimism that had marked the U.S. world outlook for much of the 1950s and 1960s had been scarred and tempered.

THE UNITED STATES REASSESSES ITSELF, 1969–1980

The U.S. trauma in Vietnam coincided with change in the American view of a bipolar world. As the 1970s opened, many Americans considered the world to be multipolar. President Richard Nixon posited that the world consisted of five major power centers: the United States, Western Europe, Japan, the Soviet Union, and China. This concept of a multipolar world dominated U.S. foreign policy throughout the 1970s.

A number of changed perceptions led to this changed world view. First, the U.S. government recognized that the communist world was no longer monolithic. The Sino-Soviet dispute had become too heated to be considered a clever ploy to throw the West off guard, and Albania, Romania, and Yugoslavia all also followed their own independent foreign policies. The Soviet Union's invasion of Czechoslovakia in 1968 to end a Czech liberalization effort clearly showed that limits existed as to Soviet willingness to accept independent Eastern European states, but the communist world, or at least the U.S. perception of that world, had changed.

Second, the U.S. government recognized that its allies were developing their own interests that sometimes did not coincide with those of the United States. West Germany initiated *Ostpolitik*, an effort to improve relations with its Eastern European neighbors, on its own initiative, and France withdrew its forces from

NATO for several reasons, not the least of which was French resentment of U.S. preeminence in that organization. Japan by the late 1960s was already a trading rival of the United States.

Third, Americans recognized the limits of their military and economic power. The Vietnam experience and the deteriorating U.S. terms of trade were fundamental causes of this recognition. In addition, the U.S. domestic political climate, again because of Vietnam, had become increasingly less tolerant of the use of military power. Thus, although U.S. military forces remained powerful, new political constraints on their employment existed.

Nixon and Detente

As the first U.S. president to formulate policy in this redefined world, Richard Nixon implemented a pragmatic foreign policy that pushed moralism to the background. Because foreign policy was no longer considered a battle between good and evil, but rather was viewed as a return to the balance of power politics of earlier eras, the United States could negotiate with former enemies and act on the basis of pragmatic national interest rather than moralistic ideological claims.[11]

The most pressing order of business for Nixon was Vietnam. Having promised to implement a "secret plan" to end the war there, Nixon began his "Vietnamization" program of increased U.S. aid to and training of South Vietnamese military forces. In 1969, he also announced the beginning of U.S. troop withdrawals. Neither the U.S. public nor Congress knew that both Vietnamization and troop withdrawals were undertaken in conjunction with extensive B-52 bombing raids against North Vietnamese forces in Cambodia.[12]

Vietnamization was part of a larger reformulation of U.S. policy known as the Nixon Doctrine. The Nixon Doctrine contained three major precepts:

> The United States will keep all its treaty commitments.
> We shall provide a shield if a nuclear power threatens the freedom of a nation allied with us or of a nation whose survival we consider vital to our security . . .
> In cases involving other types of aggression we shall furnish military and economic assistance when requested and as appropriate. But we shall look to the nation directly threatened to assume the primary responsibility of providing the manpower for its defense.[13]

American troops, then, would no longer be used to buoy up friendly governments. A risk was inherent in this policy, a risk that friendly governments would fall. The United States' new sense of its own limitations made this risk not only worth taking but also necessary to take. On the domestic level, the Nixon Doctrine was also a response to demands that the United States' role as the "world policeman" be curbed.

The Nixonian pragmatism and worldview also had a major effect on U.S. policy toward the Soviet Union and China. From the very first day of his presidency, Nixon sought to improve relations with the U.S.S.R. His policy, he declared, was to move from confrontation to negotiation.[14]

As a president with unimpeachable anticommunist credentials, Nixon was uniquely equipped to do this. Gradually, as the Nixon administration moved through its first few years, the set of policies that was to build the fabric of U.S.-Soviet detente was unveiled. Strategic arms limitation talks and negotiations on reducing military forces in Europe (the "mutual balanced force reduction," or MBFR, talks) were begun. U.S.-Soviet trade and scientific/cultural exchanges were increased. The German border problem was resolved. Summits between Nixon and Soviet leader Brezhnev became frequent. Detente was alive, and in the eyes of some a new era in superpower relations had dawned.

Later events proved them wrong. The Nixon-Brezhnev detente, even as earlier periods of U.S.-Soviet rapprochement, proved finite. Nevertheless, Nixon's worldview and pragmatic outlook made detente a more comprehensive improvement in U.S.-Soviet relations than earlier rapprochements had been. They also permitted him to alter U.S. relations with the People's Republic of China (P.R.C.).

U.S.-Chinese relations had been marked by animosity since the Korean War. During the first 30 months of the Nixon administration, however, Sino-American relations gradually warmed, culminating in Nixon's 1971 announcement that he would visit China in early 1972.

From the Nixon administration's perspective, the United States was playing a careful game of balance of power politics. Sino-Soviet antipathy had made a modicum of friendship with the United States necessary for both the U.S.S.R. and China,[15] and Nixon intended to use that need to establish a U.S. advantage. To Nixon, Sino-Soviet hostility meant that the U.S.S.R. and the P.R.C. each needed friendly relations with the United States more than the United States needed friendly relations with either. Thus, the United States could pursue friendly relations with both, even while simultaneously escalating the bombing of North Vietnam.

Ford, Carter, and the Demise of Detente

Following Nixon's August 1974 resignation from the presidency because of the Watergate affair, Gerald Ford attempted to follow Nixon's basic foreign policy outline. This became an increasingly difficult task as, to more and more Americans, it appeared as if the Soviet Union was bending detente to its own purposes. Henry Kissinger accused the Soviet Union of "breaking the rules of detente," and many Americans agreed.

The Angolan Civil War, which began following Angolan independence from Portugal in November 1975, serves as perhaps the best example to illustrate how much the United States' view of the world—and of itself—had changed since both the height of the Cold War and the height of detente.

For years before receiving independence, Angolans had struggled to oust the Portuguese colonialists. Three separate national liberation movements fought the Portuguese, and following the Portuguese departure, one another. The United States and China provided limited amounts of arms and funds to two of the movements, and the U.S.S.R. provided more substantial amounts of arms and funds to the third, the MPLA. With the Soviet-sponsored introduction of 17,000 Cuban troops in Angola in early 1976, the tide of battle swung in favor of the MPLA.

U.S. policy-makers were in a dilemma. The covert assistance the United States had been supplying the two anti-MPLA movements was meaningless in comparison with the amount of support the Soviets and Cubans provided the MPLA, so Ford and Kissinger requested additional military assistance for the anti-MPLA movements. Congress refused, claiming it feared another Vietnam. Clearly, at least in Congress, the U.S. was no longer the "world's policeman," nor was the expansion of Soviet influence in Angola considered a direct threat to U.S. interests. The old precepts of containment had been discarded.

But what of detente? Although some Americans argued that the Soviet Union and Cuba had only responded to U.S. involvement in Angola, most saw the Soviet action as proof of Soviet expansionism. The voices of those Americans who claimed that detente had been a clever Soviet ruse to throw the West off guard while the U.S.S.R. prepared to strike were correspondingly strengthened. Soviet activity in Angola did not destroy detente, but from the U.S. perspective, Soviet motives behind detente were open to question.

Detente received another blow in early 1978 when the Soviet Union helped deploy 20,000 Cuban troops to Ethiopia. To the United States, the Soviet Union had again expanded its influence in the Developing World through the use of military force.

The final blow to detente was the Soviet invasion of Afghanistan in December 1979. Americans of most political persuasions saw the Soviet action as final proof of Soviet expansionism.[16] The Carter administration believed that the U.S.S.R. because of its presence in Afghanistan now presented a major threat to Western oil interests in the Persian Gulf, and moved to create the Rapid Deployment Joint Task Force to counter the Soviet threat.

From the U.S. perspective, the high hopes of the early 1970s for U.S.-Soviet amity had been dashed. Pessimistic observers concluded that the 1980s would be a decade of renewed Cold War tension generated by Soviet expansionist tendencies. Optimistic observers hoped that a change of government or attitudes in either Moscow or Washington (or both) could reestablish cooperation in the Soviet-American relationship. These hopes and fears could not alter the fundamental fact that as far as most Americans were concerned, detente was dead.

Carter and American Morality

The United States' debacle in Vietnam destroyed the U.S. image of itself as a morally superior nation, and Nixon's belief in the primacy of objective interests over moral principle in foreign policy ran counter to long-standing U.S. rejection of overt power politics. Not surprisingly, then, some U.S. citizens called for a return to principles and morality in U.S. policy. Nixon's Watergate resignation strengthened these calls, as did worsening relations between the United States and the U.S.S.R. during 1975 and 1976. When Jimmy Carter was elected, he promised to restore a morally based U.S. foreign policy.

Carter's original foreign policy agenda was filled with issues that transcended the East–West conflict. Human rights, economic development in and economic justice for the Developing World, and global arms control and arms reductions were three key concepts. The Carter administration promised to shed the United States' obsession with communism and work for a new global order based on liberty, justice, and equity, words and concepts that fitted well with the United States' preferred self-image.

Unfortunately, they proved difficult to implement. From the very beginning, Carter's emphasis on human rights was criticized by some as being a subtle tool with which to attack the Soviet Union, and thus was considered nothing more than another instrument in the United States' anticommunist arsenal. Others criticized Carter's human rights policy as being applied unevenly.[17]

If Carter's human rights policy fell victim to inconsistency, his hope for economic development in and justice for the Developing World was frustrated by a combination of U.S. domestic politics, established economic interests, societal and institutional factors in the Developing World, and lingering perceptions in the United States that problems in the Developing World were created either by Developing World incompetence or Soviet meddling. Although the Carter administration lent a more sympathetic ear to Developing World states' interpretations of the problems that confronted them than had previous U.S. administrations, little changed in U.S. policy toward issues of development and the creation of a new international economic order.

Carter's desires to curtail the flow of weapons on the international arms market and to negotiate arms limitations agreements between the United States and the Soviet Union were also complicated by several factors. After originally linking the U.S. provisions of arms to Developing World countries to their human rights records, Carter inched his way back to a position where arms were provided to other countries on the basis of their relevance to U.S. strategic interests. Carter had discovered that if the United States refused to provide weapons to a particular country, other sources in the East and West would step into the breech. In the area of arms limitations, the Carter administration concluded the SALT II treaty with the U.S.S.R., but questions about its verifiability and possible inequities within it delayed Senate ratification. Finally, it was withdrawn from the Senate, because with the Soviet invasion of Afghanistan, its defeat had become certain. On the conventional level, no Soviet-American agreements were concluded.

Carter's efforts to reintroduce morality and principle into U.S. foreign policy were more effective on the rhetorical level than they were on the practical level. Even if inconsistencies existed in their government's human rights program, Americans could point to its avowal of fair and just principles of human behavior with pride. The U.S. unwillingness to accelerate its economic support of the Developing World was generally regarded in the United States as a justified refusal to give states something for nothing, whereas the failure of Carter's arms control efforts were more often than not attributed to the intransigence of others, particularly the Soviet Union.

THE REAGAN YEARS, 1981–1989

As the 1980s opened, the United States was beginning to overcome its so-called Vietnam hangover. Goaded by the Soviet invasion of Afghanistan, which underlined the perceived Soviet threat, and the capture of U.S. hostages in Iran, which underlined the degree to which the United States' ability to influence world events had eroded, Americans again began to support a more assertive and self-interested role for their country in the international community. Although the Carter administration moved in this direction during the last year of its rule, it was the Reagan administration that defined a new foreign policy that fit this emerging mood of national assertiveness.

Ronald Reagan entered office in January 1981, intent on rebuilding U.S. military strength and implementing a policy of "neocontainment" vis-à-vis the Soviet Union. Similarly, Reagan stressed his belief in the fundamental morality of the U.S. system and U.S. policies. In international economic affairs, Reagan emphasized free trade and the elimination of barriers to trade, and he steadfastly maintained policies that facilitated free trade despite a U.S. trade deficit that grew steadily throughout his presidency. These four precepts—building U.S. military strength, containing perceived Soviet expansionism, emphasizing U.S. morality, and maintaining an open international economic system—were pillars of U.S. policy throughout the Reagan presidency.

Building U.S. Military Strength

As part of his foreign policy, Reagan sought to increase U.S. military strength across the board. At the strategic nuclear level, Reagan proceeded with MX missiles, Trident II submarine-launched ballistic missiles, B-1 bombers, and cruise missiles. He also accelerated programs to improve U.S. ability to command and control nuclear weapons. These strategic nuclear programs were designed to eliminate the "window of vulnerability" that Reagan feared was developing between U.S. and Soviet forces. In Europe, Reagan also moved ahead with the 1979 NATO decision to deploy 108 Pershing II missiles and 464 ground-launched cruise missiles if an agreement could not be reached with the Soviets.[18]

As under previous administrations, the United States also pursued nuclear arms control efforts with the Soviet Union; despite some progress, by mid-1987 no agreement had been reached. Reagan argued that the lack of success stemmed from Soviet intransigence and the complexities of the issues. Critics asserted that the real cause of the lack of progress was U.S. intransigence, especially over the "Star Wars" strategic defense program and the opposition of some administration officials to arms control.[19] However, in late 1987 the United States and the U.S.S.R. reached an agreement to eliminate all intermediate nuclear weapons.

The U.S. military buildup under Reagan proceeded at the conventional level as well. The purpose behind the conventional buildup was both to deter Soviet conventional aggression and to enable the United States to respond better and more quickly to other regional military contingencies. One of the most visible manifestations of the conventional buildup was the effort to build a 600-ship navy. Other aspects of the conventional military buildup included prepositioning more military supplies and equipment overseas in and near areas where they might be needed, buying more aircraft and tanks, improving maintenance of equipment, and increasing the stock of munitions. In addition, the United States maintained its global military presence.

Many of these programs led to debates about national priorities, but none of the programs led to as great a debate as Reagan's proposed "Star Wars" strategic defense program. Formally titled the Strategic Defense Initiative (SDI), "Star Wars" became a major issue of debate almost from the day that Reagan proposed the idea in March 1983.[20]

Nuclear weapons, conventional weapons, and SDI all took money, and the U.S. defense budget grew immensely during the early Reagan years. Table 11–1 shows this growth and also presents U.S. defense spending as a percentage of gross national product and as a percentage of total government expenditures. Many Americans supported the Reagan administration's defense program, but others questioned whether the defense buildup was destroying American economic vitality and whether the United States had misplaced its priorities by emphasizing defense spending and deemphasizing social programs. As a result of these and other questions, the growth of the U.S. defense budget in real terms ended by 1986.

The Reagan administration also showed willingness to use military force. Indeed, the Reagan government used military force more frequently than any U.S. administration since the United States withdrew from Vietnam in 1973. Thus, in 1981, U.S. F–14 fighters shot down two Libyan fighters over the Mediterranean Sea following threatening Libyan statements about attacks against U.S. interests; in 1983, U.S. forces invaded Grenada following a coup in that Caribbean island nation; in 1983 and 1984, U.S. naval guns and aircraft bombarded Syrian and Islamic forces in Lebanon in retaliation for attacks against U.S. reconnaissance aircraft and marine units; from 1981 through 1986, a slow but steady U.S. military buildup proceeded in Central America and the Caribbean to send a message to Nicaragua and to Cuba that the United States did not accept their adventurism in other regional states; in 1985, U.S. fighters intercepted and forced down an Egyptian airliner carrying the terrorists who hijacked the Italian ocean liner *Achille Lauro* and killed an American passenger; in 1986, the United States on two occasions struck against Libyan military targets and terrorist training camps; and in 1987 and 1988, the United States retaliated for Iranian actions in the Persian Gulf.

Most Americans viewed these uses of military force favorably; the United States' pride and sense of purpose in international affairs had been restored, they felt. Others were less sure. Some criticized the Reagan administration as being too willing to use military force, and others pointed out that none of the uses of military force had been undertaken against militarily meaningful opponents. Nevertheless, as far as most Americans were concerned, U.S. military resurgence was a reality.

TABLE 11–1   U.S. Defense Budget Trends, 1965–1990

	1965	1970	1975	1980	1985	1990
Current dollars	49.6	75.5	86.2	139.3	286.7	305.6
% of GNP	7.0	8.0	5.8	5.1	7.5	5.4
% of government expenditures	38.7	39.2	26.0	22.7	30.3	25.5

SOURCE: U.S. Department of Defense statistics.

Containing Soviet Expansionism

Reagan also believed that the United States must act to contain Soviet expansionism in the Developing World. During the 1970s, Reagan believed, the U.S.S.R. had taken advantage of the United States' "Vietnam syndrome," weak U.S. leadership, and growing Soviet military strength to expand its presence and influence in the Developing World. As far as Reagan was concerned, the United States had to counter this Soviet expansionism.

Reagan summed up his attitude toward the Soviet Union in 1981 when he asserted that the Soviets reserved the "right to commit any crime, to lie, to cheat," and had undertaken "the most brazen imperial drive in history" during the 1960s and 1970s. Shortly thereafter, Reagan announced that the Soviet Union was an "evil empire" whose actions and policies had to be countered.

The U.S. military buildup was one aspect of Reagan's containment strategy, but others existed as well. Increasingly during his second term, Reagan took a page out of the Soviet book and began to support insurgencies around the world in their struggles against ruling governments; U.S. support for the Contras in Nicaragua was one case in point. The United States also sent military assistance to other guerrilla movements attempting to overthrow communist or pro-Soviet regimes. Throughout the middle and late 1980s, and in some cases earlier as well, the United States provided military assistance to Jonas Savimbi's UNITA in its effort to overthrow the pro-Soviet MPLA government in Angola; anticommunist forces in Cambodia as they tried to push the Vietnamese out of Cambodia; and most notably the Mujahadeen in Afghanistan in their fight against the Soviets themselves.

To many observers, the United States' active support of anticommunist guerrilla movements around the world combined with the U.S. military build-up and Reagan's vocal criticisms of the U.S.S.R. to create a climate of a new Cold War. Indeed, during the first Reagan administration, U.S.-Soviet relations became increasingly frigid. But in 1985, U.S.-Soviet relations began to improve, and by the end of the Reagan administration they had progressed so much that many analysts and experts speculated that the Cold War had ended once and for all.

Emphasizing U.S. Morality

Few areas of Ronald Reagan's foreign policy created as much polarized debate as his claims that the United States under his administration continued to support human rights as a "principal goal" of U.S. policy.

Critics scoffed. How could the Reagan administration honestly make such claims when it refused to move actively against apartheid in South Africa; when it supported and even caused civil war in Nicaragua; when it considered the Chilean government under Pinochet a friend of the United States; and when it used human rights only as an issue to thwart communism and mobilize opposition to the Soviets? Equally important, why were human rights violations ignored when they occurred in countries friendly with the United States?

Administration supporters responded, asserting that critics missed the sub-
tleties of Reagan's human rights policies. Under the policy of "constructive
engagement" toward South Africa, they claimed, the United States was slowly
pressuring the South African government to end apartheid. In Nicaragua, the
administration argued, it was supporting legitimate freedom fighters against growing communist repression. In Chile, according to the U.S. government, policies
did exist to push Pinochet toward democracy; the U.S. ambassador had even
demonstrated against Pinochet's extremes, it was pointed out. And, Reagan supporters asserted, it was proper to criticize Soviet human rights violations. As for
the criticism that the United States ignored human rights violations when they
occurred in countries friendly with the United States, the Reagan administration
argued that a fundamental difference existed between authoritarian dictatorships
of the right (i.e., those with which the United States was more likely to be friends)
and totalitarian dictatorships of the left (i.e., pro-Soviet and Soviet-style governments). Authoritarian governments could and would change, it was asserted, of
their own volition over time if subtle pressures were applied by the United States.
Totalitarian governments would not.

U.S. morality also meant more than human rights, the Reagan administration
asserted. It meant the fundamental correctness of other U.S. values, including
open elections, freedom of the press and of speech, and private enterprise.
Under Reagan, policies in support of these ends included verbal and some limited economic support for democratically elected governments in South America,
establishing Radio Marti to broadcast into Cuba, and applying pressure on the
World Bank to increase its lending to private businesses instead of national governments.

Other Americans viewed these policies not as proof of U.S. morality, but as
conservative ideology. The battle was joined. Few U.S. citizens disputed that
human rights and morality should be central tenets of U.S. foreign policy, but disagreement existed over what human rights and morality meant, and over how
policies should be implemented to achieve them.

Maintaining an Open International Economic System

The fourth major thrust of the Reagan administration was to create and maintain
an international economic system based on free trade. From Reagan's perspective, such a system carried with it all the benefits of competition. And during the
first Reagan administration, it appeared as if this strategy was working as the U.S.
economy expanded and inflation went down; world economic growth accelerated;
and the debt crisis in Developing World states was contained.

But by the second Reagan administration it became clear that extensive
problems continued as well. The U.S. foreign trade deficit increased, as Table
11–2 shows, and more and more U.S. jobs were lost to foreign competition. The
U.S. Congress on a number of occasions moved to introduce legislation that
would protect U.S. industry and jobs from foreign competition. High U.S. interest rates attracted foreign investment to the United States, by 1985 converting
the country into a net investment deficit country for the first time since World
War I. High interest rates also increased the dollar's value. Between 1980 and

TABLE 11–2 The U.S. Foreign Trade Deficit, in Billions of U.S. Dollars

Year	Imports	Exports	Deficit
1978	186	144	42
1979	222	182	40
1980	257	221	36
1981	273	234	39
1982	255	212	43
1983	270	201	69
1984	341	218	123
1985	353	213	140
1986	387	217	170
1987	410	250	160
1988	447	319	128
1989	475	362	113

SOURCE: 1978–1984: International Monetary Fund, *Direction of Trade Statistics Yearbook 1985*, p. 399; 1985–1989: U.S. Department of Commerce.

1984, the dollar appreciated 60–65 percent against other major currencies. Although interest rates went down from 1984 to 1986, by then large numbers of U.S. firms had already moved overseas where they could buy more and make more for the same cost. Free trade and an open international economic system, it seemed, had its costs as well as its advantages, and most Americans were unsure how to cope with them.[21]

Other potential international economic problems also confronted the Reagan administration. One was continuing U.S. resource dependence. Even though oil prices dropped precipitously during late 1985 and 1986 and somewhat lessened the urgency of the U.S. situation, U.S. resource dependency remained a problem. Table 11–3 illustrates the degree of U.S. dependence on imports of certain key strategic resources.

TABLE 11–3 U.S. Dependence on Foreign Sources of Strategic Nonfuel Minerals, 1987

Mineral	Percentage of Total Use Imported
Aluminum	90
Chromium	80
Cobalt	82
Manganese	98
Nickel	70
Platinum group	90
Tin	75
Titanium	90
Tungsten	65

SOURCE: U.S. Department of Defense, *Military Posture FY 1989* (Washington: U.S. Department of Defense, 1989), p. 13.

One solution to dependence on external resources of nonfuel minerals was to develop stockpiles and substitute materials, but the development of strategic stockpiles was frustrated by congressional hesitancy to provide funds. The Reagan administration's efforts in this regard met with little success in Congress. A second solution, decreasing dependence by developing substitutes, encountered two problems. First, for some materials, no good substitutes existed. Second, for other materials, the price of substitutes was (and is) prohibitively expensive.

Thus, U.S. citizens remained uncomfortable in light of their rather newly developed resource dependence. It was clear, however, that they were not panic-stricken by this situation.

GEORGE BUSH AND THE NEW INTERNATIONAL ORDER

George Bush assumed the U.S. presidency in January 1989, pledging to continue most of the major foreign policy directions of the Reagan years. His policies included maintaining U.S. military strength and global presence, emphasizing U.S. morality, keeping an open international economic system, and containing Soviet expansionism.

However, the rapid pace of change in Eastern Europe and the Soviet Union forced Bush to revise the fourth Reagan priority, containing Soviet expansionism, and raised questions about the continued relevance of maintaining U.S. military strength and global presence at past levels. Even before Bush assumed the presidency, it was clear that the Soviet Union was struggling with serious domestic economic, political, social, and ethnic problems; initiating radical internal reforms; and losing its hold over Eastern Europe.

Bush was therefore faced with a difficult policy dilemma. Given that trends in the Soviet Union and Eastern Europe were moving in directions that the United States preferred, and given that the future course of events in the Soviet Union and Eastern Europe remained uncertain, what policies should the United States put into place to maximize chances that events would continue to unfold in preferred directions without damaging U.S. interests or weakening U.S. security if they did not? In short, Bush's task was to formulate a postcontainment foreign policy toward the U.S.S.R. and Eastern Europe under conditions of immense uncertainty about what would happen in those countries.

At first, Bush proceeded cautiously, along with the rest of the world unsure of where the Gorbachev revolution would eventually lead. But as the Soviet Union became more and more open and posed less and less of a threat to the West, and as Eastern European states overthrew their communist regimes, the United States and the U.S.S.R. forged an increasingly cooperative relationship.

The depth of this this new cooperative relationship was illustrated by the U.S. response to the August 1991 coup in Moscow that threatened to topple the Gorbachev government and its reforms. In stark contrast to the cautious approach that had marked the early Bush approach to the U.S.S.R., the American president quickly and vocally condemned the coup attempt, praised Boris Yeltsin for his courageous stand against the plotters, and supported Gorbachev's return to the Soviet presidency.

Following the failure of the coup, Bush nevertheless faced a dilemma. Should the United States continue to support Gorbachev and the continued existence of the Soviet Union, or should it throw its support to Boris Yeltsin, who sought to dissolve the U.S.S.R.? At first, Bush opted for Gorbachev and the U.S.S.R. However, as events in the Soviet Union in late 1991 rushed onward it became clear that the U.S.S.R. would not survive. The United States switched its support to Yeltsin.

Following the collapse of the Soviet Union, the United States and Yeltsin's Russia formally declared an end to the former U.S.-Russian hostility. Obviously, with the U.S.S.R. gone, containing Soviet expansionism no longer made sense as a U.S. foreign policy objective. And the end of the East–West conflict also raised questions about how much military strength the United States still needed, about what future U.S. policy should be toward Russia, and about the future of the international system. With the Cold War over, how much should the United States cut its defense spending, if at all? How much aid should the United States send to its former enemy to help it survive its economic collapse? With the East–West conflict over, what would the new international order be?

Bush's foreign policy dilemmas were not confined to the Soviet Union and Eastern Europe. Within a year of assuming the presidency, he also had to deal with crises in China, the Philippines, and Panama.

U.S.-Chinese relations began well enough under the Bush administration, with the president traveling to Beijing in February 1989. However, during the following month, riots broke out in Tibet, and the Chinese government sent in troops. Many deaths resulted. In unrelated developments during April and May, Chinese students took to the streets in Beijing and other major Chinese cities, demanding political reform and democracy. Over 100,000 people occupied Beijing's Tiananmen Square. Simultaneously, in May, Mikhail Gorbachev visited China, signaling the end of 30 years of Sino-Soviet estrangement. The Chinese students, still in the streets, lauded Gorbachev for the political reforms he had instituted in the U.S.S.R.

At first, the Chinese government did not respond to the student demonstrations, perhaps fearing that some of the luster would be removed from Gorbachev's visit. The Chinese government appeared indecisive, perhaps even paralyzed. Then in June, just after Gorbachev left, it acted, dispatching troops into Tiananmen Square, killing several thousand students.

The Bush administration had to respond. The United States immediately criticized the Tiananmen assault, and a host of diplomatic, trade, and other contacts were put on hold. Some Americans advocated breaking diplomatic relations with the Beijing government. But on the whole, the U.S. response was surprisingly restrained. In fact, within a month of the Tiananmen assault, Bush secretly dispatched National Security Adviser Brent Scowcroft to Beijing. Throughout the rest of the year, Sino-American relations gradually edged back to where they had been before the Tiananmen massacre. Obviously, despite the revulsion of American citizens, cordial Sino-American relations remained important to the U.S. government.

The crises that developed in the Philippines and Panama were equally perplexing. In the Philippines in November 1989, Corazon Aquino faced the sixth attempt to overthrow her three-year-old government. The United States acted quickly, providing air cover to loyal Philippine military units as they put down the insurrection. Meanwhile, in Panama, the U.S. stalemate with General Manuel Noriega continued. For several years, the United States had attempted to force Noriega out of power, relying primarily on a combination of diplomatic and economic pressures, to no avail. In August 1989, the United States had not responded when dissident Panamanian Defense Force (PDF) members tried to overthrow Noriega. But in December, following a Panamanian declaration that a state of war existed with the United States and the killing by the PDF of an American serviceman, the United States invaded Panama and overthrew Noriega, who took refuge in the Vatican's embassy in Panama City. Despite movement toward a new era in international affairs, military force still had utility.

Other issues confronted the Bush administration that demanded solutions that could not be implemented by the United States alone. The U.S. trade deficit led the list. Although by 1989 the deficit had declined from its 1986 high of $170 million, Americans still bought much more from overseas than they sold. The trade deficit with Japan alone was over $50 billion. U.S.-Japanese trade negotiations continued under Bush even as they had under Reagan, but no quick solutions were in sight.

Developing World debt remained a problem as well. By 1989, Developing World countries owed over a half trillion dollars in debt. The Bush administration proposed several methods to cope with this problem, including Developing World austerity steps, debt refinancing, debt forgiveness, and debt swaps, but again, no quick solutions appeared.

The Bush administration also faced the challenge of formulating a U.S. policy in response to the European Community's single market. While the United States remained a supporter of European economic integration, it also expressed concern that the European single market would be less than open. Problem areas included agriculture, aircraft, and the telecommunications industry.

Amid these foreign policy challenges, yet another major problem erupted in August 1990 when Iraq invaded and occupied Kuwait. Bush—and other leaders throughout the world—saw the Iraqi action as a threat of immense political, military, and economic dimension. The United States—and other states—likened Iraq's invasion to Hitler's 1939 invasion of Poland, when a large powerful country launched an unprovoked attack, and took over a much weaker neighbor. At the same time, the United States and other states feared that the Iraqi action was a precursor to an invasion of Saudi Arabia, which would place Iraq's ruler, Saddam Hussein, in a position to dictate world oil prices.

The United States responded by deploying its own naval, air, and ground forces to Saudi Arabia and surrounding waters; by urging other states to deploy their forces to the region as well; and by leading the call for comprehensive economic sanctions against Iraq. U.S. actions clearly indicated that the U.S. government believed its vital national interests were threatened, and public opinion polls showed that most Americans agreed.

After several months of a massive military buildup called **Operation Desert Shield**, passage by the United Nations of a resolution authorizing the use of force to expel Iraq from Kuwait, and the U.S. Senate's vote to allow American use of its military against Iraq, the Persian Gulf War finally began. For a month, U.S. and other allied aircraft attacked Iraqi military targets and other forces virtually unop-

President George Bush and his wife Barbara visited U.S. troops deployed in the Saudi Arabian desert for Operation Desert Shield in Thanksgiving 1990. Less than two months later, Operation Desert Storm began to expel Iraq from Kuwait. (Sigma.)

posed. Then, the United States Army and the armed forces of other states launched a massive tank attack into Iraq and Kuwait. Within 100 hours, Iraq was defeated. **Operation Desert Storm**, the U.S. name for the war against Iraq, had been an immense success, and Allied forces had suffered relatively few casualties.

With the successful conclusion of the war against Iraq, and the collapse a few months later of the Soviet Union, it was clear that a new era was about to dawn for American foreign policy, and for the international system as well. George Bush was faced with the task of defining what this "new international order," as he termed it, would be.

This was a difficult task. By 1992, the United States had a mixed and multi-faceted foreign policy agenda. Old Cold War issues virtually disappeared, but as the Iraqi invasion of Kuwait, Desert Shield, and Desert Storm showed, there remained a need for the U.S. military. However, what had become more difficult than ever was deciding when to use military force. In Somalia, in 1992 and 1993, the United States, acting under United Nations auspices, used military force to help restore order and distribute food. In the former Yugoslavia, neither the United States nor any other country intervened to stop the "ethnic cleansing" campaign conducted by Serbia against Bosnia.

Meanwhile, as the United States remained mired in an economic slump and continued to run an immense foreign trade deficit, economic issues stayed near the top of the U.S. foreign policy agenda. The United States continued to pressure Japan to open its domestic markets further to foreign imports; expressed its concern that the EC might become a closed market; and attempted to find ways to make American industry more competitive in the global marketplace. In 1992, the United States, Mexico, and Canada also negotiated a **North American Free Trade Agreement** (NAFTA).

Over time, NAFTA promised to become an extremely important economic breakthrough. NAFTA's purpose was to increase trade and improve living standards in the United States, Mexico, and Canada by eliminating all tariffs and other economic and noneconomic barriers to trade between the three countries. But not everyone supported NAFTA. Many feared that U.S. capital would move to Mexico to take advantage of lower labor costs and lower environmental standards there. While NAFTA's U.S. supporters pointed to future growth of American exports under NAFTA as a source of more jobs and more exports, NAFTA's American opponents argued that in the short term, jobs would follow American capital to Mexico, the environment would worsen, and the United States would suffer.

The environment, drugs, and immigration also moved nearer the top of the U.S. foreign policy agenda following the end of the Cold War. In both its foreign and domestic approaches to the environment, the Bush administration recognized that the world's environment was deteriorating, but insisted on caution and additional study before undertaking any action. Arguing that too much emphasis on environmental protection cost jobs and hurt the U.S. and world economies, Bush refused to commit the United States to most of the environmental protection proposals put forward at the 1992 U.N. environmental summit meeting in Rio de Janeiro, Brazil. In fact, the United States more often than not tried to weaken such proposals.

On the drug issue, after first emphasizing the need to stop drug production at the source, the United States in the early 1990s moved to a more balanced three-part antidrug program. First, as earlier, the United States still sought to reduce drug production at its source, particularly by helping Colombia, Bolivia, and Peru in their efforts to reduce cocoa production and combat drug cartels. Second, the United States increased its use of American military, Coast Guard, and Drug Enforcement Agency capabilities to reduce the flow of drugs into the United States. Third, through several domestic programs, the United States tried to reduce demand for drugs within the country.

By 1992, some signs of progress in all three areas existed. Supplies had been reduced, prices had risen, and demand had fallen. Nevertheless, drugs remained an immense U.S. social problem, and critics of the administration's drug policies asserted that it was not paying enough attention to the issue, particularly in programs designed to reduce demand within the country.

Finally, in immigration policy, the United States found itself on the horns of yet another dilemma. For years, the United States had followed a general policy of accepting political refugees into the United States, but discouraging economic refugees. However, in the late 1980s and early 1990s, it became increasingly difficult to differentiate between the two. In addition, the number of people legally and illegally seeking entry to the United States continued to increase as well. The dilemma was simply stated: What should the United States do?

There was no single answer to the question even in the geographical area where the issue was most pressing, Latin America and the Caribbean. For example, large numbers of Mexicans entered the United States illegally each year, most seeking better jobs or to be reunited with family. The United States returned many to Mexico, but many remained in the United States. In comparison, large numbers of Haitians also fled to the United States, especially following the military coup in Haiti in 1991 that overthrew the freely elected government there. Many of the Haitian refugees claimed to be political refugees, but the United States said most were economic refugees, and returned them to Haiti. At the same time, Cuban immigration to the United States continued, even accelerating in 1991 and 1992 as Cuba's domestic economy deteriorated. However, since Fidel Castro and communism still ruled Cuba, Cubans were considered political refugees. They were allowed to remain in the United States.

Meanwhile, the collapse of communism and communist economies in Eastern Europe and the Soviet Union also presented difficult immigration-related issues. The leading question once again was, "Who is a political refugee, and who is an economic refugee?" However, because of geographical distance, this aspect of the immigration question was less pressing for the United States than was the Latin American and Caribbean question.

Clearly, defining the "new international order" and the American role in that order presented significant challenges for the United States. As 1993 began, it was not clear how the United States and the newly elected Clinton administration would respond to those challenges. Domestic economic problems and unexpected foreign policy crises like the Persian Gulf War presented a sobering view of reality. Most U.S. citizens recognized that the world had changed and was continuing to change. But despite having "won" the Cold War, most Americans felt little euphoria.[22]

QUESTIONS FOR BILL CLINTON

In virtually every respect, the world that President Bill Clinton faced when he assumed the presidency in January 1993 was immensely different from the world that George Bush had first faced as president in 1989. Thus, the new Clinton administration had to formulate conceptual approaches, and then specific policies, to cope with the new challenges that confronted the United States. Five conceptual questions appeared most pressing.

1. *Should the Clinton administration concentrate its efforts on solving the United States' own domestic problems, or should it concentrate on the U.S. global role and position?*

To a certain extent, this was an artificial dichotomy. It is only rarely possible in today's world to concentrate on domestic issues to the exclusion of international issues, and vice versa.

Nevertheless, many Americans strongly believed that Clinton had to center his agenda on domestic American problems, even to the exclusion of international issues. Inevitably, scarce national resources and scarce presidential time must be parceled out. As always, competition for resources and time emerge between domestic and foreign issues.

2. *What role should the United States play in the global economy?* There were at least three different answers to this question, and each had its proponents in the new Clinton administration.

Some argued that the United States should worry about its near-term domestic economic problems, and put in place programs and policies to stimulate near-term domestic job creation and economic growth.

Others maintained that despite domestic economic problems, the United States must continue to work for an international free-trade regime. Proponents of this position asserted that the United States must bear near-term and mid-term trade and balance of payments deficits, some of which were the result of unfair foreign trading practices, despite domestic American economic problems.

The third leading outlook argued that the North American Free Trade Agreement was a necessary U.S. and North American response to the European Community and to growing Japanese economic strength in East Asia. This outlook maintained that the EC and a Japanese-led East Asian trading bloc had the potential to place the United States, as well as Canada and Mexico, at a decided international economic disadvantage.

3. *When and under what conditions should the United States intervene in foreign conflicts?* Between the end of World War II and the fall of the Soviet Union, U.S. military intervention overseas usually was tied to the containment of the U.S.S.R. and communism.

But with the Soviet Union gone, this easy benchmark for deciding when to intervene overseas no longer existed. So the Clinton administration was faced instead with the job of further clarifying the task begun by the Bush administra-

Most major U.S. foreign policy decisions early in the Clinton administration were made by Secretary of State Warren Christopher (left), President Bill Clinton (middle), and Secretary of Defense Les Aspin (right).   (AP/Wide World Photos.)

tion: deciding when and under what conditions the United States would intervene militarily overseas.

4. *To what extent should the United States accede to multilateralism in its international activities?* Put differently, this question was simply, "Why should the United States go along with IGOs and NGOs when the U.S. is in the minority on an issue that is before any of these organizations in which it is a member?"

The easy response to this question was that the United States should always act to protect and promote its national interests, aligning its actions and policies with the UN and other IGOs and NGOs when possible, but not allowing those institutions to constrain U.S. actions and policies.

But in reality, this is a difficult problem. The challenge for Clinton was to find ways to make American interests and the interests of the global community coincide, and when this was impossible, to promote U.S. interests without damaging the United States' status in the global community.

5. *When all is said and done, what "new international order" is best for the United States?* Although the Bush administration began the task of clarifying the answer to this question, the answer was far from complete when Bill Clinton took office. Thus, it was left to Clinton and his administration once again to define U.S. interests; to decide whether those interests could best be achieved in a unipolar, regionally oriented, or multipolar world; and to implement policies designed both to promote those interests and help create the type of world in which they could most easily be achieved.

U.S. VIEWS OF THE WORLD: OTHER ACTORS

Policy is only partly based on self-perception. It is also based on the perceptions of others. With this rationale, we now turn to some of the more prominent U.S. outlooks on some of the more significant actors in contemporary international relations. The following section should be read not as a comprehensive description but as a selective sampling of U.S. international perceptions.

Russia and the Soviet Union

Before the Soviet Union's final collapse, U.S. perceptions of the U.S.S.R. ranged widely. During World War II, the early 1970s, and the late 1980s and early 1990s, most Americans viewed the U.S.S.R. favorably. During other periods such as the 1930s, most of the 1950s, and the early 1980s, the Soviet Union was condemned as a "godless atheistic state" or "the evil empire." In the short time that has transpired since Russia and the 14 other former Soviet republics abandoned communism and ended the U.S.S.R.'s existence, most Americans have welcomed the opportunity to develop cordial relations with the newly independent states, but nevertheless remain unsure about what the future holds for Russia and the other former Soviet republics, and for U.S. relations with them.

Until the Soviet collapse, U.S. scholars and policy-makers were split into two major schools of thought about the U.S.S.R. Some scholars and policy-makers saw the Soviet Union bent on global domination and conquest. Advocates of this

school of thought, called the "hard" school, believed that the Soviet Union operated primarily on the dictates of Marxism-Leninism, and sought expanded Soviet
influence and power. According to this school, all Soviet foreign policy behavior,
ranging from Soviet movement into Eastern Europe following World War II to
Soviet foreign policy until the late 1980s, was motivated by this Soviet desire.
Those who accepted the hard-line image of Soviet behavior generally espoused a
U.S. stance of resolute opposition to the U.S.S.R.

At the other extreme of the spectrum were scholars and policy-makers who
believed the Soviet Union acted for legitimate defense purposes in its foreign
policy. These analysts emphasized the history of Western European invasions of
first Russia and then the Soviet Union (1812, 1914, and 1941), the Western intervention in the new Bolshevik state in 1918, and the view that the United States
had to bear most of the blame for post–World War II Soviet-American antipathy.
This perspective, called the "soft" viewpoint, called on the United States to be
understanding of past and present Soviet behavior and to formulate U.S. policy
on the basis of that understanding.

At various points along the spectrum from hard to soft were scholars and
policy-makers who saw Soviet behavior as motivated by varying amounts of ideological offensive and historical defensive purposes. These scholars and policy-
makers advocated that U.S. policy toward the Soviet Union consist of differing
types and sizes of encouragements and sanctions, a sort of "carrot and stick"
approach. The closer an analyst of this mixed outlook was to the "hard" approach,
the more he or she favored sanctions including military power and economic
embargoes to influence Soviet behavior; the closer to the "soft" approach, the
more he or she favored trade, negotiations, and understanding.[23]

In the late 1980s, primarily because of Mikhail Gorbachev's domestic reforms,
the perception that Soviet foreign policy behavior had changed, and a belief that
the Soviet military threat had been reduced, the sharp distinctions between the
extremes of the "hard" and "soft" schools of thought diminished. After some doubt
within the "hard" school about whether Gorbachev's reforms were serious, almost
every U.S. analyst and policy-maker involved with Soviet affairs concluded that the
Soviet leader in fact was attempting to institutionalize radical reform in almost
every area of Soviet policy. By the early 1990s, the "hard" and "soft" schools of
thought found little to disagree on concerning Soviet policies.

The collapse of the Soviet Union in turn led to policy disagreements within
the United States about how much to help Russia and the other newly independent states, and about how much to reduce U.S. defense spending. But almost
without exception, Americans were pleased that they now had the opportunity to
cooperate with Russians and other former Soviet citizens, get to know them better, and perhaps do business with them rather than live in fear of them and their
former country. At the same time, most U.S. citizens were cautious about the
future of U.S.-Russian relations, and relations with the other newly independent
states as well. The major reason for this caution was understandable. For
Americans, as for Russians and other former Soviets as well, the future direction
of the newly independent states remained shrouded in uncertainty. Could the
newly independent states succeed in the democratic and capitalist reforms they
were undertaking, or would the reforms fail? If the reforms failed, what would
happen within Russia and the other states? What impact would this have on U.S.
relations with them? No one knew.

China

Until a few years before Richard Nixon's 1972 trip to China, many in the United States considered China a loyal Soviet satellite actively seeking to spread the communist doctrine. The United States did not recognize the Beijing government as the legal government of China, but rather called Chiang Kai-shek's government on Taiwan the rightful ruler of China. Chiang and his Kuomintang party had governed most of China until 1949, when the Chinese Communist Party under Mao Zedong finally emerged victorious in a decades-old civil war and pushed Chiang and his followers off the Chinese mainland.

Nixon's 1972 visit began a gradual normalization of U.S.-Chinese relations that culminated in the Carter administration's recognition of the Beijing government in 1979. After Nixon's visit, many U.S. citizens viewed China as a de facto ally in the struggle with the U.S.S.R. Indeed, the triangular Sino-Soviet-U.S. relationship was often viewed in the United States by the early 1980s as a relationship in which the United States and the People's Republic of China were balanced against the Soviet Union.

Such a turn of events and change of perception was truly amazing over so short a time for the United States, which up until Nixon's presidency viewed all things communist (except Yugoslavia) with loathing and considered the P.R.C. in particular to be the epitome of communist aggressiveness.

Much of the former American antipathy toward China could be traced directly to the Korean War. Before the Korean War broke out on June 25, 1950, with a North Korean invasion of South Korea, the United States had been mov-

Richard Nixon's 1972 trip to China formally ended over 20 years of U.S.-Chinese hostility. Here, Nixon is greeted by Chinese Premier Zhou Enlai upon Nixon's arrival in China. (Nixon Presidential Papers Project.)

ing slowly toward extending diplomatic recognition to Mao's new government. U.S. forces under UN auspices entered the conflict in Korea, and by October were fighting their way northward toward the Yalu River, North Korea's border with China. In late November, Chinese forces attacked the UN forces and the Korean War assumed an entirely new dimension. The war dragged on for two years, primarily between Chinese and American forces, until an armistice was finally concluded in 1953.

The die had been cast for the next 20 years of Sino-U.S. relations. For 20 years, Beijing and Washington hurled mutual charges of aggression and expansionism at each other. With the exception of sporadic ambassadorial talks in Warsaw, Poland, and negotiations in Panmunjom, Korea, over the Korean armistice, no formal contacts existed between the two countries until Henry Kissinger secretly visited China in 1971 to arrange Nixon's epochal trip one year later.[24] During the period of Sino-American hostility, the United States considered China one of the most aggressive and dangerous states in the world.

Between 1972 and 1989, the U.S. government and the American people came to view China as a useful counter to perceived Soviet expansionism in Asia. Other Americans viewed China as a potential market with over one billion consumers. Many of these Americans tended to forget that even as the United States pursued improved relations with China for its own reasons, so too did China seek improved relations with the United States for its own reasons.

The Chinese government's crackdown and suppression of the student-led democracy movement in China in 1989 had a curious effect on the U.S. government's and the American people's attitude toward China. Although both the government and the people found the Tiananmen Square massacre repugnant, the government, motivated by dictates of state and an awareness that Sino-Soviet relations were improving rapidly, tended to be more willing than the people to return to business as usual with Beijing in the aftermath of the crackdown. Conversely, many U.S. citizens viewed the Chinese government with mistrust and loathing. This apparent split between the U.S. government's policies toward China and the U.S. people's attitude toward the Chinese government continued throughout the Bush presidency. The Clinton administration warned the Chinese government that its human rights record would be closely examined, but for the most part, the Clinton administration continued previous U.S. policies toward China.

Western Europe

The United States has regarded the countries of Western Europe as its closest allies and most important trading partners since the close of World War II. Although these countries are extremely diversified both internally and as a group, many U.S. citizens nevertheless persisted in viewing them as a single regional entity.

Perhaps the best measure of the importance attached to Western Europe by U.S. policy-makers during the immediate post–World War II era was U.S. foreign policy itself; because of a fear that Western Europe would slip behind the Iron Curtain, the United States abandoned its traditional peacetime isolation and initiated the Truman Doctrine and the Marshall Plan in 1947, and two years later entered its first peacetime alliance in history, NATO. Over 40 years later, U.S. views of the importance of Western Europe to the United States' economic and security interests diminished only slightly, although U.S.-European issues of contention multiplied significantly.

U.S. ties with Europe extend beyond economic and military considerations. As most of the United States' population traces its roots to European stock, ethnic, social, cultural, and linguistic affinity further strengthen U.S.-European ties. Even with these connections, however, U.S. citizens have grown increasingly skeptical of European attitudes, objectives, and actions where the United States is concerned.

As the 1990s opened, three issues dominated U.S.-Western European relations. The first issue was relations with the Soviet Union. Whereas both Americans and Europeans saw the Eastern European revolutions of 1989 as irreversible, and concurred that Western Europe should play the primary role in reintegrating the region with Western democratic and economic traditions, they at first disagreed about the nature of change in the Soviet Union. Although Americans and Europeans alike were appreciative of the changes taking place in the Soviet Union, most U.S. citizens and their government counseled caution. In contrast, most Europeans and their governments viewed the changes in the U.S.S.R. in the same way they viewed Eastern European changes—as irreversible. The August 1991 Soviet coup momentarily lent additional credence to the American perspective, but when the coup failed and the Soviet Union shortly thereafter dissolved, Americans and Europeans agreed that the Soviet threat had disappeared.

The second issue was the future of NATO. The end of the U.S.S.R. raised questions in many minds both in Europe and the United States about whether the American military commitment to Europe should be reduced, and even about whether NATO should be disbanded. There was no single "European" or "U.S." perspective on this question, with people on both sides of the Atlantic taking different viewpoints. But it was an issue of considerable debate.

The third issue was the European Community. As already discussed, the United States supported both the Single European Act and the subsequent Maastricht Agreement for future European economic and political unity. Nevertheless, the United States expressed concern that European economic integration might exclude external producers from Europe, and that the Maastricht Agreement might lead to a breakdown in transatlantic political cooperation. Europeans assured Americans that their concern was misplaced. Even so, despite both the assurances and the problems that developed over the Maastricht Agreement in 1992, U.S. concern persisted.

Eastern Europe

The wave of revolution that swept Bulgaria, Czechoslovakia, East Germany, Hungary, Poland, and Romania in 1989 completely transformed U.S. perspectives of Eastern Europe. Until the six communist governments fell, most Americans saw the Eastern European countries as Soviet satellites. After the governments fell, most U.S. citizens believed that Western-style democracy had finally come to Eastern Europe.

Until 1989, U.S. reasons for viewing Eastern European countries as Soviet satellites were straightforward: the presence of 31 Soviet army divisions in Eastern Europe, close economic ties between the U.S.S.R. and the countries of Eastern Europe, the Soviet invasions of Hungary in 1956 and Czechoslovakia in 1968 to expunge liberal political developments, and the imposition of martial law in Poland in 1981 to crush an independent trade union movement. To most U.S. citizens, there was no doubt: Eastern Europe "belonged" to the U.S.S.R.

Events in Hungary and Poland in the early and middle 1980s did little to change this perspective. Gradually, Hungary liberalized its economy and decreased political and social censorship, but for the most part, Americans were not aware of Hungary's increasingly independent course. And events in Poland only confirmed the U.S. view that the U.S.S.R. controlled Eastern Europe. The sense of hope that developed in the United States in 1980 and 1981 that the independent trade union Solidarity could gain power and end Soviet domination in Poland was snuffed out in December 1981 with the declaration of martial law there. After this brief flicker of hope, most U.S. citizens concluded that Eastern European states would remain in the 1980s and 1990s what they had been in the 1950s, 1960s, and 1970s: Soviet satellites.

Few Americans expected the outpouring of public resentment, the collapse of leadership will, and the changes in political outlooks that combined in different ways in 1989 to topple communist governments in each of the six Eastern European states listed above. Although much of the credit for the Eastern European revolutions of 1989 must go to Mikhail Gorbachev for his refusal to use Soviet armed forces to keep the old governments in power, the revolutions themselves were undertaken and initiated by the peoples of Eastern Europe. Americans understood this and applauded them.

U.S. citizens acting as individuals, within nongovernmental organizations and through the U.S. government as well, provided assistance and support to the peoples of Eastern Europe as they attempted to reconstitute their societies. At the same time, most U.S. citizens recognized that Western Europe was in a better position than the United States to lead this effort.

Japan

Until recently, the United States perceived modern Japan as a clear and genuine victory for U.S. post–World War II reconstruction policy. U.S.-style democracy had been transplanted to Japan by a constitution written during the U.S. occupation of Japan. Japan had evolved into a staunch and loyal American ally. The Japanese economy had grown rapidly and had become strong. By all measures, U.S. citizens viewed Japan as a U.S.-inspired success story.

This U.S. perception of Japan began to alter during the 1970s as Japanese products began to appear in American markets. Japanese-produced textiles, steel, and automotive imports contributed to significant downturns in those industries in the United States. U.S. tolerance of "Japanese imitations" disappeared. The Japanese no longer were imitating. They were competing, and their products were good. Throughout the 1980s, Japan compiled large trade surpluses with the

United States, and many people believed that the United States and Japan were locked in a trade war that Japan was winning.

As seen from the perspectives of both the U.S. government and many private citizens, Japan's ability to penetrate the U.S. market and to fare so well in other export markets was the product of many of the same factors that enhanced the competitiveness of European firms relative to U.S. firms. Japanese government support for Japanese firms by insuring loans was one aspect of the perceived market advantage of "Japan Incorporated," as was the Japanese government's creation of noneconomic barriers to imports to Japan. Similarly, from the U.S. perspective, Japan's low level of defense spending (about 1 percent of the gross national product) meant Japanese efforts could be devoted to economic development, investment, and research and development, all of which directly benefited Japanese economic endeavors. Many U.S. citizens forgot that the Japanese constitution contains within it a clause that forbids Japan to arm itself with anything other than self-defense forces. The clause was inserted in the constitution at U.S. insistence during the postwar U.S. occupation of Japan.

Japan's impressive economic growth and its impact on the U.S. economy are thus the root causes of almost all the current tensions in U.S.-Japanese relations, and of the changing perceptions of Japan that many U.S. citizens have. The "Japanese economic miracle" even led some U.S. citizens to conclude that Japanese management styles and "extended family" corporate-individual relationships are the major causes of Japanese success, and should be adopted by U.S. firms.[25] Be that as it may, U.S. perceptions of Japan have changed from what might be described as condescending U.S. pride in the Japanese success story undertaken under U.S. tutelage to the outlook that the United States may now have something to learn from Japan and had best learn it rapidly because of the severity of the Japanese economic challenge.

The Developing World

Frustration. If one word could describe U.S. perceptions of the Developing World in all its disparate parts, that word would be frustration. Never having had colonial possessions on the Asian, African, or South American mainlands, U.S. citizens cannot understand how and why Developing World countries decry the United States as a neocolonialist and imperialist power. Providing a greater dollar total of economic and technical aid to Developing World countries than any other state, U.S. citizens resent the Developing World's accusation that they are not doing enough. With a political philosophy and system that they revere but which is alien to most of the Developing World, U.S. citizens are appalled by the autocracy and totalitarianism that they see as they survey the Developing World. And with their own history of economic growth and development, albeit over 200 years, Americans are convinced that economic growth and development should be proceeding more rapidly in the Developing World.

To some extent, U.S. citizens recognize the diversity that exists within the Developing World. The United States has close political, economic, and/or military relations with some states such as Thailand, and extremely cold relations with others such as Libya. The U.S. recognition of this diversity assuages the sense of frustration inherent in U.S. dealings with this group of states, but the underlying discomfiture still exists. The United States believes that it is not understood or appreciated by the Developing World for what the United States takes itself to be.

To begin with, the United States rejects the accusation that it is a neocolonialist and imperialist power. The United States correctly points out that it supported decolonization, and stresses that it has not sought or attained political control in overseas territories. The expansion of U.S. overseas economic interests is interpreted in the United States as mutually beneficial, both to the host country and to the U.S. corporation involved, because both are claimed to be advancing their own respective interests. From the U.S. perspective, U.S. need for Developing World resources and markets is balanced by the Developing World's need for U.S. products and markets. In a sense, interdependence exists as seen from the United States.

Until recently, the U.S. government and much of the U.S. population also persisted in viewing the Developing World and many of its attempted solutions to its problems in East–West terms. This outlook had far-reaching effects. In countries where violence preceded the transition from colonialism to independence, national liberation movements sought weapons wherever they were available. More often than not, the source was the Soviet Union and its allies. The United States was prone to assume that if a movement was armed with Soviet weapons, it must be pro-Soviet at best and under Soviet control at worst. The United States therefore actively opposed such movements. The United States also tended to view Developing World states that pursued a socialist path of development as pro-Soviet, and formulated policy toward them on that basis. As a result, the United States has had chilly relationships with many of them.

Perhaps most resented in the United States were charges from the Developing World that the United States did not provide sufficient quantities of economic and technical aid and assistance. These accusations were often put forward by the Group of 77 at the United Nations. Many U.S. citizens responded by arguing that the Developing World was already getting an American "free ride." Although any objective observer would find U.S. views that the United States provided the Developing World a "free ride" impossible to support, it was nonetheless a widely held perception in the United States.

Under Ronald Reagan, the United States responded to Developing World claims of insufficient aid and assistance by positing that the real problem in the Developing World was that poorer countries often looked to socialist rather than free-market solutions to solve their economic problems. To the Reagan administration, one of the prerequisites for improved economic performance in the Developing World was wider adherence to free-market models. The Bush administration also adopted this point of view.

During the late 1980s and early 1990s, more and more Developing World states began to move toward free-market economic models, many at the urging of the World Bank. At the same time, many Developing World states began to moderate their anti-U.S. rhetoric. Some, especially in Latin America, even adopted democratic political systems. The United States welcomed all three actions as long-overdue departures from past Developing World practices. These changes in the Developing World did not mean that U.S. relations with most Developing World states suddenly became warm and cordial. But at least the underlying hostility that existed in so many of the relationships was reduced and in some cases even ended.

Notably, the Bush administration even actively intervened in several Developing World countries, most notably Bangladesh and Somalia, to help distribute food and other forms of humanitarian assistance. Conversely, there were also several instances, for example in Haiti and Sudan, where the United States (and the rest of the international community) did little or nothing. For the United States and other countries as well, the question of when to intervene in Developing World states to alleviate human suffering posed a difficult dilemma. This dilemma also confronted Bill Clinton in Bosnia, Somalia, and elsewhere as well.

The United Nations

Following World War II, the U.S. government staked much of its hope for a peaceful world on a strong and vigorous United Nations. Although some opposition to U.S. membership in the new IGO existed, for the most part U.S. citizens considered the United Nations a useful if not overly successful tool for peace-keeping and for administering international social programs. Throughout the 1940s, 1950s, and 1960s, when the UN was the central forum of exchange between East and West, the United States remained favorably disposed toward the UN.

As we saw in Chapter 3, the composition of the United Nations changed as more and more former colonial holdings achieved statehood. For the most part, having had unhappy experiences with their former colonial masters and now fearing that economic control would replace political control, many of the newly independent countries opposed U.S. and Western European positions in the General Assembly. They also had the needed votes in the General Assembly and the UN's related agencies to formulate UN positions to their own liking. Gradually, U.S. and Western European ability to predominate at the UN disappeared. Not surprisingly, U.S. views of the UN became less charitable. Instead of seeing the United Nations as a hope for peace, increasing numbers of U.S. citizens viewed the UN as a seat of anti-U.S. sentiment.

It was ironic that the United States' disenchantment with the United Nations developed over North–South rather than East–West issues. Created primarily as a tool to help assure international peace and security through debate and collective security, the United Nations, to U.S. eyes, became a global forum for venting North–South issues and anti-Americanism. Indeed, it was to a great extent because of the perceived anti-Americanism of the UN's Economic and Social Council that the United States withdrew from membership in that organization in 1985. It was also resentment over anti-U.S. sentiment in the General Assembly as well as a belief that the UN bureaucracy had become too large that led the Reagan administration in 1987 to stop U.S. payments to the UN. Given that the United States funded 25 percent of the UN's operations, the U.S. action carried considerable weight.

However, by 1988, the UN had pared the size of its bureaucracy and had undertaken several other reforms demanded by the United States. Therefore, the United States resumed funding the UN, although by 1993 it had still not repaid its back debts.[26] Indeed, from the American perspective, the United Nations during the late 1980s and early 1990s began to play a useful and constructive role in contemporary international affairs, helping end the Iran-Iraq war, negotiating the Soviet withdrawal from Afghanistan, ameliorating several regional conflicts, and approving the international effort to expel Iraq from Kuwait. In addition, anti-U.S. sentiment in the UN had decreased, due in no small part to revised Developing World attitudes toward the United States and the collapse of the Soviet Union.

Perhaps surprisingly, then, by 1993 most U.S. citizens viewed the United Nations in a favorable light. To be sure, they still believed it retained many short-comings, but they had begun to see that the UN might play a useful role in the late twentieth century world.

Multinational Corporations

In the United States, both the U.S. government and private citizens often have an approach-avoidance reaction to multinational corporations. On the one hand, MNCs are viewed as contributing to international economic vitality and ex-panded U.S. economic interests. On the other hand, they are decried as being beyond the control of government and too often too devoted to economic gain at the expense of other values.

This love-hate outlook is perhaps best expressed when U.S. attitudes toward the oil industry are surveyed. Although many U.S. citizens decry the oil compa-nies for their large size, their perceived excess profits, their seeming ability to determine supply and price of oil products, and their disregard for the environ-ment (witness the 1989 *Exxon Valdez* disaster in Alaska and Exxon's response to the clean-up), they also lament that had the oil companies been influential enough to remain majority partners of the Arab states, the oil-induced economic traumas of the 1970s would have never occurred. U.S. citizens, it seems, like to have it both ways when it comes to MNCs. (This is true not only of U.S. citizens.)

The Reagan and Bush administrations' attitudes toward MNCs illustrated a similar contradiction. Reagan's strong support of private enterprise and the free market was shown to have limits when he acted to prevent private firms, includ-ing MNCs, their foreign subsidiaries, and their foreign licensees, from selling their products to the U.S.S.R. Invoking needs of national security and claiming intervention into their affairs was a matter of national interest, Reagan and Bush on several occasions both illustrated that as far as they were concerned, MNCs were not only good for the home state, but also should be used by the state to achieve its policy ends.

U.S. attitudes toward MNCs based elsewhere than the United States are more difficult to categorize. Resentment of foreign industrial production was rampant in the United States during the 1980s, particularly in the automotive, iron and steel, and textile industries, but Americans continued to buy foreign-made products at unprecedented rates, thereby worsening U.S. unemployment and worsening U.S. resentment of foreign production. Purchases, however, rarely slowed. Indeed, when Japanese and European firms invested in production plants in the United States, they were often viewed as saviors. This U.S. approach-avoidance reaction to foreign products, foreign investment, and foreign MNCs continued unabated into the 1990s.

National Liberation Movements

During the Cold War, U.S. views of national liberation movements were often colored by the propensity of such movements to adopt socialist-oriented or communist-oriented political and economic programs, to seek weapons from the Soviet Union and other Eastern countries, and to employ violence in the pursuit of their objectives. The list of movements with which the United States had cool to frigid relations is long, and includes the Palestine Liberation Organization in the Middle East, the Sandinistas and the Farabundo Marti Liberation Front in Latin America, and the Mozambique Liberation Front, the Southwest Africa People's Organization, and the Zimbabwe African National Union in Africa.

The United States, with its avid pursuit of anticommunist containment during the 1950s and 1960s, viewed national liberation movements primarily in terms of the East–West conflict. While it supported the decolonization process, the United States, because of a combination of fear of communist expansion, a desire to support its European allies, and expanding global economic interests, rarely took the lead in furthering that process. National liberation movements, often convinced of the futility of a peaceful transition to independence and aware of U.S. support for or alliances with the very colonial powers or internal governments they were fighting, affirmed the radicalness of their political outlooks and turned to the Soviet Union and its allies for arms. Interpreting these events in East–West terms, the United States concluded that all such movements were pro-Soviet or communist.

In some cases, the United States was right, but in other cases it was wrong. Although some national liberation movements were under Soviet domination and control, others after achieving independence gradually adopted a legitimately non-aligned stance between East and West as they converted themselves to governments. For them, the North–South issue became the major concern. As Robert Mugabe, the premier of Zimbabwe and head of the Zimbabwe African National Union, observed, the Soviet Union, Soviet allies, and China were often the only sources of weapons, and weapons were sought where available. Needs changed, and developmental aid and assistance was available from a variety of sources.

One last point must be made concerning U.S. views of national liberation movements. Given their willingness to use force and violence, these movements are often regarded by U.S. citizens as terrorist organizations. As pointed out earlier, one person's terrorist may be another's freedom fighter. Many U.S. citizens view any nonstate actor that uses force as a terrorist, regardless of that actor's cause. Although the accuracy or inaccuracy of this outlook is a highly personalized matter, it is a widely prevalent view within the United States today.

NET ASSESSMENT

Five times within five decades, U.S. citizens have reassessed their perceptions of themselves and their role in the world. The first reassessment came at the end of World War II as U.S. citizens, long content with their seeming isolation and their sense of moral superiority, concluded that their country's role in the world had changed. Faced with a perceived communist menace that threatened to engulf the world, the United States abandoned isolationism and took up the moral crusade of anticommunism. At least that is how most U.S. citizens pictured the situation.

The crusade of containment eventually led to Vietnam and the second major reassessment of self-image and global role. As the war dragged on with victory no closer, some U.S. citizens concluded that limits existed on U.S. power. Others questioned the morality of the U.S. involvement, and decided it was wanting. The objectives of the United States' involvement, never clearly defined, were similarly thrown open to debate.

Throughout the 1970s, the United States continued to search for a redefined role in the world. Nixon's pragmatic cynicism replaced the morality of anticommunism and containment but it was short-lived. In yet another policy reappraisal, the third since the close of World War II, pragmatic cynicism gave way to Carter's human rights and idealism.

Human rights and idealism as the foundation for U.S. foreign policy soon foundered as well, running aground on the twin rocks of the capture of U.S. hostages in Iran and the Soviet invasion of Afghanistan. These two international events, plus the election of Ronald Reagan, marked yet another new beginning in U.S. foreign policy, one based on a return to old concepts of containment: economic and military strength were to be rebuilt and wielded within the context of a world defined primarily in terms of the East–West conflict. It was a worldview with which many U.S. citizens had been comfortable once before. It was a worldview with which many U.S. citizens were comfortable again for most of the 1980s.

But as the 1980s ended and the 1990s began, U.S. citizens were forced once again, for a fifth time since World War II, to reassess their perceptions of themselves and their roles in the world. Events in the Soviet Union and Eastern Europe undermined the legitimacy of a worldview based on the East–West conflict. Increasingly, economics, the environment, immigration, drugs, and terrorism made it apparent that the United States was inextricably involved in an interdependent world. How U.S. citizens would cope with their new awareness of the complexity of international affairs, and whether they and their government could weave together a coherent view of the role the United States would play in this complex interdependent world, remained to be seen.

KEY TERMS AND CONCEPTS

isolationism
moralism
pragmatism
Truman Doctrine
containment (also in Chapter 7)
impact of Vietnam on the U.S.
   self-image
U.S. economic preeminence and
   why it declined
Vietnamization and the Nixon
   Doctrine
detente and its demise

morality and Carter's foreign
   policy
Reagan's worldview and related
   policies
Bush and the new international
   order
Desert Shield and Desert Storm
North American Free Trade
   Agreement (NAFTA)
Clinton's foreign policy questions
U.S. views of Russia/the
   Soviet Union

U.S. views of China
U.S. views of Europe
U.S. views of Japan

**U.S. views of the
Developing World**
U.S. views of the United Nations

NOTES

1. Harry S. Truman, speech before a Joint Session of the U.S. Congress, March 12, 1947.

2. Ralph K. Andrist (ed.), *George Washington: A Biography in His Own Words* (New York: Harper & Row, 1972), pp. 372–374.

3. As quoted in Norman A. Graebner et al., *A History of the American People* (New York: McGraw-Hill, 1975), p. 572.

4. For discussions of the Roosevelt Corollary, see Dexter Perkins, *The Monroe Doctrine, 1867–1907* (Baltimore: Johns Hopkins Press, 1966); and Dexter Perkins, *A History of the Monroe Doctrine* (Boston: Little, Brown, 1965).

5. Harry S. Truman, speech before a Joint Session of the U.S. Congress, March 12, 1947.

6. George F. Kennan ("X"), "The Sources of Soviet Conduct," *Foreign Affairs*, Vol. 25 (July 1947): 566–582.

7. For an interesting treatment of ethics and American foreign policy toward the Developing World, see David Louis Cingranelli, *Ethics, American Foreign Policy, and the Third World* (New York: St. Martins Press, 1992).

8. See Maurice Matloff, *American Military History* (Washington: U.S. Government Printing Office, 1969), p. 409.

9. W. S. Woytinsky and E. S. Woytinsky, *World Population and Production: Trends and Outlooks* (New York: Twentieth Century Fund, 1953), p. 394.

10. For a completely different perspective, see Henry R. Nau, *The Myth of America's Decline: Leading the World Economy into the 1990s* (New York: Oxford University Press, 1992).

11. For Richard Nixon's own conception of the state of international relations during the late 1960s and early 1970s, see Richard M. Nixon, *U.S. Foreign Policy for the 1970s*, Vols. I–III (Washington: U.S. Government Printing Office, 1970–72).

12. These raids were called OPERATION MENU. Details of OPERATION MENU can be found in *Bombings in Cambodia*, Hearings before the Committee on Armed Services, U.S. Senate, 93rd Congress, 1st Sess., 1973.

13. William P. Rogers, *United States Foreign Policy 1969–70: A Report of the Secretary of State* (Washington: U.S. Government Printing Office, 1971), pp. 36–37.

14. For a useful discussion of the origins and evolution of the concept of detente, see Michael Froman, *The Development of the Idea of Detente* (New York: St. Martins Press, 1992).

15. On March 2, 1969, the tense border situations between the two communist states exploded as Chinese and Soviet units fought on Damansky Island in the Ussuri River. Sporadic fighting continued for at least a month.

16. Some Americans such as George Kennan thought the Soviet action was defensive. For Kennan's views on Afghanistan, see *New York Times*, February 1, 1980; February 28, 1980; March 12, 1980; and March 16, 1980.

17. For discussions of the Carter "human rights" policy, see Arthur Schlesinger, Jr., "Human Rights and the American Tradition," *Foreign Affairs: America and the World 1978*, vol. 57, pp. 503–526; J. Rees, "Disastrous Foreign Policy of Jimmy Carter," *American Opinion*, Vol. 23 (May 1980): 33–39; J. J. Kirkpatrick, "Establishing a Viable Human Rights Policy," *World Affairs*, Vol. 143 (Spring 1981):

323–334; and G. D. Loescher, "Carter's Human Rights Policy and the 95th Congress," *World Today*, Vol. 35 (April 1979): 140–159.

18. For two discussions of U.S. nuclear programs under Reagan, see Walter B. Slocombe, "Strategic Forces," in George E. Hudson and Joseph Kruzel (eds.), *1985–86 American Defense Annual* (Lexington, MA: Lexington Books, 1985), pp. 77–96; and Colin S. Gray, "Strategic Forces," in Joseph Kruzel (ed.), *1986–87 American Defense Annual* (Lexington, MA: Lexington Books, 1986), pp. 67–88.

19. Details of U.S.-Soviet arms negotiations are provided in Strobe Talbott, *Deadly Gambits* (New York: Vintage Books, 1985).

20. For several different perspectives on SDI, see Daniel S. Papp, "Ballistic Missile Defense, Space-Based Weapons, and the Defense of the West," in Robert Kennedy and John M. Weinstein (eds.), *The Defense of the West* (Boulder, CO: Westview Press, 1984), pp. 157–184; Harold Brown, "The Strategic Defense Initiative: Defensive Systems and the Strategic Debate," *Survival* (March–April 1985): 55–64; John Pike, *The Strategic Defense Initiative* (Washington: Federation of American Scientists, 1985); and Office of Technology Assessment, *Ballistic Missile Defense Technologies* (Washington: Office of Technology Assessment, 1985).

21. For two excellent discussions of U.S. international economic policies under Reagan, see Jeffrey E. Garten, "Gunboat Economics," *Foreign Affairs: America and the World 1984*, Vol. 63, pp. 538–599; and Robert D. Hormats, "World Economy under Stress, *Foreign Affairs: America and the World 1985*, Vol. 64, pp. 455–478.

22. For two different outlooks on post-Cold War American foreign policy, see Kenneth A. Oye, Robert J. Lieber, and Donald Rothchild, *Eagle in a New World: American Grand Strategy in the Post-Cold War Era* (New York: Harper-Collins, 1992); and James Chace, *The Consequences of the Peace: The New Internationalism and American Foreign Policy* (New York: Oxford University Press, 1992).

23. See William Welch, *American Images of Soviet Foreign Policy* (New Haven: Yale University Press, 1970) for a typology of American views about the U.S.S.R.'s foreign policy. For a superb history of U.S.-Soviet relations during the 1970s and 1980s, see Raymond L. Garthoff, *Détente and Confrontation: American-Soviet Relations from Nixon to Reagan* (Washington: The Brookings Institution, 1985).

24. For a history of U.S.-Chinese negotiations during the 1950s and 1960s, see Kenneth T. Young, *Negotiating with the Chinese Communists: The United States Experience, 1953–1967* (New York: McGraw-Hill, 1968).

25. See T. Hamada, "Winds of Chance: Economic Realism and Japanese Labor Management," *Asian Survey*, Vol. 20 (April 1980): 397–406; and H. Sandeman, "Making It Abroad," *Economist*, July 18–24, 1981, p. 29.

26. United Nations Budget, 1993.

CHAPTER 12

Russia and the Other Former Soviet Republics

- Why did the Soviet Union collapse?
- What historical inputs might influence the viewpoints of Russia and the other former Soviet republics?
- Do any ideological inputs influence Russian and other viewpoints?
- How do Russia and the other newly independent states view each other and the world?
- What strengths and weaknesses do Russia and the other newly-independent states have?

Russia is in the midst of its second major revolution this century. The first took place in 1917, and resulted in the death of the **Russian Empire** of the czars and the birth of the Soviet Union. It had two stages. The first stage took place in March 1917 when Czar Nicholas I abdicated and was replaced by a provisional government. The second stage occurred in November 1917 when V. I. Lenin and his small band of Bolsheviks seized power. From 1917 until 1991, the communist government that Lenin instituted held sway.

The second Russian revolution of the twentieth century led to the collapse of the Soviet Union, the end of Soviet superpower status, the independence of the 15 republics that formerly made up the U.S.S.R., and the creation of a loosely linked confederation of most of these newly independent states called the Commonwealth of Independent States. This revolution was initiated in the mid-1980s by Mikhail Gorbachev, who was the General Secretary of the Communist Party of the Soviet Union (CPSU). It continues today. Where this revolution eventually will lead is not clear.

Given all the changes that they have experienced in recent years, how do Russians and the peoples of the other newly independent states view the world? How do they see their current role in the international community? Are they pleased with the opportunity to make a new future for themselves unfettered by communism? Or do they long for the return of a strong ruler, for centralized economic planning, or a return to superpower status? These are important questions, and there are as many different answers as there are citizens of the newly independent states.

The collapse of the Soviet Union was one of the most important events of the late twentieth century. For years, the Soviet Union was one of the major actors in international affairs. The U.S.S.R.'s collapse sent shock waves throughout the international system. Indeed, the Soviet collapse changed the international system completely. Despite the magnitude of the changes that have already taken place in the former Soviet Union, more will come. The situation in the 15 newly-independent states that replaced the U.S.S.R. remains fluid.

When the Soviet state was in existence, the state-sponsored ideology of Soviet Communism, also known as Soviet Marxism-Leninism, dominated all aspects of life. But with the collapse of the U.S.S.R., Marxism-Leninism was swept away as the official state ideology. The revulsion that the leaders of the newly independent states and their peoples felt toward Marxism-Leninism was so deep that in one former Soviet republic after another, communism was declared illegal.

Nevertheless, the collapse of the Soviet Union did not lead to the complete rejection of all Marxist-Leninist perspectives by everyone in today's Russia and the other former Soviet republics. Similarly, during the Soviet era, it was incorrect to assume that Lenin's revolution eliminated all memories that the Russian and other peoples had of the Russian Empire. Long before the Bolsheviks seized the reins of government in 1917, the Russian state and Russian people had developed a sense of national consciousness. The **Bolshevik revolution** did not erase the Russian people's memory of history, nor the way their view of that history influenced their perception of international affairs.

One of the many challenges that students face as they attempt to understand the realities of today's Russia as well as the realities of the other newly independent states is to determine the extent to which previous Russian imperial and Soviet viewpoints continue to influence the positions of the leaders and people of present-day Russian and the other newly independent states. Thus, before we examine either current-day Russia or the other newly independent states, we will first examine the background of the Russian Empire and the Soviet Union.

THE RUSSIAN EMPIRE

The international outlooks of the Russian Empire of the czars were influenced by many factors, but four outlooks dominated. First, Russian leaders of the imperial era believed that Russia had a messianic mission. Second, the czars and other Russian leaders believed that Russia had a responsibility and a right to expand into territories contiguous to those it already ruled. Third, the Russia of the czars had long been a major actor on the international scene. Fourth, and somewhat paradoxically, Russians were never quite sure whether their country was the equal of other European states despite its widely acknowledged great power status.

The Russian Missions

Over a thousand years ago, in A.D. 988, Prince Vladimir Svyatoslav decided to impose organization and order on his undisciplined subjects in Kiev. After examining the great religions of the day—Islam, Roman Christianity, and

Eastern Orthodox Christianity—Vladimir settled on the Eastern Orthodox religion of the Byzantine Empire as the best bet to discipline his subjects. A mass baptism of the entire population of Kiev followed, and as Kiev expanded to become the birthplace of the eventual czarist Russian Empire, a state religion was born. The church as an instrument of state power was thus a longstanding Russian tradition.

Successive Russian rulers used conversion of nonbelievers to the Russian Orthodox religion as a rationale for territorial expansion. One of the driving forces of Russian foreign policy during the eighteenth and nineteenth centuries was expansion to the north of the Black Sea to obtain access to the Mediterranean Sea. In religious terms, this thrust was put forward in terms of the third Rome (St. Petersburg) delivering the second Rome (Constantinople) from Islamic usurpers.[1]

Another mission of Russian foreign policy during the nineteenth century was the unification of all Slavic peoples under Russian rule. This theme, known as pan-Slavism, argued that the "little Slavic brothers" of Eastern Europe had been corrupted by their contact with the West, and that Russia's mission was to restore them to the true heritage of their Slavic backgrounds. The Russian mission, then, was sacred in both religious and ethnic terms.[2]

Territorial Expansion

Today's Russia began as the city-state of Kiev. Through the years and despite the humiliation of being conquered by the Mongols and ruled by them for over two centuries, the Russian people gradually acquired a national consciousness. The center of what would become Russian civilization moved from Kiev to Moscow, and eventually on to St. Petersburg.

The Russian state expanded inexorably after Mongol rule was thrown off in 1480 by Ivan III. Ivan IV (Ivan the Terrible), who reigned from 1533 to 1584 and was crowned the first Russian czar in 1547, pursued the Mongols into Kazan, and moved into western Siberia and toward the Caspian Sea. By 1689, nearly all Siberia belonged to the Russian state. The only major exception was in southeastern Siberia. However, in 1858, Alexander II annexed this region as well.

The Russian state expanded to the west as well. Peter the Great, who ruled from 1682 to 1725, defeated the Swedes, founded St. Petersburg in 1703, and absorbed Finland six years later. Catherine the Great (1762–1776) annexed much of Poland and the Crimean region on the Black Sea. The Caucasus was conquered during the nineteenth century, and by 1850 the Kazakh steppe had been joined to the Russian Empire. By 1881, the expansion of Russia was virtually completed as Islamic states in Central Asia were added to the empire.

A nineteenth-century Russian foreign minister, when asked to explain the reason behind his country's territorial expansion, responded that that which stops growing begins to die. The Russian state did not intend to die. Nevertheless, a key point of Russia's expansion that would have major propagandistic import for the Soviet state was that Russia's expansion took place in areas that were contiguous to territory already controlled by the Russian state. Thus, to Russians, the colonial imperialism of overseas empire was not part of the Russian heritage.

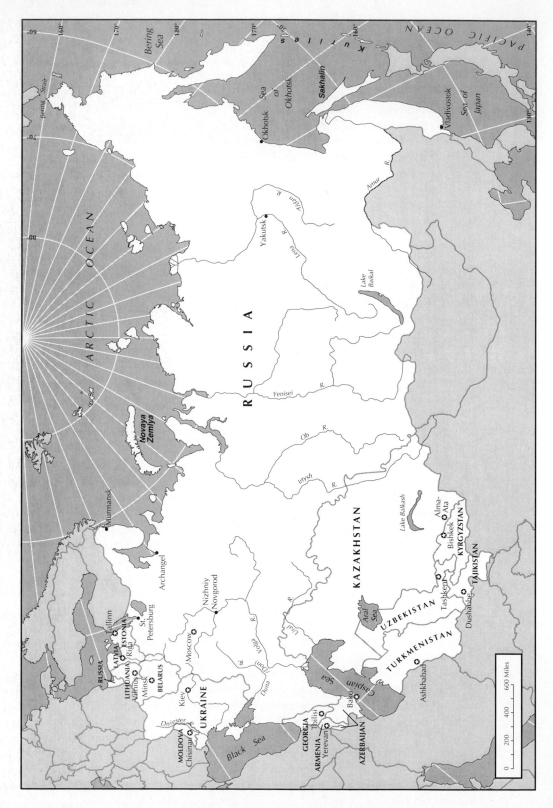

FIGURE 12–1 Russia and the Other Former Soviet Republics.

Russia as a Power

On the basis of its territorial expanse and population alone, the Russian state was a major power on the international scene in the pre-Bolshevik era. Complementing its territorial expanse and population size was its prowess in diplomacy and battle. Throughout the eighteenth and nineteenth centuries, czarist Russia was a recognized great power. It won major victories over the Swedish and Polish empires in the eighteenth century, and played a key role in Napoleon's defeat and the creation of the post-Napoleonic Concert of Europe. It struggled for influence with Great Britain throughout Central Asia, and even spread its control into China and Alaska. The czarist Empire, by almost every measure of the eighteenth- and nineteenth-century world, was great indeed.

The Russian Self-Image

Despite their country's status as a great power, many Russians never quite escaped feeling that their country was not up to the standards of the rest of Europe, particularly France and Great Britain. French was the language used in the czarist court, and French customs were widely followed in elite Russian society. Russia and its czars envied Great Britain's industrial might and its overseas empire, and eventually came to envy and fear Germany's military and industrial prowess. Those who thought Russia should adopt European practices were called **Westernizers**.

Nicholas Turgenev reflected this sense of inferiority in his 1847 commentary on his country: "Russia has had no Middle Ages; everything that is to prosper there must be borrowed from Europe; Russia cannot graft it on her own ancient institutions."[3] Another Russian admirer of European culture and society, I. Chaadaev, was even more critical of his homeland, complaining that "not one useful thought has germinated on the barren soil of our country; not one great truth has sprung up in our midst."[4]

Balancing the viewpoints of these Russians were the **Slavophiles**, who believed Russia's national salvation lay in the rejection of European thought and customs and in the emphasis of traditional Slavic culture. Other Russians had more ambivalent views. For example, the great Russian radical thinker Alexander Herzen looked to Europe during his early writings, but then rejected European culture and institutions as inferior.

Increasingly during the nineteenth century, Russians became aware of the gap between Russian aspirations and Russian capabilities. Russian reverses in the Crimean War pointed out to Slavophiles and Westernizers alike that Western European states were fast outstripping Russia. To Slavophiles, Russia's problems were caused by too close an identification with Europe. To Westernizers, Russia's problems were the result of its refusal to identify more closely with Europe.

Despite this division, the Russian Empire initiated a number of European-style reforms during the nineteenth century. These included construction of railroads, abolition of serfdom, and institutionalization of an updated legal and banking system. However, these reforms were not sufficient for the Russian state, social structure, bureaucracy, or industry to be termed truly modern. The ignominious Russian defeat in the 1905 Russo-Japanese war provided ample proof of this. Westernizers and Slavophiles were joined by other groups and movements that recognized the need for extensive change. Few agreed on the nature of the needed change.

Nevertheless, by the beginning of the twentieth century, Russians had a fairly well-defined vision of themselves and their history. Russia had historical missions, possessed vast territory, and was a great power. Its problems were great but surmountable. Few observers predicted or expected a major change in the course of Russian history. Amid the sacrifice and suffering of World War I, however, the groundwork was being laid for one of the most important revolutions of the twentieth century. In March 1917, following extensive rioting in St. Petersburg, Nicholas II abdicated, ending three centuries of rule by the Romanov dynasty. A provisional government assumed power but was overthrown by the Bolsheviks on November 7, 1917. For Russia, a new era was about to begin.

SOVIET MARXISM-LENINISM: THE ESSENTIALS

Bolshevism was one of several different versions of Marxism, which had been introduced to Russia in the late nineteenth century by Georgi Plekhanov, a Russian aristocrat. In 1898, most Marxist groups joined together in the Russian Social Democratic Labor Party (RSDLP).

However, the union was tenuous. Issues such as the editorship of the party paper, the wisdom of organizing the party along ethnic lines, and the question of whether the party should be a mass party or an elite party were the major topics of debate. The disagreements became increasingly serious, and in 1903 the internal feud became an open rupture. Lenin broke his faction, the Bolsheviks, away from the RSDLP and eventually led them to power in November 1917.

As a communist, Lenin accepted the doctrinal precepts of **Karl Marx**. However, he also reinterpreted several of the teachings of Marx in light of the needs and demands of early twentieth-century Russia and the international situation of that era. Only a lengthy study can yield a detailed understanding of Marxism, but its general outlines may be understood if two key concepts, economic materialism and historical materialism, are studied. Lenin's reinterpretation of Marx may best be understood if we look at Lenin's conception of the role of the party, the state, and the international system.[5]

Marx on Economic and Historical Materialism

To Marx, the history of humankind was the history of the struggle of economic classes. Every human society, Marx believed, reflected the economic structure dominant within it. Therefore, all human activities—politics, law, religion, sports, business, war, the arts, and so on—were products of that dominant economic structure. Even government and religion must reflect the economic realities within a state, Marx posited.

Marx argued that one economic class owned the means of production and that that class used any means at its disposal, but particularly the state, which it controlled, to maintain its ownership of the means of production. In most societies—indeed, all except a communist one—Marx's theory predicted that those who owned the means of production would not only maintain control, but also exploit those who worked for them. In all but communist societies, Marx predicted, the rich would get richer by exploiting the poor. The poor, in turn, would grow poorer—and more desperate. Class conflict was hence inevitable in all non-communist societies.

Marx interpreted the flow of human history in light of his economic theory. Human recorded history, Marx theorized, began with a primitive form of communism that dissolved into an owner/slave relationship in which the few strong men subjugated the many weak. The powerful set up a complicated system of social relationships, including the state and religion, to assure their dominance.

Gradually, however, the means of production changed. Intense agricultural use of land allowed a new class of nobility to develop, the lords and kings of the Middle Ages. Serfs and peasants worked the land and looked to landlords for protection. Land was owned by the local lord, so serfs and peasants had no recourse but to abide by the beck and call of that lord. Again, state and religion were used to make sure that the rule of lords and kings would continue.

State and church could intimidate men, women, and children, Marx believed, but could not stem the flow of history. Once again, as the means of production changed, the class relations of society changed. Industrial production replaced agricultural production, and a new class of owners, the industrial capitalists, moved to the front to replace lords and kings. Church and state were again used, Marx posited, this time by the owners of capital, the bourgeoisie, to maintain order and control in the new society.

In the new industrial society, the workers, or proletariat, sold their labor to the capitalists. Each laborer was willing to sell his labor to the capitalist less expensively than his neighbor simply to have a job so that he could survive. As a result, the capitalists could pay the workers much less than their actual work was worth. The bourgeois capitalist therefore grew wealthy off the sweat of the proletariat's brow.

Marx believed that the improved efficiency of industrial production would lead to increased ownership of the means of production by fewer and fewer capitalists. Eventually, the condition of the proletariat would deteriorate so much, Marx proclaimed, that the proletariat would rise up and overthrow the capitalists and their institutions and create a more just society. Socialism, where each worked according to ability and received according to work, would replace capitalism. Communism, where each worked according to ability and received according to need, would replace socialism.

Marx therefore viewed history as a painful but inevitably triumphant movement of people from slavery, to feudalism, to capitalism, on to socialism, and eventually to communism. Each successive stage of history would be fairer and more just than those that preceded it. Eventually, Marx predicted, "the exploitation of man by man" would end. A communist revolution would bring that perfect society, and the state, no longer needed, would wither away.

Lenin on the Party, the State, and the International System

Marx believed that the proletarian revolution would be practically spontaneous, brought about by the workers' reactions to the horrible living conditions that they endured. **V. I. Lenin** disagreed. He believed that workers left to their own devices could not initiate a successful revolution. To Lenin, workers needed a party to plan and carry out the revolution. This party had to be a small elite group of professional revolutionaries, Lenin argued. The party would be the **vanguard of the proletariat**. Lenin structured and ran the Bolshevik party on this basis.

On the issue of the party, then, Lenin was not a true Marxist. Indeed, the debate over whether the RSDLP should be a mass party or an elitist party was one of the issues over which the 1903 RSDLP rupture occurred. It is ironic to note that as early as 1904, Leon Trotsky, one of Lenin's leading opponents, wrote in his pamphlet *Our Political Problems* that Lenin's view of the party would lead increasingly to one-man rule within the Bolshevik Party.[6]

Conversely, Lenin agreed with Marx on the withering away of the state. However, he also realized that this would not be achieved until years after the revolution. During the period between the revolution that overthrew the bourgeois capitalist state and the attainment of a communist society, Lenin believed that a state would have to exist to make sure that remaining old habits of thought and action, and remaining old patterns of societal relationships under capitalism, would be eliminated. The postrevolutionary state, however, would be a state "of a new type." It would be a state that took the interests of the proletariat masses as its own and worked to eliminate remaining bourgeois habits and relationships. The state would institute the **dictatorship of the proletariat** to stamp out old ideas and ways of doing things and the state would be run by the party as the vanguard of the proletariat.

Lenin's conceptions of party and state, then, contributed an operational organization to Marxist thought that had previously been lacking. In some matters, he went beyond Marx. In other matters, he flatly contradicted Marx. Nonetheless, Lenin's contributions to Marxist theory were significant and laid the groundwork both for the Bolshevik Revolution and the prevailing pattern of party/state/society relationships that existed in the Soviet Union from 1917 until Mikhail Gorbachev launched the second Russian revolution of the twentieth century.

Lenin's analysis did not end with internal societal relationships. He also developed a theory of how and why the international system operated as it did. In his 1916 work, **Imperialism—The Highest Stage of Capitalism**, the Bolshevik oracle provided his most detailed exposition on his view of the workings of international politics under capitalism.[7]

To Lenin, international politics reflected the "internalization of the class system." The ruling class within capitalist states, having exploited the proletariat class within its own society and having grown accustomed to high rates of return on capital, turned to areas beyond the state to improve its economic position still further. This, to Lenin, explained the European states' drive to acquire colonies. Capitalists sought three objectives: control over inexpensive raw materials, external markets, and the highest possible rate of return on investment. Possible colonial holdings were finite, however, so in their struggle to attain colonies, European states went to war with each other. This, to Lenin, explained World War I. Capitalism was therefore the cause of war. From this, Lenin concluded that when the communist millennium arrived wars would be eliminated.

Unfortunately for Lenin, the Bolshevik Revolution brought socialism to only one country and full communism to none. Domestically, Lenin declared that a state, albeit an allegedly proletariat-controlled state, would be needed to combat internal enemies and guide the proletariat on its march toward communism. Internally, the fact that the Bolshevik Revolution occurred only in Russia also necessitated modifications in Lenin's view of the world. Writing in 1919, he proclaimed:

> We live not merely in a state but in a system of states, and the existence of the Soviet Republic side by side with the imperialist states for a long time is unthinkable. One or the other must triumph in the end. And before that end occurs, a series of frightful collisions between the Soviet Republic and the bourgeois states will be inevitable.[8]

In essence, Lenin created the **two-camp thesis**—one camp socialist, one camp capitalist—and prophesied that conflict between the two was inevitable, an outlook made all the more realistic to Lenin and the Bolsheviks by Western intervention in Russia during the 1918–1921 Russian Civil War. Lenin later revised his thesis of inevitable conflict to one of **peaceful coexistence**. Under Lenin's version of peaceful coexistence, war between the two camps could be delayed indefinitely, during which time the two camps could exist together in peace.

By 1918, then, Lenin and his Bolsheviks were entrenched in power in Russia. Whether their "state of a new type" would survive was an open question as civil war raged around them and as noncommunist states intervened against them. For the Bolsheviks, the coming decades were times of trials and tribulations.

THE EVOLUTION OF THE SOVIET WORLDVIEW BEFORE GORBACHEV

Between 1917 and the late 1980s, the Soviet view of the world changed considerably in some ways and very little in others. Some changes occurred because of historical experience, and others because of the preference of individual Soviet leaders. Always, however, even if it required verbal and intellectual gymnastics, Soviet leaders sought to interpret their outlooks and actions in terms consistent with Marx and Lenin.

The Civil War and the New Economic Policy

The Bolshevik/Soviet worldview was unquestionably colored by the Russian Civil War and the accompanying Western intervention. The **Civil War** and intervention followed hard on the heels of the hardships caused by Russia's involvement in World War I. Lenin, accustomed to attacking the authority of the state rather than being the authority of the state, found himself trying to cope with the problems of running the world's largest state even while he struggled against internal and external enemies to maintain Bolshevik rule.

When the Bolsheviks seized power they were a tiny band who knew only where they wanted to go, not how to get there. The first challenge they faced was maintaining themselves in power against internal counterrevolutionaries. For three long years, the Civil War raged, with the Red Army finally achieving victory in 1921.

Counterrevolutionary forces received extensive military and economic support from capitalist countries. Great Britain, France, Japan, and the United
States all sent troops to Russia. The United States sent over 14,000 troops. The
motivations of the capitalist countries varied for deploying troops in Russia. Some
countries intervened because of opposition to Bolshevism and support for counterrevolutionary philosophies. Others had dreams of creating colonial holdings in
Russia or were attempting to prevent Russian war supplies from falling into
German hands. Lenin and the Bolsheviks interpreted the intervention as ideology
instructed: Capitalist countries—all capitalist countries—sought the destruction
of Bolshevism and the Soviet state.

This perception of capitalist hostility was fundamentally correct, but stopped
neither the Bolsheviks nor certain capitalists from cooperating with each other following the Civil War. Lenin, realizing his country was in dire need of capital and
expertise to help it recover from the Civil War, turned to his capitalist opponents
for trade and aid. Capitalists, seeing opportunity for profit, responded. From 1921
to 1928, then, the Soviet Union followed what Lenin called the **New Economic
Policy** (NEP) of cooperation with capitalist states and capitalist businesses.

The Stalin and Khrushchev Years

Lenin died in 1924, and after a long internal political struggle, **Joseph Stalin**
won the reins of power. By this time (1928), the fundamental outline of action
that guided Soviet foreign policy until World War II had clearly emerged: the primacy of state objectives over revolutionary élan; the normalization of relations
with capitalist states, Germany in particular; the promotion of "peaceful coexistence"; the creation of nonaggression pacts with the Baltic and Eastern European
states; the courtship of China and, to a lesser degree, the United States, for the
purpose of countering Japanese expansionism; and finally, the use of the
Comintern to foster external support for the Soviet Union and to foment trouble
in the capitalist and colonial world.[9]

Stalin rationalized his emphasis on the expansion of Soviet power at the
expense of Soviet support for international revolution by elaborating Lenin's two-
camp thesis into his theory of **capitalist encirclement**, in which the Soviet
Union was viewed as besieged by capitalist states intent on its destruction. To
Stalin, the Soviet Union's survival depended on the U.S.S.R.'s ability to defend
itself. Hence rapid industrialization became the top priority for the Soviet state.[10]

Stalin also forced all Soviet agricultural workers to work on immense collective farms. This too brought great suffering to many Russians. Anyone who disagreed with Stalin was purged. Indeed, the purges were used by Stalin and his
supporters to eliminate anyone for any reason. At least 15 million Soviet citizens
lost their lives during **industrialization, collectivization, and the purges** in
the late 1920s and 1930s.[11]

Stalin's brutality would be monumental were it not for the carnage that followed. Stalin's fear of the external world proved well founded as, on June 22,
1941, German forces invaded the Soviet Union. World War II had come to the
Soviet Union. Before World War II was over, more than 25 million Soviet citizens
died. By contrast, the United States lost only 300,000 people.

Nazism espoused destruction not only of Soviet communism, but also of Western capitalism. As a result of both their countries' dire straits, Great Britain's Winston Churchill and Stalin buried their ideological antipathy and political hostility and worked together for the defeat of Nazi Germany. They were joined by Franklin D. Roosevelt and the United States following the Japanese attack on Pearl Harbor on December 7, 1941.

However, Stalin did not trust his anti-Nazi allies, nor did they trust him. From Stalin's perspective, Great Britain sought to have Russian and German troops kill each other off so it could move into Europe to collect the spoils of war. American intentions were also suspect. Harry Truman, at the time a U.S. Senator, commented on the Nazi invasion of the Soviet Union saying, "If we see that Germany is winning, we ought to help Russia, and if Russia is winning, we ought to help Germany, and in that way let them kill as many as possible."[12] U.S. and British actions during World War II strengthened Stalin's perception of the accuracy of his assessment of the British-American strategy, as the promised invasion of Hitler's "Fortress Europa" was delayed first from 1942 to 1943, and then put back again to 1944. Meanwhile, the Soviet Union and Germany bled each other's armies.

Stalin mistrusted his Western allies for other reasons as well. Near the end of the war, Truman, now president, abruptly terminated U.S. aid to the Soviet Union. The United States also sought to have the United Nations structured in a way that would defend U.S. interests, and opposed the Soviet removal of reparations in the form of industrial plants in Germany. U.S. complaints over the nature of the governments that the Soviet Union set up in Eastern Europe seemed similarly directed against Soviet interests; Stalin fully intended to maintain Soviet influence in Eastern Europe, both to guard against future invasions from Western Europe and to spread Soviet Marxism-Leninism and influence. U.S. objectives, Stalin believed, were clearly anti-Soviet.

The Soviet Union suffered immense damage and lost over 25 million people in World War II. (National Archives.)

The two-camp thesis, which had fallen into disuse in World War II, was formally readopted by the Soviet Union in 1946. Even so, the postwar two-camp thesis was different from the prewar version. Before World War II, the socialist camp was an outpost occupied only by the Soviet Union. Following the war the socialist camp had become a "commonwealth of nations," albeit created through force of Soviet arms.

This Soviet worldview remained unchanged until 1956, when **Nikita Khrushchev** declared that war between socialist and capitalist states was no longer fatalistically inevitable and that socialism could be developed by individual states following national paths. These revisions were fundamental. According to Khrushchev, socialism could peacefully coexist with capitalism, with the eventual peaceful triumph of socialism becoming a possibility. At the same time, socialist states no longer had to conform to the Soviet model of development. In addition, newly independent developing states, that is, states of the Developing World, could pursue "noncapitalist roads of development," which, to Khrushchev, placed them in opposition to the capitalist world. Thus, if Khrushchev so desired, nonsocialist states could be defined as pro-Soviet and anti-imperialist.

From Brezhnev Through the Triple Succession

In 1964, Leonid Brezhnev and several other Soviet Politburo members removed Khrushchev from office. Displeased over Khrushchev's "harebrained schemes" such as putting missiles into Cuba and trying to convert deserts to wheat fields, Brezhnev and his colleagues ruled the U.S.S.R. themselves for the next 18 years. During this time, Brezhnev moved from a relatively passive foreign policy in the 1960s during which the U.S.S.R. was preoccupied with the Sino-Soviet split, the U.S. involvement in Vietnam, and events in Eastern Europe through the U.S.-Soviet detente of the early 1970s and eventually on to an activist Developing World policy from the mid-1970s through Brezhnev's death in 1982.

As time progressed, Brezhnev developed a rather sophisticated logic that sought to explain the international environment in Marxist-Leninist terms. Chief among those concepts that **Brezhnev's worldview** employed were the "correlation of forces," the "world revolutionary movement," the "relaxation of tensions," and "peaceful coexistence."[13]

The *correlation of forces*, to Brezhnev, was a tool for measuring the relative capabilities of competing forces. A multifaceted concept, the correlation of forces combined socioeconomic, political, ideological, psychological, and military parameters to measure relative capabilities.

Soviet commentators argued that a significant shift in the correlation of forces occurred during the Brezhnev era. Some linked this shift to the growth of Soviet military capabilities, particularly the attainment of strategic nuclear parity with the United States. According to this view, Soviet attainment of strategic nuclear parity forced the United States to accept the U.S.S.R. as its military equal, that is, as a superpower. As a result, the Soviets contended that competition shifted from the military to socioeconomic, political, and ideological planes.

The alleged grown in strength of the *world revolutionary movement* was an important aspect of the changing international correlation of forces. According to

Soviet theorists, the movement had three major components: the Soviet Union and other socialist states, the international workers and communist movement, and national liberation movements. These streams all worked together for the defeat of imperialism.[14]

Two final components of the Kremlin's worldview under Brezhnev were integrally linked. The first, *peaceful coexistence*, referred only to relations between the two opposing social systems. It reduced the possibility of direct military conflict between the two systems, and at the same time permitted other forms of competition—economic, ideological, social, political, and so forth—to continue. As competition moved from the military plane to other planes, a *relaxation of tensions*—that is, detente—followed.

Both concepts revolved around the phrase, "between the two opposing social systems." When direct relations between the two systems were not under consideration, peaceful coexistence and the reduction of tensions were not operant. More specifically, they "[did] not extend to relations between imperialism and the national liberation movement."[15] The U.S.S.R. consequently drew a clear line between the area in which the peaceful coexistence principle operated and areas where it did not. Capitalist-socialist relations existed on one side of that boundary; capitalist-Developing World and socialist-Developing World relations existed on the other. Peaceful coexistence had the potential to "prevent imperialism from openly using force against the emergent states,"[16] but did not prevent the Soviet Union from extending verbal and material support to selected movements and states.

Leonid Brezhnev died in 1982, but his worldview continued to dominate Soviet outlooks on foreign policy for several more years. Brezhnev's two successors, Yuri Andropov and Konstantin Chernenko, did not rule long enough to change either Soviet outlooks or policies. But their successor, Mikhail Gorbachev, initiated changes in outlooks and policies so significant that they can only be described as a revolution.

THE GORBACHEV REVOLUTION

By the time Leonid Brezhnev died in 1982, the U.S.S.R. was a global superpower.[17] Wielding more military might across a greater territorial expanse than at any other time in its history, enjoying greater political influence around the world than ever before, and possessing the world's second-largest national economic base, the Soviet Union basked in its power, prestige, and influence.

But the Soviet Union also faced major problems. Economic growth had practically stopped. The U.S.S.R. was beset by declining labor productivity, a failed agricultural program, overcentralized decision-making, and graft and corruption. Communism as an ideology no longer inspired. Old men in their seventies who refused to transfer authority to the new generation dominated the political system. In short, the Soviet domestic situation was serious.

The Kremlin faced international problems as well. The U.S.S.R. remained encircled by nations either unfriendly to the Soviet Union or subservient to it only through force of Soviet arms. Relations with the United States, Japan, and Western Europe were at a low ebb, and all three were in the midst of economic booms and military buildups. Even in the Developing World, the U.S.S.R. for the most part was unsuccessful in its efforts to develop and maintain close long-term relationships.

Between 1982 and 1985, the Soviet Union's domestic and international position deteriorated further in all areas except the military. This deterioration was even more pronounced than it may otherwise have been as a result of the Soviet Union's leadership crisis. Between November 1982 and March 1985, four men—Leonid Brezhnev, Yuri Andropov, Konstantin Chernenko, and Mikhail Gorbachev—led the U.S.S.R., the first three dying in office. This turmoil prevented the implementation of new policies designed to address the U.S.S.R.'s deteriorating situation.

When **Mikhail Gorbachev** became general secretary of the CPSU in March 1985, he took over a country careening toward crisis. He realized this, and within two years instituted a series of domestic and foreign policy reforms so extensive that they could only be termed a revolution. These reforms also led directly and indirectly to the collapse of the Soviet Union, the end of Soviet superpower status, the independence of the 15 republics that formerly made up the U.S.S.R., and the creation of a loosely-linked confederation of 11 of the newly independent states in the Commonwealth of Independent States.

Gorbachev's Domestic Revolution: Glasnost, Perestroika, and Demokratizatsiya

Gorbachev's domestic revolution included major alterations in the way the Soviet Union organized and ran its social and cultural life, its economy, and its political system. In social and cultural life, Gorbachev instituted **glasnost**, or openness. In economic affairs, he implemented **perestroika**, or restructuring. And in politics, he began to put in place a certain degree of **demokratizatsiya**, or democratization. Although these reforms were integrally interrelated, each requires separate discussion.

Under **glasnost**, the Soviet people began to enjoy a greater measure of freedom of expression than they had ever experienced. The Soviet government abolished many forms of censorship; encouraged public debate on many policy issues; welcomed disclosure by private citizens of government graft, corruption, and excess; and relaxed control of literature and the arts.

Glasnost did not imply that all limitations on expression were lifted. Indeed, when in late 1989 one Soviet newspaper became extremely critical of Gorbachev, Gorbachev sought—but failed—to remove the editor. This incident taught two clear lessons. First, there were limits to openness. Glasnost did not give everyone the right to say just anything. Second, under the newly developing Soviet system, the general secretary no longer exercised complete control.

Glasnost had two primary purposes. Its first objective was to elevate the level and quality of discourse and culture in the U.S.S.R. But there was a second side to glasnost as well. As the Soviet peoples voiced displeasure with old ways of doing things, their complaints made it easier for Gorbachev to implement change. Thus, glasnost was both an objective and a tool.

Perestroika denoted the entire spectrum of change taking place in the Soviet Union, but more often than not was applied specifically to Gorbachev's economic reforms. Convinced that Soviet economic stagnation and decline resulted from the U.S.S.R.'s overly centralized economic system, Gorbachev took on a truly Herculean task: revamping the entire Soviet economy. Under the rubric of perestroika, he reduced state subsidies to industry, allowed plant managers greater decision-making discretion, permitted plants to go bankrupt, accepted unemployment, encouraged formation of cooperatives in the service sector, allowed joint ventures with foreign firms, restructured the Soviet banking system, and explored and sometimes implemented a host of other economic practices not previously known in the U.S.S.R. In 1990, private ownership of the means of production was even declared acceptable under perestroika.

These massive economic reforms aroused extensive opposition. Old-line party conservatives believed Gorbachev had abandoned communism. Privileged Soviet citizens (often senior party members) feared they would lose their privileges. Central government bureaucrats saw their power diminishing. Plant managers, trained to respond to directives, felt uncomfortable and incompetent with their new decision-making authority. Even some Soviet workers objected to Gorbachev's restructuring, having been told that if they were more disciplined and worked harder today, they would benefit tomorrow. They had heard that line before, and despite Gorbachev's charisma, it was no longer credible.

Gorbachev's efforts to institutionalize perestroika were made all the more difficult because they did not immediately succeed. Indeed, by 1990, the U.S.S.R.'s economic plight was even worse than in 1985. Nevertheless, Gorbachev forged on with restructuring, even as more and more Soviet citizens began to wonder if his cures created more problems than they solved.

Gorbachev did not content himself with glasnost and perestroika. He also sought to change the Soviet political system via **demokratizatsiya**, or democratization. Some of the most notable political reforms were connected with elections for a newly created legislative body, the Congress of People's Deputies, in March 1989.

In that election, over 3,000 candidates, at least 15 percent of whom were not communists, competed for 1,500 seats in the new congress. These statistics were important for two reasons. First, for the first time since 1917, multiple candidates could run for a single seat, and there was no requirement that the candidates had to be CPSU members. Second, candidates engaged in spirited debate over substantive issues ranging from Soviet foreign policy to food shortages to freedom of religion. Significantly, several senior party officials lost their bid for election. Many candidates were elected, most notably party maverick Boris Yeltsin, whose views differed significantly from those expressed by Gorbachev and other senior CPSU officials.

As significant as the 1989 election was, less than a year later, in February 1990, it was overshadowed by an even more impressive political reform as the CPSU renounced its monopoly political status. For the first time in Soviet history, multiple political parties became legal.

Unfortunately for Gorbachev, his social-cultural reforms, economic decentralization, and democratization efforts worsened nationality problems within the U.S.S.R. By 1990, ethnic strife and separatism threatened to tear the Soviet Union apart. National independence movements sprang up in all of the 15 republics that made up the Soviet Union, but nowhere was the push for independence stronger than in the three Baltic states, Latvia, Lithuania, and Estonia, incorporated into the U.S.S.R. by Soviet arms in 1940.

Gorbachev, then, had unleashed his revolution to solve the U.S.S.R.'s worst problems, but as the 1990s opened, the outcome was not clear. Would Gorbachev and his reforms survive? Could the Soviet Union survive the forces unleashed by Gorbachev's reforms? Indeed, by 1991, each of the 15 Soviet republics had either declared independence or stated that their own laws took precedence over Soviet laws. To many, it appeared that the Soviet Union was disintegrating.

Gorbachev's Foreign Policy Revolution: New Thinking

Gorbachev's domestic revolution went hand in hand with a revolution in Soviet foreign policy outlooks. Termed *Novoe Myshlenie*, or **New Thinking**, Gorbachev's new Soviet worldview stressed global independence rather than class conflict, and redefined traditional Soviet conceptions of security. Importantly, he also emphasized that the time for military intervention outside one's own country had passed.

Gorbachev's stress on global interdependence was particularly noteworthy. On numerous occasions, the Soviet leader declared that the countries of the world shared mutual interests and faced mutual threats that went beyond class conflict. This was a revolutionary perspective for a Soviet leader, because to a Marxist-Leninist, class conflict was the ultimate driving force behind history. Gorbachev's emphasis on global interdependence—on the need to control the arms race, to find solutions to environmental problems and drug trafficking, and to solve international economic problems of debt and underdevelopment—was thus heresy to traditional Marxist-Leninists. To them, nothing could supersede class conflict's importance, but now Gorbachev said that that was no longer true.

Gorbachev also altered old Soviet conceptions of security. Before his ascendancy, the prevailing Soviet viewpoint was that the Soviet Union was threatened militarily by the capitalist-imperialist West led by the United States, and that the Soviet military alone could protect the U.S.S.R. from the threat. Gorbachev rejected these outlooks, replacing them with new concepts such as "comprehensive security," "mutual security," "reasonable sufficiency," and "defensive defense."

Comprehensive security had two different aspects. First, Gorbachev and his supporters believed that threats besides military ones challenged Soviet security. These threats included economic decline, environmental deterioration, and related issues. This belief led directly to the second aspect of comprehensive security, that Soviet security could be guaranteed only through political means. Gorbachev therefore admitted that the U.S.S.R. had relied too heavily on its military to achieve security, and that this excessive reliance on the military had led to reduced Soviet security both in military affairs and in other fields.

Mutual security was closely tied to comprehensive security. Whereas previous Soviet leaders argued that the United States had a large military establishment because of its expansionist policies, Gorbachev acknowledged that part of the American military existed because of the U.S.S.R.'s own military buildup. This was a significant acknowledgment for a Soviet leader. In essence, Gorbachev admitted that U.S. and Soviet security was interdependent. As the general secretary said on many occasions, "The Soviet Union cannot be secure until the United States is secure."

With Gorbachev's perspective that one cause of the American military buildup was the Soviet Union's own military buildup, and his belief that security could be guaranteed only through political means, it was only logical that the Kremlin's perspectives on military posture and doctrine had to change as well. Thus, Gorbachev argued that the U.S.S.R.'s military posture would be based on "reasonable sufficiency," and its military doctrine would be changed to "defensive defense." Although the specific meaning of each term was not finalized, Gorbachev's intent was clear. From the general secretary's viewpoint, reasonable sufficiency implied that the Soviet military buildup of the 1970s and 1980s had gone beyond providing Soviet security and had become a liability. Future Soviet military expenditures would thus be based on what was reasonable and sufficient to defend the Soviet homeland. Similarly, whereas previous Soviet military doctrine was based on defending the homeland by launching an offensive before the other side could, Gorbachev argued for—and convinced the military to accept—the perspective that defense should be based on first absorbing an attack, not launching a preemptive attack. To Gorbachev, defensive defense was less provocative as a doctrine, and hence less likely to lead to Western overreaction.

But did Gorbachev's changed outlooks on global interdependence, comprehensive security, mutual security, reasonable sufficiency, and defensive defense mean anything in reality, or were they merely rhetoric? At first, there was no way to tell. Gradually, however, as changes in Soviet foreign and defense policy behavior accumulated, it became clear that Gorbachev's changed outlooks were real.

Even so, the third and final part of new thinking, that the time for military intervention outside one's own country had passed, carried with it the most impressive proof that *novoe myshlenie* was more than rhetoric. Since World War II, the U.S.S.R. time after time has made it clear that it would not permit challenges to communism in Eastern Europe to succeed, and would use military force if necessary to ensure the continuation of communist rule.

Understandably, given the long record of Soviet willingness to intervene in Eastern Europe, events unfolded slowly at first in Eastern Europe as Eastern Europeans tested whether Gorbachev was serious about nonintervention. A free election was held in Poland in 1989, and communist candidates were soundly defeated. Solidarity, the once-illegal trade union, dominated the newly formed government. Hungary opened its borders with Austria, announced that a multiparty election would be held in 1990, and changed its name, rejecting the words "People's Republic." The Hungarian Communist Party changed its name to "Socialist" as well.

By fall 1989, Eastern Europe was in turmoil. And when Gorbachev formally announced that the Brezhnev Doctrine was dead, replaced by what a Soviet foreign ministry spokesman humorously called the "Sinatra Doctrine" of allowing Eastern European states to "do it [their] way," the floodgates were opened. In rapid succession, communist governments in East Germany, Bulgaria, Czechoslovakia, and Romania all fell.

For nearly a half century, Soviet insistence on maintaining communism in Eastern Europe had been an unalterable tenet of Soviet foreign policy. To a great extent, that insistence caused the Cold War. In the course of one short year, all that had changed. Eastern Europe provided the most vivid of all proofs— Gorbachev's New Thinking was the real thing.

THE END OF THE SOVIET UNION[18]

Despite Gorbachev's reforms, the Soviet Union's international position slipped in the late 1980s as its internal problems became more serious. Indeed, it may even be argued that Gorbachev's reforms exacerbated Soviet difficulties and accelerated the U.S.S.R.'s decline. This was most apparent in nationality relations, economics, foreign affairs, and domestic politics.

The Decline of the U.S.S.R.

In several republics, but especially in the Baltic states of Latvia, Lithuania, and Estonia, the relaxation of central authority that accompanied glasnost and demokratizatsiya led to vocal cries for national independence. By 1991, the drive for increased local autonomy had become so pronounced that every Soviet republic had declared that its laws took precedence over Soviet laws. Ethnic violence broke out in several republics, including Latvia, Lithuania, Moldavia, Georgia, Armenia, and Azerbaijan. Soviet troops were used to quell ethnic unrest in the Baltic states, in Georgia, and in Azerbaijan.

The Soviet Union's economic position also deteriorated. Although the U.S.S.R. remained a major economic power, Soviet industrial and agricultural output shrank. By 1991, perestroika appeared more a series of halfhearted stop-gap measures than a well-thought out program of economic change. It failed to revive the economy, and may have accelerated the economy's decline as hard-line ideologues sabotaged programs they opposed, and as old economic relationships and methods were challenged, abandoned, and replaced by unfamiliar economic practices.

Gorbachev's foreign policy reforms also weakened the Soviet Union's international position. As we have seen, in 1989, the citizens of Eastern Europe, encouraged by Gorbachev's assurances that the time for military intervention had passed, overthrew their communist rulers. In every case, the Soviet Union did not respond. This was a far cry from Hungary in 1956 and Czechoslovakia in 1968 when the U.S.S.R. had intervened militarily to crush anticommunist movements, and Poland in 1981 when the U.S.S.R. had encouraged the Polish military to impose martial law.

Gorbachev's reforms also weakened the position of the Soviet military. With noncommunist governments in place in Poland, Czechoslovakia, and Hungary, and with Germany unified as a noncommunist state, the Soviet military's forward positions were undermined as one former communist Eastern European state after another insisted upon the withdrawal of Soviet forces.

Across the board, then, the Soviet Union was much weaker in 1991 than it had been in 1985. Instituted to reverse slow long-term decline, the Gorbachev revolution led to rapid near-term decline. Some, including Russia's Boris Yeltsin, argued that decline occurred because reforms were instituted too slowly, but others asserted that the reforms created problems that previously had never existed.

In addition, especially to senior CPSU, KGB, and military officials, Gorbachev's policies smacked of ideological blasphemy. Glasnost rejected censorship, encouraged open debate, and challenged party infallibility. Perestroika sought the abandonment of centralized economic planning and the legalization of private ownership of the means of production. Demokratizatsiya led to the abandonment of the CPSU's monopoly on political power and the movement toward the creation of opposition parties. None of this was doctrinaire Marxism-Leninism.

Worse yet from the perspective of many of the old party, the KGB and the military elite, the struggle for political power between the central government led by Gorbachev and the republics led by Boris Yeltsin and Russia resulted in the formulation of a new Treaty of Union between the republics and the central government. Scheduled to be signed on August 20, 1991, the new treaty was to transfer control over taxation policy, natural resources, and certain police forces from the central government to the republics. In essence, the new treaty would alter the power relationship between the republics and central government that had existed since the U.S.S.R. was founded.

The Coup Attempt and Its Aftermath

To forestall this and reverse other Gorbachev reforms, on August 18, 1991, an eight-man "Emergency Committee" led by senior CPSU, KGB, military, and Interior Ministry officials engineered a coup to remove Gorbachev from power. Mismanaged and poorly executed, the coup failed as thousands of Soviet citizens took to the streets, and as military, KGB, and police units refused to obey the Emergency Committee. Rallying around Russian President **Boris Yeltsin**, Soviet citizens and security forces made it clear that although perestroika may have failed, glasnost and demokratizatsiya had changed Soviet society.

Following the failure of the coup, the Soviet Union's political fabric eroded still more as the Gorbachev-led central government and the Yeltsin-led Russian government struggled to obtain the upper hand. At the same time, the complicity in the coup attempt of much of the leadership of the Communist Party of the Soviet Union (CPSU) and the organs of state coercion undermined the credibility of those organizations.

In the case of the CPSU, its role in the coup eliminated whatever shred of credibility and clout it still had. Within weeks of the coup's failure, every major Soviet republic declared the CPSU illegal.

The case of the Soviet armed forces, the KGB, and the Ministry of Internal Affairs was more complex. Although senior officials from each played central roles in the coup, other senior officials and rank-and-file officers and men staunchly opposed the coup and emerged as heroes. Nevertheless, many more Soviet citizens questioned the role of the instruments of state coercion after the coup than before it.

By the end of 1991, then, the Soviet Union was in disarray. Its economy was a shambles. Its political leadership was divided between those who wanted the U.S.S.R. to continue, and those who wanted to dissolve it. The Soviet military still had its weapons, but its credibility had been tarnished, and it was not clear where its loyalty lied. Even worse for Gorbachev and those who wanted the U.S.S.R. to continue as a state, on December 1, 1991, the people of Ukraine voted to secede from the Soviet Union.

Russian President Boris Yeltsin rallied opposition to the August 1991 coup attempt against Soviet President Mikhail Gorbachev. After the coup, Yeltsin became the most popular man in both Russia and the Soviet Union.   (Black Star.)

Thus, when the presidents of the republics of Byelorussia, Russia, and Ukraine met in Minsk in December 1991, the internal strengths and international position of the U.S.S.R. had eroded so much that they had no qualms about declaring the Soviet Union defunct. Opining that "the Union of Soviet Socialist Republics, as a subject of international law and a geopolitical reality, is ceasing its existence," the three Slavic leaders proclaimed the formation of a new Commonwealth of Independent States. A new era was about to begin.

The Soviet Union lingered on for 23 days after the declaration. Eight other former Soviet republics joined the newly created **Commonwealth of Independent States** (CIS) before the Soviet Union dissolved at midnight on December 31, 1991. But by any measure, the Soviet Union bequeathed to its successor little but an agenda of unsolved problems. It was not an auspicious beginning for the CIS.

CHALLENGES FOR RUSSIA, THE OTHER NEWLY INDEPENDENT STATES, AND THE COMMONWEALTH OF INDEPENDENT STATES[19]

The 15 new states and the ambiguous Commonwealth of Independent States that tenuously links 11 of them face many serious problems. These can best be examined under the headings of political uncertainties, economic disarray, challenges to social and cultural pluralism, and foreign and military dangers.

Political Uncertainties

The political future of the 15 former Soviet republics and the CIS is uncertain in three ways. First, the 11 former republics that joined the CIS must determine whether they truly want to remain associated with each other, and then they must overcome the serious differences that developed between and among them. (Latvia, Lithuania, and Estonia opted not to join the CIS, and Georgia applied for membership but was denied it until the republic resolved its internal human rights problems.)

In the first few weeks of the existence of the CIS, extensive bickering broke out between member states over powers, military structure, economic reform, currency, territory, and property once owned by the Soviet government. The role of the armed forces was open to question as well. Whether those issues could be resolved was an open question. Indeed, each meeting that the CIS held uncovered more differences.

Second, regardless of whether the CIS survived, the territorial integrity of several of the newly independent states was challenged by separatist movements. Russia was most vulnerable since it contained 16 "autonomous regions" based on ethnic groups. Several—including the Tartars, the Chechens, and the Yakuts—wanted independence, but Russia refused to consider this possibility.

Third, regardless of the political relationships that evolved between and among the former republics and autonomous regions, each had to determine its own form of government. With no domestic democratic tradition in any of the republics or regions, it was highly unlikely that democratic governments would develop in all cases. A considerable number of states may choose autocratic or dictatorial regimes. Indeed, the political turmoil that swept Russia in 1993 as a result of the confrontation between President Boris Yeltsin and the Congress of People's Deputies over who ruled Russia was a stark reminder that democracy in the newly independent states was fragile and extremely vulnerable. This was made even more apparent in late 1993 when Yeltsin dissolved parliament because of the deadlock that existed. In response, radical and conservative legislators and their supporters armed themselves and attacked the national television and radio station and the Moscow city government building. Yeltsin in turn ordered government forces to attack the Russian White House, which the dissident legislators had turned into their headquarters. Hundreds were killed before forces loyal to Yeltsin gained full control. Nevertheless, Yeltsin's authority was shaken.

Economic Disarray

The new states and the CIS also faced immense economic difficulties. These could best be categorized as short-term challenges and long-term problems.

Throughout the former U.S.S.R., the dominant short-term challenge was simple survival. The 1991, 1992, and 1993 harvests were poor, and the breakdown in the transportation infrastructure worsened the always-high food spoilage and loss rate. Some estimates placed this rate at 50 percent. Winters also promised to be difficult because of energy shortfalls. Oil and coal production dropped significantly because of equipment breakdowns, strikes, and disruption of the system.

Yeltsin's decision to institute an immediate free market economic system in January 1992 also contributed to the short-term challenge for many Russian people. As soon as price controls were lifted, prices for goods skyrocketed. Yeltsin gambled that production would increase as prices increased, thereby bringing more goods to the marketplace and driving prices down once again. However, if Yeltsin's gamble failed, he would most certainly lose political support, and another coup might even occur. Leaders in other newly independent states who followed Yeltsin's "shock treatment" strategy faced similar risks.

Long-term economic problems for Russia and the other former Soviet republics included the need to develop the economic institutions, attitudes, and relationships required in a market economy. This will take time. It will be difficult to create new economic institutions based on free-market principles. But it will be even more challenging to develop the requisite attitudes toward competition and the needed relationships between institutions that a free-market economy needs if it is to function well. The outlooks fostered by 74 years of communism will not disappear overnight.

Challenges to Social and Cultural Pluralism

It will not be easy to overcome the challenges to social and cultural pluralism brought about by ethnic, social, and cultural animosity. During the years of Soviet rule, these centuries-old problems were held in check by a strong central government. But with the collapse of central authority, old ethnic, social, and cultural hatreds percolated to the surface. Some have already exploded into killing and warfare.

Challenges to social and cultural pluralism have two dimensions. First, throughout the former Soviet Union, there is extensive anti-Russian sentiment. Russians in Latvia, Lithuania, Estonia, Moldavia, Ukraine, and elsewhere expressed concern over discrimination and fear for their lives. Russian President Yeltsin assured them that Russia will provide protection.

Second, many non-Russian peoples also dislike each other intensely. For example, former Georgian President Gamsakhurdia preached a "Georgia for Georgians" theme that terrified Georgia's minority groups. Ethnic fighting flared there, and elsewhere as well. None of this bodes well for domestic tranquility within or between the new states.

Foreign and Military Dangers

Future foreign and military relationships also are disquieting. Over the years, the Russian empire and the Soviet Union incorporated territory from neighboring states. International boundaries were often arbitrarily established, dividing ethnic groups between Soviet republics and foreign countries. With the demise of Soviet power, attempts may arise to redraw some of these boundaries.

The Ukraine provides an excellent example. It has territorial claims against every former Soviet republic and foreign country with which it shares borders. Although it has recently been quiet about these claims, during 1991 the Ukrainian parliament indicated that it wanted these issues to be resolved, in Ukraine's favor.

At the same time, Russia declared that it wanted to regain control of the Crimean peninsula from the Ukraine. Although the Crimea was long part of Russia, former Soviet leader Nikita Khrushchev in 1954 transferred it to Ukraine as a good will gesture between the two Soviet republics. Ukraine refused, but the issue is not necessarily over.

The future of the former Soviet military establishment and its weapons also gives cause for concern. One of the leading issues between newly independent states was whether there should be one unified CIS armed forces, or whether states should maintain separate forces. Russia strongly preferred a single unified military, but several other states including Ukraine feared too much Russian influence in a unified military and insisted on separate armed forces. Several meetings in 1992 and 1993 failed to resolve this issue.

These debates took a serious toll on military morale as soldiers and officers did not know whose orders to follow. This in turn led to serious questions about who controls weapons. At the conventional level, weapons reverted to their owners. In some cases, this meant to soldiers loyal to the CIS military structure; in other cases, to soldiers loyal to the governments of the newly independent states; and in still other instances, to local groups that overran armories and stole weapons.

The control of nuclear weapons presented a slightly different story. At the nuclear level, over 90 percent of all nuclear weapons were in Russia. Almost all of the others were in Ukraine, Belarus, or Kazakhstan, all of which declared their intention to become nuclear free. All also expressed support for the 1993 U.S.-Russian START II Treaty, under which the U.S. and Russia—and technically, Ukraine, Belarus, and Kazakhstan as well—would significantly decrease their nuclear arsenals.

However, the president of Kazakhstan, Nursultan Nazarbeyav, declared that he wanted Kazakhstan to maintain a nuclear arsenal as long as Russia remained one. The Ukrainian parliament also stated it wanted to keep some nuclear weapons. The nuclear situation therefore remains unclear.

RUSSIAN AND OTHER NEWLY INDEPENDENT STATES' VIEWS OF THE WORLD

As discussed earlier, the collapse of the Soviet Union and the elimination of communism as the state-sponsored ideology changed most perceptions in Russia and the other former Soviet republics, but not necessarily all of them. Here, we will concentrate on the predominant perceptions that can be identified in Russia and the other newly independent states, fully realizing that the range of perceptions is much broader than those that are presented here. We must also remember that in situations as fluid as those prevailing in the former Soviet republics, perceptions can change rapidly.

The Newly Independent States' Perceptions of Each Other

In almost every case, the most important new relations and perceptual outlooks that the newly independent states developed concerned each other.[20] Often, the newly independent states harbored immense mistrust about each other's intentions. The most notable of these was the mistrust between Russia and Ukraine, where ethnic dislikes, treatment of each other's minorities, territorial disputes, differences over the pace of economic reform, and disagreements about who owned the military hardware of the former Soviet Union combined to raise Russian-Ukrainian tensions.

Many of the other former Soviet republics also saw Russia as a potential threat. The major concern that most had about Russia was straightforward. Would Boris Yeltsin and subsequent Russian leaders willingly acquiesce to the final dissolution of the five-centuries old Russian empire, and to the reduction in Russian influence that those republics expected the U.S.S.R.'s collapse to bring?

In addition, with their old country disbanded and their new countries in various states of confusion, the leaders and peoples of the 15 new states often expressed widely different viewpoints about policies and political systems that could be adopted in their own and neighboring countries. Some, like Yeltsin and his supporters, wanted a free-market economic system and democratic political structures. Others, like the ultranationalist Russian movement Pamyat, advocated a centralized economic and political system like that of the czars. Some cared little what form of government or economic organization developed, as long as it was controlled by local leaders. Still others preferred a system dominated by the Soviet military. Some even argued for a return to communist political, social, and economic methods.

Clearly, then, the 15 newly independent states had different views about each other, and about what they themselves should do. Boris Yeltsin and Russia argued for independence, immediate free-market economics, and coordination of policies under the CIS. Despite concerns about Russian intentions, Ukrainian President Leonid Kravchuk agreed with Yeltsin and Russia on many issues. Nevertheless, he was concerned that the introduction of immediate free-market reforms would destabilize Ukraine's economy, and that Yeltsin's version of coordination under the CIS was a cover for continued Russian domination.

Meanwhile, Kazakhstan's President Nursultan Nazarbayev, along with most Central Asian Islamic peoples and states, harbored fears that the CIS was a formula for continued Russian dominance; expressed concerns about their own economic futures; and contemplated their own countries' directions. Given Islam's role in their own postcommunist states, should they look to the south and fundamentalist Iran as a model for their new countries, or to the west and the more pragmatic Turkey? Should they look even further to the west, to Europe, for a model for their societies? Or should they look north and maintain close ties with Russia? Throughout the former Soviet Union, policy directions and perceptual outlooks remained in flux.

The United States, Europe, and Japan

The end of the Soviet Union also led to an extensive transformation of Russian and other attitudes toward the developed West. Whereas previously the Soviet Union and communism feared the West, especially the United States, and rejected the political and economic institutions that existed there, many of the states that emerged in the aftermath of the Soviet collapse developed cordial relations with the West, and sought to institute democratic political systems and capitalist economic structures similar to those in the West.

Most former Soviet republics also saw the West as a source of economic assistance and investment, and ardently sought to attract both. However, given the economic difficulties that prevailed in the West in the early 1990s, as well as the continued unsettled situation in most of the newly independent states, none of the former Soviet republics were as successful as they had hoped to be in attracting either aid or investment.

Of course, not everyone in the former Soviet Union was favorably disposed toward this new collaboration with the former enemy. Some, remembering Marxist-Leninist teachings and seeing Western businesspeople descend by the thousands on Russia and the other newly independent states, saw the West pursuing colonial ambitions in Russia and the other former Soviet republics. Therefore, they rejected Western capitalism and democracy. Others recalled nineteenth-century Slavophile outlooks, and demanded a continued rejection of Western outlooks, values, and culture. They wanted a return to Russian roots as the source for Russia's future salvation.

The United States considered the political and economic reforms taking place in Russia to be so important that by 1993, the U.S. provided significant amounts of economic assistance to its former enemy. U.S. President Bill Clinton extended a sizeable economic aid package to Russian President Boris Yeltsin when they met at the March 1993 Vancouver Summit.   (Reuters/Bettmann.)

In addition, Russian relations with Japan continued to be troubled by the Northern Territories issues. Following World War II, the then-Soviet Union received four islands from Japan because of Soviet participation in the war against Japan. For some time, Japan had demanded these islands back. However, the Soviet Union refused even to consider such a transfer. After the Soviet collapse, even though Yeltsin appeared to be favorably disposed toward it, domestic political opposition to the transfer prevented him from actually implementing it.

Despite these difficulties, most Russians and citizens of the other former Soviet republics by 1993 considered the United States, Europe, and Japan to be friendly states. For many in Russia and elsewhere, a new era in relations with the industrialized West had dawned.[21]

China

After years of hostility, tension, and even warfare,[22] Sino-Soviet relations improved dramatically during the last several years of the Soviet era. They were capped by Gorbachev's 1989 visit to China, the first visit by a Soviet leader to China in over 25 years.

But beneath that improvement, lingering dislike, if not tension, remained. This lingering dislike arose from historical antipathy, racial animosity, and territorial disputes. Ideological rivalry and the leadership of the communist world had also been issues of contention, but even before the dissolution of the Soviet Union, they had become less important concerns both in Moscow and Beijing.

Little has changed since the Soviet Union dissolved. And given the pressing problems that leaders of the newly independent states must face, it is not likely that they will increase their involvement with China. Aside from limited amounts of cross-border trade, China can provide Russia and the other newly-independent states with little. And it appears highly unlikely that any of the newly independent states will initiate heightened tensions with China over the issues noted above.[23]

As improbable as it may seem, then, many of the newly independent states may actually downgrade their relations with China in the near and mid-term future. China has little to offer them, and none of the newly independent states needs additional foreign policy problems.

The Developing World

Over the last 20 years of the Soviet era, the U.S.S.R. developed extensive contacts with and presence in the Developing World.[24] But in the post-Soviet era, the involvement of most of the newly independent states with Developing World countries virtually disappeared. In every case, the newly independent states had much more urgent concerns to devote their time and energy to than Developing World issues. Indeed, in many cases, the newly independent states themselves were little better off than Developing World states.

To a limited extent, Russia was an exception to this rule. But whereas in the past the Soviet Union sought either political benefits or economic betterment via trade in its relations with Developing World states, Russia concentrated almost exclusively on trade. Thus, Russia maintained economic ties with Argentina,

Brazil, India, Libya, Morocco, and several other Developing World states. Notably, Russian contacts with Cuba were significantly reduced.

The Central Asian states also were exceptions, but only in regard to their relations with other Islamic states. Several of the Central Asian states developed contacts with Saudi Arabia, Iran, and Turkey to reassert their Islamic identities, to seek external funding, and to develop a better understanding about which political, economic, and social paths to follow as they charted their own independent courses.

The United Nations and Other IGOs

For most of the post–World War II era, the Soviet Union asserted that IGOs were dominated and controlled by Western Industrial powers, that is, First World states. Most IGOs were therefore considered tools of the capitalist-imperialist interests that sought to take advantage of participating Second and Third World states.

Because of this outlook, the Soviet Union was extremely unwilling to become involved in their operations. This was true even in the United Nations and its specialized agencies. The U.S.S.R. refused to support UN peacekeeping operations, participate in the UN's data collection function, submit cases to the International Court of Justice, or participate in the different economic apparatuses that are part of the UN system.[25] To a great extent, the Soviet Union managed to influence its Eastern European neighbors to follow its preferences on these matters as well.

This all changed. Gorbachev's New Thinking initiated the transformation in Soviet attitudes toward the UN and other IGOs, and the abandonment of communism by Russia and the other newly independent states completed the transformation. Even before the U.S.S.R. collapsed, Moscow paid its back debt to the UN, became a cooperative partner within the UN in resolving regional conflicts, and joined several of the UN's associated organizations. With the dissolution of the U.S.S.R., all 15 of the former Soviet republics became members of the UN, and most actively participated in it. Russian soldiers are participating in United Nations peacekeeping efforts. In addition, all 15 former Soviet republics joined or sought to join the General Agreement on Tariffs and Trade, the World Bank, and several other IGOs. In short, the approach that Russia and the other former Soviet republics now take toward the United Nations and other IGOs is indistinguishable from that taken by other states.

Multinational Corporations

Soviet perceptions of multinational corporations also changed significantly during the late 1980s and early 1990s. Whereas before the Gorbachev revolution MNCs were considered the cutting edge of capitalist exploitation and neocolonialism, Soviet spokespersons in the late 1980s came to regard MNCs as a vital source of capital investment, technical know-how, and managerial expertise. There remained a discomfort that MNCs still sought to "perpetuate and aggravate" an "unequal status" for others, but this discomfort was far overshadowed by the new favorable outlook on MNCs.

Again, the dissolution of the U.S.S.R. completed the transformation in Russian and other newly independent states' attitudes toward MNCs. Virtually without exception, each one of them now actively seeks external investment from MNCs. Given the unsettled situation in most of the former Soviet republics, most MNCs have been hesitant to invest large sums of money, but that does not alter the fact that the newly independent states now want MNC investments and operations.

National Liberation Movements

Soviet attitudes toward national liberation movements also underwent immense change in the Gorbachev years, and further evolved in the time since the U.S.S.R. collapsed. From the 1970s through the mid-1980s, most Soviet authorities argued that it was the Soviet Union's responsibilities to support these groups. But by the late 1980s, Soviet spokespersons had begun to assert that national liberation movements should be self-sufficient. In purely pragmatic terms, the Soviets realized that supporting national liberation provided them with few advantages, and also complicated their efforts to improve relations with and attract investment from the West.

Ironically, even as the Soviets were rethinking their position, they also began to have problems in foreign and domestic affairs defining national liberation movements. In foreign policy, self-defined national liberation movements in Angola, Afghanistan, Cambodia, Mozambique, Nicaragua, and elsewhere fought against pro-Soviet governments. The Soviets condemned these groups as terrorists. Similarly, in domestic affairs, when in 1989 and 1990 self-defined national liberation groups in Latvia, Lithuania, and Estonia sought peacefully to achieve independence for the Baltic republics, Moscow authorities denounced them as "illegitimate." And when at the same time a self-defined Azerbaijani national liberation movement first assaulted Armenians and then became anti-Soviet as well, Moscow sent in troops to put down the insurrection. Gorbachev himself described the Azerbaijani national movement as "terrorism."

Most ironically, it was the demand of national groups for their own independence that brought about the final collapse of the Soviet Union as all 15 of the U.S.S.R.'s republics, each based on a nationality group, declared that they no longer wanted to be part of the Soviet empire. Hence the Soviet Union passed into history.

But for leaders of Russia and the other newly independent states, the end of the Soviet Union did not end the quandary of defining which national liberation movements were legitimate, and which were not. As already noted, several of the newly independent states including Russia have nationalities included within them that are demanding independence. They too must now confront the same problem that first confronted Western leaders, and then Mikhail Gorbachev as well: when was a national liberation movement legitimate, and when was it not?

CONCLUSIONS: WHAT HAPPENS NEXT?

During 1991, the world witnessed the demise not just of 74 years of communist rule, but also the end of five centuries of Russian empire. The changes taking place are epochal, part of an ongoing process that did not begin with the failed coup attempt, nor end with the breakup of the Soviet Union.

Where, then, are the former Soviet republics and the CIS headed? Too many variables exist to answer this question definitively. But at the very least, it is evident that the failure of the coup and the dissolution of the Soviet Union did not clear the path for political stability and democratization, economic restructuring, social and cultural pluralism, or foreign policy and military stability.

Clearly, the CIS is on shaky ground. It may well be doomed. The Commonwealth's inability to solve the question of military unity as well as lingering territorial, economic, and related issues does not bode well for its future. Neither does the continuation of ethnic rivalries and animosities. It would not be surprising if the CIS proved to be a short-term transitory structure.

"Transitory to what?" is the key question. All things considered, it appears most likely that the 15 new states will jealously guard their independence, and eventually go their own separate ways. Some economic ties will eventuate, and in the Central Asian Islamic states, perhaps even a degree of political unity.

Nor would it be surprising if the process of dissolution of some of the newly independent countries continued. As we have already seen, ethnic groups in several are already clamoring for their independence, and in other cases are demanding that boundaries be redrawn.

As for Yeltsin and the leaders of other former Soviet republics, they too are on thin ice. Those like Yeltsin that are attempting to institute new economic, political, and social systems may still have a short breathing space ahead of them, but time is running out. They must have results, or demands for their removal will mount. Meanwhile, those that are attempting to hold to past ways of doing things face the challenge of making the old system work. If they do not succeed, demands for their removal will mount as well.

For the near and mid-term future, then, one of the few certainties in the territories of the former Soviet Union is the certainty of change. The peoples of the former Soviet Union are only part way through their ongoing adventure. For them, the range of possible futures has expanded immensely. With the Soviet Union dissolved and the Cold War over, the easy predictability of the last half century is gone. The hard part is just beginning.

KEY TERMS AND CONCEPTS

Russian Empire	Russia as a world power
Bolshevik Revolution	Westernizers
Russia's messianic missions	Slavophiles
Russian territorial expansion	Karl Marx

economic and historical
  materialism
V. I. Lenin
vanguard and dictatorship of
  the proletariat
Lenin's theory of imperialism
two-camp thesis and peaceful
  coexistence
Russian Civil War
New Economic Policy (NEP)
Joseph Stalin
capitalist encirclement
industrialization, collectivization,
  and purges
Nikita Khrushchev's worldview
Leonid Brezhnev's worldview
Mikhail Gorbachev

glasnost
perestroika
demokratizatsiya
new thinking
reasons for the Soviet Union's
  decline and collapse
Boris Yeltsin
Commonwealth of Independent
  States
challenges for the newly
  independent states
newly independent states' views
  of each other
Russia's views of the United
  States, Europe, and Japan
Russia's views of China and the
  Developing World

NOTES

1. Adam B. Ulam, "Nationalism, Panslavism, Communism," in Ivo J. Lederer, *Russian Foreign Policy: Essays in Historical Perspective* (New Haven, CT: Yale University Press, 1967), p. 44.
2. See Michael B. Petrovich, *The Emergence of Russian Pan Slavism 1856–1870* (New York: Columbia University Press, 1956).
3. As quoted in E. H. Carr, "Russia and Europe as a Theme of Russian History," in Richard Pares and A. J. P. Taylor (eds.), *Essays Presented to Sir Lewis Namier* (New York: Macmillan, 1956), p. 362.
4. As quoted in Robert F. Byrnes, "Attitudes toward the West," in Lederer, *Russian Foreign Policy*, p. 116.
5. One of the best-detailed explanations of these concepts is in R. N. Carew-Hunt, *The Theory and Practice of Communism* (Baltimore: Penguin, 1963).
6. For a detailed history of the development of the CPSU, see Leonard Shapiro, *The Communist Party of the Soviet Union* (New York: Random House, 1970). See also Theodore Dan, *The Origins of Bolshevism* (New York: Schocken Books, 1970).
7. V. I. Lenin, *Imperialism—the Highest Stage of Capitalism*, Selected Works, Vol. V (New York: International Publishers, 1943).
8. V. I. Lenin, *Sochineniia V. I. Lenina*, Vol. 29 (Moscow: Izdatel'stvo, 1941–1966), p. 133.
9. See Alvin Z. Rubinstein, *Soviet Foreign Policy since World War II: Imperial and Global* (New York: HarperCollins, 1992), p. 9. See also Adam B. Ulam, *Expansion and Coexistence: Soviet Foreign Policy, 1917–1973* (New York: Praeger, 1974); George F. Kennan, *Russia and the West under Lenin and Stalin* (Boston: Little, Brown, 1960); and Louis Fischer, *Russia's Road from Peace to War 1917–1941* (New York: Harper & Row, 1969).
10. See Stalin's Report to the 18th Congress of the CPSU, March 10, 1939, in I. Va. Stalin, *Problems of Leninism* (Moscow: Foreign Languages Publishing House, 1940), pp. 623–630, 656–662.

11. For one estimate, see Nikita Khrushchev, *Khrushchev Remembers* (Boston: Little, Brown, 1970), p. 583.

12. *The New York Times*, June 24, 1941.

13. A more extensive version of this discussion was published in Daniel S. Papp, "Toward an Estimate of the Soviet Worldview," *Naval War College Review*, November–December 1979, pp. 60–70.

14. For a detailed assessment of both the three streams of the "world revolutionary movement" and "imperialist intrigues" against that movement, see Daniel S. Papp, *Soviet Perceptions of the Developing World in the 1980s: The Ideological Basis* (Lexington, MA: Lexington Books, 1985).

15. *Krasnaia Zvezda*, December 20, 1973; *Izvestiia*, November 29, 1975; and *Pravda*, December 8, 1975. See also "Contemporary Imperialism in the Light of Lenin's Doctrine," *World Marxist Review*, March 1975, p. 72.

16. D. Volsky, "Behind the Conflict in Angola," *New Times*, September 1975, p. 8.

17. Much of the discussion in this section is taken from Daniel S. Papp, "The Gorbachev Revolution: A Five-Year Report Card," *Georgia Tech Research Horizons* (March 1990).

18. Most of the analysis in this section is taken from Daniel S. Papp, *The End of the Soviet Union* (Atlanta: The Southern Center for International Studies, 1992). See also Michael Ellman and Vladimir Kontorovich, *The Disintegration of the Soviet Economic System* (New York: Routledge, 1992); David Lane, *Soviet Society Under Perestroika* (New York: Routledge, 1992); and Stuart H. Loory and Ann Inse, *Seven Days that Shook the World* (Atlanta: Turner Publishing, 1991).

19. See Papp, *The End of the Soviet Union*, especially Chapter 4.

20. The material in this section has been taken primarily from interviews conducted by the author with Russian, Ukrainian, and Latvian officials and emigres in 1992 in Atlanta, Berlin, Kiev, London, Moscow, New York, and Washington.

21. For several analyses of Soviet policy toward Western Europe before Gorbachev, see Richard Pipes, *Soviet Strategy in Europe* (New York: Crane Russack, 1976); Roger Hamburg, "Political and Strategic Factors in Soviet Relations with the West: Soviet Perceptions," in Roger E. Kanet (ed.), *Soviet Foreign Policy in the 1980s* (New York: Praeger Publishers, 1982), pp. 197–230; and Thomas Wolfe, *Soviet Power and Europe 1945–1970* (Baltimore: Johns Hopkins University Press, 1970). For a discussion of the Gorbachev years, see Ray S. Cline, James Arnold, and Roger Kanet (eds.), *Western Europe in Soviet Global Strategy* (Boulder, CO: Westview, 1987). For other perspectives on U.S.-Soviet relations in the late 1980s and early 1990s, see Seweryn Bialer and Michael Mandelbaum (eds.), *Gorbachev's Russia and American Foreign Policy* (Boulder, CO: Westview, 1988); and Graham T. Allison and William L. Ury (eds.), *Windows of Opportunity: From Cold War to Peaceful Competition in U.S.-Soviet Relations* (New York: Ballinger, 1989). For a discussion of Soviet policies toward Japan in the 1970s and 1980s, see Myles Robertson, *Soviet Policy toward Japan: An Analysis of Trends in the 1970s and 1980s* (New York: Cambridge University Press, 1988).

22. For a detailed analysis of the pre-Gorbachev Soviet view of China, see Morris Rothenburg, *Whither China: The View from the Kremlin* (Miami: Center for Advanced International Studies, 1977).

23. In December 1992, Russia and China agreed to further reduce their respective armed forces on and near the Sino-Soviet border, thereby lessening the possibility of tension and confrontation.

24. For pre-Gorbachev Soviet outlooks on the Developing World, see Robert H. Donaldson (ed.), *The Soviet Union in the Third World: Successes and Failures* (Boulder, CO: Westview, 1981); several articles in Kanet, pp. 263–351; E. J. Feuchtwanger and Peter Nailor (eds.), *The Soviet Union and the Third World*

(New York: St. Martin's Press, 1981); Mark N. Katz, *The Third World in Soviet Military Thought* (Baltimore: Johns Hopkins University Press, 1982); and Daniel S. Papp, *Soviet Policies toward the Developing World During the 1980s: The Dilemmas of Power and Presence* (Montgomery: Air University Press, 1986). For Gorbachev-era outlooks, see Carol R. Saivetz (ed.), *The Soviet Union in the Third World* (Boulder, CO: Westview, 1989); and W. Raymond Duncan and Carolyn McGiffert Ekedahl, *Moscow and the Third World Under Gorbachev* (Boulder, CO: Westview, 1990).

25. See Daniel S. Papp, *The United Nations: Issues of Peace and Conflict* (Atlanta: The Southern Center for International Studies, 1990), especially Chapter 4.

CHAPTER 13

Europe, Japan, Canada, and Israel

- What led to the major political changes in Eastern European states in the late 1980s and early 1990s?
- How do Eastern European states view themselves and the world?
- What are the major economic and security problems facing Western European states, Japan, Canada, and Israel?
- How do Western European states, Japan, Canada, and Israel view themselves and the world?

During much of the Cold War, the United States and the Soviet Union dominated international affairs. It may even be argued that for much of this period, U.S and Soviet policies and perceptions determined the course of international affairs.

Obviously, this is no longer true. Indeed, even before the Cold War ended, the superpowers' dominance of their respective alliances had declined, and the importance of the policies and perceptions of other state actors had grown. Increasingly, the allies of the superpowers set their own policy directions and adopted their own perceptual outlooks. The superpowers had little choice but to accommodate themselves to the new facts of international life.

The emergence of the European Community and Japan as major international economic actors, the Eastern European revolutions of 1989, and the demise of the Soviet Union all underlined the reality that the world of the 1990s is no longer the world of the 1950s and 1960s. Indeed, it is not even the world of the 1970s and 1980s. Therefore, it is imperative that we understand how and why major state actors of the 1990s, the United States and Russia, view the world as they do.

In this chapter, we will concentrate on the perceptions of states that were the major allies of the superpowers during the Cold War. We will explore Eastern and Western European perceptions of the past, present, and future state of the international community. We will also examine Japanese, Canadian, and Israeli outlooks on the course of international affairs. The inclusion of these states together in this chapter is intended to inform students about the perceptions of these states, and to underline how diverse perceptions of the one-time allies of the erstwhile superpowers have become.

EASTERN EUROPE

The changes in governments that took place in 1989 in Bulgaria, Czechoslovakia, East Germany, Hungary, Poland, and Romania were truly revolutionary events. For nearly 50 years, communist governments ruled these six states, as well as Albania and Yugoslavia. Particularly during the 1940s and 1950s, these states were dominated by the Soviet Union. This was not surprising in view of the fact that with only three exceptions (Albania, Czechoslovakia and Yugoslavia), the governments acquired power through the presence or proximity of Soviet arms.

In many respects, the communization of Eastern Europe through force of Soviet arms is what led directly to the onset of the Cold War. What made the changes in governments in Eastern Europe in 1989 globally significant was that for the first time since World War II, the U.S.S.R. allowed events in Eastern Europe to follow their own course.

The Rise and Fall of Eastern European Communism

Before World War II, Eastern European states were governed by a variety of royalist, democratic, and autocratic governments. Albania was ruled by an authoritarian royalist regime. Bulgaria was a constitutional monarchy. Prewar Czechoslovakia was an advanced industrial democracy until Nazi Germany marched into the country in 1939. East Germany was part of Hitler's Third Reich. Hungary existed as a "kingdom without a king," that is, a titular monarchy ruled by a regent. The Polish state was ruled by a democratically elected government until Germany and the Soviet Union partitioned it in September 1939. Romania was a kingdom that sided with Nazi Germany. Yugoslavia was also a kingdom until 1941, after which Hitler partitioned Yugoslavia among its neighbors. Meanwhile, two separate guerrilla groups fought in Yugoslavia against the Germans. After initially cooperating with each other in the anti-German effort, the Chetnik forces under Draza Mihajlovic and the Partisans under Josip Broz Tito fought each other as well as the Germans in a vicious civil war that sowed some of the seeds for the violence that has ripped Yugoslavia apart again in the 1990s.[1]

As the Soviet army fought its way across Eastern Europe in the closing months of World War II, it became clear that Stalin intended to maximize Soviet power throughout the region in the postwar era. The major issue in Eastern Europe between Stalin and his U.S. and British allies was the Polish situation. At the February 1945 Yalta Conference, the three allies agreed that postwar Poland would be ruled by a Polish government selected through "free and unfettered elections as soon as possible on the basis of universal suffrage and secret ballot."[2] That government was also to be friendly toward the U.S.S.R. To the U.S.S.R., that meant a communist regime, and with the continuing presence of the Soviet Army in Poland, such a regime was established.

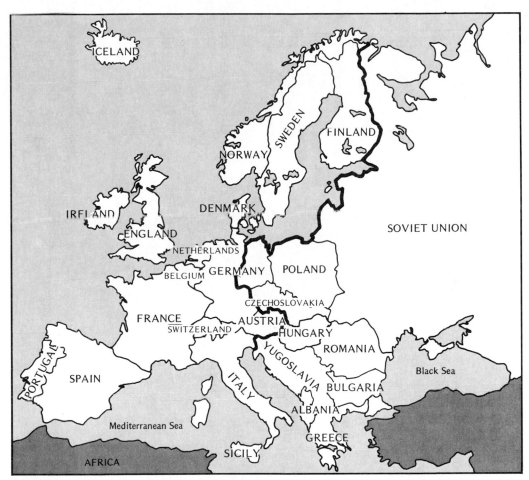

FIGURE 13–1 Western and Eastern Europe: Before the 1989 Eastern European revolutions, all the countries to the left of the heavy line were considered part of Western Europe, and all countries to the right were part of Eastern Europe, except for Greece.

Similar dramas occurred throughout Eastern Europe. By 1948, all the states of Eastern Europe had communist governments, and all had fallen under Soviet control. Each ruling communist party had close and intimate ties with the Communist Party of the Soviet Union (CPSU), with the single exception of Yugoslavia.

The rest of Eastern Europe was dominated by the Soviet Union. Bilateral defense treaties connected the U.S.S.R. to every other state in Eastern Europe, and in those states formerly friendly to or allied with Nazi Germany, the U.S.S.R. removed as much industrial capital as could be transported to the Soviet Union. The Soviet army remained in Eastern Europe, and aided the governments there in their efforts to "reeducate" the peoples of Eastern Europe about the threat of capitalism and the dangers of a capitalist-initiated third world war.

Soon, however, Soviet domination was challenged. Rioting broke out in East Berlin in 1953, Poland edged near civil war in 1956, and the Hungarian

TABLE 13–1   States of Eastern Europe: General Characteristics, 1991

Country	Land		Population					Economy — Gross Domestic Product		Government
	Sq. Km. x 10^6	% in Agriculture	Total (mil.)	Growth Rate %	Literacy Rate %	Ethnic Groups	Religion	Annual Bil.$	Per Capita	Type and Characteristics
Albania	.029	21 arable; 5 other ag.	3.3	1.8	72	Albanian 90 Greek 8	Until 1990, religion illegal; estimated 70% Islam, 20% Greek Orthodox	4.1	1,250	Emerging democracy, with significant continuing communist influence
Bulgaria	.111	41 arable; 11 other ag.	8.9	–.2	93	Bulgarian 85 Turk 9	Bulgarian Orthodox 85 Islam 13	47.3	5,300	Emerging democracy, with significant continuing communist influence
Czechoslovakia	.128	60 arable; 14 other ag.	15.7	.3	99	Czech 63 Slovak 32 Hungarian 4	Catholic 50 Protestant 20	120.3	7,700	Since 1989, democratic federal republic; split into two countries in 1993
Hungary	.093	54 arable; 14 other ag.	10.6	–.1	99	Hungarian 97 German 2	Catholic 67 Calvinist 20 Atheist 8	60.9	5,800	Since 1989, democratic republic
Poland	.313	49 arable; 14 other ag.	37.8	.1	98	Polish 98	Catholic 95 (practicing 75)	158.5	4,200	Since 1989, democratic republic
Romania	.237	44 arable; 19 other ag.	23.4	.5	96	Romanian 89 Hungarian 9	Romanian Orthodox 70 Catholic 6 Protestant 6	69.9	3,000	Moving toward democracy, with significant communist influence continuing

SOURCE: CIA, *The World Factbook 1991* (Washington: U.S. Government Printing Office, 1992).

Revolution broke out in the same year, only to be suppressed when the U.S.S.R. sent in troops and tanks. Clearly, all was not well within Eastern Europe. In each of these instances, Eastern European resentment of Soviet control played a major role in the uprisings. A new stage of intercommunist relations was about to begin.

Soviet and Eastern European writers and politicians began to discuss the evolution of the "socialist commonwealth of nations" during the 1950s, particularly following Nikita Khrushchev's denunciation of Stalin and acceptance of the concept of national paths to communism at the Twentieth CPSU Congress in 1956.[3] Numerous socialist intergovernmental organizations were formalized during this period, including the Warsaw Pact, the Council for Mutual Economic Assistance (CMEA), and the Danube River Commission. Eastern European governments took advantage of the more relaxed attitude of Khrushchev toward Eastern Europe to diverge from the Soviet model.

Throughout the 1960s and 1970s, then, Eastern European states cautiously charted their own paths within the confines of the old Eastern bloc. In some cases, a state wandered too far from a policy line that the U.S.S.R. found acceptable. Thus, in 1968, Czechoslovakia toyed with the ideas of legalizing political parties besides the communist party, eliminating censorship, and making other reforms. The U.S.S.R. found these actions too "counterrevolutionary," and intervened in conjunction with other Warsaw Pact forces to "protect socialism." Even in the intervention, however, Eastern European diversity was apparent. Romania refused to participate, Hungary participated with only a token force and expressed disapproval, and East Germany and Poland seemed more ardent advocates of intervention than even the Soviet Union itself. Only Bulgaria faithfully parroted the Soviet line.

Albania and Romania provided the most interesting and durable cases of divergence from the Soviet model during the 1960s and 1970s. Albania, closely followed a Stalinist party line until 1956, when Khrushchev denounced Stalin. Albania was shocked by the denunciation, and gradually eased out of the Soviet orbit and into a pro-Chinese stance. This occurred even as the Sino-Soviet rift worsened. By 1961, the Soviet-Albanian rift was public knowledge, and the U.S.S.R. condemned Albania as a surrogate for China.

Romania challenged the U.S.S.R. in a more subtle manner. In addition to refusing to participate in the invasion of Czechoslovakia, Romania refused to accept economic planning directives from CMEA, established diplomatic relations with West Germany despite Soviet opposition, refused to allow Warsaw Pact maneuvers on Romanian territory, refused to integrate its armed forces with the combined armed forces of the Pact, rejected the Soviet line against China, failed to implement a defense spending increase demanded by the U.S.S.R., and verbally assaulted the Soviet invasion of Afghanistan.[4]

In 1980–1981, Poland challenged Soviet interests and the Soviet model. The 1980–1981 Polish crisis was triggered by a government decision to raise food prices by 20 percent without a wage increase. This set off a massive strike wave and eventually led to the formation of an independent, noncommunist trade union, Solidarity. For over a year, Solidarity struggled to assert its influence in Poland until martial law was declared in December 1981.

For most of the rest of the 1980s, Eastern Europe remained quiet. Nevertheless, resentment of communist rule, authoritarian government, and economic privilege for communist party members simmered just below the surface.

When Mikhail Gorbachev began to institute his reforms in the U.S.S.R. in 1986 and 1987, Eastern Europeans wondered why changes could not come to their countries, too. Perhaps more important, Gorbachev in 1987 and 1988 implied on several occasions that Soviet troops would not be used to maintain governments in power in Eastern Europe.

At first, particularly in Poland and Hungary, governments and peoples gingerly tested the limits of Soviet restraint. The Polish government, bending to popular will, allowed a free election that swept the noncommunist trade union Solidarity into power. In Hungary, the government and party abandoned the term "communist" and opened the border with Austria. Hordes of East Germans seized the opportunity to defect to the West, traveling first to Hungary and then to Austria. Clearly, Eastern Europe was no longer the same. In the fall of 1989, when the Soviet Union specifically stated that it would not intervene militarily in Eastern Europe, the floodgates to revolution were opened. One after another, the communist governments in Eastern Europe tumbled.

As the 1990s began, then, an era had ended in Eastern Europe. Communism had been rejected by the people. Despite the euphoria that prevailed, many challenges remained. What types of new governments should be formed? How could economic growth be renewed? How could old ethnic and national rivalries be held in check without a uniting ideology and the threat of external military intervention? The questions were many, and the answers were not clear.[5]

Built in 1961 to end the flow of East Germans escaping to the West, the Berlin Wall came to symbolize the division between Eastern and Western Europe, between East and West as a whole. In 1989, the Berlin Wall was opened, and much of it was torn down. Less than a year later, East and West Germany united. (D. Aubert/Sygma.)

Eastern European Outlooks

For all Eastern European states before 1989, the dominant fact of international life was the reality of Soviet power. The U.S.S.R. had 27 divisions in Eastern Europe, 20 of them in East Germany alone, and another 101 divisions in the Western strategic theater of the U.S.S.R. itself.[6] Over half of the Soviet Union's foreign trade was with the CMEA states, and Eastern Europe was heavily dependent on the U.S.S.R. for many of its resource needs, including oil. Militarily and economically, with the sole exception of Albania in the economic sphere, Eastern Europe could not ignore the Soviet Union. Indeed, it had become an Eastern European "tradition" that each of the leaders of the six "loyalist" states traveled to the Soviet Union every summer for meetings with the Soviet leader.

The **revolutions of 1989** changed almost all of this. Even before Gorbachov declared that the U.S.S.R. would no longer intervene in Eastern Europe, Eastern European attitudes toward the Soviet Union were quite diverse once one moved beyond official protestations of loyalty. But the revolution—as well as the collapse of the Soviet Union—encouraged Eastern Europeans to adopt a significantly different world view than that which they previously appeared to have.

In many Eastern European states, anti-Soviet and anti-Russian attitudes emerged. Many East Germans expressed such outlooks. So too did Hungarians and Czechoslovaks, remembering respectively the invasions of 1956 and 1968. Poland and Romania lost territory to the U.S.S.R. following World War II. Besides the territorial questions, both countries have a history of conflict with Russia. Poles consider themselves a separate and distinct race, and perhaps more civilized than their Eastern neighbor. Romanians consider themselves Latin rather than Slavic. Neither has fond remembrances of the Soviet occupation of World War II. This is particularly true in Poland, where memories of the Katyn Forest massacre and the Warsaw uprising remain strong over four decades after they occurred. Only in Bulgaria does there appear to be a decent chance that hostility toward Russia will not escalate. Bulgaria originally gained its independence from the Ottoman Empire because of Russian intervention, and the country also has ethnic and social backgrounds similar to those of Russia.

Not surprisingly, sentiment also emerged throughout Eastern Europe for the withdrawal of Soviet troops. This was quickly accomplished in Czechoslovakia and Hungary, and more slowly in East Germany and Poland. Similarly, the Eastern European movement toward free-market economic systems proceeded at different paces depending on a combination of domestic politics, degree of dependence on former Soviet resources, and the ability to attract external Western expertise and investment. In every case, though, Eastern European states moved away from their former close relationship with Moscow. At the same time, in every case, Eastern European economies declined precipitously as the new governments attempted to establish new political and economic institutions, attitudes, and relationships.

These transitions unleashed other forces as well. In Yugoslavia, decades and even centuries of ethnic animosity burst forth. Yugoslavia crumbled, ripped by a civil war that pitted Serbians, Croats, Slovenians, Bosnians, and other former citizens against each other. In Czechoslovakia, Czechs and Slovaks negotiated a more peaceful dismemberment of the one time Czech and Slovak state.

In Romania, pogroms were launched against Hungarian and other ethnic minorities.

But on a more upbeat note, the revolutions of 1989 also allowed many Eastern European peoples and governments to express openly attitudes that they had previously concealed about Western Europe and the United States. Several Eastern European states expressed desires to join the European Community and NATO. Even though they were not admitted to either organization, all of the countries of Eastern Europe looked to the West for investment capital and technical know-how. Eastern Germany was the most fortunate, becoming an integral part of West Germany and thereby receiving direct access to German development funds.

Not surprisingly, Eastern Europeans adopted new outlooks on multinational corporations. Even though during the 1980s Eastern European states sought scarce capital and needed know-how from MNCs, they nevertheless officially regarded MNCs as potential exploiters. Some concern remains that the previous official outlooks were accurate, but Eastern European states without exception became much more favorably disposed toward MNCs following the revolution of 1989.

As for the UN, before 1989 Eastern European states almost always parroted the Soviet line on most issues. After the 1989 revolutions, however, all adopted independent positions on issues brought before the world body. This continued after the U.S.S.R. dissolved. The only exceptions were Albania and Yugoslavia. In Albania's case, the country continued to use the UN as a forum from which to condemn U.S. and Soviet policies until it experienced its own revolution in 1990. In Yugoslavia's case, the UN more or less stood apart from ongoing events there as Yugoslavia's ethnic groups careened toward civil war. Then, as the Yugoslavian state dissolved in 1992, the UN expelled the rump Yugoslavian state, centered in Serbia, and sent a peacekeeping force to the wartorn country in an effort to quell fighting there. Despite the UN's presence, fighting continued throughout the former Yugoslavia.

As for the Developing World, Eastern European views before 1989 generally coincided with the U.S.S.R.'s. Eastern Europeans believed that Western imperialism caused the Developing World's plight by plundering its wealth, retarding its development, and subjugating the Developing World to neocolonial exploitation that tied the Developing World to capitalism's international economic system. Eastern European states were therefore sympathetic to Developing World national liberation movements, and during the 1970s and 1980s upgraded the quantity and quality of their economic and military support to national liberation movements and revolutionary governments in the Developing World.

Now, however, most Eastern European states see the Developing World as a potential competitor for scarce investment capital and managerial know-how. Thus, Eastern Europe's own economic plight has had a significant impact on how states of the region view a major segment of the international community.

WESTERN EUROPE

Western Europe's relationship with the United States never was comparable to Eastern Europe's relationship with the U.S.S.R. Yet in certain ways, similarities existed in those respective relationships. Both relationships rested on the military and economic supremacy of one state over all others in each relationship. Although the methods and manners of expressing those relationships differed, the simple fact of preponderant U.S. and Soviet military and economic might was never in question.

Gradually, however, in both blocs, the preponderance of the great power declined. In the Eastern bloc, as we have seen, communist states slowly and hesitatingly edged out from under the shadow of the Russian bear. In the Western bloc, democratic capitalist states regained their economic vitality and self-confidence and redefined their own interests.

To a great extent, Western Europe's return to global eminence and independence is the end product of the integrative economic policy and collective security policy developed during the decades following World War II. The successes of these policies laid the groundwork for the divergent outlooks on economic matters and security policies that challenged the Western alliance during the 1980s and threaten to worsen in the 1990s.

The Growth of European Unity

Twelve of the states of Western Europe are today united in a large international governmental organization known as the **European Community** (EC). The EC is primarily an economic entity; its major constituent parts are the **European Economic Community** (EEC), **the European Coal and Steel Community** (ECSC), and the **European Atomic Energy Commission** (EURATOM). In 1979, the EC took a major political step toward integration when, for the first time, the people of Europe elected representatives to the European Parliament of the European Community.

At its heart, the EC is a customs union. By reducing and eliminating trade and tariff barriers between member countries, and by setting a common policy toward trade with external countries, a customs union seeks to create a large internal market so that firms can take advantage of economies of scale and generate production for export. Realizing this, European states have worked slowly and steadily toward reducing internal barriers to trade, capital movement, and labor mobility.

The road toward Western European unity has been a long one, and there remains a considerable way to go before economic or political unity is achieved. Indeed, many people in Western Europe and beyond argue that the divisions that remain within Western Europe are too sharp and deeply imbedded to ever allow either economic or political unity to occur. Some of the diversities of Western Europe are detailed in Table 13–2.

Even so, Western European unity has come a long way. But to appreciate exactly where Europe is today and may be tomorrow in regard to unity, it is first necessary to understand the background to the contemporary European situation.

EUROPEAN INTEGRATION: BEGINNING STEPS.   Before World War II, individual European states vied with each other for global influence, wealth, and prestige. The entire world was centered around European affairs. European states ruled vast colonial empires, and European economies dominated international trade.

TABLE 13–2 Selected States of Western Europe: General Characteristics, 1991

Country	Land Sq. Km. x 10⁶	Land % in Agriculture	Population Total (mil.)	Growth Rate %	Literacy Rate %	Ethnic Groups	Religion	Economy GDP Annual Bil.$	GDP Per Capita	Government Type and Characteristics
Austria	.084	20	7.7	.3	98	German 99	Catholic 85 Protestant 6	111.0	14,500	Federal republic
Belgium	.031	28	9.9	.1	98	Flemish 55 Walloon 33	Catholic 75	144.8	14,600	Constitutional monarchy; NATO member; EC member
Denmark	.043	61	5.1	.0	99	Danish 93	Lutheran 91	78.0	15,200	Constitutional monarchy; NATO member; EC member
Finland	.337	8 arable	5.0	.3	100	Finn 94	Lutheran 89	77.3	15,500	Republic
France	.547	34	56.6	.4	99	French 90	Catholic 90	873.5	15,500	Republic; NATO member but military forces not integrated; EC member
Germany	.357	34 arable	79.5	.4	99	German 98	Catholic 37 Protestant 44	1,157.2	14,600	Federal republic; NATO member; EC member
Greece	.132	31	10.0	.2	93	Greek 98	Greek Orthodox 98	76.7	7,650	Presidential parliament; NATO member; EC member
Italy	.301	50	57.8	.2	93	Italian 97	Catholic 99	844.7	14,600	Republic; many parties form many unstable coalition govts; NATO member; EC member
Netherlands	.401	26	15.0	.6	99	Dutch 96	Catholic 36 Protestant 27 Unaffiliated 31	218.0	14,600	Constitutional monarchy; NATO member; EC member
Norway	.324	3 arable	4.3	.5	99	Germanic 95	Lutheran 88	74.2	17,400	Constitutional monarchy; NATO member
Spain	.505	41	39.4	.5	95	Spanish 95	Catholic 99	436	11,100	Parliamentary monarchy; NATO member; EC member
Sweden	.450	7 arable	8.6	.4	99	Swedish 92	Lutheran 94	137.8	16,200	Constitutional monarchy; NATO member
Switzerland	.041	10 arable	6.8	.6	99	German 65 French 18 Italian 10	Catholic 48 Protestant 44	126.0	18,700	Federal republic
United Kingdom	.245	29 arable	57.6	.3	99	English 82 Scottish 10	Anglican 47 Catholic 9	858.3	15,000	Constitutional monarchy; NATO member; EC member

SOURCE: CIA, *The World Factbook 1991* (Washington: U.S. Government Printing Office, 1992).

316

Political changes in Europe sent shock waves around the world and with the significant exceptions of the Japanese armed forces and the American navy, European military establishments were unrivaled elsewhere in the world.

Following World War II, Europe's position deteriorated drastically. Empires were divested because of their cost and because of wider acceptance of national self-determination. Six years of warfare had devastated the once powerful European economies. European political changes, although still of great importance, could rarely produce shock waves. Militarily, the postwar world was dominated by the United States and the Soviet Union. International politics was no longer Eurocentric. Indeed, Western Europe had become the object of a power struggle between the United States and the U.S.S.R. Despite its deteriorated condition, Western Europe remained a prize of tremendous value. An industrial and technical infrastructure still existed there, and the peoples of Europe, highly educated and ambitious, could be expected to rebuild their war-shattered countries in relatively short order.

Western Europe faced not only rehabilitation, but also a perceived threat of Soviet invasion. As one Eastern European country after another formally established communist governments, and as the Soviet Army remained quantitatively numerous and on station in Eastern Europe, Western European and U.S. policymakers concluded that the Soviet Union was bent on expansion, possibly even into Western Europe itself. From both sides of the Atlantic, leaders began to wonder how the simultaneous economic and security challenges could be met.

One answer was through European integration. In September 1946, Winston Churchill urged that Franco-German reconciliation within "a kind of United States of Europe" be undertaken. To Churchill, such a reconciliation would create a political-economic counterbalance to Soviet power on the continent, would integrate French and German economies so that future conflicts between the two states would be rendered unlikely, and would lead in general to a more peaceful Europe.

Unfortunately, however, the entire continental economy continued to languish. By the end of the year, even Great Britain's situation had worsened considerably. In February 1947, Great Britain informed the United States that it no longer had the wherewithal to support the Greek or Turkish governments.

The Truman administration acted. The following month, Truman promised aid to Greece and Turkey, and promised U.S. support for "free peoples" in their struggles against internal enemies and externally sponsored subversion. In June 1947, an event of equally historic significance occurred. While delivering an address at Harvard, U.S. Secretary of State George Marshall offered American economic aid to Europe for a collective European Recovery Plan. This offer, known as the **Marshall Plan**, pumped over $15 billion of American capital into European revitalization.

Two points must immediately be made about the Marshall Plan. First, it was not an American "giveaway" program. It was undertaken as much for American economic and security interests as for European interests. Second, the Marshall Plan was predicated on European governments jointly studying their needs, jointly formulating a program to meet those needs, and jointly requesting requisite resources from the United States to implement their program. Winston Churchill's suggestion had been revitalized in a more comprehensive mode. The Marshall Plan was, in essence, the first step on the road toward European integration.

After Marshall's address, events proceeded slowly but relentlessly. In April 1948, Western European states signed a treaty creating the Organization for European Economic Cooperation to administer Marshall Plan aid. Aid began flowing the same year. In May 1950, French Foreign Minister Robert Schuman proposed that a European Coal and Steel Community be created that would place all Western European coal and steel production under a common authority. The following year, European states signed such a treaty. In June 1955, West Germany, France, Italy, the Netherlands, Belgium, and Luxembourg decided to integrate their economies even more fully as a basis for future political unification. In March 1957, representatives from these countries signed the Rome Treaties, which created the European Economic Community (EEC) and the European Atomic Energy Commission (EURATOM). In 1962, economic cooperation was extended to agriculture as well, and Greece associated itself with the EEC. Turkey achieved associate status with the EEC two years later, and by 1968, all industrial tariffs between EEC members were abolished. The EEC also removed limitation on internal movement of workers and established a common external tariff.[7] Europe had gone a long way on the path toward integration and prosperity.

Since then, the EC has expanded to 12 members with the addition of Denmark, Great Britain, Greece, Ireland, Portugal, and Spain. Equally important, in 1979, EC member states held the first direct election for the 410-member European Parliament. In addition, all 12 of the EC's members agreed to accept the European Council's decisions on certain issues even if they as states disagreed with them. This in effect transferred limited sovereignty from the 12 EC member states to the EC. The states even agreed to allow the EC to determine what each owed the EC, in effect giving the EC limited taxation powers. Clearly, European integration was proceeding apace.

THE SINGLE EUROPEAN ACT AND THE MAASTRICHT TREATY. More impressive steps on the path toward Western European integration were still to come. Fearing that the EC was lagging behind the United States and Japan economically, European leaders in 1985 passed the Single European Act. This act set the end of 1992 as the deadline by which to eliminate all barriers within the EC to the movement of goods, capital, and people between countries. About 300 different measures were identified in which action was needed.[8]

The implementation of the Single European Act made Western Europe the single largest trading market in the world. The advantages that the Act offered Europe are illustrated by a single example. In 1988, truck drivers in Western Europe needed as many as 27 separate documents to go from one country to another; in 1993—at least in concept—all they needed was their driver's license.

This is not to say that the Single European Act went forward without problems. Many states feared—and still fear—that inexpensive labor in Greece, Portugal, and Spain will attract capital there and lead to unemployment elsewhere. Some states were concerned—and remain concerned—that Germany's economic strength might give it undue clout within the EC. And many people in every EC country saw—and continue to see—a danger that European Community bureaucrats will make decisions and impose standards from their headquarters in Brussels that will eliminate local decision-making throughout Europe.

Despite these fears and concerns, European leaders met in Maastricht, Belgium, in December 1991 and concluded an agreement that went far beyond the steps envisioned in the Single European Act. The Maastricht Treaty envisioned all of the European Community's members moving toward political and economic union, adopting a single common currency, and implementing a common foreign and defense policy. In short, the Maastricht Treaty sought to create a true United States of Europe.[9]

But Europe's leaders had moved too far too quickly. Slowly at first, but then more rapidly, opposition built up to the Maastricht Agreement. In June 1992, Danish voters defeated the Maastricht Treaty. In September 1992, French voters approved it by only one percent. In November 1992, the British Parliament approved it by an extremely narrow margin. Much of the opposition to the Maastricht Treaty was the result of the very issues that had caused concern about the Single European Act—capital flight to countries where labor was inexpensive, German economic strength, EC bureaucratization, and the imposition of too many Europeanwide standards.

But another issue also played a major role in building opposition to the Maastricht Treaty: pure and simple nationalism. Many Europeans had developed a "European consciousness," that is, a sense that they were part of a greater Europe. But many others had not. To them, European unity meant the loss of separate national identity, of nationhood. Maastricht was not dead, but it had to be reworked. Even Denmark's 1993 referendum in which Danish voters reversed their 1992 rejection of the Maastricht Treaty did not alter the fact that European political and economic union, while still alive, was not a sure thing.

European Economic Perspectives

Europe has made impressive economic strides since 1945. One of the reasons for European success was American largesse provided through the Marshall Plan; another was Europe's willingness to undertake the experiment in economic integration. Not surprisingly, at least in part as a result of this economic resurgence, a distinct set of Western European perceptions on international economic matters has developed. Although significant differences of opinion exist within the EC concerning internal and external economic relations, it is possible to identify a predominant Western European attitude on at least three major issues: Euro-American trade and investment, Eastern European and Russian trade and aid, and North–South aid and trade.

EURO-AMERICAN TRADE AND INVESTMENT.   Western Europe's economic position relative to the United States has improved dramatically over the past four decades. Table 13–3 amply illustrates the role that the largest European (and Japanese) corporations now play in the international economic community. From the European perspective, this growth reflects the benefits of hard work, responsible taxation and spending policies, and the defeat of adversity.

Almost from the time they were first proposed, it was evident that plans for European revitalization and integration, if successful, would lead to a significant European challenge to the American position in the international economy.

TABLE 13–3   The World's Largest U.S., European, and Japanese Multinational Corporations, 1959–1990

Ranking	1959	1981	1988	1990
	Automotive Industry			
1.	General Motors (U.S.)	General Motors (U.S.)	General Motors (U.S.)	General Motors (U.S.)
2.	Ford Motor (U.S.)	Ford Motor (U.S.)	Ford Motor (U.S.)	Ford Motor (U.S.)
3.	Chrysler (U.S.)	Fiat (Italy)	Toyota (Japan)	Toyota (Japan)
4.	American Motors (U.S.)	Renault (Fr.)	Daimler-Benz (Ger.)	Daimler-Benz (Ger.)
5.	Volkswagen (Ger.)	Volkswagen (Ger.)	Nissan (Japan)	Fiat (Italy)
	Chemical Industry			
1.	E.I. du Pont (U.S.)	Hoechst (Ger.)	E.I. du Pont (U.S.)	E.I. du Pont (U.S.)
2.	Union Carbide (U.S.)	Bayer (Ger.)	BASF (Ger.)	BASF (Ger.)
3.	ICI (U.K.)	BASF (Ger.)	Hoechst (Ger.)	ICI (U.K.)
4.	Allied Chemical (U.S.)	E.I. du Pont (U.S.)	Bayer (Ger.)	Bayer (Ger.)
5.	Olin Mathieson (U.S.)	ICI (U.K.)	ICI (U.K.)	Hoechst (Ger.)
	Electrical Equipment			
1.	General Electric (U.S.)	General Electric (U.S.)	General Electric (U.S.)	General Electric (U.S.)
2.	Western Electric (U.S.)	ITT (U.S.)	Hitachi (Japan)	Hitachi (Japan)
3.	Westinghouse (U.S.)	Philips (Neth.)	Matsushita (Japan)	Matsushita (Japan)
4.	RCA (U.S.)	Siemens (Ger.)	Siemens (Ger.)	Siemens (Ger.)
5.	Philips (Neth.)	Hitachi (Japan)	Toshiba (Japan)	Toshiba (Japan)
	Steel and Metals			
1.	US Steel (U.S.)	Thyssen (Ger.)	Nippon (Japan)	Thyssen (Ger.)
2.	Bethlehem (U.S.)	Nippon (Japan)	Usinor-Sacilor (Fr.)	Nippon (Japan)
3.	Republic (U.S.)	US Steel (U.S.)	Krupp (Ger.)	Usinor-Sacilor (Fr.)
4.	Armco (U.S.)	Pechiney Ugine (Fr.)	Thyssen (Ger.)	Sumitomo Metal (Japan)
5.	ALCOA (U.S.)	Canadian Pacific (Can.)	NKK (Japan)	NKK (Japan)
	Banking			
1.	BankAmerica (U.S.)	Citicorp (U.S.)	Banco de Brazil (Brazil)	Citicorp (U.S.)
2.	Chase Manhattan (U.S.)	BankAmerica (U.S.)	Banco Bradesco SA (Brazil)	Suez Group (Fr.)
3.	Citibank (U.S.)	Banque Nationale de Paris (Fr.)	Citicorp (U.S.)	Sumitomo Bank (Japan)
4.	Barclay's (U.K.)	Caisse Nationale de Credit Agricole (Fr.)	Credit Agricole (Fr.)	Dai-Icohi Kangyo (Japan)
5.	Manufacturer's Hanover (U.S.)	Credit Lyonnais (Fr.)	Credit Lyonnais (Fr.)	Sanwa (Japan)

Source: 1959 and 1981—*Europe*, May–June 1982. 1988—*Forbes*, July 28, 1989. 1990—*Forbes*, July 22, 1991.

Nevertheless, the speed with which Western Europe improved its economic position and presented a challenge to the United States surprised many. The growth of Western European economic strength has led to different perspectives between Western Europe and the United States about investment and trade.

During the 1950s and 1960s, American firms invested over $20 billion in Western Europe. By 1980, U.S. direct investment in Europe surpassed $60 billion. Much of the profit from this investment was expatriated to the United States, and U.S. MNCs prospered. However, many Europeans grew resentful about the major role played in their economies by U.S. firms. From the European perspective, U.S. direct investment meant jobs, but it also meant that foreign firms might dominate European economics.

Ironically, a countertrend developed in the 1970s as European firms began to invest in the United States. Attracted by high U.S. interest rates, European investors sent capital to the United States. At the same time, attracted by high U.S. returns on investment, firms such as Volkswagen, Bayer, and Siemens opened plants in the United States. Europeans congratulated themselves on being astute businesspeople, but many Americans became resentful of foreign penetration of the U.S. economy. Even so, they were grateful for the jobs foreign investment created. On both sides of the Atlantic, then, concern mounted about foreign dominance of domestic markets.

Meanwhile, the United States became concerned that the European Community's program for economic integration in 1992 would lead to the creation of a huge market that excluded outsiders. Despite European assurances that this would not be the case, U.S. firms began to seek ways to guarantee that they would have access to the post–1992 European market. On investment, Western European and U.S. perspectives had come full circle. Transatlantic economic interdependence had become a reality, but neither side was completely comfortable with it.

Contrasting Western European and U.S. views on trade also caused problems in the transatlantic relationship. After enjoying small trade surpluses with most Western European states during the 1960s and 1970s, by the late 1970s U.S. trade with the four most industrialized Western European countries showed a substantial deficit. Most of this deficit was caused by West German exports to the United States. The United States reacted to this deficit by charging that Europeans were not carrying their fair share of defense spending and by lodging claims of unfair competition. Western Europeans countered by arguing that the United States' economic decline was caused by, among other things, inefficient energy use and ineffective leadership.

During the 1980s, as the U.S. trade deficit mushroomed, Europeans developed mixed feelings about what was happening. On the one hand, they were concerned by the United States' inability to come to grips with either its trade deficit or its budget deficit. On the other hand, Western Europe benefited from the U.S. trade deficit by selling goods to Americans. Moreover, Europeans recognized that the U.S. trade deficit was probably preferable to the most likely alternative, protectionism. Indeed, one of the best guarantees that a post–1992 Europe would not raise tariff barriers against external products was the European recognition that the United States consistently supported free trade throughout the 1980s.

Nevertheless, another serious problem remained—the issue of European Community subsidies, particularly in agriculture and the aircraft industry. To Europeans, internal politics made it necessary for European governments and the EC to subsidize certain sectors of the economy. To Americans, this unfairly lowered the price at which Europeans could sell subsidized products, and cost U.S. producers billions of dollars in sales. As a result, in 1992, the United States moved toward introducing a tariff against certain European products, including French wine. A U.S.-European trade war loomed as a distinct possibility. Hurried negotiations averted this, but U.S.-European trade tensions remained.

EASTERN EUROPEAN AND RUSSIAN TRADE AND AID.　Before the epochal Eastern European changes of 1989, Western Europeans generally had a significantly different view from most Americans about the course that East–West trade should follow. Western Europeans generally believed that trade with Eastern Europe could benefit everyone and would have few adverse effects on security, whereas the U.S. government, for security reasons, sought to place strict limitations on the types of goods that could be exported to the U.S.S.R. and Eastern Europe.[10]

There were two major reasons for this difference in perspective. First, Western Europeans tended to see a less immediate military threat coming from the Eastern bloc than did Americans. Second, Western Europe's trade with the U.S.S.R. was much more sizable than that of the United States. For example, in 1984, Western European trade with the Soviet Union and Eastern Europe totaled $48 billion, while U.S. trade with the Soviet Union and Eastern Europe totaled only $6 billion.[11] From the European perspective, continued East–West trade was desirable despite the security risks that might be entailed.

In view of the events in Eastern Europe in 1989, the differences in Western European and U.S. perspectives on East–West trade decreased and eventually disappeared as the United States moved toward a more relaxed position. Both the United States and Western Europe supported aid to and encouraged trade with Eastern European states. Both also believed that Western Europe should take the lead in providing it, and maintained that aid should be directed toward revitalizing Eastern Europe and establishing free markets there. As the Soviet Union declined and then fell, a similar situation developed, although the United States played a greater role there than in Eastern Europe.

NORTH-SOUTH AID AND TRADE.　As a general rule, most European states are more favorably disposed toward Developing States' perspectives on aid and trade than is the United States. Nevertheless, Western Europe is not prepared to alter the existing international economic order to the extent that Developing World states express in their proposals for a New International Economic Order (NIEO). Although the EC and the United States disagree on the causes of problems in their own trade, they are clearly united in their opposition to the NIEO. Several European states, France and Sweden in particular, extend considerable quantities of economic aid to the Developing World, when measured in terms of percentage of gross national product, but none have supported a restructuring of the international economic system to help Developing World interests.

Despite this, both Great Britain and France have managed to retain rather cordial economic relations and political accord with most of their former colonial holdings. Great Britain's global Commonwealth of Nations meets regularly, and the countries of the Commonwealth share the equivalent of the U.S. concept of most-favored-nation trading status. France maintains a similar relationship with the Francophone countries of Africa.

European Military Security Perspectives

Before the Eastern European revolutions of 1989 and the 1991 collapse of the Soviet Union, the possibility of war with the U.S.S.R. was the central military security issue for Western Europe. These two events eliminated that threat.

Nevertheless, a review of European security perspectives during the Cold War remains important background for contemporary European security outlooks.

During the 1940s and early 1950s, Western Europe consciously staked its security from Soviet attack on U.S. strategic nuclear superiority. According to this view, the Soviet Union was deterred from attacking Western Europe because the Soviet Union knew that if it were to attack, U.S. policy-makers would unleash long-range nuclear bombers on the Soviet Union. The Soviet Union did not have the ability to retaliate at the time, and hence was deterred.

From the European perspective, the one great unknown in this scenario was the certainty of a U.S. response. Because of this, European leaders became ardent advocates of the creation of NATO and the stationing of U.S. troops in Europe. NATO became a reality in 1949. U.S. troops thus became a sort of "trip-wire," guaranteed to bring the United States into the war in the event of a Soviet invasion of Europe. To most Europeans, NATO strengthened Europe's security and enhanced deterrence.

As the U.S.S.R. developed its own long-range nuclear delivery capabilities during the 1950s and 1960s, more and more Europeans began to ask if the United States would, in fact, use its nuclear weapons to defend Europe if the Soviets attacked, because the United States itself had become vulnerable to a Soviet nuclear strike. Would the United States risk losing Washington or New York to defend Paris or London from Soviet invasion?

French President Charles de Gaulle believed the United States would not. This, combined with French national pride and de Gaulle's fear of U.S. domination of Europe through NATO, led the French President to have France develop an independent nuclear force, and to withdraw in 1966 from NATO's integrated military command. Nevertheless, other European countries continued to rely on NATO and the protection they were afforded by the U.S. strategic nuclear umbrella. Great Britain maintained and modernized its own nuclear forces, but they were more the product of Britain's effort to maintain its self-image as a great power than the result of British mistrust of American reliability.

At the conventional level, Western European security has similarly been a matter of intense debate and disagreement. Throughout NATO's history, the organization has sought to increase its conventional military strength. The question of how much conventional military might was enough remained a pressing issue into the late 1980s, even as the Gorbachev revolution progressed. Western Europeans were increasingly torn between competing desires to strengthen conventional military forces to deter potential Soviet aggression, and to reemphasize détente and accommodation so that no new buildup would be necessary.

With the 1989 Eastern European revolutions and the end of the Soviet threat, European defense spending—East and West—has as a general rule fallen sharply. Table 13–4 illustrates this. Nevertheless, several security issues still perplex many Europeans.[12]

The first issue is whether political instability and economic hardship in Eastern Europe, the former Soviet Union, and Northern Africa might lead to a large wave of **immigration into Western Europe**. Many Western Europeans see this possibility as a significant security threat. The fear of this has led to the growth of antiforeign sentiment in several Western European states, especially Germany and France.

The second issue is **German unification**. Many Europeans recall that a uni-

TABLE 13–4   Defense Expenditures of Selected European NATO and Former
Warsaw Pact Countries, as a Percentage of Gross National Product

European NATO Countries	1984	1988	1992
Belgium	3.2	2.9	1.5
Denmark	2.3	2.1	2.0
France	4.1	4.0	2.8
Germany	3.3	3.0	1.9
Greece	7.0	5.9	1.9
Italy	2.7	2.4	1.7
Netherlands	3.2	3.1	2.7
Norway	2.8	3.3	3.2
Turkey	4.4	4.3	3.1
United Kingdom	5.5	4.7	4.2
Former Warsaw Pact Countries	**1984**	**1988**	**1992**
Bulgaria	3.9	4.7	6.9
Czechoslovakia	4.0	4.9	2.9
East Germany	7.7	8.0	—
Hungary	3.9	3.3	2.3
Poland	3.7	2.5	2.4
Romania	1.4	1.5	3.1

SOURCE: International Institute for Strategic Studies, *The Military Balance*, appropriate years and
pages.

Even in modern Europe, warfare and economic hardship have created a flood of refugees.
Here, Bosnians flee the fighting in their country in 1993.   (Magnum Photos.)

fied Germany precipitated World Wars I and II. Some retain fear that a unified Germany may again become expansionist despite nearly 50 years of peaceful relations with its neighbors.

Finally, the question of NATO's future must also be addressed. With the Soviet threat gone, many Western Europeans question whether NATO still serves a meaningful purpose. Others argue that NATO in fact retains immense importance as an institution that brings European—and American—defense establishments and political leaders together, and that it therefore serves a useful coordinating purpose. They also maintain that it provides an institution that can militarily deter threats that may develop in the future, even if such threats cannot be identified now.

Despite these issues, virtually every Western European agrees that the European continent in the 1990s is a much safer place than it has been since the 1920s.

JAPAN

Modern Japan is a nation of contradictions. Economically powerful and prosperous (see Table 13–5), its future economic well-being depends on continued access to reliable sources of external raw materials and stable markets. Militarily constrained because of its U.S.-created constitution, Japan relies on U.S. military strength and the benign intention of others to maintain its security. Pro-Western and modern in its cultural outlook, it reveres old Japanese traditions and customs. The contradictions that exist in Japan and influence its perceptions of itself and the world are a product of Japan's historical experiences.

The Making of Modern Japan

In global perspective, Japan is a unique nation. With a population half that of the United States and a gross national product 40 percent the size of the United States', Japan must import large percentages of almost every raw material that modern industrialized societies need. Since Japan's evolution to an industrial power did not begin until the late nineteenth century, and since it had no scientific technical tradition, the strides it took to transform itself into a relatively modern industrial state by the beginning of the twentieth century were truly amazing.

For two centuries before U.S. Commodore Matthew Perry used gunboat diplomacy to influence Japan to sign an 1854 trade treaty with the United States, the Japanese people lived in self-imposed isolation. However, with the signing of the treaty, Japanese-American trade relations burgeoned. It was clearly an exploitive trade, with U.S. trading companies benefiting economically and politically, and Japan receiving little in return. By the beginning of the U.S. Civil War, Japan had granted Americans the right to teach Christianity in Japan and to be tried in U.S. courts if they broke laws in Japan. Japan had also given the United States' most-favored-nation trading status.

However, Japan quickly realized that if it were to avoid the fate of colonization that had befallen China, it would have to modernize and industrialize. During the latter half of the century, traditional Japan built the industrial ground-

TABLE 13-5 Other U.S. Friends and Allies: General Characteristics, 1991

Country	Land		Population				Economy		Government
	Sq. Km. x 10⁶	% in Agriculture	Total (mil.)	Growth Rate %	Literacy Rate %	Ethnic Groups	Religion	Gross Domestic Product		Type and Characteristics
								Annual Bil.$	Per Capita	
Canada	10.0	5	26.8	1.1	99	British 40 French 27 Other Europe 20	Catholic 46 United Church 16 Anglican 10	516.7	19,500	Federal State
Israel	.002	28	4.5	1.5	92	Jewish 83 Arab 15	Jewish 82 Islam 14	46.5	10,500	Republic
Japan	.372	22	124.0	.4	99	Japanese 99	Buddhist or Shinto 84	2,115.2	17,100	Constitutional Monarchy

SOURCE: CIA, *The World Factbook 1991* (Washington: U.S. Government Printing Office, 1992).

work for a modernized Japan. With modernization, Japanese nationalism increased, and Japan began to build its own empire. Japan defeated China and took control of Korea in 1895, and expanded its influence in Taiwan. These victories were short-lived, however, for Russia, with the support of France and Germany, claimed Korea for its own. For the Japanese, the lesson was clear. Additional military strength must be developed.

Japan and Russia struggled over Korea and Manchuria once again in the Russo-Japanese War of 1904–1905. Japan learned two lessons from the war that had an immense impact on the way the island nation viewed the world. First, Japan routed Russia at sea and on land. Japan now knew that European powers could be defeated, and that territory that they claimed could be acquired. Second, the scope of the victory that Japan could have won was limited at the urging of U.S. President Theodore Roosevelt. Although the United States did not force Japan to accept a less than total victory, Japanese public opinion pictured the U.S. role in the settlement as expanding America's interests in the Far East. This perception was not entirely incorrect. Thus, as early as 1905, many Japanese viewed the United States as a rival for influence in the Pacific.

World War I provided Japan with another opportunity to assess the Western world. Germany abandoned its colonial holdings in China early in the war, and Japan moved immediately to occupy them. In 1915, Japan served China with the Twenty One Demands, a thinly veiled effort to expand Japanese influence in China. Following the Bolshevik Revolution in Russia, Japan sent its army into Siberia in an effort to dismember the old czarist empire. When European states rejected both Japanese territorial claims and Japanese requests that a declaration of racial equality be attached to the Versailles Peace Treaty, Japanese mistrust of Europe and the United States was strengthened. Although Japan received several former German holdings in the Pacific as trust territories under the League of Nations, the question of the disposition of former German holdings in China was not resolved.[13]

Following World War I, Japanese political society divided into two factions: the militarist/expansionists and the conservative/Westernizers. Gradually, the militarist/expansionists, centered in the army, won the day. In 1931, Japanese army units invaded Manchuria and soon afterward China. Throughout the 1930s, Japanese fortifications and military capabilities on its Pacific island territories were strengthened. In 1933, Japan withdrew from the League of Nations. Later

FIGURE 13–2

in the decade, Japan joined Germany and Italy in the Anti-Comintern Pact and formulated the Great East Asian Co-Prosperity Sphere on its own.

Japan was on the move. As World War II engulfed Europe, Japan's military leaders concluded that even with France removed as a barrier to Japanese expansion in Southeast Asia, and with Great Britain sorely pressed to look to its own survival, only the United States and its powerful navy, along with its forward bases in the Philippines and Hawaii, presented a meaningful threat to Japan's new empire. Given the history of U.S. opposition to a sizable Japanese role in the Pacific, at least as seen by the militarist/expansionists in Tokyo, American power would have to be neutralized. The Japanese military planned a blow designed to cripple the United States' ability to project power into the Western Pacific. It fell on December 7, 1941, at Pearl Harbor.

Four years of brutal war followed. On August 9, 1945, the war finally came to a close when the United States dropped a second atomic bomb on Nagasaki. The first had been dropped on Hiroshima three days earlier. Postwar U.S.-Japanese relations thus began under a nuclear cloud with U.S. forces occupying Japan.

Postwar Japanese Views of the United States

The U.S. occupation of Japan lasted until April 1952. During the occupation, Japan adopted a new constitution and established the political institutions and practices of a democratic government, purged the militarist/expansionists from political leadership positions, and restored a healthy industrial and agricultural economy. Washington's attitude toward Japan had meanwhile undergone a complete transformation. Whereas at the conclusion of the war the United States regarded Japan as an international pariah, by 1952 Washington considered the island nation an integral part of the U.S. security system. Mao's victory in China and the Korean War converted Japan into a crucial link in the United States' containment policy in Asia. Japan served as a valuable base for the projection of U.S. power into the Western Pacific.[14]

Japan had to pay a price for reattaining independence, and some Japanese citizens later criticized their government for its willingness to pay that price. The United States obtained bases to be used after the occupation ended, and Japan would not recognize or do business with either mainland China or North Korea, two traditional Japanese trading partners, because of its new position in the American treaty system.

Throughout the 1950s and 1960s, Japan remained an integral part of the American security system, and concentrated on building its economic strength. Under the American-inspired Japanese Constitution, Japan's military was limited to territorial self-defense forces. Thus, Japan's military expenditures remained low, and the country relied on the United States to provide its defense needs. Much of the money that otherwise would have been spent on defense was devoted to industrial investment. Indeed, between 1952 and 1971, Japan's gross national product increased at a rate nearly double that of the rest of the industrialized West.

Even so, anti-American sentiment remained strong in Japan. Japanese resentment, built up over a half-century of U.S.-Japanese mistrust, a brutal war ended by atomic weapons, and six years of occupation, did not dissipate rapidly.[15]

Japan is a country that has succeeded well in mixing modern industrial outlooks with reverence for tradition. Here, in a traditional burial ceremony, the body of Emperor Hirohito is carried by 51 Imperial Palace police during the 1989 funeral services.   (AP/Wide World Photos.)

Nevertheless, over time, it did dissipate. By the 1960s and 1970s, most of Japan's population held quite favorable views of the United States. However, two noneconomic issues complicated U.S.-Japanese relations during this period, the Vietnam War and continuing U.S. occupation of Okinawa. But the end of the U.S. involvement in Vietnam in 1972 and the return of Okinawa to Japanese rule the same year removed both issues as irritants in what had become a quite close and cordial relationship.

During the 1970s and 1980s, U.S.-Japanese relations remained cordial and close on the diplomatic and security levels with only one major exception. In 1971, without consulting the Japanese government, Richard Nixon announced he would visit mainland China the following year. The Japanese were stunned. Were they about to become less important to the United States? The answer was, "No." Japan remained the central U.S. ally in the Pacific, and over time, Japan gradually accustomed itself to the new set of relationships in the Pacific. Japan itself moved to normalize diplomatic and trade relations with China. It also, partially because of U.S. urging, increased its defense expenditures throughout the 1970s and 1980s. In 1987, Japanese defense spending for the first time since World War II exceeded 1 percent of its gross national product.[16]

U.S.-Japanese diplomatic and security relations have obviously survived the strains of the postwar era and have remained close and cordial. Equally obviously, they have been transformed in a number of ways. It is in trade and investment, however, where U.S.-Japanese relations have been most transformed. Indeed, by the 1990s, U.S.-Japanese economic relations could best be described as tense and strained.

Post–World War II U.S.-Japanese economic relations did not begin that way. In fact, during the 1950s and early 1960s, most Americans had a condescending attitude toward the island nations' economic capabilities, viewing Japan as little more than a country of copiers. The Japanese economy mimicked everything, Americans believed, and could produce little that was original. Further, Americans considered Japanese products inferior and shoddy; "Made in Japan" was a slogan of derision. The Japanese, historically a proud and able people, resented the United States' condescension.

As Japan's role in the world economy increased during the 1960s, signs of strain multiplied in the U.S.-Japanese economic relationship. When the U.S. deficit on the bilateral balance of merchandise trade passed $3 billion in 1971, the United States acted. The Nixon administration imposed a 10 percent surcharge on all imports for 90 days and threatened to invoke the "Trading with the Enemy Act" against Japan. Japan viewed these steps as a U.S. effort to push Japanese automakers out of the U.S. market and to force a revaluation of the yen.

Despite this, the U.S. trade deficit with Japan continued to balloon, as Table 13–6 illustrates. The United States continued to press Japan to restrict voluntarily its exports to the United States, to decrease nontariff barriers to U.S. imports into the Japanese market, to reduce Japanese savings rates, and to alter the structure of Japan's domestic markets, but nothing worked. The U.S. trade deficit with Japan continued to grow, and as Japanese businesspeople and corporations began to buy up U.S. real estate and industry, U.S. resentment escalated further.

From the Japanese perspective, however, much of the blame for the trade deficit rested on the United States. Japanese spokespersons argued that Japan built superior products and that the United States could not control its own spending habits. They also noted that Japan bought as many as one-third of the U.S. government notes that funded the U.S. deficit. Additionally, they maintained, there was little that could be done about the Japanese preference for Japanese products.

During the 1990s, the U.S.-Japanese relationship remained cordial, but became increasingly strained over economic issues. Indeed, given the historical uncertainties of the U.S.-Japanese relationship and the tensions that pervaded

TABLE 13–6   U.S.-Japanese Trade Balance, 1976–1988, in Millions of U.S. Dollars

	1976	**1979**	**1982**	**1985**	**1988**	**1991**
Japan exports to United States	15,888	26,452	36,546	66,684	93,168	92,200
U.S. exports to Japan	10,028	20,313	24,185	26,099	37,732	48,147
Japanese surplus	5,860	6,139	11,361	39,585	55,436	44,053

SOURCES: 1976—United Nations, *1980 Yearbook of International Trade Statistics* (New York: United Nations, 1981), pp. 1090–1091. 1979 and 1982—International Monetary Fund, *Direction of Trade Statistics Yearbook 1978–84* (Washington: IMF, 1985). 1985—International Monetary Fund, *Direction of Trade Statistics April 1986* (Washington: IMF, 1986). 1988—International Monetary Fund, *Direction of Trade Statistics May 1989* (Washington: IMF, 1989). 1991—International Monetary Fund, *Direction of Trade Statistics 1992, May 1992* (Washington: IMF, 1992).

U.S.-Japanese bilateral trade since the late 1960s, it is perhaps surprising that Japanese views of the United States have remained as favorable as they have. On the other hand, Japan knows it needs U.S. markets, and without the benefit of the U.S. security blanket, Japanese defense expenditures would undoubtedly have to be increased considerably. At the same time, it is clear that Japan is adopting a more assertive and independent set of policies vis-à-vis the United States. The Japan of the 1990s is a Japan that is not afraid to say "No" to American demands.[17]

Japanese Views of China and Russia

Japan's relations with and perceptions of China and Russia have varied widely over time. Parts of Northeast Asia, including Korea and territories currently in China and Russia, have long been subjects of dispute between Japan, China, and Russia because of resources and security concerns. Japan has not been involved in any military conflicts over these territories since World War II, but it still claims four islands currently held by Russia. These islands, called the Northern Territories, fell under Soviet control at the end of World War II as part of the peace settlement.[18] Japan has insisted that the islands be returned to Japanese rule ever since, but to no avail. The Northern Territories were thus a major irritant in Japanese-Soviet relations, and they continue to be a major irritant today.

Before World War II, Japan coveted Chinese territory for its resource wealth. Following the war, as Japan became enmeshed in the U.S. security network, Japanese relations with China were proscribed by U.S. demands. Nevertheless, Japan was careful not to undertake any actions that would alienate Mao's government in Beijing. As Japanese trade with mainland China had historically been sizable, Japan's diplomacy was understandable.

During the 1960s, Japan and China implemented tentative trade contacts, but U.S. and Chinese Nationalist objections guaranteed that these contacts would achieve little. Even the beginning of the Sino-American rapprochement in 1971 did little to improve Sino-Japanese relations, for the Beijing regime was extremely mistrustful of Japanese Prime Minister Sato, primarily because of Sato's support for Taiwan.

When Sato resigned in May 1972 immediately after the United States returned Okinawa to Japan, the situation changed. The new Japanese Prime Minister, Tanaka Kakuei, was invited to Beijing in September, and when he announced that Japan fully understood Beijing's position on Taiwan, that is, that Taiwan was and is a natural part of China, the doors opened for improved Sino-Japanese relations and trade.

Since this Sino-Japanese rapprochement of the early 1970s, Japan has had little concern about China as a threat to Japanese national security. Japan and China have no territorial disputes, and as long as Japan and the United States maintain their military security arrangement, Japan appears confident of the U.S. intent to protect it from any Chinese encroachment. Thus, as far as Japan is concerned, China is a trading partner and little more.

Japanese perceptions of Russia, and before 1992, the Soviet Union, are not so favorable. In addition to the dispute over the Northern Territories, Japan and the Soviet Union had disputes over fishing rights and over Soviet violation of Japanese air space. In the late 1970s, the U.S.S.R. moved more troops to the disputed Northern Territories islands, and stationed more of the Soviet fleet in the Pacific. To Japan, the Soviet move appeared as a potential threat to Japan's oil lifeline to the Persian Gulf. Many Japanese also saw the 1983 Soviet destruction of a Korean Air Lines 747 as an indication of hostile Soviet intent in Northeast Asia.

These modern disputes and perceived threats are, of course, additional to earlier Soviet-Japanese conflicts of this century: the 1905 Russo-Japanese War, Japanese intervention in Siberia in 1918, conflict between Japanese and Soviet troops in Manchuria during the 1930s, and the delayed Soviet entry into World War II against Japan. The latter situation was particularly galling to the Japanese; the U.S.S.R., after remaining neutral for four years, declared war on Japan on August 9, 1945, the day the second atomic bomb was dropped on Nagasaki. Five days later Japan sued for peace. Nevertheless, the Soviets demanded full reparations, and received as part of their settlement the Northern Territories.

During the late 1980s, Japanese-Soviet relations improved. The Soviets made it very clear that they were interested in obtaining Japanese investment capital for the Soviet Far East. With Japan's need for external resources and its surplus capital, and with the corresponding Soviet need for capital and desire to develop the Far East, the possibilities for trade and investment seemed real. The same situation applies to Russia after the collapse of the Soviet Union.

However, unless Russia and Japan settle the Northern Territories issue, only a limited expansion in Russian-Japanese trade and relations is probable. Japan insists that its lost islands be returned, and even if the Russian government were disposed to return them, Russian domestic politics would make such an action extremely difficult. Indeed, Russian domestic opposition to even the possibility of the return of the Northern Territories to Japan forced Russian President Boris Yeltsin to cancel two planned trips to Japan, in 1992 and 1993. If this Japanese-Russian stalemate continues, so too will Japanese resentment of Russia.

Japan and the World

After the United States, Japan has the second largest economy of any single state. Yet its economy is heavily dependent on access to foreign sources of raw materials and fuel, and on access to foreign markets. To be denied access to either external resources or markets would be a terrible blow to Japanese prosperity.

Until recently, these facts placed inevitable constraints on Japan's view of its own role in the world. But as the 1980s progressed, Japan, like Western Europe, became increasingly ready to depart on its own course in world affairs, and it gradually became more comfortable with its status as a major international actor. One measure of this comfort was Japanese Prime Minister Toshiki Kaifu's January 1990 trip to Eastern Europe, during which he pledged nearly $2 billion in economic assistance to Eastern European states.

An even more impressive measure of Japan's growing confidence in its own international role was the Japanese government's 1992 decision to deploy Japanese military forces under United Nations command in Cambodia as part of a UN peacekeeping force there. This marked the first time since World War II that Japanese armed forces were stationed outside Japan. However, this deployment also had a negative side, because in many countries in East Asia and beyond, the presence of Japanese troops overseas resurrected memories of Japan's imperial past.

Japan, then, is in curious position. It depends on external markets and resources for its economic well-being. It remains largely dependent on American armed forces for its security. But Japan is also an international economic giant that is only beginning to think seriously about its global roles and responsibilities. How Japan resolves the tension between dependence and independence, between following and leading, will be one of the major issues facing the Japanese government—and the international community—in the 1990s and beyond.[19]

CANADA

As of 1992, Canada's national economy exceeded that of all but six other states in total dollar value, and its military expenditures ranked fifteenth in the world. (See Table 13–5) If Canada's geographic location were almost anywhere else than where it is, Canada would inevitably be regarded as an important actor on the international scene. Situated on the northern boundary of the United States, Canada's role in the contemporary world is often overlooked because of its proximity to the United States. Too often, Canada's foreign policy is viewed—incorrectly—as an extension of that of the United States. Correspondingly, Canadians themselves often are unsure what perceptions they should have of themselves or their role in the world. Canadians desire a foreign policy independent from that of the United States, but little agreement exists as to what course that policy should take.

Canadian Views of America

Following World War II, the United States began to replace Great Britain as the dominant factor in Canada's worldview. Although nominally a British dependency, Canada's external economic and security ties were increasingly with the United States. Canadian resources were mined to be used by U.S. industrial firms, and Canadian soldiers fought in Korea and were stationed in Europe as part of the U.S. inspired containment policy. U.S. direct investment also poured into Canada. In 1955, U.S. direct investments in Canada were roughly $5 billion; 35 years later, they totaled over $50 billion.

This new and closer relationship with the United States caused some resentment in Canada. Some Canadians pointed to their economic ties with the United States, and argued that Canada had become an economic dependency of the United States. They discounted Canada's balance of payments surplus with the United States, reasoning that Canadian resources were being depleted for the benefit of Americans and maintaining that U.S. firms that had bought Canadian extractive industries were repatriating any profits they made to the United States. Others viewed U.S. investment in Canada and the growth of U.S.-Canadian trade ties as a threat to the very tenuous federal relationship that held Canada together as a country. As early as 1975, a greater dollar volume of trade moved north and south between British Columbia and Alberta on the one hand and the United States on the other than between the two westernmost Canadian provinces and

FIGURE 13–3

their eastern provincial neighbors. (As far as the United States was concerned, Canada as a whole had been the United States' most important trading partner for some time.) Still other Canadians were satisfied with the state of U.S.-Canadian economic ties, arguing that the Canadian standard of living was higher with the ties than it would be without them. Nevertheless, the fact of U.S. economic penetration of the Canadian economy was real, and large numbers of Canadians resented this intrusion.

At least some of Canada's overall foreign policy behavior may be attributed to Canada's self-image as a nation unsure of how closely it wishes to be to the behemoth to its south. Canada, particularly under former Prime Minister Pierre Elliot Trudeau, charted a foreign policy course for itself that consciously and intentionally differed from U.S. interests in a number of important respects. To some Canadians, Canada was simply following its own interests, interpreted in light of Canadian desires for economic independence from the United States and protection and utilization of its own resource base for Canadian purposes. Other Canadians, however, thought that Trudeau's policies were designed simply to "tweak the beak of the American eagle," that is, to assert Canadian independence from the United States simply for the sake of that independence.

Nevertheless, many Canadians consider their country to have a "special relationship" with the United States. Indeed, Trudeau's successor Brian Mulroney raised that terminology to the national policy level. And the concept of a "special relationship" was given even more legitimacy when in 1989 the United States and Canada concluded a free trade agreement that eliminated all barriers to trade and capital mobility between the two countries. Some Canadians condemned the agreement as guaranteeing the final demise of Canadian economic independence, but most supported it. The Canadian debate over the U.S.-Canadian free trade agreement continued even after the agreement took effect. Nevertheless, continuing debate did not prevent Canada from entering the North American Free Trade Agreement with Mexico and the United States in 1992.

Despite irritants in the U.S.-Canadian special relationship concerning disputes over environmental and trade issues, U.S.-Canadian relations are exceedingly good. It is an old boast, but an important one, that the two countries share the world's longest demilitarized border.

Canada and the World

Canada, with its English and French heritages and its continuing membership in the British Commonwealth of Nations, has long considered itself a European country as well as a North American one. Not surprisingly, then, Canada was among the most vocal supporters of the North Atlantic Treaty Organization when it was founded in 1949.

However, even in the early postwar years, during the very period when U.S.-Canadian economic ties were strengthening and U.S. capital investments began to penetrate the Canadian economy, it was evident that Canada sought to maintain control of its own future. Thus, although Canada was a willing supporter of NATO, Canada insisted that the alliance include political and economic, as well as military, cooperation. Canada, it was clear, did not want Cold War militarism to submerge other aspects of its relations with Europe.

Canadian policy-makers also emphasized the importance of international organizations, particularly the United Nations, much more than U.S. policy-makers. Canadian involvement in UN affairs has had two major thrusts. First, Canada has been extremely willing to have its forces participate in international UN peacekeeping efforts. Canadian forces served in Korea, the Congo, Cyprus, and the Middle East under United Nations' auspices and also participated in the international truce observer team that went to Vietnam following the 1973 cease-fire there. Canadian forces also participated in the 1992–1993 UN peacekeeping efforts in Cambodia and Yugoslavia.

Second, Canada has been more willing than most other industrialized countries to see the Developing World's perspective on international economic issues. This is not a new phenomenon. During the 1950s and 1960s, Canada regularly argued for increased aid from the First World to the Developing World. Canada's willingness to support certain Developing World proposals in the Developing World's effort to create a New International Economic Order (NIEO) has on occasion led Canada to disagree with the United States and Europe.

Canada has also followed its own foreign policy path in certain aspects of its relations with the former Soviet Union, China, and other communist countries. In some instances, displays of Canadian independence appalled U.S. policy-makers. For example, despite U.S. boycotts on grain sales to the U.S.S.R., Canada sold grain to the Soviets. Similarly, Canada developed diplomatic relations with Cuba despite the efforts of several U.S. administrations to exclude Cuba from Western hemispheric contacts.

On other occasions, Canada's independent policies toward communist countries, China in particular, led the way for subsequent U.S. policy changes. Thus, Ottawa's 1971 recognition of mainland China and subsequent large-scale wheat sales to the P.R.C. made Nixon's 1972 trip to China and gradually increasing U.S. economic ties with China less of a bombshell than they otherwise might have been. Similarly, in 1976 when Canada invited the P.R.C. to send athletes to the Montreal Olympics, the U.S. slowly came to accept the implications of an eventual diplomatic recognition of communist China.

Canada, then, has carved out its own foreign policy despite its proximity to and economic interdependence with the United States.[20] Even while it has undertaken such policy, however, it finds itself confronted by a difficulty that is both domestic and international in its implications. That difficulty is Quebec.

Quebec and the "Two Founding Nations"

Canada, like many large states, is a multilingual country. As of 1992, approximately 40 percent of Canada's population spoke English as their mother tongue, and approximately 27 percent spoke French. Of the native French speakers, most live in the province of Quebec.

During the early 1960s, Quebec underwent a so-called "quiet revolution," and French nationalism burgeoned there. Ever since, Quebec's role in the Canadian federation has been open to question, especially after the *Parti Québécois* came to power in 1976 and pledged to withdraw Quebec gradually from Canada.

The Quebec situation is a major concern to Canada and the Ottawa government. From the early 1960s through the 1980s, Ottawa attempted to satisfy French nationalism there by programs and actions designed to make Quebec and its inhabitants feel integral to Canada. Discriminatory price and wage structures were reduced, the Union Jack was removed from the Canadian flag and replaced by the maple leaf, the concept of "two founding nations"—one English and the other French—was adopted, and the Quebec government was permitted to set up overseas consulates for itself. As early as 1961, Quebec established a "Delegation Nationale" in Paris. The Canadian government also supported locating the 1967 World's Fair and the 1976 Olympic Games in Montreal, in part because of a desire to reach a modus vivendi with Quebec.

These efforts by the Canadian government to integrate Quebec more fully into the Canadian mainstream while at the same time protecting Quebec's distinct French culture quelled separatist sentiment, at least for a time. Thus, in 1980, Quebec's citizens rejected a proposal for sovereignty, opting instead to remain a part of the Canadian confederation.

But the issue was not settled. In 1990, a Canadian government constitutional reform effort designed to further strengthen Quebec's allegiance to Canada by recognizing Quebec as a "distinct society" within Canada was defeated when two other Canadian provinces, Manitoba and Newfoundland, rejected it because the reform did not provide comparable recognition to Canada's 700 thousand aboriginal peoples. The defeat of this agreement, the Meech Lake Accord, sparked another round of *Parti Québécois* demands for sovereignty for Quebec.

Thus, in 1991, Quebec's parliament passed a law demanding a referendum on independence in 1992. In response to this, Canadian Prime Minister Brian Mulroney's government, in conjunction with negotiators from all ten of Canada's provinces, carefully crafted another agreement, this one recognizing both French rights and aboriginal rights, as well as a significant transfer of autonomy to Quebec and any other province that desired it. But it still maintained Canadian sovereignty.

Canadians voted on the new confederated structures for Canada in October 1992, and soundly rejected it. Six of the ten Canadian provinces opposed the new structure, some because it gave too much power and autonomy to Quebec and Canada's aboriginal peoples, others because it gave too little power and autonomy to them, and still other because the new accord failed to address other concerns.

By 1993, the course of Canada's future remained unclear. More Quebecois than ever before desired independence, and more Canadians from outside Quebec than ever before were ready to see Quebec chart its own separate course, if only because they resented Quebec's continuing calls for special status within the Canadian confederation. Whatever the end result, it was clear that the issue of the "two founding nations" remained a major concern for Canada.[21]

ISRAEL

Although Israel is not formally allied with the United States, little doubt exists that the two countries are aligned. This observation is supported both by the historical record of Israeli policy and by the United States' willingness to support Israel's foreign policy positions in the years since the Jewish state was created in 1948. Having the only democratically elected government in the Middle East, and being a stable country in an area rent by violent and rapid change, Israel's entire international and domestic outlook has been colored by two major concerns: survival, and the maintenance of good relations with the United States to help assure survival. Israel's general domestic characteristics are presented in Table 13–5.

Survival

Compared with other major American allies, Israel's economy is small. As of 1992, 41 countries had annual economic products larger than Israel's.[22] Nevertheless, because of the severe threat to Israel's survival posed by neighboring Arab states, Israel's military expenditures ranked it the ninth most potent mil-

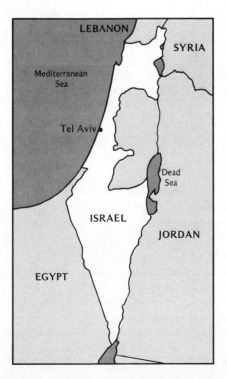

FIGURE 13–4

itary force in the world. This ranking includes only those moneys spent on Israeli defense by the Israeli government itself, and excludes moneys contributed by the international Jewish community and military aid provided by the United States. As far as capabilities are concerned, some observers ranked Israel third, after only the United States and China.

Created in 1948 out of part of the Palestine Mandate granted to Great Britain in 1920 by the League of Nations as a home for the Jews, Israel was a nation-state born in warfare and threatened by external and internal forces since its very inception. Jewish nationalists, or Zionists, began a guerrilla war against the British in Palestine even before World War II was over in the hope of obtaining an independent Jewish state. Great Britain, drained by its fight against fascism in World War II, fought back and looked for a way to resolve the situation.

After the United Nations proved to be an effective forum to cope with the international crisis brought about by the Soviet Union's continuing 1946 occupation of northern Iran, hopes were high that the UN could provide a successful stage for resolving international conflicts. In 1947, Great Britain therefore brought the Palestine question before the international body as the second test of the UN's ability to solve international dilemmas. In one form or another, that question has remained before the UN to this very day.

The UN's plan for Palestine was simple. Palestine would be partitioned into two states, one Jewish and one Arab. The United States, the Soviet Union, and 31 other states voted for the partition resolution. Thirteen states, all either Moslem or Asian, opposed it. The Jewish nation at long last had a state, and began laying the groundwork for a nation-state.

Immediately, Arab/Palestinian guerrilla forces formed the "Arab Liberation Army" and engaged Jewish settlements throughout the territory. Dissatisfied with partition and opposed to federation, Arabs internal to the territory of what would become Israel sought to eliminate the Jewish presence there. Simultaneously, five Arab states, each with its own intentions and objectives, were poised to invade Israel. On May 14, 1948, the armies of Syria, Lebanon, Iraq, Egypt, and Transjordan crossed into Israel. The first war for the survival of the Jewish state had begun.[23]

Israel won that war and subsequent fights for survival in 1956, 1967, and 1973. As a result of these conflicts, and as a result of Jewish history and Israel's struggles with the Palestine Liberation Organization, Israel developed what may be described as a siege mentality.

Israel's domestic policies are strongly conditioned by threats to Israeli survival. High taxes, high inflation, high defense expenditures, and women in combat roles in the Israeli military have all been tolerated on the domestic side because of the threat, and Israeli expansion into the Golan Heights, the West Bank, Gaza Strip, and the Sinai Peninsula were all rationalized as moves to improve Israeli security. Western intelligence services generally concede that Israel has also developed its own nuclear weapons. Throughout these difficulties, Israel has counted on, and received, American support. During the 1980s and 1990s, however, Israel increasingly undertook initiatives in the name of security that began to undermine unquestioning U.S. support for Israel. For example, in 1986, it was revealed that Israel had conducted intelligence gathering operations against the United States in the United States itself. After Palestinians in 1987

Israeli-Palestinian conflict has plagued Israel since Israel's inception. In 1987, Palestinians began the "Intifada," an uprising against Israeli occupation of the West Bank and Gaza. The intifada continued on into the 1990s. (AP/Wide World Photos.)

began the "Intifada," an uprising against Israel's occupation of the West Bank and Gaza, Israel used harsh measures to maintain control. In 1989, Israel kidnapped a mullah from Lebanon who had close ties to and probably directed terrorists. In 1991 and 1992, despite U.S. objections, the Israeli government encouraged Jewish settlers to build residences in the West Bank, thereby making the West Bank an even more integral part of Israel proper.

From the Israel perspective, all these actions were needed for security purposes. However, to many Americans, they were overreactions.

Israel and the United States

Although Israel recognizes the necessity of continued American support from the U.S. government, American Jews, and other segments of the U.S. population, Israel has not been and is not now constrained from initiating actions that it views as necessary, even if American anger is aroused. Even before the 1980s and 1990s, Israel acted as it saw fit. Thus, during Henry Kissinger's shuttle diplomacy of the early 1970s, during the Israeli Cabinet's territorial debates of the late 1960s, and during the joint Israeli-British-French invasion of Egypt in 1956, the Israeli government undertook actions that it knew would generate U.S. displeasure.

Israeli willingness to act independently of U.S. preferences has been counterbalanced by the Jewish state's recognition that in times of crisis, U.S. support is a necessity. Although Israel has developed its own internal arms industry to a degree unmatched by any similarly sized state, a sizable percentage of Israel's

armed forces is armed with U.S. weaponry. For example, of the 662 combat aircraft that Israel had in 1989, all but 150 were American-made.[24] Another indication of the importance of the United States to Israel occurred during the 1973
Arab-Israeli War, when only a massive U.S. airlift of miliary equipment averted
Israeli disaster. As former Israeli Foreign Minister Abba Eban observed during
cabinet debates over the annexation/expansion question following the 1968
Arab-Israeli War, Israel cannot afford to lose American support.[25]

From the Israeli perspective, the sizable American Jewish community,
although influential in American politics, cannot guarantee continued U.S. support. However, it can prevent rapid loss of that support. Israel realizes that U.S.
need for Arab oil has influenced the United States to adopt a more "evenhanded"
policy toward the entire region. Indications of this "evenhandedness" are the
United States' willingness to sell advanced weapons to Arab states, including
Egypt and Saudi Arabia, and occasional U.S. moves toward discussions with the
PLO. Few Israelis publicly question the commitment of the United States to
Israel or Israel's need for that continued support, but increasing numbers of
Israelis realize that Israeli views of Israeli security and U.S. views of Israeli secu-
rity are not identical. This is not a comforting thought in Israel.

Israel and the World

A combination of circumstances conspired to make Israel one of the world's most
embattled states. Arab hostility has been a given. A treaty has been signed with
Egypt; and Jordan, Saudi Arabia, and other moderate Arab states engaged more in
rhetorical bombast against Tel Aviv than military action. But threats from Libya,
Syria, and Iraq remained central features of the Israeli worldview. The inability of
Arab states to overcome differences among themselves was and is as much a factor
in Israel's survival as the superiority of Israeli weapons and military planning. Iran
under Khomeini pledged to destroy Israel and "liberate" Jerusalem. Iraq under
Saddam Hussein in 1991 launched Scud missiles against Israel in an effort designed
both to inflict as much damage as possible to Israel and to drive the anti-Iraq coalition of states participating in Operation Desert Storm apart.

Europe, one would imagine, should be a close friend of Israel's. But it has
not been. With Europe's extreme dependence on external sources of oil, much of
which is imported from Arab member states of OPEC, European governments
were, at best, neutral in the Arab-Israeli dispute. Otherwise, they faced an
embargo of oil shipments from the Arab states. Although Europe provided economic and development aid to Israel, its diplomatic and military support for
Israel has been rather limited. For example, during the 1973 Arab-Israeli War,
European NATO members refused to allow American resupply efforts to use
NATO bases on their territories.

Until the late 1980s, Israel's attitude toward the Soviet Union was one of
unabashed hostility because of the U.S.S.R.'s criticism of "expansionist Zionism,"
the Soviet Union's persecution of Soviet Jews, and the U.S.S.R.'s provision of
weapons, training, and equipment to Arab states. In the late 1980s, Soviet-Israeli
relations improved, and large numbers of Soviet Jews began immigrating to
Israel. After the collapse of the Soviet Union, Israeli relations with Russia
remained cordial, and the flow of immigrants to Israel continued.

Israel's perceptions of the Developing World have been influenced by Tel Aviv's relations with the United States. Because of the close Israeli-American connection, some Developing World states view Israel as an outpost of U.S. imperialism and react accordingly. Israel, in turn, responds to that reaction. Neither are Israeli-Developing World relations abetted by Israeli wealth (relative to the Developing World) and race (predominantly white).

During the 1960s and 1970s, Israel's position in and perceptions of the U.N. deteriorated as more and more Developing World states achieved independence and took their places in the UN General Assembly. As a result, UN positions on Arab-Israeli questions increasingly reflected the Arab/Palestinian position. On several occasions, Israel was saved from condemnation only by U.S. vetoes in the Security Council. Improved Soviet-Israeli relations in the late 1980s bettered Israel's position at the UN, but the continuation of the Arab-Israeli dispute guaranteed that Israel would still be criticized at the world body.

The End of the Arab-Israeli Dispute?

If Israel had difficulty with the world's leading IGO, it had little but open warfare with one of the world's most prominent NGOs, the Palestine Liberation Organization. Variously described as a terrorist organization, a national liberation movement, and sometimes even a government-in-exile, the PLO sought to create a Palestinian state out of the West Bank and the Gaza Strip. For years, it also sought the destruction of Israel. To Israel, the PLO was a primary enemy.

Nevertheless, because of Israel's international isolation and the burden of continual military preparedness, some Israelis argued that the Palestinian problem would have to be solved before peace could be achieved with Israel's Arab neighbors. Other Israelis rejected this view as hopelessly optimistic. However, in 1992, Israel elected a new government under Prime Minister Yitzhak Rabin, who pledged to explore more actively the possibility of peace with the Palestinians and Arabs. A series of peace talks between Israelis, Palestinians, and other Arabs were in fact begun, but progress was minimal.

Then, in September 1993, Israel and the PLO together dropped a bombshell. The PLO recognized Israel's right to exist, and called for an end to violence against Jews and the Jewish state. Israel recognized the PLO, and proposed self-rule for Palestinians in the Gaza Strip and the West Bank city of Jericho, with self-rule to be extended to more areas in the future. In every respect, this was an incredible step towards peace and the end of the Arab-Israeli dispute.

But would it be enough? Pessimists pointed to the long history of conflict that would have to be overcome, and to the hostility of hard line Arabs and Jews to peace with the other side. Optimists pointed out that many on both sides were tired of fighting and now wanted peace. Whatever the outcome, everyone agreed that the PLO-Israeli agreement was a major breakthrough.

CONCLUSIONS

The states whose perceptions we examined in this chapter at one time were all close allies of the United States or the former Soviet Union. Indeed, in the first two editions of this book, this chapter was entitled "The Perceptions of the Allies of the Superpowers."

But times change, and so do perceptions. Eastern European states now follow their own policy preferences, and Western European states, Japan, Canada, and Israel, although in most cases bound formally to the United States as allies, have moved increasingly onto independent paths of their own.

Indeed, the states whose views we examined in this chapter are the very states whose changed positions first necessitated the abandonment of the old bipolar model of how the world was organized. As the 1990s proceed, there is nothing to indicate that Europe, Japan, Canada, and Israel will alter their increasingly independent courses.

KEY TERMS AND CONCEPTS

rise and fall of Eastern European communist governments
revolutions of 1989
Marshall Plan
European Coal and Steel Community
Euratom
European Community
Single European Act
Maastricht Treaty
European-U.S. economic relations
Western European views of Russia and the East

NATO (also in Chapter 3)
European immigration issues
German unification
modernization of Japan
Japanese views of the United States
Japanese views of Russia and China
Japan's role in the modern world
Canada's views of the United States
Quebec and two founding nations
Israel's views of its neighbors
Israel's views of the United States

NOTES

1. For other looks at the Chetnik-Partisan conflict, see Jozo Tomasevitch, *War and Revolution in Yugoslavia, 1941–45; The Chetniks* (Stanford: Stanford University Press, 1975); Milovan Djilas, *Tito: The Story from Inside* (New York: Harcourt Brace Jovanovich, 1980; and V. Dedijer et al., *History of Yugoslavia* (New York: McGraw-Hill, 1974).

2. U.S. Senate, Committee on Foreign Relations, *A Decade of American Foreign Policy* (Washington: U.S. Government Printing Office, 1950), p. 30.

3. For Khrushchev's own views of these occurrences, see Nikita Khrushchev, *Khrushchev Remembers* (Boston: Little, Brown, 1970); and Nikita Khrushchev, *Khrushchev Remembers: The Last Testament* (Boston: Little, Brown, 1974).

4. See Trond Gilberg, *Modernization in Romania since World War II* (New York: Praeger, 1975); Aurel Braun, *Romanian Foreign Policy since 1965* (New York: Praeger, 1978); and Daniel N. Nelson (ed.), *Romania in the Nineteen Eighties* (Boulder, CO: Westview, 1981).

5. For additional details on the Eastern European revolutions of 1989, see Philip Longworth, *The Making of Eastern Europe* (New York: St. Martins Press, 1992); and Roger East, *Revolutions in Eastern Europe* (Pinter Publishers, 1992).

6. International Institute for Strategic Studies, *The Military Balance 1989–1990* (London: IISS, 1989), pp. 32–42.

7. For additional views on the early stages of European integration, see W. Hartley Clark, *The Politics of the Common Market* (Westport, CT: Greenwood Press, 1975); A.M. El-Agraa, *The Economics of the European Community* (New York: St. Martin's Press, 1980); Werner J. Feld, *West Germany and the European Community* (New York: Praeger, 1981); Anthony J. Kerr, *The Common Market and How It Works* (Elmsford, N.Y.: Pergamon, 1977); Uwe W. Kitzinger, *The Politics and Economics of European Integration* (Westport, CT. Greenwood Press, 1976); and Max Beloff, *The United States and the Unity of Europe: Political, Social, and Economic Forces 1950–57* (Stanford: Stanford University Press, 1968).

8. For greater detail on the Single European Act, see Michael Calingaert, *The 1992 Challenge from Europe: Development of the European Community's Internal Market* (Washington, D.C.: National Planning Association, 1988). See also David Weigall and Peter Stirk, *The Origins and Development of the European Community* (Leicester: Leicester University Press, 1992); Clive Archer and Fiona Butler, *The European Community: Structure and Process* (New York: St. Martins Press, 1992); and Brian Nelson, David Roberts, and Walter Veit, eds., *The European Community in the 1990s: Economics, Politics, Defense* (Berg Publishers, 1992).

9. The complete text of the Maastricht Treaty is available from the European Community, Brussels, Belgium (1992).

10. For an excellent discussion of East–West trade issues, as they existed in the late 1980s, see Adlai E. Stevenson and Alton Frye, "Trading with the Communists," *Foreign Affairs* (Spring 1989), pp. 53–71. See also Hélène Seppain, *Contrasting U.S. and German Attitudes to Soviet Trade, 1917–1991* (New York: St. Martins Press, 1992).

11. International Monetary Fund, *Direction of Trade Statistics Yearbook 1978–84* (Washington, D.C.: International Monetary Fund, 1985), appropriate pages.

12. For several perspectives on European military security in the late 1980s and early 1990s, see Richard K. Betts, "NATO's Mid-Life Crisis," *Foreign Affairs* (Spring 1989), pp. 37–52; Keith A. Dunn, *In Defense of NATO* (Boulder, CO: Westview, 1989); Schuyler Foerster et al., *Defining Stability: Conventional Arms Control in a Changing Europe* (Boulder, CO: Westview, 1989); J. Philip Rogers, *The Future of European Security* (New York: St. Martins Press, 1992); and Hans Gunter Brauch and Robert Kennedy, *Alternative Conventional Defense Postures in the European Theater, Volume I–III* (New York: Crane Russak, 1990, 1992, and 1993).

13. For the history of nineteenth- and early twentieth-century Japan, see Hugh Borton, *Japan's Modern Century–From Perry to 1970* (New York: John Wiley, 1970); and Edwin O. Reischauer and Albert M. Craig, *Japan: Tradition and Transformation* (Boston: Houghton Mifflin, 1978).

14. For discussion of U.S. policy toward Japan during the 1945–1952 period, see Roger Buckley, *Occupation Diplomacy: Britain, the United States, and Japan 1945–1952* (New York: Cambridge, n.d.); Grant K. Goodman, *American Occupation of Japan: A Retrospective View* (New York: Paragon, 1968); and Robert E. Ward and Frank J. Schulman, *Allied Occupation of Japan: 1945–1952* (Chicago: American Library Association, 1974). See also Nazli Choucri et al., *The Challenge of Japan Before World War II and After* (New York: Routledge, 1992).

15. See Ian Nish, "The Reemergence of Japan," in F. S. Northedge (ed.), *The Foreign Policies of the Powers* (New York: The Free Press, 1974), p. 308.

16. Many Asian countries in particular were concerned by this.

17. For a specific Japanese statement of this view, see Shintaro Ishihara, *The Japan That Can Say No* (1989).

18. The Japanese Northern Territories consist of the Habomai Islands, Shikotan Islands, Kunashiri Island, and Etorofu Island. See *Japan's Northern Territories* (Tokyo: Ministry of Foreign Affairs, 1980).

19. For other views of Japan's international role in the late twentieth century, see Mike Mansfield, "The U.S. and Japan: Sharing Our Destinies," *Foreign Affairs* (Spring 1989), pp. 3–15; Edwin O. Reischauer, *Japan: The Story of a Nation* (Hightstown, NJ: McGraw-Hill, 1990); William R. Nester, *Japan and the Third World: Patterns, Power, Prospects* (New York: St. Martins, 1992); and Eiichi Katahara, *Japan's Changing Political and Security Role* (Singapore: Institute of Southeast Asian Studies, 1991).

20. For discussions of some of Canada's most important international concerns, see Theodore H. Cohn, *The International Politics of Agricultural Trade: Canadian-American Relations in a Global Agricultural Context* (Vancouver: University of British Columbia Press, 1990); and David G. Haglund (ed.), *The New Geopolitics of Minerals: Canada and International Resources Trade* (Vancouver: University of British Columbia Press, 1989).

21. For additional commentary and analysis of Canada's difficulties with the Quebec issue and other questions of unity, see David V. J. Bell, *The Roots of Disunity: A Study of Canadian Political Culture* (New York: Oxford University Press, 1992).

22. U.S. Central Intelligence Agency, *The World Factbook 1991* (Washington, D.C.: U.S. Government Printing Office, 1992).

23. An excellent history of modern Israel is Howard M. Sachar, *A History of Israel* (New York: Knopf, 1976). See also Samuel J. Roberts, *Party and Policy in Israel: The Battle Between Hawks and Doves* (Boulder, CO: Westview, 1989).

24. *The Military Balance 1989–1990*, pp. 102–103.

25. Sachar, *A History of Israel*, p. 171.

CHAPTER 14

The Chinese Outlook

- How have Chinese history and Marxist-Leninist-Maoist ideology influenced China's view of the world?
- How does China view other international actors today?
- How has China changed since Mao died?
- How will the Tiananmen Square massacre affect the future of China?

The People's Republic of China (P.R.C.) is the world's most populous nation, with over 1.1 *billion* people, 93 percent of whom are Han Chinese.[1] This fact alone makes China a significant force in world politics. When it is also realized that China has the world's largest number of people under arms, is a nuclear power, has as one of its national objectives the creation of a modern industrial economy by the year 2000, and at one time viewed itself as a revolutionary model for the economically impoverished and politically oppressed peoples of the world, the P.R.C.'s importance in world politics is further magnified.

Despite China's importance, the P.R.C. is not a superpower. Economically, its gross domestic product is about the size of Spain's (approximately $410 billion in 1991). Militarily, its forces are equipped with few modern weapons, and have no meaningful ability to project power to regions distant from the P.R.C. Its efforts to project itself as a revolutionary model have met with limited success, and regular internal upheavals since the Communist Chinese seized power such as the Great Leap Forward, the One Hundred Flowers campaign, the Cultural Revolution, the purge of the Gang of Four, and the 1989 Democracy movement have detracted from China's efforts to modernize and industrialize.

Despite these problems, other nations recognize the P.R.C. as a great power. Although it is not now a superpower and has no hope of becoming one during the twentieth century, its potential is imposing. Table 14–1 presents several of China's more notable characteristics.

China's views of itself and the role it plays in the world have been influenced by Chinese history, geography, culture, and population, and since 1949 by Marxist-Leninist-Maoist ideology (hereafter called Maoism). China's worldview is undeniably unique. Moreover, it is a worldview that has changed several times during the twentieth century alone, both as a result of revolutions within China and as a result of changed Chinese perceptions of the external world. The

TABLE 14–1 General Characteristics of the People's Republic of China, 1991

| Land | | Population | | | | | Economy | | Government |
| | | | | | | | Gross Domestic Product | | |
Sq. Km. x 10⁶	% in Agriculture	Total (mil.)	Growth Rate %	Literacy Rate %	Ethnic Groups	Religion	Annual Bil. $	Per Capita	Type and Characteristics
9.6	10 arable; 5 irrigated	1,151	1.6	75	Han 93	Atheist	413	370	Communist

SOURCE: CIA, *The World Factbook 1991* (Washington: U.S. Government Printing Office, 1992).

FIGURE 14–1

rapidity of change in the Chinese worldview may have been disconcerting to a younger civilization, but China is not a young civilization. Indeed, the Chinese trace the origins of Confucianism, the long-dominant religious/cultural base of Chinese life, to 500 B.C. The Shang dynasty was even older, originating in approximately 1750 B.C.

Continuity and change are two major facets of Chinese consciousness. Confucius and Mao both accepted that change is the only constant, and it is at least in part because of this Chinese ability to accept a seemingly paradoxical insight that China and its people have been able to cope with two other contradictions in their worldview. First, the Chinese have had to reconcile themselves to the fact that for a century, from 1840 to 1945, they were dominated by external states, most often Western. To a people who for millennia viewed themselves as the political, economic, and social core of the universe, that century was galling and humiliating. The inevitability of change, however, proved to the Chinese that their rightful position of superiority would again be theirs. As John King Fairbank observed, the claim of Chinese superiority has been "thoroughly institutionalized and preserved as the official myth of the state for more than two thousand years."[2]

The second contradiction concerns Chinese attitudes toward the West, and is intimately connected with the century of humiliation. On the one hand, China has sought to keep Western influence at arm's length, because the West is thought to be both an inferior and a corrupting culture. On the other hand, China has found it necessary to catch up with the West in both political and economic life. It was therefore entirely plausible to the post-Maoist leadership in China that after a quarter century of reviling the West, the P.R.C. should turn to the West for support in economic and security matters.

CHINA AND HISTORY: THE THREE ERAS— AND THE BEGINNING OF A FOURTH?

The P.R.C.'s worldview cannot be understood if Chinese history is not taken into account, particularly the years of empire (to 1840), the century of humiliation (1840–1945), and the years of Maoism and revolutionary modernization

(1945–1976). In addition, following Mao's death in 1976, a wave of change and reform typified by the "Four Modernizations" swept China. Although the period of the "Four Modernizations" is too brief to be described as an era, it must nevertheless be viewed separately. Each of these four periods carries with it a separate system of thought the outlines of which must be understood if modern China's views of itself and the world are to be understood.[3]

Empire and Confucianism

Chinese call their country "Chung-kuo." Literally translated, "Chung-kuo" means "Middle Kingdom." Indeed, until the influx of Europeans consumed China midway in the nineteenth century, the Chinese knew of no other culture or society that could rival their own. The nomadic Mongols of central Asia clearly were perceived as uncultured and inferior, the civilizations of Southeast Asia were vassal possessions of the **Chinese Empire**, and the Himalaya Mountains were the "roof of the world" that filtered out much of the advanced Indian culture to the southwest. China was indeed the Middle Kingdom, and the sense of superiority that accompanied the Chinese people's perception of themselves as the center of the world was the product of historical experience and geographic isolation.

A series of dynasties ruled China throughout the classical era of empire. The emperor ruled by divine right as the "Son of Heaven." Nevertheless, throughout Chinese history, the power of emperors varied. Occasionally emperors were dethroned, but this was taken simply to mean that a particular emperor had lost his heavenly authority. In part, the political strength or weakness of individual emperors was a function of the emperor's own ability. In part, it resulted from the strength or weakness of Chinese warlords.

Warlords played major roles throughout Chinese history. Basing their power on their local popularity or military prowess within a particular region of China, warlords often challenged the authority of the emperor. Thus, during some eras of Chinese history, such as the "Six Dynasties" era from about A.D. 200 to 500, emperors ruled over China in little more than name. Effective authority was wielded by warlords, and China was more a confederation of associated kingdoms than a single empire. During other periods, however, politically effective and militarily able emperors melded China into a single centralized and organized political entity.

Chinese imperialism during the classical era took on two forms. One was outright military conquest. The other was the tribute system that required the rulers of neighboring states to send gifts and professions of loyalty to the Chinese emperor. If this tribute was acceptable, the emperor permitted neighboring rulers to stay in power.

China's political life, both domestic and international, was therefore based on a master-servant relationship. Chinese relations with external states strengthened China's self-image as the center of civilization, and the emperors' relations with warlords and other domestic political powers, although open to challenge, was theoretically based on the emperors' centrality to Chinese society.

It is a moot point to debate whether the Chinese political system reflected the Confucian religious/cultural order or vice versa. **Confucius**, who lived during the fifth century before Christ, taught that proper relations between children and parents were the basis for a moral and just society, and that this relationship had direct applicability to relations between individuals and rulers. This concept of proper child-parent relations was known as filial piety, and was explained succinctly in *Hsiao Ching (Classic of Filial Piety)*:

The filial piety with which the superior man serves his parents may be transferred as loyalty to the ruler; the fraternal duty with which he serves his elder brother may be transferred as submissive deference to elders; and his regulation of his family may be transferred as good government in any official position.[4]

Obedience was the core of Chinese society. Local officials were called "father-mother" authorities, and the emperor, with God's own mandate, was the "Son of Heaven." In classic Confucianism, a son remained a son throughout life and was expected to act as such. Similarly, a political underling remained a political underling and acted accordingly. Changes in political leadership or policy practices were rationalized as placing the government more in line with the original intention of the Confucian texts. Therefore, scholarship and education were encouraged as ways through which the meaning of the original texts could best be deciphered.

Traditional Chinese society was highly structured and authoritarian, and emphasized the role of the elder over the role of self. It was a very conservative society, inclined more to develop knowledge through the study of ancient Confucian classics than through the practical solution of problems. It was a society that was self-satisfied and confident of its place in the world. In its own eyes, it *was* the world. The West's earliest contacts with China reflected China's sense of self-satisfied superiority. Europeans went to China in the sixteenth century seeking trade, specifically silks and Chinese handiworks. Europeans were barbarians, a seventeenth-century Ming dynasty historian concluded. After all, Portugal "sent an envoy for the purpose of buying small children to cook and eat."[5] Nevertheless, the barbarians continued to come to the emperor's court, attracted by his moral example, wealth, and mandate from heaven. The emperor therefore had a responsibility to be compassionate and generous to foreigners. They, in turn, upon recognizing his mandate, had a responsibility to bring tribute to the emperor, even as rulers of countries bordering China did. The "three kneelings and nine prostrations" of the kowtow, an integral part of the tribute ceremony, made it clear to everyone that the foreigner was inferior and the emperor was superior.[6]

Humiliation and Westernization

By the early nineteenth century, Great Britain, France, Holland, and the United States were actively trading with China. To the Chinese, the Western "big noses," or "hairy ones," were tolerated but little more. All Western traders were confined to enclaves and could deal only with the government trade monopoly. The aggressive Westerners, displeased with the restrictions and convinced that more Chinese wealth was available for the taking, sought ways to expand their trade. The emperor refused to make additional concessions, few Chinese wanted Western products, and an impasse was reached. Western traders could find only one product made outside of China that the Chinese would buy in quantity: opium.

Most of the opium that was brought into China was grown in India in territories under the jurisdiction of the British East India Company. By 1840, Western sale of opium to China was a large-scale commercial activity, much of it carried out in the British enclave at Canton. When the Chinese, concerned that opium trafficking had gotten out of control, attempted to seal off Canton from the rest of China, the British government viewed the Chinese action as an impediment to free trade and sent a naval squadron to Canton. Two years later, Great Britain and China signed the Treaty of Nanking, which guaranteed British trading privileges, including trading in opium, in China.

China never fully accepted the terms of this first "unequal treaty," and Great Britain was similarly displeased by the agreement, believing it not extensive enough. A second **opium war** was fought in 1858, this time with Great Britain and France on one side and China on the other. The Europeans again dictated the terms of the treaty. This second unequal treaty was not acknowledged by the Manchu dynasty in Beijing until a joint Anglo-French expeditionary force occupied the city in 1860. Within a 20-year period, then, China had been militarily defeated, forced to accept treaties that it opposed, opened to ever-larger opium imports, and invaded, with the emperor's own capital being captured. The Middle Kingdom had begun its **century of humiliation**.

Worse was to come. By the early twentieth century, 80 Chinese ports were **treaty ports** and served as centers of trade, Western culture, religion, graft, and corruption. European intergovernmental organizations determined standards for health, sanitation, and other aspects of life in these treaty ports. Under the concept of extraterritoriality, Western merchants, missionaries, and citizens were subject not to Chinese laws but to the laws of their own home countries. Westerners took tremendous advantage of the slack that developed between law and law enforcement. All Western nations had most-favored-nation clauses inserted in their treaties with the Chinese government, and low treaty tariffs prevented the growth of China's own domestic industries. Increasingly, Western states received access not only to Chinese ports, but also to the Chinese interior.

Western customs and values accompanied Western trade into China and undermined the old Confucian order. Christian missionaries traveled throughout China, spreading both Western religion and doubt about the prevailing social order. Although the impact of these missionaries has probably been overemphasized, there is no doubt that their wide-ranging movements reflected the growing impotence of the Chinese government.[7]

The mixture of Western religion, Chinese tradition, and the collapsing authority of the Manchu dynasty led directly to the Taiping Rebellion, a civil war that swept China from 1851 to 1864 and claimed over 15 million Chinese lives. The rebels attempted to overthrow the Manchu and the Confucian religious-cultural order and substitute for it a mutated Protestant Christianity and a primitive pre-Marxist communism that included land redistribution and classless egalitarianism. At their high water mark, the Taiping rebels controlled the southern half of China and had a military force within 50 miles of Beijing, the traditional center of Manchu authority. The Western powers, meanwhile, first viewed the Taiping Rebellion as a Christian wave that would strengthen their positions in China. Gradually, however, as it became clear to Great Britain, France, Holland, the

United States, and the other powers intervening in China that the Taipings also sought a reduction of Western influence, they changed their attitudes. Western neutrality turned to Western support of the Manchus, and gradually the Taiping tide receded. The rebellion ended in 1864. From 1864 until its demise in 1911, the Manchu dynasty survived only with European support. In short, from the 1860s on, there was a Chinese government, but it did not govern China.

Territorially, China also suffered. Japan, which had successfully thrown off Western imperialism and proceeded to industrialize, defeated China in the 1895 Sino-Japanese War and acquired the Ryukyu Islands. Russia moved farther into Central Asia, and France took Indochina. Great Britain moved into Pakistan, and Korea became an international trading center. The Middle Kingdom had become the humiliated kingdom.

Understandably, many Chinese were outraged at "the foreign devils" and their role in China. In 1900, that resentment exploded in a series of attacks against Christians, missionaries, traders, and other symbols of Western presence. For two months, the foreign legations in Beijing were besieged until Western states, including the United States and Great Britain, landed troops and marched into Beijing. The revolt, led by a secret society known as the Society of Harmonious Fists, or "Boxers," proved counterproductive. For the last 11 years of the Manchu dynasty, foreigners had free reign throughout China as Europeans and North Americans alike pursued profit and wealth through an "open door" policy of free and open access.

The Manchu dynasty by this time was virtually powerless. In 1911, Dr. Sun **Yat-sen** succeeded in his tenth attempt to overthrow the old regime. Sun, however, was not powerful enough to hold China together, and once again China was ruled by warlords. The warlords reigned supreme in China until 1928, when **Chiang Kai-shek**, the new leader of Sun's **Kuomintang party**, seized power in Beijing.

The history of the Kuomintang party after Sun Yat-sen fled and before Chiang assumed power is fascinating. The Kuomintang party went underground, where it led a precarious existence, first fighting for its survival and then seeking to establish a power base for itself in the China of the warlords. In the early 1920s, the international situation lent a helping hand to the Kuomintang as the Bolshevik government in Moscow, seeking international support wherever it could find it, offered extensive aid to Sun. Sun gladly accepted Soviet support, admitted the fledgling Chinese Communist Party to the Kuomintang, and joined the Comintern. The Comintern sent **Michael Borodin** to Sun as a political-military adviser, and the Kuomintang-Comintern connection flourished.

Chiang Kai-shek did not alter this relationship after Sun died in 1925. Chiang's dream was to reunite China under his rule, and to that end Chiang's military forces launched a northern expedition against the warlords. He was highly successful. However, in April 1927, the Kuomintang-Communist alliance broke down as Chiang turned on his allies. Over 40,000 Communists were killed within a month, and the remaining few, including Mao Zedong, retreated to Kiangsi Province in central China. Chiang set up his government in Nanking, and China was united.

As a Chinese nationalist, Chiang attempted to reduce Western influence in China gradually. By 1930, tariff revision agreements had been reached with most Western powers. In addition, minor non-Chinese nationalities were once again tried under Chinese legal jurisdiction, even though the major powers—Great Britain, France, Japan, and the United States—refused to give up their "right" of extraterritoriality. Nevertheless, for only two years of work, this was an auspicious record. This promising beginning came to a grinding halt when Japan invaded China in 1932.

Meanwhile, the Chinese Communist Party (CCP) gathered strength in Kiangsi Province. The Kuomintang government, challenged both by Japan and the Communists, turned to Germany for military advice and support. Under German tutelage, Kuomintang forces launched several "Communist Extermination Campaigns" and drove the Communists out of Kiangsi in 1934. The Communists, numbering about 100,000, began the epic 6,000-mile **Long March** that by 1936 brought them to Yenan Province in China's mountainous west. By this time the CCP numbered barely 20,000, and Soviet-Comintern influence within it had declined precipitously. From here, **Mao Zedong**, who had risen to command in the CCP during the Long March, launched the campaign that would carry him and his party to victory 13 years later.

By 1937, both the Nationalists and the Communists concluded that they were threatened more by Japan than by each other. Thus, the two parties formed a second "united front" (the first having been formed during the mid-1920s), this time directed against Japan. Both sides in the uneasy political alliance fought the Japanese with one hand and held the other back for potential use against each other.

Japan's final defeat in 1945 only meant that Chiang and Mao could now turn their full forces on each other. From 1945 to 1949, yet another Chinese civil war raged, increasingly viewed from outside China as an integral part of the now dominant East–West conflict in international affairs. From the perspective of the Chinese, foreign domination of China had finally ended, and the Chinese were now struggling to determine which party and what social system would rule China.[8]

Revolutionary Modernization and Maoism

Two opposite trends marked the four-year period of the post–World War II segment of the Chinese Civil War. The first trend was the steady weakening of Chiang's Kuomintang forces. To a great extent, many Chinese viewed Chiang as a throwback to the old warlords. The fact that many Kuomintang officials were corrupt and self-serving also hurt Chiang's popularity. Often, Kuomintang officials expropriated land and property for their own personal gain. Gradually, then, popular disenchantment with and hostility toward Chiang and his party set in. One measure of that disenchantment was the steady erosion of Chiang's armed forces. On several occasions, entire divisions deserted to the Chinese Communists.

The second trend was the strengthening of Mao's Chinese Communist forces. In 1945, they numbered slightly more than a million troops. By the war's end, that force had more than doubled. Although some of the growth was undoubtedly the result of a desire on some people's part to "be on the winning side," it is impossible to deny that the Communists also emerged from World War II as national heroes. And during the civil war, they pursued politically enlightened policies in their relations with the peasants. For example, whereas

Despite the Chinese government's efforts, population pressures remain a problem in much of China. The Chinese government has undertaken a large-scale advertising campaign to slow population growth. (UN Photo/John Isaac.)

victorious Kuomintang commanders often claimed fertile land for their own, Communist leaders turned it over to the peasants. For land-starved tillers of the soil, few acts could have been politically more meaningful.

Indeed, Mao based his entire revolution on the peasant. Because of this, he has often been accused—and rightly so—of "standing Marx on his head." To Marx, the peasantry was at best a neutral political class and at worst a reactionary class. Only the industrial proletariat worker, Marx believed, could develop sufficient class consciousness to become revolutionary. To Mao, Marx's edict presented some major conceptual problems. First and foremost, China was not an industrial society, and no proletariat worker class existed. If Mao accepted Marx's views on proletariat and peasant, no revolution could take place in China. Mao therefore improvised. In Russia, Mao knew, Lenin had decreed an alliance between proletariat and peasant. Mao simply went further than Lenin. While depicting himself as an orthodox Marxist-Leninist, he revised Marxism-Leninism and based his revolution on the peasant.

If the peasant was the heart of Mao's revolution, authoritarian leadership, self-reliance, and self-sacrifice were its soul. Although many traditional Chinese familial and governmental institutions had been undermined or destroyed during the century of humiliation, traditional Confucian values that emphasized acceptance of authority and proper behavior gave Mao a strong base on which to build his social system. Even the Chinese concept of the extended family aided Mao in his effort to communize China.

Mao's efforts to assert control in China were abetted by another force out of Chinese history, China's unhappy relations with the West. As a Marxist, Mao accepted the concept of class conflict. As a Marxist-Leninist, he accepted Lenin's theory of imperialism. As a Chinese, he interpreted his country's history as proof positive of Marx's and Lenin's ideas, and pointed to Chiang Kai-shek's reliance on

U.S. military support as evidence that Chiang was an agent of U.S. imperialism. To the Chinese people, eager to escape their century of humiliation, Mao's views made sense. Thus, Mao accelerated the rate of Chiang's reduction in popularity by emphasizing class conflict and imperialism. He also built the groundwork for the next two decades of Chinese foreign policy, whose basic tenet was opposition to Western and U.S. imperialism, on the basis of Chinese history interpreted through Marxist-Leninist-Maoist eyes.

But Mao feared that the Chinese revolution would become bureaucratized and lose its fervor. Thus, in 1966, Mao unleashed the cultural revolution. For ten years, China was torn by continual ideological campaigns, factional political struggle and purges, and economic and educational turmoil as Mao and other Chinese militants sought to keep China on a "true" revolutionary path.

However, all they did was disrupt Chinese society. Economic growth ended. The political and social fabric of society was torn. And an entire generation of Chinese youth lost a decade of education. When Mao died in 1976, his militant colleagues, the so-called Gang of Four, were quickly arrested, and China was ready to begin a new period of history.

The Four Modernizations: Economic Reform, Not Political Reform

China's new course after Mao's death was charted primarily by Deng Xiaoping. Deng's conception of what China needed was simple; as he stated at the Eleventh Congress of the Communist Party of China in 1977, China needed "less empty talk and more hard work."[9]

Deng argued that China had to pursue a program of "Four Modernizations," in agriculture, industry, science and technology, and defense. To achieve these modernizations, Deng instituted a series of decidedly un-Maoist reforms. For example, in 1980, he instituted an incentive system in agriculture that allowed peasants to sell some of their crops on the open market. Deng told peasants this was their opportunity to "get rich." Chinese agricultural production jumped markedly.

During the next six years, other reforms were also instituted as central planning was deemphasized in several industrial sectors; privately owned workers' cooperatives were encouraged in light industry; and foreign investment was actively sought. The China of Deng Xiaoping was a much different place from the China of Mao Zedong.

Nevertheless, Deng insisted that China was communist. Indeed, Marx and his precepts continued to be praised as scientific and accurate interpreters of the forces of human history. Even so, the Marxism of Deng had its own unique form. Thus, according to several prominent Chinese scholars and policy-makers, Marxism as interpreted in China in the mid-1980s was a theory of history some aspects of which were true and other aspects of which were not. Their responsibility as members of the Communist Party of China, they said, was to implement policy on the basis of Marxism in those areas where Marxism was accurate, and to improvise and innovate in those areas where it was not. Reform had come to China with a vengeance.

But Deng's reforms were economic, not political. In marked contrast to the

Soviet Union's "Gorbachev Revolution," Deng intended the party to maintain political control. Thus, when in 1986 and 1987 Chinese students took to the streets to demand Western-style political democracy, Deng and the Chinese Communist Party moved quickly to quell dissent. Many Chinese officials suspected of being too lenient were removed from power, including Hu Yaobang, the head of the Communist party.

Two years later, Hu's death served as the catalyst for a wave of student demonstrations that swept China demanding political freedoms and Western-style political democracy. At first, only a few thousand students staged the demonstrations. But by early June 1989, millions of Chinese students, now joined by workers, marched in the streets of almost every major Chinese city. As many as a million students and workers occupied Beijing's Tiananmen Square alone.

The Chinese government appeared uncertain what to do. Internally divided, not sure of which course to take, and not certain of the military's support, the government was virtually paralyzed. And when it finally decided to send troops toward Tiananmen Square, the people of Beijing went into the streets to block the troop movements.

But the troops finally arrived, and when they did, they received orders to fire. No one knows for sure how many pro-democracy demonstrators died, but most estimates place the number at several thousand. The pro-democracy movement had been crushed. Across China, martial law was declared, political arrests were made, and a crackdown on noncommunist political outlooks was instituted. Economic reform could continue, but there would be no political reform.

The impact of the **Tiananmen Square massacre** on the outside world's attitude toward China was immense. Governments around the world, in varying degrees, condemned the Chinese government's actions, and businesses rethought their investments and their futures in China. Meanwhile, the Chinese government steadfastly asserted that it had acted correctly to restore public order. Thus, when in January 1990 Chinese Premier Li Peng proclaimed the end of martial law, he labeled the crackdown on political democracy a "great victory" that "quelled the counterrevolutionary rebellion."[10]

But the forces of economic and political reform in China had not been completely eliminated. Thus, in the early 1990s, moderates within the Chinese government instituted a series of free-market economic reform, and pro-democracy political reformers moved to leadership positions in the party during its September 1992 party congress. Once again, then, only three years after the Tiananmen Square Massacre, the struggle between reform and orthodoxy had been joined and the political and economic future of one-fifth of humankind hung in the balance.

THE MAOIST AND POST-MAOIST WORLDVIEWS

The Chinese Communist Party came to power in China in 1949, and for the next six years, Beijing maintained a view of the world that closely paralleled the one held by the Soviet Union at the time. The Chinese Communists' acceptance of a worldview based on a bipolar East–West construct was understandable, given both Chinese communist ideology and the Sino-American animosity gen-

Tiananmen Square, June 4, 1989. Deng Xiaoping's economic reforms did not extend into politics. Hundreds, perhaps thousands of people were killed and injured as the Chinese army occupied the Square, ending the Chinese students' sit-in demanding political democracy.   (AP/Wide World Photos.)

erated by the Korean War. Mao further denied that a neutral stance was possible in a world characterized by the struggle between capitalism and communism; the infant nonaligned movement was not crucial to world politics, Mao believed, and the Developing Third World would soon join either the First or the Second.

China's worldview began to change around 1955 as Mao realized that China's interests diverged from the U.S.S.R.'s despite their shared acceptance of communism. As **Sino-Soviet tension** increased in the late 1950s and early 1960s, each communist power charged the other with "revisionism," that is, with adulterating orthodox Marxism. As we have already seen, both sides were right. A major part of this ideological struggle was China's effort to win the support of the socialist Second World, an effort that split the block but yielded insignificant returns for China. Only Albania became a true Chinese ally. Other communist states remained tied to the U.S.S.R., or as in the cases of North Korea and North Vietnam, moved to a position more or less equidistant from China and the Soviet Union. The P.R.C. picked up significant support from left-wing and communist parties not in power, but the Soviet Union remained in firm control of the world communist movement. Nevertheless, throughout the late 1950s and early 1960s, China continued to view the Western world in general and the United States in particular as its primary enemy.

During the middle 1960s, worsening Sino-Soviet relations led to another fundamental revision of the Maoist view of the outside world. To Mao, the United

A lone man blocks the advance of a column of tanks against Tiananmen Square on June 5, 1989. Bystanders eventually pulled the man away to safety.   (AP/Wide World Photos.)

States and the Soviet Union had become equally despicable hegemonistic powers that sought to divide the world into two spheres of influence, much as China itself had been divided into spheres of influence during the century of humiliation. Soviet and American allies were no different than their superpower providers, only weaker. What others called the First and Second Worlds were, to Mao, two sides of the same coin, each bent on global domination.

China's hope and the world's future, Mao believed, rested with the poor states of the world, what others called the underdeveloped Third World. Portraying itself as the champion of opposition to Soviet and American colonialism, neocolonialism, and imperialism, the P.R.C. actively extended its diplomatic contacts throughout the Developing World, offered economic aid and political advice, and supported global revolution. To Mao, the same strategy that led him to victory in China would lead the impoverished and exploited countries of the world to victory over the Soviet-American conspiracy. Mao had based his forces in the countryside of China and encircled and engulfed Chiang's forces in China's cities. So, too, would the poor rural countries of the world, with China at their head, encircle and engulf the rich urban Soviet-American alliance. The world's countryside would defeat the world's cities, even as had happened in China.

Central to this strategy was self-reliance. Despite China's willingness to extend economic and military support to governments and movements that it favored, the P.R.C. was a poor country that could not compete effectively with, especially, U.S. largesse. Revolutionary self-sufficiency was thus both a virtue and a necessity, just as it had been in Mao's victory over the Kuomintang.

During the Cultural Revolution, which began in 1966, China's relations with the external world were curtailed as purge and reform swept across China.[11] As the Cultural Revolution proceeded, China faced yet another changed international situation that predicated yet another changed Maoist worldview. The U.S. threat was clearly receding as the Vietnam War took its toll on the United States' international position, and the Soviet threat was clearly worsening as the U.S.S.R. built its military strength along the Sino-Soviet border and condemned Chinese policies. Finally, in 1969, warfare broke out between Soviet and Chinese forces along the Ussuri River.

Slowly but surely Mao invoked the old Chinese proverbs that "the enemy of my enemy is my friend," and that the wise leader "befriends the far enemy and fights the near." Mao now condemned Soviet "social imperialism" as the primary threat, although not the only threat, to world peace. He also attempted to contain Soviet expansionism by building a global united front that consisted of China, capitalist countries including the United States, and the poor countries of the world. The key elements in the implementation of Chinese policy based on this new view of the world were Richard Nixon's February 1972 trip to the P.R.C. and the November 1972 normalization of Sino-Japanese relations. Chinese support of global revolution was correspondingly relegated to an extremely low priority, although not abandoned.

With Mao's death in 1976, China's worldview continued to change. Although Beijing still recognized fundamental contradictions between capitalism and communism and between rich and poor, it did not see the world divided along communist-capitalist lines or even rich-poor lines. Rather, it was divided along pro-Soviet, anti-Soviet lines. This remained true for most of the 1980s despite a gradual improvement in Sino-Soviet relations. Equally important, as the 1980s progressed, the Chinese no longer claimed that their model of society was universally applicable. Rather, they argued that each country had to develop and follow its own model.

Even this worldview changed in the late 1980s and early 1990s as the Soviet Union was first weakened and then dissolved, and as China continued to emphasize economic reform and post-Maoist political orthodoxy. By the early 1990s, with the Soviet threat gone and the United States considered meddling but benign, the Chinese worldview saw fewer external threats to Chinese security than ever before under communist rule. Indeed, the Chinese government still claimed to base its worldview on communism, but it was a worldview significantly different from that of Mao Zedong.

CHINA'S VIEWS OF THE ACTORS

Not surprisingly, given the major shifts that have taken place in the Chinese outlook on the international system since 1949, Chinese views of the actors in international politics have also changed considerably. Former friends have become enemies, and enemies friends. The phenomenon is not unique to the Chinese outlook.

Despite these changes, an observer must be careful not to overlook the impact of history on China's current perceptions. Memories of empire and Confucianism, and of humiliation and Westernization, linger on even during the current era of revolutionary modernization. All these factors combine to produce Chinese perceptions of individual actors in today's world.

Russia

Even with the demise of the Soviet Union, the "Russian bear" still looms large in contemporary Chinese outlooks. The Chinese people have long had territorial disputes and simmering disagreements, with first the czarist government and then the Soviets. Indeed, it is not inaccurate to say that the 11 years of cordial Sino-Soviet relations extending from Mao's assumption of power in 1949 to the open Sino-Soviet rupture in 1960 was a peaceful aberration in a 300-year history of conflict.

Russia and China first faced each other as enemies during the 1650s as the Russian Empire spread into Siberia and Central Asia. By 1689, Russians and Chinese had fought a series of battles that finally led to the Treaty of Nerchinsk, signed in that year. The Treaty of Nerchinsk was the first treaty that China signed with a European state, and although both sides claimed it as a victory for their diplomacy, Russia's expansion to the east was stopped for 170 years.

In the 1840s and 1850s, Russia again expanded at Chinese expense, gaining over 185,000 square miles of Chinese land. In 1860, Russia acquired still more Chinese territory in the Treaty of Beijing, which gave Russia all lands between the Ussuri River and the Pacific Ocean. This territory covered 133,000 square miles. In 1864, another treaty yielded 350,000 additional square miles of Chinese territory to the czar. Meanwhile, Russian traders and merchants within China benefited from the same unequal treaties that other Europeans enjoyed.

The Chinese government railed against Russian expansion, but could do little about it. Following Sun Yat-sen's revolution in 1911, the Russians again intervened in Chinese affairs, this time encouraging Mongolia to revolt against Chinese rule. The czar aided the Mongols with 15,000 rifles, 7 million cartridges, and 15,000 sabers.[12] Again, the Chinese government could do little.

The history of Bolshevik and Comintern support for the Kuomintang party has already been detailed, but the fundamental fact remained that the Russians, despite later Soviet aid, were a central part of China's century of humiliation. In at least one way, they were worse than other Europeans when seen from the Chinese perspective because they took and kept for their own over 650,000 square miles of Chinese territory.

Soviet exploitation of China occurred in the aftermath of World War II as well. The U.S.S.R. removed almost all available industry from Manchuria in the years immediately after the war. Mao, following his victory in 1949, spent three months in Moscow trying to convince Stalin to extend reparations for the removed plants and to offer additional aid, but met with little success. A long-term Sino-Soviet treaty was signed, but in retrospect this appears more cosmetic than was realized at the time. Mao hid his disappointment and resentment from the outside world for over a decade.

Mao's resentment of Stalin was strengthened even more by Stalin's claims of substantial Soviet support for the Chinese Communist Party during World War II and before. Most Soviet aid had in fact gone to Mao's mortal enemy Chiang Kai-shek. The Soviet leader had even recommended that the Chinese Communists *not* accelerate their struggle against the Kuomintang in 1945–1946. If Mao had followed Stalin's advice, there might never have been a communist revolution in China.

Mao undoubtedly hoped that Stalin's death in 1952 would open the way to improved Sino-Soviet cooperation and additional recognition of Mao as an authoritative spokesman for world communism. If so, he was sorely disappointed. Khrushchev guarded the mantle of Soviet centrality to the world communist movement jealously. Sino-Soviet ideological disagreements worsened as China attempted a Great Leap Forward to full communization and as Mao urged Khrushchev to apply greater military pressure on the imperialist West. One of Mao's purposes in the Great Leap Forward was to wrest leadership of the communist movement from Moscow, and the Soviets resented it. Mao's objectives in urging the Soviets to adopt a more hard-line posture against the West were twofold. First, Mao was convinced that the United States and the West were "paper tigers," and that additional pressure would accelerate world revolution. Second, Mao realized that if he urged the Soviets to pressure the West and they did not, he could charge them with having abandoned their revolutionary ideals, a useful criticism to make in the struggle for leadership in the communist world. Khrushchev responded to Mao by reminding him that "nuclear weapons do not know class distinctions," and Mao called Khrushchev a revisionist, a dirty word in the Marxist-Leninist political lexicon.

Territory and ideology were thus two of the leading causes of Sino-Soviet hostility. This remained true into the 1960s, 1970s, and 1980s. When, following the Soviet invasion of Czechoslovakia in 1968, the U.S.S.R. postulated in the Brezhnev Doctrine that socialist states had the right to keep other socialist states in the socialist camp through military force if necessary, China believed that the Soviet threat to its northern areas had escalated tremendously. As the U.S.S.R. built up its military forces on the border and as tension mounted between the two communist giants, Mao reassessed his global strategy and found it wanting. China's subsequent rapprochement with the United States and the West did not take place soon enough to prevent outright Sino-Soviet fighting along the Ussuri River in 1969, but it did give pause to any more adventurous plans that the Kremlin may have had vis-à-vis China. Nevertheless, sporadic border incidents occurred throughout the 1970s and 1980s between the two countries.

By 1982, China viewed the Soviet Union as an implacable enemy intent on pursuing policies of anti-Chinese containment in Asia and expansion throughout the world. From the Chinese perspective, the Soviet military buildup on the Sino-Soviet border, Soviet stationing of naval vessels in Vietnam, Soviet economic and military support for the Vietnamese government itself, continual and increased Soviet attempts to improve relations with India, and the Soviet invasion of Afghanistan were all links in the same chain of Soviet containment directed against China. The Chinese also condemned other Soviet activities in Asia, Africa, Europe, and Latin America as proof of Soviet global "social imperialism."

Nevertheless, from 1982 on, the Chinese also sought to improve relations with the U.S.S.R. Gradually, especially after Gorbachev's accession to power in 1985, Sino-Soviet relations did in fact improve. From China's perspective, the Kremlin by the end of the 1980s had substantially changed the three aspects of

Soviet foreign policy that concerned China the most, namely, the Soviet occupation of Afghanistan, Soviet support for the Vietnamese occupation of Cambodia,
and the Soviet military buildup along China's northern border. Indeed, by 1989
conditions had changed so much that Gorbachev visited Beijing, the first time
that a Soviet leader had done that since the 1950s. Clearly, as the 1990s opened,
Sino-Soviet relations had improved dramatically.

Following the collapse of the Soviet Union, China breathed even easier
about its relations with its neighbor to the north. Nevertheless, with the Russian
future uncertain, the Soviet collapse did not eliminate Beijing's concern about
Russia. Despite Russia's clear economic and political decline, Chinese leaders in
the mid-1990s did not forget that the Russian bear and the Chinese dragon have
had a long history of tension.

The United States

Since Richard Nixon's 1972 trip to China, Sino-American relations have undergone a breathtaking transformation. Diplomatic relations have been established,
trade has expanded, tourism has increased, and hesitant discussions of economic
and military aid have been undertaken. Significant problems still remain, specifically the resolution of the Taiwan question and the fallout from the 1989
Tiananmen Square massacre, but the fact remains that the difference between
Sino-American relations of the 1970s and 1980s on the one hand and the Sino-
American relations of the 1950s and 1960s on the other were like the difference
between day and night. As the 1990s opened, Sino-American relations were
clouded by the aftermath of the Tiananmen Square massacre, on the American
side by the U.S. view that the Chinese government had brutalized its citizens and
on the Chinese side by Beijing's view that the United States had meddled in
Chinese domestic affairs, but it was nevertheless evident that both governments
wanted to preserve a relatively close relationship.[13]

Until the Sino-American rapprochement began in the early 1970s, Sino-
American relations were frozen in mutual hostility since the Korean War. In the
months before the June 1950 North Korean invasion of South Korea, the United
States had been moving hesitantly toward recognition of the new Chinese
Communist government. The Korean War halted that movement, and China's
entry into the war ended all possibility of recognition.

To the Chinese, America's involvement in Korea and threats against China
confirmed to Mao that the United States was a typical Western imperialist power.
On a personal level, one can only speculate about the impact that the war had on
Mao, whose son was killed by United Nations' fire.

Following the Korean War, the United States established a treaty system
designed to contain communist expansion. From the Chinese perspective, all the
treaties with the exception of NATO were directed wholly or partly against
China. CENTO, SEATO, ANZUS, and bilateral American treaties with Japan
and Taiwan proved in Mao's mind the continued fact of American hostility toward
China, and the Beijing government reciprocated. As the American involvement
in Vietnam escalated during the 1960s, the Chinese increasingly were confronted
with the possibility that the Vietnam War might spill over into a Sino-American
conflict.

The winding down of the Vietnam War in the late 1960s reduced the possibility of such a conflict, and the Sino-American rapprochement all but eliminated the possibility. Nevertheless, one issue has remained intractable in Sino-American relations throughout the years of confrontation and rapprochement alike. That issue is Taiwan.

The Taiwan question is a residual issue from the Communist-Kuomintang Civil War of 1945–1949. As Mao's forces drove the Kuomintang off the Chinese mainland, the Kuomintang retreated to the island province of Taiwan. The Kuomintang established their government there and claimed to be the rightful government of all China. The Communists, meanwhile, claimed that Taiwan was a province in revolt against the central government in Peking. Both parties agree that Taiwan is an integral part of China, so the central issue is: Which is the rightful government of China?

Having supported Chiang in the Civil War and viewing Mao's government as little more than a Soviet minion, the United States strongly supported Chiang's Nationalists on Taiwan. Between 1949 and 1972 the United States provided Taiwan with almost all of its military equipment and supported Taiwan diplomatically at the United Nations as well. Taiwan's economy boomed as Western aid flowed to Taiwan and Western corporations found cheap labor, an industrious people, and a favorable tax structure an attractive combination. The Nationalists were pleased. The Communists, however, had another perspective: The United States and the West were meddling in internal Chinese affairs.

Despite some progress, the issue has not yet been resolved. The Shanghai Communique, issued as a joint statement at the conclusion of Nixon's 1972 trip to China, outlined American and Chinese positions on the issue. For its part, China put forward its claim that as the "sole legal government of China," the "liberation of Taiwan is China's internal affair in which no other country has the right to interfere." The United States' circumspect position was that the United States reaffirmed its interest "in a peaceful settlement of the Taiwan question by the Chinese themselves." Further, the United States indicated it would "progressively reduce its forces and military installations on Taiwan as the tension in the area diminishes."[14] That reduction has since been completed. In addition, in 1979, the United States transferred diplomatic recognition from the Taiwan government to the Beijing government. The Taiwan issue has bristled to life on occasion since then, most recently in 1992 when the United States decided to sell advanced fighter aircraft to Taiwan, but even this did not dissuade Beijing or Washington from maintaining a relatively close relationship.

Even with problems with Washington over Taiwan, the Chinese see the United States as a source of investment capital as China strives to industrialize. Deng Xiaoping charted a path for external investment in China that would modernize China's industry and agriculture and at the same time keep China in control of its own economy. U.S. multinational corporations suddenly became desired sources of external knowledge and investment rather than the pariahs they had been in Chinese eyes. Trade between the two countries also expanded considerably, as Table 14-2 indicates. In all cases, however, the Chinese were careful to establish strict guidelines on and control over foreign investment and trade procedures.

If there is one area where China grew increasingly concerned about the United States during the 1970s, it was in the area of security. Surprisingly, China's

TABLE 14–2　Chinese-U.S. Trade, 1979–1991, in Millions of U.S. Dollars

	1979	**1981**	**1983**	**1985**	**1988**	**1991**
U.S. exports to China	1,857	4,682	2,753	5,050	5,039	6,287
Chinese exports to United States	595	1,505	1,713	2,284	9,270	6,192
U.S. surplus	1,262	3,177	1,040	2,766	−4,231	95

SOURCE: International Monetary Fund, *Direction of Trade Statistics*. various editions.

concern was that the United States had grown too pacifistic as a result of its Vietnam experience and could not provide a counterbalance to Soviet expansion. As we have seen, China's entire global strategy rested on that counterbalance. As a result, China continually stressed the necessity of the maintenance of a global U.S. presence.

Sino-American relations received a serious setback in 1989 as a result of the Chinese crackdown on the pro-democracy movement in China. For the most part, before the Tiananmen Square massacre, the United States maintained a restrained attitude toward the movement. Nevertheless, the Chinese government considered this to be U.S. meddling. Following the massacre, the Chinese government adopted a pronounced anti-American posture and blamed the United States for fomenting revolution. Although over subsequent years much of the tension resulting from the assault dissipated, efforts by the U.S. Congress throughout the Bush presidency to deny China most favored nation trading status led the Chinese government to continue its charges that the U.S. meddled in domestic Chinese affairs. With Bill Clinton during the 1992 presidential campaign expressing an intention to monitor Chinese human rights violations more closely and apply sanctions against China in response to violations, the Beijing government's concern over U.S. "meddling" escalated once again in 1993. Even though Clinton extended most favored nation status to China, the Beijing government remained concerned about U.S. attitudes and policies. In addition, many Chinese believed that the United States played a major role in influencing the International Olympic Committee to award the 2000 Olympics to Sydney, Australia, instead of Beijing—all because of U.S. concern over China's human rights record.

Japan

Next to Russia and the United States, Japan is the most important external state to the P.R.C. For most of the period from 1949 to 1972, Mao viewed Japan's economic progress and alignment with the United States with almost as much distrust as he viewed the United States. History and ideology were the reasons for Mao's suspicion; during China's century of humiliation, Japan was one of the primary exploiters of China. Interpreted in Marxist terms, Japan's need for raw material sources and expanding markets drove it to expand during the 1895–1945 period in particular, and the rapid postwar economic growth that Japan enjoyed implied that both resources and markets would be needed once again. From the Chinese perspective, Japan's military association with the United States appeared to carry with it potential for resurgent Japanese militarism.

It was therefore not surprising that China's rapprochement with the United States led rapidly to a Sino-Japanese rapprochement. Japanese Prime Minister

Tanaka visited Beijing in September 1972, only a half-year after Nixon's historic visit, thereby ending the nominal state of war between the two countries and laying the groundwork for diplomatic recognition. Sino-Japanese trade expanded rapidly as well, as Table 14–3 indicates. Japanese investment in China also increased rapidly.

The post-Mao Chinese leadership had made it clear that it intends to forge close but not constricting economic ties with Japan, and it is succeeding. With China's resources and need for capital and Japan's capital and need for resources, it is a trading marriage made in heaven. In all probability, the Chinese will try to keep it there.

The Developing World

The Developing World, or as Mao termed it, "the world countryside," has played a major role in Communist China's foreign policy since 1956.[15] Before that time, Mao viewed the Developing World as little more than a holding ground for states that had not yet decided which of the major power blocs they wished to join. Since that time, as China itself moved away from the Soviet bloc, the P.R.C. elevated the importance of the role that the "world countryside" plays in the world. By the 1960s, China viewed the Developing World as the key element for the future defeat of Soviet-American global domination, and through the 1970s and 1980s as a major part in the Chinese-Western-Developing World united front against Soviet "social imperialism." In the 1990s, China's emphasis on the Developing World centered on the need for cooperative economic relations.

China's approach to the Developing World has been seductively subtle. The P.R.C. regularly asserted that it, too, had been the victim of colonial exploitation and that it, too, was underdeveloped and impoverished. Therefore, Mao continued, the P.R.C. itself was a developing state, a member of the "world countryside." Further, Mao offered, the P.R.C. had a revolutionary model of self-reliance that was guaranteed to work, and China was willing to offer some limited amounts of aid and assistance to help others down the revolutionary road. Zhou Enlai's famous maxim, "China will never be a superpower," was directed as much toward Developing World ears as toward American and Soviet listeners.

There is no doubt that since 1956, China has seen the Developing World as the central theater of confrontation between, first, itself and Western imperialism, and then, between its tripartite united front and Soviet social imperialism. Chinese policies toward the Developing World have varied over time and by area and are too complex to detail here other than in broadest outline. During the late

TABLE 14–3　Chinese-Japanese Trade, 1979–1991, in Millions of U.S. Dollars

	1979	1981	1983	1985	1988	1991
Japanese exports to China	3,674	5,076	4,918	12,590	9,486	8,605
Chinese exports to Japan	2,933	5,283	5,089	6,534	9,861	10,265
Japanese surplus	741	–2,073	–171	6,056	–375	–1,660

SOURCE: International Monetary Fund, *Direction of Trade Statistics*. various editions.

1950s, the P.R.C. concentrated on expanding its diplomatic contacts in Africa and the Middle East, initiating diplomatic relations with Yemen, Syria, Lebanon, Iraq, Ghana, Guinea, Tanganyika (which soon became Tanzania), and Congo-Brazzaville by 1960. The P.R.C. expanded its support of Developing World national liberation movements during the early 1960s, but the combined impact of its own Cultural Revolution and the American threat in Vietnam influenced China to reduce its Developing World presence in the late 1960s. China for the most part urged advocates of change and revolution in Africa and the Middle East to fight on with "revolutionary self-reliance."

In Asia, China sees India as a major regional rival. China and India have territorial disputes in Tibet, and the P.R.C. perceives India as meddling in Chinese internal affairs there. In 1962, China and India fought a small border war along their Tibetan boundary because of both territorial disputes and Chinese claims of Indian interference in Chinese internal affairs. Sino-Indian relations cooled even further during the 1960s and 1970s because of India's intimacy with the U.S.S.R. and the Chinese perception that the Soviet Union was using India as part of its anti-Chinese containment barrier. With all these sources of dispute, it was understandable that China "tilted" toward Pakistan during the 1971 Indo-Pakistani War. During the 1980s, Sino-Indian relations were not particularly tense, but neither were they friendly.

To reiterate, by the 1990s, China had begun to concentrate on developing cooperative economic relations with the Developing World. Beijing no longer asserted that the Chinese model of economic development or political organization were necessarily appropriate for developing states, but maintained that pragmatic mutually beneficial economic relations were the central hallmark of Chinese–Developing World relations. Whether either China or Developing World states could benefit significantly from this relationship remained to be seen.

The United Nations

The Chinese view of the United Nations coincides with its broader worldview.[16] Frustrated in its efforts to join the United Nations until 1971 by adamant U.S. opposition to Communist Chinese membership and by the United States' equally strong insistence that Taiwan retain its membership in the General Assembly and its permanent seat on the Security Council, China saw the United Nations as little more than a U.S. tool of world domination. This Chinese perception was strengthened by the Korean War, when a predominantly U.S. force under putative United Nations command threatened to invade China. In addition, the United States influenced the United Nations to implement an economic boycott of the P.R.C.

Nevertheless, China considered UN membership to be a useful tool for its international purposes and continued to seek admission. Finally, in 1971, the United States acceded to China's entry, and the P.R.C. took what it considered to be its rightful seat at the UN. The P.R.C. refused to participate actively in UN affairs, however, until Taiwan's presence had been eliminated from all UN organizations with which the P.R.C. intended to be affiliated.

In the years since then, China's record at the UN reflected the world outlook it adopted at a given time. On most issues, China has sided and continues to side with the Developing World. It interpreted and continues to interpret social and economic issues from a Marxist-Leninist perspective, and until the late 1980s, often found itself in agreement with the Soviet Union on these issues despite Sino-Soviet hostility. In contrast, China expressed strong concern at the United Nations throughout the 1970s and on into the late 1980s over Soviet expansionism. Thus, on political and security issues, it frequently voted with the United States and the West. At the same time, China often criticized the West.

On the basis of its UN activities and voting record, it is clear that the UN has become an important part of China's foreign policy. Indeed, on the basis of China's UN activities and voting record alone, one might even conclude that China is exactly what it claims to be: an underdeveloped Marxist-Leninist state still fearful of possible Western neocolonialism.

CHINA AND THE FUTURE: AN OVERVIEW

China's perceptions of the world and its own role in the world have changed several times since the Communist party came to power. Undoubtedly, these perceptions will change again in the future. Economic development, national security, and political control, however, will remain major concerns of the Chinese leadership throughout the rest of the twentieth century. Major debates will inevitably take place within the Chinese hierarchy about how best to achieve all three.

In the economic sphere, China's problems can be solved only through a combination of effective leadership, hard work, population control, large-scale investment, and good luck. The first three inputs can be provided only by the Chinese, and the last is beyond anyone's control. Large-scale investment, however, can be obtained only from capital-rich external sources such as Japan. The Japanese connection in particular must appear attractive to China's leaders; geographical proximity, complementary needs and resources, and no major outstanding political differences are the major items adding to Japan's attractiveness.

Economic reforms begun in 1980 catapulted China's economic growth rate to over 7 percent per year for the entire decade of the 1980s and on into the 1990s. This astounding growth rate was fueled by a contract incentives system that allowed peasants to sell their above-contract production on the open market; by reduced but not eliminated central planning in the industrial sector; and by small worker-owned collectives that produced primarily consumer goods.

This economic growth and other accompanying social reforms had a downside as well. Inflation, crime, and unemployment were increasingly parts of the Chinese socioeconomic landscape as well. Within the Chinese political elite, debates and deliberations continue about how best to modernize China.

Closely related to these debates and deliberations over economic matters are debates and deliberations over how to maintain political control. The prodemocracy movement of 1989 shocked and appalled many senior Chinese leaders. Deng never intended for his economic reforms to spill over into the political sphere, and when they did, he made it exceedingly clear that democratization, to him, was out of the question.

Deng Xiaoping's "Four Modernizations" have brought more consumer goods to more Chinese than ever before.   (Laffont/Sygma.)

Obviously, the Chinese government's crackdown on the pro-democracy movement set the movement back considerably. But the return of political and economic reformers to positions of prominence at the 1992 Communist Party of China Congress made it evident that reform sentiment had not died. However, the extent to which reforms could be instituted remained an uncertainty. So too did the question of whether a reinstitution of reform might lead to another round of repression as had occurred in 1989.

As for security, the dissolution of the U.S.S.R. in 1991 eliminated Beijing's fear of that state, but lingering uncertainty about Russia and Russian intentions remained. The growth of instability along the borders with the newly independent states of Central Asia, especially relating to ethnic issues, also became a concern to Beijing following the Soviet collapse. Nevertheless, despite these concerns, China's external security environment was better by 1992 than it had been since the beginning of its century of humiliation in the 1850s.

Nor did the Beijing government any longer have difficulties in finding international recognition of its legitimacy. By 1993, over 120 governments had recognized the Beijing government, while the corresponding figure for Taiwan had dropped to 21.[17] China is no longer the isolated state it was in the 1950s and 1960s.

But this does not mean that China's future is any more certain. It continues to be too populated, and despite its impressive economic growth of the 1980s and 1990s, it remains underdeveloped. Forces of political and economic reform continue to clash with forces of orthodoxy and autocracy. For China, much has changed, but much remains the same.[18]

KEY TERMS AND CONCEPTS

China's era of empires
Confucianism and Confucius
Opium Wars
century of humiliation
treaty ports
Sun Yat-sen
Kuomintang Party
Chiang Kai-shek
Michael Borodin
Long March
Mao Zedong and Maoism

Four Modernizations
Tiananmen Square massacre
Sino-Soviet split
China's Maoist and post-Maoist
   worldview
Chinese views of Russia
Chinese views of the United States
Chinese views of Japan
Chinese views of the
   Developing World

NOTES

1. U.S. Central Intelligence Agency, *The World Factbook 1991* (Washington: U.S. Government Printing Office, 1992), p. 63.

2. John King Fairbank, "China's Foreign Policy in Historical Perspective," *Foreign Affairs*, Vol. 51 (October 1972): 456.

3. For a good overview of China and China's past, see Lucian W. Pye, *China: An Introduction* (New York: HarperCollins, 1991).

4. Richard H. Solomon, *Mao's Revolution and the Chinese Political Culture* (Berkeley: University of California Press, 1971), p. 28.

5. John King Fairbank, *The United States and China* (Cambridge: Harvard University Press, 1967), p. 112.

6. For other interpretations of classical Chinese history, see Charles O. Hucker, *China to Eighteen Fifty* (Stanford: Stanford University Press, 1978); Oun J. Li, *Ageless China* (New York: Charles Scribner's Sons, 1978); J. D. Langlois, *China under Mongol Rule* (Princeton, NJ: Princeton University Press, 1981); and John Ross, *The Manchus, or the Reigning Dynasty of China* (New York: AMS Press, reprint of 1881 edition).

7. One estimate concluded that by 1884, only 60,000 Chinese had been converted to Christianity! See Fairbank, *The United States and China*, p. 147.

8. For details of the 1911–1945 period, see James E. Sheridan, *China in Disintegration: The Republican Era in Chinese History, 1912–1949* (Exeter, NH: Heinemann Educational Books, 1974); and Barbara Tuchman, *Stillwell and the American Experience in China 1911–1945* (New York: Bantam Books, 1972).

9. For an excellent study of Deng Xiaoping's first decade of rule, see David Wen-Wei Chang, *China Under Deng Xiaoping: Political and Economic Reform* (New York: St. Martins Press, 1991).

10. Li Peng, as quoted in *Time*, January 22, 1990, p. 39.

11. For an analysis of the Cultural Revolution, see Simon Leys, *The Chairman's New Clothes: Mao and the Cultural Revolution* (New York: St. Martin's Press, 1978); L. Culman, *Cultural Revolution in the Provinces* (Cambridge: Harvard University Press, 1971); and David Milton and Nancy D. Milton, *The Wind Will Not Subside: Years in Revolutionary China 1964–69* (New York: Pantheon Books, 1976).

12. Harry Schwartz, *Tsars, Mandarins, and Commissars* (Garden City, NY: Doubleday, 1973), p. 88.

13. For discussions of Sino-American relations since 1949, see Michel Oksenberg and Robert B. Oxnam (ed.), *Dragon & Eagle: United States-China Relations* (New York: Basic Books, 1978); Robert G. Sutter, *China Watch: Toward Sino-American Reconciliation* (Baltimore: Johns Hopkins University Press, 1978); and John Garver, *Foreign Relations of the People's Republic of China* (New York: Prentice Hall, 1993).

14. *Peking Review*, March 3, 1972, pp. 4–5.

15. For detailed views of China's Developing World policies under Mao, see H. S. Behbebeni, *China's Foreign Policy in the Arab World* (Boston: Routledge & Kegan Paul, 1981); Cecil Johnson, *Communist China and Latin America 1959–1967* (New York: Columbia University Press, 1970); Devendra Kaushik, *China and the Third World* (Mystic, CT: Verry-Lawrence, 1975); and Bruce D. Larkin, *China and Africa* (Berkeley: University of California Press, 1971).

16. See Samuel S. Kim, *China, the United Nations, and World Order* (Princeton, NJ: Princeton University Press, 1979), for a treatment of China's attitudes and policies toward the UN under Mao.

17. U.S. Department of State statistics, 1992.

18. For two experts' interpretations on the future of China, see David S. G. Goodman and Gerald Segal, *China in the Nineties: Crisis Management and Beyond* (New York: Oxford University Press, 1992).

CHAPTER 15

Outlooks from the Developing World

- Why is the Developing World so different from the First World?
- How does the Developing World view the international system?
- In what ways does the Developing World want to change the international system?

Before we begin our discussion of the Developing World's outlooks on the international arena, it may be useful to again define the Developing World. Often, as Chapter 8 pointed out, the Developing World is described by interchangeable terms—the Third World, the South, the Developing World, and the Less Developed Countries (LDCs), to name a few. In some cases, these terms create confusion. Should impoverished communist states such as Cuba, Vietnam, Cambodia, and Laos be considered Developing World states, or should they be excluded because they are communist states? What about China, whose size and population erroneously lead some people to consider the P.R.C. a superpower? Do the rich OPEC states still qualify as Developing World and Southern states, or have they, because of their oil wealth, moved to another category?

These definitional questions are serious ones, and they will be answered here as they were in Chapter 8: The Developing World excludes the United States, Canada, Europe, Israel, Japan, Russia, and the other newly independent former Soviet republics (although this may be a matter of debate), China, South Africa, Australia, and New Zealand. All other states—more than 110—are Developing World states.

These 110 countries are separated not only by national boundaries, but also by differences in political leadership, social structure, economic organization, and standard of living. Before the 1990s, some states, such as Ethiopia and South Yemen, were decidedly pro-Soviet without being formally communist, whereas others, such as Chile and Egypt, were pro-Western without being democratic. Indeed, diversity has abounded within the Developing World, as Table 15–1 illustrates.

TABLE 15–1   General Characteristics of Eight Selected Developing World States, 1991

| Country | Land | | Population | | | | | Economy | | Government |
| | Sq. Km $\times 10^6$ | % in Agriculture | Total (mil.) | Growth Rate: % | Literacy % | Ethnic Groups | Religion | 1991 Gross Domestic Procut | | Type |
								Bil. \$	Per Capita	
Angola	1.247	2 arable	8.7	2.7	42	Ovimbundu 37 Kimbundu 25 Bakongo 13	Indigenous 47 Catholic 38 Protestant 15	7.9	92.5	In transition from Marxist people's republic to multi-party democracary
Bolivia	1.099	3 arable	7.2	2.4	78	Indian 55 Mestizo 30 White 15	Catholic 95	4.9	690	Republic
India	3.288	55 arable	866.4	1.9	48	Indo-Aryan 72 Dravidian 25	Hindu 83 Muslim 11 Christian 2 Sikh 2	254.0	300	Federal republic
Nigeria	.924	34 arable	122.5	3.0	51	Hausa, Fulana, Ibo, Yoruba (total 65)	Muslim 50 Christian 40 Animist 10	27.2	230	Military
Panama	.077	8 arable	2.5	2.1	88	Mestizo 70 West Indian 14 White 10	Catholic 93 Protestant 6	4.8	1,980	Republic
Saudi Arabia	2.150	1 arable	17.9	4.2	62	Arab 90 Afro-Asian 10	Muslim 100	79.0	4,800	Monarchy
Solomon Islands	.030	1 arable	.3	3.5	NA	Melanesian 93 Polynesian 4	Christian 99 Variants	.2	500	Parliament
Somalia	.638	2 arable	6.7	3.3	24	Somali 85	Muslim 99	1.7	210	Government control no longer exists, anarchy

SOURCE: CIA, *The World Factbook 1991* (Washington: U.S. Government Printing Office, 1992).

The diversity of the Developing World is only part of the picture. Many Developing World states share the experiences and heritages of a colonial past; sharply opposed internal social and economic classes; and economic underdevelopment and poverty. These shared experiences and heritages often influence Developing World states to have similar if not identical outlooks on issues as diverse as the New International Economic Order and multinational corporations. Even if the diversity of the Developing World is immense, this similarity of outlooks is one of the factors that legitimizes labeling this group of states the Developing World.

UNITY IN DIVERSITY: A COLONIAL PAST, SHARPLY DIVIDED CLASSES, AND ECONOMIC UNDERDEVELOPMENT AND POVERTY

Before we turn to the individual perceptions that a few Developing World states have of the international system, it may first be worthwhile to examine how shared experiences and heritages unite many of the states that make up the Developing World. Again, the student must be cautioned that not all Developing World states shared these experiences, and thus although unity often does exist within the Developing World, diversity is also a frequent fact.

A Colonial Past

One of the factors that unifies the Developing World is a shared colonial past. Most states in South America achieved independence during the early nineteenth century. Similarly in Africa and Asia, Ethiopia, Liberia, Saudi Arabia, Thailand, and a few other states avoided colonialism. But for most of what is today the Developing World, colonialism was a fact of life until well into the twentieth century.

It was not a pleasant life. European states that held colonies held them for a specific reason: to extract wealth from them and to better their own economies. Few European states considered it wise or necessary to improve living conditions or economic standards in their colonies for more than a very few of the local peoples. For example, after 70 years of French rule in Vietnam, by 1940 there were only 14 high schools and one university in the entire country.[1] In the Belgian Congo (what is today Zaire), fewer than a dozen local people held university degrees when the country received independence in 1960. Throughout the colonial world, hunger, disease, and poverty were widespread. Some colonial holdings fared better than others, and certain colonial powers paid more attention to improving the lot of local peoples than others, but as a general rule the pattern was clear. Colonies existed to contribute to the economic betterment of the colonial powers.

For local peoples, choices about what to do were few. Faced by superior military firepower and, after colonial states were established, a preferential system of laws and values that gave all rights and privileges to Europeans and few if any to local peoples, local peoples could submit to European hegemony, move on to new locations, or fight. The choices were not appealing. Some of those who submitted became field hands on colonial plantations, miners in European-owned mines, houseboys and servants, or otherwise entered the employ of Europeans at extremely low wages. Many remained as peasants, subservient to the European overlords who supplanted local overlords. A very fortunate few were selected to be educated either locally or in Europe. Those who moved on to new locations had their lives disrupted, and often came into conflict with other local peoples whose territories they were moving into. And those who fought, faced by superior European firepower, died.

From the perspective of Developing World states, then, it is not surprising that strong resentment and hostility against European states remain about their colonial experience. When seen from the viewpoint of Developing World states, Queen Victoria's definition of the imperial mission to "protect the poor natives and advance civilization" was little more than a cover to allow Europeans to exploit. And those Europeans who took the "white man's burden" seriously also contributed to the problem, for they gave colonialism a veneer of humanity. As one writer in the Malaysian newspaper, *The Straits Times*, said in a 1986 review of the movie, *Out of Africa*, the movie "distorts history by focusing on the show-piece colonials while obscuring the deeds of the more Philistine types who were more commonplace."[2]

Nevertheless, ties were created and remain even today between former colonial holdings, new states, and the European colonizers. English is spoken and cricket is played around the world within the British Commonwealth of Nations. French is the official language and schooling follows the French system in many countries in Africa. These are all ties that arose from the colonial period, which in some cases ended during the 1940s for Developing World states, and in other cases during the 1980s. Even as we recognize these ties, however, we must also recognize the darker legacy that colonialism left, for in many respects it is this darker legacy that predominates.

Sharply Divided Classes

Most Developing World states also share the heritage of a sharply divided internal class structure. Very few people hold political power and enjoy most of the wealth of the country. Table 15–2 illustrates the disparity of the distribution of wealth in a few Developing World states.

By far the largest group of people in most Developing World states is the **peasantry**. In some Developing World states, peasants made up as much as 95 percent of the population during the colonial era, and in many countries even today peasants make up more than 75 percent of the population. Peasants till the land, often for an absentee landlord; seldom have any education; and often survive at bare subsistence levels. For the peasant, the future has traditionally been the same as the past and present: There is no hope for a better life, because there is no thought of a better life. The peasant's greatgrandparents, grandparents, and parents were peasants, and the peasant's children will be peasants, too.

European colonialism did not invent peasantry. Peasantry was a global phenomenon avoided by only a few fortunate countries such as the United States,

TABLE 15–2   Wealth Distribution in Selected Developing World States

Country	Year	% National Income to Richest 10%	% National Income to Poorest 20%
Bangladesh	1985–86	23.2	10.0
Brazil	1983	46.2	2.4
Egypt	1974	33.2	5.8
India	1983	26.7	8.1
Indonesia	1987	26.5	8.8
Ivory Coast	1985–86	43.7	2.4
Panama	1973	44.2	2.0
Philippines	1985	32.1	5.5
Sri Lanka	1985–86	43.0	4.8
Zambia	1976	46.3	3.4

SOURCE: The World Bank, *World Development Report 1992*, pp. 222–223.

Canada, Australia, and New Zealand. According to many historians, peasantry as an institution had its roots in the feudal system that placed political, economic, and military power in the hands of a very powerful few people. Fortunately for Europe, the Renaissance ended most of the more extreme vestiges of feudalism in Europe during the fourteenth and fifteenth centuries. For the rest of the world, feudalism as an institution remained, and was not truly disrupted until the second round of European empire began in the nineteenth century.

For most peasants, European colonialism simply meant that local lords with familiar customs were replaced by foreign lords with unfamiliar customs. However, to the former ruling class, European colonialism brought immense change. Some cooperated with the Europeans, some became traders and merchants, some fought the Europeans, and most were simply supplanted by the Europeans. The key point, however, is that local rulers were replaced by Europeans.

Meanwhile, in Latin America, a rigid class structure developed following the early nineteenth-century attainment of independence by most of that region. This class structure often placed Europeans who owned land in positions of power and influence over those who did not. Thus, even though Latin America's experience with colonialism was different from that of most of Asia and Africa, a large peasantry and a small ruling class developed.

During the colonial era, two phenomena took place that had an immense impact on the Developing World once it obtained independence. The first was the development of **anticolonialism** among local peoples, especially the dispossessed former ruling class. Some of the dispossessed former ruling class espoused returning to old precolonial ways, to the reinstitutionalization of the rule of the privileged local few over the peasantry. Their thinking in many ways reflected the thinking of the peasants, but from a considerably different perspective: Our greatgrandparents ruled, our grandparents ruled, our parents ruled, and had the Europeans not arrived, we would have ruled, too. Therefore, when the Europeans leave, we will rule again, or our children will.

But other anticolonial attitudes came from other sources, from European concepts such as freedom, justice, independence, and equity. Very slowly, as a fortunate few local individuals received European educations and religious train-ing, these European values filtered to local peoples, often members of the intelli-gentsia, the military, and even the dispossessed ruling class. Gradually, these individuals evolved into a class of revolutionary modernizers who asserted that freedom, justice, independence, and equity were as valid for colonial peoples as for Europeans. In many countries, these revolutionaries and modernizers played a major role in ending colonialism.

The second phenomenon was **urbanization**. Urbanization was caused by many factors, but the most important were the growth of rural unemployment brought about by European expropriation of land and limited updated farming methods; population growth brought about by limited application of European medical knowledge; and the hope for some form of employment in the cities. Table 15–3 shows some of the dimensions of this urbanization trend since 1960. More often than not, hopes for urban employment never materialized. Thus, an entirely new class of people emerged, the urban unemployed.

But some did find jobs, occasionally in the few industries that developed, sometimes in the government or colonial bureaucracies, frequently in the military or as servants, and sometimes in other pursuits. Although not many in these groups truly prospered, all were better off than the urban unemployed whom they saw begging every day. And so, although the urban employed may not have been as well as off as the privileged, they were better off than the urban unem-ployed or the peasants. They had developed a stake in the system.

By the end of the colonial era, and continuing on to the present day, most Developing World states have a dizzying array of opposed classes. The peasantry with its ties to the soil are quantitatively most numerous, but politically weak and economically poor. However, in some countries, segments of the peasantry are beginning to ask why life cannot be improved. In Latin America in particular, the theology of liberation encourages peasants to ask this question. The peasantry is juxtaposed in many countries to the traditional elite, who consider it their right by birth or by military power to retain political and economic control over other groups within the country. Their objective remains their own betterment, and the betterment of their families. Still other individuals and groups see themselves as rightful rulers because of superior moral or ethical values. These individuals and groups have opted for revolutionary modernization through Marxism, arguing that they understand the needs of society, especially the peasantry and the urban unemployed, better than others, and therefore are the right people to run the government and implement policy. In other Developing World countries, other revolutionary modernizers attempt to hold elections, improve the economy, and run the government in a more Western-oriented way. All must also cope with the facts that the urban unemployed is an abiding underclass, and that the urban employed see efforts to improve the lot of the peasantry and the urban unem-ployed as threats to their own well-being.

Economic Underdevelopment and Poverty

Sharply divided classes within Developing World states is one reason why eco-nomic underdevelopment and poverty have persisted in those states. In many states, this intense conflict between classes has frustrated and even stopped eco-

TABLE 15–3 Urbanization Trends of Selected Developing World Countries

Country	Urban Population as Percentage of Total Population		Population in Cities Over 1 Million as percentage of Urban Population		Population in Capital as Percentage of	
	1965	1990	1965	1990	1990 Urban Population	1990 Total Population
Algeria	38	52	24	23	23	12
Bangladesh	6	16	50	47	38	6
Bolivia	40	51	28	33	34	17
Brazil	50	75	48	47	2	2
Egypt	41	47	53	52	37	17
India	19	27	32	32	4	1
Kenya	9	24	41	27	26	6
Libya	26	70	55	65	n/a	n/a
Nigeria	17	35	23	24	19	7
Panama	44	53	n/a	n/a	37	20
Phillipines	32	43	28	32	32	14
Saudi Arabia	39	77	23	29	17	13
Zaire	26	40	17	25	24	9
Zambia	23	50	n/a	n/a	24	12

SOURCE: The World Bank, *World Development Report 1992*, pp. 278–279.

nomic development. Continual civil strife has thus been a major detriment to economic development.

The Developing World's heritage of exploitation by Europe also continues to complicate economic growth and the reduction of poverty in many Developing World states. As previously pointed out, European states held colonies specifically for the purpose of increasing their own wealth, and rarely took significant steps to develop extensive technical, communications, transportation, and educational infrastructures within their colonies. When Developing World states received their independence, few local people had been trained to operate and maintain those infrastructures that had been developed, and many Europeans who lived in newly independent Developing World states returned to Europe. Thus, at the outset, Developing World states were saddled with difficulties that complicated economic development.

Other problems also complicated economic development and reduction of poverty. High birth rates, often brought about because of better health care, meant that economic growth had to remain at the same level as birth rates just to maintain standards of living. This was (and is) often a difficult task, as Table 15–4 shows.

Many Developing World governments attribute their economic problems to the existing system of international economic relations. They see the system as a method through which industrialized states exploit Developing World states. For example, the price of a barrel of Saudi oil fell from $2.18 in 1947 to $1.80 in 1970.[3] Although it is true that in the case of oil the 1970s witnessed astronomical increases in price, the price of other raw materials that Developing World countries exported to the West increased at rates below that of the global inflation rate. Some prices, such as those for sugar and copper, fell. From the Developing

TABLE 15–4 A Comparison of Economic Growth Rates and Population Growth Rates in Selected Developing World States, 1990–1991

Country	Population Growth Rate in %	Economic Growth Rate in %
Angola	2.7	2.0
Bangladesh	2.3	4.0
Bolivia	2.4	2.7
Brazil	1.8	−4.6
Egypt	2.3	1.0
India	1.9	4.5
Indonesia	1.8	6.0
Kenya	3.6	4.0
Nigeria	3.0	2.7
Panama	2.1	5.0
Philippines	2.1	2.5
Saudi Arabia	4.2	.5
Zaire	3.3	−2.0
Zambia	3.5	−2.0

SOURCE: CIA, *The World Factbook 1991*, appropriate pages.

Note: Economic growth rate must surpass population growth rate for the absolute standard of living in a country to improve.

World's perspective, then, Western economic exploitation continues even though the West's political control has passed.

Nor can it be overlooked that some Developing World states such as Chad, Mali, Somalia, and Bangladesh suffer from a dearth of natural resources. They simply have too little arable land, too little water, and too few minerals to have an opportunity to develop.

Some Developing World states made unwise decisions. In some cases, Developing World governments sought to industrialize too rapidly and neglected agriculture, with disastrous results. Other Developing World governments borrowed too heavily, and now face immense external debts. Still others did not seek to diversify their economies; some tried, and failed. Some Developing World states spent too much on their militaries, as Table 15–5 suggests. And overriding all this is the fact that no one is quite sure how economic development actually proceeds.[4]

Thus, economic underdevelopment and poverty remain pervasive in most of the Developing World. OPEC states have used their oil wealth to initiate development. South Korea, Hong Kong, Taiwan, Singapore, Thailand, Malaysia, and several other states have made impressive enough strides that they are now labeled "newly industrialized countries" (NICs). But economic underdevelopment and poverty continue to unify most of the rest of the Developing World.

Even so, economic schisms are developing within the Developing World. This had led some analysts to conclude that the concept of the "Third World" should be replaced by that of "Third World," "Fourth World", and "Fifth World" divisions. The "Third World" would be defined as those states that have sufficiently developed economic infrastructures, resources, and/or skills of the population so that they could become industrialized in the foreseeable future. The "Fourth World" would be defined as those states that have potential for future economic development. Finally, the "Fifth World" would include those states that have few or no resources, infrastructures, or current skills.

Despite this differentiation, Developing World states—or if one prefers Third, Fourth, and Fifth World states—all need economic development and amelioration of poverty. This fact alone legitimizes grouping them together in a single category.

SELECTED DEVELOPING WORLD STATES AND THEIR OUTLOOKS

How do Developing World states view themselves and the international community? There are as many answers to this question as there are Developing World states. Most Developing World states agree on issues such as support for a New International Economic Order, the necessity to control the activities of multinational corporations, and the sanctity of international borders, but extensive disagreement exists on many other issues. These disagreements spring from a host of local and regional differences in history, values, cultures, and experiences.

In this section, the backgrounds and viewpoints of four widely divergent Developing World states will be presented. Two are new states, and two are old. One has a government that was democratically elected in an election overseen by an international team of United Nations observers. Another has a president installed by a foreign power, but elected by his own people. A third is a monarchy

TABLE 15–5 Developing World Military Expenditures, Selected Countries

Country	Total in Millions of Dollars		Dollars per Capita		% of GNP	
	1978	1991	1978	1991	1978	1991
Algeria	628	971	35	36	2.4	1.4
Bangladesh	113	234	1	2	1.3	1.3
Bolivia	91	122	17	16	2.4	2.0
Egypt	1,586	3,582	40	63	11.2	7.5
El Salvador	50	201	11	37	1.6	2.4
India	3,784	7,990	6	9	3.2	2.9
Indonesia	2,036	1,739	14	9	4.0	1.3
Jordan	310	594	107	135	16.5	14.1
Kenya	12	283 (1990)	.8	12 (1990)	.2	3.5 (1990)
Malaysia	712	1,670	53	92	4.5	3.7
Mexico	556	917	9	10	.5	.5
Philippines	794	843	17	13	3.3	2.2
Syria	1,214	3,095	152	235	14.6	13.0
Tanzania	302	313 (1990)	17	12 (1990)	3.4	3.9 (1990)
Thailand	794	1,761	17	30	3.4	2.5
Venezuela	615	1,525	47	74	1.5	3.6
Zaire	179	41 (1988)	7	1 (1988)	2.7	1.6 (1988)
Zambia	252	61	46	8	9.3	2.6

SOURCE: International Institute for Strategic Studies, *The Military Balance*, appropriate years and pages.

that in 1992 instituted limited constitutional reform. And the fourth has a parliamentary system. One is rich, one is "lower middle class," and two are poor. Three are strategically significant, all for different reasons; one is insignificant in almost every sense of the word. In short, they are four states that well represent the diversity of the Developing World.

Angola

As a southern African colony of Portugal, Angola did not receive independence until 1975. However, even before independence, movements within Angola fighting for independence from Portugal were drawn into the maelstrom of the Soviet-U.S.-Chinese triangle as the Soviet Union helped the Kimbundu-based MPLA, and the U.S. and Chinese supported the Bakongo-based FNLA and the Ovimbundu-oriented UNITA. (The Kimbundu, Bakongo, and Ovimbundu are Angolan tribes.) A change in government in Portugal led to Angolan independence, and what had been a revolutionary war against Portugal turned into the Angolan Civil War.

Even before the civil war broke out, many of the Portuguese colonists, fearful of what independence would bring, left the country, carrying with them the wealth and skills that an independent Angola would need. The civil war accelerated that flight and further undermined Angola's economy. In the civil war itself, Soviet aid to the MPLA outstripped U.S. and Chinese aid to the FNLA and UNITA, and when 20,000 Cuban troops entered the fray, the MPLA emerged victorious.

Not surprisingly, the leader of the MPLA, Agostinho Neto, adopted a pro-Soviet stance in foreign policy and signed a Treaty of Friendship and Cooperation with the U.S.S.R. Nevertheless, Neto steadfastly refused to turn the MPLA into a communist party, and maintained that Angola was in reality a nonaligned state. Ever the pragmatist, Neto turned to the Soviets and Cubans for military aid, and sought economic aid from the West. The Angolan leader also attempted to attract private investment to Angola from MNCs and other Western firms, but the unstable political climate in the Angolan hinterlands where civil war still raged frustrated his efforts.

The United States presented a particular problem for Angola. The United States refused to extend diplomatic recognition to Angola or provide Angola with any aid until Cuba withdrew its troops. Worse yet from the Angolan perspective, the United States in the 1980s also began to provide Jonas Savimbi's UNITA, still fighting against Angola's MPLA government, with limited amounts of military aid.

To the MPLA government, U.S. actions represented unwarranted and illegitimate meddling in Angola's internal affairs. As leaders of a sovereign state, Angolan officials argued that they had the right to request the presence of whomever they pleased to help defend their government, and rejected U.S. claims that the Cubans were interlopers.

Indeed, to Angola's leaders, Cuban troops were needed for two reasons: to fight in the continuing struggle against UNITA, and to guard against South African attacks against Angola. As one of the so-called Front Line States in the struggle to bring majority rule to South Africa and Namibia, Angola served as a

base for the Southwest African People's Organization (SWAPO), a national liberation movement struggling to free Namibia from South African control. During
the 1970s and 1980s, South Africa launched raids into Angola against SWAPO
bases. The MPLA saw these raids as violations of Angolan sovereignty, and
declared that it needed the continued presence of Cuban troops to deter further
South African adventures.

Gradually, however, as the civil war took a greater and greater toll on Angola,
and as the Soviet Union became less and less willing in the late 1980s to support
the Angolan/Cuban war effort, Angola and Cuba became increasingly willing to
negotiate Cuban withdrawal. At the same time, as the cost of keeping Namibia as
the equivalent of a colony mounted, South Africa also became increasingly flexible. Finally, then, under American, Soviet, and United Nations tutelage, Angola,
Cuba, and South Africa signed an agreement in December 1988 that achieved a
Cuban withdrawal and laid the groundwork for Namibian independence. Cuban
troops began to leave Angola in 1989. Later the same year, preliminary elections
were held in Namibia for an independent government.

Despite this, in Angola itself the civil war between the MPLA government
and Jonas Savimbi's UNITA raged on. Savimbi had begun to receive U.S. military
assistance in 1985, and he continued to receive it into the 1990s. Gradually, however, both the MPLA and UNITA tired of the ongoing conflict. In 1991, the
United Nations convinced both sides to adopt a ceasefire, and in 1992, again
under U.N. auspices, countrywide free elections were held in Angola for the first
time. The MPLA won the election, but unfortunately for Angola, UNITA
reneged on its agreement to participate in a new coalition government. As 1993
began, civil war and violent fighting once again raged throughout Angola. It
remained to be seen whether a coalition government could be successfully
formed.

The years since independence have been neither peaceful nor prosperous for
Angola. A tribally based civil war became a forum for superpower confrontation,
and the ensuing destruction further undermined what had been a precariously
functioning economy to begin with. Despite Angola's natural wealth in oil, dia-
monds, iron ore, and coffee, its road to economic growth has been plagued by
internal divisions and a dearth of external assistance and aid. Thus, even if the

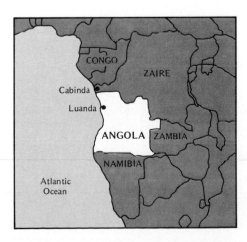

FIGURE 15–1

1992 elections eventually lead to the establishment of a coalition government, Angola still has a long way to go.

Angola's postindependence history is not unique. Although it achieved independence later than most other states, has had a more violent history since independence than most other states, and has more potential wealth than most, the problems it faces are similar to those of many other Developing World states. Internal division, inadequate capital, and an oppressive colonial past color the way that Angola, and many other states, look at the external world today.[5]

Panama

Without doubt, the state of Panama owes its independence to U.S. willingness in 1903 to support residents of Panama, then a segment of Colombia, in achieving their independence. The United States made it clear to the Colombian government that it was not to challenge Panama's declaration of independence. For its part in aiding this early twentieth-century national liberation movement, the United States received "in perpetuity the use, occupation, and control" of a 10-mile-wide, coast-to-coast territory that divided Panama in two.[6] That territory became the Canal Zone, the site of the Panama Canal. No Panamanian ever signed the treaty.

However, Panamanian nationalism was not the product of an American desire to build a canal. Throughout much of the nineteenth century, Panamanians revolted against their Colombian masters. On at least one occasion, in 1884–1885, American troops were landed to aid Colombia in quelling the revolt.[7]

Nevertheless, Panamanian independence was eventually achieved through U.S. intervention, with the United States receiving what eventually became a profitable property for its efforts. Panamanians understandably felt ambivalent about the outcome, even in the early twentieth century. On the one hand, without U.S. intervention, the fight for independence would have been bloody at best and futile at worst. On the other hand, the United States had extracted a valuable concession from Panama "in perpetuity."

Panamanian ambivalence toward the United States continued throughout the years. Although U.S. residents in the Canal Zone and Panamanians employed

FIGURE 15–2

there pumped millions of dollars into the Panamanian economy, U.S. control of the Canal galled and irked the Panamanians. Anti-Americanism was further fueled by the extreme differences in living standards between the Canal Zone and the rest of Panama. Periodic anti-American violence erupted. Finally, in 1974, Secretary of State Henry Kissinger agreed to turn over the Canal to Panama "in principle." It was left to the Carter administration three years later to finalize a treaty that, in the year 2000, guarantees Panama full control of the canal and the Canal Zone. Despite criticism of the treaty from the left and right in both countries, one of the major irritants to U.S.-Panamanian relations was thus removed.

But other problems soon arose. After the Canal Treaty was signed, U.S.-Panamanian relations warmed considerably. However, in 1981, Panama's President, General Omar Torrijos, died in a plane crash. Shortly thereafter, General Manuel Antonio Noriega shouldered his way to control in Panama. Noriega and his henchmen then rigged the 1984 Panamanian election to assure their hold on power. Soon after, reports surfaced that Noriega was heavily involved in drug dealing, money laundering, and spying for Cuba. In 1988, a U.S. grand jury indicted him on drug-running charges.

U.S.-Panamanian relations deteriorated rapidly over the next year and a half as the United States tried to force Noriega from power. The United States blocked withdrawal of Panamanian funds from U.S. banks, withheld payment of canal fees, and ended trade preferences for Panama. Meanwhile, Noriega nullified an election in 1989 in which his presidential candidate lost, and survived two coup attempts. By November 1989, the Panamanian economy was in a shambles, but Noriega was as solidly entrenched as ever as Panama's dictator.

Apparently confident in their position, Noriega and his sympathizers stepped up harassment of Americans living in Panama in December 1989. Finally, U.S. forces invaded Panama and after a short struggle subdued the Panamanian Defense Forces. The Americans installed Guilermo Endara, who had won the annulled election earlier in 1989, as Panama's new president. As for Noriega, he first took refuge in the Vatican embassy in Panama City. After a short stay there, he surrendered to U.S. forces and was brought to the United States to stand trial for drug trafficking and money laundering. He was convicted in 1992, and sentenced to 40 years in prison.[8]

Meanwhile, Panama continued to languish. The combination of Noriega's leadership, the U.S. economic sanctions, and the U.S. invasion had played havoc with the country's economy, and the limited amount of economic assistance that the United States provided Panama in the early 1990s was not sufficient to overcome the country's economic problems. Nevertheless, throughout the early 1990s, it was clear that a fundamental fact of Panamanian history had been reasserted. Panama's view of the world and its role in it remained closely tied to the United States.

Saudi Arabia

Saudi Arabia's existence as a self-ruling political entity began in 1744 when the head of the House of Saud allied himself with Muhammad ibn Abd al Wahhab, the founder of an Islamic reform movement, and began to expand throughout the

Arabian peninsula. The alliance between Wahhabism—basically a return to the fundamental principles of Allah as revealed in the Koran—and the Saud family still holds today, and is the basis for the present-day Saudi Arabian state.[9]

The Saud family's influence in and control of the Arabian peninsula contracted and expanded on several occasions during the past two and a half centuries. By the beginning of the 1800s, Saudi warriors had captured almost the entire peninsula. Reasoning that any people who did not accept the puritanical reform Islam of Wahhabism were infidels, the Saud family had a ready rationale to launch holy wars, or jihads, against their neighbors. By 1811, the sultan of the Ottoman Empire became outraged at the growth of this new Moslem state, and more particularly over its control of all the shrines and holy places of Islam. Muhammad Ali, viceroy of the semiautonomous Ottoman province of Egypt, sent a major expeditionary force against the Sauds and defeated them.

For the next 20 years, the Saud family slowly rebuilt its old empire as Ottoman power receded. Riyadh was chosen as the capital for the renewed Saud/Wahhabi state. The new state was never as powerful as the one overrun by Muhammad Ali, and for the next 50 years of its existence, it fought internecine battles with the rival Rashidi family. Finally, in 1891, the Rashidis captured Riyadh, and the Sauds fled to Kuwait.

The Sauds remained in Kuwait for 11 years. In January 1902, Ibn Saud led an attack force of only 30 men into Riyadh, captured the city, and once again began restoring the Saud empire. By 1913, Ibn Saud had conquered most of the peninsula for his family and his religion, with the significant exceptions of the Persian Gulf coastal area and some areas of western Arabia. On the gulf, from Kuwait in the north to Oman in the south, British influence predominated. In western Arabia, the weakened Ottoman Empire held sway.

Following World War I, the Ottoman Empire was carved up by the victorious European powers, particularly Great Britain and France. The Najd, as Ibn Saud's realm in Arabia was called, had supported the Allies during the war, but was considered strategically and economically unimportant. It therefore retained its independence, at least in part as a token of Great Britain's and France's goodwill toward the Arabs and Moslems. The Hejaz, the western section of Arabia, was also granted its independence. By 1925, Ibn Saud had added it to his realm.

Throughout these years, the Saud realm was poor. The desert produced little. Hence, the major sources of revenue for the Saud family were from Muslim pilgrims who made their way to the holy places of Islam under Saudi control, and a British subsidy of 60,000 pounds a year. Ibn Saud undertook some limited service and development projects, such as schools, sanitation improvements, and medical services, but even these were cut back when Great Britain ended its subsidy and as the Great Depression cut pilgrimage rates from an average of 100,000 persons per year during the 1920s to 20,000 in 1933. By 1931, the financial situation had become so bad for Ibn Saud that his minister of finance declared a moratorium on all the kingdom's debts.

Saud's Arabian Kingdom was a Developing World state in every sense of the word, with little realistic chance to escape poverty. Ibn Saud, a devout Muslim, had serious reservations about allowing Western investment and technology into his traditional society. Nevertheless, when in May 1932 the Bahrain Petroleum Company struck oil in Bahrain, only 20 miles off Arabia's coast, Ibn Saud had a change of heart. Given his kingdom's abject poverty, Ibn Saud quickly signed an

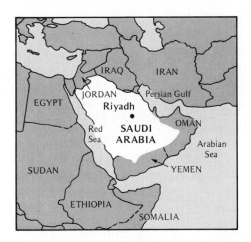

FIGURE 15–3

agreement with Standard Oil of California, granting the American company concessions for drilling rights in return for a 50,000-pound cash advance, 5,000
pounds in gold, and future royalties, if any. Although no one realized it, a new era
was about to begin in Saudi history.[10]

Standard Oil, operating in Saudi Arabia as the California Arabian Standard
Oil Company, or CASOC, struck oil in 1938. Forty-two years later, the Saudi
ambassador to the United States proudly estimated that his country alone had
"one-fourth of the planet's proven oil reserves and a third of all the oil in the
world internationally available."[11] CASOC and Ibn Saud had found a veritable
gold mine.

Standard Oil of California brought three other American oil firms, Texaco,
Standard Oil of New Jersey, and Mobil, into the CASOC consortium, changing its
name to the Arabian-American Oil Company, or ARAMCO. The role and influence of ARAMCO in Saudi Arabia spread as oil wealth flowed into the formerly
poverty-stricken country. Although ARAMCO kept most of the oil profits itself,
Saudi Arabia was a country whose future appeared assured.

For the first two decades of the postwar era, Saudi Arabia remained an
inward-looking country, concerned with its Muslim heritage and with keeping
political power firmly in the hands of the Saud family. A "special relationship"
developed with the United States, primarily through the auspices of ARAMCO.
To a great extent, ARAMCO conducted the United States' foreign policy toward
Saudi Arabia and defined U.S. and Saudi interests in nearly identical terms. The
Saud family, content with its role as caretaker of the holy shrines of Islam, politically secure internally, and comfortably wealthy from its oil revenues, saw its role
in the world defined within those parameters.

Nevertheless, the external world was changing, and Saudi Arabia changed
with it. Concerned that it maintain its place as the world center of Islam, and
aware that pan-Arabism was beginning to reemerge throughout the Arab world,
the Saud family began to seek more control over its oil wealth. ARAMCO, concerned primarily with maintaining access to oil, readily accepted most Saudi
claims. In 1950, Saudi Arabia requested and received 50 percent of all ARAMCO
profits. In 1952, Saudi Arabia demanded that Saudis be appointed to ARAMCO's
Board of Directors and that company headquarters be moved from New York to

The Ka'ba in the Great Mosque of Mecca is Islam's holiest shrine and strengthens Saudi Arabia's claims to be the center of Islam. (Aramco World Magazine.)

Dhahran. ARAMCO acceded. By 1972, Saudi Arabia owned 25 percent of ARAMCO's assets, and by 1974, 60 percent. In 1981, Saudi Arabia received all ARAMCO's assets.

Of even greater importance than Saudi Arabia's ownership of assets was Saudi Arabia's ability to determine oil output levels and prices. Saudi Arabia was the only "swing producer" in the Organization of Petroleum Exporting Countries (OPEC), that is, the only country that could, by determining its own production level, affect the global oil market by itself. During the 1970s and 1980s, Saudi Arabia on several occasions threatened to expand production to hold oil prices down in the face of more extreme demands for price increases from radical OPEC members. And in 1985 and 1986, Saudi Arabia played a major role in bringing about a steep reduction in oil prices, insisting that market share was more important than maintenance of price.

The Saudi view of the contemporary world is most heavily influenced by four factors: oil, Islam, Iraq, and Israel. Oil is the core of Saudi Arabia's continuing "special relationship" with the United States. The United States, and even more certainly the Western world, needs Saudi oil. The Saudis are aware that this gives them leverage in the capitals of the West. At the same time, they are aware that their leverage is tempered by Saudi Arabia's vast holdings of dollars, its reliance on the Western-controlled international monetary system, and the more than $50 billion of investments it has in the United States alone. Stated simply, the Saudis are as dependent on the United States and the West as the United States and the West are on the Saudis.

Saudi Arabia's oil-generated wealth led to two other major connections with the United States. First, Saudi Arabia implemented a major economic development program. Most of Saudi Arabia's development program is planned and managed by American businesses. Second, because of the threat that the Saudis perceive from the several radical states that have sprung up in the Middle East, the Saudis have turned to the United States for arms. With their oil wealth and their leadership position in the Middle East, they have requested and received some of the most modern and potent American weapons as part of the "special relationship." The depth of this "special relationship"—in both directions—became exceedingly evident in 1990 when Iraq invaded Kuwait, one of Saudi Arabia's neighbors to the immediate north, and posed a military threat to Saudi Arabia as well. The United States immediately sent sizable contingents of air, land, and naval forces to Saudi Arabia and surrounding waters to deter an Iraqi attack on Saudi Arabia, defend the Saudi regime, and maintain access to Saudi oil.

Islam remains the core of the Saud family's political legitimacy. As we have seen, the Islam/Saud alliance is an old and powerful one, but it is challenged from two directions. First, within Saudi Arabia, modernization has created social and political strains that threaten the traditional values of Islam, including the role of women, sobriety, and piety. The Saud family has attempted to keep modernization within the limits of what is acceptable to Islam, but strains exist. For example, in 1992 Saudi ruler King Fahd issued a series of decrees that created a 60-person Consultative Council to advise him on governance; the king subsequently guaranteed many personal freedoms to Saudi citizens, and altered the way that future kings would be chosen. Modernizers praised Fahd's actions, but Islamic traditionalists and fundamentalists within the kingdom condemned the changes.[12]

Second, outside Saudi Arabia, the Saudi government sees a threat from the fundamentalist Islamic movement, most notably in Iran. Saudi Arabia believes it must arm itself against that threat and, as noted above, has turned to the United States and other Western states for support in that effort.

In addition to oil and Islam, Iraq has risen to prominence in the Saudi worldview. The 1990 Iraqi invasion of Kuwait had an immense impact on the Saudi sense of security. As a result, Saudi Arabia was willing to serve as the primary staging base for the massive U.S.-led military buildup that led to Operation Desert Storm, the expulsion of Iraq from Kuwait, and the destruction of much of Iraq's military capabilities. Nevertheless, despite the Iraqi defeat, Saudi Arabia remains immensely concerned about the possibility of continuing Iraqi expansionist intentions.

To a certain extent, then, oil, Islam, and Iraq produce a community of interests between the United States and Saudi Arabia. Shared economic needs and security concerns yield similar outlooks on a number of issues that are complicated by the fourth major determinant of the Saudi worldview, Israel.

Until recently, Saudi Arabia, like most other Arab and Islamic states, did not accept the legitimacy of the existence of Israel. Although Saudi Arabia stopped short of calling for Israel's destruction, it nevertheless made known its sympathy for the Palestinians and the PLO. Saudi Arabia thereby could argue that it was defending Arabs and Islam, and also protecting its position as a leader in the Arab world. But with the 1993 accord reached between Israel and the PLO, Saudi Arabia, as other moderate Arab states, moved to improve its relations with Israel.

Even so, Saudi Arabia's views on Israel often impacted its relations with the

United States. With the U.S. being Israel's strongest supporter in the international arena, Saudi Arabia's close relationship with the United States often was questioned in the Arab world. Saudi Arabia, on occasion, was pressured by other Arab states to use its "oil weapon" to force the United States to moderate its support for Israel and to adopt a more evenhanded policy in the Middle East in general. Indeed, during the 1973 Arab-Israeli War, Saudi Arabia joined other Arab OPEC states in their boycott of oil shipments to the United States and other countries that supported Israel.

The second impact of the Israeli situation on Saudi–U.S. relations has been on U.S. weapons sales. Saudi Arabia believed it needed advanced weaponry to fend off threats from the radical left and radical right states in the area, but some segments of the American body politic feared that weapons sold to Saudi Arabia for that purpose would be diverted to anti-Israel use. Although Saudi Arabia obtained F-15 fighter-bombers, Maverick air-to-ground missiles, Sidewinder air-to-air missiles, and AWACS radar planes from the United States, Saudi patience with the United States wore thin on several occasions over arms sale questions. By the 1990s, Saudi Arabia therefore had begun to buy arms from other sources, primarily Western Europe.

Saudi Arabia's relations with and attitude toward the rest of the world, that is the non-Western and non-Islamic world, is one of restraint. With the Saudi abhorrence of communism, relations with the U.S.S.R. were generally low-key even though the Soviet Union was the first country to recognize Ibn Saud's 1926 claim as the rightful trustee of Islam's holy places. At the time, the Soviets believed Ibn Saud would be anti-imperialist and anti-Western. Since the collapse of the U.S.S.R., Saudi Arabia has actively sought to expand its ties with the newly independent Central Asian Islamic states that emerged from the former Soviet Union. As a leader of the Islamic world and a major economic power, Saudi Arabia sees itself in a struggle for influence there with Iran and possibly Turkey.

Meanwhile, Saudi Arabia's attitude toward black Africa has been quietly supportive. Indeed, the Riyadh government initiated its own foreign aid program to all of Africa, sending about 5 percent of its oil revenues to less fortunate states in Africa. Black African states, however, claim that most aid has gone to Arab and Islamic states.

As far as Saudi Arabia is concerned, its position in the world has improved at an astronomical rate in the last 60 years. The Saudis are a proud people who trace their government back almost 300 years, and with their prestige, wealth, and global importance, they expect to be treated as such. Nevertheless, a variety of external threats and internal challenges make the Saudis less sanguine about their current role and place in the contemporary world. The "special relationship" with the United States is still special, but it no longer guarantees Saudi security. The U.S. response to the heightened Iraqi threat to Saudi Arabia in the wake of Iraq's 1990 invasion of Kuwait increased Saudi confidence in American reliability, but it could not alter the fact that Iraq threatened Saudi security as it rarely before had been threatened.

Because of its high per capita income, it is sometimes difficult to remember that Saudi Arabia is a Developing World state in the early stages of industrialization. Its two major strengths remain Islam and oil. Islam has supported the Saud family for three centuries, and oil for only a half-century. At current rates of extraction, its oil will last for another century or more. Thus, Saudi Arabia's economic future appears secure for the foreseeable future, even though it faces serious domestic social and external military problems.

The Solomon Islands

Admittedly, the Solomon Islands is a political entity significant to few other than its 347,000 residents. It has no oil and no industry, has not been the scene of major domestic or international strife since World War II, and is largely forgotten. As an independent parliamentary state within the British Commonwealth, it is nonetheless an independent actor in the international arena. It is included in this study only in that it is representative of a burgeoning phenomenon in the international arena—the **microstate**.[13]

The list of Developing World microstates with populations of fewer than one million is a long one, including at least 31 states. Many other microstates that belong to the UN have slightly more than one million citizens. Others do not belong to the UN. Some microstates such as Barbados and the Bahamas are renowned vacation sites; others such as Brunei and Qatar are significant oil or mineral exporters. Cyprus has been the object of a major disagreement between Greece and Turkey. Others became prominent because of the East–West conflict. For example, in October 1983, Grenada catapulted to international prominence when a violent leftist coup precipitated U.S. military intervention, and in 1985, when Kiribati signed a fishing rights agreement with the U.S.S.R., U.S. interest in Kiribati escalated markedly. Some microstates such as Vanuatu and the Bahamas also have become bustling international banking centers. At one time, such "offshore banking activity" was notable primarily as a way that the wealthy could avoid paying taxes in their home country, but in the 1980s and 1990s, it became a way to launder illicit drug money. As the 1990s progress, it would not be too surprising to see antidrug efforts direct attention toward banking activities in microstates.

For the most part, however, most microstates, including the Solomon Islands, are important only in that they are voting members of the General Assembly of the United Nations. Most are also members of the Group of 77, and

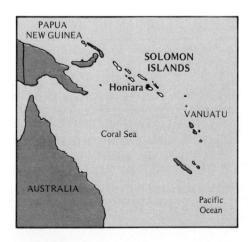

FIGURE 15–4

hence are supporters of the New International Economic Order. In the General Assembly, their votes are as significant as those of the United States, Russia, Japan, China, and the Western European states.

Little more can meaningfully be said about the Solomon Islands. They exported $75 million worth of copra, timber, and fish in 1989, and imported $117 million worth of assorted goods in the same year. They received about $16 million of aid in 1989.[14] The Solomons have no known economically exploitable natural resource. As an independent political entity, they are representative of a number of small states that are politically unimportant and relatively stable, but economically poor with no real prospects for development. Most are indeed in the backwaters of international life.

THE DEVELOPING WORLD IN PERSPECTIVE

Obviously, even among the preceding limited sample, Developing World states are diverse. They disagree about and have different perspectives about a variety of local, regional, and global issues. In Chapter 8, we examined differing Developing World interpretations of the concept of nonalignment. In this chapter, we have encountered territorial disputes between Developing World countries, political rivalry over regional leadership positions, disagreement over the generosity and direction of OPEC aid to other Developing World countries, religious conflicts, and a variety of other disagreements. The Developing World is as much at conflict with itself as it is with the industrialized West.

Again, however, this diversity should not block out the unity of the Developing World that was addressed earlier in this chapter. Equally important, the Developing World sees itself as substantially unified by its colonial heritage and economic underdevelopment. Industrialized market economies are the ready targets of Developing World countries as the causes and perpetuators of the Developing World's plight. Further, in one way or another, rightly or wrongly, most Developing World states feel that the current international system, even in its current state of flux, relegates them to a permanently inferior position.

KEY TERMS AND CONCEPTS

a colonial past
sharply divided classes
peasantry
anticolonialism
urbanization
economic underdevelopment
Angola's perspectives on
   the world

Panama's perspectives on
   the world
Saudi Arabia's perspectives on
   the world
Solomon Island's perspectives on
   the world
microstates

NOTES

1. George McTurnan Kahin and John W. Lewis, *The United States in Vietnam* (New York: Dell, 1969), p. 10.

2. *The Straits Times*, April 5, 1986.

3. Peter Mansfield, *The New Arabians* (Chicago: J. G. Ferguson, 1981), p. 204.

4. For good discussions of a variety of developmental theories and concepts, see Gavin Kitching, *Development and Underdevelopment in Historical Perspective* (New York: Methuen, 1982).

5. For additional assessments of Angola's situation and its outlook, see Gerald Bender, *Angola under the Portuguese* (Berkeley: University of California Press, 1978); John Marcum, *The Angolan Revolution*, Vols. I and II (Cambridge: MIT Press, 1969, 1978); and Douglas Wheeler and Rene Pelissier, *Angola* (New York: Praeger, 1971). See also Abiodun Williams, *In Search of Peace: Negotiations and the Angolan Civil War* (Washington, D.C.: United States Institute of Peace, 1992); and I. William Zartman, *Ripe for Revolution: Conflict and Intervention in Africa* (New York: Oxford University Press, 1989).

6. Walter LaFeber, *The Panama Canal: The Crisis in Historical Perspectives* (New York: Oxford University Press, 1978), pp. 38–39.

7. Kenneth J. Hagan, *American Gunboat Diplomacy and the Old Navy, 1877–1889* (Westport, CT: Greenwood Press, 1973), pp. 170–188.

8. See Margaret E. Scranton, *The Noriega Years: U.S.-Panamanian Relations 1981–90* (Boulder, CO: Lynne Rienner Publishers, 1991) for greater details.

9. Much of the following Arabian history is based on J. B. Kelly, *Arabia, the Gulf and the West* (New York: Basic Books, 1980); and Peter Mansfield, *The New Arabians* (Chicago: J. G. Ferguson, 1981). See also Ragaei El Mallakh, *Saudi Arabia: Rush to Development* (Baltimore: Johns Hopkins University Press, 1982).

10. According to one observer, Ibn Saud explained his change of heart by saying, "if anyone would offer me a million pounds, I would give him all the [oil] concessions he wanted." Mansfield, *The New Arabians*, p. 66.

11. *Ibid.*, p. 206.

12. King Fahd's decrees are available from the Saudi Embassy, Washington, D.C. See also *The New York Times*, March 2, 1992.

13. For studies of the role of small states and microstates in the contemporary international arena, see Marshall R. Singer, *Weak States in a World of Powers: The Dynamics of International Relations* (New York: The Free Press, 1972); August Schon and Arne Olav Brundtland, *Small States in International Relations* (New York: John Wiley, 1971); and Elmer Plischke, "Microstates: Lilliputs in World Affairs," *The Futurist*, Vol. 12 (February 1978): 19–25. Only the last of these discusses microstates specifically.

14. These figures are from *The World Factbook, 1989*, p. 268.

PART FOUR

The Instrumental Framework

THE TOOLS OF POWER IN INTERNATIONAL POLITICS

International politics, like all politics, is a struggle for power. Whatever the ultimate aims of international politics, power is always the immediate aim.
—*Hans J. Morgenthau*

Power confuses itself with virtue and tends also to take itself for omnipotence. Once imbued with the idea of a mission, a great nation easily assumes that it has the means as well as the duty to do God's work.
—*J. William Fulbright*

In the preceding two frameworks, we examined international actors and their interests, and the views that those actors hold of themselves and others in the international arena. This framework analyzes the major instruments that the actors use in their relations with one another as they attempt to achieve their objectives. In short, this framework discusses power and its constituent elements.

Everyone recognizes and respects power, but few can define precisely what it is, or what its exact ingredients are. It is a means to an end, and an end in itself, the primary tool and chief objective of domestic and international political processes. Power is anything but a universal constant. Someone who is a powerful individual in one situation may find his or her power greatly diminished in another situation. For example, Mikhail Gorbachev had the power to decide to cut the U.S.S.R.'s defense budget in 1990 and to choose whether or not he should meet with George Bush. Yet during the same time, he could not convince Lithuanians that they should not try to secede from the Soviet Union, nor could he persuade Soviet citizens to work harder. In an equally pointed example, George Bush could order the American military into Iraq and Somalia,, but he could not convince

Japan to abandon restrictive trade practices or American voters to reelect him president.

Power depends on the context in which it is used. This is as true for state and nonstate actors in international politics as it is for individuals, whether they be major international actors or lesser known individuals. The United States, for all its military and economic power, found itself virtually powerless in its relations with Iran during the hostage crisis. Nuclear and conventional weapons and economic strength were meaningless in effecting the hostages' eventual release. Similarly, poorly armed Afghan guerrillas fought against Soviet nuclear-capable armed forces, and a group of economically deprived states decided that they would attempt to extract higher prices for their only resource, oil, from the wealthy and powerful industrial countries. Afghan guerrillas and OPEC states both succeeded in standing up to their more powerful antagonists.

This framework examines the instruments of power in international politics. Chapter 16 presents an overview of power in its international context, how it comes into being and is measured, and how it can and cannot be used. The subsequent three chapters examine the most prominent parameters of power—economic strength, military capabilities, and sociopolitical measures of power. The final chapter in this framework discusses international law and diplomacy as inputs to power in the international arena. Some of the most important issues examined in this framework are

- What are the constituents of power?
- What are the differences among military, economic, and sociopolitical parameters of power?
- Why is one type of power useful in one instance but not in another?
- What constrains the employment of power?
- How do international law and diplomacy add to an international actor's power?

CHAPTER 16

Power

- What is power?
- What contributes to power?
- Why is one type of power useful in one situation but not in another?
- How can power be measured?

Power has been studied from earliest recorded time. In the West, Aristotle, Plato, Socrates, Machiavelli, Hobbes, Montesquieu, and thousands of other writers, philosophers, and analysts turned their thoughts to the elusive concept of power. In the East, Kautilya, Lao Tzu, Confucius, and thousands more did the same. In our effort to understand what power means and what power is, we are following a long and illustrious line of thinkers.

Unfortunately, nearly as many definitions of power exist as there are writers. Some writers define power as physical force;[1] others see it as a more broadly based concept that includes military, economic, psychological, and social dimensions. The concept of power that we will use is broadly based, but first we will examine some views of power that prevail today.

VIEWS OF POWER

Hans Morgenthau's classic text, *Politics Among Nations: The Struggle for Power and Peace*, elevated the study of the role of power to a new level of respectability in international affairs.[2] Morgenthau's basic thesis in *Politics Among Nations* was simple: Power is a psychological relationship between those who exercise it and those over whom it is exercised.[3] To Morgenthau, those who exercise power influence the decisions of those who have less power because the weaker individual, group, or state expects benefits, fears retribution, or respects the individuals and/or institutions exercising power. Morgenthau even went so far as to define national interest in terms of power; to Morgenthau, any action or policy that maximized a nation's power was in the national interest, and actions or policies that did not maximize power were not in the national interest. Power, to Morgenthau, was both a means and an end.[4]

Morgenthau also drew four distinctions about the role of power in international affairs. First, power and influence were not synonymous. Power denoted the ability to determine outcomes; influence implied the ability to affect the decisions of those who could determine outcomes. To use Morgenthau's example, a secretary of state advises the president to choose a policy option, but only the president makes a decision. Thus, the secretary of state has the potential to be influential, but is influential only if the president follows the secretary of state's advice. Conversely, the president is powerful regardless of whether or not secretarial advice is followed.[5]

Second, Morgenthau differentiated between power and force. To Morgenthau, force meant physical violence, which eliminated the psychological implications of power. A powerful actor, to Morgenthau, employed force as a threat and did not need to employ it as a reality. Thus, "armed strength as a threat or a potentiality is the most important material factor making for the political power of a nation."[6]

Third, Morgenthau identified a difference between usable and unusable power. Nuclear capabilities and the threat of their use was and is a credible element of national power in certain situations but not in others. Thus, nuclear weapons may be either usable or unusable additions to a nation's power potential. In other words, power was contextual.

Fourth, Morgenthau claimed a distinction between moral power, or legitimate power, and immoral power, or illegitimate power. Political ideologies, whether they be bourgeois democracy, Marxism-Leninism, Nazism, or something else, endowed national actions with the cover of legitimacy. This legitimacy in turn made it acceptable to them to employ their power.

Morgenthau's conception of power has been criticized by many. Some critics observed that Morgenthau and other proponents of the realpolitik school of international relations emphasized the coercive aspects of power and minimized its attractive aspects. Although Morgenthau stressed that power permitted one actor to force another actor to act as the first desired and prevented other actors from forcing the first actor to act as they desired, critics of Morgenthau's emphasis on coercion pointed out that certain actors enhanced their power by attracting the loyalty or allegiance of other actors. These analysts argue that power must therefore be viewed as having both coercive and attractive components.

The complexities of the concept of power have led many analysts to maintain that power is essentially a qualitative concept that can not be precisely measured. At best, these analysts assert, power can be gauged in broad qualitative terms, but not in precise quantitative terms.

Others disagree. For example, Ray S. Cline, former Director of Intelligence and Research at the Department of State and former Deputy Director of Intelligence for the Central Intelligence Agency, developed a formula to measure the **perceived power** that a country has.[7] According to Cline:

$$P_p = (C + E + M) \times (S + W)$$

where

P_p = perceived power
C = critical mass: population and territory
E = economic capability
M = military capability
S = strategic purpose
W = will to pursue national strategy

Cline's first three elements of power $(C + E + M)$ are tangible elements that can be objectively quantified. The last two elements $(S + W)$ are intangibles, and may be only subjectively quantified.

However, an astute observer will realize that a degree of subjectivity also enters an assessment of tangible elements. Relative skills and education levels of a country's people are major factors to be considered when population is being assessed. So too is the physical topography of a country when territory is being considered. A skilled and educated people in many respects must be rated more highly than a quantitatively more numerous unskilled and uneducated population. Similarly, a country with few or no navigable rivers has certain transportational disadvantages to overcome. In the area of military capabilities, quantitative and qualitative parameters of the international military balance are often subjects of heated debate. In certain instances, quantitatively more numerous weapons will overcome qualitatively superior weapons. In other cases, quality will defeat quantity. Economically, debates over questions of the wisdom of developing one's own expensive resource base or relying on relatively less expensive foreign resources are legion. Is the country that pays less for foreign resources, and is therefore dependent, in a better position than a country that pays more to develop its own resources, but is therefore self-sufficient? These and similar other economic questions make an assessment of the economic parameters of power extremely uncertain. Nevertheless, when compared to $S + W$, $C + E + M$ is a more objective set of criteria of power, at least in a relative sense.

Some specific examples may clarify these points. In 1980, Cline calculated U.S., Soviet, and Chinese power potentials as shown in Table 16–1.

By early 1990, however, much had changed. Inflation had decreased in the United States, economic growth had accelerated, the United States had put new weapons into its arsenal, and had become more assertive in international affairs. In the U.S.S.R., the economy had decayed, nationalities fought for their independence, and the Communist party was in disarray. In China, economic growth continued, submarines with ballistic missiles had entered the arsenal, and despite the horror of the Tiananmen Square massacre, China followed a resolute strategy. These situations are reflected in Table 16–2.

But was this the way things really were? Had the United States actually moved from a position 50 percent behind the U.S.S.R. to one 50 percent ahead of the U.S.S.R. in ten short years? Had China really moved from being one-sixth as powerful as the U.S.S.R. in 1980 to one half as powerful in 1990? Or was the situation even more strikingly different than Table 16–2 implies?

As subsequent events showed, the situation in the Soviet Union had deteriorated even more than Table 16–2 indicates. In reality, "critical mass" was far

TABLE 16–1   Perceived Power of the United States, U.S.S.R., and China, 1980

	Critical Mass	Economic Capability	Military Capability	Partial Total	Strategy and Will	Total
United States	100	146	188	434	.7	304
U.S.S.R.	100	85	197	382	1.2	458
China	75	23	41	139	.6	83

TABLE 16–2   Perceived Power of the United States, U.S.S.R., and China, 1990,
                  Version 1

	Critical Mass	Economic Capability	Military Capability	Partial Total	Strategy and Will	Total
United States	100	155	200	455	1.0	455
U.S.S.R.	100	75	200	375	.8	300
China	75	30	45	150	1.0	150

below 100; virtually every nationality group in the U.S.S.R. wanted its independence. Economic capability and military capability had also declined far more
than Table 16–2 implies. And strategy and will had also eroded more than indicated. A more accurate assessment of the U.S.S.R.'s real situation, as borne out
by the course of events there in 1991 and 1992, appears in Table 16–3. But yet, in
the world of 1990, it would have been virtually impossible to convince anyone
that the Soviet Union's power potential had sunk to a level virtually the same as
that of China.

Obviously, assessing power even when a formula is provided remains quite
subjective. To Cline, the bottom line is the capacity of a state to wage war.[8] In situations where political or economic dialogue breaks down, this view is exactly
correct. In other situations, the case may be overstated. In some instances, the
relational and contextual aspects of power render the superior ability of one state
over another to wage war virtually meaningless. We explore these seemingly contradictory facts in the next section.

RELATIONAL AND CONTEXTUAL ASPECTS OF POWER

Power defines relations between or among states. A "powerful state" may force or
influence a "less powerful state" to change its policies or objectives, and that less
powerful state may in turn force or influence a "weak state" to alter its policies or
objectives. By implication, the powerful state also can influence or control decisions made in the weak state. The weak state, in turn, is prevented from forcing
or influencing the less powerful state to change its policies or objectives by its
inferior power position, and the less powerful state, in turn, cannot force or influence the powerful state to alter its policies or objectives. Again by implication,

TABLE 16–3   Perceived Power of the United States, U.S.S.R., and China, 1990,
                  Version 2

	Critical Mass	Economic Capability	Military Capability	Partial Total	Strategy and Will	Total
United States	100	155	200	440	1.0	455
U.S.S.R.	80	60	175	315	.6	189
China	75	30	45	150	1.0	150

the weak state cannot influence the powerful state. Thus, power defines the relationship.

This simple relational aspect of power is immeasurably complicated by the contextual aspect of power. Put simply, the "right kind" of power must be used in the "right kind" of situation. Arguments made at the United Nations about the folly of war may influence the behavior and attitudes of those delegates who hear the arguments. They may even lead the UN to deploy peacekeeping forces. However, those same arguments made to combatants in the field would probably prove meaningless. Words may be appropriate tools of power in the United Nations' chambers, but they rarely are on the battlefield.

Particular types of weapons may also be appropriate or inappropriate tools of power, depending on circumstances. Nuclear weapons, the extreme tools of violence, are inappropriate instruments for use against terrorism and other types of low-intensity conflict. Even in the case of open war between a nuclear-capable country and a nonnuclear country, nuclear weapons, so far, have been deemed inappropriate. American military actions in Korea in the 1950s, Vietnam in the 1960s and 1970s, Grenada in 1983, Panama in 1989, and the Persian Gulf War in 1991 all offered proof that in certain contexts, nuclear weapons and the power they provide are not meaningfully useful. Soviet military actions in Afghanistan in the 1970s and 1980s, Chinese actions against Vietnam in 1979, and British actions against Argentina in 1982 also proved the same point.

The contextual nature of power therefore frustrates any simple measure of the relationships that exist between international actors. Using our previous example, the "powerful state" (hereafter A) had the ability to force or influence the "less powerful state" (hereafter B) to change its policies or objectives, and B could in turn influence or force the "weak state" (hereafter C) to alter its policies or objectives. A has power over B and C, and B has power over C.

But given the different contextual attributes of power:

1. C may in some contexts be able to resist B's power, and may be able to resist A's power as well.
2. C may in some contexts be able to influence or force B's policies or objectives to be changed, and may be able to influence or force changes in A's policies or objectives as well.
3. B may in some contexts have a greater ability to influence or force C to change its policies or objectives than does A.
4. A may in some contexts be totally powerless to influence either B or C.

Other scenarios are possible as well. But these examples may be more meaningful if actual countries are used to illustrate them. For example, no one would deny that the United States is a more powerful actor across a wide spectrum of capabilities than China, and that China is in turn generally more powerful than Vietnam. Yet in several instances during the 1970s and 1980s, this simple relational ordering of power was negated by the contextual aspects of power. Using the same contextual relationships as were just listed in points 1–4, we note the following:

(1) In 1978, Vietnam invaded Cambodia despite clear signals from the United States and China that they opposed such an action. Despite being more

powerful in general than Vietnam, neither the United States nor China were able to prevent the Vietnamese action.

(2) As Vietnam fashioned a military alliance with the Soviet Union in the early 1980s, Vietnam forced China to pay more and more attention to the defense of China's southern borders and southern sea lines of communications. Similarly, Vietnam successfully withstood the U.S. war effort earlier in the 1970s. Both China and the United States therefore had to change their policies as the result of the actions of Vietnam, a "less powerful" state.

(3) Two months after the Vietnamese invasion of Cambodia, China launched a "punishment operation" against Vietnam, and throughout the 1980s, China supported the Khmer Rouge, the Cambodian Communist party that Vietnam had expelled from power, in their effort to retake Cambodia. Meanwhile, for most of this period, the United States refused to become involved in the continuing Cambodian conflict. Because of the Chinese actions, Vietnam was forced to maintain large numbers of combat troops on station in Cambodia to keep the government that it installed there in power. China thus had a greater ability to force Vietnam to change its policies than did the United States, even though the United States in general was more powerful than China.

(4) In the late 1980s, the United States supported the Chinese democracy movement, but could do nothing to prevent the Tiananmen Square massacre of 1989. Similarly, from the early 1970s until the early 1990s, the United States demanded a full accounting from Vietnam about U.S. prisoners of war and missing in action. However, when Vietnam refused to cooperate, the United States could do nothing to force Vietnamese cooperation.

Numerous other examples of the contextual nature of power exist. Despite their military capabilities, the United States and NATO could not prevent Serbia from launching its "ethnic cleansing" campaign against Bosnia-Herzegovina in 1992. U.S. military strength also was of limited use in rescuing American hostages from the Middle East throughout the 1980s and on into the 1990s. Britain's ownership of nuclear weapons was not sufficient to deter Argentine occupation of the Falkland Islands in 1982, and the very destructiveness of those nuclear weapons made them inappropriate for use against Argentina. Cuba has regularly pulled the beard of Uncle Sam, seemingly with impunity, despite the United States' geographic proximity, military capabilities, and economic wealth. Even with its superior overall power position, the United States' could not influence its European allies to allow U.S. planes to use NATO bases for refueling and maintenance during the 1973 Arab-Israeli War. The United States' overall economic and military strength proved less influential on European decision-makers than the threat of loss of access to oil. Oil was thus more powerful than military and economic strength and more powerful than the bonds of alliance solidarity. Finally, for over a decade, Ayatollah Khomeini with his version of Shiite fundamentalism was little more than an academic curiosity. By the 1980s, however, Khomeini's fundamentalism struck terror in the hearts of less fundamentalist Muslims and disrupted calculations of the United States and the Soviet Union. Khomeini's fundamentalism had not changed, but the context in which he used it had.

The contextual nature of power introduces even more complications into our study of power when the diversity of actors in the international system is taken into account. Some actors respond more willingly to one parameter of power than to another. For example, multinational corporations respond to economic parameters of power more rapidly than a national liberation movement. Negotiations and appeals to morality may prove more powerful at the United Nations than in the corporate boardroom or in the bush. Allegiance of an uneducated people in a newly independent country may render a national liberation movement more powerful, yet be meaningless for a multinational corporation or the United Nations. Power, then, is contextual not only as it applies to states, but also as it applies to other actors. The power of any actor rises and wanes depending on the context in which constituents of power are employed.

The relational and contextual aspects of power even complicate the concept of the balance of power that we discussed in Chapter 2. How can "balance" be determined when constituent elements of power are weighed differently by different observers? How can "balance" be assessed when different elements of power come into play—or do not come into play—in different contexts? These are difficult questions, and no widely accepted answer has yet been found.

CONSTITUENTS OF POWER

What, then, is power? For our purposes, we may define it as the ability of any actor to persuade, influence, force, or otherwise induce another actor to undertake an action or change an objective that the latter would otherwise prefer not to do. It is also the ability of one actor to persuade, influence, force, or otherwise induce another actor to refrain from an action that it would prefer to undertake. One actor may achieve power over another actor through persuasion, coercion, force, or dependence. An actor may have its power enhanced as other actors enter willingly into alliance with it. Power is both subjective and objective, although its constituent elements vary from time to time and place to place. Its contextual nature complicates the ordered relations that a simplistic definition of power yields.

Power is nevertheless a product of many inputs. The power potential of an actor is best estimated by examining each input individually.

Population is one of the most important determinants of power. Here, population refers not only to numbers but also to the training and expertise of a population. China's immense population is one reason why it is considered a major power, yet the advantages that China could derive from its population are reduced by the level of training and expertise of that population. Outside the realm of states, other actors benefit from the number, training, and expertise of their populations as well. IBM employs few people in comparison with the population of the major national actors, but the training and knowledge of IBM's "population" enhances IBM's power. Similarly, national liberation movements increase their power as their cadre grows more numerous and better trained.

The role that population plays in enhancing or reducing the power of an actor cannot be divorced from other parameters of power, such as organization, leadership, and industrial base. For example, Indonesia has a population of 193 million, but its internal diversity and its island geography have complicated its leadership's efforts to coordinate the country's human and material resources. Bangladesh, with a population of 116 million, has had organizational and leadership problems, and has too few natural resources.

Geography also plays a role in determining the power of an actor, although the importance of geography remains a matter of debate. Geography is almost exclusively relevant for determining the power potential of state actors. As discussed in Chapter 1, during the early twentieth century the geopolitical school of international analysis emphasized the role of geography to the exclusion of other factors in determining national power potential. The advent of nuclear weapons and other high technology armaments led most analysts to minimize the importance of geography during the first three post–World War II decades, but geography's importance was again reemphasized during the 1980s when the U.S.S.R. moved into Afghanistan.

Sheer size is a major geographical contributor to a country's power potential. The immense distances of the czar's Russia played a major role in defeating Napoleon in 1812 and in frustrating the Kaiser during World War I. Soviet Russia was similarly saved by its size during World War II. The incredibly cold Russian winters, a product of Russia's geographical location, contributed mightily to the defeat of all three invading armies. Switzerland's mountains have played an invaluable role in Swiss defense, and the United States has been blessed with two immense buffer zones that shielded it from invasion—the Atlantic and Pacific Oceans.

Size, terrain, and location need not be advantages, however. Russia is a good example. Russia does not have an ocean port that is ice-free year round. Russian foreign trade and ocean-borne freight are thus limited. Similarly, all major Russian rivers run north and south and, with the exception of the Volga, provide limited service as internal transportation arteries. Finally, because of its size and location, Russia finds it necessary to have four separate fleets. During times of war these four fleets, one in the Pacific, one in the Black Sea, another in the Baltic, and the fourth in the north, would not be able to link up.

A country's geography may also deny it access to the sea. A landlocked state that has the economic ability and desire to engage in trade must depend on its neighbors to provide it access to the sea. In some cases, this presents little problem. Bolivia has had few difficulties exporting its mineral production through Peruvian or Chilean ports. Conversely, Zambia's copper exports could no longer reach the Angolan port of Benguela when the Angolan Civil War erupted, and Zambia's political relations with white-controlled Rhodesia (now Zimbabwe) precluded egress on Rhodesian railroads.

Nonstate actors, with the significant exception of national liberation movements, rarely count geography as elements of their power. National liberation movements may be fortunate enough to benefit from geographically or topographically provided advantages. Thus, the Vietcong used Vietnam's jungle to good advantage, thereby increasing their power, and Afghan mujahadeen used Afghanistan's rugged terrain both to provide shelter and to ambush Soviet troops.

Natural resources are a third element of power. At least four levels of importance—possession, exploitation, control, and use—may be attached to resources. Obviously, an actor that has large quantities of resources is in a potentially advantageous position compared with an actor that has few or none. But an actor must also be able to exploit those resources. For example, the Russian Far East and Siberia have large quantities of minerals, but Russia cannot exploit them because they are located in areas of extremely inhospitable climate and terrain. Similarly as we have seen, Zambia has rich copper deposits, but when the Angolan Civil War closed the Benguela railroad, Zambia was unable to export its copper except through Rhodesia, which Zambia refused to do for political reasons. The Chinese-built Tanzam railroad has since given Zambia a third egress alternative.

Control is a third level of importance of resources. It does little for an actor's power if the actor possesses resources that are being exploited by another actor. Here, the oil-producing states of the Middle East are a prime example. Until they were able to coordinate their oil policies with each other through OPEC and wrest control of production and pricing decisions from the multinational oil companies to which they had earlier granted lucrative long-term concessions, the oil-producing states were important, but impotent, actors on the international scene. However, when they obtained control over their abundant and exploitable oil fields, they emerged to a new powerful position in the international order of states.

Use is a final level of importance of resources. Unless an actor can put its resources to effective use for its own purposes, it adds little to its power. Use is primarily a function of an actor's level of industrial and economic development. Brazil has immense deposits of exploitable resources that it controls, yet it is only slowly developing an industrial and economic base that takes full advantage of its abundant resources. Zaire and Zambia are also resource rich, but do not have industrial or economic bases. In Zaire's case, multinational corporations still enjoy extremely favorable concessions there, so the question of control remains pertinent for Zaire. In Zambia, use is complicated by its being denied access to ports.

Other than states, multinational corporations are the most prominent actors that derive power from natural resources. MNCs are dependent on states to grant access, but on many occasions, because of the human expertise and financial income they provide, particularly to Developing World states, MNCs may exercise a disproportionate amount of influence within a state because of that state's reliance on an MNC to provide expertise and capital for resource exploitation.

Industrial capabilities are also major inputs to a country's power potential. Particularly during major wars, the record of the nineteenth and twentieth centuries indicates that countries with superior industrial bases and the wealth to support those bases generally emerge victorious in war. Quantitative studies tend to confirm this general observation.[9] Caution must be exercised in reaching this conclusion, however. In wars of less than major scale, industrial capabilities provide a less effective source of power. France, the former Soviet Union, and the United States encountered tremendous difficulties in their struggles against nonindustrial nonstate actors in Algeria, Afghanistan, and Vietnam.

Industrial capabilities are major contributing elements to a country's economic power during peace. Industrial strength contributes directly to the standard of living, which, if acceptable to a population, may lead that population to be more amenable to its government's policies. For example, the German people willingly supported Adolf Hitler's policies as he nationalized German industry, improved its efficiency, and raised Germany out of the quagmire of the Great Depression. Hitler's industrial successes and the support they won for him within Germany enhanced the power of the German state and led directly to the tragedy of World War II.

For many countries, industrial capabilities carry with them the necessity for access to external resources. Thus, industrial capabilities add to a state's power, but also make it potentially dependent on other actors. Europe's and Japan's industrial bases make them powerful actors, but their power is somewhat qualified by their extreme energy dependence, Great Britain and Norway excepted.

Military capabilities are important to an actor's power potential. In fact, some analysts of the role of power in international affairs argue that military capabilities are the only real determinants of an actor's true power. This is an extremely narrow outlook that may be legitimate during times of war, but is overly restrictive during peace. For example, Japan has limited its military capabilities because of its constitutional restriction on armed forces, but it is a powerful country in economic terms. Similarly, few actors other than states and national liberation movements have military capabilities, but depending on the context of a particular situation, many have power.

Nevertheless, the military capabilities of a state are fundamental constituents of power for state actors. Qualitative and quantitative aspects of military power are variously measured, as are the varying utilities of conventional and nuclear forces. The ability to project military power far from a national homeland is one measure of military capabilities, as is the ability to defend one's homeland. Numerous other questions also must be addressed when the military might of an actor is examined: How well are an actor's military forces prepared for war during time of peace? How long would it take for an actor to mobilize for war? How self-reliant is an actor on its own resources and industry? How supportive of the leadership are the people? How solid an alliance system does an actor have?

Obviously, the factors that determine an actor's military capabilities are complex and extend far beyond counting the number and quality of planes, tanks, ships, and troops. Although it is an extreme oversimplification to argue that military capabilities and the power of an actor are synonymous, one must neverthe-

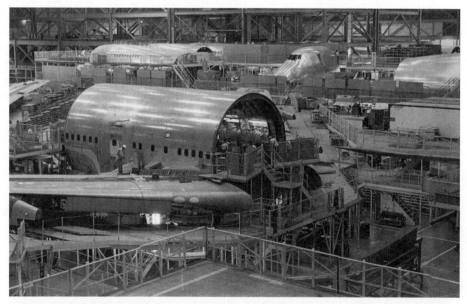

Industrial capabilities have been major contributing elements to economic power and military power since the industrial revolution. Here, aircraft are assembled in the Boeing aircraft plant in Seattle, Washington.   (Stock, Boston.)

less conclude that in the anarchistic and competitive world of the 1990s, military capabilities are still a major component of power.

So, too, is *will*. Regardless of the quantity or quality of the more objective, tangible elements of power that an actor may have, an absence of will to use those elements renders them virtually meaningless. Indeed, many analysts rank will as one of the most, if not the most, important determinants of power.[10] Without will, even a massive state-of-the art military can achieve little.

Yet will is difficult, if not impossible, to measure. It cannot be quantified, and may only be estimated. Will may refer either to the intention of a particular set of decision-making elites to achieve a particular goal, or it may refer to the willingness of the population to support the decision-makers' decision. During the Vietnam War, for example, the U.S. political and military elite remained committed to the maintenance of an independent South Vietnam much longer than the general population of the United States. Eventually, the population's attitude influenced the elite's attitude as well. By 1975, when North Vietnam overran South Vietnam, neither the U.S. population nor the U.S. elite had the will to become reengaged in Southeast Asia. By contrast, in 1982 when Argentina captured the Falkland Islands, Great Britain's population and government alike surprised the world by displaying a firm will to push the Argentines from the islands.

Will may also be ephemeral; that is, it may appear and disappear quickly. Thus, when the United States invaded Grenada in 1983 and Panama in 1989, a groundswell of support quickly developed in the United States for the U.S. actions. In both examples, the United States achieved its objectives quickly with very few losses. Would U.S. will in Grenada or Panama have remained strong if the two actions had taken several years or if U.S. losses had been high? The question cannot be answered, but the U.S. experience in Vietnam implies that long wars with large losses may reduce the U.S. population's will to support conflict.

Leadership plays a major role in establishing will, and it also often influences how well an actor takes advantage of other parameters of power. Leadership may be either jointly managed or undertaken individually, but in either case it is a key. Particularly during time of peace and prosperity, decision-makers often prefer leadership roles to be widely shared, or at least to have the appearance of being widely shared. In many strongly authoritarian or dictatorial societies, leadership elites seek to create the image of a broad sharing of power. Despite the fact that communist "People's Republics" rarely allowed the people to share in decision making, the decision-making elite considered it necessary to maintain the fiction of popular participation. Conversely, during periods of economic and military crises, actors often opt for a more centralized form of leadership. This phenomenon occurs in democratic as well as authoritarian societies. Franklin Roosevelt presided over an unprecedented accumulation of power in presidential hands during the Great Depression and World War II.

Additionally, the occasional importance of single individuals in determining the course of history has led to the development of the "Great Man" theory of history. According to this concept, the exploits of Alexander the Great, Caesar, Napoleon, Bismarck, Lenin, Roosevelt, Hitler, Churchill, and Mao occurred not because of a fortuitous combination of circumstances, but because a "great man" was in a position to take advantage of circumstances.

Leadership also influences the amount of societal cohesion that exists within a society. Although *charisma* is an overworked term, who can deny that a John Kennedy or a Franklin Roosevelt was able to mobilize large segments of the U.S. population behind him by force of personality? On other occasions, particular ideas or concepts may be used by leaders to achieve or seek to achieve societal cohesion. After the trauma of Vietnam, Americans responded willingly to Jimmy Carter's call for a reemphasis on human rights in U.S. foreign policy. Thereafter, as the image of U.S. impotence grew in the wake of the hostage crisis in Iran and the Soviet invasion of Afghanistan, U.S. citizens responded favorably to Ronald Reagan's call for a rearmed United States. In all cases, effective leadership abets power.

Although our discussion of leadership's role in power has centered on the state, leadership is of equally great importance in multinational corporations, IGOs, and nongovernmental organizations. Effective leadership can enhance power, and ineffective leadership can reduce power. ITT became a rich MNC under the leadership of Sosthenes Behn, and Dag Hammarskjold's skills in guiding the United Nations enhanced its power in the international community.

Nevertheless, even with skillful leadership, other parameters of power are also needed. It is doubtful if any leader or leadership elite, regardless of skill, could significantly enhance the power of Chad, Niger, or Mali, three state actors that are among the world's most impotent and powerless.

A country's *diplomacy* must also be considered an element of its power. Skillful diplomats can influence other countries to act in ways that will promote their own country's interests, can weave together alliances that will help defend their country, and can help establish an international climate that will abet their country's efforts to achieve its international objectives. Conversely, unskilled diplomats can allow other countries to improve their positions relative to the diplomats' own country by inattention to detail, by failing to think through implications of an agreement, by not staying attuned to ongoing events, and in many other ways.

Internal organization is also a constituent of power. An actor whose internal organization is rigidly stratified or which disperses too many rewards to too few of its members may reduce the allegiance of its people to that actor. Power potential is correspondingly reduced. Similarly, extreme internal political fractionalization can reduce a country's political stability, thereby reducing if not its power, then at the very least others' perceptions of its power. In Italy, for example, at least six major political parties exist. Governments must be formed by coalition.

Internal organization is also important within nonstate actors in the international arena. The United Nations, for example, permits any of the "Big Five" to veto Security Council resolutions; it is not surprising that the United Nations rarely undertakes an action that will adversely have an impact on the interests of China, France, Great Britain, Russia, or the United States. Similarly, "mother-daughter" organizational structures reduced the ability of MNCs to take advantage of changes in the international economic environment, and reduced the economic power of MNCs.

The role of *strategy* in determining an actor's power has been the subject of considerable debate. As defined by Ray Cline, strategy is "the part of the political decision-making process that conceptualizes and establishes goals and objectives designed to protect and enhance . . . interests in the international arena."[11] To some analysts, strategy flows from an actor's elite and therefore must be analyzed in conjunction with the outlooks of an actor's leadership. In this view, current U.S. strategy is the product of the predominant U.S. emphasis on pluralistic political democracy and a free-market economy. An opposed perspective argues that population, geography, resources, and other factors determine strategy. In this view, U.S. strategy flows from the United States' economic interdependence, peaceful borders, and continuing concerns about world peace.

However, all concede that strategy is important. The manner in which a leadership organizes and directs capabilities toward a specific goal can add to or detract from an actor's power as much as any of the other parameters of power we have discussed. Capabilities without strategy are nearly as meaningless as strategy without capabilities.

The final major input to a country's power potential is *perception*. Because power is both a relational and a contextual concept, its utility lies not only in what it *can* do, but also in what others *think* it can do. An actor that is "weak" but is perceived by others as being "strong" has much greater leeway for action than an actor that is weak and is perceived as being weak. During the late 1950s and early 1960s, the Soviet Union was in the position of a weak state perceived as a strong one. Despite the reality of pronounced nuclear inferiority in comparison to the United States, the combination of the U.S.S.R.'s success in being the first country to orbit an artificial earth satellite and of Khrushchev's "missile-rattling" influenced many people to perceive that Soviet power was nearly equal to U.S. power. Somewhat paradoxically Soviet power *was* nearly equal to U.S. power, *simply because others perceived it to be so*.

Here, it may be useful to discuss the difference between the **declaratory policy** of a state and the **actual policy** of a state. The declaratory policy of a state is what a state says that it will do in a given situation; the actual policy of a state is what it really does, or really intends to do.

Why do differences sometimes exist between declaratory policy and actual policy? In part, it is because states—and other actors—seek to add to their own power by convincing others that they will do something that they do not intend to do. If states or other actors can succeed in doing this, then another state or another actor may change its own policies.

An example may help clarify this. During the 1950s, the United States had a declaratory policy for nuclear weapons called "massive retaliation." This declaratory policy of "massive retaliation" stated that if communist forces anywhere in the world attempted to increase the amount of territory under their control, the United States would reserve the right to use nuclear weapons at times and places of the United States' own choosing, including massive nuclear attacks against the Soviet Union. The intent of the U.S. declaratory policy was to influence the Soviet Union and other communist states to end whatever plans they had to expand.

U.S. leaders, however, did not actually intend to use nuclear weapons in every and all cases. They simply made such statements in an effort to influence Soviet and other communist policy. The actual policy of the United States remained much as it had been—conventional weapons would be used in most instances of conflict, and nuclear weapons only in extreme cases. A clear difference existed between U.S. declaratory policy and U.S. actual policy, a difference that existed because of an effort on the part of U.S. policy-makers to influence the perceptions that Soviet and other communist leaders had of what the United

States would do in the event of Soviet or other communist expansion. By trying to change the perception of what Soviet leaders thought the United States would do, U.S. leaders sought to change Soviet and other communist actions. Perceptions, then, are major inputs to power potential, and international actors often use declaratory policy as a way to manipulate other actors' perceptions.

Of course, when differences exist between actual power and perception of power, the actor perceived to be more powerful than it actually is, or that perceives itself to be more powerful than it actually is, may be in for a rude awakening. During the early twentieth century, Russia was generally recognized as one of the leading powers in the world. It also considered itself to be such a power. The czar and the rest of the world were shocked when the Japanese administered a humiliating defeat to the Russians in the 1905 Russo-Japanese War. Europe and Russia had deluded themselves into overestimating Russia's military prowess, a delusion that added strength to Russian power until that power was actually tested. So, too, 75 years later Soviet leaders deluded themselves into believing that their military power was sufficient to defeat the mujahadeen in Afghanistan. The entire world believed this to be true as well—until year after year passed, with Soviet forces mired ever more deeply in Afghanistan. Thus, at first, the U.S.S.R.'s power was enhanced by the prevailing perception that it had the will to use its military capabilities to achieve its objectives, but as Soviet military capabilities proved unequal to the task, the perception of the power of the Soviet Union dwindled appreciably.

CONCLUSIONS

Measuring power is more art than science. Given the relational nature of power, the contextual quality of its application, and the difficulty of assigning an objective value to even its most tangible elements, it is not surprising that one of the major debates in the American body politic has been over power, specifically whether the United States is a "declining power" or whether it remains preeminent. Other countries also debate their relative power position in the world. Thus, political elites throughout the world search for answers to the questions of where their state stands relative to the power of other regional and global actors. It was not without pride that Margaret Thatcher's government announced that it had "put the Great back into Britain" following the Falkland Islands War. Power can be measured accurately only when it is used, and for the first time since the Suez intervention in 1956, Great Britain had an opportunity to gauge the military parameters of its power.

The struggle to gauge power has led some analysts to adopt broadly based subjective judgments of global and regional balances of power, and has led others to develop concepts such as Cline's "Politectonics." The former accept measures of power as an art; the latter attempt to make it more of a science. All are attempting to answer the question, who, if anyone, will dominate whom?

Given the uncertainties inherent in the study and use of power in international affairs, only one specific conclusion may be reached: "Real power—the ability to affect others—seems in fact more widely dispersed than perhaps at any time in the world's history."[12] With the end of the Cold War and the East–West conflict, that reality has become increasingly evident for all to see.

With this in mind, the next four chapters analyze some of the more important tools of power in contemporary international relations.

KEY TERMS AND CONCEPTS

Hans Morgenthau's ideas
   about power
perceived power
relational aspects of power

contextual aspects of power
constituents of power
declaratory policy
actual policy

NOTES

1. Inis L. Claude, Jr., *Power and International Relations* (New York: Random House, 1962), p. 6.
2. Hans J. Morgenthau, *Politics Among Nations: The Struggle for Power and Peace* (New York: Knopf, 1973). The first edition was published in 1948. For a more recent and extremely useful study of the concept of power, see John M. Rothgeb, Jr., *Defining Power: Influence and Force in the Contemporary International System* (New York: St. Martin's Press, 1993).
3. Morgenthau, p. 28.
4. Ibid., p. 5.
5. Ibid., p. 29.
6. Ibid.
7. Ray S. Cline, *World Power Trends and U.S. Foreign Policy for the 1980s* (Boulder, CO.: Westview, 1980).
8. Ibid., p. 13.
9. Bruce Russet, *International Regions and the International System* (Chicago Rand McNally, 1967); Harvey Starr, *War Coalitions* (Lexington, MA.: D.C. Health, 1973); and Rudolph Rummell, "Indicators of Cross-National and International Patterns," *American Political Science Review*, Vol. 68 (March 1969): 127–147.
10. See Cline, *World Power Trends*, p. 143.
11. Ibid.
12. William P. Bundy, "Elements of National Power," *Foreign Affairs*, Vol. 56 (October 1977): 1–26.

CHAPTER 17

Economic Parameters of Power

- How does economics contribute to power?
- Why is there a new awareness of economics as a parameter of power?
- Why is international trade so important?
- How do exchange rates work?
- Why is international finance so important?
- How has the international economic system evolved?

Few people would disagree with the observation that economic strength is a vital constituent of power. Economic strength allows those who have it, whether they be individuals, corporations, states, organizations, or any other type of international actor, to purchase goods and services, to influence decisions and outlooks of others, to produce many or most of one's own needs, and to maintain control of much of one's own future.

None of this argues that international actors necessarily must have extensive economic strength to be powerful. Indeed not, for as we have seen, a variety of different parameters can provide power to an actor. But at the same time, economic strength is often one of the most significant constituents of power.

Perhaps surprisingly, this fundamental reality was overlooked for much of the post–World War II era, at least at the state level. Although economics was never ignored as an input to power, it was frequently relegated to a second-order or even third-order priority.

There were at least three reasons for this. First, World War II and the bipolar international system that emerged from it placed a primacy on military capabilities. Economic capabilities usually were and are required before military capabilities can be obtained, but given the emphasis on military capabilities that accompanied the bipolar international system, it was perhaps unavoidable that economic parameters took a backseat to military concerns.

Second, the end of World War II ushered in a new age, the nuclear era, in which many people wrongfully concluded that old truths no longer applied. Even in the military arena, many analysts at first concluded that nuclear weapons made conventional arms obsolete. So, too, many analysts somehow concluded that in the nuclear era, economic parameters of power would be less important than before.

Third, at the end of World War II, the United States enjoyed unchallenged global economic superiority. As the only major country whose industrial base had not been ravaged by the war, the United States and its dollar reigned economically supreme. Little wonder, then, that few Americans or their Western allies felt an urgency about international economics once European and Japanese reconstruction began. Peoples and governments in the Second and Developing Worlds had different views about the level of urgency of economic issues, but even there, many had been persuaded that military parameters of power now reigned supreme. Thus, economics became the stuff of low politics, a significant but not dominant input to international power equations.

THE REEMERGENCE OF ECONOMICS: PRESENT AND PAST

However, as time passed, national governments in the West began to reassess the lower priority they had placed on economics. Governments in the Second and Developing Worlds did the same. Indeed, by the 1990s, economics had reemerged as a first-order priority for most international actors.[1] What led to this fundamental reassessment, to the reemergence of economics as a first-order parameter of power? Four closely related factors played a role.

First, the United States no longer dominated the global economy. During most of the 1950s and 1960s, the United States had been the world's only economic superpower. However, as the 1960s ended and the 1970s wore on, chronic American balance of payment and balance of trade deficits led many observers throughout the world to conclude that the United States had entered a period of economic decline even though American military capabilities remained strong. As the U.S. national debt mounted during the 1980s and U.S. payment and trade deficits continued, it became evident that the era of American global economic dominance was over.

Second, even as American economic dominance declined in the 1960s, 1970s, and 1980s, other economies gathered strength. The economies of Western Europe and Japan surged ahead, and despite a variety of domestic problems, China also experienced sizable economic expansion during the 1980s. Similarly, a host of smaller countries on the Pacific rim, the so-called "newly industrialized countries" (NICs), including South Korea, Taiwan, Singapore, and other states, enjoyed impressive growth during the 1980s. By the opening of the 1990s, the center of the world's economic activity had moved from the Atlantic to the Pacific basin.

Third, the collapse of the Soviet Union also helped make it evident that economic strength remained a vital constituent of national power. Extensive Soviet emphasis on military strength to the detriment of economic strength had taken its toll. The Soviet government under Mikhail Gorbachev attempted to reverse the U.S.S.R.'s economic decline with extensive domestic reforms, but made little progress. Indeed, the Gorbachev reforms may even have accelerated the Soviet Union's economic collapse.

The fourth source of the international community's new awareness of the importance of economic strength was the emergence during the 1970s and 1980s of oil-rich states to positions of international prominence. Oil-derived economic wealth flowed into Saudi Arabia, Iran, Iraq, Libya, Algeria, and elsewhere. Although some states squandered their wealth on wars or ill-conceived development projects, others used their new wealth wisely. Even the downturn in the world's oil market in the middle and late 1980s did not erode significantly the positions of prominence that many oil-rich states found in the international community. Indeed, the extensive world-wide opposition to Iraq's 1990 takeover of Kuwait was the result not only of the blatant nature of Iraq's aggression, but also the concern that Iraq, in control of large reserves of oil and with a military that it clearly could and would use to assert its will, might try to dictate world oil prices. Thus, by the 1990s, there was no doubt that economics played a major role in determining national power.

As stated above, this relationship between economic strength and power was an old reality newly discovered. Mercantilist theorists of the fifteenth through eighteenth centuries believed that a country's strength depended directly on how much gold and silver it had; this was the theory of **mercantilism**. Consequently, during the mercantilist era, states placed strict controls on the movement of gold and silver and on transactions in exchange markets, intervened in trading structures to attempt to develop favorable balances of trade, subsidized exploration in the hope of adding to national wealth, established tariffs and quotas, and prohibited some types of trade.

During the early nineteenth century, the European balance of power and Great Britain's control of the seas allowed Great Britain to establish an international economic system centered on Britain, based on **free trade,** that is, the ability to engage in commerce wherever one wanted without restrictions or taxes. Britain slowly reduced its **tariffs** (taxes on imports) as it developed an exchange system of domestic manufacturing for overseas raw materials. London became the world's banking and financial center so that the exchange system could be effectively and efficiently funded and overseen.

However, as the second wave of empire swept the world during the late nineteenth century, free trade was abandoned. Colonial empires were again integrated into the economic systems of the various metropoles, as during the mercantilist era. Once again, colonies existed to improve the economy and enhance the power of the ruling state.

The strains of World Wars I and II undermined and then destroyed the old colonial empires. And as we have seen, a bipolar international system based on the primacy of military capabilities, the nuclear stalemate, and the economic dominance of the two superpowers in their respective blocs emerged after World War II. Therefore, economic issues became a lower-level priority.

Even so, policy-makers of the day recognized that the collapse of the international economic system prior to World War II had played a major role in beginning the war. They could not allow that to happen again. Consequently, even though economic concerns were perceived as less urgent than military ones, the construction of a stable and productive international economic system became one of the most important agenda items for the allies even before World War II drew to a close.

However, before one can understand the postwar economic system or the evolution of that system to what it is today, it is first necessary to provide the theoretical perspectives on which that system is based. We turn to that now.

THEORETICAL PERSPECTIVES

International actors become involved in the international economic system because they believe they benefit from doing so. How actors engage the system can best be approached at five different levels.

The first level is the internal economic strength of an actor. Industrial base, skills and training, internally available resources, access to external resources, accumulated wealth, organization, strategy, and leadership must all be considered here. To an extent, internal economic capabilities determine the roles that international actors play in international affairs. This level is crucial for understanding how an actor's own economic capabilities and constraints influence its mesh with the international economic system.

The second, third, and fourth levels are the stuff of traditional international economics: international trade, monetary policy, and finance policy. All are key elements in actors' attempts to supplement their internal economic capabilities. International trade allows actors to acquire that which they do not have, or to acquire more cheaply that which they do have. Thus, astute traders can use trade to enhance their power. International monetary policy is the mechanism that allows trade to take place. It too can add to an actor's strength, if used wisely. International finance is the vehicle that generates investment and capital accumulation in one or another actor. International finance is also a critical component of economic strength.

The fifth level consists of the major subsystems of international trade. It includes the following: (1) trade within the First World; (2) trade between the First World and the Developing World; and (3) trade within the Developing World. Before the collapse of communism in the Soviet Union and Eastern Europe, First World–Second World trade, Second World–Second World trade, and Second World–Third World trade were also important international trading subsystems. However, with the collapse of communist governments in the U.S.S.R. and Eastern Europe, these trading subsystems disappeared.

Domestic Economies and International Economics

Economic capabilities of international actors are a major factor in determining how powerful an actor is in international affairs. A single individual with limited economic resources cannot hope to build effective modern weapons systems, and economically underdeveloped states cannot hope to have political clout equivalent to IBM. The United Nations, aided in part by virtue of its $1 billion budget, dwarfs all other IGOs in its international operations. Internal economic realities of international actors do influence an actor's international role.

Yet given the relational and contextual nature of power, one must be careful not to overemphasize the role of economics in international affairs. A single terrorist armed with a $30 weapon nearly assassinated Pope John Paul II in 1982. Another lightly armed would-be assassin attacked Ronald Reagan the same year. Had either been successful, the course of international affairs may have been altered almost as assuredly as if a new world power had arisen.

The combination of an actor's economic capabilities and the political out-looks of its decision-making elite determine to what extent and in what ways an actor will involve itself in the international economy. Some actors have greater need than others to involve themselves in international economic transactions. Some need resources, others need markets, and still others seek to provide their populations with products not produced domestically or produced less expensively externally. For example, Europe and Japan have little choice but to seek external sources of resources. They also need external markets for their products. On the other hand, with its great domestic resource base and emphasis on heavy industry for internal use, the U.S.S.R. for much of its history minimized its inter-action with the international economic community. However, viewpoints of the Soviet elite changed, and by the late 1980s the U.S.S.R. actively sought interna-tional trade, exporting sizable quantities of raw materials and importing Western technical know-how and capital.

In the industrialized West, with its emphasis on free enterprise and market economics, domestic and international economic questions often combine to cre-ate volatile political issues. For example, as Japanese and European automobile manufacturers acquired a larger and larger market share of U.S. automotive sales in the 1980s, sales of U.S.-made cars plummeted. U.S. automobile manufacturers and U.S. auto workers unions joined forces and demanded protection from for-eign imports. The same chain of events occurred in textile, electronics, steel, and other industries. By the end of the 1980s, the U.S. Congress had introduced sev-eral bills calling for quotas, domestic content (the requirement that finished products have a certain percentage of their total value produced domestically), and other retaliatory and protectionist measures designed to protect American industries and jobs.

Similarly, many U.S. citizens are also concerned that the creation of a North American Free Trade Area (NAFTA) will lead to a flow of jobs out of the United States into Mexico where labor costs are lower. They consequently oppose NAFTA.

Concerns about the interrelationships between domestic and international economic questions are not unique to the United States. Indeed, one of the most urgent fears of the international trading community is that states would bow to protectionist pressure and restrict free trade. Domestic political criteria are thus mixed with economic criteria as decision-makers formulate their policy on the desired interrelationship of their internal economy with international markets. Often, economically irrational decisions are politically motivated and politically necessary within an individual actor. Consequently, the political and economic sit-uations within countries and other international actors are crucial elements in understanding the dynamics of international political economy.

Indeed, one of the most volatile political issues facing decision-makers in states and other international actors throughout the 1990s and on into the twenty-first century will be the proper blend between **economic interdepen-dence** and **economic independence**. The political implications of this simply phrased issue are immense, for interdependence, whatever its economic advan-tages, compromises national sovereignty and the ability to make decisions free of externally created constraints. The interdependence/independence issue is cen-tered around the most basic of all questions concerning domestic economies and international economics: Why is trade economically advantageous?

Trade and Trade Theory

During the early nineteenth century, English economist David Ricardo formulated the **law of comparative advantage**. In its simplest form, this law asserts that the distribution of the factors of production (land, labor, capital, and entrepreneurship) are best determined by freely operating economic exchanges. For example, Great Britain should use its land, labor, capital, and entrepreneurial abilities to produce whatever it makes most efficiently (rugby balls?), and Argentina should use its factors of production to produce whatever it makes most efficiently (bolos?). With each country specializing in what it makes most efficiently, more rugby balls and more bolos will be made than if both countries had tried to make both items. When a British need for bolos and an Argentine need for rugby balls developed, the two countries would trade bolos for rugby balls, and everyone would have more of both.[2]

The law of comparative advantage requires several preconditions before it operates well. First, both supply and demand must exist. If Britain never develops a need for bolos, British-Argentine trade will not occur even if Argentina needs rugby balls. Second, products must be able to move across borders freely without economic barriers such as tariffs and import taxes or nontariff barriers such as quotas and discriminating environmental protection measures. Such barriers artificially raise the price of products and reduce or eliminate the advantages of trade. Third, competitive markets and reasonable transportation costs must exist. The intrusion of monopolies and oligopolies into international trade distorts the free trading system, and high transportation costs reduce the incentive to trade.

International trade has improved living standards in many countries around the world. In addition to the jobs that exports create, international trade also provides work for many people in the shipping industry in ports like Hamburg, shown here.   (Magnum.)

Advocates of free trade point out that free trade would allow the standard of living in involved countries to improve since all would buy their goods wherever they were produced most inexpensively, and produce the goods that they could make most efficiently. Opponents of free trade point out that all the preconditions needed for perfect free trade do not exist, and that the advantages allegedly derived from free trade are therefore a theoretical nicety at best. Free trade opponents further posit that the concept leads to excessive and extreme dependence on external sources for too many products. Trade, they argue, can be used as a weapon, and in extreme cases, extreme dependence on external products in key areas could adversely affect national security and national survival. Opponents of free trade sometimes conclude that no state can allow itself to become dependent on others for vital needs if it wishes to protect its own security and control its own decisions.

Free trade opponents also point out that an influx of cheap products from overseas can undercut the price of locally manufactured products, thereby reducing demand and leading to unemployment. In developed countries where labor unions are strong, labor often acts as an anti-free trade spokesman. Labor fears that in the event of an open economy without trade restrictions, multinational corporations will relocate to less developed countries to take advantage of cheaper nonunion labor costs. "Job flight" is thus viewed as a cost of free trade, at least by labor.

Conversely, in Developing World states, governments themselves often oppose free trade, arguing that infant industries in their states must be protected from predatory trade of more efficient industries in already industrialized states. From the Developing World's perspective, this is both a political and an economic argument. It is political in the sense that Developing World states seek to escape the lingering vestiges of colonialist and neocolonialist dependence on the industrialized West, and it is economic in the sense that Developing World states are seeking to allow their own industries time to become efficient producers. By the 1990s, this argument was used less frequently by Developing World states than in the past, but it has not completely disappeared from the international community as a rationale for restricting free trade.

In opposition to these arguments, free traders accept the arguments that inefficient industries are driven out of business by free trade and that dependence on external actors increases in a free trade regime, but posit that both are advantages rather than disadvantages. Supporters of free trade suggest that governments should step in with labor retraining programs and unemployment compensation for those workers who lose their jobs because of foreign competition. They also argue, as do managers of multinational corporations, that mutual dependence leads to interdependence, and that interdependence leads to peace, thereby reducing national security concerns. The rationale that interdependence leads to peace flows directly from the belief that as countries rely more and more on external sources to fulfill their needs, they will be less and less likely to undertake actions that would jeopardize their access to those sources of need fulfillment.

But what happens if a country continually buys more from overseas than it sells overseas? Obviously, to pay for its imports, it must transfer some of its own wealth to the country from which it imported goods, or borrow money to purchase its imports. This situation is called a chronic balance of trade deficit, and it is the situation the United States has been in for most of the 1970s, 1980s, and 1990s.

Balances of trade are different from balances of payment. Whereas a country's **balance of trade** is the receipts garnered from its exports minus the cost of its imports, a country's **balance of payments** is the total exchange of currencies that one country has with others. It includes receipts and payments for trade, tourism, travel, transportation, military expenses, foreign aid, emergency relief, capital transactions, stock and bond transfers, and savings account movements. The balance of payments is much more inclusive than the balance of trade.

If one country over time builds up a large balance of payments deficit, it gradually drains its wealth. This too has been the United States' situation in recent years. Conversely, when a country has a balance of payments surplus, it adds to its wealth. In a simplistic sense, chronic balance of payment deficits can thus lead to a decline in national power, whereas chronic balance of payment surpluses can add to national power.

International actors may or may not become international traders for the specific purpose of enhancing their power. But when all is said and done, at the end of a trading transaction, all trading partners should have more than they could have produced on their own, at least if they traded rationally and intelligently. Thus, international actors who trade wisely have the potential to increase mutually both their wealth and their power, even if the intention of trade has nothing to do with power.

International Monetary Policy

International trade is rarely undertaken on a barter basis. Rather, countries use their own currencies, or widely accepted currencies of other countries, to buy the goods that they wish to import from foreign sources. Consequently, a standard must be established to determine the rates of exchange between currencies of different countries. This standard is the exchange rate.

The exchange rate is either "floating" or "fixed." **Floating exchange rates** exist when governments allow the market forces of supply and demand to determine the relative price of national currencies. Most exchange rates today are floating. Table 17–1 illustrates how exchange rates have changed over time against the U.S. dollar.

By comparison, **fixed exchange rates** result when two or more governments agree to set the price of their currencies in relation to each other. For

TABLE 17–1   Exchange Rates of Several Selected Currencies Against the Dollar

Country	1950	1960	1970	1980	1990
France (franc)	.29	.20	.18	.24	.18
Germany (mark)	.20	.25	.27	.55	.63
Great Britain (pound)	2.80	2.80	2.40	2.32	1.76
Japan (yen)	—	—	.003	.004	.007
Mexico (peso)	.12	.08	.08	.04	.0004

SOURCE: 1950–1980—United Nations, *1980 Yearbook of International Trade Statistics* (New York: United Nations, 1981), pp. 1076–1079. 1990—American Express.

example, during the 1950s, the U.S. and German governments agreed that one dollar equaled five marks, and during the 1960s, they agreed that one dollar equaled four marks.

The value of a country's exports and imports is thus determined not only by the direction and volume of a country's trade, but also by the exchange rate. For example, in 1960, a bottle of German beer that sold for 4 marks in Germany, if exported to the United States, would have sold for about one dollar in the U.S. In 1990, that same bottle of beer still may have sold for 4 marks in Germany, but because of the changed dollar–mark exchange rate, between 1960 and 1990, it would have sold for about $2.52 in the United States! Germany would have exported one bottle of beer to the United States in 1960 and in 1990, but in 1990, Germany (or more accurately, the German company that exported the bottle of beer) would have received $1.52 more for the bottle of beer!

In theory, floating exchange rates over time make sure that a country's balance of payments balance out. How a floating exchange rate achieves this is simple. When citizens of country A want to purchase goods or services from country B, they must first buy the currency of country B. If citizens of country A want to purchase more goods and services from country B than citizens of country B want to purchase from A, then the demand for country B's currency will be greater than the demand for country A's. The price for country B's currency will therefore go up, in turn making the price for its goods and services higher for people in country A who want to purchase them. The higher prices for country B's goods and services should therefore reduce demand for them in country A. Over time, this mechanism of a floating exchange rate should bring the value of a country's externally purchased goods and services more or less in line with the value of those it sells to foreigners.

Unfortunately, things do not always go as smoothly in reality as in theory. Four problems complicate the operation of floating exchange rates. First, floating exchange rates can take a long time to correct trade and payments imbalances. Thus, a country can develop chronic balance of trade and balance of payments deficits, sliding deeper and deeper into debt as it transfers its wealth overseas to pay for its imports.

Second, for floating exchange rates to work effectively, impediments to free trade and free movement of exchange rates must be removed. Despite progress in that regard, tariffs, quotas, and noneconomic barriers to free trade and free movement of exchange rates continue to exist.

Third, floating exchange rates encourage currency speculation. Speculators buy foreign currency when it is cheap, and sell it when it is expensive. This skews the exchange rate beyond what the balances of trade and payments imply it should be.

Fourth, because of uncertainties associated with a floating exchange rate, a floating exchange rate usually discourages investment between countries. As we will see in the next section, this slows and may even stop economic growth.

Because of the problems associated with floating exchange rates, governments devised fixed exchange rates, as defined above. Fixed exchange rates ended speculation in currencies and accelerated international investment because of the certainty they introduced to international exchange markets. But like floating exchange rates, they could not cope effectively with chronic balance of trade and payments deficits.

Indeed, fixed exchange rates accentuated the problem of chronic balance of payments deficits. Under a fixed exchange rate, countries that have chronic balance of payments deficits eventually run out of foreign currencies to pay their debt, whereas under a floating exchange rate system, the value of the currency of the country in debt theoretically continues to go down until the growth of debt stops.

Another method that states use to settle their foreign debts is **Special Drawing Rights** (SDRs), created by the International Monetary Fund (IMF) in 1968. The value of an SDR is based on the average value of several currencies of Western industrial states. When countries experience large unwanted declines in the value of their currency in floating exchange markets, they can borrow SDRs from the IMF to help shore up the value of their currencies. SDRs are not really money and cannot be used for purchases. Rather, they are bridging mechanisms that allow countries to overcome short-term runs on their currency.[5]

International Finance

Closely related to international trade and monetary policy is international finance. International finance is the movement of money among countries for the purpose of investment, trade, and capital accumulation.

During the 1970s and 1980s, more and more barriers collapsed in the international community to the mobility of capital and other wealth. Moreover, electronic banking and other technological advances enabled investors to transfer funds around the world in seconds instead of days. Indeed, by the beginning of the 1990s, much of the world had become a single integrated financial market.

To attract this newly mobile capital, those who need funds—usually businesses and countries—issue bonds, stocks, and other financial instruments. Investors keep a close watch on which stocks, bonds, and other financial instruments offer the best rates of return, then move their money to where the best rates are. With the speed that electronic banking and other technologies afford, international finance has become a highly volatile undertaking. (Here, it should be pointed out that rate of return on investment is not the only variable investors consider. They also look for factors such as political stability, future opportunity, tax structure, and related items.)

The implications of the real-time integration of a global financial market are extensive. Rises and falls in a major stock market can trigger rises and falls in stock markets half a world away almost instantaneously. Increases in interest rates in one country could attract investors overnight, while decreases in interest rates could send them scurrying around the globe to find better rates of return elsewhere. Quarterly economic reports by major Western industrial countries in turn cause interest rates and exchange rates to rise and fall, sometimes with investors themselves not knowing what specifically led to the increases and decreases.

International mobility of capital is not a new phenomenon, but what is new is the magnitude and speed of its mobility. The United States is a key player in this drama. As the United States moved from creditor nation to debtor nation status in 1985 (for the first time since 1917), foreign investment flowed into the United States, buying up both debt and real property. By 1988, non-Americans held 16 percent of the $1.7 trillion in bonds and other securities sold by the U.S.

government to finance the national debt. At the same time, foreigners owned $1.6 trillion in real property in the United States. Obviously, the movement of foreign capital into the United States was a critical factor in maintaining U.S. economic prosperity in the 1980s.

But as the 1990s opened, the U.S. economy slowed and interest rates went down in the United States, making the United States a less attractive place for non-Americans to invest their money. At the same time, again because of the slowdown in the U.S. economy, fewer foreign firms wanted to buy U.S. businesses. As a result, the flow of non-American capital into the United States slowed down, thereby worsening the United States' economic problems.

The Japanese role in international finance during the 1980s and 1990s is particularly instructive. Enjoying a booming economy, Japan between 1985 and 1990 exported an incredible $596 billion in long-term investment capital throughout the world. Between 1988 and 1990, Japanese sources invested an average of about $17 billion per year in the United States alone. But in 1991, as Figure 17–1 shows, Japan, driven by a combination of lower overseas interest rates, the slowdown in the global economy, and the growth of economic problems in Japan, moved from being a net exporter of capital to being a net importer of capital. Much of the capital moving to Japan in 1991 and 1992 was capital that Japan exported during the 1980s.

The worldwide impact of this changed direction in the flow of Japanese capital investment was immense. With investment moving into Japan rather than out of it, there was less money for investment in the United States, Europe, Asia, and elsewhere. For example, after averaging $17 billion per year investment in the United States for each of the three preceeding years, in 1991 Japanese sources invested only about $3 billion in the United States. And by 1992, Japanese investors, who had as recently as 1990 been the largest purchasers of securities sold by the U.S. government to finance the U.S. national debt, became net sellers of U.S. government securities.[4]

Meanwhile, in the late 1980s and early 1990s, U.S. capital also moved out of the United States as some individuals and industries found better investment opportunities elsewhere. By 1988, U.S. holdings in other countries totaled $1.2 trillion, and they continued to rise in subsequent years. U.S. overseas investment by 1993 was less than foreign investment in the United States, but neither U.S. investment overseas nor foreign investment in the United States came to an inconsequential sum.

Nevertheless, the key point here is that by the 1990s, the international financial market was more open than ever before. Individuals, corporations, and governments all took advantage of this to find the best opportunities for their investments in a global financial marketplace.

This international mobility of capital is both a blessing and a curse. It is a blessing because investors can move their money rapidly to the best opportunities available to them. Theoretically, this should accelerate growth. But at the same time, it is a curse. Easy, rapid mobility of funds can lead to extremely volatile financial markets that rise and fall precipitously on little more than rumor and momentary perception. Over time, such volatility could actually lead to a growth of investor fear and reduction in the rate of global economic growth.

But how does international finance affect power? The answer to this question is both straightforward and exceedingly complex. Clearly, countries, corpora-

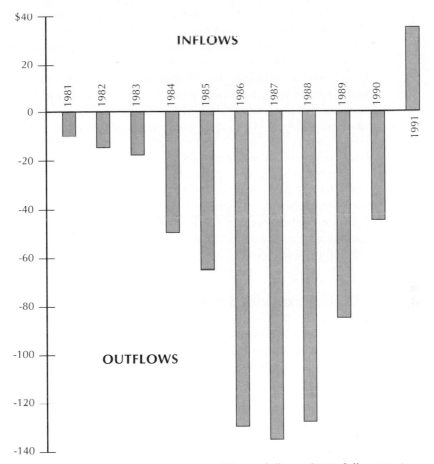

FIGURE 17–1 Japan's long-term capital flow, in billions of U.S. dollars. Figures reflect the purchase of real estate, stocks and bonds, company investments, building, and long-term lending. (SOURCE: Bank of Japan. From *The New York Times*, March 22, 1992.)

tions, individuals, and other organizations that have sizable financial assets have an ability to influence decisions. This does not mean that decisions are made in any arena for exclusively economic reasons, but it does imply that all other factors being equal, those with greater financial assets involved in a decision will often have a greater degree of influence on that decision. Power results.

At the same time, access to financial assets, not just ownership of assets, can enable international actors to enhance their power, at least for a period of time. For example, much of the U.S. military buildup of the 1980s was financed by deficit spending. The debt accumulated by this deficit spending was substantially bought up by Japanese investors. In a simplistic sense, American access to Japanese financial assets made the American military buildup possible. At the same time, Japanese investment in U.S. firms strengthened the U.S. economy and kept U.S. workers employed. The tradeoffs, of course, are that borrowed Japanese capital will have to be repaid, and business decisions affecting certain U.S. firms will be made outside the United States.

Similar issues affect North–South financial relations. Because many Developing World states owe much money to Western banks and other financial institutions, Western states and banks sometimes find themselves in the position of recommending and even dictating policy to Developing World states. Conversely, some Developing World states owe so much money that if they were to default or suspend payment on their debts, significant segments of the international financial community would be shaken. Of course, such actions on the part of any Developing World state would virtually guarantee that it not receive loans in the future. Thus, it is in the interests of international lending institutions and borrowing states to find ways that debts can be paid.

International finance, then, is tied directly to issues of power and influence, but often the tie is more complex than it appears. This is true at the individual, corporate, national, and organizational level. As the 1990s progress, the impact of real-time global mobility of financial assets on the international system will undoubtedly grow and become an even more critical component of contemporary international affairs.

The Three Global Economic Subsystems

To complicate matters even more, most analysts of contemporary international economics recognize three global economic subsystems.[5] The first subsystem functions among developed Western industrial states. It is the most important economic subsystem in terms of total trade. The United States, Western Europe, and Japan are willing members, whereas Developing World states are peripherally associated. The degree to which Developing World states belong to this first subsystem is a function of both economic relationships and perceptions, and is discussed later in this chapter.

The second economic subsystem functions between the industrialized West and most of the Developing World. In the first subsystem, the dilemma is whether mechanisms can be created to manage mutually beneficial economic relations. In the second subsystem, the dilemma is whether mechanisms can be formed to *create* mutually beneficial economic relations.

Western industrial states perceive a common advantage in preserving the current system. Developing World states see no such advantage in preserving the current North–South economic relationship, and therefore actively strive for the creation of a New International Economic Order (NIEO). From the Western industrialized states' perspective, Developing World states and Western states participate in a single international trading system on the same basis, with equal access provided to all economic institutions on the basis of wealth and capability. From the Developing World's perspective, developing states enter international trade in a clearly subservient position and therefore are not part of a Western system, but rather are unwilling partners in a separate subsystem, that of North–South economic relations.

Three major schools of thought exist concerning North–South trade and monetary relations.[6] The first school, the **liberal school**, sees trade as a tool for growth. Trade leads to specialization, which, under the theory of comparative advantage, improves a state's economic position. An improved economic position in turn leads to savings, which can be translated into investment. Investment leads in turn to further economic growth. Foreign trade and foreign investment, in the liberals' view, accelerate economic growth.

The second school is the **Marxist trade school**, which received a serious setback as a result of the collapse of communism in Eastern Europe and the Soviet Union, but which is still influential in some quarters in the West and in the Developing World. Marxism asserts that the superior economic position of industrialized Western powers allows them to determine international trade patterns and rates of exchange. Marxists maintain that prices for raw materials from developing countries are artificially deflated by Western market-economy countries and that prices for finished goods produced in industrialized countries are artificially inflated. Thus, through its international trade and exchange system, the West exploits the Developing World economically even though political independence has been achieved by the Developing World. Further, foreign investment adds to local unemployment by introducing capital-intensive productive means and actually leads to a new flow of wealth from South to North as profits are repatriated. Foreign aid is similarly exploitive because "strings" are often attached to it, thereby perpetuating Developing World dependence on the West.

The third school of thought is the **structuralist trade school**. It argues that, as in Marxist analysis, the international trade and exchange system perpetuates the South's backwardness and dependence on the West. Gunnar Myrdal was a leading structuralist who posited that the market tends to favor "have" states more than "have not" states. Therefore, according to Myrdal, the gap between rich and poor tends to increase so that even in the best of all worlds, the lot of the poor improves only marginally.[7]

Structuralists further observe that although foreign investment and trade help Developing World states improve their economic status, only a small sector of a developing country's economy is aided, the export sector. Therefore, in Developing World states, investment and trade create a dual economy, one part of which is relatively developed, the export sector, and the other of which is underdeveloped. Indeed, according to structuralists, the advanced export sector takes investment moneys away from the underdeveloped sector, thereby rendering the underdeveloped sector even more backward.

The debate over North–South trade and exchange relations has been long and heated. Where one comes to rest is a product of perspective and ideology. Extreme proponents of the Western subsystem of trade and exchange deny that a North–South subsystem even exists. Extreme opponents of the Western subsystem theorize that not only does a North–South subsystem exist, but that it was designed and is run by the industrialized Western states with the specific intention of exploiting the Developing World.

The third major global economic subsystem exists between Developing World states. In comparison to the first two subsystems, it is relatively minor in terms of total trade turnover. Indeed, some analysts even argue that it is so small that it should not be considered an economic subsystem, but be appended to one of the larger subsystems.

Nevertheless, the fact remains that although trade between Developing World states is relatively small, the nature of trade between Developing World states is often significantly different than the trade that takes place within either of the two larger economic subsystems. Often, it is trade in natural resources, raw materials, handmade products, or unfinished products in both directions.

Frequently, it is undertaken on a barter basis. And often, despite its relatively small value in relation to the trade that takes place in the other subsystems, it is extremely important in economic terms to the states that are involved.

INTERNATIONAL ECONOMIC POLICY SINCE WORLD WAR II

Internal economic strength; international trade, monetary, and financial policy; and the place in which an international actor fits within the three major subsystems of international economic relations are all important factors that affect an actor's power. How well an international economic system is crafted can also influence whether economic growth or stagnation will occur, and can play a role in establishing political stability or unrest. Realizing this, and at the same time understanding the complexities of international economics, the leaders of the Western Alliance following World War II made the construction of a productive and stable international economic system one of the most important items on their agenda. Thus, even before World War II was over, representatives from 44 nations met in July 1944 at Bretton Woods, New Hampshire, to try to construct such a system. By December 1945, most states at the conference accepted the conference's plans for the postwar international economic system. For the next 26 years, the international economic system of the noncommunist world was based on the plans developed at Bretton Woods.

The Bretton Woods System: IBRD, IMF, and GATT

The Bretton Woods negotiations established two international governmental organizations, the **International Bank for Reconstruction and Development** (IBRD, also known as the World Bank) and the **International Monetary Fund** (IMF), to undertake central banking functions for the management of international monetary policy.[8] The **General Agreement on Tariffs and Trade** (GATT) was not specifically a part of the Bretton Woods negotiations. Rather, GATT evolved from the wreckage of the International Trade Organization (ITO), a body proposed by the United States to negotiate tariff reductions in an effort to create a free trade regime. GATT, unlike IBRD and IMF, was designed as a temporary measure until the ITO began functioning. By default, GATT became as permanent as the World Bank and the IMF.

Bretton Woods provided for an international financial structure based on fixed exchange rates. Most delegates to the conference were convinced that the system of floating exchange rates that existed between World Wars I and II contributed directly to the collapse of the international economic system during the 1930s and the growth of economic nationalism that, in part, led to World War II. At Bretton Woods, stability was a chief objective.

Under the Bretton Woods system of fixed exchange rates, all countries agreed to establish the value of their currencies in terms of gold and to maintain that exchange rate within a plus or minus one-percent range. Signatory states agreed to the convertibility of their currencies into other currencies and accepted in concept free trade. The IMF was to oversee the management of the system. As the world's strongest economic power, the United States received the preponderance of influence within the IMF. The IMF had to approve any changes in exchange rate, and had at its disposal a fund of $8.8 billion of gold and currencies of member countries that it could credit to countries experiencing chronic balance of payments deficits. Although the IMF credits were an innovation in international economics, the Bretton Woods system nevertheless placed primary emphasis on national solutions to monetary problems. Even with IMF credits and rules, it was expected that states over time would reduce imports or expand exports if they had a balance of payments or trade deficit, and increase imports or reduce exports if they had a surplus.

The national representatives at Bretton Woods also recognized that economic recovery was needed before the IMF could operate successfully. Consequently the World Bank was created. IBRD was to make loans from its $10 billion account funded by member states to underwrite private loans and to issue securities to raise new funds so additional loans could be made to speed recovery.

By 1947, however, the Bretton Woods system was near collapse. Europe's balance of payments deficit in 1947 alone amounted to $7.6 billion; the American balance of trade surplus the same year totaled $10.1 billion. IBRD and IMF funds were barely capable of sustaining one year of operation, much less a long-term system. In light of this bleak economic picture, and in light of unstable political situations in Italy and France; Britain's impending withdrawal from India, Palestine, Greece, and Turkey; and the establishment of communist regimes under Soviet domination throughout Eastern Europe, the United States stepped in to rescue the Bretton Woods system.

U.S. Intervention and Domination: 1947–1960

In simplest terms, the international economy's major problem by 1947 was that too many people wanted U.S. goods, and too few dollars were in non-American hands to pay for them. World War II had shattered the economic base of most of the world, the United States excepted, and there were too few foreign products to be imported by the United States. Therefore, U.S. dollars stayed in U.S. hands, and increasing quantities of foreign currencies came into U.S. hands as well. The key question was, "How could more dollars be placed in foreign hands?"

The answer was obvious—the United States deliberately created a balance of payments deficit for itself via foreign aid programs that allowed foreign countries to buy U.S. products with dollars. U.S. aid programs were many and varied—support for Greece and Turkey under the Truman Doctrine, Point Four program aid to underdeveloped countries, and most important, Marshall Plan aid, under which 16 Western European countries received over $17 billion in grants from the United States between 1948 and 1952. U.S. military forces overseas also contributed to the outflow of dollars, both through personnel and base operations costs. Between 1949 and 1959, U.S. gold assets declined from over $24 billion to slightly under $20 billion, and dollars held abroad climbed from $7 billion to over $19 billion.[9]

On the surface, the Bretton Woods system began to operate, but it was an operation based on the strength of the dollar. Indeed, the dollar in a certain sense was better than gold; the dollar earned interest, and gold did not. For all practical purposes, the dollar became the noncommunist world's currency.

Many of the other objectives of Bretton Woods changed as well. The United States encouraged Japanese and European discrimination against the dollar and supported trade protectionism. The U.S. intent in supporting discrimination and protectionism was to revive the Japanese and European economies. Over time, it was expected that Japanese and European recovery would increase demand for U.S. exports. Thus, the United States willingly endured chronic balance of payments deficits. It was rich enough to do so, and it expected long-term benefits. Equally important, Western Europe and Japan accepted and encouraged the U.S. role. In the words of one analyst, the modified Bretton Woods system developed by the United States in the late 1940s and accepted by Europe and Japan had three primary political bases, the concentration of power in a small number of states, a cluster of interests shared by those states, and U.S. willingness to provide leadership.[10] However, by 1960, the system was in trouble.

The Weakening of the System: 1960–1971

International confidence in the dollar provided the base for the international economic system of the 1950s. Confidence was assured because of the United States' vibrant domestic economy, the United States' large gold and currency reserve, the U.S. commitment to convert dollars into gold, and the global reach of U.S. economic and military power. Gradually, however, people began to wonder just how long the United States could absorb such significant balance of payments deficits without eroding the strength of the dollar. As more and more dollars became available outside the United States, the shortage of dollars turned into a glut. In 1948, $7.3 billion were held abroad; by 1959 that figure had climbed to $19.4 billion. More important, the excess of U.S. gold and currency reserve holdings over foreign-held dollars declined from $18.1 billion in 1948 to $.5 billion in 1959. In 1960, for the first time, more dollars were held outside the United States than the United States had gold and currency reserves to cover.

Not surprisingly, Europeans, Japanese, and others who held large quantities of dollars began to convert their dollars into gold. Confidence in the dollar had been shaken. A shared perception of a necessity for cooperation still existed, but the United States could no longer manage the system alone.

Two separate groups took on the task of managing the evolving multilateral international economic structure. Following the dollar crisis of 1960, the United States joined the monthly meetings of European bankers held at the Bank for International Settlements in Basle, Switzerland. The meetings served as forums from which financial crises could be managed. Accession of the U.S. Federal Reserve Bank to this "Basle Group" tremendously increased the group's clout and its ability to manage international monetary crises successfully.

A second self-selected group of industrial countries, the "Group of Ten," created a separate fund of $6 billion to be used to extend loans to the IMF in time of IMF need. The "Group of Ten"—Belgium, France, Germany, Italy, the Netherlands, Sweden, Great Britain, Canada, Japan, and the United States—created this new "General Arrangement to Borrow" specifically to maintain control over the funds in it. From the European perspective, the arrangement was made to keep the new fund free of U.S. control, which predominated in the IMF. To the Developing World, the arrangement was clearly aimed against it.

Meanwhile, the United States actively attempted to reduce its balance of payments deficit. The Kennedy administration implemented an interest equalization program designed to make foreign borrowing in the United States less attractive, and the Johnson administration passed capital restraint legislation on U.S. foreign investments. U.S. foreign aid was tied to the purchase of U.S. products, and the dollar value of duty-free tourist allotments was reduced.

Emphasis was also placed on expansion of U.S. exports. Primarily under U.S. urging, six multilateral trade negotiations were conducted under GATT auspices between 1947 and 1967. The last round of negotiations, the so-called Kennedy Round, sought overall tariff reductions by percentage rather than item-by-item reduction. It also sought to limit discrimination against American exports. By the end of the Kennedy Round in 1967, tariffs on nonagricultural products were cut to 9.9 percent in the United States, 10.7 percent in Japan, and 8.6 percent in the EEC. GATT also used the concept of most-favored-nation (MFN) status. MFN simply means that a state that imports a particular product grants to all countries terms of import that are as favorable as the most favored nation's terms of import. MFN helped reduce tariff barriers considerably.

However, even with these trade devices, the U.S. balance of trade continued to deteriorate. Between 1964 and 1971, with the exception of only one year, the U.S. balance of trade worsened annually, finally becoming a deficit in 1971. This steady deterioration combined with the glut of dollars in the international economy to further weaken the dollar's position.

The dollar weakened because of other reasons as well. In 1968, as a result of the seemingly uncontrollable flow of dollars out of the United States, the United States announced that it no longer would support gold at $35 an ounce on the free market. Gold would be allowed to rise to find its own value. This announcement had two effects. First, to maintain the value of their own currencies, other foreign governments and banks had to absorb dollars that private investors made available. Second, the United States, for all practical purposes, had abandoned the Bretton Woods agreement. Many people feared that the next U.S. step would be devaluation.

Another reason for lower confidence in the dollar was Western European and Japanese economic revitalization. By the 1960s, Western Europe and Japan again had dynamic economies. Both had less need for dollars and U.S. products. Indeed, some Europeans and Japanese viewed the abundance of dollars as an infringement on their sovereignty.

Other causes of the weakened dollar were the U.S. adventure in Vietnam and the improvement in Eastern European–Western European relations during the late 1960s. The Vietnam War led many to question the perceived wisdom of U.S. leadership, and better East–West relations lessened the need for the U.S. military arsenal. Rightly or wrongly, many Europeans believed that U.S. leadership had outlived its usefulness, and this outlook had direct impact on foreign willingness to hold dollars. U.S. accusations that Germany and Japan in particular undervalued their currencies, thereby leading to increased U.S. consumer demand for German and Japanese products, were rejected as unfounded in those countries. It was apparent to everyone that the international monetary and trade system, despite multilateral management under U.S. predominance, was in serious straits. During the spring and summer of 1971, another run on the dollar occurred, and action became inevitable.

Shock: NEP and OPEC

Faced with a seemingly uncontrollable outflow of dollars into the international economy and an equally uncontrollable inflation domestically, the U.S. government resorted to unilateral action in August 1971 by suspending the dollar's convertibility to gold and levying a 10 percent surcharge on all dutiable imports to the United States. Domestically, the Nixon government instituted a wage-and-price freeze as part of its so-called **New Economic Policy** (NEP). Bretton Woods had been abandoned by the United States.

Nixon's NEP devalued the dollar in relation to both gold and other currencies. A Group of Ten meeting at the Smithsonian Institution in Washington in 1971 hammered out temporary guidelines for a revised Bretton Woods system that included realignment of exchange rates relative to gold (and also to each other), and acceptance of a floating parity rate of plus or minus 2.25 percent. The Smithsonian Agreement failed on at least two counts. First, the role of the dollar within the international economic system was not solved, and the dollar therefore remained inconvertible against gold. Second, American leadership in the international economic system was no longer acceptable to the Europeans, nor was it wanted by the United States. Within 15 months, the Smithsonian Agreement had unraveled, and every major currency floated against gold.

During 1972, attempted reforms of the international monetary system were frustrated by global double-digit inflation and the collapse of the international system of monetary management. Hopes of reinstituting some form of management received another major setback on October 16, 1973, when members of the **Organization of Petroleum Exporting Countries** (OPEC) unsheathed the oil weapon and initiated an international flow of currencies beyond control. By instituting production cutbacks, embargoing oil shipments to the United States and Holland, and quadrupling the price of oil from about $2.50 per barrel in early 1973 to $11.65 per barrel in 1974, OPEC states signaled the world that they were a force to be reckoned with in international monetary matters. In 1974 alone, over $70 billion flowed from the industrial world to OPEC.

The flow of dollars—now called "petrodollars"—to OPEC created new problems for the seriously troubled international monetary system. Developing World countries were particularly hard hit by the increased price of oil. With their oil imports costing more and their few exports not selling well, these countries found it increasingly difficult to get loans to finance development and oil imports. As a result, their economies suffered even more than did the economies of industrialized countries. The dollar played a central role in the continuing drama as the United States, to finance its own oil purchases, pumped still more dollars into the hands of OPEC. For those non-Americans who held dollars, this proved both a bane and a blessing. On the one hand, the continued outflow of dollars from the United States further depressed each dollar's value; more dollars meant less demand for dollars and hence less value. On the other hand, with oil being priced in dollars and usually paid for in dollars, OPEC countries were more than ever tied to the dollar as their base currency. Thus, some degree of stability existed in the unhinged international economic system.

By far the major problem created by the flow of money to OPEC countries was the **recycling problem**. The recycling problem was similar to the problem that confronted the United States and Western Europe immediately after World War II: How does money return to the hands of those who need it to purchase products when insufficient balancing demand exists? During the late 1940s, Western Europe bought U.S. products, but Americans bought little from Europe. Consequently, a massive flow of currency moved from Europe to the United States. During the early 1970s, Europeans, Japanese, and Americans bought OPEC oil, but the flow of dollars to OPEC states was so great that even after they had purchased their imports in return, large quantities of dollars remained in OPEC hands. According to one estimate, OPEC surplus income in 1974 alone totaled $70 billion; for the 1974 to 1979 period $200 billion; and for the 1980s it was estimated to be $500 billion.[11]

As we have seen, the recycling problem was solved during the 1940s by U.S. balance of payments deficits engineered through aid programs such as the Marshall Plan and through maintenance of overseas military bases and presence. Immediately following the 1973 oil shock, a number of methods were developed to address the recycling problem. None proved immensely successful. OPEC states placed sizable percentages of their surpluses in bank deposits, treasury bills, bonds, and loans in the industrialized states, particularly Great Britain and the United States. Private banks in the industrialized states then lent money to Developing World and other needy states to help them finance their oil and other purchases. Increasingly, however, as the deficits of Developing World and other needy states climbed, and as the ability of the borrowing states to repay loans grew more tenuous, private banks hesitated to make loans to high-credit-risk borrowers. In addition, OPEC states distributed their surplus to a special IMF oil fund, to be used by states to help them ride out short-term deficits caused by higher oil prices. The World Bank received development moneys from OPEC states as well. Finally, Arab OPEC states directed grants and loans to Developing World states through an Arab Development Fund. Non-Arab and non-Islamic states complained, however, that they received little support, and in some instances accusations were made that OPEC states through their foreign aid programs meddled in the internal political and economic affairs of recipient countries.

Anarchy and Interdependence: 1974–Present

Since 1974, industrialized and developing states alike have sought to fashion an acceptable international economic order. Depending on whom one talks with and listens to, these efforts have been colossal failures or moderate successes. No one asserts that a solution has been found. Developed industrialized states have concentrated their efforts in the areas of exchange rate management and development of international reserve assets. Developing states have pushed for the creation of a new international economic order that would facilitate the transfer of wealth to Developing World states for developmental purposes and create preferential trade arrangements for products of Developing World states.

As a result of the problems of international trade and finance, and of the collapse of consensus on leadership in the system, little organization exists in today's international economic system. Exchange rates, for the most part, are determined by supply and demand, although an informal agreement does exist in which central banks and governments will intervene to keep exchange rates within broadly defined and imprecise limits. In addition, the currencies of some countries, particularly those in the European Community, remain pegged to one another.

During the 1980s, several major economic issues continued to buffet the international community. The first major problem was the continued large flow of petrodollars to OPEC coffers, at least until oil prices fell precipitously in 1986. This flow of dollars benefited not only the OPEC states but also those industrialized countries that imported relatively little oil or that attracted OPEC moneys to their banking system.[12]

A second major problem resulted from U.S. efforts to cut back inflation during the early 1980s. As the U.S. Federal Reserve system kept interest rates high to decrease borrowing within the United States, foreign investors moved their money to the United States. This drove up the value of the dollar and made U.S. exports more expensive for foreign consumers. U.S. exports thus decreased relative to imports, and the U.S. balance of trade declined precipitously. The negative U.S. balance of trade was also worsened by restrictive trade practices of some industrialized countries, most notably Japan. These changes are shown graphically in Figure 17–2.

Matters were made worse by the huge U.S. budget deficit. Brought about primarily by a significant decrease in the tax structure in the early 1980s, the U.S. budget deficit helped keep U.S. interest rates high, attracted large quantities of capital to the United States as foreign investors bought up the U.S. debt, and kept the price of U.S. exports high.

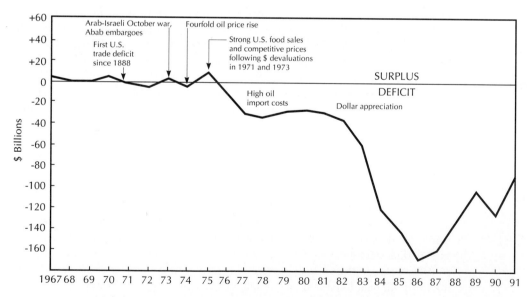

FIGURE 17–2   The U.S. balance of trade, 1967–1991.   (SOURCE: U.S. Department of State, *Atlas of United States Foreign Relations* [Washington: U.S. Government Printing Office, 1985], p. 52. Figures for 1985–1991 are from the U.S. Department of Commerce and the International Monetary Fund, *Direction of Trade Statistics 1992*, p. 402.)

Throughout the 1980s and on into the 1990s, leaders of the Western world met at a series of economic summit meetings held annually to discuss petrodollars, discriminatory trade practices, the excessively strong U.S. dollar and high U.S. interest rates, exchange rates, international debt, and other related international economic problems. Although these economic summits found no solutions, by 1987 the industrialized world's economic problems had eased somewhat. High oil prices, set at over $30 a barrel as recently as 1985, tumbled to less than half that level by early 1986. U.S. interest rates also dropped significantly, as did the value of the dollar. And Japan again promised to reduce restrictions on imports. Nevertheless, throughout the Western world, protectionist sentiment remained high. In the United States, it was particularly strong in the automotive, steel, and textile industries.

East–West and North–South economic issues also were major areas of concern at the economic summits of the leaders of the industrialized West. On East–West issues, the U.S. position throughout the 1980s was that stricter measures had to be taken on East–West trade to reduce the flow of technology, some of which was militarily significant, to the U.S.S.R. European states generally were less concerned about technology transfer to the U.S.S.R., arguing that the flow was not as significant as the United States maintained. As political and economic reform swept through Eastern Europe and the Soviet Union in the late 1980s and early 1990s, differences between the United States and the rest of the industrialized West on East–West trade issues diminished significantly.

The disagreements that existed among Western industrial states during the 1980s were mild by comparison with the discord that existed between the developed and developing worlds. The combination of the oil shocks of 1973 and 1979–1980, the decreased demand for raw material exports, global inflation, and massive debt repayment schedules seriously damaged economic development efforts in most Developing World states throughout the 1980s. Not surprisingly, Developing World states called loudly for a restructuring of the international economic system to help alleviate their problems. Specific demands included debt rescheduling and forgiveness, a new pricing structure for finished products and raw materials, and preferential treatment for their exports. Not surprisingly, faced by their own economic problems, few industrial states responded favorably.

As the 1990s progressed, it became increasingly clear that the international economic system bordered on anarchy. It was highly volatile, with immense possibilities for rapid change of great proportions. At the same time, the worldwide economic slowdown of the early 1990s was accompanied by a shortage of investment capital needed to restructure the former Soviet and Eastern European economies, rebuild the economic infrastructures of the United States and other developed Western states, and help the Developing World cope with the many economic challenges facing it. In virtually every regard, the remaining years of the twentieth century promised to be years of global economic problems.

Finding solutions to the problems of the system is rendered urgent by global economic interdependence. Global economic interdependence means that the economies of almost every state rely on goods, products, raw materials, and information produced in other countries. Without this interdependence, standards of living would decline, and economic dislocation would occur. In some

The Western Heads of State meet in Tokyo, Japan in July 1993 for their annual G-7 Summit Meeting.   (Sygma.)

countries, production would grind to a halt. Admittedly, interdependence means that decisions taken in one country influence events in another, and as a result national sovereignty is challenged. But proponents of interdependence, who are often advocates of free trade, argue that its benefits outweigh its negative effects.

And economic interdependence is a documentable fact of international economic life in the 1990s. High U.S. interest rates (relative to those overseas) in the early 1990s helped keep the price of the U.S. dollar high. This meant lower demand in Europe and Japan for American-made products, and higher demand in the United States for European and Japanese products. This in turn meant fewer Americans in certain industries had jobs, but more Europeans and Japanese in those same industries had jobs. And when an economic downturn occurs simultaneously in Europe, Japan, and the United States, its effects are felt in the Developing World as demand for raw materials and even finished goods produced there goes down.

Yet another indication of global economic interdependence occurred in October 1987 when a 22.6 percent freefall in stock market prices in New York sent stock market prices in London, Tokyo, Hong Kong, Sydney, and elsewhere tumbling as well. The global collapse in stock market prices amply underlined that interdependence is a reality that has disadvantages as well as advantages.

To reiterate, the international economic system of the 1990s is interdependent, volatile, and anarchic. And for the first time since shortly after World War II, economic capabilities are widely recognized as a major parameter of power in the international arena. But that does not mean there is agreement on where the international economic system is headed or should be headed, as the following section makes clear.

VIEWS OF THE INTERNATIONAL ECONOMIC SYSTEM

No doubt exists that economic capabilities contribute to an international actor's power. Yet despite this agreement, little consensus is apparent about the equity of the distribution of power resulting from economic capabilities. We have already examined disagreements between types of actors over this distribution; states fear that their sovereignty has been and is jeopardized by the economic wherewithal and flexibility available to MNCs, whereas MNCs chafe over the economic limitations that states place on them. Other types of actors without sizable economic bases recognize that their power to influence international events has been circumscribed by their economic shortcomings. Questions of economic equity and justice exist as well.

Because in the present international environment states create the economic systems in which all other actors function, we are inevitably driven toward an analysis of views held by states of the relationship between the international economic system and power. We turn to that now.

The Industrialized West

When seen from the perspective of developed Western industrial states, free trade, a predictable system of international monetary exchange, and economic interdependence carry with them a multitude of advantages: increased production because of efficient division of labor, incentive to invest because of a certain and relatively "knowable" future, and the probability of fewer serious political confrontations. Such an international economic system is often referred to as "open" because of the relatively free flow of goods and services that exist in it. Certain disadvantages, such as decreased levels of control in their own economy, potential national security shortfalls, and other challenges to national sovereignty also accrue to the accounts of those states that pursue "open" policies. However, from the perspectives of most industrialized Western states, such costs are small when compared with the benefits that an open system offers.

No country has a completely open economic system. But to most industrialized Western states, openness is an ideal to be striven for, subject to qualifications rendered necessary by demands of national security, domestic politics, and related considerations. As far as developed Western industrial states are concerned, Second World communist states until the late 1980s excluded themselves from the advantages of an **open international economic system** for erroneous ideological reasons, and Developing World states are subject to the same advantages, disadvantages, and whims of the market as any industrialized state.

First World states recognize that their industrial base gives them a powerful instrument with which to pursue their foreign policy objectives both in the economic sphere and beyond, but they also maintain that this is an advantage that any state can achieve if it develops its economic capabilities. Further, developed industrial states allege that an open international economic system provides opportunities, but not necessarily exactly equal opportunities, for other states to develop their economic potentials.

Nevertheless, disagreement does exist between industrialized Western states about the degree of opportunity provided developing states by current international economic relationships and about the equity and justice inherent to the system. For example, the European Community during the early 1980s was particularly anxious to initiate negotiations with Group of 77 states on a range of North–South issues. The United States opposed such talks.

Agreement need not exist within a given First World state about the equity and justice of the international economic system or about particular segments of the system. Domestic U.S. disagreement over the proposed Law of the Seas Treaty provides a good example. The Carter administration devoted extensive time and effort to negotiating what it viewed as an acceptable treaty under the auspices of the United Nations' Conference on the Law of the Seas (UNCLOS). One aspect of the treaty was the establishment of an international authority to govern deep seabed mining rights, including dispensation of profits. After the Reagan administration took office, it asserted that the proposed deep seabed mining regime discriminated against those states (read: the United States) that had the technical know-how to engage in deep seabed mining. In 1982, the Reagan administration rejected the treaty. Obviously, Carter and Reagan disagreed about the level of equity and justice in the treaty despite their both having been chief executive of the same state.

The effect of U.S. opposition to the UNCLOS treaty was devastating. Without U.S. adherence, the treaty meant little. This simple fact illustrated a truth of the current international economic system, a truth that is recognized though seldom admitted publicly in the West—economically powerful states have disproportionate shares of political power. This fact was and is recognized in the composition of the IMF and World Bank, each of which gives additional voting powers to large shareholders.

The economic parameter of power, and the industrialized West's recognition of the utility of this parameter, may be illustrated by U.S. emphasis under the Reagan and Bush administrations on "the magic of the marketplace" as the engine for economic development. Both administrations suggested that the World Bank and other regional development banks not emphasize public sector projects at the expense of private sector projects, and supported use of World Bank and regional bank funds to attract other investment capital. The clear implication was that unless the World Bank and regional banks altered their lending policies and reassessed their lending criteria, U.S. contributions to the various banks would be curtailed. Since the United States is the largest single contributor to the World Bank, such an implied threat carried weight. Thus, U.S. economic power influenced global development strategy.

The Former Second World

With the collapse of the Soviet Union and the rejection of communism by the people of Eastern Europe, most of the major international actors of the Second World of communist states passed into history. So too did much of the international importance of the perspectives on the international economy that they held. Nevertheless, a brief overview of Second World perspectives on the international economy is in order, primarily because of the stark contrast it presented for so long with that of the First World.

Until the Soviet Union began its economic restructuring programs under Gorbachev, most communist states saw the international economic system of the noncommunist world as merely an extension of domestic political economic relations; that is, they believed that the economically advantaged exploited the economically disadvantaged. Although the U.S.S.R. and other communist states accepted that the more odious forms of political colonialism for economic exploitation had ceased, they posited that a more insidious form of economic exploitation, neocolonialism, had replaced the older, more blatant exploitive relationship. Thus, even though the First World no longer politically controlled the Developing World, communist states alleged that the same exploitive result was achieved through Western economic institutions such as the World Bank, the IMF, exchange rate variations, and unjust terms of trade. An "open" economic system was thus a Western excuse to permit Western penetration of underdeveloped economies.

As a result of Gorbachev's reforms, the Soviet Union and Eastern European communist states before their collapse had fundamentally changed their perspective on the Western economic system. All avidly sought investment, managerial expertise, and technical know-how. As more and more Western money, managers, and technology—Japanese, Western European, and American—moved into the Soviet Union and Eastern Europe, the possibility increased that the old Second World International economic system would become fully integrated with and indistinguishable from that of the First World. The collapse of communism in the U.S.S.R. and Eastern Europe further increased the possibility that this would happen.

China deserves separate mention here, even though it does not fit smoothly within a Second World categorization. The P.R.C., with its unique perspective on international affairs, condemned both the Western international economic system and the old Soviet-led system as imperialist and exploitive. Chinese assessments of both systems used standard Marxist-Leninist rhetoric. The West was condemned as being neocolonialist, whereas the U.S.S.R. was charged with social imperialism. Even so, China avidly sought Western investment throughout the 1980s and on into the 1990s in an effort to modernize its economy. To the Chinese, the objective was to attract Western investment so that modernization could occur, but to make sure that such investment did not carry with it any potential to influence or control China's own political decision-making process.

The Developing World

Throughout most of their years of independence, many Developing World states considered contemporary international economic relations to be based on an inequitable system foisted on the world by economically powerful countries and designed by those countries to assure their continued economic preeminence. Many Developing World states maintained that they remained economically dependent and politically subservient to developed states because of the inequities built into the system. These inequities included low valuation for the currencies of the Developing World, poor terms of trade for the primary products produced by Developing World states, and too much international emphasis on who has wealth as opposed to who needs wealth. In addition, many developing countries viewed the First World's emphasis on an open international economic regime as a First World effort to use its economic might to penetrate and control Developing World economies. Often, multinational corporations were considered extensions of First World states. To many Developing World states, economic strength was both desired and feared.

Developing World states held these perceptions for several reasons. Some were rooted in historical memory. Few could deny that developed states exploited their colonies during the colonial era. Only rarely did colonial powers improve the living conditions and economic standards in their colonial territories. These memories colored many Developing World perceptions of realities, as well as reality itself.

There was more to the Developing World charges than resentments and hostilities stemming from historical memory alone. As already noted, the International Monetary Fund and World Bank granted preferential voting rights to wealthy states, a fact widely condemned in the Developing World. In addition, as the International Monetary Fund itself has observed, import prices for the world's most underdeveloped countries climbed throughout the 1980s, whereas the prices of their exports fared much more poorly. Even though the issue is not directly linked to trade, Developing World states also charged that the industrialized West refused to extend sufficient economic assistance. In the eyes of leaders of many Developing World states, these facts indicated that the international economic system was biased in favor of developing states.

In addition, in many Developing World states, reliance on one or two primary products for export earnings worsened trade and finance problems. During times of high demand and high prices, such states experienced economic booms. But longer and more frequent periods of low demand and low prices often prevented any real economic growth. Developing World states recognized this problem, and therefore moved to diversify their exports and to move away from primary product exports.

These sentiments led Developing World states in the Group of 77 to propose the Declaration on the Establishment of a New International Economic Order, adopted by the Sixth Special Session of the United Nations General Assembly in 1974. The NIEO Declaration particularly emphasized home-nation control of internal natural resources and economic activity. Later in 1974, the General Assembly, again with Group of 77 urging behind it, passed the Charter of Economic Rights and Duties of States. In addition to reaffirming the NIEO Declaration, the charter addressed issues such as control of multinational corporations, foreign investment and property ownership, and primary producer cartels.

The United Nations Conference on Trade and Development (UNCTAD) played a central role in the Developing World's effort to create an international economic system more favorable to its needs and wants. UNCTAD emphasized several different programs of economic benefit to Developing World states. The generalized system of preferences (GSP), for instance, is an UNCTAD-initiated system under which Developing World products are imported to developed countries with little or no duty. An obvious departure from the old Bretton Woods system, GSP was proposed at the first UNCTAD conference and was finally accepted fully by developed states at the 1979 Multilateral Trade Negotiations in Geneva. By then, however, most industrialized Western states had operationalized duty charges preferential to Developing World imports on a state-by-state basis. UNCTAD has also had some success convincing developed states to reschedule and cancel Developing World debt repayments. It has been less successful in areas such as commodity price stabilization, product price indexation, and trade liberalization.

Developing World states also used other forums to push their economic demands. The World Bank, IMF, various regional organizations such as ASEAN, OAU, the Inter-American Development Bank, the United Nations Law of the Seas Conference, and the Multilateral Trade Negotiations all provided stages for Developing World demands.

But the bottom line is that not much has actually been done to redress Developing World grievances or implement Developing World programs. Efforts to improve the Developing World's plight have been undertaken for the most part on terms preferred by the First World.

Nor may the international debt of Developing World states be overlooked. When seen from the perspective of Developing World states, the debt itself plus the interest that accrues on the debt are additional ways in which the present international economic system assures continued Developing World dependence on industrialized Western states. Although individual debt payments have often been rescheduled and sometimes forgiven, many Developing World states believe that their economic development has been frustrated by the international economic system.

Nevertheless, in the late 1980s and early 1990s, more and more of Developing World States changed their outlooks on and policies toward foreign direct investment, cooperation with international lending and development institutions, and domestic economic strategies. Many Developing World states became increasingly willing to allow multinational corporations to invest capital with few or no state controls. Some Developing World states also adopted the recommendations of the World Bank, the IMF, and other international financial institutions about how development could best be pursued, and many Developing World states moved away from reliance on centralized government-controlled domestic economic development strategies.

There were at least three reasons for these changes. First, in most Developing World states, old outlooks and policies simply had not worked. Therefore, many Developing World leaders concluded that it was time to change. Second, with the Soviet Union and Eastern European communist states experiencing extreme economic difficulties that contributed eventually to the collapse of communist governments, the model of "developed socialism" that the U.S.S.R. and it erstwhile allies preached no longer looked attractive or possible. Third, Western industrialized states (including Japan), international lending and financial institutions that were oriented toward the free market, and MNCs had become the only possible sources of development and investment capital.

Even so, despite these changes in outlooks and policies, many people in the Developing World remain convinced that today's international economic system is in the hands of the wealthy Western industrialized states, and that the system is intentionally structured to favor the wealthy. And as seen through many Developing World eyes, economic might breeds political power and control.

As a result, despite the clear move toward cooperation with and inclusion in the contemporary international economic system that began in the late 1980s and is continuing today, many Developing World states still believe that the international economic system must be restructured. However, they desire restructuring of the economic structure of the current state system, not of the state system itself. Indeed, one of the great paradoxes of Developing World development is the clash between growing international economic interdependence and the continuing Developing World desire for full national sovereignty.

POWER AND ECONOMIC CAPABILITIES

This chapter began with the observation that recently, the international community has increasingly recognized the role of economic strength in international affairs. As we conclude, we must offer a word of caution. Given the relational and contextual nature of power, we must also remember that economic capabilities alone do not determine an actor's power potential. Therefore, despite the again-acknowledged importance of economic parameters of power, economic capabilities are only one of a number of measures of power in the international arena.

For the foreseeable future, questions about the relationship between power and wealth will be at the forefront of the international agenda.[13] In the First World, the United States is plagued by its chronic national debt and balance of trade and payments deficit. Western Europe hopes that the further development of the European Community via EC 92, the Maastricht Treaty, and economic reforms subsequent to the Maastricht Treaty will fuel an economic boom. Japan seeks a way to rekindle its export-driven prosperity boom of the 1980s. And oil-importing First World states, still shaken by Iraq's 1990 invasion of Kuwait, remain concerned about the prices of and access to imported oil.

Meanwhile, in what once was the Second World, Eastern European states strive to develop market economies and economic ties to the West. Russia and the other newly independent states that emerged from the former Soviet Union struggle with their own immense economic and other problems. Leaders in virtually all these countries push economic reforms in efforts to revitalize their economies, but there is little agreement about how to do it. None of these states will succeed quickly in their revitalization efforts, and additional diminution in their power and influence appears inevitable.

In the Developing World, despite a new willingness to accept foreign direct investment, to cooperate with international lending and development institutions, and to adopt free-market domestic economic development strategies, calls for a new international economic order less stacked in favor of First World states continue. A few fortunate Developing World states will become the "NICs of the Nineties," but most Developing World states will remain economically weak. For most, change will come slowly, if at all.

But inevitably, just as the past brought economic shocks that affected the power potential of international actors, so too will the future. Few people expected American global economic domination to wane as rapidly as it did, and few people predicted either the oil shocks of 1973–1974 and 1979–1980 or the oil price collapse of 1985–1986. Nor did many people expect the Eastern European and Soviet economic crises of the late 1980s, or the collapse of the Soviet Union and its economy in 1991.

Already, as we saw in Chapter 9, there is extensive speculation that the international system that is emerging as the twentieth century draws to a close will be based on three major international trading blocs, one centered in North America led by the United States, another based in Europe led by the European Community and Germany, and a third focused in East Asia led by Japan. It remains to be seen whether this theory is true.

Even if these trading blocks do emerge, questions remain. Will these blocs, if they develop, be led by—or be dominated by—the countries named above? Will these blocs strive for economic cooperation with one another, or will relationships between them degenerate into destructive trade wars?

These are important questions, but they are presently unanswerable. In the future, as in the past, the direction and shape of the international economy, and of the power derived from economic capabilities, is anything but certain.

KEY TERMS AND CONCEPTS

reemergence of economics in international affairs
mercantilism (also in Chapter 2)
free trade
tariffs
interrelationship of domestic economies and international economics
economic interdependence vs. economic independence
law of comparative advantage
balance of trade
balance of payment
floating exchange rate
fixed exchange rate
special drawing rights
international finance
international mobility of capital
global economic subsystems
liberal trade school
Marxist trade school

structuralist trade school
International Bank for Reconstruction and Development (IBRD)
International Monetary Fund (IMF)
General Agreement on Tariffs and Trade (GATT)
Bretton Woods system
evolution of international trading system after World War II
U.S. New Economic Policy (NEP)
Organization of Petroleum Exporting Countries (OPEC)
recycling problem (monetary)
open international economic system
industrialized West's views of international economics
Developing World's view of international economics

NOTES

1. International economics also reemerged as a primary concern of the academic community. For several excellent studies of international political economics, see Jeffrey A. Frieden and David A. Lake, eds., *International Political Economy: Perspectives on Global Power and Wealth* (New York: St. Martin's Press, 1991); Robert Gilpin, *The Political Economy of International Relations* (Princeton: Princeton University Press, 1987); Thomas D. Lairson and David Skidmore, *International Political Economy: The Struggle for Power and Wealth* (New York: Harcourt Brace Jovanovich, 1993); Joan Edelman Spero, *The Politics of International Economic*

Relations (New York: St. Martin's Press, 1990); and Robert S. Walters and David H. Blake, *The Politics of Global Economic Relations* (Englewood Cliffs, NJ: Prentice Hall, 1992).

2. Ricardo's example used Portuguese wine and English cloth. See David Ricardo, "The Principles of Political Economy and Taxation," as quoted in William R. Allen (ed.), *International Trade Theory: Hume to Ohlin* (New York: Random House, 1965), p. 63.

3. For further discussions of special drawing rights, see J. G. Ruggie, "Politics of Money," *Foreign Policy*, No. 43 (Summer 1981): 139–154; *The Economist*, September 26–October 2, 1981; *The Economist*, March 22, 1980.

4. *The New York Times*, March 22, 1992.

5. See again Lairson and Skidmore, Spero, and Walters and Blake.

6. See Gilpin and Spero. For other discussions of North–South economic relations, see Jeffrey Hart, *The New International Economic Order: Conflict and Co-operation in North–South Economic Relations 1974–77* (New York: St. Martin's Press, 1983); David Apter, *Rethinking Development: Modernization, Dependency, and Post-modern Politics* (Beverly Hills: Sage, 1987); and James Caporaso (ed.), *A Changing International Division of Labor* (Boulder, CO: Lynne Rienner, 1987).

7. Gunnar Myrdal, *Rich Lands and Poor: The Road to World Prosperity* (New York: Harper & Row, 1957). See also Raul Prebisch, *The Economic Development of Latin America and Its Principal Problems* (New York: United Nations, 1950).

8. More detailed views of the Bretton Woods system may be found in Fred L. Block, *The Origins of International Economic Disorder: A Study of U.S. International Monetary Policy from World War II to the Present* (Berkeley: University of California Press, 1977); Richard N. Gardner, *Sterling-Dollar Diplomacy in Current Perspective: The Origins and Prospects of Our International Economic Order* (New York: Columbia University Press, 1980); and W. M. Scammell, *The International Economy since 1945* (New York: St. Martin's Press, 1980).

9. Spero, *The Politics of International Economic Relations*, p. 37.

10. Ibid., p. 24.

11. United States Department of the Treasury, Office of International Banking and Portfolio Investment, January 17, 1980; and Rimmer de Vries, "The International Monetary Outlook for the 1980s: No Time for Complacency," *World Financial Markets*, December 1979, p. 5.

12. See Robert Solomon, "The Elephant in the Boat?: The United States and the World Economy," *Foreign Affairs: America and the World 1981*, Vol. 60 (1982): 577.

13. For an excellent discussion of possible future relationships between power and wealth, see Lairson and Skidmore, pp. 315–332.

CHAPTER 18

Military Parameters of Power

- What role does military power have today?
- How have nuclear weapons affected the international balance of power?
- Are conventional weapons useful in a nuclear world?
- How effective is arms control?
- Which countries spend the most on the military?
- In the post-Cold War world, how great a danger is the spread of advanced weapons technologies and weapons of mass destruction?

In the classic early nineteenth-century analysis of political-military affairs, *On War*, Carl von Clausewitz observed that "war is a continuation of politics by other means." Clausewitz further argued that although war was the ultimate form of political persuasion, the military forces so requisite during war have utility during peace as well.[1] The Prussian general was correct. During war or peace, the military capabilities of international actors make up a significant portion of an actor's power potential.

In objective terms, the power that an actor derives from its military capabilities can be determined only in actual combat. During the Cold War, the U.S. Department of Defense told its troops in Europe that superior training and superior equipment would allow them to fight outnumbered and win. Whether this was fact or fiction could have been tested only on the battlefield. So, too, with Great Britain and Argentina in the Falklands War. The British scoffed when Argentina warned that it would take over the islands if the dispute over their sovereignty was not concluded in Argentina's favor, but learned to their chagrin that the Argentine military had the capability and will to undertake such an action. Argentines scoffed when Britain sent a naval armada to retake the islands, but discovered that Britain's capability and will were sufficient for the task as well. Conversely, by assessing the volume of firepower that the United States brought to bear on Vietnam and that the Soviet Union unleashed in Afghanistan, both superpowers should have emerged victorious in short order. Neither did.

The interrelationship of military capabilities and power has both **objective and subjective components**. Quantity of military equipment alone does not determine the outcome of a battle, nor does it determine how much power an actor's military capabilities add to its overall power potential. The same is true for quality of equipment. Quantitatively numerous and qualitatively advanced military equipment adds little to an actor's power if the actor has no inclination to use its military to achieve its objectives, and if the other actors are aware of that lack of inclination. However, if an actor has both numerous and modern weapons, and is perceived as willing to use its weapons to achieve its objectives, then its military does in fact enhance its power *regardless* of whether the actor in reality has any inclination to use its military. From the perceptual vantage point of other actors, its power has been enhanced. Obviously, the interrelationship of military capabilities and power is an issue of some complexity.

It is an issue that is not limited to the quantity and quality of men and equipment that can be placed in the field or the real and perceived level of will. Other factors also impinge on the interrelationship of military capabilities and power. How well can the leadership command, control, and communicate with its forces? How well can the forces be supplied, and for how long? How rapidly can losses be replaced? All these questions—and others—are important when the interrelationship of military capabilities and power is being analyzed.

Traditionally, at least since the Treaty of Westphalia, states have been the repositories of military capabilities. However, during the twentieth century and particularly since World War II, other actors have increasingly developed their own military capabilities. IGOs such as the United Nations and the Organization of African Unity have requested and received military forces from states to make up their own international peacekeeping forces, and multinational corporations have in some cases strengthened their own security forces so that they may be considered in-house paramilitary organizations. On one occasion during the Iranian hostage crisis, fearing that several of his employees might also be taken hostage, U.S. businessman (and 1992 presidential candidate) Ross Perot used his corporation's security forces to rescue employees from Teheran. NGOs such as national liberation movements and terrorist organizations use their military capabilities to strive for their desired ends, and mercenaries have again become a recognized, although not honored, segment of the international community. Since 1980, mercenaries have played roles in Angola, Nicaragua, and Mozambique, to name just a few conflicts. Indeed, Frederick Forsythe's novel, *The Dogs of War*, was based on an attempt by a mercenary band to take over a West African state. Even in the Bahamas, plots developed on Abaco and elsewhere, where separatist groups funded mercenary units to aid individual islands in efforts to secede.

The power that military capabilities impart to an actor is thus the product of a variety of factors. For the purposes of our study of the interrelationship of military capabilities and power, we will examine military capabilities from several different perspectives. Because states are the primary possessors of military capabilities, we will begin our analysis with separate discussions of state-related military capabilities at the nuclear and conventional levels. The role of arms control efforts will also be discussed. Finally, we will conclude with an analysis of the interrelationship of nonstate actors and military power.[2]

NUCLEAR WEAPONS AND WORLD POLITICS

As of 1993, six international actors, all states, had exploded nuclear devices. The United States exploded the world's first atomic device near Alamogordo, New Mexico, in 1945. The Soviet Union joined the nuclear club in 1949, and Great Britain followed in 1952, but it was not until the 1960s that the next countries, France (1960) and China (1964), became members. India exploded a nuclear device in 1973, but declared that the explosion was "peaceful" and would not be used for military purposes.

In addition, South Africa revealed in 1993 that it had had six nuclear weapons but disassembled them in 1991. Also, most experts believe that Israel has the material and expertise to make nuclear weapons and could assemble one in a few days at most. Other countries such as Argentina, Brazil, Iran, Iraq, North Korea, Pakistan, South Korea, and Taiwan may also be capable of building nuclear weapons.

The United States is the only state that has ever used an atomic bomb in anger. On August 6, 1945, the *Enola Gay*, a U.S. B-29, dropped an atomic bomb on Hiroshima, leveling much of the city. Three days later, a second bomb destroyed Nagasaki. The nuclear age had arrived.

The U.S.–U.S.S.R. Nuclear Arms Race

The **nuclear arms race** started slowly. The United States retained a nuclear monopoly until 1949, when Soviet scientists conducted their first nuclear test. Despite the end of the American nuclear monopoly, the United States enjoyed a significant lead in delivery capabilities. American aircraft technology was far ahead of Soviet technology, and remained so throughout the early years of the nuclear arms race.

Soviet-American nuclear rivalry soon moved from developed **fission weapons** to developing fusion weapons. The bombs dropped on Hiroshima and Nagasaki were both fission weapons, that is, atomic bombs whose destructive power was considerably greater than that of conventional weapons. But as the postwar U.S. strategic bombing surveys revealed, 210 conventionally armed B-29s could have inflicted the same amount of damage on Hiroshima as did the *Enola Gay*. And 120 conventionally armed B-29s could have wreaked havoc on Nagasaki similar in scope to that caused by the atomic bomb.[3] Raids of this size were commonplace during the last months of the Pacific war.

Fusion weapons yielded a tremendous increase in destructive potential beyond fission weapons. The destructive potential of a fusion weapon, or hydrogen bomb (also called an H-bomb or a thermonuclear bomb) was several orders of magnitude beyond a fission weapon (an A-bomb). The United States exploded its first fusion device in late 1952, and the Soviets followed suit less than a year later.

Still, the United States continued to enjoy its lead in delivery vehicles. By the time sizable numbers of fusion weapons began to enter the U.S. arsenal in 1954, the B-52 had been operationalized. The B-52 remains one of the primary U.S. strategic bombers today.

Another aspect of the nuclear arms race was the effort to make small nuclear weapons that could be used close to one's own conventional fighting forces in the field. The United States and its NATO allies viewed the development of theater nuclear forces (also called tactical nuclear forces; in either case, TNF) as a key element for the defense of both Western Europe and South Korea, given the U.S.S.R.'s preponderance of conventional weaponry. The United States reasoned that TNF would be used against hostile forces in the event that conventional defense proved futile. The United States obtained the lead in TNF development and began moving those weapons to Western Europe and South Korea during the mid-1950s.

The Western world as a whole, and the United States in particular, were shocked when in October 1957 the U.S.S.R. launched *Sputnik I*, the world's first artificial satellite. *Sputnik* delivered a blow to American scientific-technical prestige, and it also carried with it military implications. The degree of technical sophistication needed to launch a satellite was roughly equivalent to that needed to deliver nuclear weapons by missile across intercontinental distances. The marriage of fusion weapons and **intercontinental ballistic missiles (ICBMs)** forced major reevaluations of all preceding strategic thought. In the United States, the fear of a "missile gap" became an accepted political reality.

In actuality, the Soviet Union never operationalized significant quantities of ICBMs until the mid-1960s. Thus, despite the American fear of strategic inferiority, the United States remained superior to the U.S.S.R. in all aspects of the nuclear arms race throughout the 1950s. The nuclear strike ability of U.S. strategic forces was supplemented by U.S. aircraft carriers in the Mediterranean Sea and Pacific Ocean, by intermediate-range ballistic missiles (IRBMs) in Italy and Turkey, and by dual-capable intermediate-range aircraft at bases on the Soviet periphery.

In this light, the 1962 **Cuban Missile Crisis** may be viewed as a Soviet effort to reduce or eliminate American nuclear superiority by deploying IRBMs at sites from which they could reach the United States. Following the failure of Khrushchev's effort to deploy Soviet missiles in Cuba, the U.S.S.R. began to accelerate its deployment of ICBMs.

Meanwhile, in response to the alleged missile gap, the United States accelerated deployment of its own ICBMs and began operationalizing submarine-launched ballistic missiles (SLBMs). A new generation of U.S. ICBMs, the *Minuteman*, was deployed in underground silos, making them impervious to anything but a direct hit. SLBMs were also safe from attack because of the mobility and stealth of submarines. By the middle 1960s, U.S. nuclear superiority was greater than it had ever been or has been since.

However, the degree of American superiority began to diminish as the United States decided to hold its force levels relatively constant and the Soviet Union continued to try to catch up. By the late 1960s, the U.S.S.R. had virtually eliminated U.S. quantitative nuclear superiority, as Table 18–1 indicates, although the U.S. qualitative lead in accuracy and reliability remained considerable. Throughout the 1970s, the Soviets whittled away at the American qualitative lead as well. The era of "essential equivalence" had arrived.

Perhaps the major technical breakthrough of the 1970s was the development of the **multiple independently targetable reentry vehicle (MIRV)**. A MIRVed ICBM had several warheads atop it, each of which could be guided to a

(a)

(b)

Despite the end of the Cold War, the United States nuclear Triad is an important element of U.S. defense policy. Views of the U.S. nuclear Triad: (a) a B-2 Stealth bomber (Sygma); (b) a test launch of an MX ICBM (U.S. Department of Defense); and (c) "Ohio" class ballistic missile submarines, built to carry "Trident" missiles, under construction (U.S. Department of Defense).

(c)

TABLE 18–1   The Growth of the U.S. and Soviet Strategic Nuclear Arsenals°

	1966	1970	1974	1978	1982	1986	1990
U.S.A. ICBM	904	1054	1054	1054	1052	1018	1000
SLBM	592	656	656	656	520	616	608
Long-range bombers	630	550	437	366	316	240	360
U.S.S.R. ICBM	292	1299	1575	1400	1398	1398	1451
SLBM	107	304	720	1028	989	979	942
Long-range bombers	155	145	140	135	150	170	195

SOURCE: International Institute for Strategic Studies, *The Military Balance* (London: IISS, appropriate years).

°Chart does not include other significant quantitative and qualitative measures of strategic importance such as number of warheads, yield of warheads, reliability and survivability of systems, and accuracy.

separate target. Thus, a single ICBM or SLBM could destroy several enemy targets. The United States began to deploy MIRVed Minuteman ICBMs in 1970, and the Soviet Union followed with its own MIRVed systems five years later.

In 1972, Soviet and American leaders reached agreement on the first **Strategic Arms Limitation Treaty (SALT I)**. SALT I placed a cap on the quantity of Soviet and U.S. delivery vehicles, and an accompanying protocol limited the number of antiballistic missile systems (ABMs) each side could deploy. However, no limits were placed on qualitative improvements, and the nuclear arms race continued. A SALT II agreement that effected some limitations on qualitative improvements was negotiated by 1979, but the U.S. Senate never ratified it.[4]

By the early 1980s, the U.S.-U.S.S.R. nuclear arms race had reached a virtual stalemate as each side sought to obtain advantage in one aspect or another of the race. Some Americans, including Ronald Reagan, concluded that the Soviet Union had opened a "window of vulnerability" on the United States, and that the United States was vulnerable to a disarming Soviet first strike. Such analysis emphasized Soviet superiority in throw-weight, total number of launch vehicles, and cold-launch capabilities. Other Americans argued that American forces were as safe as ever and deterrence was as assured as ever because of U.S. superiority in total numbers of warheads, submarine technology, and aircraft technology.[5]

By the late 1980s, the nuclear arms race had become a confused arena for sophisticated arguments, expensive weapons systems, and bewildering acronyms. The relatively simplistic deterrence arguments of the 1950s ("if you attack me, I will attack you, and you cannot then hope to win") had been replaced by sophisticated discussions of dynamic equilibrium, pindown, and fratricide. In the American arsenal expensive B-52s and Minutemen were to be replaced by more expensive B-1s, Stealth, and M-X. ICBMs, SLBMs, MIRVs, ABMs, and SALT were joined by ALCMs, GLCMs, SLCMs, MaRVs, ASAT, SDI, and START. Older strategic terminology like mutual assured destruction, counterforce and countervalue, and damage limitation were complemented by newer terms such as pop-up, precursor bursts, and interactive discrimination. Questions about nuclear superiority and inferiority, about nuclear strategy and tactics, became as complicated as the weapons themselves.

Nuclear Strategy and Policy

Despite the development of cordial East–West relations in the late 1980s and the collapse of the Soviet Union in 1991, most of the nuclear weapons of the former Soviet Union remain in place. In addition, more and more countries have the ability to produce nuclear weapons, and some may have attained nuclear know-how or nuclear weapon components from sources in the former U.S.S.R.. Thus, questions about nuclear deterrence and related issues remain extremely important today.[6] Here, we will concentrate on only five of the questions.

(1) What is the logic behind **deterrence, mutual deterrence, and mutual assured destruction**? The concept of nuclear deterrence is a simple one. Stated briefly, nuclear deterrence relies on the certainty that one country has sufficient military capabilities to convince another country that it would not be worth its while to attack.

Military analysts identify three types of deterrence: deterrence by denial, deterrence by punishment, and deterrence by defeat. Under deterrence by denial, the country that might wish to initiate a war would not do so because it is convinced that it could not obtain its war objectives. Thus, it would have no reason to begin a war. Under deterrence by punishment, the country that might wish to initiate a war would not do so because it would believe that the country that is attacked could inflict unacceptable damage (punishment) to the attacking country. Obviously, the higher the level of cost tolerance that an attacking state is willing to accept, the higher the level of damage that the attacked state must be capable of inflicting if deterrence by punishment is to be effective. Under deterrence by defeat, the state that might wish to initiate a war would not do so because of the certainty that it would be defeated.

Deterrence deals in subjective aspects of military capabilities. The truth of deterrence is that if weapons are used, deterrence has failed. Thus, under any of the three versions of deterrence, the country that may be contemplating an attack must be convinced of the futility of its efforts before it initiates an attack. Under mutual deterrence, both sides in a potential war must be convinced of the futility of attack-initiation. This is particularly true at the nuclear level where the stakes of miscalculation are so high.

Mutual assured destruction (MAD) is a variant of mutual deterrence by punishment. MAD dictates that *both* sides in a potential nuclear war must be convinced even before a war begins that the other could absorb a first strike and still have enough nuclear weaponry left to destroy the initiating side as a functioning modern society. Assuming rationality on the part of national decision-makers in such a situation, no incentive to attack other than suicide could exist.

Efforts to deliver an assured second strike led U.S. and former Soviet planners to place their ICBMs in hardened underground silos and influenced U.S., Soviet, British, and French planners to place sizable portions of their nuclear strike capabilities in submarines. China has also developed SLBM capabilities. The more convinced that a state is of the invulnerability of its own nuclear forces, the more stable are deterrence, mutual deterrence, and mutual assured destruction. Any of the types of deterrence are in danger of disintegrating as soon as a state believes that it has been put in a position to "use it or lose it."

In the curious world of nuclear strategy, nuclear weapons exist so that they will never be used. They deter not only nuclear war but also, it is hoped, large-scale conventional war.

(2) What is the **Triad** and what is its rationale? U.S. deterrence has been and still is based on the Triad, that is, three separate delivery systems for U.S. nuclear weapons. The three separate delivery systems are ICBMs, SLBMs, and manned planes. Its rationale is simple: If a potential aggressor were to achieve a defensive breakthrough against one or even two of the systems, the remaining system(s) would continue to deter the potential aggressor.

Since at least the late 1970s, the American Triad has been challenged from two quarters. On the one hand, increased accuracy of Soviet missiles rendered the survivability of U.S. ICBMs less certain. Critics of U.S. land-based missiles therefore question the wisdom of maintaining current ICBMs or building new ones. On the other hand, development of cruise missile technology has led some analysts to believe that a fourth leg of U.S. strategic forces has been deployed. Nevertheless, the Triad remains the core of American deterrent forces.[7]

(3) Why is accuracy so important when nuclear weapons are so destructive? In the event of a large nuclear exchange, accuracy probably would not be of extremely great importance. However, in the event of a small exchange, accurate delivery vehicles would enable a national command authority to tailor a response to a conventional or nuclear attack in whatever way it sees fit. Targets in such a partial exchange probably would not be cities (called countervalue targets, or soft sites) where accuracy of attack would have little meaning. Rather, targets would probably be individual command, control, or communication sites or individual enemy silos (called counterforce targets, or hard sites) that demand high accuracy. According to current American strategy, hard sites would be targeted in response to a partial first strike in an effort to prevent escalation to a total exchange.[8]

Additionally, given the improved hardening capabilities of all nuclear powers, accuracy is required to assure target destruction. Furthermore, as miniaturization capabilities improve, more and more MIRVs could be placed aboard each delivery vehicle, each of which must be highly accurate if it is to destroy its target.

(4) Before the Soviet Union broke up, both it and the United States had sufficient nuclear weapons to destroy the other several times over. Why did both sides have so many weapons?

There are at least three answers. First, because the objective of deterrence was (and is) to prevent anyone from ever employing nuclear weapons, both sides sought to convince the other through sheer quantity of weaponry that a nuclear attack was futile. Here, it should also be stressed that until recently both the United States and the U.S.S.R. claimed they were convinced that the other was seeking nuclear superiority, and therefore each continued its buildup to avoid inferiority.

Second, successful deterrence is predicated on the certainty of retaliation. As all nuclear-capable states claim to be building their forces for retaliation rather than for first strike, the prudent planner must assume that all of nuclear forces will not survive an enemy's first strike. Nevertheless, that planner must be able to convince potential enemies that in a post-first strike environment, a sufficient number of operational weapons will be available to destroy the attacker as a functioning society. Given the uncertainties inherent in any war, much less nuclear war, quantity appears the most effective means to provide certainty and hence assure deterrence.

Third, nuclear weapons provide states a certain aura of power. This aura may not necessarily be deserved, but it is nonetheless there; it is part of the psychological baggage that nuclear weaponry carries with it. Indeed, at the nuclear level as well as at the conventional level, a certain sense of "more weapons, more power" prevails. At the nuclear level as well as at the conventional level, this sense is not necessarily accurate.

(5) Are nuclear weapons too powerful and too destructive to have political utility? Stated differently, at the nuclear level, have we moved beyond Clausewitz' dictum that war is the continuation of politics by other means?

This question must be answered in several ways. As we saw in our discussion of the subjective aspects of military capabilities, a country that has a particular military capability adds nothing to its power potential if it does not have the intention to use that capability and if other states realize it does not have the intention to use that capability. Conversely, at the other extreme, if a state has the intention to use a particular capability and other actors realize that it will, that state may have significantly enhanced its power potential.

These observations have immediate relevance for nuclear weapons and for the power that they bestow on actors that have them. It was widely accepted that the United States and the Soviet Union would use their nuclear weapons against the other in the event of an attack on the other's homeland. Both sides had the intention of using their nuclear weapons in this situation, and both sides realized that the other would do so. Deterrence was thus assured, and both sides used their nuclear capabilities to influence potential actions of the other. Nuclear weapons thus added a degree of power to the United States and the Soviet Union.

In other cases, however, nuclear weapons added little or nothing to Soviet or American power potential. The United States never seriously considered using nuclear weapons in Vietnam, and as far as is known, the Soviet Union never seriously considered using them in Afghanistan. Both the Vietcong and the Afghan guerrillas realized this. Nuclear weapons therefore contributed nothing to U.S. power potential in Vietnam nor to Soviet power potential in Afghanistan. The use of nuclear weapons was simple not credible; they were too powerful to be militarily—or politically—useful, and all involved actors realized it.

This paradox is not limited to the U.S. and former Soviet strategic arsenals. When China, a nuclear power, launched its "punishment operation" against Vietnam in 1979, few analysts believed that China would use its nuclear weapons. The Vietnamese certainly did not. Thus, given China's own unwillingness to use them, nuclear weapons added nothing to Chinese power. Similarly, in 1982, if Argentina had expected Great Britain to drop a nuclear weapon on Buenos Aires, Argentina probably would not have taken over the Falklands. Argentina's estimate of Britain's willingness to use its nuclear arsenal was correct, even though Argentina's estimate of Britain's commitment to take back the Falklands was not. Argentina therefore went ahead with its invasion. British use of nuclear weapons was simply not credible, and therefore nuclear weapons added nothing to Britain's power.

Nuclear weapons, then, are situationally meaningful additions to the power that a country has at its disposal. In some cases, because of the level of destruction that they cause, nuclear weapons add little or no power to a state's account. In other cases, nuclear weapons add considerable quantities of power to a state's account. Obviously, the examples here cited are at opposite extremes of a continuum along which more uncertain situations lie.

Constraints on employment of nuclear weapons are both psychological and material. Following the American attacks on Hiroshima and Nagasaki, the world was shocked, awed, and revolted by the damage caused by two single-weapon attacks. As nuclear weapons became even more destructive with the advent of fusion weapons, people's fear of nuclear war increased. Today, most states accept that nuclear weapons will not be used except in response to a nuclear attack or except to assure their own survival or the survival of allies. This is a psychologically imposed constraint stemming both from the revulsion of mass destruction and the fear of a hostile response by the world community.

At the same time, material constraints exist. Using nuclear weapons could bring nuclear retribution, thereby causing immense damage even to the first user. In addition, a large-scale nuclear exchange could cause immense damage to the environment, bringing about, among other things, large decreases in global temperature levels. Although later studies of the climatological consequences of nuclear war suggested that the original studies of "nuclear winter" were overstated,[9] the phenomenon nevertheless still raised the level of concern about nuclear war. In still other cases, impoverished actors with little to lose may be much more willing to risk a nuclear exchange than wealthy actors with much to lose. Thus, the power that nuclear weapons add to an actor's capabilities is both relational and contextual. In certain contexts, nuclear weapons do have political utility and therefore do add to the power potential of international actors. In other contexts, however, nuclear weapons may add nothing to the power potential of an international actor.

The Nuclear Proliferation Problem

The debate over nuclear strategy is as pressing as the problem of **nuclear proliferation**. Although nuclear proliferation has long been a major concern of the international community, the discovery in 1991 of how advanced Iraq's nuclear weapons program was and the breakup of the Soviet Union in the same year elevated international concern over nuclear proliferation to a new level of global urgency.

Six states currently have known nuclear capabilities, and a seventh, South Africa, claims to have developed a nuclear arsenal but then voluntarily disarmed itself. By the end of the century, the most pessimistic estimates are that as many as forty states may have nuclear capability. Although some states with nuclear expertise will doubtless eschew production of nuclear weapons, all will not. The nuclear club will therefore be joined by a variety of states that, one can only hope, will be as responsible with nuclear weapons as those that currently have them have been. Table 18–2 lists those countries with nuclear energy programs that have not accepted international safeguards on their programs, as well as many of those countries with nuclear energy programs that have accepted safeguards.

But no room for complacency exists. Accepting nuclear safeguards does not necessarily mean that they will be followed, as international inspectors found in

TABLE 18–2 Countries Without Nuclear Weapons That Have Nuclear Energy Programs, 1993

Those That Have Not Accepted International Safeguards	Those That Have Accepted International Safeguards
Brazil	Argentina
Chile	Canada
Israel (may already have nuclear weapons)	Cuba
North Korea (rejected safeguards in 1993)	Czechoslovakia
Pakistan (may already have nuclear weapons)	Germany
	Iran
	Iraq
	Italy
	Japan
	Mexico
	Spain
	Taiwan
	Vietnam
	Yugoslavia

Iraq in 1991 and 1992 when they investigated Iraq's nuclear programs. They found that despite assurances to the contrary, Iraq was far advanced in its nuclear weapons programs.

And there is always the concern that nuclear weapons once developed will be used. If Iraq had had nuclear weapons in 1991, would it have used them against U.S. and other forces during Operation Desert Storm? If Argentina had had nuclear weapons in 1982, would the Argentine government have used them to eliminate the British fleet off the Falklands? If Libya had had nuclear weapons in 1986 when the United States launched two air attacks against Libya, would Libya have used them against the U.S. Sixth Fleet—or even the United States? If Pakistan had had nuclear weapons in 1971, would they have been used in Pakistan's conflict with India, when Indian intervention in a civil war led to East Pakistani independence from West Pakistan as Bangladesh? In future years, would another Arab-Israeli War lead Israel to use nuclear weapons against its Islamic neighbors, or influence Libya, Iran, Iraq, Pakistan or some other potentially nuclear-capable Islamic state to use them against Israel?

These are not academic questions. All the states mentioned above will have the potential to develop nuclear weapons before 2000. Some may already have them.

How have these states come close to or developed the ability to make nuclear weapons? There are several answers. In some cases, these states developed some or even most of their nuclear capabilities on their own. However, more frequently, nuclear-capable countries knowingly or unknowingly provided potential nuclear states with their nuclear know-how. In some cases, businesses and individuals worked their way around or ignored international limitations on the sale of nuclear materials and components. Some potential nuclear states stole nuclear know-how, parts, and components. But the bottom line is nevertheless easy to see. Nuclear know-how and capabilities have proliferated immensely.

The impact of the dissolution of the Soviet Union on nuclear proliferation warrants special mention here. With the end of the U.S.S.R., the Soviet Union's nuclear arsenal was divided between four states: Belorus, Kazakhstan, Russia, and Ukraine. All agreed that the nuclear weapons that they inherited from the former Soviet Union would eventually be transferred to Russia, with most then being dismantled. However, this has not yet occurred. Forebodingly, Kazakhstan and Ukraine have on occasion expressed hesitancy about giving up their nuclear weapons.

Equally unsettling is the possibility that with the collapse of the Soviet Union's nuclear command and control structure, former Soviet nuclear weapons, components, or materials may have been sold to countries that want to develop their own nuclear capabilities. There is also the possibility that former Soviet nuclear scientists, now unable to make a living in the financially destitute former Soviet Union, may have gone to work for nonnuclear countries that want to develop nuclear capabilities. Unfortunately, it is highly likely that international efforts to stem the flow of nuclear components, materials, and know-how following the Soviet collapse have been less than completely successful.

Why do nonnuclear countries want to acquire nuclear weapons? In most cases, the drive to attain nuclear weapons comes from psychological and security considerations. Nuclear-capable countries are generally regarded as great powers simply because they possess nuclear weapons. This adds psychological importance to the possession of nuclear weapons. In addition, regional rivalries may push states to develop nuclear weapons. It is generally accepted that a major impetus to Pakistan's nuclear program was the Indian nuclear explosion, and Nigeria has declared it would develop nuclear capabilities if South Africa did.

It is not only at the state level that nuclear proliferation presents potential threats. With the expertise to build nuclear weapons easily attainable, only the availability of materials frustrates would-be nuclear-capable nonstate actors. Western leaders have long feared that terrorist groups of one type or another would gain access to a nuclear device and then engage in nuclear blackmail. A terrorist group, with little to lose, may well be able to achieve its demands if it placed a nuclear weapon in New York City or London, and threatened to detonate it if its demands were not met. For the terrorist group, a nuclear weapon would clearly have an immense political utility and would tremendously enhance the power potential of that group.

Nuclear proliferation, then, is a real and growing problem. Although most of the nations of the world signed the 1968 nuclear nonproliferation treaty (NPT), several of those countries that are most likely to achieve nuclear status did not. No nonstate actor signed the treaty.[10]

A final chilling observation must be added to our discussion of nuclear proliferation. In many respects, those international actors that have the least to lose may be the most willing to use nuclear weapons. Historically, those actors have also had the most difficult task achieving nuclear status. However, as the twentieth century draws to a close, this cold solace may be less and less true.[11]

CONVENTIONAL WEAPONS IN A NUCLEAR WORLD

During the first few years of the nuclear era, some analysts speculated that the role and influence of **conventional weapons** in a nuclear world would diminish. They were wrong. Conventional weapons have retained nearly all the utility they ever had, and in most cases remain a more accurate measure of a country's military power than nuclear weapons. Nuclear weapons, as we have seen, lose much of their political-military influence because of their extreme destructive capabilities. Conventional weapons, because their use can be tailored more easily to meet the demands of a given situation, and because they do not carry with them the psychological revulsion of nuclear weapons, therefore remain extremely important measures of an actor's power potential even in a nuclear era.

This does not mean that the power afforded by conventional military capabilities is not relational or contextual. It is. U.S. conventional military capabilities are virtually meaningless as tools of power in U.S. economic disputes with Europe, Japan, or Canada, but in U.S. disagreements with Iraq, they clearly add to U.S. power potential. Again, however, it must be stressed that the subjective and objective aspects of military capabilities make it extremely difficult to estimate the relative amounts of power that states acquire because of their conventional military capabilities. Not surprisingly, many states have responded to this insecurity of uncertainty by expanding their expenditures on conventional military arms and weaponry.

Dimensions of Military Expenditures

Between the end of World War II and the mid-1980s, military expenditures of states expanded astronomically. Very few states did not contribute to this explosion. As Table 18–3 indicates, between 1969 and 1984 alone, world military expenditures in current dollars expanded nearly four times. Even when constant dollars are used, military expenditures throughout the world during the Cold War grew by roughly 3 percent per year. On a global scale, the stark fact was that by the mid-1980s, more than $1 out of every $20 was spent on the military.[12] Since then, global military expenditures have declined, but not significantly.

By 1985, in order of their own expenditures, the Soviet Union, the United States, France, West Germany, Great Britain, Japan, and China accounted for almost 75 percent of the world's military expenditures. This remained true until 1992 when the Soviet Union broke apart. These countries, other than Japan, were also the sources of much of the Developing World's arms and weaponry, as Table 18–4 indicates. This also remained the case until the Soviet Union's 1992 demise, when Russia replaced the Soviet Union as a major arms supplier. And as Table 18–5 shows, industrialized states embroiled in the East–West conflict

TABLE 18–3 The Growth of World Military Expenditures, 1969–1984, in Billions of Current Dollars

	1969	1974	1979	1984
Developed World	197	263	405	665
Developing World	39	57	109	170
Total	236	320	514	835

SOURCE: U.S. Arms Control and Disarmament Agency, *World Military Expenditures and Arms Transfers* (Washington: U.S. Government Printing Office, appropriate years).

TABLE 18–4　International Arms Transfers in the Early 1980s: Leading Exporters and Importers, in Billions of U.S. Dollars

Total Arms Exports to Developing States, 1981–85		151.1
U.S.S.R.	49.1	
United States	28.9	
France	18.9	
Great Britain	7.0	
West Germany	6.7	
Total Arms Imports of Developing States, 1981–85		**151.1**
Iraq	23.9	
Saudi Arabia	14.8	
Libya	10.5	
Syria	8.9	
Egypt	7.1	
Iran	6.4	
India	6.1	
Cuba	4.1	
Algeria	3.9	
Jordan	3.8	
Angola	3.0	

SOURCE: U.S. Arms Control and Disarmament Agency, *World Military Expenditures and Arms Transfers 1986*, (Washington: U.S. Government Printing Office, 1987), pp. 143–146.

tended to devote a higher percentage of their gross national product to defense than did other states.

As Cold War tensions lessened during the late 1980s, the upward spiral in world military expenditures slowed. Indeed, in the late 1980s, military expenditures of many Developing World states outside the Middle East even declined, both as a result of reduced superpower rivalry there and as a result of the declining ability of Developing World states to bear such high rates of military expenditures. And when the Cold War ended in the early 1990s, developed states also began to reduce their military budgets, again as Table 18–5 shows. Throughout the world, this trend toward lower defense expenditures became known as "the peace dividend."

Nevertheless, it must also be stressed that in the Middle East and in several other locations as well, there was no significant reduction in military expenditures in the late 1980s and early 1990s. In some regions and countries, the growth in military expenditures even continued.

Dimensions of Increased Conventional Military Capabilities

Increased levels of military expenditures have over time permitted a quantitative growth and qualitative improvement of conventional military forces throughout the world. This proliferation of conventional military quality and quantity carries with it some implications that are often overlooked. First, however, let us examine the dimensions of that proliferation.

Quantitatively, African states fielded approximately 1.1 million people in their collective armed forces in 1991, and Latin American armed forces totaled 1.5 million. Asian states excluding China, Japan, and India placed 5.3 million

TABLE 18–5   1985 and 1991 Military Expenditures, in Billions of 1985 Dollars and as a Percentage of Gross National Product

	1985		1991	
	Total	**%GNP**	**Total**	**%GNP**
First World States				
France	20.1	4.0	18.0	2.8
Germany (1985—West;				
1991—Unified)	19.9	3.2	16.5	1.9
Great Britain	23.8	5.2	22.4	4.2
United States	258.2	6.5	227.1	5.1
Former Second World States				
Czechoslovakia	4.9	4.7	2.8	2.0
Hungary	2.4	3.6	1.2	2.3
Poland	5.8	3.0	2.2	2.4
Soviet Union	241.5	16.1	91.6	11.1
Selected Developing World States				
Algeria	.9	1.7	.9	1.4
Argentina	1.9	2.9	1.2	1.7
Bangladesh	.2	1.2	.2	1.3
Brazil	1.7	.8	1.1	.8
China (People's Republic)	10.6	3.6	12.0	3.2
Egypt	4.1	8.5	3.6	7.5
Guatemala	.2	1.8	.2	1.2
India	6.3	3.0	8.0	2.9
Iran	14.2	8.6	4.3	7.1
Iraq	12.9	25.9	?	?
Philippines	.5	1.4	.8	2.2
Saudi Arabia	17.7	19.6	35.4	33.8
Tanzania	.3	4.4	.3	3.9
Thailand	1.5	4.1	1.8	2.5
Zambia	.3	4.1	.1	2.6

SOURCE: International Institute for Strategic Studies, *The Military Balance 1992–1993*, pp. 218–221.

people in their armed forces. China had 3.0 million soldiers, sailors, and aviators under arms, India 1.3 million, and Japan .2 million. Western European states fielded 2.8 million people in their armed forces, whereas the United States had approximately 1.9 million military personnel. Eastern European states had 1.3 million men in their militaries, and the Soviet Union had 4.0 million men.[13] These numbers were all lower than they had been during the 1980s. Nevertheless, no region of the world lacks soldiers, sailors, and aviators.

Increased military expenditures have also led to the creation of more lethal conventional weapons to arm these men. Some conventional weapons are powerful enough to destroy a square kilometer of a city. Nine of these could wreak the same nonradiation damage that the Hiroshima A-bomb did. Other weapons are dropped by parachute and suspend tiny droplets of flammable chemicals in the air over a distance of one kilometer. A spark then lights the chemicals, incinerating everything in the area. Cluster bombs with over a thousand tiny bombs each were used with devastating effect by the Israelis during their 1982 assault on Beirut. Biological and chemical weapons are increasingly available, and according to some reports, are used.[14] More and more countries also have ballistic missiles, as Iraq so vividly demonstrated with its use of Soviet-made and Iraqi-modified "Scud" missiles during the 1991 Persian Gulf War. In many ways, these and other conventional weapons of mass destruction increasingly erase the distinctions that separate conventional and nuclear weapons.

Conventional weaponry is also becoming more sophisticated, thanks to breakthroughs in a variety of technical areas. Multimach aircraft are now commonplace; "smart weapons," including bombs, missiles, and torpedos, are guided to their targets by television, lasers, computers, and microscopic wires. The U.S. Phoenix missile system can track six targets and simultaneously guide missiles to each one of them, with virtual certainty of destruction at ranges up to 50 miles and more. Other systems are equally impressive—or frightening—depending on one's perspective.

And it must be reemphasized that these more capable weapons are becoming available to more and more countries. The United States sold F-14s with the Phoenix missile system to the Shah's Iran, and sophisticated AWACS radar planes to Saudi Arabia. Modern antitank guided munitions are widely available in the Developing World, as are relatively advanced surface-to-air missiles. The former Soviet Union sold its most modern battle tanks and state-of-the-art aircraft to a host of countries in the Middle East and South Asia. France sold deadly Exocet air-to-surface missiles to Argentina, and the Argentines destroyed two British ships with them during the 1982 Falklands War. Iraq also used an Exocet missile in the May 1987 accidental attack against the U.S. Navy frigate *Stark*. Moreover, the United States delivered shoulder-fired antiaircraft missiles called Stingers to anticommunist guerrillas in Afghanistan, Angola, and Nicaragua, and China sold Silkworm surface-to-surface missiles to Iran. Meanwhile, the Soviet Union sold Scud surface-to-surface missiles to Iraq. By 1993, at least 20 Developing World states either had their own or were developing the capability to build ballistic missiles.

The implications of large military forces armed with better and more deadly conventional weapons are several. First, regional conflicts will become more dangerous not only to the combatants but also to other states as the dangers of escalation increase. Increased range of aircraft and greater destructiveness of weapons also increase the chances that states not immediately involved in a conflict may be drawn in. Second, the great powers of the world will find their ability to control and influence events in other parts of the world reduced. Easily available modern weaponry will enable militarily weak states to exact a certain toll from more powerful states even though the weaker states would undoubtedly lose in the end. However, the great powers may think twice about undertaking coercive activity if they realize that they would accrue inevitable losses. Finally, as more states acquire modern weapons, even more may be expected to attempt to attain them either through arms transfers or development of internal weapons capacity.

Most modern weapons reach the nonindustrial world via arms transfers from the industrialized world. After reaching a high of $57 billion in 1984, First and Second World arms transfers to Developing World states dropped during the late 1980s and in the 1990s. Nevertheless, in 1992, First World states and former Second World states still sold at least $30 billion in weapons to Developing World states. The United States and, before its demise, the Soviet Union, were far and away the major exporters of arms. The United States remains a major arms exporter today, and perhaps ironically, so too does Russia, despite the changes that have taken place there. Indeed, Russia maintains that it must export arms today simply to survive; arms exports are one of its few sources of export earnings. In addition to the United States and Russia, China, Great Britain, France, Germany, and even Brazil also export sizable quantities of weapons.

There are several **reasons for the international arms trade**. Until recently, as far as the former Soviet Union and the United States were concerned, the struggle for global advantage played a major role in arms sales. Both countries sought to expand their influence through arms sales, and both feared that if they did not offer weapons, the other would step into the void. Historically, at least the second part of their rationale was accurate. On a number of occasions when the United States refused to sell arms to Peru, Egypt, Ethiopia, and others, the Soviet Union stepped in. On other occasions, when the Soviets refused to continue arms aid to Egypt and Somalia, the United States stepped in. However, little persuasive evidence exists that either side over the long run enhanced its influence in one or another country by extending military aid and assistance.

Another strong motivating factor for arms transfers is money, particularly insofar as sales to the Middle East are concerned. Former Secretary of Defense Donald Rumsfeld put it quite bluntly, declaring that "most of these customers are ready to pay cash. They ask no gifts from the U.S." And as we saw previously, after the collapse of the Soviet Union, Russia has continued to play a major role in the international arms market because of economic needs.

Cost and obsolescence also contribute to international arms traffic. The more units of a weapon made, the more the costs of research, development, and production startup can be amortized. Thus, per unit cost for weapons is reduced as

During the 1991 Persian Gulf War, Iraq used Scud missiles to attack Israel and Saudi Arabia. Three people were killed in this Tel Aviv building by a Scud. Iraq's use of Scuds provided ample proof that some developing countries had weapons that posed real threats to military units even of advanced industrial countries. (Reuters/Bettmann.)

production increases. One way to increase production, and therefore bring down costs, is to sell weapons overseas. Additionally, given the fact that the technological imperative drives technically advanced states to replace their weapons with still more modern weapons, foreign sales provide a convenient dumping ground for older weapons. Old weapons thus provide income, as part of their cost is recovered through foreign sale.

The flow of arms to Developing World states has been further accelerated by the widespread desire of those states to improve their military forces. The reasons for this are several. First, many Developing World states see security challenges on or near their borders. India and Pakistan eye each other with uneasiness, as do China and India. Despite promises not to rearrange their international boundaries, many African states fear their neighbors do not intend to keep their promises. In the Middle East, Iraq's defeat in the 1991 Persian Gulf War has not eliminated its neighbors' concerns over its intentions, and the Iranian military buildup that began in the early 1990s once again raised concerns about Iran's intentions. Nor has South America been immune to regional rivalries. Venezuela claims territory in Guyana, and Guatemala and Belize have territorial disputes as well. The list could continue. Europe and North America, for their parts, allowed their regional disputes in this century to become world wars.

If regional rivalries provide one motivation for arming, internal security—which, in many cases, may be translated to mean the maintenance of authoritarian or dictatorial regimes—provides another. Weapons can be put to many purposes, not the least of which is suppressing dissent.

A third reason developing states seek strengthened military forces is that, historically, the military has been the measure of a nation. Prestige thus plays a role. The more powerful a military, the more prestigious is the country, or so it is believed.

Closely linked to prestige as a motivating cause is the effort to escape vestiges of the colonial past. To many Developing World states, having one's own military forces is viable and tangible proof of independence, even if one's economy is controlled or influenced by others. Several Developing World states nonetheless resent their continuing dependence on external sources for military equipment and arms and have therefore begun to develop their own domestic arms industries despite higher costs of limited production. Some, such as Brazil, have even become weapon exporters.

Even in a nuclear era, then, states continue to recognize the utility of conventional arms and weapons and continue to purchase more and more weapons to add to their inventories. Although the additional power that such purchases add to a state's power potential may not be precisely defined, it is nonetheless evident that even in the nuclear age, conventional weapons are major instruments of power for states.

The Global Impact of Conventional and Nuclear Military Capabilities and Expenditures

Unfortunately, large-scale purchases of military capabilities carry with them sizable social costs. Critics of high levels of military expenditures point to several problems they claim are exacerbated by high levels of military expenditures. First, and most obviously, moneys spent on weaponry are not available for other socially useful expenditures. As all states operate more or less on budgets, moneys that are made available to the military are not available for other uses.

Second, the military produces little if anything. Soldiers and sailors, to be sure, may add to a state's security, but they do not add capital or consumer goods to a state's economy. The same is true for defense industries. Defense industries may produce hardware requisite for a state's defensive or offensive purposes, but they produce nothing that adds capital to a state's economy. In a certain sense, then, defense expenditures draw people and material away from economically expansive endeavors and may therefore retard economic growth.[15]

In part, inflation also may be linked to military expenditures. Members of the armed forces and employees of defense industries draw their pay and consume products, yet they do not produce a single consumer-oriented good. Thus, more money is injected into the economy, whereas the quantity of consumer goods remains constant. Therefore, prices are bid upward, and a classical inflationary situation occurs.

A corollary of this line of reasoning is that ever-higher levels of defense expenditures may in fact *undermine* the power of a state. During Dwight Eisenhower's presidency, he made exactly this point on several occasions. Eisenhower observed that the sinews of national strength were based on a variety of inputs and that emphasizing the military too much meant that other aspects of national strength would be starved. As a result of this reasoning, Eisenhower actually sought to reduce defense spending during his presidency.[16] Critics of the U.S. defense buildup during the Reagan presidency also used this argument. Significantly, many economists and policy analysts both within and outside the former Soviet Union believe that too much defense spending was one reason that the Soviet economy collapsed in the late 1980s and early 1990s.

The growth of military expenditures and the spread of advanced military technologies have had major noneconomic consequences as well. One of them, the increased ferocity of regional conflicts, has already been mentioned. Although the increased lethality of modern weapons may lead to more killing and destruction in a single war, a number of studies have concluded that the frequency of war has not increased.

Although no noticeable link exists between lethality of weapons and frequency of war, most analysts agree that increased lethality could lead to escalation of small regional wars to large ones. The rationale for such feared escalation is simple: As larger regional powers see their allied or client states suffer higher and higher casualty rates and levels of destruction, they may be more likely to step in to assist their ally/client. Indeed, before superpower relations improved so dramatically in the late 1980s, some analysts even speculated that such escalation could lead to a global conflict between superpowers.

Fortunately, this escalation claim remains pure speculation. However, the so-called **Nth country problem** is more than speculation; it is demonstrable fact. Although the Nth country problem generally is restricted to the nuclear level, the concept may also be used at the conventional level. Put simply, the Nth country problem refers to the attitude of many states that they must have military capabilities sufficient to meet all potential threats to their security. For example, if country A considers itself threatened by countries B and C, it may conclude that it needs military capabilities sufficient to defend itself from both threats. Country B, in turn, feels threatened by A and C, and begins a buildup to meet both threats. Country C sees a heightened threat from A and B and thus builds to off-set those threats. Country A once again must add weapons to its arsenal to meet the suddenly greater security challenges posed by B and C, and so the spiral con-tinues. Although contemporary arms races are not explained in totality by the Nth country problem, it does provide some of the rationale for increased levels of military expenditures and for the spread of modern conventional and nuclear weapons.

The heightened lethality of Developing World arsenals may also in some cases lead to increased unwillingness on the parts of the world's Great Powers, including the United States, to invervene in the Developing World when their interests are challenged. Because of increased lethality, the costs would be high-er. National decision-makers may thus decide that the benefit of intervention would be less than the cost.

The final paradox of the awesome growth of global military capabilities—both conventional and nuclear—since the end of World War II is that few if any countries have enhanced their security. More is being spent, more states have weapons and can use them, and the weapons are more deadly than ever, but the perturbing reality is that, almost without exception, states and their citizens feel more threatened than ever by the military might of potential foes. States them-selves have expanded their abilities to destroy, and in so doing have expanded the absolute level of their power potential, but it is less than certain that any has meaningfully increased its relative ability to achieve its objectives with military force. Indeed, as Figure 18–1 suggests, it may even be possible that after a cer-tain point additional military expenditures add nothing to a state's military power. National experiences throughout the world indicate that once a state develops an effective fighting force, a point is reached where each new division, tank, plane, or ship adds less to a state's power potential than the one that preceded it.

To their credit, some national leaders have recognized this paradox of decreasing security. Because of this recognition, because of their cognizance of the economic drain caused by military expenditures, and because of political pressures and other reasons, the world since 1968 has witnessed a historically unequaled series of efforts to control arms both quantitatively and qualitatively.

ARMS CONTROL: NAIVE FUTILITY OR HUMANITY'S LAST CHANCE?

Efforts to control arms and armaments are not new. As early as 431 B.C., Athens and Sparta argued over Athens' decision to extend its walls. To Athens, the exten-sion was purely defensive in nature. However, Sparta reasoned that the Athenian walls would render Athens invulnerable to land attack, thereby removing the only check on Athenian imperialism that other Greek city-states had. Sparta hence saw the walls as offensive. Efforts to negotiate failed, and the Peloponnesian War resulted.

Later, papal decrees of the Middle Ages attempted to define how and when certain weapons could be used. Following Grotius' arguments during the early seventeenth century about the necessity for laws to govern relations among nations, international law devoted much of its efforts to controlling the use and misuse of weapons during war and peace.

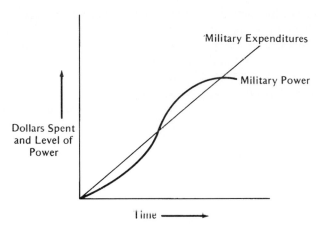

FIGURE 18–1   Military power as a function of military expenditure: a hypothetical representation.

Modern efforts to control arms and armaments are generally traced to the Hague Conference of 1899 and 1907. Both conferences presented excellent examples of good intentions complicated by military realities and uncertainties. At the 1899 conference, land bombardment of undefended towns was proscribed, but no agreement could be reached on sea bombardment, so the question was deferred. It was also agreed that reprisals were permissible if the enemy breached the rules. In 1907, poison gas and dum-dum bullets were outlawed.[17] Despite those and other efforts, states viewed arms control efforts with misgiving, as affronts to their sovereignty and as unwanted limits on their potential power. Thus, although few states were as bold as Germany, which in a 1904 military manual declared that the "law of necessity" would sanctify breaches in international laws of war,[18] most state leaderships held similar attitudes.

During the period between World Wars I and II, a variety of efforts were undertaken to limit arms and outlaw war. The Washington Naval Conference of 1921–22 set fixed tonnage ratios for major surface combatants at a formula of 5–5–3–1.75–1.75, respectively, for the United States, Great Britain, Japan, Italy, and France. Although the formula limited tonnages, it did not limit firepower, so a technical race began to improve naval firepower capabilities. More important, the treaty covered neither aircraft carriers nor submarines, the two major naval weapons of World War II. Other interwar arms control efforts proved equally futile.

Following World War II, new efforts were again made to limit arms and armaments. At first, these efforts were aimed at nuclear weapons, but as it became gradually evident that conventional war could escalate to the nuclear level and that conventional war itself was growing ever more destructive, these efforts expanded into nonnuclear areas as well. As in earlier years, all arms control efforts met with less than resounding success.

Nuclear Arms Control

In 1946, the United States advanced the first concept for the control of nuclear weapons. Under the Baruch Plan, a UN body, the Atomic Development Authority, would be created to control global nuclear energy programs, including weapons. Given the composition of the UN at the time, and the Soviet view of the UN as an American foreign policy tool, Soviet rejection of the plan was preordained. To the Soviet Union, international control of nuclear energy should have followed rather than preceded nuclear disarmament. The United States, of course, had a monopoly on nuclear weapons in 1946.

Subsequent nuclear arms control negotiations faltered on the issue of verification of compliance. The United States regularly proposed on-site inspections, which the Soviet Union always rejected as spying. At the 1955 Eisenhower-Khrushchev Geneva Summit meeting, the U.S. president offered his famous "Open Skies" proposal for reciprocal air inspections. Khrushchev countered with his own proposal for ground sensor stations at areas remote from test sites, which the United States rejected as inadequate.

The 1959 Antarctic Treaty was the first major success in nuclear arms control. Eighteen states, including the United States and the U.S.S.R., agreed under the treaty to ban deployment of nuclear weapons in Antarctica. The next breakthrough came with the 1963 Limited Test Ban Treaty, in which most UN member states agreed not to set off nuclear explosions in space, under water, or in the atmosphere. 1967 was a banner year for nuclear arms control, with two separate treaties banning nuclear weapons from outer space and from Latin America.

In 1968, 98 states signed what was the most promising, and has become the most frustrating, treaty in the history of efforts to control nuclear weapons, the **Non-Proliferation Treaty** (NPT). Signatory states agreed not to transfer nuclear weapons to any state that did not have them, and opposed the development of nuclear weapons by those states. Monitored by the International Atomic Energy Agency, the NPT promised to be a useful tool to halt nuclear proliferation. Unfortunately, several states, most of which had either just joined the nuclear club or which were projected to develop a nuclear capability before the end of the century or sooner, chose not to sign. France, China, India, Israel, and South Africa were all nonsignatory states that claimed the treaty either abridged national sovereignty or allowed the United States, the U.S.S.R., and Great Britain to maintain their nuclear supremacy relative to the rest of the world. Given this, the NPT may well be rendered virtually meaningless in the future.

The centerpiece of U.S.-Soviet detente during the 1970s was SALT I. Although not specifically a nuclear arms control treaty, SALT I did seek to set an upper limit on Soviet and U.S. strategic delivery systems. SALT I, agreed to in 1972 for a period of five years, was completely successful in its efforts to limit the quantitative growth of SLBM and ICBM delivery vehicles. Unfortunately, however, SALT I had several flaws. It did not limit bombers or cruise missiles, nor did it limit qualitative improvements to existing or new SLBMs or ICBMs. Thus, during the five years when SALT I was in force, the U.S.-Soviet nuclear arms race continued virtually unabated, but on the qualitative rather than quantitative plane. Accuracies improved, MIRVs were deployed, and mobile land-based systems were developed on both sides. In addition, SALT I contained a political flaw. Because of lower reliability rates of Soviet ICBMs and because of shorter on-station times for Soviet ballistic missile submarines, SALT I permitted the Soviet Union a numerical advantage in both ICBMs and SLBMs. From the viewpoint of many U.S. citizens, SALT I appeared to be a treaty of negotiated inferiority.

SALT II attempted to rectify many of the real and perceived flaws in SALT

I. Emphasizing controls on qualitative as well as quantitative aspects of the nuclear arms race, SALT II set an equal maximum level for combinations of Soviet and U.S. delivery vehicles, including strategic bombers, ICBMs, and SLBMs. MIRVs on ICBMs were limited to 10 per launch vehicle, and on SLBMs to 14. Each side could also deploy only one new ICBM during the duration of the treaty.

Nevertheless, critics found flaws. Verification of the treaty was one major concern, and the fact that the U.S.S.R. was permitted to retain over 300 heavy ICBMs was another. The treaty was submitted to the U.S. Senate in 1979 but was withdrawn following the Soviet invasion of Afghanistan. Had the Soviet invasion of Afghanistan not occurred, SALT II may have been ratified by the Senate. With the Soviet invasion, its defeat was certain.

Before Ronald Reagan assumed the presidency, he condemned SALT II as "fatally flawed." Nevertheless, after taking office he promised that the United States would abide by the terms of SALT II until a new treaty was negotiated. Reagan was as good as his word, at least until May 1986 when he declared that unless Soviet noncompliance with SALT ended, the United States would reassess its own position. In late 1986, after concluding that the U.S.S.R. had ignored treaty provisions, the United States itself exceeded SALT II limits.

As for new arms control negotiations, U.S.-Soviet strategic arms reduction talks began in June 1982, but made no headway. They were suspended in December 1983 following U.S. deployment of **intermediate nuclear forces** (INF) to Europe, but resumed in March 1985 under a different format. Three separate tracks of negotiations were pursued, one covering INF, a second on space and defensive weapons, and the third on strategic weapons.

The INF negotiations were a major success. These talks continued negotiations that began formally in 1981, whose objective was to reduce the number of "Eurostrategic" nuclear weapons deployed in Europe. (Eurostrategic weapons did not have intercontinental range but could reach the Soviet Union from Western Europe, and vice versa.) Eurostrategic systems included the U.S.S.R.'s SS-20 and the United States' Pershing II and ground-launched cruise missiles.

The INF negotiations were incredibly complex, and both sides on occasion changed their negotiating positions. Issues of disagreement included whether U.S. aircraft carriers and tactical aircraft should be counted (the so-called "forward-based systems" issue); whether British and French systems should be counted; and whether because of the SS-20's mobility the count on this system should include only those SS-20s deployed in Europe or be global. Table 18–6 details the tortuous path these talks took following their initiation.

Eventually an INF agreement was forged, and it probably was more comprehensive than either side thought possible. In simplest terms, under the INF agreement the United States and the Soviet Union agreed to eliminate all their INF weapons, regardless of where they were based. Never before had the superpowers ever agreed to so comprehensive an arms control step. The INF treaty was concluded in December 1987, and the following year Soviet and U.S. inspectors each journeyed to the other's country to watch INF weapons be destroyed, and to monitor plants that formerly had made them to make sure that production had stopped. All INF weapons are now destroyed.

Progress at the space and defensive arms talks was slow. The Soviets first linked success in these talks to the INF and strategic arms talks, saying that no progress could be made elsewhere on arms talks unless the United States

TABLE 18–6   The Tortuous Course of Intermediate Nuclear Force Arms Negotiations

Events	U.S. Proposal/ Response	Soviet Proposal/ Response
1976—Soviet SS-20 deployment begins		
Dec. 79—NATO "Two Track" decision: Negotiate and deploy INF		
Oct. 80—Preliminary INF talks begin and end		Soviets demand U.S. forward-based systems be included
	U.S. says this is out of the question; missiles only to be discussed; Soviets can move weapons into Europe quickly	1981—U.S.S.R. says if NATO suspends INF deployment, U.S.S.R. will reduce SS-20 numbers
Nov. 81—INF talks begin	U.S. says this assures Soviet superiority	
	Zero Option: No U.S. INF, no Soviet INF	This removes old Soviet SS-5 missiles, too, but leaves British and French forces; NATO gets superiority
	This ignores Soviet planes in U.S.S.R., and hence gives U.S.S.R. big advantage; also U.S. does not speak for France or Britain	Feb. 82—Reduce all systems to 600 by 1985 and 300 by 1990, including French and British
Mar. 82—Soviets freeze SS-20 deployment at about 300	U.S. stays with Zero Option; Soviet freeze a ploy that gives U.S.S.R. superiority	Dec. 82—U.S.S.R. to reduce INF to number possessed by France and Britain; no NATO INF
July 82—"Walk in the Woods" agreement reached by U.S. and Soviet negotiators; then disavowed by both sides	Feb. 83—U.S. does not speak for France and Britain; this gives U.S.S.R. superiority	
	Mar. 83—"Interim Agreement" of phased INF reduction to zero, with equal numbers on a global basis until then	This ignores French, British, and U.S. forward-based systems

Events	U.S. Proposal/ Response	Soviet Proposal/ Response

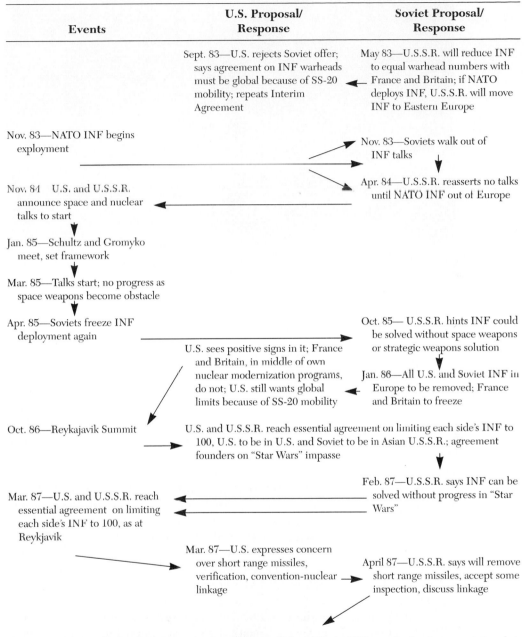

| | Sept. 83—U.S. rejects Soviet offer; says agreement on INF warheads must be global because of SS-20 mobility; repeats Interim Agreement | May 83—U.S.S.R. will reduce INF to equal warhead numbers with France and Britain; if NATO deploys INF, U.S.S.R. will move INF to Eastern Europe |

Nov. 83—NATO INF begins exployment

Nov. 83—Soviets walk out of INF talks

Apr. 84—U.S.S.R. reasserts no talks until NATO INF out of Europe

Nov. 84 U.S. and U.S.S.R. announce space and nuclear talks to start

Jan. 85—Schultz and Gromyko meet, set framework

Mar. 85—Talks start; no progress as space weapons become obstacle

Apr. 85—Soviets freeze INF deployment again

Oct. 85— U.S.S.R. hints INF could be solved without space weapons or strategic weapons solution

U.S. sees positive signs in it; France and Britain, in middle of own nuclear modernization programs, do not; U.S. still wants global limits because of SS-20 mobility

Jan. 86—All U.S. and Soviet INF in Europe to be removed; France and Britain to freeze

Oct. 86—Reykajavik Summit

U.S. and U.S.S.R. reach essential agreement on limiting each side's INF to 100, U.S. to be in U.S. and Soviet to be in Asian U.S.S.R.; agreement founders on "Star Wars" impasse

Feb. 87—U.S.S.R. says INF can be solved without progress in "Star Wars"

Mar. 87—U.S. and U.S.S.R. reach essential agreement on limiting each side's INF to 100, as at Reykjavik

Mar. 87—U.S. expresses concern over short range missiles, verification, convention-nuclear linkage

April 87—U.S.S.R. says will remove short range missiles, accept some inspection, discuss linkage

Further negotiations lead to INF Agreement that eliminates U.S. and Soviet INF completely; Agreement signed at Third Reagan-Gorbachev Summit, Washington, D.C., December 1987; U.S. and Soviet inspectors began to oversee destruction of each other's INF weapons in 1988.

In January 1993, George Bush and Boris Yeltsin signed the START II Treaty, which when completely implemented will drastically reduce the strategic nuclear arsenals of the United States and the former Soviet Union.   (Reuters/Bettmann.)

stopped its SDI work. Gradually, the Soviets moderated their position, but by 1990, the two sides still disagreed over several issues, and no treaty on space and defensive weapons was in sight. By 1991, the United States had begun to contemplate deploying what it called a "Global Protection Against Limited Strikes" (GPALS) system, and the Soviet Union and the United States occasionally talked about cooperation in strategic defensive research. However, with the dissolution of the U.S.S.R. and Russia's ensuing economic and other problems, by 1993 nothing had come of these talks.

Progress was also slow at the strategic arms talks, at least at first. As the 1990s opened, no agreement had been reached. However, Soviet-American differences gradually narrowed and in July 1991, the United States and the Soviet Union signed the first **strategic arms reduction treaty**, also called START I. Under START I, each side was limited to a total of no more than 1,600 ICBMs, SLBMs, and strategic bombers. Combined, these delivery vehicles were not permitted to carry more than 6,000 "START-countable" warheads.

The breakup of the Soviet Union caused serious problems for START. Following the collapse of the U.S.S.R., Belarus, Kazakhstan, Russia, and Ukraine all inherited some of the Soviet Union's strategic weapons. Careful negotiations between these four states and the United States led to an agreement that all nuclear weapons of the former Soviet Union would be returned to Russia, with most being destroyed. All the involved states agreed that the START treaty would remain in force. But it remained to be seen whether all the new nuclear powers would be as good as their word.

Nevertheless, the United States and Russia continued to negotiate further strategic nuclear weapons reductions, and in January 1993, the two countries reached a START II accord that, among other things, would reduce the total number of strategic nuclear warheads in each country's arsenal to 3,500 or less by

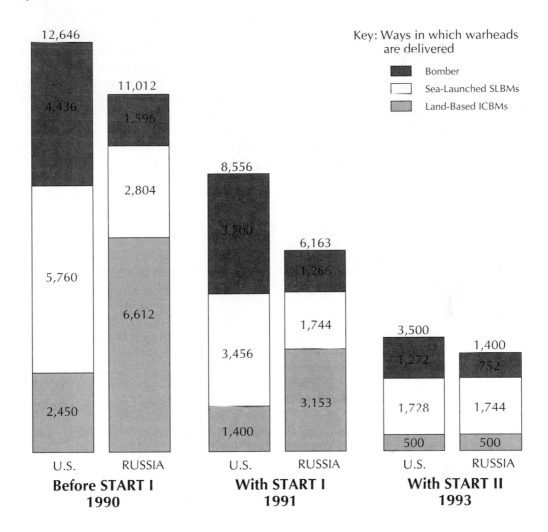

FIGURE 18–2   The impact of the START I and II treaties on the number of strategic nuclear warheads in the U.S. and Soviet/Russian strategic nuclear arsenals.
(SOURCE: START I and II treaties, 1991 and 1993, respectively; and the Arms Control Association.)

2003, and which banned multiple warhead missiles. Nuclear arms reductions negotiations had indeed made tremendous progress in a short period of time, and this progress is shown in Figure 18–2.

Conventional Arms Control

The record of conventional arms control closely parallels the record of nuclear arms control. A few conventional arms control agreements such as a multilateral treaty banning biological weapons (1975) and environmental modification (1978) have been signed, and the 1972 ABM treaty may possibly be considered a conventional arms agreement.[19] But as a rule, treaties that were completed had little impact, and most conventional arms negotiations achieved little or nothing. Thus, conventional arms transfer talks in the 1970s were suspended shortly after they began, the Indian Ocean talks met a similar fate, and the mutual and balanced force reduction discussions in Europe dragged on for almost two decades without achieving a breakthrough.[20] Conventional weapons remained too precious commodities and objects of too much disagreement for states willingly to accept, other than in rare cases, limitations on their sovereign right to determine for themselves the proper levels of armament.

As with nuclear arms control negotiations, conventional arms control negotiations took a pronounced turn for the better in the late 1980s and early 1990s, especially in East–West relations. Beginning in 1989, two new sets of negotiations opened in Vienna within the framework of the Conference on Security and Cooperation in Europe, which first met in 1972. The first set, the Negotiations on Conventional Armed Forces in Europe (CFE), covered all NATO and Warsaw Pact territory from the Atlantic Ocean to the Ural Mountains. Twenty-three countries were involved. The second set, the Negotiations on Confidence and Security-Building Measures (CSBM), involved 35 European and North American states, and sought to create structures and mechanisms to lower East–West tensions and increase trust.

As a result of these negotiations, and as a result of the major changes in Eastern Europe in 1989 and 1990, two major East–West agreements were signed in 1990, both of which were either partially or completely related to conventional arms control. The first agreement, the so-called "Two Plus Four" treaty, was concluded in September 1990. This treaty concluded terms for German unification and the withdrawal of Soviet troops from what was East Germany by the end of 1994.

The second agreement, the **Conventional Forces in Europe (CFE) Treaty**, was signed in November 1990. Under the terms of CFE, the U.S.S.R. was required to undertake a massive reduction in the quantity of military equipment it had based west of the Ural Mountains. CFE required less sizable but still significant reductions in NATO's European based military equipment as well.[21]

As was the case with nuclear arms control agreements, the collapse of the Soviet Union complicated several aspects of the treaties. Fortunately, however, all sides agreed to proceed with the treaties as negotiated. By 1993, Europe was no longer the armed camp that it had been just a few short years before.

Nevertheless, the haunting reality remains that despite the brightening future for conventional arms control, states retain greater military capabilities than at any other time in history. Although the East–West conflict is over, other centers of conflict remain. Thus, states may continue to find it difficult to create and implement conventional and nuclear arms control regimes. We turn now to some of the more prominent difficulties.

Problems of Arms Control: An Overview

Compliance is one of the greatest bugaboos of arms control agreements. Stated differently, how can country A verify what country B is doing to make sure it is not cheating? Throughout most of the postwar history of arms control efforts, the United States advocated on-site inspections, which the U.S.S.R. rejected as espionage. The U.S.S.R. generally proposed nuclear free zones and complete nuclear disarmament; to the United States, these were unacceptable concepts because of the alleged Soviet conventional military edge. The verification dilemma remained unsolved.

The advent of the space age, advanced telemetry, and high-grade communications systems provided both the United States and the U.S.S.R. with new potential for verification of arms control agreements through so-called national technical means of verification. In more workable terms, spy satellites with high resolution cameras and other equipment allowed national authorities to see exactly where and how many nuclear delivery vehicles the other had. Both SALT I and SALT II were based on national technical means of verification. Even so, verification problems persisted, particularly when mobile missiles, MIRVs, and qualitative limits were set. Mobile missiles can be more easily hidden, the number of MIRVs on an ICBM can be shielded, and qualitative limits, in many cases, are not outwardly discernible.

National technical means of verification have even more serious problems at the conventional level. Counting tanks and soldiers is a difficult task, especially when they are so many and so mobile. Indeed, one of the major difficulties at the MBFR talks was that the United States and the Soviet Union could not agree on what force levels were. Clearly, without agreement on existent force levels, negotiations were frustrated from the start.

In addition, arms control negotiations are too often concerned with current weapons capabilities and too rarely concerned with future capabilities. Once a weapon system becomes operational, it takes on a life of its own; procurement moneys have been spent, strategy and tactics may have been altered to incorporate it, and in a psychological sense, parting with a new military capability may be difficult.

This reality began to change in the late 1980s and the 1990s as the INF treaty, the CFE agreement, and the two START treaties all led to significant reductions in the number of deployed weapons. Nevertheless, with the exception of the ABM treaty, negotiations virtually always are carried out about weapons already in the field, even while newer and more deadly weapons are being tested and developed—and ignored by the negotiators. Thus, in SALT I, MIRVs were ignored; they had not yet been deployed. By the early 1980s, MIRVed ICBMs presented the greatest threat to the security of both the United States and the U.S.S.R.; would that farsighted negotiators had included them in SALT I. Today, the same scenario may be seen in its early stages with lasers and other exotic weaponry.

With these and other difficulties, and given the sketchy-at-best record of arms control attempts throughout history, skeptics might be forgiven if they ask why national leaders continue to make arms control a part of national policy. Several answers are possible, not the least of which are public pressure and genuine concern on the leaders themselves about the potential destructiveness of contemporary war. Here, one need only remember Ronald Reagan's originally slow, but then increasingly rapid acceptance of the principle of negotiations with the U.S.S.R.

At least two other reasons also exist for continued efforts to reach arms control agreements. The first is cost. Although spokesperson after spokesperson in both the Reagan and Bush administrations warned that negotiations, if successful, would not by themselves lead to reduced defense expenditures, the question as it should be posed is somewhat different. How much more *would* have been spent if no agreement had existed? Thus, for example, the U.S. Department of

State estimated in 1979 that by 1985, the U.S.S.R. would have approximately 2,500 more reentry vehicles without SALT II than with it. The comparable U.S. figure was about 5,100. SALT II may not have led to expenditure decreases, but it slowed the rate of increase.

Indeed, in addition to the transformation in the international political landscape that occurred in the late 1980s and early 1990s, the primary reason that arms control has become more successful is because many countries face severe economic difficulties and hope to develop a "peace dividend" from reduced military spending that will help them cope with their other economic difficulties.

Finally, when a verifiable agreement is in place, states may more effectively plan their own defense needs in relation to those of other states. Predictability is part of the intellectual baggage of arms control. States know how many of at least some weapons a potential enemy has and what its future procurement pattern must be to stay within treaty restrictions. Security planners may thus predict the future with greater accuracy, at least in the narrow area of arms control. And despite the failures, this is a step in the right direction.

MILITARY CAPABILITIES OF NONSTATE ACTORS

Traditionally, at least since the Treaty of Westphalia, states have been the primary repositories of military capabilities. So far, this chapter has followed a traditional approach and examined only those aspects of military capabilities that are directly controlled by states themselves. By itself, such analysis yields an incomplete view of the dimensions of military power in international affairs. Not only states have enhanced their power potential by attaining military capabilities. Other actors have followed and will continue to follow the path that states took. Ethnic/national liberation organizations, terrorist groups and movements, and even religious movements and political parties have consciously attempted, on occasion, to increase their power by acquiring additional military capabilities. A few nongovernmental organizations, certain intergovernmental organizations, and some multinational corporations have also yielded to the attraction to influence actors and events through military power. So too have other international economic interests. For example, in 1990, rumors circulated throughout the Americas that South American drug interests had offered a $30 million contract for the assassination of President George Bush.

With the exception of a few IGOs designed specifically or primarily as military alliances and an occasional transnational religious movement or political party, nonstate actors rarely possess the wherewithal to procure and maintain military forces of great size or power. Nevertheless, the military capabilities that these other actors do possess enable them to engage in various types of nontraditional violence, including civil wars, terrorism, and other types of low-intensity conflict. Often states, or more precisely governments of states, are the targets of nontraditional violence.

It is difficult, if not impossible, to determine objectively the boundary between the wanton destruction and death caused by terrorists, the guerrilla war (sometimes called "low-intensity conflict") pursued by weak national liberation movements, and the civil war fought by stronger national liberation movements. Yet in each of these cases, the user of military capabilities as a tool or potential tool of violence is not a state. Nontraditional violence, then, may be most simply defined as violence between any two international actors at least one of which is a nonstate actor.

Despite the fact that nonstate actors rarely have the military capabilities at their disposal that major state actors have, their ability to influence the course of world events is sometimes considerable. George Washington and the Continental Army fought against the world's premier military power, and neither Washington nor his army represented a state actor. They won, and in so doing changed world history. Lenin and his Bolsheviks were little more than a splinter political party when they used their military capabilities to seize the Russian state in 1917; despite their limited military capabilities, they succeeded in maintaining control of the state, in part because of weak and divided opposition and in part because of Lenin's skilled leadership. Some 40 years later, Fidel Castro used military force to take over Cuba, again with startling effects for the international community. Indeed, many of the states that were formed out of the old European empires received their independence because indigenous nonstate actors, generally national liberation movements, used their military prowess to prove to their colonial masters that the costs of administering an empire were too great to bear. From Jomo Kenyatta in Kenya to Robert Mugabe in Zimbabwe, leaders of ethnic or national liberation movements have often resorted to their military arms to enhance their power. Only Mahatma Gandhi, the Indian independence leader, successfully resorted to nonviolence and passive resistance to achieve independence for his country from a colonial power that, at the outset of the struggle, preferred to maintain control.

It is a statement of the obvious that military capabilities are key ingredients of civil wars. Nevertheless, civil wars have also had tremendous impact on international affairs and must be included here since at least one side, and possibly both sides (or more), are nonstate actors. For example, the Chinese Civil War pitted Chiang Kai-shek's governmental forces against Mao Zedong's communist forces. The repercussions of this epic confrontation, civil in character, continue today. Here it would also be proper to note that at the height of the Chinese Civil War, Mao fielded an army of over 1 million men. Obviously, the military capabilities available to nonstate actors can sometimes be large.

Washington, Lenin, Castro, Kenyatta, Mugabe, and Mao were all leaders who used the military capabilities at the disposal of the nonstate actors they led to enhance the power of their respective movements. In each case, military capabilities played a decisive role in aiding the respective movements to attain their objectives. In other cases, however, the use of military capabilities by nonstate actors has strengthened the actor temporarily, even though final objectives may not be attained. Biafran secessionists, El Salvadorian guerrillas, and the PLO all turned or turn to the military as an instrument to increase their ability to influence events.

Terrorist use of military capabilities may also have great impact on world politics. (Again, the student should recall the difficulty in defining terrorism. The PLO, the IRA, the Mau-Maus, the Red Brigade, and a variety of organizations and groups are sometimes described as ethnic or national liberation movements, political parties, or religious movements, but are viewed by many others as terrorists.) Efforts to assassinate prominent world leaders such as Pope John Paul II have shocked the global community; if those efforts had been successful, the shock would have been magnified many times. The 1981 assassination of Anwar Sadat by religious dissidents within the Egyptian army threw much of the Middle

East into turmoil and uncertainty, at least until Sadat's successor, Hosni Mubarak, clarified his policy intentions.

For the most part, nonstate actors have rather basic military arsenals. They do not fly high-performance aircraft, use state-of-the-art land equipment, or have access to other advanced military capabilities. This, of course, detracts from their military potential. However, as they rarely seek to fight their opponent or enemy in a standing battle, this diminution of power is not so serious as may at first be supposed.

On some occasions, though, modern weaponry has been obtained by nonstate actors. The PLO has heavy tanks, artillery, and armored personnel carriers; the Zimbabwe Patriotic Front had surface-to-air missiles; Mao's People's Liberation Army had heavy artillery and other main force weapons; and the Afghan guerrillas acquired Stinger surface-to-air missiles. Since these and similar groups and organizations had neither the industrial capacity nor the economic base to produce these weapons, where do they come from?

Four answers are possible. First, states sometimes furnish sizable quantities of military equipment to selected nonstate actors. These arms transfers rarely appear in official statistics on international arms transfers. For example, the Soviet Union provided the PLO with virtually all of its tanks, artillery, and armored personnel carriers. Especially during the 1980s, the United States also provided extensive support to guerrillas fighting against pro-Soviet governments in Afghanistan, Angola, Cambodia, and Nicaragua. (In the case of Nicaragua, at least some of the aid was provided illegally, as was discovered during the 1987 Iran-Contra hearings.) The purpose of these U.S. actions, as was and is the purpose of other state actors who provide weapons for nonstate actors, is straightforward: to help the nonstate actor achieve its objectives, which inevitably coincide with the objectives of the aid donor, and to strengthen political ties between donor and recipient. In more extreme cases of state support to nonstate actors, the phenomenon of state-supported terrorism develops; the state that supplies the nonstate actor in these instances may deny that it is supporting a terrorist organization, but from the perspective of the state whose interests are attacked by the nonstate actors, things look different.

A second source of weapons and arms for nonstate actors is through defection. Mao's forces were greatly strengthened by men—and the weapons they brought with them—from the Kuomintang. In Afghanistan during the 1980s, anti-Soviet forces were also strengthened by defections from the army of the pro-Soviet Afghan regime.

The international demand for arms has also led to the development of a large, illicit trade in weapons, a sizable percentage of which are purchased by nonstate actors. States have attempted to control arms trade by issuing end-user certificates and by implementing arms export control legislation, but arms dealers have used many methods ranging from forged certificates to refusing to report exports to circumvent the legislation. Illicit arms traffic to nonstate actors accelerated during the 1970s and 1980s, and continues in the 1990s.

The final major method nonstate actors employ to acquire arms is through theft and capture. Particularly in the Developing World, theft of military equipment from state military forces presents a major problem; however, it is a problem not restricted to the Developing World. Thus, when in 1990 civil war broke out in Soviet Azerbaijan between Armenians and Azerbaijanis, both sides raided Soviet army depots to obtain weapons. Furthermore, opponents' weapons are often used by nonstate actors. The Vietcong, for example, used old French and new American weapons that they had captured during much of the Vietnam War, at least until Soviet aid was accelerated.

Perhaps the greatest fear related to nonstate actors' military capabilities is at the nuclear level. This potential problem was discussed earlier in this chapter, but must be addressed here again. Although nuclear proliferation at the state level is an issue of extreme concern throughout the world, an equal concern exists about the potential for terrorist groups to steal a nuclear weapon. If it was true at the state level that those having the least to lose may be the most willing to use nuclear weapons, then it is even more true at the nonstate level. The threat of nuclear terrorism is a real one.

At the other extreme from terrorist groups and organizations are intergovernmental organizations. Whereas terrorists seek to undermine state governments and social structures with their military capabilities, IGOs—at least those that have a military arm—attempt to defend and further the interests of member states. IGOs receive whatever military capacity they have from member states. UN peacekeeping forces, NATO, the Warsaw Pact, and OAU peacekeeping forces are all composed of units from member states. The units are generally employed only when widespread agreement exists within the IGO about the proposed employment. Obviously, this creates a major constraint on the use of military capabilities by IGOs. NATO countries will not designate forces for use outside European theater areas, the OAU had difficulty funding a peacekeeping force in Chad, and the United Nations Secretariat must develop not only funding sources and a political consensus in the UN before peacekeeping can begin, but also find states willing to have their troops participate in proposed peacekeeping efforts.

Quantitatively and qualitatively, the aggregate military capabilities under the control of nonstate actors is probably less than military capabilities in the arsenal of a midrank power such as Great Britain or France. (This observation excludes NATO and other defense- or security-related IGOs.) Nevertheless, because of the types of objectives nonstate actors pursue and the methods that they choose to use, the power they acquire from their weapons capabilities is disproportionately large. They rarely have territory or complex ecotechnical infrastructures to defend, and the threat of the use of force is, for them, perhaps even more effective than the actual use of force. At the level of nonstate actor, then, military capabilities continue to have subjective and objective components, even as they did at the state level. With few economic tools at their disposal, military capabilities remain the major parameter of power for many nonstate actors.

POWER AND MILITARY CAPABILITIES

Despite the increased complexity of international affairs during the 1990s, the military capabilities of an international actor continue to supply a major—and possibly *the* major—input to an actor's power potential. Even though in the light of the end of East–West tensions and increased efforts to solve regional conflicts, some analysts argue that military power is becoming irrelevant, there is little to suggest that this conclusion is true. Granted, the likelihood of the use of military force under certain conditions has decreased, and the conditions under which resort to force is likely are changing. Nevertheless, contemporary international actors regularly find resort to force necessary even in the 1990s. They must and do prepare themselves for that contingency, even if the ethics and morality of using force or threatening to use force are sometimes open to question.

This chapter has traced the major trends in the relationship between power and military capabilities. More states are acquiring more weapons, and the quality and lethality of the weapons they attain is rising as well. Militarily speaking, states are becoming more powerful in absolute terms but rarely improving their power potential in relative terms. The great powers of the 1990s—France, Great Britain, China, and a very few others—would have been superpowers in the 1940s or 1950s if they had had then the armaments and weapons they have now. Today, none are military matches for the world's one remaining military superpower, the United States.

Another comparison may be more telling. Before the Persian Gulf War, Iraq could put 5,500 tanks and 689 combat aircraft into the field. These totals were more than Hitler used to invade France in 1940. And their capabilities dwarfed those of Hitler's weapons. Nevertheless, in 1990, Iraq was not even considered a great power.

Even with these major trends, military capabilities do not translate directly into increased power potential. Powerful weapons used unintelligently add little to a state's power; certain types of weapons are not useful in certain situations; and the will to act must be present as well. For example, France had what was arguably the world's finest tank in its arsenal in 1940 but deployed it as an infantry support vehicle. Because of its style of deployment, it proved virtually useless. Similarly, U.S. nuclear weapons were useless in Vietnam, and Soviet tanks proved of limited utility in Afghanistan. In the U.S. case, nuclear weapons were inappropriate because of the scale and type of damage they caused, and in the Soviet case, tanks proved poorly suited for use in Afghanistan's mountainous regions. Finally, concerning will, United States armed forces were meaningless assets to effect the rescue of the U.S. hostages in Teheran once the hostages' safe return was elevated to the highest national priority. The will to use force did not exist.

The question of will returns us once again to the subjective and objective components of military capabilities. It cannot be emphasized enough that the degree of power that an actor acquires from its military abilities is a function not only of relatively objective qualitative, quantitative, and organizational parameters, but also of completely subjective parameters such as morale, cohesion, and will. These subjective parameters are rendered even more abstract since they are measured and assessed not only by the actor, but also by those that the actor is attempting to influence. Thus, the power that an actor acquires from its military capabilities is seen differently by different actors. Power, in the military sphere as elsewhere, is thus as much perceptual and reputational as actual.

Above the assessments of power and military capabilities hovers the reality that humans in their quest to influence others by force of arms and to prevent others from influencing them by force of arms have created and are dispersing military capabilities unrivaled in recorded history. It is disconcerting to realize that despite the death and destruction that twentieth-century wars have caused, humanity has come no further than it has on arms control and arms limitation efforts.

Given the immense destructive capacity of nuclear weapons, it is even more frightening to realize that the next global war, if there is one, may end civilization as we know it. Albert Einstein once observed that although he did not know what types of weapons would be used in World War III, he could predict what weapons would be used in World War IV: sticks and stones.

Power and military capabilities, then, remain integrally related. Before the late 1980s, nothing indicated that state or nonstate actors were slowing their efforts to acquire those capabilities, both in hope of enhancing their own power and in fear that unless they improved their own capabilities, they would fall behind. But in the late 1980s and early 1990s, East–West tensions ended, several efforts to resolve regional conflicts proved successful, and several major arms control agreements were successfully concluded. So there is a glimmer of hope that despite the outbreak of new and serious regional conflicts in many regions of the world, the mad momentum to acquire more and better arms has slowed. Nevertheless, we must also recognize that this glimmer of hope may be only a respite before international actors once more begin their pursuit of more and better weapons, even while their security, paradoxically, decreases.

KEY TERMS AND CONCEPTS

objective and subjective
   components of military power
nuclear arms race
fission weapons
fusion weapons
intercontinental ballistic
   missile (ICBM)
Cuban Missile Crisis
multiple independently targetable
   reentry vehicle (MIRV)
Strategic Arms Limitation
   Treaty (SALT)
deterrence and mutual deterrence
mutual assured destruction (MAD)
triad
nuclear proliferation
conventional weapons
dimensions of international
   defense spending

reasons for international
   arms trade
impacts of military capabilities
   and expenditures
Nth country problem
arms control
Non-Proliferation Treaty
   (NPT)
intermediate nuclear forces
   (INF) treaty
strategic arms reduction
   treaty (START)
Conventional Forces in Europe
   (CFE) treaty
military capabilities of
   nonstate actors

NOTES

1. Carl von Clausewitz, *On War* (Princeton.: Princeton University Press, 1976).
2. For an excellent series of articles on the relationship between military capabilities and power, see Robert J. Art and Kenneth N. Waltz, eds., *The Use of Force: Military Power and International Politics* (New York: University Press of America, 1993).
3. As reported in Coral Bell, *Negotiations from Strength* (New York: Knopf, 1963), p. 141.
4. For the full texts of SALT I and SALT II, and other related materials, see U.S. Arms Control and Disarmament Agency (ACDA), *Arms Control and Disarmament*

Agreements: Texts and Histories of Negotiations (Washington: U.S. Government Printing Office, 1982), pp. 148–157, 239–277.

5. See Alton Frye, "How to Fix SALT," *Foreign Policy*, No. 39 (Summer 1980): 58–73; Edward L. Rowny, "Soviets Are Still Russians," *Survey*, Vol. 25 (Spring 1980): 1–9; and J. Muravchik, "Expectations of SALT I: Lessons for SALT III," *World Affairs*, Winter 1980–81, pp. 278–297.

6. For more detailed discussion of these and related issues, see Michele A. Flourney, *Nuclear Weapons After the Cold War: Guidelines for U.S. Policy* (New York: Harper-Collins, 1993).

7. For a brief official discussion of U.S. strategic nuclear forces, see Organization of the Joint Chiefs of Staff, *United States Military Posture FY 1991*.

8. Jimmy Carter changed the public U.S. targeting posture to this position during the fall of 1980 with Presidential Directive 59. Ronald Reagan continued and expanded upon this posture.

9. For discussions of "nuclear winter," see Carl Sagan, "Nuclear War and Climatic Catastrophe: Some Policy Implications," *Foreign Affairs*, Vol. 62, No. 2 (Winter 1983–84): 257–292. See also A. B. Pittock et al., *Environmental Consequences of Nuclear War* (New York: John Wiley, 1985); and Dennis M. Drew, *Nuclear Winter and National Security: Implications for Future Policy* (Maxwell Air Force Base: Air University Press, 1986).

10. For the text of the NPT and other related information, see ACDA, pp. 82–99.

11. For detailed discussions of the nuclear proliferation problem, see Peter A. Clausen, *Nonproliferation and the National Interest: America's Response to the Spread of Nuclear Weapons* (New York: HarperCollins, 1993); and David Fischer, *Stopping the Spread of Nuclear Weapons: The Past and the Prospects* (New York: Routledge, 1992).

12. *World Military Expenditures and Arms Transfers 1988* (Washington: U.S. Government Printing Office, 1988), p. 27.

13. International Institute for Strategic Studies, *The Military Balance 1992–1993*, pp. 218–221.

14. The Soviet Union reportedly used gas in Afghanistan, and there is no doubt that Iraq used gas against Iran in 1987 and 1988. In 1990, Iraq implied it would use gas against U.S. and other forces deployed against it in Saudi Arabia, but did not.

15. For critiques of military expenditures, see Ruth Leger Sivard, *World Military and Social Expenditures 1989* (Leesburg, VA: World Priorities 1989); Seymour Melman, *The Permanent War Economy* (New York: Simon & Schuster, 1976); and Geoffrey Best and Andrew Wheatcroft (eds.), *War, Economy, and the Military Mind* (Totowa, NJ: Rowman & Littlefield, 1976).

16. For Eisenhower's own thoughts on the subject, see Dwight D. Eisenhower, *The White House Years* (Garden City, NY: Doubleday, 1963–1965).

17. See James B. Scott, *Hague Conference of 1899 and 1907* (New York: Garland, n.d.) for a discussion of the Hague Conferences.

18. Richard A. Preston and Sydney F. Wise, *Men in Arms: A History of Warfare and Its Interrelationships with Western Society* (New York: Holt, Rinehart and Winston, 1978), p. 219.

19. For the texts of these agreements, see ACDA, *Arms Control and Disarmament Agreements*, pp. 120–131, 190–200.

20. See John G. Keliher, *The Negotiations on Mutual and Balanced Force Reductions: The Search for Arms Control in Central Europe* (New York: Pergamon Press, 1982).

21. For discussions of the relationship between arms control and the evolving security situation in Europe, see David Dewitt and Hans Rattinger, *East-West Arms Control* (New York: Routledge, 1991); and Hans Gunter Branch and Robert Kennedy, eds., *Alternative Defense Postures in the European Theater*, Vol. 3 (Washington: Crane Russak, 1993).

CHAPTER 19

Sociopolitical Parameters of Power

- Why does the militarily or economically strongest international actor not always get its way?
- What internal and external factors besides economics and the military add to or detract from a state's power?

Discussions of the power potential of international actors too often are limited to the subjective and objective aspects of economic and military capabilities. Although economic and military capabilities are demonstrably important, other parameters are also crucial in determining an actor's power potential. If one had measured solely the economic and military capabilities of North Vietnam and the Vietcong during the late 1960s, one would have been driven to the conclusion that the North Vietnamese-Vietcong tandem could not successfully stand up to U.S. economic and military might. One would also have been wrong. Similarly, a comparison of solely the Soviet and Afghan guerrilla economic and military capabilities would lead one to conclude that the U.S.S.R. would win in a conflict. One would have again been wrong. Numerous other examples exist of seemingly superior economic and/or military actors being defeated by, losing influence to, or having their policies frustrated by seemingly less capable economic and/or military actors.

Why? What enabled Mao to overcome Chiang Kai-shek, when Chiang, at least at first, had at his disposal the wealth and productive capacity of all of China's cities and the military capability of most of China's men and weapons? What enabled Gandhi to drive the British from India, and how did Khomeini undermine the shah? What gives the United Nations so prominent and persuasive a voice in international affairs when its economic and military capabilities are virtually nonexistent? Why does the Pope command such respect and allegiance throughout the Catholic and non-Catholic worlds? Why couldn't the United States win in Vietnam, and why couldn't the Soviets win in Afghanistan? There are no easy answers to these and other similar questions, but it is clear that the answers lie beyond the realm of economic and military parameters of power.

SOCIOPOLITICAL COMPONENTS OF POWER: AN OVERVIEW

Those aspects of power that helped Gandhi drive the British from India, that enabled Mao to attract more and more Chinese to his cause, and that give the United Nations such prestige as it has may best be described as sociopolitical components of power. Sociopolitical components of power are intangible elements such as will and morale, character, and the ability to attract external support for one's own causes. In many cases, these intangible components of power are more important factors in determining an actor's power potential than more tangible elements of economic and military capabilities.

Determinants of sociopolitical strength are diverse: ethnic and religious identity, legitimacy of cause, linguistic background, reputation, will and morale, character, ability to attract external support, cultural or conceptual integration or diversity, leadership, political strategy and tactics, and lifestyle are just a few of the more readily identifiable determinants.

They are also ever-changing. For example, Americans have become much more willing to accept cultural diversity in the United States during the last decade than they were during the 1950s. During the 1950s, cultural integration was extremely important. Cultural diversity was often viewed as "un-American," and therefore shunned. Diversity was also believed to reduce U.S. sociopolitical capabilities. By the 1980s, however, cultural diversity was considered natural and even desirable, at least within certain bounds. Cultural integration became less important, and the prevalence of diversity was believed by all but the extreme political right to have little adverse impact on U.S. sociopolitical strength. What, then, is the **nature of sociopolitical parameters of power**?

Sociopolitical parameters of power are psychological in nature. The role of ethnicity as a determinant of sociopolitical power offers perhaps the best example. Ethnic *uniformity* has often been alluded to as a factor that enhanced national identity and hence national will in Germany, France, and Japan. Even today, citizens of these countries point to their ethnic uniformity as a symbol of national pride. Yet in the United States, ethnic *diversity* is often presented as an element of U.S. strength. Clearly, the part that ethnic uniformity or diversity plays in the international arena as a sociopolitical parameter of power is far from well defined.

Sociopolitical parameters of power are also often ephemeral; that is, they may appear and then disappear rapidly. U.S. will in Vietnam during the 1960s and U.S. will to rearm during the 1980s provide classic examples of the ephemeral nature of sociopolitical parameters of power. Following attacks on U.S. destroyers in the Gulf of Tonkin in August 1964, U.S. sentiment strongly supported U.S. military action against North Vietnam. Within three years, however, mounting U.S. losses and growing uncertainty about U.S. war objectives led many U.S. citizens to question the wisdom of the war effort. The Johnson administration had lost one of the most crucial elements of power available to a democratic government: support of the population for its international policies. Although the loss of popular support did not preordain the failure of American policy in Vietnam, it did seriously erode the ability of the U.S. government to continue its preferred policy in Vietnam.

Similarly, in the case of the Reagan rearmament program of the 1980s, domestic support for rearmament grew rapidly in the wake of the capture of U.S. hostages in Teheran and the Soviet invasion of Afghanistan. Ronald Reagan used this sentiment to good advantage during the 1980 presidential elections and during his first year in office, but discovered by 1982 that public support for large increases in defense expenditures was soft. Many U.S. citizens began to question whether the United States could afford the massive defense expenditure increases Reagan proposed, and others questioned both the need for and wisdom of such increases in light of significant reductions in U.S. governmental social expenditures. Reagan thus found it necessary to nurture the intangible sociopolitical element of popular support for his defense program so that the more tangible military elements of power could be acquired. For the most part, his efforts to maintain popular support for his defense program succeeded, as evidenced not only by continued widespread pro-defense spending sentiment, but also by public support for his policies during and following the 1983 destruction of a Korean airliner by Soviet fighters, the bombing of a U.S. marines barrack in Lebanon, the U.S. invasion of Grenada, and the 1986 air attacks against Libya. But even Reagan was not completely successful, as shown by Congress's willingness not only to lower his defense budget requests, but also to question his fondest defense dream, SDI.

However, sociopolitical parameters of power are not confined to ephemeral and diverse domestic concerns. Actors also gain—and lose—sociopolitical strength in the international arena. The United States and the Soviet Union again offer excellent cases for study.

Through most of the post–World War II era, the United States prided itself on its reputation of being a fair and stalwart ally, opposed to communism and external interference in the internal affairs of others. Whether this was a legitimate and accurate reputation is beyond the scope of this chapter; what is relevant is that that was the U.S. image and reputation held both by the United States of itself and by many other international actors. U.S. prestige and U.S. power were enhanced by this image and reputation. However, with Vietnam, this began to change. Increasingly, the United States took on the reputation of a traditional imperial power, seeking to influence and control lesser actors to its own advantage, and the U.S. image increasingly became one of a state willing to use napalm against women and children. As a result, U.S. prestige and power throughout the world were undermined. A change in intangible sociopolitical parameters of power, image, and reputation had contributed to an overall decrease in the United States' overall global position.

The Soviet Union was a short-term beneficiary of this deteriorating U.S. image and reputation. During the 1960s and early 1970s, the U.S.S.R. moved rapidly to cement its reputation throughout the world as a proponent of nonintervention and disarmament, and as an opponent of imperialism, militarism, and expansionism. Globally, the Soviet message sold well, particularly in the Developing World. The U.S.S.R.'s reputation and image improved tremendously, and the U.S.S.R's ability to influence world events expanded. Although the Kremlin's military capabilities grew rapidly during this period as well, it is an arguable point that, because of the U.S.S.R.'s improved reputation and image in the Developing World, the sociopolitical parameters of its power had grown equally rapidly. In short, the U.S.S.R. had done well in its efforts to win the hearts and minds of the global community.

It also began to overplay its hand during the 1970s, and to consume the sociopolitical parameters of power it had acquired. Certain intangible elements of Soviet power, image and reputation among them, began to deteriorate as one country after another told Soviet advisers to leave. Egypt, Nigeria, Sudan, Iraq, and Somalia were some of the more prominent ones. Other countries asked for Soviet support and assistance. Nevertheless, Zambian President Kenneth Kaunda's warning that "the marauding tiger with cubs" (i.e., the Soviet Union and Cuba) should not be allowed to enter the African back door while other dangers (the United States and Europe) were being barred from the front pointed to new Developing World uncertainties about the legitimacy of the U.S.S.R.'s reputation and image. The Soviet invasion of Afghanistan added to these uncertainties as the Soviet Union was increasingly viewed by the Developing World as just another great power pursuing its own selfish interests. Probable Soviet use of chemical and bacteriological weapons in Afghanistan, Laos, and Cambodia, and the U.S.S.R.'s September 1983 destruction of an unarmed Korean Air Lines passenger plane further undermined the Kremlin's efforts to present itself as a reasoned, fair, and compassionate international actor. As a result, the Soviet image and reputation were tarnished, and an important sociopolitical element of Soviet power was compromised.

INTERNAL SOCIOPOLITICAL FACTORS

Of the many factors that may be included among those elements that constitute sociopolitical parameters of the strength of international actors, we concentrate on only four: will and morale, character, leadership, and degree of integration. These four factors have been selected for two reasons. First, they apply to all the actors we have examined. Will and morale taken together are as important for an IGO as for a state in the eventual success or failure that it has in attaining its goals. Similarly, an IGO or an MNC with ineffective leadership is less likely to achieve its objectives, and the same is true for a state or NGO. The same may be said for both character and degree of integration.

Second, each of these four factors includes diverse items that may be important for one set of actors, but less so for another. Will and morale include internal public opinion, a factor of considerable importance for a democratic government or an IGO that needs unanimity of opinion before action can be taken; public opinion is of less importance, but not inconsequential, in an autocratic state or an MNC. The character of an international actor may be the product of its historical experiences, its geographical and environmental location, or its technical orientation. Although history is important for all actors when character is discussed, geographical and environmental location may be expected to be more important for a state than an MNC, whereas technical orientation may be more important for an MNC.

So, too, for leadership. Leadership may include type and style of government or control, the ability of decision-making elites to mobilize internal support, and the ability of elites to plan and implement plans successfully. One or another of these elements may be more important for one type of actor than for another. Similarly, degree of integration may refer to cultural, ethnic, religious, technical, or organizational integration, or lack thereof. As we have already seen, in some actors integration of one or another element is valued highly, whereas in another, it may be considered irrelevant.

It should further be noted that these divisions between sociopolitical factors are somewhat artificial. Will and morale influence character, leadership, and integration, even as each of the other three influences all. Nevertheless, for clarity, their interrelationships have been minimized in the following discussions.

Will and Morale

Hans Morgenthau defined national morale as "the degree of determination with which a nation supports the foreign policies of its government in peace or war."[1] For our purposes, this definition is accurate, but overly restrictive. Will and morale are viewed here as the degree of determination that any actor has in the pursuit of its internal or external objectives.

Within a given international actor, will and morale need not be identical at all levels of society. Leadership will and morale (as apart from leadership capability) may be strong, as was the case in Russia during 1916 and early 1917, whereas the masses may be defeatist. The Russian nobility and military continued to plan for and believe in new offensives against the Germans even while Russian troops were laying down their weapons and walking away from the front. Similarly, the final withdrawal of the United States from Vietnam resulted primarily from a conviction on the part of U.S. citizens that the war should be terminated; only slowly did the U.S. decision-making elite adopt this attitude. Differentiated levels of will and morale also exist in other actors. The chief executive officer and board of a multinational corporation may bask in the confidence and assurance generated by a record profit year for the MNC as a whole, while at the same time a single division may be laboring under loss, impending leadership changes, and layoffs.

Differences between elite and nonelite levels of will and morale may be further differentiated by different degrees of determination extended to internal and external objectives. Here, the Johnson administration in the United States provides an extremely useful example. Although it is an oversimplification to say that the most vocal critics of Johnson's Vietnam policies were some of the most ardent supporters of his Great Society domestic efforts, a not insignificant degree of truth is in the statement. Conversely, Johnson's Vietnam policy supporters were often among the most adamant critics of his domestic efforts. The combination of disagreements between and within U.S. elite and nonelite groups over both domestic and foreign Johnson administration policies clearly indicated that U.S. will and morale were in disarray.

But what creates will and morale? No one can say with any degree of certainty. The will and morale of the British, the Germans, the Japanese, and the Vietnamese remained strong, according to most estimates, despite the large-scale conventional bombing raids they experienced during World War II and the Vietnam War. Would they react the same way to similar experiences today? Would other peoples react with heightened will and morale if they were subjected to similar bombing? How would any society react to a nuclear bombing exchange as opposed to a conventional one? The answers are unknown.

Here, the role of **nationalism** as a significant input to the will and morale of state actors must be stressed. As discussed in Chapters 1 and 2, nationalism has been and remains an extremely important force in bonding people together within the modern nation-state. By psychologically providing people with a sense of attachment to an entity beyond themselves as individuals, and by providing people with a sense of pride in their nation, nationalism often adds an immense measure of will and morale to the capabilities of state actors in the international arena. Indeed, as we have previously seen, nationalism was one of the primary factors that led to the creation of many of the states that constitute such a significant part of today's international community.

Nevertheless, nationalism, like all aspects of will and morale, is a psychological phenomenon. Why do so many East Europeans and former Soviet citizens still have high hopes for the future, when their economic situations are disastrous and their political systems are in disarray? The answer is that despite their problems, they believe that the future will be better than the past. Similarly, why during the height of the Cold War did so many members of the UN's Secretariat continue to have high hopes for the future of the organization as a peacekeeping body when time after time states appealed to their sovereign rights and frustrated UN peacekeeping efforts? They too believed the future would bring better times, and events of the late 1980s and early 1990s proved them right. And why do the employees and management alike of some MNCs maintain appearances of high dedication to the company under even the most trying circumstances? The answers, again, are not known, but are clearly psychological in nature.

Character

The character of an international actor is a subject of somewhat more debate than will and morale. Some analysts deny the existence of a national, organizational, or corporate character. Others argue that certain emotional, intellectual, or human qualities occur more frequently and are valued more highly in one actor than in another. Germans are more philosophic and militaristic than the French, who are in turn more emotional and sensual than the English. Russians are stoic and persistent; Americans are industrious and pragmatic. UN employees are idealistic internationalists, whereas IBM employees are efficient and methodical. Critics of the concept of character dismiss these and other categorizations as meaningless stereotypes. Adherents to the concept accept them as generalizations that may have many exceptions.

Given the insights to societies and organizations provided by cultural anthropology and related disciplines, it is difficult to dismiss the concept of national, organizational, or corporate character in totality.[2] Russian mistrust of the external world is historically documentable. Regardless of whether its cause is the centuries of Tatar rule, three invasions from Western Europe in little more than a century, or something else, it is a part of the Russian character. Russian stoicism, regardless of whether caused by Russian Orthodox Christianity, communism, or long and cold Russian winters, is equally real. Similarly, regardless of whether the successful "IBMer" is fashioned by the demands of the corporate environment or selected for employment because his or her character fits the employer's preferences, a certain style of corporate personality emerges. Again, many exceptions exist, but enough evidence exists to accept a generalized rule.

How does character relate to power? Stated simply, certain policies, strategies, or tactics may be favored or proscribed by character. For example, Americans are ever impatient for results, or so the North Vietnamese believed. As seen by the North Vietnamese, the United States could not successfully fight a protracted war, and at least in Southeast Asia, events proved them right. Obviously, American impatience effectively reduced U.S. power, at least in the eyes of the Vietnamese.

Similarly, U.S. citizens like to justify their actions. Thus, the United States did not enter World War I until after U.S. ships and U.S. lives were being lost, World War II until after Pearl Harbor, or Vietnam until after the alleged attack on U.S. destroyers. More recently, the United States invaded Grenada in 1983 only after internal order in that Caribbean island country dissolved and the lives of U.S. students there were allegedly endangered. The United States also sent troops into Panama in 1989 only after General Noriega's forces stepped up harassment of U.S. citizens living there, and killed a U.S. citizen. In 1990 and 1991, the United States did not move against Iraq after Iraq invaded Kuwait until the United States obtained United Nations approval. And in 1992, the United States intervened in Somalia, once again only after the UN requested U.S. action. There are, of course, other examples that can be used to show that the United States acts independently when it so desires, but there is nevertheless an undeniable U.S. desire to justify U.S. actions. This desire significantly reduces the United States' ability to initiate truly preemptive action.

British determination provides another useful example. This national trait, so often mentioned in assessments of individual Britons, was somehow overlooked by both Hitler in 1939 and Argentina in 1982. This determination, according to some, was the sole factor that allowed Great Britain to fight on, alone, against the Nazi juggernaut for over a year, and was a major factor in convincing the Thatcher government to undertake an expensive, long-range military operation for the purpose of recapturing a few bleak South Atlantic islands. Russian stoicism and persistence may in turn be best exemplified by Soviet Marshal G. K. Zhukov's response to the question of how the Soviet army would clear a minefield: by marching a division across it!

As in the case of will and morale, constituent parts of and sources behind character cannot be clearly and specifically delineated. Historical experiences and traditional values undoubtedly play a role, as do geographical location, environment, organizational structure, and a country's economic and technical base. Other sources undoubtedly exist as well. But in the final analysis, character's contribution to the sociopolitical parameters of power can be only roughly estimated.

Leadership

Few analysts deny the necessity of effective leadership. Effective leadership permits an actor to take advantage of its economic and military capabilities, and in some instances may allow an actor to overcome shortcomings in one or another parameter of power. An absence of leadership inevitably detracts from an actor's ability to achieve its ends.

Three separate aspects of leadership must be discussed. First is the organizational structure of an actor, for it is within this milieu that leadership must function. Different types of organizational structures have certain strengths and certain weaknesses, whereas other structures have different strengths and weaknesses. At the state level, for instance, a totalitarian system cripples individual freedom and initiative, but permits formulation of a highly organized state strategy. Totalitarian systems rarely can rely upon significant levels of popular support for their policies, if simply because the decision-making process is tightly controlled and does not permit interchange of ideas. Democratic systems, by comparison, require policy formation by consensus building and persuasion. A policy, at least initially, may have significant support from wide segments of the state's population. However, it is extremely difficult, to develop and implement a long-range state strategy, or to change policy direction. Clearly, although both the totalitarian and democratic systems have their advantages, the type of leader that each system demands is quite different, at least if he or she is to be successful.

Hitler's Germany and Churchill's Britain provide excellent examples of the strengths and weaknesses of both systems. With the power to make decisions in the hands of Hitler alone, and with Hitler having complete power of decision throughout Germany, the Third Reich found little difficulty in reaffirming its alliance with the Soviet Union one month and initiating war against it the next. Churchill's Britain could never have altered policy so rapidly and extremely, given its organizational structure. Germany clearly enjoyed a latitude of policy that Britain did not. Nevertheless, Hitler launched Operation Barbarosa against the U.S.S.R. against the advice of most of his senior military staff and experienced no diminution in his authority. In Britain, Churchill could have undertaken policy against the advice of most of his staff as well, but would have experienced extreme criticism. Indeed, Churchill himself was removed from office via an election before the end of the war in Asia, although the causes were not disagreements with his staff. Obviously, a democratic system increases the possibility that more voices will be heard in the policy process, although it does not guarantee the wisdom of those voices.

Quality is a second aspect of leadership. Put simply, the power potential of an international actor is increased in proportion to that actor's leadership capability. A mesh between type of system and type of leader is important, but quality of leadership also is important. Thus, Franklin Roosevelt could not only operate effectively in the U.S. political environment, but he could also make that environment serve his purposes. By exercising his leadership gifts and position, he not only succeeded in building his own personal prestige, and therefore power, but also strengthened U.S. morale and will. Roosevelt's ability to mobilize the American people behind his policies proved a tremendous asset. Under Roosevelt, then, presidential leadership and U.S. will and morale were integrally related both during the depression and during World War II.

Ronald Reagan played a similar role in his administration. Whatever the criticisms that may be levied against Reagan's policies or his grasp of the issues, few can deny that Reagan's leadership helped rekindle U.S. patriotism and rebuild a sense in many U.S. citizens that the United States had an important and assertive role to play in world affairs. Once again, leadership was demonstrably important.

Roosevelt and Reagan, impressive successes in the U.S. system, would probably have been colossal failures in the Soviet system where Joseph Stalin so ruthlessly succeeded. By contrast, Stalin would have failed in the U.S. system.

Nevertheless, Stalin's ruthlessness provided the Soviet people with a strong central authority in the tradition of Ivan the Terrible, the Romanov dynasty, and Lenin. His methods proved workable and successful within the Soviet system.

The same may be said for Iraqi President Saddam Hussein and his methods. Many people in the Arab world, particularly among the lower classes, viewed Saddam's invasion of Kuwait and his willingness to fight both non-Arabs and rich Arabs not as aggressive or reprehensible behavior, but as fighting for the Arab birthright. Whatever Saddam's shortcomings, as a leader he succeeded in bringing many others into line with his intentions.

The ability of a leadership to formulate and implement a strategy to achieve its objectives is a third aspect of leadership. Although this third point is a subset of quality of leadership, it is significant in its own right. Regardless of the quality of leadership, if a strategy is not formulated that is meaningful and workable in relation to an actor's objectives, leadership quality means little. A national leadership may be capable enough to tap all the measures of economic, technical, and sociopolitical parameters of power, but if it has no strategy, its chances of success are considerably diminished.

Even though he failed to achieve his objective of a more humane and efficient Soviet Union, Mikhail Gorbachev and his efforts to revitalize the Soviet Union provide a useful example. Early on, Gorbachev concluded that the changes that would have to take place in the U.S.S.R. to renew the country were so significant and would arouse so much opposition that he would have to launch a comprehensive revolution that would change Soviet political, economic, social-cultural, and foreign policies. He implemented this strategy of comprehensive revolution first via glasnost, and then in economic restructuring, political democratization, and foreign policy New Thinking. Although the tactics he employed were ad hoc, and the changes that eventuated were not those that he envisioned, he nevertheless had an overall strategy to bring about change within the U.S.S.R.

Leadership is also important in the world of diplomacy, which in its most elemental form is simply the art of conducting relations between governments of independent states. Although diplomacy is sometimes viewed with derision, effective leadership can transform diplomacy into a meaningful instrument of state power. Effective leadership defines for diplomacy the objective that it is to pursue, the strategies that it is to employ, and the instruments that are available. Without effective leadership, diplomacy can achieve little; with effective leadership, it can enhance a state's power.

An example or two may help clarify the importance of leadership for diplomacy. During the nineteenth century, Otto von Bismarck strengthened Germany by weaving a subtle pattern of alliance across Europe. Without an overall strategy, Bismarck could never have created his treaty system. Between 1969 and 1974, Richard Nixon and Henry Kissinger also formulated U.S. foreign policy toward China and the Soviet Union on the basis of a comprehensive strategy. Nixon and Kissinger forged a policy that made China and the Soviet Union consider cordial relations with the United States to be of paramount importance. Such a policy increased U.S. freedom of action in the international community and limited Chinese and Soviet options.[3]

Leadership is also important within international actors other than states. Dag Hammarskjold's optimism about the United Nations, his ability to convince others that peacekeeping was a legitimate function of the UN, and his willingness to have the UN accept international responsibilities were all trademarks of his secretariatship; they have remained trademarks of the UN to this day. With a lesser leader, the UN may not have acquired the prestige that it has. Similarly, at the corporate level, Sosthenes Behn mapped out a global strategy for ITT that he implemented with iron will. ITT prospered under the Behn leadership to become one of the world's most influential MNCs.

Degree of Integration

Will and morale, character, and leadership are clearly important elements in an actor's sociopolitical strength, but another factor, degree of integration, adds a significant dimension to sociopolitical strength as well. Stated differently, degree of integration refers simply to the sense of belonging and identification of an actor's people. At the state level, this often translates into nationalism. In many ways, degree of integration contributes to will and morale, to character, and to acceptance of a particular leader. As pointed out earlier in this chapter, it is difficult, and sometimes misleading, to isolate these intangible sociopolitical parameters of power.

In most cases, the greater the degree of homogeneity and uniformity, the greater the degree of perceived integration. This, in turn, contributes to a sense of belonging, of citizenship. Homogeneous ethnic, religious, linguistic, or cultural backgrounds add to a sense of identity and integration. Shared values are also important. For states, national liberation movements, and other actors whose members share one or more of these identities, a significant parameter of power has been acquired. Technical and organizational identity are also important, particularly for MNCs, IGOs, and certain NGOs. An MNC whose employees are unsure of the contribution they make or role that they play in the company's overall operations is less likely to have the allegiance of its employees than is an MNC whose employees recognize that their abilities are valuable assets to the MNC, and that the MNC appreciates those assets. The same is true for IGOs and NGOs.

Although it is generally true that great integration leads to an enhanced sense of identity between an actor and its people, a lack of integration need not necessarily imply a lack of identity. For example, France has a high degree of integration. Ethnic origins, language, religious preference, cultural heritage and values, and historical background are all widely shared. The same is also true of Japan. Switzerland, by contrast, has little integration. Shared values are offset by ethnic diversity, disparate languages and religious preference, different cultures, and in many cases, different historical backgrounds. Yet the Swiss view themselves as a separate entity as surely as the French view themselves as a separate entity.

There are, of course, numerous cases where a low degree of integration leads to an uncertain or questionable degree of unity. Yugoslavia and the Soviet Union are two cases in point. In both countries, immense internal diversity led many citizens in each country to identify more with their own ethnic group than with the state itself. In Yugoslavia, Serbs, Croats, Bosnians, Macedonians, and others all insisted on their own national identity. Similarly, in the Soviet Union, Latvians, Lithuanians, Estonians, Moldavians, Armenians, Azerbaijanis, Georgians, and others wanted their own national identity, too. In both Yugoslavia and the

U.S.S.R., this sense of allegiance to a group other than the Yugoslav or Soviet state led to secession, the collapse of the Yugoslav and Soviet states, and warfare between ethnic groups. Both cases prove that too low a degree of integration can be disastrous for a state.

It is impossible to specify how and why a sense of identity develops, or what the key factor or factors are in leading to a sense of belonging. In some cases, a low degree of integration across a wide number of variables will be sufficient to lead to a sense of belonging. In other cases, a high degree of integration in a single area will be sufficient. In either case, the sense of identity may be long-lived or ephemeral. To use the Swiss as an example again, Swiss unity has continued across the centuries despite low degrees of integration in ethnicity, language, religion, and so on. The Angolan national liberation movements by comparison had a shared enemy in Portugal, but little else. They shared the objective of driving the Portuguese out of Angola, but, with that single integrative factor removed, they plunged into civil war. Japanese multinational corporations provide yet another type of example. Japanese industrial workers identify themselves as much with their corporation as with their nation; although several causes for this identity exist, it is nonetheless a unique phenomenon.

All the sociopolitical parameters of power addressed to this point—will and morale, character, leadership, and degree of integration—evolve from considerations internal to an international actor. All also are important aspects of an actor's overall power potential, but are at the same time intangible elements whose composition cannot be precisely defined or measured. The sociopolitical parameters of an actor's power are not, however, limited to internal considerations.

EXTERNAL SOCIOPOLITICAL FACTORS

Many international actors appeal to the "good of the people" to justify their international actions. The Soviet Union claimed that it was fighting against imperialism for the "good of the Afghan people" when it sent its combat forces into Afghanistan in 1979, and the United States argued that it was opposing communism and supporting freedom for "the good of the Vietnamese people" during the long years of war there. Ayatollah Khomeini overthrew the shah for "the good of the Iranian people," and the UN sent relief and developmental teams into Somalia for "the well-being of those who have little." The World Council of Churches sends money for food and medical aid, some of which is diverted into weapons purchases, to a variety of national liberation movements, all in the name of humanity, whereas those national liberation movements fight for independence for "the good of the peoples" of a variety of territories. Even multinational corporations justify their global reach by arguing that they will bring better living conditions to more people than ever before, if only they can operate unfettered by national and international restrictions. "The good of the people," it seems, is everywhere.

"The good of the people" plays a dual role in international affairs. It may serve as either the ultimate objective of an actor, or it may serve as a pretext behind which an actor pursues its real objectives, one of which may or may not be "the good of the people." "The good of the people" is variously defined by various actors to mean national independence, improved living conditions, equitable distribution of resources, freedom of religion or dominance by a specific religion, or any of a variety of other "goods." In addition, actors have found that they are able to broaden their own appeal and therefore add to their own power if they can convince not only their own citizens, but also those of other actors, of the accuracy of their own interpretation of good and of their own honesty in pursuing it.

Examples of this abound. The Soviet Union represented the vanguard of communism for years, and as a result of its preeminence, won the allegiance of communist parties throughout the world. As a result, Soviet power was enhanced. When Mao took power in China with his own variant of communism, Soviet preeminence in the international communist movement was challenged. The ensuing Sino-Soviet ideological dispute hence revolved around more than esoteric interpretations of Marxist dogma. To an extent, it was a dispute over sociopolitical parameters of power. Clearly, if a large number of communist parties adopted pro-Chinese as opposed to pro-Soviet stances, the external sociopolitical parameters of Soviet power would have been diminished.

Religious movements and organizations also depend on their **supranational** appeal, that is, their appeal that extends beyond a single state to several states, to strengthen their international positions. The Vatican, Israel, and Iran are three examples in which religions have combined their spiritual aspirations with the secular realities of a state. The Vatican, the heart of Catholicism and the earthly seat of power of the Pope, is a microstate not unlike the Solomon Islands in terms of its economic and military capabilities. Yet because of its religious importance and historical background, it plays a role in international affairs far above what its economic and military capabilities would imply. The Pope may not have many earthly divisions, but he wields considerable influence.

Israel, by comparison, is the strongest military power in the Middle East. But even its military capabilities are enhanced by its stature as the Jewish state, the spiritual home of the Jewish people. Jews throughout the world extend their moral support and financial aid to Israel, and on occasion actively seek to influence the policy of other actors on issues that concern Israel. Thus, Israel's power is strengthened by its supranational appeal as the Jewish homeland. This is obviously a sociopolitical factor contributing to Israeli power.

Iran is similar. Revolutionary Iran purports to be a fundamentalist Shiite Islamic state that follows Allah's teachings in the Koran precisely. The Iranian clerics hope to attract fundamentalist Shiites throughout the Islamic world to their revolutionary cause. Moderate Arab states, including Saudi Arabia, Jordan, Oman, and the United Arab Emirates, fear that Iran's call for revolution may fall on receptive ears. Iran, then, has become a potentially powerful center for revolution in the Middle East, not necessarily because of its economic or military capabilities, but because of religion.

Communism and religion are not the only sources of supranational strength. Other concepts, like human rights, noninterference, nonalignment, and economic betterment, also attract external support for those actors that claim to support them. Jimmy Carter's human rights policy was undoubtedly a sincere statement of Carter's beliefs, but it also allowed the United States to assert that it was on the side of justice and morality. Although the concrete results of Carter's human rights policy are open to debate, no one can deny the international appeal of human rights as being for "the good of the people."

As another example from the Carter era, the Georgian condemned interference in the internal affairs of others as an un-American activity. Although Carter clearly did not consider demands for human rights in other countries to be interference, he did lay out his concern for America's international appeal in no uncertain terms:

> The moral heart of our international appeal—as a country which stands for self-determination and free choice—has been weakened. It is obviously un-American to interfere in the political processes of another nation.[4]

Carter's concern for the United States' international appeal revolved around his belief that the United States' Vietnam adventure had adversely affected its external sociopolitical parameters of power. He was, of course, correct. Even for a superpower, such parameters of power are important.

International public opinion is thus an important element of an actor's sociopolitical strength. Some actions, such as withholding food from a starving population to prove a political point or using nuclear weapons when anything less than national survival is threatened, are usually viewed by international actors as so certain to evoke an international backlash that they are usually excluded as policy options. Similarly, for multinational corporations, international public opinion is a critical variable. Fear of adverse public opinion was a major reason that baby formula producers curtailed their marketing efforts in the Developing World in the early 1980s. The involved MNCs concluded that the long-term impact of adverse international public opinion was more important than the short-term economic advantage that might be gained by continuing sales. Consequently, favorable international public opinion may be seen as a critical component of sociopolitical power for MNCs as well as states and other international actors.

Sometimes, international actors who have no clear claim to external sociopolitical appeal through ideology, religion, human rights, or the like, seek to enhance their stature by claiming to be leading spokesmen for other concepts of international appeal. Yugoslavia and India both did this with nonalignment, and both states acquired sociopolitical strength and prestige that they had not previously had.

Again, we have to this point concentrated on states and their efforts to acquire external sociopolitical parameters of power. Other international actors also attempt to improve their power potential by seeking external support. There are many examples. Multinational corporations seek to persuade others not associated with MNCs that they bring economic advantages not available elsewhere. Nongovernmental organizations regularly appeal for support for their causes from external sources. The World Council of Churches asks others to remember their religious morality, hoping that such remembrances will yield additional support for WCC causes. Greenpeace begs others to observe the brutality against whales, hoping that such observers will become more opposed to the slaughter. The United Nations Charter is the source of much of the UN's reputation as an international beacon of morality and justice. National liberation movements the world over claim their struggle is a just one against colonial oppression, hoping to acquire added external support and legitimacy.

It is in this light that the eventual success of South African blacks in their struggle against the white South African government's policy of apartheid can be understood. Over time, much of the international community accepted the morality of the blacks' cause: the elimination of apartheid and the institutionalization of majority rule in South Africa. This acceptance added a significant but immeasurable amount of sociopolitical power to calls by the African National Congress, Nelson Mandela, Bishop Desmond Tutu, and others to change the system in South Africa. Gradually, under a combination of internal and external sociopolitical pressures, the South African government began to dismantle apartheid.

External sociopolitical parameters of power are obviously no more easily defined or categorized than are their internal counterparts. It is equally obvious that no guarantee exists that they will be long-lasting or easily regained if lost. The United States squandered much of its international appeal in Vietnam; Carter's calls for human rights and noninterference only regained a portion of what had been lost. Before its collapse, the Soviet Union too found its external sociopolitical parameters of power rendered less persuasive by a combination of poor economic performance, adventurous foreign policy, and ideological stultification.

Nevertheless, international actors of all types are aware that their overall power potential can be increased if they influence others to support their causes. As we move toward 2000, efforts to enhance one's external sociopolitical parameters of power will not diminish, and may well increase.

Nelson Mandela, shown here with his wife Winnie shortly after his 1990 release from a South African prison, came to symbolize the struggle of Black South Africans against apartheid. Mandela's leadership of the African National Congress, even from prison, played a major role in gaining international recognition for the ANC's cause.   (Patrick Durand/Sygma.)

SOCIOPOLITICAL CAPABILITIES AND POWER

For the most part, sociopolitical capabilities of an international actor are psychological factors. As psychological factors, they are difficult to categorize and quantify. How an actor's will and morale will hold up under adverse conditions cannot be predicted, and how well an actor's leadership will respond to a crisis is similarly unknown. Although an actor's character may provide an observer with some clue as to how the actor will react in a given situation, it is usually impossible to predict with any certainty whether an actor's degree of integration will add to or detract from its overall power. And the power that an actor acquires through its external appeal is even more difficult to gauge.

One of the most frustrating aspects of sociopolitical parameters of power is that, in many cases, they are more significant factors in determining an actor's overall power potential than the actor's more tangible economic and military capabilities. As an example, Ray Cline's work on "politectonic" measures of national power that we examined in Chapter 16 extends most importance to strategic purpose and national will, two elements that we have termed sociopolitical parameters of power.[5]

Outside the world of academia, in the so-called "real world," evidence supports this conclusion. The United States was, for all practical purposes, defeated in Vietnam by the North Vietnamese–Vietcong tandem. The Soviet Union was defeated by undermanned and outgunned Afghan guerrillas. Mao's forces continually grew, whereas Chiang's shrank. Gandhi drove the British from India without recourse to violence. Khomeini overthrew the Shah. UN resolutions and papal declarations are listened to, if not followed, the world over, even though neither the UN nor the pope has economic clout or military divisions. In South Africa, after years of struggle, apartheid finally is being dismantled, less because of military or economic parameters of power, but more because of sociopolitical parameters of power.

In each case, one or another aspect, or a combination of aspects, of sociopolitical strength explains what otherwise would be incomprehensible results. Sociopolitical parameters of power are difficult if not impossible to quantify, but nevertheless, their strength is evident.

KEY TERMS AND CONCEPTS

nature of sociopolitical parameters
   of power
will and morale
nationalism (also in Chapter 2)
character

leadership
degree of integration
external sociopolitical factors
supranational
international public opinion

NOTES

1. Hans J. Morgenthau, *Politics Among Nations: The Struggle for Power and Peace* (New York: Knopf, 1973), p. 135.
2. See R. P. Anand, *Cultural Factors in International Relations* (Columbia, MO: South Asia Books, 1981); Frederick H. Hartmann, *Relations of Nations* (New York: Macmillan, 1978); Hans J. Michelmann, *Organizational Effectiveness in a Multinational Bureaucracy* (New York, Praeger, 1979); Luc Reychler, *Patterns of Diplomatic Thinking: A Cross National Study of Structural and Social-Psychological Determinants* (New York: Praeger, 1979); and Kenneth N. Waltz, *Man, The State, and War* (New York: Columbia University Press, 1959).
3. For Nixon's and Kissinger's views on global strategy, see Henry Kissinger, *The White House Years* (Boston: Little, Brown, 1979); Henry Kissinger, *Years of Upheaval* (Boston: Little, Brown, 1982); Henry A. Kissinger, *Nuclear Weapons and Foreign Policy* (New York: Norton, 1969); Richard Nixon, *The Real War* (New York: Warner Books, 1980).
4. Jimmy Carter, "Address to the Chicago Council on Foreign Relations," March 15, 1976.
5. See again Ray S. Cline, *World Power Trends and US Foreign Policy for the 1980s* (Boulder, CO: Westview, 1980), pp. 16–25.

CHAPTER 20

Other Parameters
of Power

INTERNATIONAL LAW AND DIPLOMACY

- How effective is international law?
- What types of international law exist?
- Who interprets and enforces international law?
- What is diplomacy?
- How has diplomacy changed over time?
- How does diplomacy contribute to an international actor's power?

Two additional parameters of power—international law and diplomacy—deserve separate attention. Depending on how they are used, both international law and diplomacy can be seen as concepts that constrain or add to an actor's capabilities. This chapter emphasizes how law and diplomacy strengthen an actor's capabilities. First, however, we will discuss law and diplomacy as constraints, and explain how law and diplomacy can be both a constraint on and a constituent of power.

As a constraint, international law attempts to limit how an international actor may act. Admittedly, international law is not always effective. Laws of war exist but are sometimes ignored. Likewise, it is supposedly illegal to invade and take over an embassy, but such invasions have occurred.

Yet law also often limits the international use of power. States trade for what they want more often than they simply take it. Most international agreements are in fact respected rather than ignored. Thus, although not always effective, international law can constrain power.

So, too, can diplomacy. Diplomacy, defined here in only its most general sense as the implementation of an international actor's policies toward other actors, establishes a set of expectations about what an international actor will and will not do. (More often than not, diplomacy refers to state-to-state policies.) To the extent that expectations by others about what an actor will do limit what that actor can do, diplomacy may act as a constraint on power. Diplomacy creates expectations, and expectations can be ignored only at a cost.

If international law and diplomacy can be seen as constraints on power, how may they be viewed as elements of power? International law, if adhered to, inserts a certain amount of predictability into the international arena. Assuming that tenets of law are followed, predictability enables international actors to plan and rationalize policies, thereby enhancing power. At the same time, international law adds to a state's power by its defense of national sovereignty, the very basis of today's international state system.

Similarly, skillful diplomacy enables international actors to implement policies toward others in the most effective way. Admittedly, not all states are equally skilled in diplomacy. However, this should not detract from the fact that skillful diplomacy can add great strength to a state's international power potential.

As noted above, our emphasis here is on international law and diplomacy as constituents of power. However, this emphasis should not obscure their roles as constraints.

INTERNATIONAL LAW

International law may best be viewed as a system of agreements between international actors, usually states, that defines how relations between and among them will be conducted. International law is not new. Rudimentary international law can be traced back to the fourth millennium B.C., when warring parties agreed to stop conflicts for holiday and celebration periods, and to send and receive emissaries from each other. Ancient Greece and Rome furthered the practice of establishing rules of conduct to be followed between political groupings. Homer's *Iliad* and Thucydides' *The Peloponnesian Wars* have many references to truces, acceptance of heralds, and other standards of accepted behavior between peaceful or warring parties. (The *Iliad* and *The Peloponnesian Wars* are equally filled with instances of agreements being violated).

The Evolution of International Law

Modern international law evolved as the modern state system developed. **Hugo Grotius**, a Dutchman, is commonly considered the father of modern international law because of his 1628 publication, *On the Law of War and Peace*. Grotius' work laid the intellectual foundation for the rights and responsibilities of states to each other. It is on Grotius's work that the entire contemporary system of international treaties, tribunals, and codes of conduct is built. Not only states but also IGOs, MNCs, and certain NGOs, accept and follow these precepts.[1]

At least four different interpretations of international law exist.[2] The **naturalist school**, exemplified by Samuel Pufendorf (*The Law of Nature and Nations*, 1672), argued that all law was derived from God's law, and that law was therefore universal and unchangeable. In many ways, the naturalist school found its intellectual and philosophical heritage in St. Augustine, who argued that war was justifiable in self-defense or to punish evil. Naturalists sought a universally acceptable code for international law, but accepted the possibility that war could occur.

A problem with the naturalist interpretation of international law was that someone must determine what God's law is. This was no easy task. Given the record of European religious wars and the diversity of religions, cultures, and moralities that exist in the world, it was evident that those who sought to implement international standards based on natural law faced a formidable task. Unfortunately, naturalism also provided a ready rationale for those who wished to appeal to a higher authority to justify blatant territorial expansion and other aggressive behavior.

These problems of naturalist law led to the development of the **positivist school**. Led by Cornelius van Bynkershoek (*Forum for Ambassadors*, 1721, and *On Questions of Public Law*, 1737), positivists rejected divine authority as the basis for law and argued that the only law that existed was what its subjects agreed to. Positivists stressed that rights and responsibilities of international actors were protected by laws and standards of behavior that they themselves accepted.

The positivist position was and is criticized from two perspectives. First, states or other international actors could reject law simply by saying that they no longer agreed with it. Second, international actors could, in the absence of higher principles, declare whatever they desired to be law as long as mutual consent existed. To the naturalist, positivist law was amoral and immoral.

Not surprisingly, a third school evolved that attempted to bridge the gap between naturalists and positivists. Known as the **eclectic school** and led by Emmerich de Vattel (*The Law of Nations*, 1758), the third school posited simply that two levels of law existed, one of which was God-given, timeless, and universal, and the other of which was man-made, finite, and voluntary. To the eclectic, man-made law was the natural result of man's effort to understand and interpret the meanings of natural law. To the eclectic, naturalist law and positivist law were simply different sides of the same coin.

A fourth major school of international law was the **neorealist school**, which asserted that rules were irrelevant, but policy and values were important. To the neorealist, international law was simply the product of the desires of the prevalent power(s). It was not timeless. It was not universal. And it might be imposed by power. In this view, international law is a product of power.

Basic Concepts of International Law

Despite the debate over the basis for international law, little disagreement exists about its sources. Article 38 of the Statute of the **International Court of Justice** lists four separate sources of law—international conventions, international customs, general principles, and subsidiary sources of law.[3]

International conventions are either bilateral or multilateral treaties and agreements that specifically commit a signatory actor to a particular type of conduct or to a particular set of standards. Of the four Article 38 sources of international law, it is the most explicit type and is valid only when two or more actors agree to abide by treaty or agreement provisions.

International customs refer to the general standard of behavior and action accepted by actors. It is a precept of international law that any widely accepted behavior or action over time becomes a part of the body of international law.

Laws governing diplomatic and consular immunity and privilege as well as ocean law and high seas law evolved from the principle of international custom.

General principles of law are even more vague than international customs. Expectation of reciprocal fair treatment and nonpersecution of foreign nationals, equal application of laws, and protection of personal property and life are included as "general principles of law recognized by civilized nations." They, in some interpretations, are said to be international customs. The distinction between custom and principle is difficult to draw, but may best be described as follows: Custom is practice, and principle is ideal.

Subsidiary sources are still more vague. They are generally considered to mean interpretations of international law adopted by various courts, and particularly by the International Court of Justice (ICJ). Here, a distinction between national law and international law must be made. Under most national legal systems, judicial precedence, or *stare decisis*, prevails. *Stare decisis* means that legal opinions and interpretations handed down in one case have relevance to other cases, and should themselves be treated as law. Although most international tribunals accept *stare decisis*, the ICJ specifically does not.

Who are the subjects of international law? Originally, only states were. Over time, this has changed. Consequently, the current answer is more complicated. For example, although states have always been subject to international law, some states in certain situations declare that special circumstances prevail and that they therefore are exempt from the provisions of international law. For example, when the United States filed suit against Iran before the ICJ for the 1979 Iranian takeover of the U.S. embassy, Iran refused to recognize ICJ jurisdiction.

Other states have also ignored ICJ rulings. Thus, in 1984, the ICJ decided that it would accept a case filed by Nicaragua against the United States in which Nicaragua charged that the United States was arming and training rebels who sought to overthrow the Sandinista government of Nicaragua. Nicaragua requested the ICJ to order the United States to end that support. The United States responded to the ICJ in 1985, declaring that it would not participate in the Nicaragua case because the case was "a misuse of the court for political and propaganda purposes." Later in 1985, the court reaffirmed its position that it had jurisdiction in the case, and the United States immediately reaffirmed its rejection of the court's position. Finally, in 1986 the ICJ ruled on the case itself, deciding in Nicaragua's favor and ordering the United States to stop arming and training of the Contras. The United States rejected the ICJ's ruling, declaring that the court was "not equipped" to handle "complex international issues."

The Iran and Nicaragua cases raise the question of what issues that court can meaningfully decide. The obvious answer—and the correct answer—is those issues between states that states are willing to allow the court to decide. But in recent years, the jurisdiction of the ICJ has expanded to include international governmental organizations and multinational corporations. Even so, international organizations have on occasion flouted international law, but generally only with prior approval from their member states. Multinational corporations have only received widespread standing under international law since World War II. MNCs have been more successful gaining standing before regional legal bodies such as the Court of Justice of the European Community than before the ICJ.

The status of individuals under international law remains ill-defined. Before the twentieth century individuals were accountable to and protected by international law only through their governments. Following both World Wars, however, individuals were tried before international tribunals for acts of state and crimes against humanity, including initiating "aggressive war." A precedent was thus established for granting international tribunals jurisdiction over individuals. Whether individuals can initiate cases before the ICJ and other international courts is less certain. Here, Europe again leads the way with its European Court of Human Rights. However, the granting of standing to individuals before European international courts did not occur until after Europe opted for increased integration. Thus, courts of the European Community have both domestic and international characteristics.

Other nongovernmental actors—terrorists, national liberation movements, transnational ideological and religious movements, and other NGOs—still have little access to global legal institutions, although their individual members may be subject to individual trials. At the regional level, somewhat better access exists. However, some NGOs such as terrorists and ideological or religious movements may deny the legitimacy of current international legal practice. For them, access to the international legal system is irrelevant, as is the system itself.

What happens if an international actor won't comply with international law? Obviously, the situation is considerably different from that of domestic law. In a domestic case, the overriding ability of the state to apply sanctions prevails. In an international case, no entity has such overriding ability.

Traditionally, sanctions for breaches of international law have been left to the aggrieved party. In the most extreme cases, the ultimate sanction is war. But other types of sanctions have also been applied. Israel's 1982 attack on the PLO in Lebanon was publicly explained as a reprisal for PLO attacks on Israel and the Israeli ambassador to Great Britain. The "Flaming Dart" U.S. bombing raids against North Vietnam in February 1965 were reprisal raids for Vietcong attacks on U.S. and South Vietnamese personnel and bases in South Vietnam. (The "Flaming Dart" raids were conceptually separate from the later massive "Rolling Thunder" attacks.)

Economic sanctions are also often used. OPEC refused to sell oil to the United States in retaliation for American support of Israel in 1973, and the United States applied economic sanctions to Iran in 1979 and 1980 because of the hostage crisis and to the Soviet Union in 1980, 1981, and 1982 because of the Soviet invasion of Afghanistan and the declaration of martial law in Poland.

International organizations have on occasion attempted to apply sanctions when international law has been breached. Often, however, IGO-initiated sanctions fail because individual states place their own interests above those of international law. Under the League of Nations, for example, collective security was to be the guarantor of universal security. Collective security called for universal action against an aggressor. When Italy invaded Ethiopia, however, the international community conveniently found excuses to avoid action. Collective security failed, and the economic sanctions implemented instead proved ineffective.

The United Nations also has means at its disposal to institute sanctions, but it too must rely on member states to implement them. The United Nations Command in Korea became operational only because the United States footed the bill and provided most of the forces, and other UN peacekeeping missions live in continual jeopardy of supplier-nation withdrawal. UN economic sanctions have been implemented in a number of cases, notably against China in 1951 for its role in Korea, Southern Rhodesia in 1967 for its racial policy, Iraq in 1990 for its invasion of Kuwait, Serbia in 1992 for its "ethnic cleansing" campaign against Bosnia, and Khmer Rouge-held regions of Cambodia in 1992 for the Khmer Rouge's refusal to disarm as they had agreed to under the terms of a Cambodian peace settlement. These sanctions have proved of different value in different cases as UN member states pursued the policies they deemed appropriate. In the Chinese case, the Soviet Union and other communist states continued trade with China. In the Southern Rhodesia case, the United States defined the sanctions to mean that ongoing trade was permissible whereas new trade was not. (The United States, it should be pointed out, imported most of its chromium from Rhodesia in 1967.) In the Iraqi case, almost all nations complied with U.N. sanctions against Iraq, and a naval and air blockade was imposed by several states, including the United States, to help enforce it. In the case of Serbia, many states enforced UN sanctions, but some did not. In the case of Khmer-held Cambodia, the dependence of Khmer-held regions of Cambodia on external trade was so small that the sanctions had virtually no impact.

Obviously, sanctions that are available in the event of noncompliance with international law are weak. The decentralized mode of application of sanctions is the major drawback. And in some cases, it must be admitted that no meaningful sanctions can be applied. For example, when the United States decided that it would not comply with the ICJ's ruling that the United States must end its aid to the Contras in Nicaragua, there was little Nicaragua's Sandinista government could do to apply sanctions to the United States.

Yet to leap to the conclusion that the weakness of sanctions means that international law does not exist or is irrelevant is erroneous. Although many of the breaches of international law that become public knowledge are headline news, compliance with international law is by far the prevalent type of behavior in the international community. On a daily basis, far more treaties are kept than broken, whether they be extradition treaties or START treaties. For every day that an embassy staff is held hostage in contravention of international custom, thousands of days pass at embassies around the world without incident. The principle of freedom of the seas is only rarely challenged during peacetime. International law, despite it shortcomings, provides extensive predictability to today's international community.

Sovereignty, Statehood, and the Law of War

Despite the advantages that predictability affords to the international community, few states would accept international law if it undermined national sovereignty. Sovereignty under international law promises many rewards for states, for example, independence of action, jurisdiction over internal matters, freedom from external interference, and equality of legal standing. These rewards are sometimes more theoretical than actual, but their promise is significant, nonetheless. Paradoxically, the freedom of action that sovereignty promises reduces the possibility of guaranteeing other rewards that sovereignty may offer.

Sovereignty is bestowed only on political entities that have acquired statehood. What, however, does statehood denote? Although we examined this question in some detail in Chapter 2, the question is again relevant here. When did the United States become a state, before or after it received formal independence from Great Britain? Was Guinea-Bissau a state before 1974, when it received formal independence from Portugal, simply because 81 states recognized it as independent? When did Mao's China formally join the family of states: when Mao seized power in 1949, when China joined the UN in 1971, when the United States recognized it in 1979, or some other time? When did Latvia, Lithuania, and Estonia cease to be states, or did they ever cease to be states? Conversely, if they did cease to be states during their time as Soviet republics, when did they become states again—when they declared their independence, or when the Soviet Union dissolved? When Key West, Florida, declared its independence from the U.S., did it really become an independent state called "the Conch Republic"?

There is no single answer to these questions under international law. The Montevideo Convention of 1933 attempted to establish rules for statehood. It said that any political entity seeking statehood required a permanent population, a government that could rule that population, the ability to conduct relations with other states, and a defined territory. Other requirements also existed, including that the prospective state be recognized by other states.

Thus, the question of statehood is closely tied to the issue of recognition. One of the major theories of recognition and statehood is the **constitutive theory**, which argues simply that a state or new government is not a legal entity until it is recognized. However, a problem exists with this theory of recognition and statehood: How many states must recognize the new government or state? International law responded by answering a "reasonable" number of states, but even that response clarified nothing. In a world with over 170 states, is a majority reasonable? Is a majority still reasonable if the majority consists primarily of ministates?

A more politically oriented answer, called the **declarative theory**, rejects the Montevideo Convention's requirement for external recognition for new governments and states. Under the declarative theory, the key element to statehood is a government that can effectively rule the indigenous population. This approach solves the problem of governmental legitimacy. Under the declarative theory, if a government can maintain control over its population, its legitimacy is proven.

Critics of the declarative theory of statehood and recognition argue that it relies too heavily on considerations of governmental power and too little on considerations of governmental quality. Some Western democrats and humanists argue that no dictatorial or repressive regimes should ever be recognized or be declared states. Others posit that no communist government should ever be recognized. In the past, strident communist states such as Albania rejected the legitimacy of Western governments and refused to recognize them. Other communist states extended recognition even though they denied the long-term legitimacy of the Western governments.

In practice, states may exist as sovereign entities despite a lack of formal diplomatic recognition, as China and Southern Rhodesia both did for so long. Conversely, states may disappear even when they have extensive diplomatic recognition. Latvia, Lithuania, Estonia, and South Vietnam were proof of this proposition. At a somewhat less extreme level, a widely recognized government in one state may disappear overnight, only to be replaced by a new government that gradually legitimizes itself by acquiring extensive international diplomatic recognition. The history of Bolivia is proof of this. Statehood, in short, is both a pragmatic and a political concept.

Nevertheless, once statehood is acquired—either through territorial and population control or recognition—international law bestows sovereignty on the new state or government. The new entity therefore enjoys the same freedom of action that old ones do, including the freedom to follow or breach international law, to apply or ignore sanctions, and to make war. With war being the ultimate sanction, it is not surprising that international law devotes much of its effort to providing rules for starting, stopping, and fighting wars. We turn to those efforts now.

Jus belli, or the **law of war**, evolved as an eminently sensible result of the conclusion reached by international legal scholars and jurists that if war was unavoidable, then its destructiveness and brutality should be limited as much as possible. International law set itself the task of creating those limits. As a result, international lawyers of the nineteenth and early twentieth centuries created wide-ranging laws of war. Wars should be declared, combatants should be in uniform, noncombatants should be given safe conduct out of combat areas, open cities should not be attacked, merchant vessels of noncombatants should not be attacked unless they carried military goods, prisoners of war should be treated humanely, mercy and medical personnel and equipment should be exempted from attack—the list continued. Laws of war also sought to limit the types of weapons that could be used. Dumdum bullets, mustard gas, poison darts, and other weapons were ruled illegal by the Hague Conferences of 1899 and 1907. However, as technology advanced and weapons became more lethal, the efforts to limit the brutality and destructiveness of war through international law proved futile.

The law of war also concerned itself with defining **bellum justum (just war)** and **bellum injustum (unjust war)**. Increasingly, however, jurists recognized the futility of their efforts to draw clear distinctions between the two. The concepts of just and unjust war relied heavily on an adequate and acceptable definition of aggressive war, and no widely accepted definition of aggressive war could be formulated. Indeed, during the twentieth century the distinction between peace and war has become increasingly blurred.

International law creates a contradictory situation when sovereignty, statehood, and the law of war are viewed together. Professor J. L. Brierly summed up this contradiction concisely, observing that international law's acceptance of state sovereignty created an international system in which states were "legally bound to respect each other's independence and other rights, and yet free to attack each other at will."[4]

Alternate Views of International Law

Given the diversity of viewpoints that exist in the international community on every subject, it should come as no surprise that international law is itself the subject of debate. Because contemporary international law is almost totally a product of Western European and North American civilization and culture, one of the most prominent charges levied against it is that it seeks to protect the privileged positions that Western states and institutions enjoy in the international community. International law has consequently been an issue in both the East–West and North–South disagreements.

THE WESTERN OUTLOOK.   Although differences of opinion and interpretation exist between the states of the West on issues of international law, these differences are slight when contrasted to the West's—including Japan's—basic similarities in outlook. With the source of much of modern international law being Europe, it was natural that much of that law coincided with the European view of how the world should be ordered. Thus, state sovereignty became an overriding concern of international law, just as it was a primary concern of France, Great Britain, Germany, and other European states. Noninterference in the internal affairs of other states was used not only to protect sovereignty in Europe, but also to preserve the European state system. The law of the seas protected shipping and free passage on the high seas. Obviously, European states benefited tremendously from these and other tenets of international law.

However, following World War II, with the old bastions of European order crumbling and with strong challenges emerging to Western dominance from within the communist bloc and the newly independent Developing World, Eurocentric international law was increasingly questioned. In Marxist terms, it was considered part of the bourgeois capitalist superstructure used to shore up colonial exploitation. In non-Marxist realpolitik terms, it was considered a tool of state power used to keep the weak weak and make the strong stronger.

At U.S. urging, the United Nations and its associated bodies, then dominated by the United States and Western Europe, took on a larger and larger role in formulating international law. But even this effort to create a truly supranational legal forum was recognized by 1950 as being only marginally useful in achieving a global legal order, and the United States retreated to the old standard of sovereignty to achieve its ends. Thus, even though the United Nations eventually supported and aided the U.S. effort in Korea against the North Koreans and Chinese, the United States doubtless would have kept forces in Korea even if no UN support had been forthcoming.

Little change occurred in Western attitudes toward international law at the global level during the 1950s and 1960s. However, at the regional level, the pace of European integration quickened. Its implications for international law in Europe were awesome, for states were in the process of gradually acknowledging the supremacy of a supranational body over their own sovereignty. This was almost unheard of in international law. In addition, the European supranational legal bodies liberalized traditional rulings of who could enjoy standing before an international court.

A more subtle change also took place in European attitudes toward international law, a subtle change that by the early 1980s threatened to drive a wedge between the United States on the one hand and Europe and Japan on the other. As Europe and to a lesser extent Japan became increasingly cognizant during the 1970s of their economic vulnerabilities created by dependence on external resources and the potential of resource boycotts, Europe and Japan became increasingly willing to discuss restructuring international economic and trade relations with Developing World states. Canada also supported such negotiations, not out of fear of a Canadian resource shortfall but out of sympathy with the Developing World's economic plight, a sympathy created by Canada's own proximity to and interdependence with the American economic behemoth. In concrete terms, Canada, Western Europe, and Japan were all more willing than the United States to accept a new international economic order and a new law of the seas, both of which were to be more favorably disposed toward Developing World states than were the old structures.

A similar area of disagreement between First World states developed during the 1980s over issues that had political content. Although most First World governments agreed that political issues fell outside international law, the United States adopted an increasingly broad view of what "political issues" meant. Of course, the wider the definition of "political issues," the narrower the applicability of international law. The wide definition of "political issues" that the United States employed thus, for example, allowed the United States to argue that the ICJ had no jurisdiction in the Nicaragua case of 1984–1986. Most other First World states disagreed. Obviously, Western consensus on international law is not universal.

THE OUTLOOK OF THE FORMER SOVIET UNION. Since the collapse of the Soviet Union, the Russian perspective on international law has gradually moved toward coincidence with standard Western outlooks. Nevertheless, as a contrast, it remains instructive to examine briefly the perspectives on international law held by the former Soviet Union.

Before Gorbachev, the U.S.S.R. maintained a rather traditional Marxist-Leninist view on international law. To the pre-Gorbachev Kremlin, international law was divided into three categories. The first category was international socialist law, which was just and fair, and had the interests of the people at heart rather than the interests of the exploiting classes. The second category was that of international law in the capitalist world. To the Soviets, capitalist international law was exploitive, as was, the Soviets argued, the capitalist system itself. The third category of international law governed relations between the capitalist world and the communist world. For a variety of economic and political reasons, the U.S.S.R. found it advantageous to undertake legal and legalistic transactions with Western states in the interests of peaceful coexistence. To Soviet leaders, the West continued to attempt to gain advantage over the U.S.S.R. and other communist states through international law, but was prevented from doing so by Soviet strength and vigilance.[5]

As Gorbachev's New Thinking took hold, these outlooks changed. By 1990, although Soviet discussions of Western international law still evidenced concern with class conflict, most Soviet commentary detected worthwhile elements in the Western international legal system. These elements included fostering trade and international economic interaction, preserving national sovereignty, and redressing certain grievances. Notably, Soviet commentary also began to point to problems within socialist internationalist law, especially in the area of sovereignty.

Under traditional Soviet conceptions, sovereignty was limited, not absolute. This differed markedly from the Western view of absolute sovereignty. The U.S.S.R.'s doctrine of limited sovereignty was advanced in the so-called Brezhnev

Doctrine following the Soviet invasion of Czechoslovakia in August 1968. Under the Brezhnev Doctrine, communist states had the right to determine their own course of internal and economic development, but only up to the point where other communist states considered aberrations to be a threat to the international communist system. When other states believed that such a point had been reached, they had the right and responsibility to intervene, militarily if necessary.[6]

Under Gorbachev's New Thinking, however, signals were sent out, slowly at first, that the Brezhnev Doctrine no longer applied. Then in 1989, the Soviet government announced that the Brezhnev Doctrine had been renounced formally. A Soviet foreign ministry spokesman declared that the U.S.S.R. had accepted the "Sinatra Doctrine"—that each state now was free to do things its own way. Thus, a central part of Soviet international law was brought into line with Western thinking.[7]

THE CHINESE OUTLOOK. China's views on international law in many ways were and are similar to those of the traditional Soviet view, at least as far as the class nature of law was concerned. However, although China agreed with the U.S.S.R. about the exploitive character of Western international law, the P.R.C. also grouped Soviet-style international law in the exploitive category. China pointed both to Soviet economic relations with Eastern Europe and the Developing World and to the Brezhnev Doctrine as proof that the Soviet version of international law was no better—and probably worse—than the capitalist version.

Perhaps surprisingly, China was not very favorably disposed toward the new Soviet outlook on international law either. From China's perspective, Gorbachev's new thinking and its impact on international law brought the U.S.S.R. dangerously near a Western perspective. However, Beijing was pleased that Moscow renounced the Brezhnev Doctrine.

China's attitude toward Western international law remains driven by Marxism-Leninism. This remains true despite China's improved and improving relations with the West in general during the 1970s and 1980s. China has found it advantageous in a number of sectors, particularly economics and trade, to accept Western legal tenets, but still views them as products of exploitive capitalism.

Often China's criticisms of Western-dominated international law coincide with Developing World criticisms. This is understandable in view of the facts that Chinese history and Chinese economic development in many respects parallel Developing World history and development. From the Chinese perspective, Western international law was used as a vehicle to legitimize the partition of China and much of the rest of the world into colonial empires to the economic benefit of the West and the economic detriment of the rest. Thus, China has been most supportive of Developing World desires for a new international order.[8]

THE DEVELOPING WORLD'S OUTLOOK. As might be expected, the Developing World's views of international law have generally been critical. Some are more critical than others, but almost all chastise Western-dominated international law as granting economic preference and advantage to those very states that created most of the tenets of international law, the states of Western Europe and North America.

The Developing World is extremely supportive of the concept of sovereignty but argues that because of the strictures of prevailing international law,

Developing World sovereignty is abridged by economic dependence on and penetration by the developed Western world. Under prevailing international law, the Developing World believes, such neocolonialism is not prevented. Rather, it is encouraged.

Further, Developing World states often perceive that the institutions of the international community are established by and for the Western world to protect its own interest. Thus, the Developing World has regularly sought to create new forums from which to argue for a restructuring of the international legal and economic order. UNCTAD is perhaps the most prominent single forum. As more and more Developing World states achieved independence and entered the UN General Assembly, the assembly became a center for Developing World action as various declarations and charters calling for international change were passed. The Declaration on the Establishment of a New International Economic Order, the NIEO Program for Action, and the UN Charter of Economic Rights and Duties of States are chief among them. So far, however, redress of grievances imposed by international law against industrialized states has been painstakingly slow, at least from the Developing World's perspective. Neocolonialism to the Developing World, remains a major problem.

Developing World jurists themselves have advocated changes in international law such as the "clean slate doctrine," which argues essentially that once a new state or government comes into being, all obligations of previous states or governments are ended. Developing World jurists have also supported the doctrine of nationalization without compensation. These doctrines have been rejected by the West.

During the late 1980s and early 1990s, as noted earlier, many Developing World states have become more favorably disposed toward the West and toward the international economic system. This more favorable attitude has carried over into outlooks concerning international law as well. Nevertheless, it would be incorrect to assume that Developing World states and Western states now see eye-to-eye on most issues in international law. As a result, it is probable that the dialogue between the Developing World and the West on changing the international legal structure will proceed, but slowly.

DIPLOMACY

Defined earlier in this chapter as the implementation of an international actor's policies toward other actors, **diplomacy**, if skillful, can immeasurably enhance an actor's power potential. Conversely, inept diplomacy can weaken an actor's international position. Economically or militarily weak actors can and do strengthen their international positions with skillful diplomatic initiatives, and economically or militarily strong states can and do lose standing as a result of diplomatic blundering.

For the most part, diplomacy refers to the efforts that a state undertakes to implement its policies. However, nonstate actors conduct diplomacy as well. For example, a diplomatically skillful leader of a national liberation movement may convince others that his or her cause is so just that the group receives much more support than it otherwise would receive. Here, however, we concentrate on diplomacy as a tool of state actors.[9]

The Evolution of Diplomacy

Diplomacy is an old activity, dating back to ancient Greece and Rome. As we have seen in our discussion of international law, Homer's *Iliad* and Thucydides' *The Peloponnesian Wars* contained many references to diplomatic missions, treaties, negotiations, and other concepts associated with diplomacy. Ancient Rome also engaged in extensive diplomacy, although the Roman Empire is more noted for its military conquests.

As far as is known, the first professional diplomatic corps appeared in the Byzantine Empire following the collapse of Rome. Byzantium established the world's first department of foreign affairs, developed strict and complex diplomatic protocols, and actively sought intelligence about friend and enemy alike. Surrounded by enemies, Byzantium needed all the skill in diplomacy it could muster.

The art of diplomacy was carried to the next higher (some might say lower) plane in Italy during the fifteenth and sixteenth centuries. The Italian city-states of the era engaged in constant intrigues against each other. During this era, diplomacy became identified with behind-the-scenes scheming, duplicity, and double-dealing. Niccolo **Machiavelli** of Florence, whom many consider the father of realpolitik views of the international system, stressed in his book *The Prince* (1532) that rulers should use whatever means they had at their disposal to stay in power.

Western European diplomacy continued to evolve in the seventeenth and eighteenth centuries, particularly in France. Under Louis XIV, the minister of foreign affairs became an important adviser to the King. Louis XIV also established embassies with permanent ambassadors who served as his official representatives in all major foreign capitals. For the first time, international treaties and agreements also required exact and specific wording.

The next stage in the evolution of Western diplomacy began at the end of the Napoleonic Wars with the 1815 Congress of Vienna. Throughout the nineteenth century, diplomatic practices were formalized and regularized. Ambassadors and their embassies attained an immense international importance, often creating and implementing their country's foreign policy on the scene with little control from their home capital. Diplomats were drawn almost exclusively from the nobility. Most diplomacy was conducted in secret. More often than not, diplomacy was bilateral, directly between two countries.

For the most part, nineteenth-century diplomacy sought to preserve the European balance of power as diplomats tried to maintain a rough status quo in Europe and in the colonial empires. Generally speaking, nineteenth-century diplomacy worked well, but it also planted the seeds for World War I.

World War I is frequently viewed as the watershed between "old" diplomacy with its emphasis on elitism, secrecy, bilateral agreements, and the importance of the embassy, and "modern" diplomacy with its emphasis on competency, openness, multilateral agreements, and personal conduct of affairs. With many people believing that nineteenth-century diplomacy's practices had caused World War I, it was perhaps inevitable that old diplomatic practices would change.

Following World War I, more and more countries began to emphasize competency as opposed to class connections in their diplomatic corps. Increasingly, diplomats came from a wider cross section of society. This democratization of the diplomatic corps came in part from the belief that elitist diplomacy had lost touch with reality, and as a result had spawned World War I. Competency—at least in theory—replaced class connections as a prerequisite for the diplomat.

In theory, **open diplomacy** also replaced secret diplomacy. Many people, particularly U.S. President Woodrow Wilson, believed that secret treaties concluded by secret diplomacy had been a primary cause of World War I. Wilson and others therefore called for "open covenants, openly arrived at." Thus, following World War I, open diplomacy became an ideal of modern diplomacy.

So, too, did **multilateral diplomacy**, in which many countries would participate in diplomatic activity. Woodrow Wilson again led the way, with his appeals for a League of Nations. Even after the league failed, the world's statesmen eventually created the United Nations. The states of the world also began to meet more frequently in conferences to discuss specific issues. Importantly, however, beyond these world bodies and multilateral conferences, an immense network of multilateral contacts developed between states following World War I, as we saw in our earlier discussion of IGOs.

After World War I, personal diplomacy on the part of leaders of states also replaced reliance on ambassadors and embassies as a hallmark of diplomacy. One criticism of "old" diplomacy's reliance on ambassadors who operated relatively independently of control from their home government was that an ambassador might be working at cross-purposes to the home government. Some experts believed that this was one cause of World War I. Following World War I, in part because of this belief, and in part because of technical breakthroughs in transportation and communications, many governments placed tighter reins on ambassadors and embassies. They relied more and more on personal diplomacy conducted by senior members of the government, usually the president and secretary of state in the United States, and their equivalents in other countries. These changes led to a new emphasis on summitry and public diplomacy, both of which are discussed below.

"Modern" diplomacy did not emerge overnight, and it did not completely replace "old" diplomacy. Even today, diplomacy often retains vestiges of elitism, secrecy, bilateralism, and ambassadorial and embassy independence. Indeed, a strong case can be made that effective diplomacy needs a certain degree of each of these. Elitism under certain conditions may abet competence, and secrecy sometimes can assist negotiations. On some occasions, bilateralism can achieve diplomatic breakthroughs that multilateralism cannot. Similarly, ambassadorial initiatives can yield results that the personal diplomacy of senior government officials cannot.

In reality, "modern" diplomacy is a mix of new elements and old, with competency and elitism coexisting; openness and secrecy both serving their purposes; multilateral and bilateral diplomacy occurring simultaneously; and personal diplomacy and ambassador/embassy diplomacy blending together. The world of modern diplomacy is complex indeed, and it is to some of its specific purposes we now turn.

The Purposes of Modern Diplomacy

Modern diplomacy has at least six purposes, all concerned with the implementation of a state's policies toward other actors. These purposes are representing the state, gathering and interpreting information, signaling and receiving positions, conducting negotiations, managing crises, and influencing international public opinion. Each purpose demands separate commentary.

REPRESENTATION.   When diplomats are overseas, their official duty is to represent their country and its policies. Skillful diplomats project a favorable image of their country, and in so doing, aid their country in its efforts to achieve its objectives. Skillful diplomats also explain their country's policies and positions in ways that are both comprehensible and acceptable to the governments and peoples of the country to which they are assigned. When they find it impossible to present their country's policies and positions in acceptable ways, skillful diplomats attempt to minimize points of disagreement, emphasize points of agreement, and otherwise seek to further their country's policy objectives. Obviously, in their representational capacity, skillful diplomats are a tremendous asset for a country to have.

INFORMATION GATHERING AND INTERPRETING.   Because good policies are usually based on good information, diplomats often find themselves gathering and interpreting information for their country. This does not mean that all diplomats are spies. Rather, it is accepted throughout the world that one purpose of diplomats is to acquire and interpret information about the country to which they are posted.

There is a vague boundary between what is acceptable information gathering in the overt diplomatic community and unacceptable spying in the covert world of espionage. This is not the place to explore the dimensions of that boundary. Indeed, many embassies of many countries have personnel attached to them who have one overt responsibility, but whose primary responsibility is in fact the gathering of covert, clandestine information.

Here, however, the emphasis is on the overt information gathering and interpreting function that all diplomats at all embassies have. It is accepted within the international community. Given the advantages that good information accurately interpreted gives to a country as it makes its own policies, a country whose diplomats are skilled information gatherers and interpreters is fortunate indeed.

SIGNALING AND RECEIVING.   Sometimes, diplomats are vehicles through which their government communicates new and sometimes subtle position shifts to other countries. Similarly, diplomats sometimes are asked to float "trial balloons" to their opposite numbers to see how their opposite numbers' countries might respond to a policy or position change. Diplomats operating in this capacity are serving as signaling agents for their country.

Diplomats also often serve as receivers, as when a foreign government wishes to communicate information back to a diplomat's home country. Signaling and receiving are essentially opposite sides of the same coin of diplomatic communications. Seasoned diplomats frequently have well-developed signaling and receiving skills.

NEGOTIATING.   All diplomats must engage in negotiations to some extent. At the highest levels, presidents and foreign ministers negotiate the final details of weighty international issues like arms control agreements and free trade agreements. At the lowest levels, consular officials decide who will receive travel documents. In between, diplomats negotiate a host of other issues as well. But in all cases, diplomats must be able to negotiate.

Sometimes even the efforts of skilled negotiators are not sufficient to end warfare. UN mediators Lord Owen and Cyrus Vance tried for months to find a way to stop the fighting in Bosnia, including splitting Bosnia up into safe havens for Bosnian Moslems, but nothing they suggested ended the warfare.   (The United Nations.)

International negotiating is an art and a skill in which representatives from two or more countries meet to find or create areas of agreement among two or more different positions. Most international negotiating is done by ambassadors and their staffs, by senior government officials, or by national delegations with expertise on specific issues who attend international conferences, talks, and meetings. Often, international governmental organizations play important roles in organizing, sponsoring, and even moderating or mediating such conferences, talks, and meetings.

A country whose diplomats are capable negotiators often finds itself in an advantageous position relative to other international actors, even when the strengths of its other parameters of power imply that it should be weaker. Negotiating is thus a key element of diplomacy, and of national power.

CRISIS MANAGEMENT.   When international crises break out that affect their own country and the country to which they are posted, diplomats sometimes find themselves on the front line of crisis management. In these situations, diplomats must use all their skills to the fullest as they seek to defuse the crisis, while simultaneously achieving their country's objectives.

As a general rule, the more serious a crisis is, the more likely it is that a senior official in the home capital, perhaps the national leader, the minister of foreign affairs, or even the entire senior executive branch, will focus on the problem and assume primary responsibility for crisis management and resolution. But even then, the role of diplomats remains crucial. Even in crises, it is frequently through the ambassador or the embassy staff that representation, information gathering and interpreting, signaling and receiving, and even negotiating take place. In times of crises, these functions are collectively elevated to a higher level of importance.

PUBLIC DIPLOMACY. Finally, public diplomacy has become a critical part of the diplomatic repertoire. As a result of the communications and transportation revolutions, diplomats from national leaders on down can be seen and heard by more people in more places than at any previous time. Skillful public diplomacy can influence public opinion beyond one's own country to support one's country's policies and positions, and can influence foreign peoples to have a favorable view of one's country. Conversely, blundering public diplomacy can undermine even well-conceived policies and positions, and can project an extremely negative image of a country.

At the highest level, superpower summitry must be viewed as the epitome of public diplomacy. Whatever the substantive content of such summits, most negotiations have been concluded by lower-level diplomats before the summit takes place. Without denying the importance of personal relationships that develop at superpower summits (both the Nixon-Brezhnev and Reagan-Gorbachev relationships come to mind), and recognizing that only national leaders can untie certain policy knots that may exist, one of the primary purposes of summitry is public diplomacy. Both sides seek to project a favorable image of themselves and their policies to domestic and international publics through summitry.

Public diplomacy is important at other levels as well. Diplomats often seek and accept speaking engagements, media interviews, and other ways in which they can obtain the opportunity to influence others to view their country and its policies favorably. At some times, such public diplomacy may be considered by host countries as meddling in their internal affairs. At other times, such public diplomacy may be virtually identical to a diplomat's representation function.

Nevertheless, regardless of the level, there is no doubt that in the 1990s, public diplomacy has become a central part of the function of diplomacy and diplomats.

INTERNATIONAL LAW AND DIPLOMACY AS PARAMETERS OF POWER

As we saw in our study of sociopolitical parameters of power, not all dimensions of power can be categorized or quantified easily. The contributions that international law and diplomacy make to a country's power potential are such parameters.

International law's relationship to power is complex. On the one hand, it limits power by establishing certain standards of behavior. If adhered to, international law thus constrains the application of power. But on the other hand, international law also provides a certain degree of predictability for the international community, thereby enabling international actors to rationalize their policies. International law thus enhances power by helping to create an international environment in which actors can plan and implement future-oriented policies.

At the same time, for state actors, national sovereignty is rooted in international law. Obviously, states benefit immeasurably, although not equally, from the concept of national sovereignty.

Meanwhile, skillful diplomacy also enhances an international actor's power potential. Although our discussion in this chapter has centered on the importance of diplomacy for states, all international actors can benefit if their diplomats represent their policies and positions well, gather and interpret information effectively, signal and receive communications accurately, negotiate persuasively, manage crises intelligently, and engage in effective public diplomacy.

Too often, because they are not easily categorized or quantified, both international law and diplomacy are ignored or overlooked as elements of power. International actors that ignore or overlook either one weaken their own international standing.

KEY TERMS AND CONCEPTS

Grotius
naturalist school
positivist school
eclectic school
neorealist school
International Court of Justice (ICJ)
(also in Chapter 3)
sovereignty
constitutive theory
declarative theory
law of war
just and unjust war

diplomacy
diplomacy's evolution
Machiavelli
open diplomacy
multilateral diplomacy
representation
information gathering and
interpreting
signaling and receiving
negotiating
crisis management
public diplomacy

NOTES

1. For a recent study of Grotius's work, see Hedley Bull, et al., eds., *Hugo Grotius and International Relations* (New York: Oxford University Press, 1990).
2. For more detailed explanations, see J. L. Brierly, *The Law of Nations: An Introduction to the International Law of Peace* (New York: Oxford University Press, 1963), especially Chapter 1.
3. See S. Rosenne, *Documents on the International Court of Justice* (Dobbs Ferry, NY: Oceana, 1979); and R. Bernhardt et al. (eds.), *Digest of the Decisions of the International Court of Justice, 1950–1975* (New York: Springer-Verlag New York, 1978). See also Paul Reuter, *Introduction to the Law of Treaties* (Leicester: Leicester University Press, 1992).
4. For more extensive discussions of the law of war, see William Ballis, *Legal Position of War: Changes in Its Theory and Practice from Plato to Vattel* (New York: Garland, n.d.); Julius Stone, *Legal Controls of International Conflict* (New York: Garland, n.d.); and Peter D. Trooboff (ed.), *Law and Responsibility in Warfare: The Vietnam Experience* (Chapel Hill, NC: University of North Carolina Press, 1975). See also Peter Rowe, ed., *The Gulf War and International Law* (New York: Routledge, 1993).

5. A discussion of the pre-Gorbachev Soviet view of international law may be found in T. A. Taracouzio, *The Soviet Union and International Law* (Millwood, NY: Kraus, 1935); H. W. Baade (ed.), *Soviet Impact on International Law* (Dobbs Ferry, NY: Oceana, 1965); and Alvin Z. Rubinstein, *Soviet Foreign Policy since World War II: Imperial and Global* (Boston: Little, Brown, 1981).

6. See Helmut Schmidt, "Consequences of the Brezhnev Doctrine," *Atlantic Community Quarterly*, Vol. 7 (Summer 1969): 184–195.

7. See Gorbachev's October 7, 1989, speech in East Berlin in which he told East German and other Eastern European communist leaders that they could no longer count on Soviet military power to keep their parties in control of the government.

8. Good explanations of Chinese international legal outlooks may be found in Jerome A. Cohen (ed.), *China's Practice of International Law: Some Case Studies* (Cambridge: Harvard University Press, 1973); and Jerome A. Cohen and Hungdah Chiu, *People's China and International Law* (Princeton, NJ: Princeton University Press, 1974).

9. For a more detailed view of diplomacy, see Adam Watson, *Diplomacy: The Dialogue Between States* (New York: Routledge, 1992).

PART FIVE

The Argumentative Framework

ISSUES OF INTERNATIONAL POLITICS

If present trends continue, the world in 2000 will be more crowded, more polluted, less stable ecologically, and more vulnerable to disruption than the world we live in now. Serious stresses involving population, resources, and environment are clearly visible ahead. Despite greater material output, the world's people will be poorer in many ways than they are today.

—The Global 2000 Report

> Man to man is so unjust
> You don't know who to trust
> Your worst enemy could be your best friend
> And your best friend, your worst enemy.

—Bob Marley

Many of the issues that confront the international community—that is to say, humanity—cannot be fully understood in local or regional contexts. Issues such as population growth, food shortages, resource availability, technical capabilities, economic development, skewed distribution of wealth, trade issues, environmental problems, drugs, health, war, peace, violence, and conflicts in value systems have local and regional impacts, it is true, but they are problems that can be fully understood only on the global level.

To this point, we have examined different types of international actors and their interrelationships, the system in which the actors operate, the dominant perceptions those actors hold, and the major instruments with which those actors pursue their objectives. We have not analyzed the preceding issues in their global contexts. This framework makes that analysis.

Global issues may be categorized in many ways. In this framework, we examine them in five different chapters. Two chapters concentrate on issues of international political economy. The first, Chapter 21, examines basic inputs to the global standard of living, namely, population, food, resources, and technology.

The second chapter on international political economy, Chapter 22, explores questions about economic development and the global distribution of wealth. Emerging global problems of the environment, drugs, and health issues are examined in Chapter 23. Problems of war, peace, and violence are presented in Chapter 24, and problems emerging from conflicts of values are discussed in Chapter 25.

This framework by no means pretends to present a comprehensive discussion of each of the preceding issues, nor does it maintain that it covers all potential and real issues. Rather it highlights several of the international community's major concerns. How well the international community resolves these concerns will determine how well—indeed, whether—humanity lives in the twenty-first century. This framework examines such questions as

- How serious are the world's population and food situations?
- Why do resource shortages exist, and can their impacts be reduced?
- What role does technology play in today's world, and why do some countries have developed technical capabilities, while others do not?
- Why are there such skewed distributions of wealth throughout the world?
- How does economic development take place, and can it be accelerated?
- How serious are the world's environmental problems, and what is the international community doing about them?
- What can be done about the international drug and health problems?
- What causes war, and can war be avoided?
- What types of conflicts of values exist, and why?

CHAPTER 21

International Political Economy I

POPULATION, FOOD, RESOURCES, AND TECHNOLOGY

- What are the implications of the world's rapid population growth?
- Is world hunger caused by an absolute shortage of food or by poor distribution of food?
- How long will the world have adequate mineral resources?
- What role does technology play in today's world?
- Why have some countries advanced in technological terms, while others have not?

Throughout history, but particularly since World War II, international actors—especially states—have been joined in what may be called a "standard-of-living race." Disagreements over which state had the best quality of life and over which socio-political-economic system provided higher standards of living and better quality of life to more people were central to the East–West conflict throughout the Cold War era, and disagreement over the causes and cures of the economic gap between North and South remains a major international issue today.

Beyond the narrow parochial economic concerns of individual state and nonstate actors loom issues of importance for the international system at large. On a local and regional basis, international actors continue to undertake policies that run contrary to what most analysts would consider to be the global interest. Global population continues to grow, but some states continue to provide economic and noneconomic incentives for large families. World food production barely meets need, yet some governments pay their farmers to produce less. Governments pursue economic development in different ways, but no one is really sure how and why it occurs. And the simmering resentments caused by uneven distribution of wealth may explode into violence at any time.

Much of the debate and disagreement that the "standard-of-living race" has generated intertwines international political issues and international economic issues. Indeed, this intertwining is so complex that most analysts and policy-makers now term the issues that are included in the debate and disagreement issues of **international political economics**. Although no single definition of international political economics is universally accepted, there is general agree-ment that factors as diverse as population growth, food shortages, resource avail-ability, technical capabilities, skewed distributions of wealth, economic development, and trade are all included within the term.

These are just some of the issues included in the international political econ-omy of the global standard of living. Each is significant enough to warrant vol-umes, but in this chapter, we concern ourselves with four basic inputs to the international political economy of the global standard of living—namely, popula-tion, food, resources, and technology. In Chapter 22, we will examine the deriva-tive international political economic issues of economic development and the global distribution of wealth.

POPULATION

The central problem for the twenty-first century may be nothing so esoteric as international control of exotic laser weapons and charged particle beams or meth-ods to cope with information overload and accelerated obsolescence. Twenty-first century humanity may be faced with the mundane problem of assessing the earth's carrying capacity for human beings, and then determining how to stay within that capacity. The population explosion may have only begun.

In quantitative terms, the earth's **population growth** has been accelerating for some time. Humankind did not reach the one-billion-person level until 1830, but within another century, it had passed the 2-billion mark. The third billion came by 1960. By 1975, over 4 billion people lived on the earth. The World Bank projects global population by 2000 to be over 6 billion people. Some projections for 2100 place the world's population at 9 billion people! Most of this rapid growth has been the result of impressive improvements in health and medical services throughout the world. Death rates declined precipitously, but birthrates remained relatively constant. Inevitably, population totals grew rapidly.

The overall problem of explosive population growth is compounded by the location of that growth. According to the UN Population Fund, about 95 percent of the world's population growth between 1992 and 2042 will take place in the Developing World. By 2000, five billion of the world's six billion people will live in the Developing World. At least 37 countries will not be able to feed their own populations.[1]

Equally distressing, most of the Developing World's population by 2000 will also be in or near their offspring-producing years. Thus, barring an unexpected and precipitous drop in birthrates, rapid population growth will continue. This has important political and economic implications, as we will see later. Table 21–1 illustrates these projections.

Population growth has historically been accompanied by urbanization. Table 21–2 gives both historical trends and future projections for the urbanization phe-nomenon in 11 Developing World cities. By 2000, all will be larger than the New York of 1993. Rapid large-scale urbanization means that urban sanitation, water, health, and food delivery systems will have to be substantially upgraded. More

TABLE 21–1 Population Projections for the World by Major Regions, in Millions of People

Region	1987	2000	2020
Africa	601	880	1,479
Asia	2,930	3,598	4,584
North America	270	296	326
Latin America	421	537	712
Europe	495	507	502
Soviet Union	284	312	355
Australia, New Zealand, and South Pacific Islands	25	29	35
TOTALS	5,026	6,159	7,993

SOURCE: Population Reference Bureau, 1990.

housing must be constructed, and more jobs must be created. Particularly for Developing World governments that find themselves hard-pressed to maintain satisfactory living conditions in urban areas today, this task may prove insurmountable. Most distressingly, the rural areas of Developing World states are often less well off than the urban centers.

Population pressures, along with warfare, are also primary causes of a growing world refugee problem. Some estimates place the world's refugee population at over 20 million people, and others go as high as 40 million. In some locations, warfare is the chief cause of the refugee problem. In others, population has simply grown so rapidly that land can no longer support the number of people that are present. Thus, as we will see later, population pressure leads to overuse of land, which in turn leads to land degradation and desertification, which in turn forces population migration. Hence, more people are added to the world's refugee population. This can lead to international tension and conflict as refugees seek to move across national boundaries to seek better land or more food.

All is not necessarily gloomy, however. During the 1950s, population experts predicted global population would top 7.5 billion by 2000. Current projections

TABLE 21–2 Urban Populations in Twelve Major Developing World Cities, in Millions of People

	1960	1975	1992	2000
Calcutta	5.5	8.1	11.1	12.7
Mexico City	4.9	10.9	15.3	16.2
Bombay	4.1	7.1	13.3	18.1
Cairo	3.7	6.9	9.0	10.8
Jakarta	2.7	5.6	10.0	13.4
Seoul	2.4	7.3	11.6	13.0
Delhi	2.3	4.5	8.8	11.7
Manila	2.2	4.4	9.6	12.6
Karachi	1.8	4.5	8.6	11.9
São Paulo	NA	NA	25.8	28.0

SOURCE: 1960–1975, *Global 2000 Report*, Table 13–9. 1992 figures and projections for 2000 are from the Population Division of the UN Secretariat, January 1993.

are for 6.2 billion people.[2] Clearly, a population growth slowdown has occurred. Several possible reasons exist for this slowdown. One explanation is that population growth rates are declining because of artificial or natural birth control methods. Government policy is often integrally involved in such efforts. In Cuba, for example, birthrates fell 47 percent between 1965–1970 and 1970–1975, and in China, birthrates fell 34 percent between the same two periods. The governments of both countries have pursued aggressive birth control policies. Indeed, throughout the Developing World, the rate of contraceptive use climbed from 40 percent in 1980 to 49 percent in 1990.[3]

Often, however, birth control is opposed by religious, social, or cultural custom. The depth of this opposition to birth control is well illustrated in China, where in 1989 the Chinese government concluded that despite its birth control efforts, China's population would exceed its planned population target of 1.2 billion people in 2000 by at least 100 million people.[4] And in some Developing World countries, efforts to control population growth are also viewed as neocolonial plots designed to maintain Developing World subservience to the First World.

Opposition to birth control is not confined to Developing World states. The Catholic Church has long opposed birth control efforts. Indeed, it was primarily because of the Catholic Church's opposition to birth control that the issue of population was not directly addressed at the UN's 1992 "Earth Summit" in Rio de Janeiro.[5] And during the Reagan presidency, the United States government also ended its support for international birth control programs that supported abortion as a method of population control. Both the Catholic Church's position and the Reagan administration's position raised an extremely difficult moral and ethical issue: at what point, if any, does it become ethical to limit population growth because of low or deteriorating standards of living?

Social revolution may also bring lower birthrates as women begin to control more of their own lives. Sri Lanka and Thailand attribute at least some of the decline in their birthrates to this factor. In addition, as old attitudes about the superiority of male children over female children are displaced, fewer and fewer couples may be expected to continue to have children simply to assure a male heir.

The education level of women also has a direct impact on population growth. UN data from many countries indicates that where women receive no secondary school education, the average woman has seven children. But in countries where 40 percent of all women have had secondary school education, the average drops to three children.[6]

Historical data also shows that higher standards of living lead to lower birthrates. For example, in Western Europe, Austria, Belgium, Finland, France, Germany, Great Britain, Greece, Italy, and Sweden all have population growth rates under one half percent per year, and Denmark has a zero population growth rate. Japan's population growth rate is .4 percent, and the United States' growth rate, while higher than most developed states, is still only .8 percent.[7]

Indeed, under the Reagan and Bush administrations, the **United States' population policy** was based on the argument that the best form of birth control was economic growth driven by private enterprise. However, many Developing World states considered this U.S. position absurd. Even under the best conditions, they point out, economic growth takes many years to occur. With large population growth rates, many Developing World countries believe that they do not have many more years before disaster strikes. The Clinton administration has indicated that under it, the United States will take a more activist position on international family planning issues.

More pessimistic reasons for lower population growth rates in the future have also been advanced. Extreme poverty and malnutrition may in themselves be cause for lower future population growth rates. Historical data indicates that Indonesian fertility declined between 10 and 15 percent and Brazilian lower-class fertility fell between 15 and 20 percent between 1970 and 1976.[8]

Despite this, the world population is continuing to grow. Even this fact, however, does not concern some people. Technological optimists maintain faith in the ability of science, technology, and humanity to provide for the world's population, almost regardless of number. Religious optimists express a similar faith in God's ability to provide for humankind. These optimists are offset by population pessimists who predict a future of Malthusian pestilence, famine, and war, all brought about by rising population pressure. Even the experts disagree about whether the earth has a finite capacity to support human beings, and if it does have one, what that capacity is.

 # FOOD

The world's population problem is closely linked to questions about food. This linkage and the concern that it evokes are not new. Indeed, as early as the eighteenth century, British clergyman and economist **Thomas Malthus** postulated that global food production would expand arithmetically, whereas global population would grow exponentially. The disparity in growth rates of food and population would lead to disease, hunger, and conflict on an unprecedented scale, Malthus believed.[9]

Although Malthus's dire prediction did not happen, continued population growth and a falling rate of growth of world food production during the early 1970s resurrected this fear. In 1972, for the first time since World War II, the global food supply actually decreased. Global grain reserves fell from 223 million metric tons in 1971, sufficient for 70 days of consumption, to 186 million metric tons in 1972, sufficient for 57 days of consumption. Although global grain reserves were rebuilt by 1974, they plummeted again in 1988 to a 54-day reserve. Table 21–3 illustrates this. Clearly, humanity is perched on a precarious balance between food scarcity and food sufficiency. While global famine is not imminent, the world's margin of safety is such that one or two years of drastically reduced food production could spell disaster.

Disturbingly, as Table 21–3 makes clear, world grain production fell in the late 1980s after reaching a record high in 1986. In the 1990s, world grain production increased again, but not at the rates of the early 1970s and early 1980s. The temporary decline in global grain production in the late 1980s raised questions about earlier projections that world food production would continue to increase during the remainder of the century.[10] Nevertheless, since most of the world's arable land outside North America is already in agricultural use, little increased production may be expected from increasing the area under cultivation. Much of the future's expanded agricultural production must come from more extensive and intensive use of fertilizer, herbicides, pesticides, and irrigation. But as we will see in Chapter 23, all these efforts to increase food production often damage the environment.

Other solutions may also be available to increase the world's food production.

TABLE 21–3   World Grain Production, Utilization and Reserves
(in million metric tons)

Year	Production	Consumption	Stocks	Days of Consumption
1969/70	1078	1094	228	76
1971/72	1194	1169	217	68
1973/74	1272	1260	192	56
1975/76	1250	1230	220	65
1977/78	1337	1339	279	76
1979/80	1428	1441	316	80
1981/82	1499	1478	309	76
1983/84	1487	1539	304	72
1985/86	1664	1596	433	99
1987/88	1615	1670	408	89
1989/90	1685	1701	300	64
1991/92	1697	1726	305	64

SOURCE: U.S. Department of Agriculture, Foreign Agricultural Services, "World Grain Situation and Outlook," (Washington, D.C.: U.S. Government Printing Office, 1992).

Bioengineering may provide new strains of disease-resistant and insect-resistant crops that have higher yields than present-day crops. More fallow land may be put into production for a short time to help lessen short-term food shortages. But to reiterate, humanity has only a narrow margin of safety in its food supply situation.

The total level of global production is not the only food-related problem the world faces. Distribution is also a problem. As Table 21–4 shows, in 1988 only Europe, North America, Australia, and New Zealand were grain surplus areas. This pattern has not changed in the years since then. Indeed, if North American figures are excluded, the world's grain situation appears dire. And it is extremely perplexing that most of the countries in the food deficit areas are economically underdeveloped. Many will be forced to rely on aid and assistance from wealthier states to import food. In the absence of such aid and assistance, or even in the event of insufficient aid and assistance, food shortages in deficit areas are inevitable. Indeed, as we have already seen, the United Nations predicted in 1992 that at least 37 countries would not be able to feed their populations by 2000.

In some countries, famine has already been and is now present. During the

TABLE 21–4   World Grain Trade, 1950–1988 (in million metric tons)

Region	1950	1960	1970	1980	1988
North America	+23	+39	+56	+131	+119
Latin America	+ 1	0	+ 4	− 10	− 11
Western Europe	−22	−25	−30	− 16	− 22
E. Europe and Soviet Union	0	0	0	− 46	− 27
Africa	0	− 2	− 5	− 15	− 28
Asia	− 6	−17	−37	− 63	− 89
Australia and New Zealand	+ 3	+ 6	+12	+ 19	+ 14

SOURCE: Lester R. Brown et al., *State of the World 1989* (New York: Norton, 1989), p. 45.
Note: Plus sign = exports; minus sign = imports

1970s and 1980s, famines killed somewhere between 2 and 3 million people.[11] In the early 1990s, famine struck again in Ethiopia, Mozambique, Somalia, and Sudan. In Somalia alone, as many as 3 million people were in danger of starving to death. Before the UN-authorized U.S.-led military intervention took place in December 1992 to create a secure situation in which emergency food rations could be distributed, as many as 200 people per day were dying of hunger and malnutrition.

What is worse, in all four states listed above, governments, other political authorities, and gangs used hunger and famine as weapons of war to increase their own power, control, and influence.[12] Although most people would condemn the use of hunger and famine as a weapon of war, it is an undeniable fact of international life that such actions occur.

Obviously, the uneven global distribution of food leads to uneven levels of food consumption throughout the world. Even so, the magnitude of this unevenness is surprising. For example, North Americans consume about 1 ton of grain per capita per year, 200 pounds directly in grain and the remainder indirectly through livestock and dairy products. In Developing World countries, average annual per capita consumption is about 400 pounds of grain per year, most as grain. According to the UN Food and Agricultural Organization (FAO), individual Developing World caloric intake during the 1970s and 1980s averaged 94 percent of the minimum FAO requirement. When internal skewing is taken into account, that is, when it is realized that the rich eat much better than the poor in Developing World states, the 94 percent figure appears greatly overinflated.

With global hunger a fact, one of the supreme ironies of the twentieth century is that the U.S. government, despite global hunger, pays its farmers to take land out of production for the purpose of maintaining higher agricultural prices so U.S. farmers can make a decent living. However, even if additional food were

Too often, U.S. citizens think hunger and homelessness is "only" a Developing World problem. They are wrong. It is also a U.S. problem, as this recent photo taken in Manhattan illustrates.   (U.N. Photo/P. Sudhakaran.)

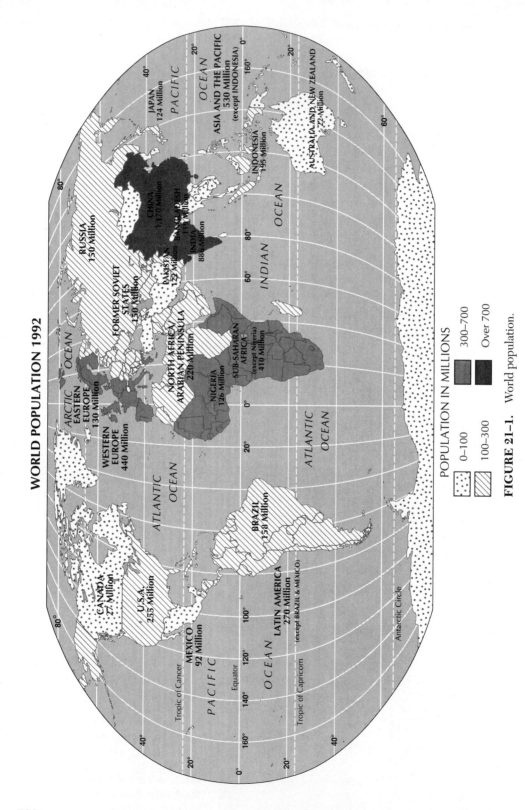

WORLD POPULATION 1992

POPULATION IN MILLIONS

| 0–100 | 300–700 |
| 100–300 | Over 700 |

FIGURE 21–1. World population.

produced, the most needy states could attain little except through aid because of their shortage of hard currency.

Undernourishment carries with it a hidden cost. Underfed youth never develop their full mental or physical capabilities. For example, in Africa, over 40 percent of the children under age five are malnourished to the degree that they experience actual physical or mental damage. For a continent seeking to modernize and industrialize, this is indeed a considerable blow. Undernourishment in no uncertain terms hampers economic development.

Questions of food are clearly among the most important that humanity will face in the remaining years of the twentieth century and on into the twenty-first century. The international political economy of food is obviously complex, and the complexity of the food equation is a large part of the reason why global maldistribution of food remains a problem. Others regard food exports as one of the tools of foreign policy that they can exercise at their own free will.[13]

In addition to political and economic issues, population and food issues pose moral dilemmas. Is it moral to practice birth control? If so, what method(s) is (are) acceptable and successful? If not, is it moral to bring a child into the world if the world's population is nearing its limits and insufficient food supplies appear a possibility? Is it moral to deny a hungry person food for political or economic reasons? How accurate in a moral sense was Willy Brandt, former chancellor of West Germany, when he declared that, "morally, it makes no difference whether a man is killed in war or is condemned to starve to death by the indifference of others"?

These and related questions have no universally accepted answers. Nevertheless, as the world's population increases and its food situation becomes more precarious, humankind must begin to address and solve such questions.

RESOURCES

For centuries, humans have used and abused nature's resources as if these resources were limitless. When one valley was overhunted, tribal man simply moved on to the next valley. Slash-and-burn agricultural methods destroyed acres of forestland. Wide areas of forestland and savannahs were stripped of wood for construction and fuel. These and other cases of human assaults to nature pale in comparison with the ravishes visited upon nature following the industrial revolution. Strip mining, industrial production, sedentary agriculture, and extensive fishing tremendously improved life either directly or indirectly for millions, even billions, of people, but it has only been during the last three decades in particular that humans became widely aware that resources were not limitless. By the late 1970s and early 1980s, resource depletion was an issue of widespread global concern, especially in the industrialized countries of Western Europe, Japan, the United States, and the former Soviet Union. For our purposes, resource concern may be examined as concern over energy resources and nonfuel mineral resources.

Energy

Global energy consumption expanded tremendously with the industrial revolution, and has continued to expand ever since. Some analysts have been predicting for years that humanity's rabid consumption of fossil fuels would deplete those resources, but few paid serious attention to their prediction. However, following the 1973 OPEC price increases and boycott, the Western world listened anew to those who foresaw future fuel shortages. For the first time, widespread segments of the West saw their visions of a future utopia clouded by the prospect of an energy shortage. For most, that energy shortage revolved around oil.

The rise of oil to the central position in the world's energy picture is a relatively recent phenomenon. At the beginning of the twentieth century, coal occupied the dominant position; at the onset of World War I, as much as 75 percent of the world's energy consumption came from coal. Coal's preferred position deteriorated rapidly during the next 40 years, however, as more and more oil was found in exploitable locations. Given oil's relative cleanliness, ease of production, and relatively low cost during this period, and given the invention of the internal combustion engine, oil gradually surpassed coal as the world's dominant energy source. By 1950, oil accounted for one-third of the world's energy consumption. Fifteen years later, oil had supplanted coal as the world's most important energy source, and 15 years after that, by 1980, oil met nearly one-half of the world's energy needs.

The specter of oil depletion arises from the simple fact that, until the worldwide economic recession of 1981–1982 reduced demand for oil, global petroleum producing capacity was not increasing as rapidly as demand. In addition, fewer oil reserves were being discovered. On the positive side, more efficient use of petroleum and petroleum products during the 1980s and 1990s lent credence to the technological optimists' claims that global petroleum reserves could be extended. Nevertheless, even to the optimist, it was clear that the earth's oil reserves were finite. Table 21–5 shows estimates of oil reserves in a number of locations, and gives their expected life at current rates of production.

Impending oil scarcity was not the only reason oil became a source of concern. Much of the Western world's prosperity of the 1950s and 1960s was built on the availability of inexpensive oil. Indeed, from the late 1940s through the early 1970s, oil declined in price relative to most other commodities. Depressed oil prices for this 25-year period may be attributed both to favorable concessions gained by the major oil companies from their sources of production, and to their success in keeping independent producers out of the market. When OPEC, whose member states had recently gained control of production and pricing decisions over the oil they produced, quadrupled the price of oil during 1973–1974, the entire noncommunist world economy felt the shock. OPEC raised prices again in 1979–1980. Not until 1985–1986 did oil prices fall significantly, from roughly $30 per barrel to about $15.

However, this respite proved short-lived. Following the Iraqi invasion of Kuwait in 1990, world oil prices shot up temporarily to over $35 per barrel as Iraqi and Kuwaiti oil disappeared from the market and as fears of war swept world oil markets. Following the 1991 Persian Gulf War, oil prices dropped to about $20 a barrel.

Even so, this was about ten times higher than oil prices had been only twenty years earlier. This meant that even with inflation factored in, oil importing countries had a larger economic burden to bear for energy imports than they had in the early 1970s. In addition, the habits, technologies, and investment patterns that had been established during the postwar era of cheap oil could not be changed overnight. In the United States, for example, the automobile played a dominant role in social, cul-

TABLE 21–5 Global Oil Reserves and Production Rates

Region/Country	Estimated Proven Reserves Jan. 1993 (1000 bbl)	Estimated Oil Production in 1992 (1000 bbl/day)	Years of Production Remaining at 1992 Rate
Total Asia–Pacific	*44,572,328*	*6,484*	*19*
China	5,291,630	2,834	5
India	6,049,068	573	29
Indonesia	5,779,000	1,370	12
Malaysia	3,700,000	661	15
Total Western Europe	*15,828,836*	*4,486*	*10*
Norway	8,802,734	2,098	12
United Kingdom	4,143,630	1,828	6
Total Middle East	*611,791,002*	*17,421*	*96*
Abu Dhabi	92,200,000	1,891	134
Iran	92,860,000	3,415	74
Iraq	100,000,000	417	657
Kuwait	94,000,000	845	305
Oman	4,483,000	729	17
Qatar	3,729,000	415	25
Saudi Arabia	257,842,000	8,207	86
Total Africa	*61,872,424*	*6,319*	*27*
Algeria	9,200,000	771	33
Egypt	6,200,000	871	20
Libya	22,800,000	1,469	43
Nigeria	17,889,820	1,887	26
Total Latin America	*123,810,674*	*7,384*	*46*
Argentina	1,569,987	544	8
Brazil	3,030,000	641	13
Mexico	51,298,000	2,776	51
Venezuela	62,650,000	2,329	74
Total North America	*29,973,630*	*8,755*	*9*
Canada	5,291,630	1,618	9
United States	24,682,000	7,137	9
Total Eastern Europe and C.I.S.	*59,192,880*	*9,181*	*18*
C.I.S.	57,000,000	8,898	18
Romania	1,568,754	140	31
Total World	*990,041,774*	*60,029*	*45*

Source: *Oil & Gas Journal*, Dec 28, 1992, pp. 44–45, vol. 90; 52.

tural, and economic life; to some, the entire American style of life was based on the habit of the car. In industry, cheap oil had led to lack of concern about efficient energy use; industrial technologies took time to regear themselves to emphasize efficient energy use. Perhaps most perplexingly, the long availability of cheap oil had discouraged investment in other nonoil sources of energy. Only gradually did the sudden surge in oil prices lead to energy substitution. Wind power, geothermal power, solar power, and other sources of energy consequently grew in importance during the early 1980s, but the drop in oil prices in the mid-1980s slowed the movement toward nonoil sources of energy.

Political uncertainty was also a factor in reducing the attractiveness of oil as an energy source. Arab OPEC states had shown themselves willing to use "the oil weapon" if a proper set of circumstances presented itself, and all OPEC states knew that, given the inevitably increasing scarcity of oil, the more oil they left in the ground now, the wealthier they would become in the future. To Western states in particular, the threat of reduced availability of oil was like a knife pointed at their collective economic throats. Table 21–6 illustrates this point, contrasting the total oil produced by selected Western states with the total amount of oil they consume. In many cases, severe economic disruption would result from a sizable reduction in the amount of oil imported. This fear was one reason that the United States and other Western states reacted so quickly and so emphatically when Iraq invaded Kuwait in 1990.

Impending scarcity, increased prices, and politically induced disruption of oil

TABLE 21–6   Oil Consumption and Domestic Production for Selected Developed Countries (in million metric tons)

Country	1971	1978	1987	1991
Australian				
Consumption	25	32	31	32
Domestic production	14	22	27	27
Canada				
Consumption	74	89	74	73
Domestic production	71	75	80	81
France				
Consumption	102	118	84	91
Domestic production	little	little	little	little
Germany				
Consumption	145	161	129	133
Domestic production	little	little	little	little
Italy				
Consumption	91	98	90	93
Domestic production	little	little	little	little
Japan				
Consumption	216	264	209	246
Domestic production	little	little	little	little
United Kingdom				
Consumption	104	93	75	83
Domestic production	little	54	123	91
United States				
Consumption	727	900	764	758
Domestic production	528	482	462	411

Source: International Energy Agency, *Oil and Gas Information 1989–1991* (Paris: OECD, 1992), p. 72.

supply also played havoc with the economies of Developing World countries. Although scarcity and politically induced disruption of supply are of relatively minor import to most of them, increased prices proved particularly painful despite efforts by Arab OPEC states to lessen the shock through programs such as the Arab Development Fund, money set aside to help Developing World states pay for their oil needs. Higher oil prices necessitated that scarce hard currencies formerly available for food purchases or investment instead be used to pay higher oil import costs.

Oil problems exist in Russia, the other newly independent states that emerged from the Soviet Union, and Eastern European states as well. Although the U.S.S.R. remained the world's single largest oil producer up until its final demise, Soviet oil production did not meet planned totals for most of the U.S.S.R.'s last decade of existence. Since the collapse of the Soviet Union, the oil industry in Russia and the other newly independent states has continued to be plagued by problems, and production has lagged. As for Eastern European states, most received their oil at subsidized prices from the Soviet Union before the revolutions of 1989. Since 1989, they have had to pay world market prices for oil. This has had a serious negative impact on Eastern European economies.

Often, government policies have a major impact on national and world energy situations. For example, the United States deregulated the price of oil and gas in an effort to spur more production, whereas France opted to emphasize nuclear power. Japan stressed conservation. The former Soviet Union sought to bring more oil and gas production sites into production in the Soviet Far East and Siberia. Although few of these efforts proceeded independently of other energy-related efforts, it is nonetheless evident that energy decisions made in the recent past and being made today will play a major role in determining the world's energy future.

Humankind's quest for energy has led to adverse environmental consequences. We examine those consequences later, but here it must be pointed out that such consequences are both global and local in nature. Global consequences of humankind's energy use can be seen primarily in concerns over global warming, but on a local basis the quest for energy has already had sizable impact. For example, wood is used as a major fuel throughout much of the Developing World today. Local scarcities of fuel wood already exist, particularly in West Africa's Sahel region, in India's Ganges plain, and in regions of South America's Andes Mountains. Deforestation will inevitably continue, making fuel-wood gathering a major task in many areas of the world. Environmental degradation will assuredly accompany deforestation.

The shape of humankind's energy future may also go a long way in determining how international actors, particularly states, define their international interests. For Japan and Western Europe in particular, and to a lesser degree the United States as well, the Middle East must be a central area of concern as long as it remains the source of so much oil. Thus, the United States, Europe, and Japan were all vitally concerned throughout the 1980–1988 Iran-Iraq war that oil production in and around the Persian Gulf not be closed down. Similarly, in 1990, Iraq's takeover of Kuwait raised concerns in industrialized countries—and in other states as well—that Iraq could determine both the price and production level of Middle Eastern oil.

One last point must be made about the world's energy and oil situations—

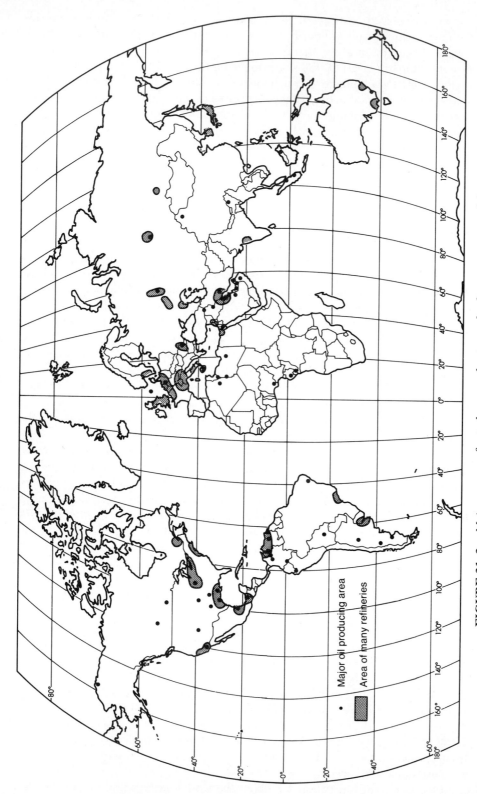

FIGURE 21–2. Major sources of petroleum production and refinery operations of the world. (Reprinted with the permission of Macmillan Publishing Company from *Geography* by Arthur Getis, Judith Getis, and Jerome Fellman. Copyright © 1981 by Macmillan Publishing Company. Updated in 1993 by the author.)

Major oil producing area

Area of many refineries

namely, that global energy consumption is extremely skewed. Western industrialized countries led by the United States use far more energy than do Developing World states. Table 21–7 illustrates this. Much of the industrialized West's higher rate of energy use is both a product and a cause of the West's high standard of living, so at least two questions must be asked concerning that energy use. First, in an ethical sense, one must question the morality of so few of the world's inhabitants using so much of the earth's scarce energy resources. Second, in a pragmatic sense, one must wonder where additional energy will come from if energy and development are as integrally linked as they appear to be. Both the moral and pragmatic questions have within them the seeds for future conflict over energy.

However, conflict over energy is far from certain. As we have seen, the world's energy future is murky at best. How well will government policies, technical innovations, and changed living habits succeed in making alternate energy sources more attractive? Can efficiency and conservation extend the time that currently utilized energy sources, particularly oil, can be exploited? How much more oil, gas, and coal remain to be discovered? How much will the Chernobyl nuclear disaster influence countries to turn away from nuclear energy? These questions are unanswerable, but their answers hold the key to the world's energy future.

Nonfuel Minerals

Worldwide consumption of nonfuel mineral resources has steadily increased throughout the twentieth century except during economic recessions. Between now and 2000, nonfuel mineral consumption is expected to increase about 2 percent annually. Thus, many of the same concerns addressed in the previous discussion of energy resources—depletion, cost, and access, to name three—are relevant for nonfuel mineral resources as well.

TABLE 21–7   Global Energy Consumption (in Quads)°

Country	1985	World Total (%)	1990	World Total (%)	Est. 1995	World Total (%)	Est. 2000	World Total (%)
United States	76.6	24.7	84.4	24.3	90.0	24.1	95.5	23.8
Japan	15.8	5.1	18.3	5.3	20.9	5.6	22.8	5.7
W. Germany[†]	12.3	4.0	12.5	3.6	13.5	3.6	14.3	3.6
Other OECD	56.1	18.1	63.6	18.3	67.6	18.1	72.4	18.0
Developing Countries	48.9	15.7	59.8	17.2	67.8	18.1	74.9	18.6
Former USSR	54.9	17.7	58.9	16.9	56.6	15.1	59.3	14.8
Other Former CPE's	23.4	7.5	24.6	7.1	24.7	6.6	25.9	6.4
China	22.5	7.2	26.4	7.6	32.4	8.7	36.8	9.2
World Total	310.5		347.7		373.6		401.9	

Source: World Energy Projection System, 1991.

°A quad is one quadrillion British Thermal Units (BTUs).

[†]These data are for western Germany only. Data was compiled in 1991, before unification.

NATIONAL LEVELS OF ELECTRICITY PRODUCTION 1992

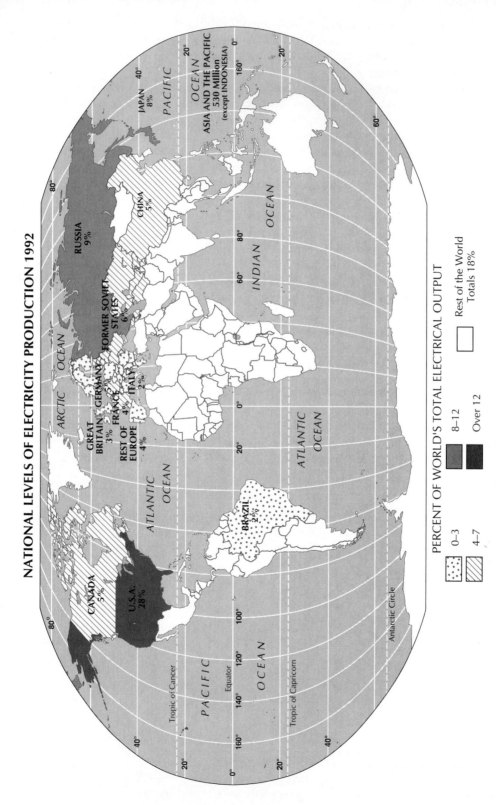

FIGURE 21-3. National levels of energy consumption, rated by kilograms per capita.

Mineral depletion is a particularly vexing issue, if only because it is so difficult to come to terms with. Depending on the resource examined and the assumptions made, enough reserves are available for centuries—or barely enough for a decade. The severity of the problem presented by those minerals that may be depleted is difficult to gauge. Resource substitution (of copper for silver in wires, for example) and improved efficiency of use may tremendously alter consumption rates for various minerals.

Although conclusions about mineral depletion are difficult to reach, conclusions about resource location and the political implications that may be derived from them are more obvious. Table 21–8 shows that sources of several minerals are concentrated in a very few countries or regions. Australia, North America, the former Soviet Union, and southern Africa are four of the major locations for many nonfuel mineral resources. Many industrialized states, particularly Japan and those in Western Europe, are highly dependent on nonfuel mineral imports. Thus, as in the case of oil, a very few areas of the world are of critical importance to mineral-importing states.

Because production of several of the most important nonfuel minerals is concentrated in a few locations, fears are occasionally expressed that mineral resource cartels modeled after OPEC may be formed to control mineral production and prices. To date, no successful mineral cartel has been formed. Mineral substitutability is one reason for the failure of mineral cartelization; few nonfuel minerals are as critical to industrialized societies as oil. Thus, in the event of cartel-induced price increases or production cuts, less expensive minerals may in many

TABLE 21–8 Percentage Share of the World's Production for Selected Minerals Among the Five Major Mineral-Producing States, 1988

Country	U.S.	Canada	Australia	South Africa	USSR	Total
Metal						
Platinum Group	W	4	—	50	43	97
Vanadium	W	9	—	57	29	95
Nickel	W	30	9	4	23	66
Potash	5	26	—	—	34	65
Chromium	W	—	—	35	28	63
Manganese	—	—	8	14	40	62
Phosphate	30	—	—	2	26	58
Diamond	—	—	31	10	13	54
Molybdenum	40	13	—	—	—	53
Iron Ore	6	4	11	2	27	50
Bauxite	1	—	37	—	5	43
Tantalum	—	10	32	—	—	42
Lead	11	11	14	3	—	39
Copper	17	8	3	—	8	36
Sulfer	19	12	—	3	—	34
Zinc	4	20	10	—	—	34
Silver	10	10	—	—	11	31

Source: Kenneth A. Kessel, *Strategic Minerals: U.S. Alternatives* (Washington, D.C.: National Defense University Press, 1990), p. 207.

W = Withheld.

cases be substituted for the cartelized one. A second reason that mineral cartels have not been successful is that many production sites are still under the control of foreign firms by virtue of concession. Host states have as a result denied themselves a voice in production and pricing decisions, at least until concessions expire. Stockpiling is a third reason that nonfuel mineral cartels have been less than successful. For example, the United States has maintained strategic stockpiles of a variety of minerals since 1939. U.S. stockpiles have rarely reached levels the U.S. government wanted, but the stockpile program nevertheless serves as a buffer against price and supply disruptions. A final cause of the futility of nonfuel mineral cartels is recycling. Oil, when it is used, is gone, but many minerals may be used again and again. And even in the case of OPEC, as the 1986 collapse of oil prices indicated, holding a cartel together once it is formed is an extremely difficult task.

As has been true in all facets of our examination of the international political economy of resources, Western industrialized states consume and use a disproportionately large percentage of the world's nonfuel minerals. The same ethical and pragmatic questions that were asked about food, wealth, and energy could be asked about nonfuel minerals, but the points will not be belabored further. Suffice it to say once again that they are serious questions.

TECHNOLOGY

Too often, the role that technology plays in the political economy of international relations is overlooked, or restricted only to the role of technology in military affairs. This is unfortunate, for in nonmilitary issue-areas of international political economics as well as in military issue-areas, technology's role is vitally important.[14]

The role of technology in military affairs is discussed elsewhere in this text, and its military importance will not be belabored here. But beyond military affairs, technology is critical in domestic economic production—for example, in agriculture and manufacturing. Indeed, the degree to which a country uses technology in agriculture, manufacturing, and other sectors of its domestic economy is a major factor in determining the level of production and often the standard of living that a country has. More often than not, the use of modern technologies by a country's labor force will increase the productivity of the labor force. As a result, production increases, and the country's standard of living rises. As a general rule, the greater the quantity of technology that a country uses and the more sophisticated its technology is, the higher a country's standard of living will be.

Unfortunately, there are several downsides to technology. For example, technology is often expensive, and not all countries have the wherewithal to acquire the types of technology that they need. Thus, the use of technology can sometimes lead to greater differences in the standard of living both within and between countries. At the same time, under some conditions, increased use of technology can also lead to unemployment as technical advances reduce the number of people needed to perform an industrial or agricultural function.

In addition, to be effectively employed, technology more often than not requires an educated and disciplined labor force. Not all countries have or can develop such a labor force. Indeed, as we will discuss in the next chapter when we explore issues relating to economic development, the combination of the cost of technology and the requirement that many technologies have for an educated and disciplined labor force goes a long way to explaining why advanced technologies in particular are so unevenly distributed around the world.

Also, technology frequently disrupts traditional social relationships and patterns of behavior. Therefore, those who wish to defend traditional values and ways of life sometimes oppose technological advance. Indeed, much of the conflict between tradition and modernization is driven by efforts to apply technology to society. Nor can it be overlooked that some types of technology degrade the environment, again as we will discuss later. Nevertheless, despite the possible drawbacks of technology, virtually every country in the world has sought and continues to seek to introduce more and more technology to its economy, and to develop and apply new technical breakthroughs.

International actors do not limit their efforts to acquire technology to developing their own technologies. Because of the advantages that technology can bring, all types of international actors, especially states and multinational corporations, seek to acquire technical know-how from others. Consequently the flow of technology between and among international actors has become an issue-area of major importance in contemporary international affairs. This flow of technology between and among international actors is called **international technology transfer**.

Sometimes, international actors acquire foreign technology openly and legally. Other times, they engage in covert or illegal efforts to acquire foreign technology. Indeed, even outside military affairs, the importance of technology as a factor in international economic competitiveness has led many international actors to spy on others to acquire technical secrets from their competitors.

Not surprisingly, because of the advantages that technological superiority may impart to those who have it, some international actors including the United States have sought to restrict international technology transfer in certain critical areas. The extent to which these efforts have been successful is a matter of debate.

Beyond the impact that technology has had and is continuing to have on individual international actors, technical breakthroughs and applications have altered the way in which the entire international system is shaped and has operated. For example, as we already have seen, the advent of nuclear weapons played a major role in the creation of the bipolar system that existed between the late 1940s and the early 1990s. Nonmilitary technologies have played an equally important role in shaping the international system and influencing how it operates as well.

Breakthroughs and applications of transportation and communication technologies perhaps lead the way. The ability to travel to any point on the globe in short periods of time and to know almost immediately what is happening half a world away have revolutionized the way many people look at the world, creating a sense of a "global village." Transportation and communications advances have also given a sense of immediacy and urgency to events in the most remote corners of the world. A few years ago, many events could have gone unheeded for months, perhaps permanently. Now they become headline news almost as they occur.

Transportation and communication breakthroughs have also changed political, social, and economic relations within and between international actors. New transportation technologies enable major countries to intervene rapidly in far-distant places, and allow countries throughout the world to trade with one another. New communications technologies make it almost impossible for a government to cut its citizens off from information from and about the outside

New communication technologies enable us to see events on the other side of the world as they happen, as CNN's reports of the Persian Gulf War showed. Will instantaneous global communications change the way we look at the world?   (Black Star.)

world, and the pervasiveness of the international news media has influenced the behavior of some governments toward their people. For example, the presence of the international media played a major role in the failure of the 1991 coup attempt against then-Soviet President Mikhail Gorbachev. And as we have seen, the failure of the coup played a major role in the collapse of the Soviet Union.

Transportation and communication breakthroughs have also altered perceptions of peoples around the world about other peoples and events. People-to-people contacts lessened U.S. views of Russians as enemies, and lessened Russian views of Americans as enemies, as well. Advances in transportation technologies helped make this possible. Advances in communications technologies allowed anyone who had a television set to see what life is like in other countries, to witness the bombing of Baghdad at the beginning of the Persian Gulf War even as it occurred, and to observe the horror of famine in Somalia.

Nor can we overlook the impact that the international media has had on the behavior of nonstate international actors such as terrorist groups, national liberation movements, and others. The availability of worldwide publicity via the international media on at least some occasions has served to goad certain international actors to action.

Transportation and communications breakthroughs have also revolutionized diplomacy by tying ambassadors more closely to their home capitals. In earlier eras, ambassadors often acted on their own discretion. But today, with rapid transportation and instantaneous communications, ambassadors often are called home for consultation, receive immediate instructions from their home government, or both.

Other scientific-technical breakthroughs, sometimes even the potential of breakthroughs, can also alter political, social, and economic relations among international actors. The emergence of technical capabilities to initiate deep seabed mining made that issue one of the most bitterly contested items in the United Nations Law of the Seas negotiations in the late 1970s and early 1980s. Developing World states feared American hegemony over the seabed, whereas the United States feared Developing World appropriation of U.S. technology. Thus, a scientific-technical advance became an issue that separated the United States and the Developing World.

But scientific-technical breakthroughs need not be the source of discord. The Green Revolution allowed many countries to avoid famine, and improvements in health care and immunization have increased life expectancy throughout most of the world. Manufacturing throughout the world benefited from a multitude of new technical innovations, and information processing has improved immensely with the advent of silicon chip technologies. Computer capabilities have improved so much that information on a variety of subjects is now almost instantaneously available from anywhere in the world. Several developing nations such as Taiwan and South Korea have based much of their economic growth on these new industrial technologies.

There is little doubt that the importance of technology in contemporary international relations will continue to expand. However, the issues that emerge from the international political economy of technology are not simple. Technology has tremendous potential to bring great benefits to humankind. Unfortunately, technology and its imbedded issues also carry potential for great risks.

INTERIM CONCLUSIONS: THE INTERNATIONAL POLITICAL ECONOMY OF POPULATION, FOOD, RESOURCES, AND TECHNOLOGY

In this chapter, we have examined only what may be described as the primary inputs to issues of the international political economy. As we have seen, the questions that flow from these primary inputs are exceedingly complex. What are the implications of the world's population growth? Can the world's population growth be controlled? If it can be, should it be? Why is there hunger, and can hunger and starvation be prevented? How long will the world have adequate fuel and mineral resources? What role does technology play in today's world? The answers to these questions are subjects of considerable debate and disagreement. It is likely that there will be no simple or widely accepted answer to any of them.

These questions are only the beginning. In the next chapter, we will again explore issues of the international political economy, this time concentrating on what may be described as derivative issues of international political economics—that is, issues that flow from a combination of factors, including the primary inputs that we examined in this chapter. The questions that flow from economic development and the global distribution of wealth are exceedingly complex, and they too have no simple or widely accepted answers.

Nevertheless, at the risk of disclosing the next chapter's concluding observations too soon, we may state that finding answers to the questions posed in this and the next chapter—and then beginning to implement them—may well be the most important task for humankind as the twentieth century draws to a close.

KEY TERMS AND CONCEPTS

international political economics
population growth
U.S. population policy
Thomas Malthus
trends and patterns in global food
    production and consumption
role of oil in world energy picture
trends and patterns in global
    energy production and consumption

trends and patterns in global
    mineral production and
    consumption
role of technology in
    international affairs
international technology transfer

NOTES

1. 1992 UN Population Fund data.
2. This is the 1992 World Bank projection. See also the Population Reference Bureau information from 1990 in Table 21–1.
3. The World Bank, *World Development Report 1992* (New York: Oxford University Press, 1992), p. 29.
4. Ann Scott Tyson, "China, UN Join Forces to Reshape Population Policy," *Christian Science Monitor*, January 27, 1989, pp. 1–2.
5. "Population Control: The Issue that Got Scuttled," *The Atlanta Journal*, May 23, 1992, p. E1.
6. *World Development Report 1992*, p. 29.
7. U.S. Central Intelligence Agency, *The World Factbook 1991* (Washington: U.S. Government Printing Office, 1992), appropriate pages.
8. Ronald Freedman, "Theories of Fertility Decline: A Reappraisal," in Philip M. Hauser (ed.), *World Population and Development* (Syracuse: Syracuse University Press, 1979); and John C. Caldwell, "Toward a Restatement of Demographic Transition Theory," *Population and Development Review* (September/December 1976). See also Gerald O. Barney et al., *The Global 2000 Report to the President*, Vol. 1 (Washington: U.S. Government Printing Office, 1980), p. 12.
9. See Thomas Malthus, *First Essays on Population, 1798* (New York: St. Martin's Press, 1966).
10. See National Defense University, *Crop Yields and Climate Change to the Year 2000* (Washington: U.S. Government Printing Office, 1980).
11. "Not By Bread Alone," *The Economist*, January 13, 1990, p. 65.
12. "Hunger as a Weapon of War," *The Economist*, December 2, 1989, pp. 50–52.
13. For other studies of the international food situation, see Jean Dréze and Amartya Sen, eds., *The Political Economy of Hunger*, Vols. 1–3 (New York: Oxford University Press, 1991); and Peter Uvin, "Regime, Surplus, and Self-Interest: The International Politics of Food Aid," *International Studies Quarterly* (September 1992), pp. 313–329.
14. For further discussion, see Dominique Foray and Christopher Freeman, *Technology and the Wealth of Nations: The Dynamics of Constructed Advantage* (Pinter Publishers, 1992). See also Dennis Pirages, *Global Technopolitics: The International Politics of Technology and Resources* (Pacific Grove, CA: Brooks/Cole Publishing Company, 1989); and John A. Alic, et al., *Beyond Spinoff: Military and Commercial Technologies in a Changing World* (Boston: Harvard Business School Press, 1992).

CHAPTER 22

International Political Economy II

ECONOMIC DEVELOPMENT AND DISTRIBUTION OF WEALTH

* How does economic development happen?
* Why is economic development so difficult?
* Why are some states so rich, and others so poor?
* What are the dimensions and implications of uneven distribution of wealth within and between states?

Questions about economic development and distribution of wealth are integrally linked to the international political economy of the global standard of living. During the last half century, these issues have moved near the front of the agenda of the international community.

Economic development and distribution of wealth have not always been high priority issues for the international community. During the colonial era, industrialized powers were rarely interested in bringing the advantages of economic development to their colonies. Beyond the basic question of how colonies could be exploited to increase the wealth of the imperialist state, industrialized states rarely concerned themselves with questions about the distribution of wealth within and between themselves and their colonies. Indeed, the primary purpose for having colonies was to increase the wealth, power, and prestige of colonial states.

In most peoples' eyes, this situation has changed. As the decolonization process accelerated after World War II, more and more people throughout the world, in former imperial states, former colonial states, and other states as well, began to recognize that questions about economic development and distribution of wealth were central issues to the well-being and stability not only of individual states, but also to the international community. As a result, economic development and distribution of wealth have become important issues for the entire global community.

ECONOMIC DEVELOPMENT

States and other international actors find economic development attractive for many reasons. On a very basic level, economic development improves living standards. More often than not, economic development allows people to live longer, and to live more comfortable and more fulfilling lives. For states and other types of actors, economic development also may provide a sense of power and prestige. Until relatively recently, economic development also tended to provide a sense of independence and the ability to control one's own destiny. However, with the growth of economic interdependence between and among states and other international actors, the provision of independence is fading as a rationale for economic development.

Unfortunately, however, no one knows for sure how the economic development process proceeds. Many developmental theories have been advanced. Some stress the creation of a technical infrastructure such as roads, harbors, and communications as a necessary first step. Others stress the necessity of an educated population. Some assert that external investment is required, while others argue that external investment brings external control and external exploitation. They counter that economic development can best proceed without external investment, with all developmental needs including investment being supplied locally. Marxist-Leninists advocate centralized control to bring about the elimination of the exploitation of human by human as a necessary corequisite to economic development. No one has the complete answer.

Theories of Economic Development

Over the years, several distinct schools of thought emerged out of the debate over economic development. Here, we will examine only two of them: *modernization theory* and *dependency theory*. Both are widely accepted, but as we will see, their views on economic development are significantly different.

Modernization theory has as its basic premise the belief that economic development requires the rejection of traditional patterns of behavior, value, and organization, and the acceptance of new patterns of behavior, value, and organization more conducive to economic development.[1] For the most part, modernization theorists argue that those patterns of behavior, value, and organization that are required for economic development to occur are those that have emerged in countries that are economically developed—that is to say, the countries of Western Europe, the United States, Canada, Japan, and a very few others.

Modernization theorists do not unanimously agree on the requirements for modernization. However, more often than not, they point to the need for an educated population; widespread acceptance of science, technology, and the scientific method throughout society; increased secularization and the decline of religious tradition; urbanization; division of labor in the productive sectors of society; rule by law rather than edict; the development of a system of social and economic rewards based on merit rather than station of birth or place in society; greater social mobility between and among people and classes; and a tolerance for diversity, innovation, and change as critical elements needed for economic development to take place and prosper. Not coincidentally, these are the same

traits that are often viewed as required for the development of the capitalist market economies that are prevalent in Europe, North America, Japan, and a few
other countries as well.

Similarly, modernization theorists do not unanimously agree on what characteristics must be eliminated from traditional societies for modernization to take
place and prosper. Nevertheless, there is widespread agreement among proponents of modernization that for economic development to occur and prosper, the
percentage of the population engaged in agriculture and living in rural areas
must decline; feudalist social and economic organization of society must be
replaced; the dominance of restrictive religious authority must be reduced; arbi-
trary political decision-making must be eliminated; and political, economic, and
social decision-making must become less centralized.

Modernization theorists proceed from the elementary argument that since
these or similar changes are what preceded or accompanied economic development in countries that are today economically developed, these same changes are
logically what must precede or accompany economic development in countries
that are today underdeveloped economically. For modernization theorists, there
may be many paths toward economic development, but all are paved by the abandonment of traditional ways of doing things, and the acceptance of modern—that
is, Western—ways of doing things.

Modernization theory has been challenged from a number of perspectives.
Some critics point out that there may be other ways for economic development to
occur that simply have not yet been tried. Others maintain that modernization
theorists have an ethnocentric perspective and are too ready to dismiss and reject
valuable dimensions of traditional societies. Still others argue that modernization
theorists misunderstand economic development completely. Many who make this
argument adhere to the **dependency theory** of economic development.[2]

To dependency theorists, modernization theorists miss two key points. First,
dependency theorists point out that the late twentieth-century world bears no
resemblance to the world in which economic development began and proceeded
in its early phases in Europe, North America, and Japan.[3] They observe that
industrialization began in these locations in the absence of external competition,
whereas in today's world, countries that are attempting to industrialize and develop economically face immense external competition. To dependency theorists,
this competition prevents economic growth in the Developing World. What is
more, they argue, the differences between the international conditions under
which European, North American, and Japanese economic development proceeded and those of today are so great that the developmental experiences of the
past are irrelevant to the world of today.

Second, and equally important, many dependency theorists also argue that
the First World's economic development was underwritten by the inexpensive
raw material and labor of the Developing World.[4] Put simply, Europe and the
capitalist system that developed there exploited less developed parts of the world.
More extreme proponents of dependency theory even argue that industrialization
in Europe and elsewhere as well could not have taken place without this exploitation. All dependency theorists agree that the present-day international economic
system remains heavily stacked in favor of the industrialized West, and that the
industrialized West owes an immense debt to the Developing World for its own
economic development that it is not repaying.

Dependency theorists identify many mechanisms through which industrialized states continue to take advantage of poor states. According to dependency theorists, these mechanisms include many issues and actors that we have already studied, such as unequal exchange rates, which keep the prices of resources low and manufactured products high; the international banking and financial system, which provide loans at high and unfair rates; and multinational corporations, which repatriate profit and drive local competitors out of business.

Dependency theorists also frequently argue that exploitation has occurred and continues to occur on two levels. The first level is within individual businesses, where the owners exploit and profit from the labor of their workers. In many respects, this level of analysis is similar and in some cases identical to Marxist interpretations. The second level of exploitation is then between states that are economically developed and those that are not. Many dependency theorists express this relationship between economically developed states and underdeveloped states as a relationship between "the core" of economically developed states and "the periphery" of those states that are poor and dependent.

Like modernization theory, dependency theory has its critics. Some critics of dependency theory maintain that it overemphasizes the role that the international system plays in constraining development, and underemphasizes the impact that policies implemented in Developing World states have on economic development. Other critics observe that dependency theory fails to explain why some states such as South Korea, Thailand, Malaysia, Singapore, and others are enjoying rapid economic growth, while others are not. Clearly, then, neither modernization theory nor dependency theory provides answers to all aspects of the question, "Why and how does economic development happen?" Both provide insights to the economic development process, but both also have their shortcomings.

Despite the shortcomings of our current understanding of the economic development process, it is encouraging to note that scholars and analysts are continuing to try to develop new ways to understand economic development more thoroughly. For example, some have begun to ask why different countries facing similar situations have chosen different developmental strategies, and to explore on a comparative basis what can be learned from the experiences of these countries with their different strategies.[5] Others are investigating the role that international trade plays in economic development. There is still much to be learned about how and why economic development takes place, and how and why it does not.

Policy Realities of Economic Development

Beyond the realm of theoretical debate over economic development, numerous everyday policy disagreements about economic development have existed and continue to exist. For example, developed states that provided funds for foreign aid and assistance often disagreed over whether they should provide their assistance unilaterally or multilaterally through international organizations. The first option had the advantage, from the donor state's perspective, of allowing it to maintain some control over the direction of that aid and assistance; conversely, it had the disadvantage of appearing neocolonialistic. Multilateral aid through

IGOs, on the other hand, rendered the impression of a donor state interested primarily in economic development rather than political aggrandizement.

Tied aid and assistance also became an issue of some importance. In its simplest form, tied aid and assistance referred to a donor state's requirement that aid and assistance be used only in conjunction with donor state products, equipment, and so on. To donor states, this appeared a logical policy. If aid and assistance were extended, why then should a requirement not exist that it be expended in the donor country? To Developing World states, this again smacked of neocolonialism.

Other developmental issues abounded. Some issues involved governments and private companies. For example, the United States was particularly concerned about formulating a policy on aid and assistance for states that nationalized U.S.-owned private property; the Hickenlooper amendment prevented the extension of aid and assistance to states that nationalized property owned by Americans. Other issues were state-related. European states, France and Great Britain in particular, targeted most of their aid to countries in their respective commonwealths. Some Americans and Europeans argued that all developmental aid and assistance should be sent to those states that had the best chance for development. Other states were to be "written off", at least for the time being. A sort of economic triage would occur, with the states least capable of economic development fending for themselves until additional aid and assistance became available, possibly from the states that were themselves but recently developed.

The private sector also involved itself heavily in developmental policy. This involvement most often took one of two forms. The first was investment. Investment presented the private sector, particularly MNCs, with possibilities for profitable return, but risks were high. Nationalization and political or economic turmoil presented constant risks, and host states often viewed external investors as exploiters and colonialists (not always incorrectly). Credit was a second major form of involvement. Private banks and some Western state-owned banks extended massive credit to Developing World states during the 1970s and 1980s. In 1992, Western banks had over $1 trillion in outstanding loans to Developing World countries.[6]

Inevitably, problems developed as Developing World states found it difficult to repay loans. Only emergency action by the Mexican government prevented default in 1982 on Mexico's $80 billion in outstanding loans, and the 1986 drop in oil prices slashed Mexico's earnings from oil exports to the point that Mexico in 1986 once again faced **default** on loans. Other Developing World borrowers such as Argentina, Brazil, and the Philippines were in equally precarious straits for most of the 1980s and on into the 1990s. Even though the IMF and World Bank had strict performance and reporting criteria for those states to which they extended loans, default potential remained in several states.

Implications of defaulting on foreign loans are sizable. Countries near default find it difficult to import needed goods because they can rarely pay for those goods; if a country defaulted, it might well find it impossible to import what it needs. Investors as well as lenders are leery of states that are near default; an actual default would make it almost impossible to attract any external investment. One of the major impacts of defaulting, then, is that external sources of all types of money would disappear. This in turn would retard economic development and growth even more in the state that defaulted.

(a)

In much of the world, agriculture
has not been mechanized.
 (a) Planting, care, and harvesting of
crops often remains a by-hand
activity.   (U.N. Photo/John Isaac.)
(b) In other cases, animals help work
the fields.   (United Nations Photo.)

(b)

Defaults would also affect lending nations. One can only imagine the turmoil
that would occur in Western financial markets if Developing World states
defaulted on a sizable percentage of the loans outstanding to them. Probably
because of this, Fidel Castro in 1986 urged Latin American leaders to default on
their loans. None did, although the thought must have appeared temporarily
attractive to some. Rather, during the late 1980s and early 1990s, several Latin
American states suspended payment on their debts.

In a technical sense, this was not default. Indeed, if a default occurred, both
lender and borrower would lose; lenders would lose their money, and borrowers
would lose their ability to borrow. Thus, both borrowers and lenders in the international arena have sought ways to reschedule debts, to initiate payment morato-

riums, and employ other tactics to avoid default. These methods have successfully averted disaster, but the debt problem remains. Table 22–1 shows the largest external debts owed by Developing World countries and also shows how those debts have grown over time as a percentage of gross national product.

Politics and ideology also enter into development decisions, both in donor and recipient states. For example, during the 1950s, U.S. Secretary of State John Foster Dulles refused to send U.S. aid and assistance to any country that would not join an American alliance. His reasoning was that only those states willing to declare themselves American allies should receive the benefits of American largesse.

Although U.S. policy on aid and assistance has since changed several times, politics and ideology still play a role. For example, Ronald Reagan complained that the World Bank was extending too many loans to public sector projects in Developing World countries and that the United States would consider reducing its commitment to the World Bank if it did not expand its private sector loans. The former U.S.S.R. also interjected politics and ideology into its aid and assistance policies, limited though they were, by arguing that capitalist colonialism caused Developing World underdevelopment and that capitalism should therefore correct it. In addition, within the Developing World, political considerations often influence decisions to accept or reject aid. Pakistani President Zia, for example, rejected Jimmy Carter's $400 million aid package as "peanuts" in 1980. His rejection was based more on his assessment of the political liabilities that would accompany the package than on the limited nature of the package.

The debate and uncertainty over how development can best be accomplished and the intrusion of political considerations into the developmental process have been important factors in limiting the success of efforts such as the

TABLE 22–1   1990 Largest Developing World External Debt Burdens in Billions of U.S. Dollars, and Debt Burdens as Percent of Gross National Product

Country	1990 Debt in Billions of U.S. Dollars	Debt as a Percentage of GNP	
		1970	1990
Brazil	116.2	8.2	3.0
Mexico	96.8	8.7	45.1
India	70.1	14.7	23.6
Indonesia	68.0	25.2	50.9
Argentina	61.1	8.6	79.8
Egypt	39.9	22.5	127.6
Nigeria	36.1	3.4	107.3
Venezuela	33.3	5.7	66.0
Philippines	30.5	8.8	67.9
Algeria	26.9	19.3	52.0
Thailand	25.9	4.6	32.7
Morocco	23.5	18.2	98.6
Peru	21.1	12.0	83.8
Pakistan	20.7	20.6	48.5

SOURCE: The World Bank, *World Development Report 1992*, pp. 258–259.

United Nations' "Decade of Development". Another factor that has retarded international developmental efforts is insufficient funding. Absolute levels of economic aid and assistance to Developing World states have rarely kept pace with real and perceived need. Table 22–2 shows the official development assistance that Developing World states received between 1965 and 1990 both in dollars and in terms of percent of gross national product of donor states.

Whatever the reasons, it is evident that economic development has not proceeded on a global basis as rapidly as had been hoped during the euphoric days of the early 1960s. Nor does agreement exist on the future course or rate of development. Meeting in Lagos, Nigeria, in 1980, the economic summit of the OAU heard a report from the United Nations Economic Commission for Africa that posited that by 2000, the OAU may find that only 14 of its 50 members could function economically. More optimistically, the *Global 2000 Report* projected a 2000 global gross product more than double the 1975 level, even in terms of constant 1975 dollars ($6,025 billion in 1975; $14,677 billion in 2000). That conclusion was promptly criticized as being "15–20 percent too high".[7] The famous 1972 Club of Rome report, *The Limits to Growth*, foresaw large global increases in food and per capita income until 2020 at which time either food or resource scarcity would lead to a precipitous downturn. The 1982 World Bank *World Development Report* offered a cautiously optimistic conclusion that world developmental problems could be overcome, but only if cautious and intelligent policies were adopted by poorer countries in conjunction with economic assistance

TABLE 22–2　　Official Development Assistance from Selected OECD States and OPEC Members, 1965–1990

	1965		1975		1985		1990	
	Millions of Dollars	**% GNP**	**Millions of Dollars**	**% GNP**	**Millions of Dollars**	**% GNP**	**Millions of Dollars**	**% GNP**
OECD States								
Austria	10	.11	79	.21	248	.38	394	.25
Britain	472	.47	904	.39	1,530	.33	2,638	.27
France	752	.76	2,093	.62	3,995	.79	9,380	.79
Germany	456	.40	1,689	.40	2,942	.48	6,320	.42
Japan	244	.27	1,148	.23	3,797	.29	9,069	.31
Netherlands	70	.36	608	.75	1,136	.90	2,592	.94
Switzerland	12	.09	104	.19	302	.31	750	.31
United States	4,023	.58	4,161	.27	9,403	.24	11,394	.21
All OECD	6,480	.48	13,847	.35	29,429	.35	55,632	—
OPEC Members								
Algeria	—	—	31	.21	54	.10	7	.03
Libya	—	—	270	2.39	57	.58	4	.01
Nigeria	—	—	14	.04	45	.06	13	.06
Saudi Arabia	—	—	2,665	7.50	2,630	2.86	3,692	3.90
Venezuela	—	—	31	.11	32	.07	15	.03
All OPEC	—	—	6,230	2.92	3,614	—	6,341	—

SOURCE: The *World Development Report* 1992, pp. 254–255.

from wealthier ones. The World Bank stressed that economic development efforts in agriculture should take precedence over efforts in industry. Many African states eventually opted for such an approach, but by 1993, there were few success stories.

Even more distressingly, as the world's environmental situation has deteriorated, it has become increasingly clear that economic development is not necessarily a friend of the environment. This is not to say that economic development is necessarily an enemy of the environment. But it is exceedingly evident, as *World Development Report 1992* makes clear, that future economic development undertakings will have to take their impact on the environment into account much more than earlier economic development efforts did.[8]

Indeed, concerns have risen so much about the extent to which economic development is ravaging the environment in Developing World states—both because of Developing World efforts and the industrialized West's demand for resources—that a new school of developmental thought has emerged. Termed **sustainable development**, this school of thought argues that economic development must "meet the needs and aspirations of the present without compromising the ability of future generations to meet their own needs."[9] Advocates of sustainable development argue that economic development can proceed, indeed must proceed, but that it must be carefully planned and thought out so that the environment is not further degraded, and so that future generations will also be able to provide for their needs.[10]

Proponents of sustainable development, as well as the authors of all of the reports alluded to above, agree on one major item: governments and other international agencies must develop and adopt long-range, intelligent policies to deal with issues of global development. All agree that with effective developmental policies, the world's situation in the early twenty-first century will be much better than it would be without such policies. This agreement, however, is of little utility given continuing disagreement over what effective policies are and the probability that many governments would not enact them even if policy agreement existed.

THE GLOBAL DISTRIBUTION OF WEALTH

In addition to economic development, the global distribution of wealth is an immense issue in international political economy. As discussed in Chapter 8 and again in our exploration of the dependency theory of economic development, there are two different levels to this issue, one within countries and the second between countries. In the context of our study of contemporary international relations, we will here concentrate only on the second level.

As we saw in our discussion of the North–South controversy, most of the world's gross national product is produced in industrialized countries. A relatively small percentage of the world's population lives in industrialized states. By comparison, much of the world's population lives in nonindustrialized states where little is produced. Obviously, this means that the people who live in these countries have small annual per capita incomes. Table 22–3 illustrates this.

Even more perplexingly, when projections for future population growth are viewed in conjunction with projection for future gross national product increases, it becomes clear that, although the gross national product in several developing

TABLE 22–3   GNP, Population, and Per Capita Incomes in Selected Countries, 1990

Country	Million Population	GNP (Billion $)	Per Capita Income (in Dollars)
Algeria	25.1	52	$2,060
Bangladesh	106.7	22	$210
Brazil	150.4	403	$2,680
Chad	5.7	1	$190
China	1,133.7	419	$370
France	56.4	1,100	$19,490
India	849.5	297	$350
Japan	123.5	3,141	$25,430
Mozambique	15.7	1	$80
Nigeria	115.5	33	$290
Philippines	61.5	45	$730
Somalia	7.8	1	$120
United States	250.0	5,448	$21,790
All OECD States	776.8	15,218	$19,590

SOURCE: The World Bank, *World Development Report 1992*, pp. 218–219.

states is expected to expand more rapidly than that of developed states, their lower starting points and more rapid rates of population growth will actually lead to a larger gap in per capita income between developed and developing states. The most significant exception to this is China, but it remains to be seen if China can maintain the astounding growth rates that it achieved in the 1980s and early 1990s.

The bottom line, then, is that although the standard of living in some developing states in absolute terms may be higher in the future than it is now, in relative terms, it will have deteriorated vis-à-vis the industrialized world. Even under conditions where Developing World economic growth takes place, sizeable disparities in wealth between rich countries and poor countries will continue to exist.

What led to the development of such immense disparities in wealth between countries? Depending on which model of economic development one prefers, there are different answers to the question. For example, if one adopts a simple outlook on development, then the answer is **industrialization**. There can be no debate whatsoever that countries with the highest standards of living today are those that are industrialized. Historically, there is no doubt that the immense disparity in wealth between rich countries and poor countries first began to develop as industrial methods of production increased productivity in Europe.

But if one delves deeper and asks, "What allows industrialization to take place?" then the answer becomes more complex. As we saw in our study of economic development, if one accepts the perspectives of modernization, then an educated population; widespread acceptance of science, technology, and the scientific method throughout society; increased secularization and the decline of religious tradition; urbanization; division of labor in the productive sectors of society; rule by law rather than edict; the development of a system of social and economic rewards based on merit rather than station of birth or place in society; greater social mobility between and among people and classes; and a tolerance for diversity, innovation, and change are all needed for economic development to take place.

Conversely, many proponents of dependency theory argue that the economic gap between rich and poor states grew to its current size either because of the industrialized world's exploitation of less fortunate regions of the world; the unfair advantages that early economic development provided European states and other industrialized states; or some combination of these two reasons. Indeed, if one accepts the most radical versions of the dependency theory, then the only reason that industrialization proceeded in Europe to begin with is because European states began to exploit others.

In any event, it is clear that depending on which theory of economic development one adopts, the driving forces behind the development of today's immense disparities in wealth between rich states and poor states are considerably different. It should then come as no surprise that different **policies** have been **proposed to balance the distribution of wealth**.

For example, industrialized states, more often than not adopting the modernization perspective, have generally stressed the need for change in Developing World states to be effected primarily by proper market-oriented policies in Developing World states; changed attitudinal, organizational and operational methods in Developing World states; and encouraged hard work. Economic assistance from the industrialized West would play an important role in assisting these changes, but the primary force behind economic development and the eventual reduction of the economic gap between rich and poor would be the effort of the people of Developing World states themselves.

By contrast, Developing World states, although not opposed to such efforts, argue that the prevailing international economic order, as well as past and present exploitation, frustrates all but the most fortunate among them from realizing economic growth that would, over time, reduce disparities in wealth. Therefore, many Developing World states have sought more radical changes in the international system to achieve economic development and a more balanced distribution of wealth. Approaches advocated by Developing World states include direct transfers of wealth from rich states to poor states to make up for past exploitation and to speed future development; creation of a new international economic order to end present inequities and prevent future ones; debt relief, repayment delay, or debt forgiveness; and recognition of the wealth of the sea, including mineral assets on the deep seabed, as the common heritage of all humankind, with any profits made by exploitation of the sea to be shared by all states.

It should also be noted that in the early 1980s, frustrated by their inability to win the industrialized West's acceptance of what they considered meaningful concessions to speed economic development and to reduce the economic gap between rich states and poor states, some Developing World states began calling for "collective self-reliance," that is, cooperation among Developing World states to achieve economic development and a reduction in the global disparity of wealth. However, by the mid-1990s, collective self-reliance remained little more than a theoretical concept.

One final question must also be asked, namely, "So what? Does it really matter if there is an immense difference in wealth between rich states and poor states?" There are both pragmatic and moral reasons to have **concern about unequal distribution of wealth**.

Pragmatically, if economic development and a more even distribution of global wealth are not achieved, political and economic tension between "have" and "have-not" states will escalate. While it is far-fetched to imagine that Zambia or Chile would take on the United States or France in a military conflict over economic development or the distribution of wealth, other types of action are both feasible and plausible. For example, resource-rich Developing World states could form resource cartels, imitating OPEC. If successfully formed and operated, such cartels could be disastrous for resource-dependent states. Alternately, at the extreme, terrorist actions against First World interests could be undertaken by groups or nongovernmental organizations not directly related to Developing World states, but sympathetic to their arguments.

Moral issues must also be raised. Regardless of the source of their wealth, what responsibilities do developed states have or should developed states have in assisting less fortunate states out of their economic difficulties? In 1960, for example, OECD countries gave .51 percent of their GNP to foreign aid. By 1990, as Table 22–2 shows, foreign aid as a percentage of GNP among OECD states had fallen to .36 percent despite the fact that they had agreed to raise official development assistance to .7 percent of their GNP. Domestic concerns, it seemed, had triumphed over humanitarian concerns.

Or another moral and ethical dilemma: How just is the world order when industrialized states extend assistance less on the principle of need than on the principle of securing their own advantage? Little morality and few ethics are involved when states regularly extend their economic aid and assistance for their own aggrandisement. However, politics has always defined and will always define its own interests.

In many Developing World countries, animal power is frequently used instead of machine power.   (© Orde Eliason/Impact Visuals.)

Indeed, although at the one extreme advocates of moralism and ethics call for extensive transfers of wealth to Developing World states and large-scale reorganization of the international system, the other extreme is held down by those who advocate **lifeboat ethics**. In its simplest form, lifeboat ethics argues that because of population pressures, food uncertainties, and impending resource constrictions, states should fend for themselves as best they can without concerning themselves about the less fortunate. If there is not enough for everyone, lifeboat moralists argue, keep what is available in the lifeboat so that the few there may survive.[11]

This pessimistic outlook does not take into account the waste, duplication, and senselessness of much of the world's current lifestyle. Defense spending provides one example. One B-2 bomber costs over a billion dollars, roughly one tenth of the total U.S. foreign aid package in 1993. Although the exact figures are unknown, it is estimated that the former Soviet Union spent more on its intelligence gathering efforts in North America in one year than it spent on its entire foreign aid and assistance program. Developing World states perform little better. For example, as recently as 1987, African states spent $14.3 billion on their militaries. This was over 13 percent of their total central government expenditures. Meanwhile, again in 1987, Middle Eastern states spent $67.5 billion on their militaries. This was 32 percent of their total central government expenditures.[12] Thus, even though Developing World expenditures on the military declined in the late 1980s and 1990s, if blame for resources diverted from development is to be parceled out, there is enough to go around.

Net Assessment

Issues of economic development and the global distribution of wealth will be with the global community for the forseeable future. No easy answers to these difficult issues are apparent. Indeed, as we have seen throughout this chapter, finding answers to these issues is rendered even more difficult because of the extensive disagreement about the causes of the problems. Such is the stuff of international political economy in the late twentieth century.

Despite these disagreements, one conclusion appears undebatable. As long as humans continue thinking in parochial local, national, or regional terms, Spaceship Earth will do much more poorly in solving its developmental and distribution problems than it has potential to do.

KEY TERMS AND CONCEPTS

modernization theory
dependency theory
tied aid and assistance
default and its implications
the politics and ideology of
    foreign aid
sustainable development

industrialization and wealth
methods proposed to balance the
    distribution of wealth
concerns about unequal
    distribution of wealth
lifeboat ethics

NOTES

1. For several classic discussions of modernization theory, see Gabriel Almond and James S. Coleman, *The Politics of Developing Areas* (Princeton: Princeton University Press, 1960); Cyril Black, *The Dynamics of Modernization* (New York: Harper & Row, 1966); Alex Inkeles and David H. Smith, *Becoming Modern: Individual Change in Six Developing Countries* (Cambridge: Harvard University Press, 1974); and Myron Weiner, ed., *Modernization: The Dynamics of Growth* (New York: Basic Books, 1966).

2. For several classic studies of dependency theory, see C. Furtado, *Development and Underdevelopment* (Berkeley: University of California Press, 1964); Andre Gunder Frank, *Capitalism and Underdevelopment in Latin America* (New York: Monthly Review Press, 1967); and Immanuel Wallerstein, *The Modern World System: Capitalist Agriculture and the Origins of the European World Economy in the Sixteenth Century* (New York: Academic Press, 1976).

3. Some trace the early phases of the capitalist international system as far back as the sixteenth century. See for example Wallerstein in the work cited above.

4. This outlook is similar to that put forward by V. I. Lenin in *Imperialism: The Highest Stage of Capitalism*, as discussed in Chapter 12.

5. See for example Stephen Haggard, *Pathways from the Periphery: The Politics of Growth in the Newly Industrialized Countries* (Ithaca: Cornell University Press, 1990); and Sylvia Maxfield, *Governing Capital: International Finance and Mexican Politics* (Ithaca: Cornell University Press, 1990). For other recent studies of development and development theory, see Stuart A. Bremer and Barry B. Hughes, *Disarmament and Development: A Design for the Future* (Englewood Cliffs, NJ: Prentice-Hall, 1990); Charles L. Clark, ed., *A Guide to the Theories of Economic Development* (New Haven: Human Relations Rea Files Press, 1982); Christopher Colclough and James Manor, eds., *States or Markets? Neo-Liberalism and the Development Policy Debate* (New York: Oxford, 1991); and Lee A Travis, ed., *Rekindling Development: Multinational Firms and World Debt* (South Bend, IN: University of Notre Dame Press, 1989).

6. The World Bank, international debt data for 1992.

7. *The Global 2000 Report*, p. 45.

8. *World Development Report 1992*, entitled "Development and the Environment," is devoted completely to the impact of development on the environment.

9. This is the definition of sustainable development adopted by the World Commission on Environment and Development in 1987.

10. For example, see Olav Stokke, ed., *Sustainable Development* (London: Frank Cass, 1991); and Walter V. C. Reid, "Sustainable Development: Lessons from Success," *Environment* (May 1989), p. 709.

11. For the "lifeboat" argument, see Garrett Hardin, "Lifeboat Ethics: The Case Against Helping the Poor," *Psychology Today*, Vol. 8 (September 1974), pp. 38–43. For an opposing viewpoint, see Marvin Soroos, "The Commons and Lifeboat as Guides for International Ecological Policy," *International Studies Quarterly*, Vol. 21 (1977), pp. 647–674.

12. U.S. Arms Control and Disarmanment Agency, *World Military Expenditures and Arms Transfers 1988*, pp. 28–29.

CHAPTER 23

Emerging Global Issues

THE ENVIRONMENT, DRUGS, AND HEALTH

- How serious are the world's environmental problems?
- Can anything be done to stop and reverse environmental degradation?
- Can the international flow of drugs be curtailed?
- Can global health be improved?

The questions and issues explored in the preceding two chapters have been with humankind for some time. But during the late 1980s and early 1990s, another set of global issues emerged that had potential to affect international affairs and the future of humankind significantly. In this chapter, we examine the outlines of three of the most important emerging global issues: the environment, drugs, and health.

THE ENVIRONMENT

Population growth, increased food production, and accelerated energy and non-fuel mineral use have all taken their toll on the world's environment. The earth enjoys an amazing capacity to replenish itself, but that capacity is not limitless. Several unalterable facts exist: The environment has a finite capacity to absorb pollution and to overcome pollution-caused damage; most resources are not renewable, and those that are require time to replenish themselves; no one knows what the earth's limits are; and environmental damage often does not appear until long after the damage-inducing agent is placed in the environment.

Humanity's degradation of the environment is not new, but its pace has accelerated both as humans multiplied and as the industrial revolution proceeded. As more human beings consumed more food and needed more resources, more land was tilled, more animals were killed, and more resource sites were more heavily exploited. The industrial revolution led to an explosion of per capita energy use and resource consumption in the industrialized areas of the world, accompanied by new and previously unknown types of environmental pollution.

For our purposes, humanity's assault on the earth may be viewed under four categories: (1) land degradation and desertification; (2) water degradation; (3) atmospheric pollution and climate change; and (4) species and gene pool extinction. Many of these phenomena are interrelated, but for ease of analysis, they are treated separately here.[1]

Land Degradation and Desertification

Most U.S. citizens are familiar with the stories of the erosion and the dust bowls that ravaged U.S. farmlands during the 1920s and 1930s. Most also know that erosion and dust bowls were the result of, among other things, overfarming and poor land-use practices. Fortunately for the United States, a combination of luck, good weather, and improved land use resurrected American farmlands. By 1982, the United States alone accounted for 60 percent of the world's grain trade and 17 percent (by value) of the world's total agricultural trade.

This stunning U.S. recovery pushed the ominous reality of global soil loss and deterioration into the back of most U.S. citizens' minds. But the appalling fact is that soil loss, soil deterioration, and even desertification are proceeding more rapidly now than at any other time in recorded history. Thus, the International Center for Arid and Semiarid Land Studies concluded that each year desert claims land roughly the extent of Denmark (43,000 square kilometers). Table 23–1 shows the dimensions of desertification in Africa. More insidiously, even where desertification is not a problem, erosion continues and topsoil depth decreases. In certain areas of Nebraska and Kansas, topsoil loss exceeds one-half inch per year, giving rise to fears that in their foreign sales efforts, U.S. farmers, in effect, are exporting their most important commodity, their topsoil.

In most cases, soil-related problems are directly traceable to population growth and poor soil use. More people need more food, and hence even marginal agricultural areas such as the former Soviet Union's "Virgin Lands" territory of Central Asia must be brought into production. More extensive use of rich croplands degrades the soil, and in many areas of the world neither chemical fertilizers, crop rotation, nor fallow-year practices are used to replenish it. Urbanization presents another threat to good cropland. Major urban and industrial centers are often located near rivers. The rich alluvial river valley soils therefore fall victim to the concrete, asphalt, and high population densities that accompany urbanization.

Forest degradation is a serious problem as well. Deforestation occurs because of urbanization, farming, industrial and private consumption of wood, and the need for fuel. In many cases, deforestation leads to desertification or destabilized water flow, which in turn causes siltation of streams, intensified flooding, and worsened water shortages during dry periods. According to many estimates, forests in South and Southeast Asia will be reduced by half by 2000. The impact of deforestation on food production areas is expected to be severe. Table 23–1 shows those countries in Africa where deforestation has become a problem.

As Table 23–2 illustrates, land degradation is a global phenomenon, existent

TABLE 23–1   Desertification Trends in Selected African Countries, 1977–1985

Country	Sand Dune Encroachment	Worsening Rangeland	Forest Depletion	Worsening Irrigation	Rain Shortfalls
Botswana	+	+	Stable	Stable	Stable
Burkino Faso	Stable	+	+	+	++
Cameroon	Stable	+	+	Stable	+
Chad	++	++	+	++	++
Ethiopia	+	++	++	+	+
Guinea	Stable	Stable	+	+	++
Kenya	Stable	++	+	Stable	+
Lesotho	Unknown	+	++	Stable	++
Mali	+	++	++	+	+
Mauritania	+	++	++	+	+
Niger	+	++	+	++	+
Nigeria	Stable	+	++	Stable	+
Senegal	+	++	+	+	++
Somalia	+	+	+	++	+
Sudan	++	+	+	+	Stable
Swigiland	Unknown	+	++	Stable	++
Tanzania	Unknown	++	+	Unknown	++
Uganda	Stable	++	Stable	Stable	+
Zambia	Unknown	Unknown	Unknown	+	+
Zimbabwe	Unknown	++	+	+	++

Source: Adapted from Leonard Barry, "Desertification: Problems of Restoring Productivity in Dry Areas of Africa," as presented in Lester R. Brown et al., *State of the World 1986* (New York: Norton, 1986), p. 27.

Key: + some increase; ++ major increase.

on every continent. Although many of the technologies and practices needed to slow, halt, and even reverse land degradation exist today,[2] until recently, land degradation has seldom been a major international issue. In the one case where it has, Brazil's destruction of the Amazon rain forest, Brazil has charged developed countries with seeking to slow its development, and the international community has been powerless to act.

One reason that land degradation and desertification have so rarely become major international issues is that many of those people who are immediately affected by land degradation and desertification are at the lower end of international society's structure; they are pastoralists and subsistence farmers, for the most part outside the channels of local, national, and regional political influence. But there is little doubt that land degradation and desertification is occurring, and at some point it will become a major international concern.

Can anything be done about land degradation and desertification? First, sufficient concern must be developed so that there is awareness of the problem. However, even if this occurs, another major difficulty exists. Many of the causes of land degradation and desertification cross national boundaries, and the cures for the problems must cross national boundaries as well. Thus, before solutions can be implemented to cope with land degradation and desertification, it may be necessary for humankind to recognize and accept the need for transnational solutions to at least some of the causes. That promises to be difficult to achieve.

TABLE 23–2   Land Degradation in Selected Countries and Regions

Country/Source	Observation
Mali Patricia A. Jacobberger, geologist, Smithsonian Institution, 1986	"On the Landsat maps, there is now—and there wasn't in 1976—a bright ring of soil around villages. Those areas are now 90% devoid of vegetation, the topsoil is gone, and the surface is disrupted and cracked."
Mauritania Sidy Gaye, *Ambio*, 1987	"There were only 43 sand-storms in the whole country between 1960 and 1970. The number increased tenfold in the following decade, and in . . . 1983 alone a record 240 sandstorms darkened the nation's skies."
Tunisia UNEP, 1987	"Rangelands have been overgrazed with three heads of cattle where only one could thrive . . . Two-thirds of the land area of Tunisia is being eaten by desertification."
China *Beijing Review*, interview with Zhu Zhenda, Chinese Academy of Sciences, 1988	"Unless urgent measures are taken, desertification will erode an additional 75,300 square kilometers . . . by the year 2000, more than twice the area of Taiwan."
Indonesia Ronald Greenberg and M. L. Higgins, U.S. AID Jakarta, 1987	"Thirty-six watersheds . . . have critical erosion problems . . . In Kalimantan, the silt load in streams has increased 33 fold in some logging areas."
Thailand D. Phantumvanit and K. S. Sathirathai, Thailand Development Research Board, 1988	"The pace of deforestation has been accelerating since the early 1900s, but it has moved into a higher gear since the 1960s . . . [Between 1961 and 1986,] Thailand lost about 45 percent of its forests."
Brazil Mac Margolis, interview with geologist Helio Penha, *Washington Post*, February 1988	"Every year, rains slash deeper into the bared soil, dumping tons of silt in waterways, causing rivers to overflow into the city's streets. Now people flee the drought in the Northeast only to die in floods in Rio."

SOURCE: Sandra Postel, "Halting Land Degradation," in Lester R. Brown et al., *State of the World 1989* (New York: Norton, 1989), p. 24.

Water Degradation

Water pollution is a significant problem throughout the world, although its causes often differ. Urbanization creates major problems for water-table levels, and widespread use of pesticides and industrial use of water for cooling and waste disposal pollute large quantities of water daily, although First World countries, since about 1970, have reduced use of long-lived "persistent pesticides" and have sought to limit industrial water damage. Nevertheless, in many Developing World states, persistent pesticides are still used widely, and planners there show little predilection for water-quality control measures. Irrigation also adversely affects water quality. In areas downstream from extensive irrigation projects water salinity often climbs to levels unacceptable for agricultural use. In addition, coastal ecosystems are important to fisheries, but development of coastal communities and offshore oil drilling have put many coastal ecosystems at risk.

Water degradation is not limited to Developing World states. In the United States, industrial pollution and irrigation have put American water resources at risk. In Russia, several major lakes and other water resources have been seriously damaged by industrial waste. Irrigation has also used so much of the water from the tributaries to the Aral Sea that it lost one-third of its total surface area between 1960 and 1990.[3] Japan has also polluted many of its water sources. And in Western Europe as well as elsewhere, industrial emissions into the atmosphere have led to acid rain, which is poisoning many lakes, rivers, and streams.

As was the case with land degradation and desertification, many of the causes of water degradation cross national boundaries. Thus, once again, successful actions by individual states to solve water degradation can be undertaken only rarely. More often, regional or even global solutions may be necessary. But to reiterate, humankind must begin to recognize and accept the need for transnational solutions to problems of declining water quality. Again, such a fundamental reorientation of thinking may be difficult to achieve.

Atmospheric Pollution and Climate Change

During the 1980s, it became increasingly clear that the large quantities of nitrogen dioxide, carbon monoxide and dioxide, sulfur dioxide, chlorofluorocarbons, and other gases and particulates that humankind was releasing into the atmosphere were beginning to have an effect on the atmosphere and on climate. Industrialization, the industrial processes that go with industrialization, and the internal combustion engine are the chief culprits in atmospheric pollution and climate change. Although these culprits may have additional effects on the atmosphere and climate, here we concentrate on only two, the so-called "greenhouse effect" and the deterioration of the ozone layer.

The **greenhouse effect** refers specifically to the dangers of global warming brought about by greater concentrations of carbon dioxide and other "greenhouse gases" in the atmosphere. These gases, produced primarily by burning coal and other carbon-based fuels such as oil, hold heat in the atmosphere. Deforestation also contributes significantly to the quantity of carbon dioxide in the atmosphere. Other greenhouse gases like methane, nitrous oxide, and chlorofluorocarbons (CFCs) enter the atmosphere from other sources, but in all cases, the rate of emission of the greenhouse gases into the atmosphere has risen steadily.

Although some debate remains over the degree of seriousness of the greenhouse effect,[4] it is striking nevertheless that the five warmest years of the past century occurred during the 1980s. Figure 23–1 illustrates the gradual climb in the world's average temperature since the late nineteenth century. The consequences of global warming brought about by the greenhouse effect are consider-

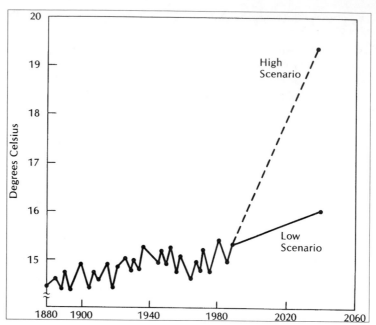

FIGURE 23–1   Observed global average temperatures, 1880–1987, with projections to 2040. (SOURCE: Lester R. Brown et al., "A World at Risk," in Lester R. Brown et al., *State of the World 1989* [New York: Norton, 1989], p. 10.)

able. Glaciers will melt, oceans will rise, rainfall patterns will alter, crop locations will shift, and climate will change. These consequences will be accompanied by social problems and human dislocations.

Indeed, 37 island states, home to 23 million people, have already expressed their fears to the United Nations that unless global warming is curtailed, they may disappear altogether. They fear that global warming will melt the polar ice caps, raising the level of the oceans. If this occurs, this aspect of global warming will also have an immense impact on nonisland states. For example, a 3-foot rise in ocean levels would drive 72 million people from their homes in China, 11 million in Bangladesh, and 8 million in Egypt.[5] Clearly, even a slight rise in global temperatures has significant implications for humankind.

Closely related to the greenhouse effect is **ozone depletion**, caused primarily by CFCs used as refrigerants, propellants, solvents, and insulators. CFCs rise into the upper atmosphere and attack ozone molecules that reside there, molecules that shield the earth's surface from too much ultraviolet solar radiation. During the last half of the 1980s, scientific observations confirmed that the release of human-made CFCs into the atmosphere had created a "hole" in the earth's ozone layer over the South Pole. Subsequent observations verified that the earth's overall ozone layer was thinning as well.

The consequences of a weakened ozone layer are also severe. With more ultraviolet radiation able to reach the earth's surface, the incidence of cancer and other skin diseases is likely to increase. Equally unsettling, CFCs are extremely stable gases; even if production were stopped tomorrow, it would take a century for CFCs to settle out of the atmosphere.

Can anything be done about the greenhouse effect and the deterioration of the ozone layer? Under the auspices of the United Nations Environment Program, 45 countries and one international organization signed the **Montreal Protocol** on Substances That Deplete the Ozone Layer, which took effect in 1989 and requires a 50 percent reduction in consumption of CFCs by 2000. But there are many loopholes in the Montreal Protocol, and there is concern that despite it, CFC consumption may increase by as much as 10 percent.[6] Subsequent international negotiations have led to additional agreements to lessen CFC and other greenhouse gases, with the most notable breakthrough being a multinational agreement in 1990 to eliminate production of CFCs by 2000. Nevertheless, there is still a considerable way to go.

Once again, though, it is evident that the world's atmospheric pollution and climate change problems cannot be successfully approached on only a local or country basis. Solutions to these problems must be undertaken on a regional or global basis. It is encouraging that the international community appears to recognize this, but extensive work remains to be done.

Species and Gene Pool Extinction

Species and gene pool extinction is often overlooked when human impact on the environment is addressed. When it is examined, it is often viewed in terms of an aesthetic or moral loss, as were the extinction of the passenger pigeon and the dodo bird, and the near-extinction of the whooping crane.

These were tragedies in their own right, but today, species and gene pool extinction is proceeding faster than at any time in history. Environmental scientists estimate that before the twentieth century, species became extinct at the rate of about 10 per year. By 1972, the rate had climbed to about one per day. In 1992, according to environmental scientists' estimates, 100 to 300 species died out. About one-fourth of the earth's remaining species are under risk of extinction by 2025 as the result of human activities.[7]

Many environmentalists—and others as well—believe that the accelerated rate of species and gene pool extinction indicates both that the ability of the earth to support life is diminishing, and that the decline in the number of species carries immediate dangers for humankind as well. Their point of view can be easily illustrated in agriculture.

For example, in the 1990s, as much as 80 percent of the world's food comes from fewer than two dozen plant and animal species. Subspecies variation within these species assures some degree of survivability in the event of disease or sickness, but the movement toward monoculture high-yield varieties of grains in particular reduces the number of subspecies available, and increases the chance of crop blight. The blight that ravaged U.S. corn production in 1970 is ample proof that high-yield monocultural agriculture carries with it some significant dangers. Therefore, it should not be overlooked that monoculture is taking place concurrently with the extinction of many genetic variants. The dangers this portends for the future are clear.

Solutions to species and gene pool extinction problems are as difficult to find as with any of the preceding environmental problems we discussed. First, a political consciousness must be built to convince people that a problem exists, and then transnational action must be decided upon, implemented, and enforced. But in the area of species and gene pool extinction, there remains debate. This was shown by the United States' original refusal under the Bush administration to sign the Biodiversity Treaty concluded at the June 1992 Earth Summit in Rio de Janeiro, and the reversal of the U.S.' position less than a year later by the Clinton administration.

The Rio Earth Summit

Slowly, however, the nations of the world are beginning to recognize that the earth's environment is in trouble. In addition to the international agreement phasing out CFCs discussed earlier, the clearest indication of this was the June 1992 Rio Earth Summit. Held under United Nations' auspices, the Earth Summit brought together thousands of delegations and representatives from hundreds of states, IGOs, and NGOs. Over one hundred heads of state attended, including President George Bush of the United States, Chancellor Helmut Kohl of Germany, and Prime Minister John Major of Great Britain. According to one observer, the Earth Summit was "the largest and most complex conference ever held—bigger than the momentous meetings at Versailles, Yalta, and Potsdam."[8]

But did the Rio Earth Summit accomplish anything? To a great extent, the answer to this question depends on one's perspective. Over 150 states attending the conference signed each of two treaties, one treaty calling for countries to reach agreement on climate improvement and the reduction of carbon dioxide emissions, and the other treaty pledging protection of biodiversity and endangered species. In addition, the conference issued a sweeping declaration on balancing the needs of man and nature, which in at least a declaratory sense, committed the international community to pursuing sustainable development. The Earth Summit also adopted a vaguely worded pledge on protecting the earth's forests and woodlands. In addition, it adopted *Agenda 21*, a 700-page document that stressed the need for international cooperation to combat environmental deterioration, the requirement for changed patterns of consumption in developed countries, and the necessity of transferring appropriate technology from First World states to developing states to aid in sustainable development. Finally, the Earth Summit also created the Commission on Sustainable Development to help implement the actions agreed to at Rio.

Some participants and observers considered the conference a success. They rightfully pointed out that so many people from so many parts of the international community, including many heads of state, had never before assembled to discuss a particular issue. In this respect, the Earth Summit was a tremendous success in raising global consciousness about environmental issues. They also pointed out that industrialized countries of the world pledged over $11 billion to help clean and protect the environment, $7 billion from Japan over five years and $4 billion from the European Community. Germany by itself pledged to increase its overseas development assistance from a 1992 rate of .42 percent of its gross national product to .7 percent, most of the increase directed toward sustainable development. This meant that Germany alone would increase its developmental efforts by as much as $6 billion per year.[9]

But others believed the conference accomplished little. They pointed out

Rain forests in many developing countries are being destroyed by economic development efforts. The 1992 Rio Earth Summit proved unable to overcome the difference in perspectives between developing countries, which seek economic development, and developed countries, which seek to protect the rain forests.   (Sygma.)

that because of U.S. insistence, the climate treaty was so diluted that it had no meaningful effect on reducing carbon dioxide emissions. They also noted that the United States, even though it later changed its position, at first refused to sign the Biodiversity Treaty. From the U.S. perspective, both treaties might have an adverse effect on the U.S. economy. Meanwhile, the agreement on forest and woodland protection was also watered down, this time because of the insistence of many Developing World states who feared that stronger wording might adversely affect their economies. Throughout the Rio meeting, a conflict between environmental protection and economic development was evident.

Critics of the Rio meeting even minimized the importance of the new commitments for environmental programs and sustainable development taken on by Japan, Germany, and the rest of the European Community, noting that the United Nations estimated that as much as $125 billion per year were needed for the next decade for environmental clean-up efforts on a global basis. While every little bit helped, they asserted, the new environmental aid was much too little to have any meaningful impact. They also noted that the United States pledged only $150 million in new money for global environmental improvement, to protect forests.

It remains to be seen whether the Rio Earth Summit was a success or a failure. Nevertheless, one final point must be made not only about the Earth Summit, but also about all of the solutions to the environmental problems we examined earlier. In the past, most if not all the environmentally related problems in the categories that we examined here were localized or national in scope. Within the last decade or two, however, they have been increasingly recognized as international in scope. Acid rain caused by Russian industrial production damages Norwegian as well as Russian lakes and streams. U.S. topsoil loss threatens not only U.S., but also Japanese, nutrition. French industrial production brings smog and air pollution to Germany, and German industrial production brings smog and air pollution to France. Dam construction and irrigation in the Sudan affect Egyptian agriculture, and deforestation in the Ivory Coast, Ghana, Togo, and Benin accelerates desertification in Mali, Upper Volta, and Niger. Environmental challenges have become international in scope, and solutions to them must also be international in scope.

DRUGS

Like the environment, drugs emerged as an international problem during the 1980s. They remain an immense international problem today.[10] But unlike with the environment, the contemporary era is not the first time that drugs have created problems in the international community.

During the nineteenth century, European powers sold large quantities of opium to China, disrupting the normal functioning of Chinese society. When the Chinese government tried to stop the opium trade, Great Britain and France went to war with China to force China to continue to allow the import of opium. Indeed, opium addiction remained a significant problem in East Asia until well into the twentieth century. And in the United States, today's drug problems are not the first time society has shown concern about addictive substances. In the early twentieth century, many U.S. citizens developed a cocaine habit, using cocaine imported from South America. New food and drug laws and changed societal outlooks helped reduce cocaine use in that earlier era, but new laws did not succeed in decreasing U.S. citizens' love for alcohol during prohibition in the 1920s. Many people made millions of dollars smuggling alcohol into the country, and U.S. relations with several states, notably Canada, became strained because of the U.S. government's attempts to stem the flow of illegal liquor.

Today's drug problems are immense in scope and global in nature. Although it is difficult to measure the magnitude of drug problems, the United States probably has the worst one, followed by Western Europe. However, drug addiction does not stop there. Russia, Japan, Eastern Europe, and most Developing World states admit that drug addiction is on the rise there as well.

The sources of drugs are also widespread. Cocaine comes primarily from South America; marijuana from South America, the Caribbean, and North America; heroin and opium from Southeast Asia and the Middle East; and other drugs from elsewhere, as well. Interestingly, however, many of these drugs, and especially cocaine, must first be processed. In a fascinating twist that points out the complexities of the international drug trade, American businesses provide up to 90 percent of the ethyl ether and acetone needed in South America to make cocaine out of coca leaf.

International drug traffic is big business. Some estimates place the earnings of international drug traffickers at between $10 billion and $20 billion per year. In some countries like Peru, Colombia, and Bolivia, drug profits allow drug barons to fund private armies, bribe public officials, and otherwise operate as if they were sovereign rulers. Their great wealth allows the drug barons to extend their influence beyond their home countries, keeping people on their payrolls in the United States and Europe and buying property there as well.

In many instances in Latin America, Asia, and elsewhere, drug lords rely on local peasants to provide them with the labor power to grow, harvest, and process drug-producing crops. Living on the edge of subsistence, peasants frequently view drug traffic as the only way to earn a livelihood. Thus, an intricate relationship exists between drugs and economic underdevelopment. Without the substitution of crops whose payoff is better than drug crops, there appears little hope of stemming the flow of drugs at their sources. But the difficulty of relying on crop substitution as a cure for the drug problem was well underlined by the 1989 collapse of the 74-nation international coffee agreement. This collapse depressed coffee prices—one of Colombia's primary nondrug exports—and cost Colombia as much as $500 million per year. Ironically, lower coffee prices probably pushed more Colombians into the drug industry.

At the same time, in Peru and Bolivia, an alliance of sorts has developed between drug lords and local revolutionary groups. The drug barons provide money and weapons to the guerrilla bands for protection, and the revolutionary groups then both protect drug production and run their military campaigns against the national governments. In some cases, national governments find themselves less well financed than either the guerrillas or the drug barons.

Not surprisingly, the flow of drug money into several countries provides a major engine to maintain a functioning economy in those states. This is especially true in the Andean countries of South America. For example, in Colombia alone, the Medellin and Cali drug cartels in the late 1980s brought between $2 billion and $4 billion per year into the Colombian economy.[11] This is an impressive figure, especially in view of the fact that the entire Colombian gross national product in 1987 was only $33 billion.[12] Thus, just by themselves the Medellin and Cali cartels controlled income which is the equivalent of as much as 10 percent of the entire Colombian economy.

International traffic in drugs has also had an impact on a number of smaller countries, for example, the ministates of the Cayman Islands, the Bahamas, and Vanuatu, in which prosperous banking industries have sprung up. Often, these banks also launder drug money. Although most of the banks in these countries operate legally, and most were established for the purpose of providing tax shelter locations for large "offshore" investors, large quantities of drug money move through these so-called "offshore banking sites."

Can anything be done about international drug traffic? Given the scope and magnitude of the problem, it is evident that only multifaceted international cooperative efforts have a chance to have a serious impact. Within user countries, demand-reduction programs must be put in place. Within producer countries, economies must be strengthened and alternate crops must be established to reduce drug sources and profits. Governmental institutions in producer states must be strengthened as well. And interdiction efforts must be undertaken with an understanding of national sensitivities about neocolonialism and imperialism. Indeed, when in 1990 the United States announced its intention to deploy an aircraft carrier off the Colombian coast in international waters to help that country in its ongoing war against drugs, almost every sector of the Colombian body politic denounced the U.S. move as an unwarranted intrusion into Colombian affairs. The deployment did not take place.

Nevertheless, military cooperation between the United States and the governments of Colombia, Peru, and Bolivia to combat the drug industry and drug trade has grown significantly. For the most part, U.S. forces provide information and act as advisers to local militaries in coca crop eradication, processing plant destruction, and interdiction efforts. In 1990, the United States promised to provide these governments with $2.2 billion over five years in military and economic aid to help combat drugs and improve local economies.

Thailand's experience with its campaign against drugs is also noteworthy. Long a source of the poppy plant from which heroin and opium is made, Thailand with U.S. help began a campaign in the 1980s to eradicate poppy cultivation. The campaign met with considerable success, at least until those who were growing the plant simply moved their fields across the border into Myanmar, formerly Burma. As a result, and in the absence of Myanmar's cooperation, the poppy crop in 1992 was virtually undiminished.

Obviously, multifaceted international cooperative efforts to combat drugs are needed. For a variety of political and economic reasons, this has been difficult to arrange. When and if such efforts are arranged, they take a long time to produce the desired effect. They will also be costly in terms of money, time, lives, and property. Much of the cost in money will have to be borne by developed states, including the United States; the poverty-stricken states of South America and elsewhere have few spare resources to provide in the war against drugs. But unless such steps are taken, it is likely that the international drug problem will only grow worse. Over time, it is a problem as dangerous and deadly as a major military conflict.

HEALTH

The emergence of acquired immune deficiency syndrome (AIDS) as a global health problem has cast a spotlight on global health issues. As Table 23–3 shows, countries around the world have reported over 600 thousand cases of AIDS. As Table 23–4 shows, the increased frequency of AIDS in many countries between the late 1980s and early 1990s has been immense. And as Figure 23–2 shows, over 10 million people around the world are infected with the human immunodeficiency virus (HIV) that causes AIDS.

AIDS is not the first disease that has had widespread and even global implications. When Europeans moved to the western hemisphere during the fifteenth, sixteenth, and seventeenth centuries, they brought with them measles, typhus, yellow fever, and smallpox, diseases which were until that time unknown in the western hemisphere. These diseases ravaged much of the western hemisphere's

TABLE 23–3   Reported AIDS Cases, by Continent, as of 1992

	Countries with One or More Cases	Total Number of Cases
Africa	52	211,032
Americas	45	313,083
Asia	33	2,582
Europe	31	80,810
Oceania	12	4,082
Totals	173	611,589

Source: Global Program on AIDS, World Health Organization, 1993.

TABLE 23–4   The Global Growth of AIDS, as Reported in Selected Countries, 1988
and 1992

	Number of Cases	
Country	1988	1992
United States	78,985	242,146
Uganda	5,508	34,611
Brazil	4,436	31,364
Kenya	2,732	31,185
Malawi	2,586	22,300
France	4,211	21,487
Italy	2,556	14,783
Mexico	1,502	11,034
Germany*	2,580	8,893
Rwanda	987	8,483
Canada	2,156	6,889
Zambia	1,056	6,556
Burundi	1,408	6,052
Congo	1,250	3,482
Haiti	1,455	3,086
Switzerland	605	2,691
Japan	90	508
French Guiana	113	232
Bermuda	81	199
China	3	11

SOURCES: Global Program on AIDS, World Health Organization, 1993.
*1988 figure is only for West Germany.

indigenous population. More recently, extensive international health campaigns have been undertaken against smallpox and malaria under the auspices of the World Health Organization (WHO). The WHO campaign eliminated smallpox throughout the world and had a major role in reducing the frequency of malaria.

In fact, WHO was specifically created by the nations of the world to monitor, treat, and prevent a host of diseases and health problems that confronted the international community. Given that today's rapid transportation capabilities and mobile populations make it possible for diseases to spread very quickly, there is a demonstrable need for WHO and similar bodies. Highly infectious and new diseases without known antidotes have a greater probability of affecting more of the world's population than in years past, and the international community has already taken some steps to meet this challenge.

In the case of AIDS, WHO in 1987 formed the Global Program on AIDS (GPA), which by 1992 had grown to a program of over 200 professionals with a budget of over $100 million. With GPA's encouragement and support, at least 119 countries developed short-term anti-AIDS plans, and at least 48 countries have developed three- to five-year plans to combat the disease. No cure for AIDS has been found, and much remains to be done, but the global community has clearly made a start in responding to the international AIDS crisis.

Given rapid transportation and mobile populations, global health problems in certain ways parallel global environmental and drug problems—the most

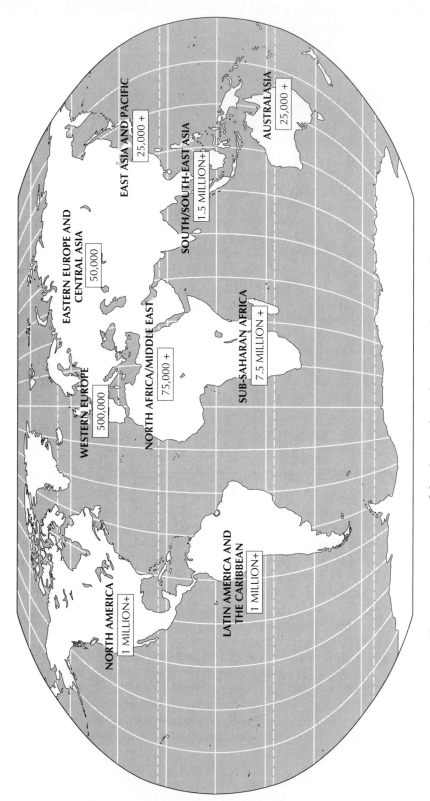

FIGURE 23–2 Estimated distribution of cumulative HIV infections in adults, by continent or region, late 1992. (SOURCE: Global Program on AIDS, World Health Organization, January 1993.)

The following labels appear on the map:

NORTH AMERICA — 1 MILLION+

WESTERN EUROPE — 500,000

EASTERN EUROPE AND CENTRAL ASIA — 50,000

NORTH AFRICA/MIDDLE EAST — 75,000 +

EAST ASIA AND PACIFIC — 25,000 +

SOUTH/SOUTH-EAST ASIA — 1.5 MILLION+

SUB-SAHARAN AFRICA — 7.5 MILLION +

AUSTRALASIA — 25,000 +

LATIN AMERICA AND THE CARIBBEAN — 1 MILLION+

In the past, global health problems have included malaria, the plague, smallpox, and polio. Today, AIDS presents an immense threat to worldwide health. It is a global problem that is particularly severe in the United States and several countries in Africa and the Caribbean.

effective approach is a transnational approach. And it is clear that the international community has been willing, on at least a limited basis, to respond to health problems in this manner. At the same time, lest the international community be too proud of its record in global health, it has also exhibited some glaring blind spots; each year, over 5 million children die of chronic diarrhea and 3 million people fall victim to tuberculosis.[13]

The lesson to be learned is clear. Even when countries recognize the need to respond to a problem on a transnational basis, this is sometimes not enough. There also must be a political will to do something about the problem at hand, whether it be health or some other emerging global issue.

CONCLUSIONS

It is apparent that several global issues are emerging that may force the international community, and particularly states, to think in terms that transcend national sovereignty. The interrelationships among population, food, economic development, resources, the environment, drugs, and health are exceedingly complex, and few of the problems associated with any of these issues can be contained completely within national boundaries.

One of the challenges for the rest of this century and the beginning of the next is for humankind, on at least some issues, to make the transition from narrowly defined parochial thinking and solutions to more broadly defined globalist thinking and solutions. The extent to which this transition is successful may determine not only the quality of life in this and the twenty-first century, but also whether *Homo sapien* as a specie survives into the twenty-second century.

KEY TERMS AND CONCEPTS

land degradation
desertification
water degradation
greenhouse effect
ozone depletion
Montreal Protocol
species and gene pool extinction

Rio Earth Summit
role of drugs in international
   affairs
trends and patterns in global
   AIDS problem
mobility, political will, and the
   global health situation

NOTES

1. Unless otherwise noted, most of the following discussion comes from Jessica Tuchman Mathews, "Redefining Security," *Foreign Affairs* (Spring 1989), pp. 162–177; David A. Wirth, "Climate Chaos," *Foreign Policy* (Spring 1989), pp. 3–22; Norman Myers, "Environment and Security," *Foreign Policy* (Spring 1989), pp. 23–41; Thomas A. Sancton, "The Fight To Save the Planet," *Time* (December 18, 1989), pp. 60–61; and Martin W. Holdgate, "Planning for Our Common Future," *Environment* (October 1989), pp. 15–41.

2. See Sandra Postel, "Halting Land Degradation," *State of the World 1989* (New York: Norton, 1989), pp. 21–40.

3. See William S. Ellis, "A Soviet Sea Lies Dying," *National Geographic* (February 1990), pp. 73–93.

4. See, for example, Eugene Linden, "Now Wait Just a Minute," *Time*, December 18, 1989, p. 68. See also *Science*, March 30, 1990.

5. *The New York Times*, February 16, 1992.

6. Wirth, "Climate Chaos," p. 14.

7. *The Atlanta Journal-Constitution*, May 16, 1992.

8. Philip Elmer-Dewitt, "Rich vs. Poor," in *Time*, June 1, 1992, p. 42.

9. *The New York Times*, June 14, 1992.

10. Much of this section is developed from 1991, 1992, and 1993 news reports. For more academic-oriented assessments of the international drug situation, see "Assessing the Americas' War on Drugs," a special edition of the *Journal of InterAmerican Studies and World Affairs* (Summer/Fall 1988); and Bruce Michael Bagley, "Dateline Drug Wars: Colombia: The Wrong Strategy," *Foreign Policy* (Winter 1989), pp. 154–171.

11. "Heavy Flak in the Drug War," *U.S. News and World Report*, December 18, 1989, p. 17.

12. U.S. Central Intelligence Agency, *The World Factbook 1989*, p. 66.

13. As reported in Lori Heise, "Responding to AIDS," *State of the World 1989* (New York: Norton, 1989), p. 113.

CHAPTER 24

War, Peace, and Violence

- What causes war?
- Are there different types of war?
- Where are the boundaries between war and peace?
- Can war and violence be avoided in international affairs?

No issues present greater challenges to humankind than war, peace, and violence. Energy and resource shortfalls present the unwelcome alternative of a deteriorated global standard of living, and environmental deterioration, in its most extreme form, offers the specter of a future earth made unlivable by humans. War and violence, however, present the threat of immediate death and destruction. Although the end of the East–West conflict and the breakup of the Soviet Union immensely reduced the possibility of large-scale nuclear war, the hard reality remains that thousands of nuclear warheads still exist, any one of which could devastate an entire city. Thus, without minimizing the severity of problems relating to international political economics or other emerging global problems, humankind must successfully address the issues of war, peace, and violence, both on a short-term basis and over the long term.

War and violence are nothing new to the human experience. The fourth chapter of the Bible records man's first murder, and the ancient Hindu classic, *The Bhagavad Gita*, opens with a chronicle of the "heroic warriors, powerful archers, . . . and the chariots of war" of two great armies about to lock in combat.[1] Man's violence against man has ranged from confrontations between individuals armed only with their bare fists to confrontations between armed forces several million strong, equipped with nuclear weapons capable of destroying civilization. Violence and war, it would seem, are part of the human condition. Indeed, over 13 million people have been killed in wars since 1960 alone.

Historically, war and peace have been viewed as mutually exclusive. Cynics considered peace to be merely a respite between wars, simply a period of time to prepare for war. Other analysts were more optimistic, arguing that war was the aberrant condition. To optimists, peace could be preserved only if the right combination of factors could be found. And so, at least until recently, a distinction was drawn between peace and war. By definition, war was the absence of peace, and peace the absence of war.

567

During the twentieth century, this overstated dichotomy between war and peace has been relegated to the dustbin of history as extended periods of **neither war nor peace** became increasingly common. Leon Trotsky's famous dictum may have been considered ridiculous by Germany in 1918, but in a curious way, it is an apt description of the state of much of international relations since World War II.[2]

Indeed, if only industrialized states are examined, none have been formally at war since World War II. Nevertheless, many instances of First and Second World violence and threatened violence were evident during the period. Throughout the Cold War, for example, the United States and the U.S.S.R. each feared violence would be unleashed by the other and built their militaries accordingly. On a more active plane, the United States fought in Korea, Vietnam, Grenada, Panama, and the Persian Gulf; bombed Libya and supplied the Contras in Nicaragua; and participated in a number of covert actions throughout the world. Even so, the United States never declared war. Similarly, the former Soviet Union fought in Afghanistan, sent troops into Eastern European states on two occasions, supported national liberation struggles throughout the world, and funded terrorist organizations, but never declared war.

Examples of the "neither peace nor war" status of contemporary international relations are not limited to the superpowers. Since World War II, Great Britain has fought in Malaya and the South Atlantic, and France has fought in Indochina, Algeria, and sub-Saharan Africa. China has struggled with the United States, India, the former Soviet Union, and Vietnam, but never declared war. Additional examples abound.

The distinction between war and peace in the twentieth century is made even more difficult by the proliferation of international actors. Under traditional international law, war was described as a condition of conflict between two state actors. However, as different actors rose to prominence during the twentieth century, and as those actors gained access to military equipment and weapons, an increased frequency of "new styles of warfare" became inevitable as states' interests conflicted with the interests of nonstate actors. Indeed, among those examples just listed, only the British struggle in the South Atlantic with Argentina and the four conflicts that China was involved in were fought between two traditional state actors.

Terrorism deserves special mention here. Whether it is a form of warfare is a matter of debate, but no doubt exists that it is a type of violence that has come to play an increasingly large role in contemporary international relations. Perhaps more than any other form of conflict, terrorism blurs the distinction between war and peace.

The difficulty in distinguishing between war and peace in the twentieth century is more than a semantic problem emanating from the proliferation of nonstate actors and the growing reluctance of states formally to declare war. Indeed, low-intensity conflicts have multiplied in number and scope. Greater availability of weaponry, ease of travel, and the disruption of consensus in the international community have been major contributing factors to the increase in violence in the international arena. Thus, to be accurate, questions of war and peace must be realistically discussed as questions of war, peace, and violence.

Diplomats, theologians, military officers, academics, and other men and women from all walks of life have regularly addressed themselves to issues of war, peace, and violence. On occasion, their efforts to reduce or eliminate the incidence of war and violence have succeeded. More often, they have not. War and violence continue to plague humankind, seemingly without respite, and peace often seems the aberrant condition. Nevertheless, with the awesome growth in destructive power of modern nuclear *and* conventional weapons, and with increased availability of those weapons throughout the world, the urgency of reducing or eliminating the incidence of war and violence has acquired a new poignancy. Man's very survival as a species may be in the balance.

However, efforts to enhance the prospects for peace must be predicated on an accurate appraisal of what causes war and violence, and how war and violence fit within the international community. Therefore, before we examine the potential to reduce or eliminate war and violence and achieve greater peace, we first must examine the causes of war and violence and the types of conflict they bring with them.

THE CAUSES OF INTERNATIONAL CONFLICT

What causes war and international violence? The question is as old as recorded history. Not surprisingly, the answer has been and remains a matter of dispute. Academicians, politicians, theologians, philosophers, and others have debated the causes of war and violence for centuries, and today consensus is no nearer than it was in ancient Greece or Rome or elsewhere.

Nevertheless the question persists, and it is more than a mere academic or philosophic query. To provide an answer is to imply that certain actions should be taken or policies adopted to reduce, minimize, or eliminate the possibility of war and violence. Different answers therefore imply different actions or policies. Thus, the quest for resolution continues.

Many answers to the question "What causes war and international violence?" have been advanced, but almost all may be grouped into five broadly defined categories: (1) the nature of human beings; (2) perceptual limitations of humans; (3) poverty and disparities in wealth; (4) the internal structures of states; and (5) the international system itself.[3]

Human Nature

Perhaps the most widely accepted interpretation of the cause of war is human nature. Western intellectuals as diverse as St. Augustine, Reinhold Niebuhr, and Benedict de Spinoza all concluded that the source of international conflict springs from within people. Outside the West, Confucius and the unknown authors of the sacred scripts of Hinduism, among others, reached similar conclusions. Although these and other similarly disposed thinkers disagreed as to the type of fatal flaw within us, they all concurred that human nature caused war.

For example, St. Augustine posited that wars were but a manifestation of original sin. "Perfectly good men," St. Augustine argued in *City of God*, "cannot war." Unfortunately, however, perfectly good men do not exist, at least if one accepts the concept of original sin, and therefore wars were inevitable. Existing hand-in-hand with original sin in St. Augustine's worldview was human fear of death, our inability to reason logically, and our flawed will. The contradiction between our fear of death and our willingness to wage war was explained by our inability to reason logically. At the same time, although humans were cognizant of the immorality of warlike behavior, St. Augustine maintained that their flawed will rendered it impossible for them better to control their actions even on the occasions when they were aware of the immorality of their behavior and feared their own death. Thus, to St. Augustine (and many others in the classical Christian tradition), our "love of vain and hurtful things" was the source of human conflict, whether it was on the individual scale of murder or the state-sanctioned scale of war.

Benedict de Spinoza argued that people were led by simple passion to undertake acts that defy reason. People are slaves to their passions, Spinoza argued, and because of this, conflicts have occurred as individuals and groups of individuals sought to assuage the demands of their passions. In Spinoza's view, passion and reason were continually at odds within us. If we were to follow reasonable courses of action, passion would become slave to humans, and wars would be less frequent. Spinoza, however, was no naive idealist. Whoever believed that people could be "induced to live according to the bare dictate of reason" was himself "dreaming of the poetic golden age, or of a stage play," as Spinoza said in *Political Treatise*. One of the roles of the state, Spinoza maintained, was to promote peace. Not surprisingly, however, inasmuch as states were subject to the conflict between passion and reason that rages within humans, they could become warlike as they fell prey to human passion.

Spinoza's dualism of passion and reason was specifically rejected by Reinhold Niebuhr. Nevertheless, Niebuhr's view of international conflict still placed its cause within human nature. To Niebuhr, people were flawed. As he said in *Beyond Tragedy*, war stemmed from "dark unconscious sources in the human psyche." Niebuhr further argued in *Christianity and Power Politics* that exploitation, class division, conquest, and intimidation stemmed from "a tendency in the human heart." Indeed, to Niebuhr, human nature was the cause of war.

Such conclusions were also reached in Asia. In China, Confucius concluded that "there is deceit and cunning in man, and from these wars arise." Wars could arise between feudal barons or between emperors and kings, but Confucianism still attributed them to human "deceit and cunning." In *The Bhagavad Gita*, the answer to the question of what caused war and violence was pronounced to be a fatal flaw in human character. As Krishna revealed to Arjuna, people are driven to act sinfully and to conduct war by "greedy desire and wrath, born of passion . . . wisdom is clouded by desire, the everpresent enemy of the wise . . . which like a fire cannot find satisfaction."

Perceptual Limitations

As we discussed in Chapter 10, humans are limited beings. They are limited in their ability to comprehend natural phenomena, to understand and relate data, and to perceive from more than a single viewpoint. These facts of human existence have led some to conclude that war and violence are more than anything the result of human perceptual limitations.

John G. Stoessinger's *Nations in Darkness* is one of the most thoughtful and thought-provoking discussions of the role of human perceptual limitations in war and international violence. In *Nations in Darkness*, Stoessinger posits that because people are limited in their ability to comprehend and perceive, they most naturally seek to justify that with which they are most familiar and that with which they are identified. This, in turn, leads to their rejection of and opposition to less familiar and less identifiable elements of life. In the context of human relations, this rejection and opposition leads to conflict. Using case histories from the U.S.-Soviet-Chinese triangle, Stoessinger argued that perceptual limitations have led to various conflict and near-conflict situations.

Taken in total, this second outlook on the cause of war is less optimistic than the first. In the first outlook, at least in the eyes of some of its proponents, human reason could succeed in overcoming human passion, thereby limiting warfare. However, in the second outlook, human perceptual limitations are unavoidable and inevitable, given the biophysical capabilities of the species. People are victims of their own perceptual limitations, and war and violence therefore result.

Poverty and Disparities in Wealth

In his classic 1942 work, *A Study of War*, Quincy Wright presented evidence that industrialized states with relatively high standards of living were generally less likely to initiate war than were poorer states.[4] Significant exceptions to this rule, such as Germany in 1939, existed during Wright's time, but it is noteworthy that almost 40 years later, Ruth Leger Sivard made a similar observation—poorer states are more prone to initiate war and violence. Sivard concluded that of the more than 120 instances of armed conflict that occurred between 1955 and 1979 all but six involved developing states.[5]

To some, this is persuasive evidence that poverty, either in a relative or absolute sense, induces war. Poverty-stricken countries, frustrated in their efforts to "keep up with the Joneses" of the international community, may lash out at neighbors in an effort to meet needs or to overcome a sense of impotence. Alternatively, war in the Developing World may be brought about by poverty-produced political instability. Governments of Developing World states, seeking to quell domestic hostilities brought about by poverty, may cast about for an external enemy in an effort to defuse resentment directed at the government itself. A key point in the argument that poverty leads to war and violence is that either absolute or relative poverty may generate hostilities. Thus, the point is more aptly phrased that poverty and disparities in wealth cause war. Several Developing World states have used this theme not to argue for the legitimacy of their war objects, but to argue for the necessity of a more equitable distribution of global wealth.

The Internal Structure of States

Another explanation for the existence of wars and violence in the international arena traces causality to the internal governmental, social, cultural, and economic structure of the state. Optimistically, many proponents of this outlook assert that people can determine state structure and therefore reduce or eliminate the cause of war and violence. V. I. Lenin, Immanuel Kant, and Woodrow Wilson, to name a few, all posited that people could within certain limits construct the internal relationships of a state, and in so doing, minimize and even eliminate the possibility of a military conflagration.

For example, Lenin looked to private ownership of production as the cause of class conflict within a state and of international conflict between states. To Lenin, the elimination of capitalist society and the creation of socialist society would not only eliminate the exploitation of man by man within a state, but also eliminate the external thrusts of capitalist states that lead to war. Thus, to Lenin, socialism brought peace.

Immanuel Kant defined the "good" state as one that sought to promote abstract principles of right. The duty of the state, Kant argued, was to make people act morally. The state, however, was neither wholly good nor wholly bad, and thus wars were inevitable. Kant argued in *Eternal Peace and Other International Essays* that states must actively seek to improve themselves internally. The ideal state structure, one for which all states must strive, was the republic, a state form "unable to injure any other by violence."

Woodrow Wilson, on the other hand, advocated that those states that had achieved what he deemed superior statehood should actively encourage establishment of internal structures in other states based on national self-determination and modern democracy. The enemy of peace, to Wilson, was neither private ownership nor conflict between the senses and reason, but rather the absence of political democracy. To enhance the opportunity for the spread of political democracies, Wilson urged a world confederation of states that would itself operate on a democratic basis and provide collective security. The key to success of Wilson's plan, however, was widespread acceptance of the legitimacy of the principle of political democracy, and that acceptance was not forthcoming. Even so, to Wilson, the willingness of a state to give its own citizens the right to choose their political leaders was a major step in reducing the probability of the outbreak of war.

The International System Itself

According to another outlook, the existence of an anarchical international system in which each state must fend for its own survival was the primary cause of war. States, or more accurately the leaders of states, were bound by no code of conduct other than that which they established for themselves and then chose to follow. Despite international law, no established pattern of international behavior existed that was both universally applicable and universally enforceable. Thus states, and the leaders of states, sought to achieve their goals and objectives through whatever means they deemed appropriate, including force of arms. This outlook, of course, flowed directly from the realpolitik interpretation of international politics advocated by Hans Morgenthau.

Morgenthau had many predecessors. In his *History of the Peloponnesian War*, Thucydides observed that Agamemnon "raised the force against Troy" simply because he was "the most powerful of the rulers of his day." In the ancient world, Thucydides believed, might made right, and the anarchy of the international system permitted and encouraged the outbreak of conflict.

Jean Jacques Rousseau viewed the Europe of his era in a similar light. European laws were simply contradictory rules from "which nothing but the right of the stronger" could produce peace. Self-interest, Rousseau claimed in *A Lasting Peace*, would produce wars as long as nations sought to preserve their identities and expand their powers. The culprit, Rousseau maintained, was neither humans, their perceptions, nor the internal structure of states, but rather the international system of states itself. An imperfect international community existed in Europe, and "the imperfections of this association make the state of those belonging to it worse than if they formed no community at all." To Rousseau, inasmuch as no authority existed above the state to control the state, states could and did act in their own selfish interests to promote their own self-defined objectives. War was the end result.

To those who see the international system as the primary cause of war, the structure of that system is of paramount importance. A first viewpoint argues that an international system that has one dominant power is the least likely to lead to war. Others maintain that such a system, in the absence of a benevolent dominant power, would lead to exploitation of all other international actors by the dominant power. A second point of view asserts that a bipolar system with two dominant powers is the least likely to lead to war, as long as rough parity of power exists between the two. This type of system existed for most of the period since World War II, as we saw in Chapters 7 and 9. A third point of view maintains that a multipolar system with many centers of power is the most stable and the least likely to lead to war. Here, the rationale is that international actors will maintain flexible policies and attitudes so that a rough balance of power will always exist, and war will be avoided.

For our purposes, it is worth noting once again that the 1990s appear to be a period during which the international system is moving from a bipolar system to a regionalized or a multipolar system. Despite disagreements over which system tends to be the most stable and the least likely to lead to conflict, the transition of the international system from one type to another appears beyond any single actor's control.

TYPOLOGIES OF INTERNATIONAL CONFLICT

Despite the obvious disagreement over the causes of international conflict, analysts have identified certain broad categories of types of war and violence. Until the fall of communism in Eastern Europe and the Soviet Union, two typologies of conflict predominated, one Marxist and the other traditionalist. With the demise of Soviet-style communism, only the traditionalist school still maintains widespread international credibility. We turn to the five major categories within the traditionalist school now.

International Crises

Sometimes we seem to live in an age of continual crisis. For example, during the 1990s, news accounts have applied the term *crisis* to a wide variety of international events: The Persian Gulf crisis, the Somali crisis, the Bosnian crisis, the debt crisis, the food crisis, and the environmental crisis are a few examples. Some included violence, as in the Persian Gulf and Bosnia. Others did not, as in the debt crisis and the food crisis.

For our purposes, a more restricted definition of crisis is requisite. One of the most useful definitions demands that four sets of circumstances prevail: (1) high priority goals of an actor must be threatened; (2) a limited amount of time is available before action must be taken; (3) the situation must be for the most part unanticipated; and (4) the situation must not escalate into armed conflict.[6] When many of the benchmarks of East–West relations since World War II are listed— for example, the Formosan Straits crisis, the Berlin crisis, and the Cuban missile crisis—it is evident that crisis was central to the East–West relationship.

But crises were not limited to East–West relations, even under the restrictive criteria just set forth. The Iranian hostage crisis, for example, met the require- ments for a true crisis: A high-priority U.S. objective, the safety of its diplomatic legation in Iran, was threatened; the Carter administration believed the situation was time-sensitive; the capture of the hostages was generally unanticipated; and the situation did not escalate into armed conflict.

Because crises, under the definition we have adopted, preclude war and most types of violence, the question may legitimately be asked, "Why are crises included in a typology of war?" The answer is because a large percentage of crises escalate into war and violence. Although quantitative evidence suggests that crisis escalation to warfare has become less frequent, possibly because of the increased cost of war, crises nevertheless must be viewed as a special stage in the relation- ships between international actors. They are, in a classic sense, manifestations of a condition of "neither war nor peace."[7]

International crises may be considered a type of negotiation or communica- tion between international actors that arises when neither side desires war or vio- lence, but considers its own goals important enough to risk war or violence. John Foster Dulles's concept of "brinkmanship" offers a useful description of crisis; it is the art of being willing to move closer to the brink of war than one's potential opponent. The more skilled an actor is in practicing "brinkmanship," the more successful he will be in resolving crises to his advantage.[8] Crises may in this light be viewed as situations in which one's resolve and intent are communicated to potential opponents.

This method of negotiation or communication carries with it the danger of sliding over the brink into war and escalating into violence. Often, as in World War I and the Vietnam conflict, no sharp distinction between crisis and conflict is apparent; the "brink" may in fact not be a brink, but rather an ever-steeper incline that precludes a reversal of policy. Negotiation by crisis is therefore an extremely risky way to achieve one's objectives.

Nevertheless, international actors and states in particular continue to be will- ing to engineer crisis situations in efforts to achieve their objectives. For example, in 1982, Argentina did not expect Great Britain to mount an effort to recapture the Falkland Islands following the Argentine takeover. Great Britain in turn mis- calculated the Argentine seriousness of purpose. Both sides sought to move closer to the brink of conflict, without actually initiating conflict, in an effort to make the other side back down. Both sides failed. By the time the British task force reached the Falkland Islands, the brink—or was it an ever-steeper incline?—had been passed, and armed conflict broke out.

In the West, and particularly in the United States, some analysts have devel- oped a degree of confidence in human ability to "manage" crisis. **Crisis manage- ment** has become a major conceptual tool of Washington's national security community. Basing its appeal on the assumption that war and violence are not, in the end, rational or cost-effective responses to disagreements between international actors, crisis management theorists have developed techniques of bargaining, signaling, and nonverbal communication that, they hope, will prevent actors from taking the last step into war and violence. Little evidence suggests that their methods have been successful. Indeed, by wrongly assuring decision-makers that their lines of logic are clearly evident to others, and by incorrectly persuading decision makers that a particular action will send an unambiguous signal to others, crisis management techniques may have precipitated the transition of some situations from crisis to war and violence.[9]

Low-Intensity Conflict

Relations between and among state and nonstate actors are often marred by small skirmishes along borders or at sea, by individual or small-group violence, or by other forms of sporadic conflict. Violence as diverse as Sino-Soviet border incidents, Thai and Cambodian attacks on Vietnamese "boat people," South African incursions into Angola to destroy Southwest African Peoples' Organization camps, and exchanges of gunfire along the 38th parallel between North and South Korea fit within the broad heading of low-intensity conflict. Crises may escalate to low-intensity conflict, or move beyond low-intensity conflict directly to full-scale warfare.

Low-intensity conflict may be limited either in frequency or in level of violence. Fighting along the Sino-Soviet border, for example, occurred rarely after the two communist powers had their falling out, and with the exception of a period during 1969, has not been large-scale. Similarly, the signing of the Korean Armistice ended main force engagements between North Korea and United Nations forces, but gunfire often erupts along the demarcation line, often with no damage and no loss of life.

Low-intensity conflict has long been a part of international affairs, but its importance has only been recognized in the relatively recent past. A number of reasons exist for its newfound notoriety. First, low-intensity conflict presents the danger of escalation to a more destructive level of violence. Once violence of any type has been perpetuated, a significant psychological inhibition has been overcome, and escalation to more extreme levels of violence becomes more probable. Second, with the spread of modern weapon capabilities, low-intensity conflict has the potential to become extremely destructive. Closely related to this, and the third reason for the notoriety of low-intensity conflict, is global interdependence. In an interdependent world, the effects of a temporary disruption of peaceful activity in one location ripple out to other areas. For example, during the 1980s, South African raids into Angola not only weakened SWAPO, but also raised tensions between South Africa and other front-line African states, complicated U.S.-Angolan relations, and strengthened Cuba's role in Africa.

Low-intensity conflict may be used as a tool of policy by a state actor or a nonstate actor, or it may on some occasions spontaneously erupt. As a tool of state policy, it may be employed to drive home a point; North Korea's capture of the USS *Pueblo* in 1968 was North Korea's way of asserting its claim to its territorial waters, and driving home its point to the United States. (The *Pueblo* incident was a situation that conceivably could be termed a crisis rather than a low-intensity conflict; few rounds were exchanged, and no aftermath of violence resulted.) Nonstate actors may use low-intensity conflict in the same way; the Palestine Liberation Organization, for example, vowed to continue its attacks on Israel and Israeli personnel overseas following Israel's 1982 invasion of Lebanon to prove that the PLO continued to exist and would continue to fight. Spontaneously erupting low-intensity conflict can result from the flow of events rather than conscious policy; some evidence indicates that skirmishes along the Sino-Soviet border were the result of neither Soviet nor Chinese policy, but rather local military responses to local stimuli. The same is true of some of the sporadic gunfire and shelling between North and South Korea.

In any event, low-intensity conflict is one of the most prevalent forms of violence in the international arena. In the eyes of some, terrorism is one form of low-intensity conflict. Given the specific objective of terrorism, however, and its increased use as a peculiar form of international violence, terrorism is here categorized as a distinct form of international violence.

Terrorism

V. I. Lenin summed up the objective purpose of terrorism as concisely as anyone: "The purpose of terrorism is to inspire terror." Despite the fact that the political, economic, or social objectives of terrorists range across all fields of human endeavor, terrorism must be listed in any typology of war and international violence, either as a subset of low-intensity conflict or as a separate category. The problem with terrorism is defining it. As we saw in Chapter 5, in many cases the difference between a freedom fighter and terrorist depends on one's perspective. Yet Lenin's stark description of terrorism permits certain distinctions to be drawn even within the shadowy world of the terrorist. Thus, if a PLO artillery piece fired from southern Lebanon into Israel against an Israeli army depot, that action probably was not classified as terrorism. But if that same artillery piece fired into a kibbutz, the case was less clear; an Israeli would immediately label the action terrorism, and a Palestinian would probably describe it as low-intensity conflict. However, if two groups of extremists from a PLO faction armed with Soviet and U.S. weapons purchased with Libyan money launched attacks on airports, indiscriminately firing into the check-in area, that would unarguably be terrorism. This is exactly what happened in December 1985 at Rome and Vienna airports when PLO extremists raced into the airport check-in areas and started killing people. As Lenin said, the purpose of terrorism is to inspire terror.

As a form of international violence, terrorism actually causes relatively few casualties, as Figure 24–1 makes clear. Nevertheless, terrorism has a psychological impact far beyond the death and destruction that it causes. One excellent example of this was the 40 to 50 percent drop in U.S. tourism to Europe that took place in 1986 following a number of terrorist attacks in Europe and the U.S. retaliatory strikes against Libya. Another excellent example is the increased level of tension evident throughout New York City in 1993 following the terrorist bombing of the World Trade Center, which killed six people.

Terrorism is an extremely useful tool for those elements of international soci-

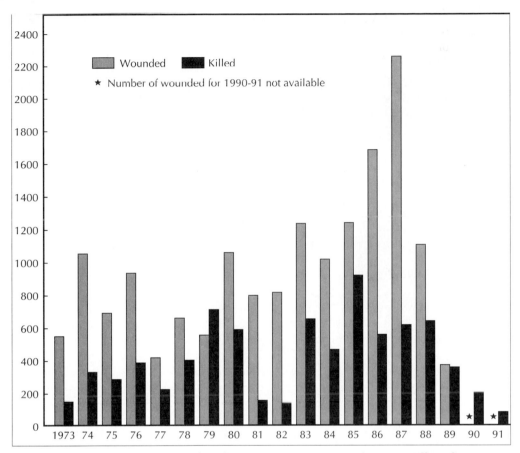

FIGURE 24–1 Casualties from terrorism, 1973–1991. (SOURCE: Office of Counterterrorism, U.S. Department of State, 1992.)

ety that find themselves unable to influence events in the way they desire. For the most part, terrorism is therefore a tool of violence used by nonstate actors against state authority.

During the 1980s, however, the United States and the Soviet Union exchanged charges that the other supported terrorist activity, giving rise to speculation that when the superpowers' objectives coincide with objectives of weaker actors, the superpowers were willing to aid terrorists because of the coincidence of objectives. The attempted assassination of Pope John Paul II by Mehmet Ali Agca in May 1981, for example, was tenuously linked to the U.S.S.R. through Bulgaria.

Many states besides the superpowers have been accused of abetting terrorist activities. Among the more prominent supporters of state-supported terrorism are Iran, Libya, and Iraq. All deny they support terrorism, but all defend their right to fight "U.S. imperialism" and "Zionism" in any way they see proper. Indeed, by the late 1980s and on into the 1990s, the concept of "state-supported terrorism" had become one of the hallmarks of late twentieth-century international life.

Terrorism is so common in contemporary international affairs because of a number of reasons. The first is the widespread availability of arms. It is not at all difficult to purchase or steal arms in most international cities. A second cause of terrorism is the growth of international interdependence; with more and more economic, social, and political events and endeavors being connected to each other, terrorists see many secondary targets that can be attacked in the hope of bringing pressure to bear on their primary target. Third, the lack of international consensus about the future of the international community may also lead to terrorism; ideology and frustration can serve as powerful goads to violent action. And a fourth major cause is the communications revolution; with global communications via satellite and microwave, the impact of terrorist actions is worldwide whether it results from murder at the Rome and Vienna airports, a bomb in the World Trade Center in New York or in a Pan American jet over Scotland, or assassination attempts in Vatican City. Terrorism as a form of international violence has come of age.

Civil War and Revolution

In general terms, civil wars are conflicts within a state between two or more groups fought because of disagreements over the future of that state. At least one of the groups at war must be a nonstate actor; the other group(s) may be either the state's government or additional nonstate actors. Civil wars may be massive upheavals including millions of men and women, as were the American Civil War and the Chinese Revolution, or they may be more limited in scope. All levels of violence may also be included. The American Civil War was fought between full armies, as was the Chinese Revolution during its later phases. Guerrilla warfare must also be considered a type of civil war, for movements internal to a country are here seeking to overthrow a government. At the opposite extreme from conflicts such as the American Civil War, certain forms of terrorism may be described as low-intensity civil war. The terrorist, after all, has a different view of the desired future of the state structure he or she is attacking.

The frequency of civil war appears to be increasing. One study analyzed the wars that occurred between 1900 and 1941, and found that over 80 percent of them were traditional wars between the armed forces of two or more states. Another study examined wars that took place between 1945 and 1976, and discovered that over 85 percent of them were either "internal antiregime" or "internal tribal" wars, that is, civil wars. This study did *not* include terrorist-oriented activity.[10] The conclusion to be reached is simple—since World War II, state authority has been challenged more often from *inside* the state than from *outside* it.

Civil wars often have international dimensions, either because one or another of the parties involved in the war receives support from external sources or because an external actor is vitally concerned with the outcome of the war. This is not a new phenomenon, but a rediscovered one. The two "civil wars" that the United States has fought provide ample proof of the international relevance of civil wars. During the American Revolution (a civil war in the sense that British subjects were fighting for their independence from British rule), France helped the revolutionaries because of a French desire to weaken the British Empire. Poles and Germans also came to the aid of the North Americans on an individual basis because of their support for the ideals that the revolution espoused. During the War Between the States, Great Britain lent support to the South, primarily because Britain saw its economic interests tied more closely to Southern cotton and timber than to Northern industry.

During the twentieth century, ideology, economics, power, and religion have internationalized virtually every civil war. The Russian Civil War saw British, French, American, and Japanese intervention. The Spanish Civil War included elements from Italy, Germany, France, Great Britain, the Soviet Union, and the United States. The Chinese Revolution also was internationalized. During the Cold War, internal conflicts without fail were analyzed by Washington and Moscow on the basis of which side was more "democratic" or more "procommunist." Even during the height of East–West detente, the Angolan Civil War, the Ethiopian conflicts, and the racial strife in Zimbabwe, all of which began as civil wars, rapidly took on significant international import. The United States often interpreted Latin American events in light of their East–West implications. The Nicaraguan, Grenadan, and El Salvadoran situations, to Washington, presented a threat of communist penetration of the western hemisphere, and the frequent government changes in Bolivia and Peru caused consternation in Washington and elsewhere whenever a too radical public policy line was adopted by the new government.

Since the end of the Cold War, several "old" civil wars that once were interpreted in East–West terms have continued, such as the conflicts in Afghanistan, Angola, and Cambodia. Several "new" civil wars have broken out as well, as in Somalia and Yugoslavia. In all of these cases—and others as well—there was a significant international component. A civil war contained solely within the confines of one state, it would seem, is nearly impossible in the late twentieth century. All civil wars, in Pierre Hassner's term, have become potential "International Civil Wars."[11]

Civil wars occupy a curious place in any typology of wars and violence. On the one hand they are quite often destructive. One study concluded that 10 of the 13 "most deadly conflicts" of the nineteenth and twentieth centuries were civil wars.[12] Because of their inordinate violence, civil wars have been condemned as needless and senseless destroyers of life and treasure. Advocates of "evolution, not revolution" base their arguments on a solid body of evidence as to the destructiveness of even limited civil war. On the other hand, civil wars have been defended as the last recourse of action against corrupt, outdated, or unyielding social systems and governments. The American, French, Russian, Chinese, Cuban, and other revolutions all have been defended on exactly these grounds— the entrenched order refused to permit orderly change, and the violence of civil war and revolution was the only recourse available.

International War

International war is conflict between or among states carried out by their armed forces.[13] It is an accepted form of conducting relations between and among states, and has been accepted by international law as an inevitable if not desirable element of state interaction. It is distinct from low-intensity conflict only in its level of violence. However, in some cases this may be misleading. "The Phony War" period of World War II, for example, was a period of extremely low-

As recently as the late 1980s, Yugoslavia was a country where Bosnian Moslems, Croats, Serbs, and Slovenes lived with each other in peace. Civil war erupted there in the 1990s, leading to thousands of deaths and immense destruction, such as this mosque in Bosnia. (Sygma.)

intensity conflict as each side prepared for battle, and yet it was also a period of war inasmuch as Great Britain and France had declared war on Germany, and vice versa. Conversely, the Korean conflict was officially labeled a "police action" by the United States and the United Nations despite its extreme level of death and destruction; it was a war in everything but name.

For our typology, all declared wars and all periods of extensive military engagement between and among states even if not declared as war will be considered war. A state may have a number of reasons for not declaring a major military conflict a war. A declaration of war may break treaties a state is committed to, prove constitutionally illegal or politically unpopular within the initiating belligerent state, reduce or eliminate the element of military surprise, draw forth neutrality and neutrality regulations from other states, or widen rather than localize a conflict. If one examines those military confrontations fought by the major world powers since World War I, it is startling how seldom war was declared. Instead, terms such as intervention, reprisal, embargo, pacification, blockade, and police action were all used as euphemisms to describe military conflicts as diverse as the Japanese campaign against China between 1931 and 1941, the Soviet actions in Afghanistan between 1979 and 1989, the U.S. involvement in Vietnam between 1965 and 1973, and the Chinese and Indian border conflict of 1962. Although none were formally declared wars, they all must be viewed as wars.

Similarly, at least in theory, wars may be "just" or "unjust." Humanity has long struggled with the question of what constitutes a just war. Plato thought that just wars were those fought for the benefit of the state and that war against non-

Greeks was acceptable regardless of purpose. Aristotle accepted three types of wars as just—wars of self-defense, wars to control others for their own benefit, and wars against peoples that deserved to be enslaved. Early Christianity rejected all wars as unjust, but gradually changed its viewpoint as it became the state religion of many European courts. Following the 1648 Treaty of Westphalia, war increasingly was regarded as the right of all states, and questions about the "justness" or "unjustness" of war gradually were relegated to the background.

The twentieth century has witnessed a resurgence in interest over the distinction between just and unjust wars. A major reason for the increased interest is the destructiveness of modern weapons and the inability of those weapons (or more accurately, the users of those weapons) to discriminate between military and civilian personnel and targets. The Covenant of the League of Nations and the United Nations Charter both include efforts to allow states to judge whether an international conflict is just or unjust, and the Tokyo and Nuremburg trials at the end of World War II both attempted to define "just" and "unjust" actions by individuals and states during war. In 1983, Catholic bishops in the United States concluded that any use of nuclear weapons was unjust. Nevertheless, no consensus has been reached as to the definition of just and unjust wars.

TOWARD PEACE AND STABILITY

This chapter has examined disagreements over the causes of war and violence, and analyzed disputes over how best to categorize war and violence. Issues of war and international violence are clearly complex. But given the urgency of the matter, humankind must be more successful than ever before in finding solutions to the problems posed by war and international violence. The costs of failure are increasing almost daily.

Unfortunately, however, such solutions remain elusive. Agreement on how to assure a just, lasting, and stable peace is as remote as agreement on what causes war and violence. Some prescriptions predict peace through purchase of more arms, whereas others advocate arms limitation and disarmament measures. One school of thought maintains that peace can be attained only if a balance of power exists between potentially hostile forces. World order through a world state has its advocates, too, as does world peace through world law. St. Augustine, Spinoza, Niebuhr, and Krishna all prescribed religion in one form or another as an antidote to the problem of war and violence. Others assert that equitable distribution of wealth will lessen the tendency toward war and violence, whereas Marx, Kant, and Wilson all believed that a particular type of social structure within states would lessen human willingness to visit death and destruction on fellow human beings.

A **world state** is one of the more enticing prescriptions for world peace. If an international organization such as the United Nations were given authority over global affairs, and were also given the ability to enforce that authority, it is sometimes argued that war and violence would be curtailed, regardless of cause. A world government would theoretically be able to prevent human flaws (if those are the causes of war) from leading to conflict and would eliminate international anarchy (if that is the cause of war). Global standards of equity and justice could also be enforced, as could global standards of perception. In many respects, a world state appears an ideal solution to the problems posed by war and violence.

But many problems exist with such a solution. Aside from the obvious difficulty of how states can be persuaded to renounce their sovereignty and the independence of action that it affords them, no guarantee exists that war and violence will be eliminated by a world government. Since World War II, it will be remembered, over 85 percent of all wars were civil wars. Governments of states in today's world have clearly shown their inability to eliminate domestic strife; why would a world state be any different?

Advocates of world peace through a world state or world law also often assume that a global order of either type would find most people willing to accept international law and that those who would not accept it would be easily and readily apprehended. This again may not be the case. Again using current states as examples, what guarantee is there under a world state or world law that a lawbreaker would, for example, resign his office as Richard Nixon did? Is not the Indian experience equally plausible? In India, when a court ruled that Prime Minister Indira Gandhi had violated election laws and requested that she resign, she refused, and imprisoned her opposition.

Even with a global state or world law, it appears that some degree of coercive capability would be needed to assure peace. Again, one must ask how states are to be made willing to yield their coercive capabilities to the proposed world order, particularly given the animosities that exist among states. Although the experience of the European Community gives some hope, it is a limited hope.

Many globalist proposals to reduce or eliminate the incidence of war and violence also carry with them the distinct risk of increasing the probability of war and violence as attempts are made to implement them. Barring a tidal change in human attitudes, efforts to establish a world government to assure peace almost certainly would engender armed conflict and hostility. On an equally pessimistic note, efforts on the state level to assure peace may also send incorrect signals to potential enemies. Extreme emphasis on arms control and disarmament may signal a collapse of will as much as a desire for peace, and thereby lead to war. Conversely, a military buildup undertaken to deter may appear as preparation for attack, and thereby invite preemption. Whether one examines globally-oriented proposals or state-oriented proposals to limit war and violence, no guarantees exist for success.

Nevertheless, the search for reliable methods to assure peace continues. Often, this pursuit of peace proceeds on several tracks simultaneously and seemingly contradictorily. In many cases, these contradictions may be less real than apparent. Advocates of military preparedness and disarmament may be equally committed to the pursuit of peace; they simply have different views on how it can be achieved. Military preparedness advocates argue that if one wants peace, one must prepare for war; disarmament advocates maintain that the chances for peace are diminished by the existence of arms and weapons. Similarly, both balance of power proponents and world government proponents desire reduced international conflict; they simply disagree on how best to achieve it. Balance of power proponents see a match of countervailing capabilities as the best guarantee of peace; world government advocates rest their hopes for peace on the creation of a transnational body that will overcome petty parochial disagreements and enforce peace.

At one time, globalists hoped that the United Nations would be the foundation for a world government. Shown here is United Nations headquarters in New York City.   (United Nations Photo.)

Peace and stability, then, remain elusive goals. World order, whatever its form, is no nearer a reality now than it was at the beginning of the century. With the proliferation of international actors and the breakdown of bipolarity, one may argue it is further from reality now than earlier. Nevertheless, the search for peace and stability continues. As long as the search continues, there is reason for optimism that humankind may someday successfully meet the challenges raised by war, peace, and violence.

KEY TERMS AND CONCEPTS

neither war nor peace
causes of international conflict
international crises
crises management
low-intensity conflict

terrorism
civil war and revolution
international war
world state

NOTES

1. *The Bhagavad Gita* (New York: Penguin Books, 1962), pp. 43–47.
2. In 1918, Leon Trotsky proclaimed that a condition of "neither war nor peace" existed between Germany and the new Bolshevik government of Russia. After some hesitation, Germany attacked Bolshevik Russia despite Trotsky's slogan, and the Bolsheviks were forced to accept the humiliating Treaty of Brest-Litovsk.
3. For another set of views on the causes of war, see Greg Cashman, *What Causes War? An Introduction to Theories of International Conflict* (New York: Lexington Books, 1993).
4. Quincy Wright, *A Study of War* (Chicago: University of Chicago Press, 1942).
5. Ruth Leger Sivard, *World Military and Social Expenditures 1979* (Leesburg, VA: World Priorities, 1979).
6. For varied discussions of crises, see Charles F. Hermann (ed.), *International Crises* (New York: The Free Press, 1972); and Richard Ned Lebow, *Between Peace and War: The Nature of Individual Crisis* (Baltimore: Johns Hopkins University Press, 1981).
7. See Gerald W. Hopple, Paul J. Rossa, and Jonathan Wilkenfeld, "Threats and Foreign Policy: The Overt Behavior of States in Conflict," and Robert B. Mahoney, Jr., and Richard P. Clayberg, "Images and Threats: Soviet Perceptions of International Crises, 1946–1975," both in Patrick J. McGowan and Charles W. Kegley, Jr. (eds.), *Threats, Weapons, and Foreign Policy* (Beverly Hills, CA: Sage, 1980), pp. 19–53, 55–81, respectively.
8. According to John Foster Dulles, brinkmanship was "the ability to get to the verge without getting into the war . . . if you are scared to go to the brink you are lost." See James Shepley, "How Dulles Averted War," *Life*, January 16, 1956, p. 70.
9. For a further discussion of "crisis management," see A. N. Gilbert and P. G. Lauren, "Crisis Management: An Assessment and Critique," *Journal of Conflict Resolution*, Vol. 24 (December 1980): 641–682.
10. Wright's *A Study of War* contains the data on traditional wars, whereas the "internal antiregime" and "internal tribal" data are from Istvan Kende, "Wars of Ten Years (1967–1976)," *Journal of Peace Research* Vol. 15 (1978): 227–241. See also William Eckhardt and Edward Azar, "Major World Conflicts and Interventions, 1945 to 1975," *International Interactions*, Vol. 5 (1978): 75–110; Evan Luard, *Conflict and Peace in the Modern International System* (Boston: Little, Brown, 1968); Melvin Small and J. David Singer, "Conflicts in the International System, 1816–1977; Historical Trends and Policy Futures," in Charles W. Kegley, Jr. and Patrick J. McGowan (eds.), *Challenges to America* (Beverly Hills, CA: Sage, 1979), pp. 89–115; and Melvin Small and J. David Singer, *Resort to Arms: International and Civil Wars, 1816–1980* (Beverly Hills, CA: Sage, 1982).
11. Pierre Hassner, "Civil Violence and the Pattern of International Power," *Adelphi Papers No. 83* (London: IISS, 1971), p. 19.
12. Ted Robert Gurr, *Why Men Rebel* (Princeton: Princeton University Press, 1970).
13. For a more detailed definition, see Wright, *A Study of War*, pp. 8–13.

CHAPTER 25

Conflicts of Values

- Why do conflicts of values cause international strife?
- What happens when some countries value individual freedom and others value collective rights?
- How do material values and spiritual values lead to international conflict?
- Must conflict between modernization and traditionalism, and between centralization and decentralization, necessarily cause international problems?
- Can the conflict between political democracy and political authoritarianism/totalitarianism be resolved?
- What happens when people disagree on fundamental moral values?

The diversity of the world's assorted languages, societies, lifestyles, foods, and music is often praised as one of the most valuable and worthwhile assets of humanity. Few would deny that the overall quality of human life is greatly enhanced by this variety. Nevertheless, despite the advantages the world community derives from diversity, that diversity is sometimes the source of considerable hostility and disagreement. This is particularly true when international diversity includes differences in the value systems that prevail within and between individual actors. Several of the major clashes between value systems in the international arena have already been discussed in some detail: capitalism versus communism, one national viewpoint versus another, debates over the global standard of living, issues of war and peace and violence, and others. However, a number of other major conflicts of values in the international arena have not yet been discussed. Indeed, in many introductory international relations texts they are ignored. This is unfortunate, in that many of the less discussed international conflicts of values play prominent roles in shaping the current and future world.

In this chapter, six of the most prominent global conflicts of values are discussed: individualism versus collectivism, materialism versus spiritualism, modernization versus traditionalism, centralization versus decentralization, political democracy versus political authoritarianism/totalitarianism, and moral value versus opposed moral value. Often these conflicts are closely interrelated. For example, in Western Europe, Japan, and the United States, individualism and materialism are closely related, whereas in the former Soviet Union, Eastern Europe, and China, until recently, collectivism and materialism were closely connected. Certain forms of collectivism may also be categorized as traditionalist, as in many African states, whereas other forms of collectivism are termed modernist, as in China. Similarly, spiritualism and traditionalism are often equated in Christian, Islamic, Buddhist, and Hindu societies, whereas materialism is viewed as a force of modernization. Decentralization and individualism are also often considered to be integrally related, as are centralization and collectivism. However, despite these and other interrelationships, this chapter examines each of the six major conflicts of values individually.

INDIVIDUALISM VERSUS COLLECTIVISM

Throughout the many human societies, tensions exist between value systems that emphasize the responsibility of individuals to themselves, and those that emphasize the responsibility of the individual to society. In simplistic terms, this tension may be described as the conflict between individualism and collectivism. Throughout the world, in developed and developing states alike, tensions exist between these two opposed concepts of value, often with important ramifications for the conduct of international relations.

The conflict between individualism and collectivism takes many forms. Throughout most of the post–World War II period, East–West rivalry, with the East emphasizing collectivism and the West individualism, was perhaps the most celebrated. That conflict pitted the West's emphasis on self against the East's emphasis on society. In the context of the East–West struggle, this was an ideologically derived conflict.

Beyond the East–West clash over individualism and collectivism, other aspects of the conflict between individualism and collectivization have important ramifications for international affairs. In a certain sense, the struggle to impose some form of world order on the anarchic international system may also be viewed as a form of conflict between individualism and collectivism. State actors, seeking to protect their individual claims to national sovereignty and independence, have been historically unwilling to subordinate their individual desires and actions to the needs of the broader global community. International governmental organizations such as the United Nations, to their chagrin, have discovered this on regular occasions. But conflict between individualism and collectivism need not exist only at the international system level to have an international impact. State and nonstate actors throughout the world find themselves torn by internal tensions between individualism and collectivism. Only rarely have international actors achieved an apparent internal balance between collectivism and individualism, with Japan being perhaps the best example.

Developing World states are often caught in the individualism/collectivism clash. In the traditionalist societies of many Developing World states, life revolves around a collective body. In some cases that body is the tribe or village; in other cases it is the extended family. In all cases, however, the desires of individuals, as well as their rights and needs, are subordinate to the interests of the collective. Often, rigid formal or informal rules and customs have been developed to assure primacy of the collective. In societies such as these, Western conceptions of individualism often have little relevance. This has portentous implications for Western relations with Developing World states.

But traditional societies are breaking down, succumbing to pressures of urbanization and development. Together, urbanization and development disrupt traditional collective societies by challenging or rejecting old rules and customs and by weakening or destroying links within the collective. Within many Developing World states, masses of the population are adrift, their old traditional collective attitudes disrupted and replaced by little or nothing.

Developing World governments have reacted to this phenomenon in various ways. Some, such as Tanzania, Nigeria, and Ghana, have sought to transfer the old uprooted traditionalist collective consciousness to the state, thereby developing what may be termed a "new national collectivism." Such efforts continue, but to date have yielded limited success. A few states such as Kenya and Sri Lanka have attempted to instill a degree of Westernized individualism, at least within their urban populations. Their success has also been slight. Other states like Cambodia and Iran have tried to reinculcate old collective values, often agrarian in form. The Cambodian effort resulted in what some observers regarded as genocide, and the Iranian effort remains embroiled in strife. Most Developing World governments followed a fourth pattern and appeared unsure what steps, if any, to take concerning the contradictions between individualism and collectivism.

Developing World states are not alone in their quandary. In the industrialized West, with its emphasis on individualism, concern is often expressed that excessive individualism may undermine the societal cooperation that is so necessary in an industrialized society. Although few advocate an abandonment of individualism, many believe that more social consciousness, that is, a greater sense of collectivism, must eventuate if Western societies are to overcome the challenges that confront them. Collectivism is rarely held up as a model in industrialized Western states, but its ideal of social cooperation is often praised.

In the pre-1989 communist world, collectivism was the idealized objective of the various governments, but among the populations, considerable sentiment existed for individual fulfillment and identity. A large number of youth in Eastern Europe asserted their individualism through Westernized dress and manner, and the former Soviet Union's *stilyagi* (Soviet youth who adopted "stylish" Western patterns of dress and action) offered a more subdued version of Western individualism. Soviet and Eastern European governments condemned these displays of individualism as "decadent" and "antisocial," but despite government condemnations—and in some cases, more severe penalties—the displays continued.

The depth of rejection of collectivism as a value in the former Soviet Union and Eastern Europe became increasingly apparent in the late 1980s and early 1990s as revolution and change swept these countries. Individualistic social, political, and economic behavior became increasingly accepted and increasingly apparent. The collapse of communism in Eastern Europe and the U.S.S.R. accelerated this trend.

But even in Eastern Europe and the former Soviet Union, the collapse of communism did not eliminate collectivism. And in many other countries throughout the world, collectivist values continue to either hold sway or play an important role. Indeed, conflicts between individualism and collectivism remain in most societies. These conflicts have been sources of both mistrust and animosity among international actors, and tension and instability within particular actors. Aside from the other nationalistic and ideological baggage included in the

East–West conflict, the governments on both sides fundamentally disagreed on the value of individualism and the value of collectivism. Individuals on both sides of the East–West boundary, however, identified elements of attraction in the value that the other side espoused. Not surprisingly, the governments on each side often viewed those individuals as threats to the dominant internal value system. Thus, before Gorbachev, ideologues on both sides of the East–West boundary saw internal and external threats to their own existence, and in a certain sense, they were correct.

But what of the Developing World? In many respects, the impact of the conflict between individualism and collectivism in the Developing World has had an even more profound impact on the Developing World's international role. Although Developing World states may individually be deciding whether to cast their lots with individualism or collectivism, or to follow their own line of thought to resolve the individual/collective dilemma, they are at the same time seeking to establish their own internal identities, called into question by the disruption of their traditional collective societies. With their traditional collective heritages disrupted, a natural response to that disruption may in many cases be an effort to institutionalize an allegedly "modern" version of collectivism—socialism or communism. In a certain sense, developing societies may therefore be predisposed to adopt a more socialistic, that is, collectivist, social organization than the West would prefer.

This observation is far from an ironclad rule, but it is sufficiently valid to argue that some Western disagreements with Developing World states are in part the result of a clash in values—individualism versus collectivism—as well as products of the colonial past, outside subversion, and disparities in wealth. Although empirical proof for this line of reasoning is difficult to provide, it does merit careful consideration by policy-makers and students alike.

MATERIALISM VERSUS SPIRITUALISM

Like the conflict between individualism and collectivism, the conflict between materialism and spiritualism is global in scope and affects internal and external dimensions of international actors. In Iran, Ayatollah Khomeini condemned U.S. capitalism, Soviet communism, the shah's modernism, and most of the rest of the Islamic world's version of Islam as perversions of the true spiritualism of Allah. In the United States, Ronald Reagan reached back to the Cold War rhetoric of the 1950s to chastise "Godless communism," even while critics in the Developing World, and in the United States and Western Europe as well, criticized the U.S. for being too materialistic. Several Developing World states such as Zambia and Tanzania that had opted for collective approaches to societal organization also stressed a need to remember spiritual values.

Materialism had its proponents as well. Marxist states throughout the world, including China, continued to stress materialism as the preferred value. Even in these societies, however, the old Marxist mandate that spiritualism in general and religion in particular were nothing more than the "opiate of the proletariat" and therefore to be shunned was increasingly abandoned as spiritual values and religious beliefs became more acceptable in the early 1990s. Meanwhile, some Developing World states, Angola and Mozambique included, emphasized materialism at the expense of spiritualism, although no economic improvement resulted. And in the United States and Western Europe, materialism remained the dominant feature of life for many.

How does the conflict between materialism and spiritualism affect international relations? The East–West struggle again provides a useful example. U.S. criticism of Soviet materialism did little to raise Soviet ire against the United States; the Soviets probably viewed such criticisms as compliments. U.S. criticisms of Soviet materialism, however, raised in some quarters U.S. consciousness of the differences between the two systems, and therefore made a Soviet-U.S. modus vivendi more difficult to arrange. This same observation applied to Soviet criticism of spiritual values in the West and elsewhere. Although spiritually oriented and religiously oriented people regarded such criticisms as compliments, Soviet attacks on religious and spiritual values raised consciousness of intersystemic differences. These observations should be regarded neither as supportive of nor opposed to U.S. or Soviet pronouncements on materialism and spiritualism.

Probably the best and most poignant recent examples of the impact of the conflict between materialism and spiritualism on international relations are events of the late 1970s and throughout the 1980s in Iran. Here, an ascetic fundamentalist Muslim cleric, exiled from his home country for his criticisms both of his government's blatant materialism, and its modernization program (we will return to this aspect later), appealed to Allah's higher authority to restore Iran to a straight and narrow Islamic path. While factors additional to Khomeini's spiritualism were also at work, the Iranian people accepted Ayatollah Khomeini's arguments, overthrew the shah, and brought Khomeini to power. Although Khomeini's actions while in power left many both inside and outside Iran uncertain about the sincerity of his spiritualist appeals, no doubt existed that the inherent conflict between materialism and spiritualism was manipulated brilliantly by Khomeini and his lieutenants in their pursuit of political power. The impact of the success of their spiritual appeal was immense—ruptured U.S.-Iranian relations, the hostage crisis, an abortive rescue mission, possibly the Soviet invasion of Afghanistan, the seizure of the Great Mosque in Mecca, the Iran-Iraq War, and worsened U.S.-Western European relations, to name but a few. Accuracy dictates pointing out that the conflict between materialism and spiritualism was not the only cause of these events, but had the shah's government not fallen to Khomeini's spiritual appeal, the course of events in Southwest Asia would doubtless have been considerably different.

Without doubt, the late twentieth century has witnessed a resurgence of the role of spiritualism and religion in the international community. The self-immolation of Buddhist monks in South Vietnam sent searing images of the meaning of religious commitment to materialistic Americans in particular, and less than 30 years later the Catholic Church played significant roles in bringing down a communist government in Poland and challenging a right-wing government in El Salvador. Khomeini's Islamic revival has already been discussed, but even it is only a part of a broader global resurgence of Islamic vitality. In the United States, the spiritual revival manifested itself during the late 1970s and 1980s in the conservative politics of the Moral Majority; in Europe, many of the clergy used their spiritual appeal to lend weight to their support of nuclear disarmament. In the United States, Catholic bishops also threw their weight behind

the antinuclear movement, maintaining that no Christian could support the annihilation of humanity. And with revolution sweeping the U.S.S.R. and Eastern
Europe, many observers noted increased interest in religion and greater atten-
dance at churches. Indeed, in 1990, the Soviet government granted freedom of
religion, a freedom which continued in Russia and most of the other newly independent former Soviet republics.

During the 1980s, then, searches for and adherence to spiritual values grew
noticeably. There is nothing to indicate that this trend will dissipate in the 1990s.
The implications of this trend for international relations are several. Appeals to
higher moral authority were used on several occasions during the 1980s to justify
wars, to support calls for peace and disarmament, and to legitimize demands for
alternate economic systems and pleas for more equitable social orders. In many
cases, spiritual and religious explanations were also used to justify traditionalist
positions in struggles against modernization. Every one of these phenomena has
already appeared in the 1990s as well.

Thus, the struggle between materialism and spiritualism continues. In many
societies, materialism remains or is becoming the dominant force, but in others,
spiritual values are gaining strength and becoming dominant. As we near the year
2000, the potential for conflict between materialist and spiritualist values remains
high. If present trends continue, the potential for conflict will increase.

MODERNIZATION VERSUS TRADITIONALISM

The conflict between modernization and traditionalism takes on many faces and
has many impacts in contemporary international affairs. In Poland before 1989,
the Catholic Church defended what it considered traditional Polish respect for
church, family, and state, and often found itself in conflict with the Polish
Communist Party, which viewed itself as a force for modernization. The implications of this church/party conflict—which may be viewed as either a moderniza-
tion/traditionalism struggle or as a materialist/spiritualist conflict—extended far
beyond Poland to Moscow, Washington, and the Vatican. In Japan, proponents of
traditional Japanese customs and values decry the Westernization that has sped
forward throughout society. Old customs and values have been lost, they say, and
disservice to Japan's heritage has been committed. Other Japanese argue that the
post–World War II Japanese economic miracle would have been impossible had
not forces of modernization swept aside old Japanese traditions. The fact that
modernists retain the upper hand in Japan has had tremendous importance for
international economic affairs, at least if their explanation of the cause of Japan's
economic successes is accurate. And in other states along the Asian periphery, in
the Philippines, Indonesia, Singapore, Malaysia, and Hong Kong, governments in
the 1980s had either restricted or banned the use of video games because, as one
Malaysian newspaper said, "video games [were destroying] traditional games and
children (were) no longer interested in flying kites or top spinning." In 1986,
Burma banned rock music and Malaysia outlawed public kissing because they
undermined traditional values. And in 1990, the Malaysian government refused
to allow LaToya Jackson to give a concert in Kuala Lumpur, the capital city,
because her songs "promote values alien to Malaysian traditions."[1]

Obviously, modernization and traditionalism as concepts have several meanings. Modernization may mean "progressive" change; it does not necessarily mean change alone. On many occasions, modernization implies opposition to entrenched religion, if only because religion often defends traditional values. In preindustrialized societies, modernization is regularly defined as the series of processes that lead to industrialization, whereas in industrialized societies, it is often viewed as the introduction of state-of-the-art productive capabilities or the transformation of society from an industrial to a postindustrial phase.

By contrast, traditionalism may best be defined as the desire to maintain values, customs, mores, and living patterns that have been established over time. Traditions usually take centuries to develop, although sometimes their history is much shorter. Many Jewish traditions, for example, are twenty or more centuries old; by comparison, the U.S. tradition of two political parties is barely two centuries old. At the short-term end of the scale, cartoons on Saturday morning and college football on a fall Saturday afternoon are verging on becoming U.S. traditions, although a purist would argue that both phenomena are much too recent to be called traditions.

In its more extreme forms, traditionalism dictates continuation of the past. Extreme traditionalism is therefore unalterably opposed to all forms of modernization simply because modernization may challenge or change established societal values, relationships, and patterns of behavior. "Conservative" governments that seek to maintain established values may therefore find themselves in conflict with other segments of society that seek change. Ethiopia's Haile Selassie opposed modernization in Ethiopia, and found opposition to his rule steadily mounting. Eventually, he was driven from his throne by forces that labeled themselves "modernists." China's Sun Yat-sen led modernist forces against traditional

The conflict between modernization and traditionalism is frequently strong and sometimes violent, but sometimes old and new can coexist in harmony. Here, modern conveyances meet traditional garb in Lahore, Pakistan.   (U.N. Photo/Viviane Holbrooke.)

Chinese society and unleashed a revolution that continues today. In Africa, Julius Nyerere sought to create a modern state by transferring the traditional collectivist attitude of the Tanzanian citizenry from the tribes to the newly created government in Dar es Salaam.

Governments that emphasize modernization find themselves in conflict with traditional elements of their own societies. Khomeini's opposition to the shah stemmed not only from conflict between Khomeini's spiritualism and the shah's materialism, but also from conflict between their visions of what Iran's future should be. To the shah, the Iran of 2000 would be a modern, Westernized, industrial state. To Khomeini, the Iran of 2000 would be a traditional, fundamentalist Islamic state. Similarly, in Cambodia, Pol Pot's opposition to Lon Nol's government was a product not only of ideological antipathy, but also of Pol Pot's desire to return Cambodia to its rural agrarian past. Lon Nol, by comparison, accepted Westernization and urbanization.[2] Traditionalism and modernization were again in conflict.

Some states have sought to balance pressures for adherence to traditional values, relationships, and patterns of behavior with policies of modernization in industry and other sectors of society. Saudi Arabia is perhaps the leading example of those states that have attempted to balance traditionalist/modernist tendencies in this way. The future of the Saudi and other similar experiments is not certain.

In most cases, the conflict between traditionalism and modernization has greatest impact within a state. But the conflict can and does have at least two types of relevance for international relations as well. First, when transnational religious, ideological, or other movements assume for themselves the mantle of traditionalism or modernization, the international community is immediately affected. Thus, the Islamic revival—and not only Khomeini's version of it—supports traditional values, relationships, and patterns of behavior and is therefore a force that all Islamic states must reckon with. Similarly, for decades, Marxism purported to be a force for modernization, given its claim to be a higher form of social organization. Therefore, states wishing to "modernize" sometimes looked to Marxism or one of its variants.

Second, the conflict between traditionalism and modernization has relevance for international relations when traditional/modernization struggles within a state affect external actors. This occurs often. Indeed, every example used in this section falls within this category, with the two exceptions of Southeast Asian attitudes toward video games and U.S. views of cartoons and football. In Poland, Japan, Israel, the United States, Ethiopia, China, Tanzania, Iran, Cambodia, and Russia alike, domestic tensions between traditionalist and modernist forces spill into the international community. Some are more explosive and more important than others, but they cannot be overlooked as conficts that help shape contemporary international affairs.

CENTRALIZATION VERSUS DECENTRALIZATION

In most cases, international actors have developed internal organizational structures to enable them better to make and implement policy decisions. States have their governments, multinational corporations have their corporate organizations, and intergovernmental organizations have their own structural forms. Nongovernmental organizations usually have internal decision-making and policy-implementing structures as well. However, despite the diversity of internal organization in all these actors, a common issue confronts all: How much authority should be concentrated in a single central location, and how much should be dispersed to secondary and tertiary sites?

Many arguments have been advanced to defend both centralization and decentralization. Advocates of centralization argue that more efficient decision-making and policy-implementation can be achieved if authority is concentrated. If need be, decisions can be reached quickly, and policy can be implemented with fewer people working at cross-purposes. Under a centralized regime, international actors can more readily function as a single unit, thereby displaying unity of purposes and allowing pursuit of a single goal. Centralization also frustrates any tendencies toward actor fragmentation, or so centralization proponents assert.

Advocates of decentralization counter with the argument that decentralization is more democratic because it brings more people into the decision-making and policy-implementing processes, thereby frustrating the potential for dictatorship and/or authoritarianism that centralization carries with it. Moreover, decentralization advocates argue, expanding the number involved in the decision-making process multiplies the perspectives from which an issue is viewed, thereby minimizing the possibility of a decision-making error. Proponents of decentralization concede that their preferred system is less efficient than a centralized one, but maintain that the advantages their preference carries with it outweigh its decreased efficiency. In addition, decentralization enhances the probability of grass-roots support for a particular decision because more people are involved in arriving at that decision.

Clearly, many of the arguments advanced by both centralists and decentralists are diametrically opposed and rest on considerably different sets of assumptions and expectations. Generally speaking, centralists value efficiency more than do advocates of decentralization. Similarly, decentralists fear dictatorship more than do advocates of centralization. Proponents of both schools of thought have numerous historical examples to prove the superiority of their preferred model. Centralists may point to Stalin and his ability to rally the Soviet people to the anti-Nazi cause as proof of the advantages of centralized authority; conversely, decentralists may point to the national consensus of the American people that built slowly but relentlessly in support of Great Britain during 1940 and 1941 as proof that a less centralized system has certain advantages.

The clarity of the debate between advocates of centralization and advocates of decentralization is often clouded by the fact that defenders of both positions may seek nothing more than to strengthen their own positions. Some centralization–decentralization debates are therefore more related to questions of power than of value. It should also be evident that when centralization and decentralization are at issue, two extremes on a spectrum are being discussed. Many degrees of difference exist between those two extremes. Indeed, it is doubtful whether a totally centralized or a totally decentralized system ever existed. Nevertheless, as concepts, the impact on international affairs of the conflict between centralization and decentralization is considerable. Generally, that impact is more evident within actors than between them.

At the level of the state, many separatist movements interpret alleged usurpation of authority by a central government as a primary cause of their struggle for autonomy. Many separatists maintain that the central government that they oppose has taken decision-making powers unto itself; separatists therefore claim that they are seeking a return of centralized power to local authorities. Thus, a struggle between centralization and decentralization is joined.

And it is a struggle that is joined on every inhabited continent in the world. French-speaking Canadians in Quebec decry the control that Ottawa has over their lives, even as Western Australians argue for fewer rules and regulations from Canberra. Basque separatists threaten to assassinate the pope to make known their displeasure with Madrid's rule, and Eritreans fight the armies of whoever controls the seat of government in Addis Ababa. In both India and Brazil, state governors make known their opposition to the powers wielded in New Delhi and Brasilia. And demands for sovereignty on the part of Latvia, Lithuania, Russia, Estonia, Georgia, and other Soviet republics in the late 1980s and early 1990s tore the U.S.S.R. apart. Similar demands for sovereignty and independence on the parts of different ethnic groups in Yugoslavia and Czechoslovakia also led to the dissolution of those countries. Obviously, when the conflict between advocates of centralization and decentralization becomes severe, the internal stability of a state may be destroyed, often with international ramifications.

Debates over the proper degree of centralization and decentralization also take place in transnational political and religious movements. Such debates may play a significant role in shattering the unity of those movements. Soviet insistence that only the Communist party of the Soviet Union could provide accurate ideological guidance to the world communist movement was one of the factors that alienated the Chinese, Yugoslav, and Albanian Communist parties. Although the CPSU eventually accepted the inevitability of decentralized decision making in the international communist movement by recognizing "national paths to communism," its recognition came too late to repair the damage done by what was essentially a debate over degree of centralization. Interestingly, the CPSU's 1990 abandonment of its insistence on its own monopoly of political power also came too late for the CPSU to maintain its legitimacy as a political party within the U.S.S.R.

IGOs, MNCs, NGOs, and other international actors are not immune to conflicts over centralization and decentralization. Should the UN Secretariat strictly oversee the operations of UN field operations? If it does, rapid response to changing needs in the field may be stifled. If it does not, individual field operations may be directed to purposes other than those for which they were intended. Should IBM run its foreign subsidiaries from corporate headquarters? If it does, individual initiative within the subsidiary structure may be reduced, but if it does not, subsidiary managers, not knowing the global picture of operations, may undertake actions not in the company's overall economic interest. The centralization/decentralization question may be most critical for NGOs. As essentially voluntary organizations, too much decentralization could lead to the dissolution of an NGO. Paradoxically, too much centralization could have the same effect.

POLITICAL DEMOCRACY VERSUS POLITICAL AUTHORITARIANISM/TOTALITARIANISM

In some respects, the clash between political democracy and political authoritarianism/totalitarianism is essentially a subset of the clash between centralization and decentralization.[3] As a concept, political democracy argues for a decentralized political system in which all citizens in a society have a say in decisions that affect them, whereas political authoritarianism/totalitarianism argues that only one person or a small portion of the citizens of a society, either because of birth, control of the elements of power, or an allegedly superior view of the direction in which society should be heading, should make decisions for that society. Nevertheless, despite the nature of the democracy versus authoritarianism/totalitarianism conflict as a subset of the centralization versus decentralization conflict, it is of sufficient importance in the 1990s to be examined separately here.

The democracy versus authoritarianism/totalitarianism conflict is exceedingly old, going back at least as far as the wars between Athens and Sparta in ancient Greece. More recently, much of the East–West conflict was centered around the clash between political democracy and political authoritarianism/totalitarianism. The United States and its industrialized allies claimed to be democratic, and chastised the U.S.S.R. and its allies for being authoritarian or totalitarian states controlled exclusively by a small portion of society, the Communist party. The U.S.S.R. and its allies rejected the Western charges, claiming in turn that Western political democracy was a sham and a coverup of the fact that the wealthy few dominated Western political processes. Further, Communist parties maintained that only they spoke for all the working class even though only a few of the working class were actually party members.

The collapse of communism in Eastern Europe and the Soviet Union eliminated one of the most visible clashes between political democracy and political authoritarianism/totalitarianism, but it did not mean that the conflict between political democracy and political authoritarianism/totalitarianism had ended. In China, the Communist party of China insisted on maintaining a monopoly of political power. This insistence led directly to the Tiananmen Square massacre of 1989. And in many Developing World countries, authoritarian or totalitarian regimes continued to rule.

Interestingly, however, in one Developing World region, Latin America, political democracy during the 1980s and early 1990s won victory after victory over political authoritarianism/totalitarianism. Politically democratic governments came to power via open elections in Argentina, Bolivia, Brazil, Ecuador, Guatemala, Honduras, Nicaragua, Peru, and Uruguay, whereas in Panama a government that had been voted into office via an open election but that was not allowed to assume power because of military force was eventually put into office by a U.S. military intervention. During the 1980s and early 1990s, the forces of political democracy were clearly ascendant in Latin America.

But given the serious economic problems and social cleavages that dominated the region, how long could political democracy survive there? Indeed, the same question could be asked about the new democracies that emerged from the wreckage of communist governments in Eastern Europe and the former Soviet Union as well. Although there could be no doubt that the 1980s and early 1990s witnessed a pronounced growth in strength of political democracy over political authoritarianism/totalitarianism, that growth was far from a final victory. Thus, the struggle between democracy and authoritarianism/totalitarianism, as old as recorded history, will undoubtedly continue, both within and among the various international actors.

MORAL VALUE VERSUS OPPOSED MORAL VALUE

On other occasions, conflict in national and international communities is more elemental, stemming from disagreements over what is morally right and what is morally wrong. Many white South Africans, for example, believe that they are in fact a superior race, and therefore should rule; to them, nothing was wrong with apartheid. Most of the rest of the international community disagree, believing that apartheid was morally repugnant. There can be few starker contemporary examples of opposed moral values than this.

Other examples of conflict resulting from opposed moral values abound. Until after World War II, few Europeans saw anything wrong with the imperial system. Similarly, throughout the world, authoritarian and totalitarian leaders find it completely acceptable to imprison those who disagree with them; they feel that it is a right that comes with the position. On an economic level, in many states, bribery and payoffs are accepted and acceptable ways of conducting business; the people in power there feel that nothing is wrong with these practices.

From the prevailing North American and Western European perspective of the 1990s, however, apartheid, imperialism, political imprisonment, and bribery are not acceptable. They are morally wrong. Even so, the fact remains that in some areas of the world apartheid is considered morally acceptable; imperialism is morally legitimate; political imprisonment is not a moral issue; and bribery is a way of life. These conflicts of moral value versus opposed moral value sometimes serve as a cover for other conflicts, but no analyst can deny that few universal moral standards exist.

The West itself receives its share of moral criticism from the Developing World. What right does the West have to challenge and criticize the moral values of others when people are unemployed, without adequate food, and in need of shelter even in the richest Western state? How can Western states speak of morality when Western consumers each year spend three times as much on cosmetics as their governments do on food aid and technical assistance to developing states?

Obviously, opposed moral values raise difficult questions. And the answers are even more difficult.

CONFLICTS OF VALUES AND WORLD ORDER

Assume, for a moment, that all the world's outstanding problems had somehow been solved—that population pressures and food shortages had dissipated, that all states were satisfied with their respective levels of economic development, that economic dependence and resource scarcity had been overcome, and that the problems of war and violence had been solved. Assume further that individuals and societies continued to disagree over individualism and collectivism, materialism and spiritualism, modernization and traditionalism, centralization and decentralization, political democracy and political authoritarianism/totalitarianism, and the legitimacy of opposed moral values.

How long would the idyllic world depicted above last?

The definitive answer, of course, will never be known, because such an idyllic state of world affairs will probably never exist. Nevertheless, the scenario should provide considerable food for thought. How long would a near-perfect world exist if men and women as individuals and in groups continued to have different values, different approaches to life, and different ideas about what was right and wrong? The answer, in all probability, would be, "Not long at all."

This is a chilling realization that reaffirms the oft-made assertion that humankind's technical accomplishments have outstripped its ability to deal with social relationships. But it is a realization that must be dealt with in realistic terms. The question, of course, is, what those terms will be.

Many different proposals have been advanced to enable humankind to deal more effectively with social relationships at the international level. Some proposals stress a unitary world government. Some suggest an international federalist governmental structure. Others suggest world law as a solution to international problems. Still others call for universal social justice as a prerequisite for improving our ability to live with one another.[4]

The objectives of all these proposals are laudable, but they all ignore the fundamental conflicts of values that continue to divide humankind. Is it realistic to propose a unitary world government when proponents of decentralized government remain influential throughout the world? How likely is it that any government, particularly those that are militarily or economically strong, would accept even a federated world governmental structure? What foundation exists for world law when forces of modernization oppose forces of traditionalism, and vice versa? How can universal social justice be achieved when some people advocate individualism and others collectivism? In short, given the many conflicts of values that exist in today's world, how can we move from where we are to where we want to be, when no consensus exists on where we want to be?

These are pessimistic thoughts, but they at least offer an insight to one of the major problems confronted by all forms of world order proposals: Given the diversity of human values, comprehensive global solutions to humankind's international problems stand little chance of success until greater global consensus on values exists. Building that consensus may be humanity's most important—and most challenging—future task.

KEY TERMS AND CONCEPTS

individualism	centralization
collectivism	decentralization
materialism	political democracy
spiritualism	political authoritarianism/
modernization	totalitarianism
traditionalism	conflict of moral values

NOTES

1. "An Asian Assault on Video Games," *Newsweek*, October 11, 1982, p. 38; *Atlanta Journal-Constitution*, January 19, 1986; and *The Indonesian Observer* (*Jakarta*), April 14, 1986. For other interesting articles on these and related issues, see "East

Asia Spurns West's Cultural Model," *International Herald Tribune*, July 13, 1992; and "Why Is Black Africa Overwhelmed While East Asia Overcomes?" *International Herald Tribune*, July 14, 1992.

2. See Gareth Porter and G. C. Hildebrand, *Cambodia: Starvation or Revolution* (New York: Monthly Review Press, 1978); Francois Ponchaud, *Cambodia: Year Zero* (New York: Holt, Rinehart and Winston, 1978); and Norodom Sihanouk, *War and Hope: The Case for Cambodia* (New York: Pantheon Books, 1980).

3. As used here, *authoritarianism* refers to a government that exerts extensive control over society. *Totalitarianism* refers to a government that exerts extreme control over society. These definitions may thus be viewed as different points along a continuum depicting governmental control of society. Authoritarianism at some point may therefore evolve into totalitarianism, as the government in question exerts greater and greater control over society. These views of authoritarianism and totalitarianism are fundamentally different from the views that argue that authoritarianism refers to "right-wing dictators who can be influenced to accept democratic principles," and totalitarianism refers to "communist dictators who will never accept democratic principles."

4. See Louis René Beres and Harry R. Torg, *Reordering the Planet: Constructing Alternative World Futures* (Boston: Allyn & Bacon, 1974); Howard O. Eaton (ed.), *Federation: The Coming Structure of World Government* (Norman, OK: University of Oklahoma Press, 1944); Lester R. Brown, *World without Borders* (New York: Random House, 1972); Philippe de Seynes, "Prospects for a Future Whole World," *International Organizations*, Vol. 26 (1972): 1–17; Grenville Clark and Louis B. Sohn, *World Peace through World Law* (Cambridge: Harvard University Press, 1966).

PART SIX

The Futuristic Framework

WHERE IS THE WORLD HEADING?

The question at issue is therefore the ultimate end of mankind.
—*Hegel*

Man had acquired a past, and he was beginning to grope toward a future.
—*Arthur C. Clarke*

The twentieth century has been a century of immense change for the international community. As the century opened, a few states and their empires dominated the international landscape. Today, over 180 states exist, and overseas empires are gone. Only a few decades ago, states were the sole actors of international consequence. Today, so many other types of actors exist and wield so impressive an array of capabilities that several serious observers question whether states will remain viable entities very far into the twenty-first century. Economic and military issues remain as important now as they were at the turn of the century, but they have become increasingly complicated. Economically, questions of dependence, interdependence, distribution, depletion, and development demand answers. Militarily, nuclear proliferation and increased destructiveness and availability of conventional weapons have called into question the continued political utility of military solutions to the world's problems. Even so, the frequency of violence has not diminished.

All these changes also altered the international system. As we saw in Chapter 9, the twentieth century opened with international affairs organized into a balance of power system. World War I—and the changes in international actors and their relationships that preceded and accompanied that conflict—brought the balance of power system to an end, and the international actors of the day then created an international collective security system that proved ineffective and unstable. It too ended in a global conflict. And at the end of World War II, yet another international system formed—a bipolar system—that went through various shapes and forms, but for the most part survived intact until the beginning of the 1990s.

599

Now the international community is experiencing another period of systemic change. The East–West conflict ended. Economic issues are gaining a newfound prominence as additional centers of economic power gain strength. New sets of global issues are emerging to join older transnational concerns. Old ways of looking at the world and the international community in many cases are outdated.

Can a new international system emerge without the international community resorting to global violence? What will its shape and form be, and how will it affect international actors and their interactions? How can the actors influence the shape and form of that system as it emerges?

These are difficult questions, made all the more problematic by the fact that indications are that the rapidity of change will increase as the year 2000 nears. Present-day international actors find themselves increasingly challenged. The international economic system is in turmoil. The arms race has been globalized. Scientific and technical advances have the potential to revolutionize international affairs. Conflicts of values remain as prominent, perhaps more prominent, than ever.

The impact that these and other forces will have on international affairs will be immense, and the shape that the future world will take is not yet evident. Will increased economic interdependence accelerate a trend toward world order, or will it precipitate a move toward increased protectionism? Will affordable energy and materials alternatives be found, or will energy and materials availability decrease, thereby heightening the chances of "resource wars"? Will scientific and technical breakthroughs enable the Developing World to accelerate its pace of development and reduce the North–South gap, or will the industrialized world reap most of the advantages of future advances and widen the gap still further? Will the state, today's dominant international actor, survive the challenges presented from within and without? Even more centrally, will humankind survive, given existing stockpiles of nuclear weapons and the virtual inevitability of nuclear proliferation?

Answers to these questions are at best speculation. But even so, given our understanding of the past and present international system and the forces that shaped and are shaping it, such speculation may prove useful in preparing us for change. This concluding chapter is a primer on "future shock" in the international system. Although future shock cannot be avoided, it can be prepared for, even if projections of change prove less than totally accurate. In this final chapter, we look at some of the most important issues we need to examine:

- Where is the international community heading?
- Where do we want it to go?
- How can we help it get there?

CHAPTER 26

Toward 2000 and Beyond

- What forces are changing today's international system?
- What type of international system do we want?
- How can we use forces for change to create the international system we want?

International actors rarely remain static. Neither do the systems that they help create, the perceptions that they hold, the instruments that they use, or the issues that they face. In the last 10 years alone, all have undergone major changes. Obscure actors have attained prominence, and prominent actors have become obscure. Allies have become enemies, and enemies allies. Resources increase and decrease in value, weapons change, and the world economy surges and falters. Equitable distribution of resources, economic dependence and interdependence, and nuclear proliferation and the environment have joined more traditional issues on the agenda of the international community. Indeed, the international arena is a world of change.

On occasion, these changes individually and collectively may be quite unexpected and go in directions few imagined or planned for. As aware as people were in 1941 that World War II would bring incredible change to the international arena, few predicted that events and inventions would shift the center of world power from Europe within six short years. Yet that is exactly what happened. In the early 1960s, many knowledgeable people predicted "an American century" that would rival the eras of Roman and British global dominion. Thirty years later, U.S. citizens wondered what had happened to their clear-cut economic and military preeminence. And in the first two years of the 1990s, the Soviet Union, one of the world's two superpowers, came apart at the seams, altering the world that we live in in ways that are still not completely clear. Major change can truly come rapidly and unexpectedly to the international arena.

CRITICAL AREAS OF INTERNATIONAL CHANGE

Although the exact nature of future change cannot be foretold, several critical areas of international change are evident. Each could have immense and unpredictable impact on international affairs. Here, six of the most significant areas of potential change are discussed, not with the purpose of projecting the shape of the world to come, but with the purpose of outlining possible alternative futures. The importance of such an outline is best deduced by paraphrasing management consultant Peter Drucker: Planning the future does not deal with future decisions, but with the future of present decisions.

Present-Day Actors Under Assault

This book opened with a detailed analysis of the most prominent categories of actors in the international arena: states, intergovernmental organizations, multinational corporations, nongovernmental organizations, and individuals. Although it was pointed out on several occasions throughout the opening framework, a rather startling fact may nevertheless have been overlooked: Several of the categories of actors, and even more specifically several prominent actors, are under internal and/or external assault. Although their survival may not currently be in question, their legitimacy and raison d'être are.

States provide the leading example. In most cases no longer as able to provide as much economic independence or to offer as much physical security as it has in the past, the state has seen two of its fundamental reasons for existing thrown open to question. Some states have sought to overcome their problems by adhering to supranational alliances or economic communities, whereas others seek to enhance their own military credibility or attempt to erect trade barriers. But the fundamental fact remains that the state, as Henry Kissinger said, is "inadequate" to meet many of the challenges of the late twentieth century.

Other actors realize this, and seek to turn this to their own advantages. Executives of multinational corporations promise higher living standards and eschew state protectionism. The secretariats of IGOs seek to strengthen their own organizations' positions vis-à-vis states. A variety of nongovernmental organizations, particularly national liberation movements that seek to break away from existing states and transnational movements that purport to have supranational appeal, similarly argue that the state in its present form is obsolete. They propose respectively to replace states with more localized forms of governance or with large governmental units, perhaps even a world government.

The decline and fall of the former Soviet Union deserves special mention here. Recognized as one of the primary actors in the international arena for half a century, the U.S.S.R. proved unable to cope with the combination of the need for internal political and economic reorganization and the demands by internal national movements for their own independence. Despite its global military reach, it was unable to survive as an international actor. Similarly, Yugoslavia and Czechoslovakia were also unable to survive internal ethnic, political, and economic tensions, and also dissolved as states.

What of the states of Western Europe as they unite in a continentwide economic union? Will national identities remain, or over time will a supranational identity emerge, a type of "citizen of Europe" regional mentality that will overshadow old national identities? Despite the setback that "European consciousness" received as a result of the cool reception Europeans gave the Maastricht Treaty, the possibility is there.

The state is not the only international actor under assault. Multinational corporations, viewed by their advocates as purveyors of economic plenty, are criticized by state governments, national groups, IGOs, and other NGOs alike for their perceived efforts to dominate the economies of others. Several states have taken active steps to limit activities of MNCs within their borders and to prohibit the export of profits. National groups, some of which seek independence from the state taking such action, have applauded these restrictions, as have a variety of IGOs, including the UN. NGOs, as would be expected given the variety within the category, hold disparate views.

As the most prominent IGO, the United Nations has received its fair share of criticism as well. Developing World states resent the great powers' ability to veto in the Security Council, and the United States in the 1980s evidenced similar resentment toward the General Assembly and several of its associated agencies. Indeed, in 1985 the United States ended its participation in UNESCO because of that agency's tolerance and even encouragement of criticism of U.S. and Western policies and values. Although by the 1990s many of the UN's agencies had adopted attitudes and outlooks more favorably disposed toward the United States and the West, North–South tensions still pervaded the UN, often frustrating its ability to accomplish its appointed tasks.

States, MNCs, and IGOs are thus all under assault from internal and/or external forces. None of this is to say that any category of actor or individual actor is in danger of extinction. However, it is to point out that the precarious balance of capabilities, power, influence, and importance that exists among and between these actors is by no means a given. The state will maintain its position of preeminence. Nevertheless, since few states exclusively control their own destiny, even that is a statement of faith.

The International Economic System in Turmoil

Few actors are pleased with the condition of the contemporary international economic system. Developing World states call for a New International Economic Order, claiming that the industrialized world enjoys unfair advantages under the present system. The industrialized world, itself internally riven by disputes over protectionism, dumping, and interest rates, asserts that free trade and market access would solve many of the Developing World's economic problems. Developing World states respond that this is little more than a cover for industrialized economic interests, represented primarily by MNCs, to further penetrate and dominate their economies. Meanwhile, the debt that Developing World states owe Western banking institutions mounts steadily.

International economic problems also exist between and among industrialized states, which accuse one another of enacting unfair trade laws, instituting nontariff barriers to free trade, dumping, and other practices designed to generate economic advantage. Threats of protectionism abound. And in Eastern Europe, Russia, China, and elsewhere as well, governments search for ways to attract external capital to accelerate economic growth there. Meanwhile, capital and stock markets around the world become increasingly bound together because of the ability of investors and speculators to shift funds from one location to another on virtually a moment's notice.

This turmoil and tension in the contemporary international economic system is even more striking because of the growth of global economic interdependence.

What will happen in a world where interdependence exists, but where disagreement exists over the advantages that each side derives from that interdependence? What will happen if one side believes it is overcharged for resources that it desperately needs? How will international actors react when their needs are increasingly met by uncertain external sources of supply? This is the type of world that increasingly will exist as we move toward 2000, and at least three scenarios seem probable.

First, international actors may realize that global interdependence dictates that precepts of cooperation and mutual advantage be followed. From this perspective, negotiations and discussions will gradually supplant conflict as means of resolving disputes, simply because each actor will realize its own welfare depends on the welfare of others in the international system. Indeed, the Nixon-Kissinger detente strategy of the early 1970s was substantially based on this belief. It is a strategy that has a rational appeal. If everyone is better off because of cooperation, is it not rational to cooperate? Unfortunately, however, rationality must be seen from a number of different perspectives.

Second, international actors, particularly states, may see increased interdependence as a threat to economic well-being and physical security and may seek to reduce dependence on outside sources to satisfy internal needs. This phenomenon has already taken place in many areas of the world. For example, dependence on imported oil led the French government to emphasize nuclear power. Similarly, the Japanese government has also decided to expand its nuclear power program to decrease its dependence on imported oil.

At the same time, during the late 1980s and early 1990s, sentiment grew within industrialized countries for protectionist economic measures. For example, in the United States, Congress introduced legislation for domestic content of finished products, and quotas in iron, steel, and automotive products were negotiated. U.S.-Japanese trade negotiations in the late 1980s and early 1990s became particularly rancorous as the United States accused Japan of unfair trade practices and Japan accused the United States of overconsumption and inattention to its economic base. Protectionist sentiment proliferated in Europe as well. Meanwhile, Developing World states argued that they must develop indigenous industry before they can participate in anything other than a dependent economic relationship. Therefore, they often attempted to insulate their economies from the outside, usually with limited success.

The third and final scenario is the most frightening, particularly in a world made more dangerous by more and more powerful weapons. Given the continuing differences in perceptions and conflicts of values that exist throughout the world, the possibility exists that international actors may decide to meet their needs by using armed might. Resource-starved actors may engage in "resource wars" to satisfy their requirements, and capital-starved actors may opt for terrorism to meet their needs. This is not a pleasant scenario. But in a world where national sovereignty and freedom of action remain chief objectives of the still preeminent category of actor, it is a realistic one.

The Global Availability of Advanced Weaponry

Despite the end of the East–West conflict and a slowdown in the growth of spending throughout the world on arms, in 1993, states still spent about $1 trillion on weapons. This amounted to over $1.6 million a minute. These expenditures bought more weapons than ever before, and many of the weapons are more powerful than ever before. In addition, more countries have access to highly sophisticated and lethal weaponry than ever before. This is true at the nuclear as well as conventional level. The U.S. government estimates that by the turn of the century, nearly forty countries will have the ability to make nuclear weapons if they so desire.

Clearly, the availability of greater quantities of increasingly lethal conventional and nuclear weaponry will make the world a more dangerous place in which to live as we move toward 2000. More hands will be on more triggers. Optimists hope that the increased lethality of the weapons in various arsenals will introduce elements of caution and restraint into the foreign policies of newly potent states. Pessimists fear that more weapons in more hands will merely add more deaths to the over 15 million that occurred in wars fought between 1960 and 1993 alone.

Wider availability of more lethal weapons will inevitably make wars more costly in terms of human life. Will that realization act as a deterrent, or will it be an irrelevant consideration to policy-makers caught in the web of past practice and history? No one knows the answer to that question, but if the answer is the former, international affairs could be transformed by the very lethality of modern war. Even as nuclear war has been avoided because of its lethality, conventional war may become obsolete.

Unfortunately, events suggest otherwise. During 1993, conflicts raged on every inhabited continent except North America and Australia. Nor has the frequency of wars and the number of casualties they cause declined. In 1993, as Table 26–1 shows, at least 19 major conflicts were under way. Clearly, suggestions that military force had lost its importance in contemporary international affairs were premature.

Nuclear war is, of course, the greatest threat. Although the United States and Russia will continue to have nuclear arsenals that dwarf all others by 2000, the probability of nuclear proliferation threatens to transform international affairs into a system even more anarchical than it currently is, especially if countries with small nuclear forces become embroiled in regional conflicts. If Iraq had had nuclear weapons during the 1991 Persian Gulf War, or Egypt or Israel in the early 1970s, or India or China in the early 1960s, the gravity of those conflicts for the international community would have taken on new dimensions. By 2000, these countries could all have nuclear weapons, if they do not have them already.

Military research and development could further alter international relations

TABLE 26–1 Locations of Ongoing Conflicts, 1993

Afghanistan	Moldova
Angola	Mozambique
Armenia	Northern Ireland
Azerbaijan	Peru
Bosnia	Philippines
Cambodia	Somalia
Chad	South Africa
Georgia	Sri Lanka
Iraq	Sudan
Lebanon	

in ways not even dreamed of, just as the atomic and hydrogen bombs and long-range aircraft and missiles did. Lasers in space may be practical before the end of the century. Their impact on international affairs could be immense. "Hold the high ground" could take on an entirely new meaning if domination of space meant domination of earth. On earth itself, improved remote control and sensing capabilities could give rise to a true automated battlefield that would be extremely expensive but result in few casualties. Defense against ballistic missiles may become a possibility. The United States under the Strategic Defense Initiative has already worked on lasers and other defensive technologies. The list could continue.

But here, the point to be made is a simple one. With many countries spending large sums of money on their militaries, and with revolutionary new military capabilities on the horizon, the possibility of military induced change in the international system remains great.

Scientific and Technical Changes—Their Potential to Revolutionize International Affairs

When the roles of science and technology in international affairs are discussed, their impacts are too often restricted to their military implications. Although scientific-technical contributions to military advances cannot be overlooked, neither should they be overstressed, for scientific-technical breakthroughs and applications have altered the conduct of international affairs in many other ways as well.

Agricultural, health, transportation, and communication advances perhaps lead the way. All have been discussed in earlier chapters, and that discussion will not be repeated here. Advances in these and other scientific-technical areas have allowed more people to eat better and to live longer than ever before, to travel faster and further than any previous generation, and to know more about what is going on in the world than their forebears.

Scientific-technical advances often create problems as well. The population explosion and the arms race are at least partially attributable to scientific-technical advances. Science and technology drove the industrial revolution onward, but industrial pollution has also contributed extensively to environmental degradation. Whether science and technology can be harnessed to improve the environment is likely to be one of the major issues of the 1990s and beyond. Furthermore, industrial processes remain potentially dangerous, as proved by the explosion at a chemical storage tank in Bhopal, India, in 1984 that killed over 2,000 people. In 1986, the U.S.S.R. and the rest of the world suffered through the Chernobyl nuclear disaster.

Even when science and technology bring potential for benefit to humanity, questions must be asked about the use that will be made of scientific-technical advances. Will they be used to improve the living standards of the billions of Developing World citizens who live in poverty, or will they lead to increased concentration of wealth and capital in the hands and countries of the affluent? In international affairs, as in domestic affairs, scientific-technical advances do not occur in a vacuum. The Green Revolution provides a perfect example. On the one hand, it allowed many people to avoid starvation. On the other hand, it also led to greater concentration of wealth in the hands of a few in several countries.

Improvements in health care and immunization also provide poignant examples. These improvements not only lengthened lives, but they also increased population, thereby resulting in a decreased standard of living in those countries in which economic growth rates fell behind population growth rates. Scientific-technical advances may therefore be seen as a mixed blessing.

Again, however, the emphasis here is on change. No doubt exists that scientific-technical advances, innovations, and breakthroughs have major effects on international affairs. They will continue to do so. Imagine, for a minute, a major breakthrough in alternate energy sources. Such a breakthrough could significantly degrade the importance of Persian Gulf oil to Western Europe, Japan, and the United States. How different would the foreign policies of all these states be in the absence of need for external sources of oil? No specific answer is possible, but major changes in their foreign policy would inevitably occur. Or contemplate for a moment an even more revolutionary advance, a breakthrough in simultaneous translation and language education capabilities. What would happen if leaders and peoples could communicate across language barriers without need of extensive training or translators? How would the conduct of international relations be changed? Again, we can only speculate, but scientific-technical change opens a multitude of possibilities. Where these possibilities could lead is an open question.

Resurgent Conflicts of Values

The preceding chapter detailed some of the major conflicts of values prevalent in the world of the 1990s, and on more than one occasion concluded that the potential for increasingly severe conflicts of values was possible. The consequences of worsened conflict are discernible: multiplied instances of civil strife within countries, increased senses of nationalism and economic protectionism, jingoism, and a general decrease in international cooperative efforts.

In many ways, each pole of the conflicts of values that we observed may be considered an ideology. All are belief systems that maintain a degree of internal consistency and assert their own primacy. This is an important realization in that many intellectuals speculated during the 1960s and 1970s that the world was entering an era that would see the end of ideology. The collapse of communism in the 1980s and 1990s has given rise to such speculation once again.

The prediction that ideologies would soon die away was premature in the 1960s and 1970s, and it is probably premature once again today. A more accurate assessment may well be that specific ideologies are less and less able to hold sway over masses of peoples, but other ideologies remain of major importance. Ideologies have fragmented and mutated, but they have not disappeared.

Ideologies—and conflicts of values—therefore remain potent forces for change in the international arena. But as we saw in the cases of the other forces for change discussed here, the shape of ideologically or value-induced change is not predictable. Who would have predicted in the early 1970s that revolutionary Islam would be a major force in world politics only 10 years later? Who in the early 1980s would have predicted that only 10 years later, communism as an

(a)

(b)

(c)

Scientific-technical breakthroughs have the potential to revolutionize international affairs.
(a) The U.S. space shuttle at liftoff. Will easier access to space lead to greater incentives to
cooperate internationally, or greater military rivalry in space? (b) An earth station for
satellite communication in Barbados. West Indies. Will better international communications lead to a greater sense of global community, or make humankind more aware of
the differences that separate it? (c) An artist's rendition of NASA's "Landsat" in orbit.
Will the ability of remote sensors in space to identify resources lead to international
agreements on resource identification and use, or to greater rivalry to exploit newly
identified resources?   (NASA.)

ideology would have been rejected throughout Eastern Europe, and that nationalism as an ideology would tear the Soviet Union apart? Ten years from now, conflicts of value may be less important international causes of change, but for the present, they cannot be ignored.

The International System in Transition

One of the major themes running throughout this text has been that the international system is changing to a new system, as yet undefined, whose broad outlines are a multiplication of international centers of power and a proliferation of types of power. When a new international system emerges, it will be the fourth major system of the twentieth century, following on the heels of first a balance of power system, second a collective security system, and third and most recently, a bipolar system, which itself changed over time.

Because the international system is not only formed and shaped by international actors and their interactions, but also in turn helps form and shape those actors and their interactions, the views that the major actors hold about the constraints and opportunities they will have in the emerging international system will be critical variables in determining what that system is like. For example, if the major economic powers see the emerging international system as one in which economic well-being mandates cutthroat economic competition and protectionism, the emerging system will doubtlessly have those characteristics. Conversely, if the major economic powers see the emerging international system as one that requires cooperation for economic well-being, the emerging system will probably have those characteristics.

The key point here is that in the midst of systemic change, old expectations and patterns of behavior of international actors are themselves more likely to change. This does little to help us predict in which direction systemic change will move. But it is beyond question that systemic change is taking place. However, developing an international consensus on the direction of preferred change remains an immense challenge.

CHALLENGES FOR 2000

Too many forces for change are at work in the international system to allow anyone realistically to believe that the current global status quo will be preserved. Similarly, given the uncertain nature of change, no one can accurately predict the world's future. Despite the proliferation of communication and information technologies that allow us to know more and more about the world we currently live in, the shape of the world in 2000 is increasingly unknown and unknowable.

Nevertheless, a number of clear challenges confront the human race. These challenges range across a wide spectrum of issues: Population growth, food production, nuclear and conventional arms races, the environment, drugs, health, equitable distribution of wealth, trade and exchange, mineral and energy scarcity, development and developmental aid, and value conflicts are just a few. Failure to initiate actions that come to grips with any single one of these challenges could seriously degrade the quality of life on earth in the twenty-first century. Efforts to come to grips with these challenges must be initiated now, or in the relatively near future, and they must be undertaken on a widespread and even a global basis.

A skeptic might ask, what actions could be undertaken now or in the relatively near future on a widespread basis to cope with the challenges that face the world? With so many international actors of so many different types, each of which perceives its own interests as special, can any global solutions to global challenges ever be implemented? Is not the anarchy of the current global system severe enough to preclude any widespread consensus on how best to cope with global issues?

Indeed, as we have seen, the current international system, with its variety of actors and interests, its diversity of perceptions, its imbalance of capabilities, and its multitude of issues, gives cause to be skeptical about the feasibility of instituting solutions to global problems. Remember, however, that actors are under assault, that the very legitimacy and utility of states, IGOs, MNCs, and NGOs are being questioned. All may survive as actors, but all may also change. Although the possibility of a global government appears as remote as ever, regardless of whether one be created by force or by agreement, the possibility of actors recognizing the severity and the scope of the challenges they confront is increasing. Leaders and peoples throughout the world acknowledge the necessity of avoiding nuclear war; perhaps someday they will acknowledge a need to avoid all war. They also avow desire to improve the economic and human conditions of everyone on earth; perhaps someday they will agree on how to attempt to do this. And increasingly, international actors recognize environmental issues as global problems that often need international solutions.

So there is room for optimism about the future. Some significant advances have been made in the recent past—for example, only a half-century ago, colonialism and imperialism were accepted and respectable; today, they are almost universally decried and reviled—and there is reason to hope that today's problems and challenges will be met and overcome as well.

Change, then, is inevitable. Nothing can escape its far-flung net. What the world will be in 2000 is not what the world is today. Change will come, and it can come rapidly. Its impact can be immense. Our responsibility is to be ready for change, and to shape it so that the challenges the world faces can be met better in the future than they are being met today.

KEY TERMS AND CONCEPTS

assaults on present-day actors
turmoil in international economics
increased availability of advanced
   weapons

impacts of scientific-technical
   change
resurgent conflicts of values
international system in transition

Index